quiet nibble on the
Cavalry skirmish line —

An Orderly

MILLS COLLEGE
LIBRARY

Henry Steele Commager, Professor of American History at Columbia University and onetime Pitt Professor of American History at Cambridge University, is a lifelong student of the Civil War. Among the many books in the fields of American political, social and intellectual history of which he is author are *The American Mind, Majority Rule and Minority Rights, Theodore Parker, The Growth of the American Republic* (with S. E. Morison), and *America: The Story of a Free People* (with Allan Nevins). He is editor of *Documents of American History, America in Perspective,* the forty volumes in process of *The Rise of the American Nation,* and other books.

THE BLUE AND THE GRAY

Currier and Ives

The Second Battle of Bull Run

The Blue
and
the Gray

THE STORY OF THE CIVIL WAR
AS TOLD BY PARTICIPANTS

EDITED BY

Henry Steele Commager

VOLUME

I

THE BOBBS-MERRILL COMPANY, INC.

publishers

INDIANAPOLIS   NEW YORK

First Edition

To
the memory of

HENRY STEELE COMMAGER
Colonel, 67th Ohio

DAVID HEDGES COMMAGER
Captain, 184th Ohio

JAMES ALEXANDER WILLIAM THOMAS
Captain, 21st South Carolina

DUNCAN DONALD MCCOLL
1st Heavy Artillery, North Carolina

JAMES THOMAS CARROLL
North Carolina Volunteers

and to
my children

HENRY STEELE
NELLIE THOMAS MCCOLL
ELISABETH CARROLL

That they may remember their forebears
and the causes for which they fought

FOREWORD

Many hands filled the storehouse from which Henry Steele Commager drew the treasures that appear in the fascinating pages of this long-desired collection. Some survivors wrote of the eighteen-sixties because they had tarnished reputations to repolish or grudges to satisfy. Other participants set down the history of their old Regiment to please comrades who met annually at a G.A.R. encampment or at a Confederate reunion to live again in memory their great hours. In a few instances, most notably that of General Grant, memoirs were prepared because the public literally demanded them. Hundreds of books and brochures were the work of those who sought, consciously or otherwise, to associate themselves with the mighty men and the decisive conflict of their generation. The failure of some Southern writers to find a publisher was responsible for the private printing of numerous books and for the allegation, never justified, that the North would not give Southern writers a hearing. One forgotten phase of this had its origin in the persistent effort of certain schoolbook publishers to procure the "adoption" in the South of texts on American history written in partizan spirit for Northern readers. This salesmanship was met repeatedly with pleas for the establishment in Richmond, Atlanta or New Orleans of a publishing house that would be "fair to the South." Where a response was made to this appeal, the fruit sometimes was a text as extreme as the one that provoked it. A long-popular Southern school history contained 590 pages, of which more than 200 were devoted to the preliminaries of the War Between the States and to the events of that struggle. A study of the disputes of the eighteen-nineties involving rival books of this type would startle a generation that assumes an author's non-partizan approach as a matter of course.

Many contrasts are offered in the literature of the American war of 1861-65, and most notably in what Mr. Commager remarks in his introduction—that "the Confederate narratives seem to be of a higher literary quality than the Federal." This is meant, of course, to be subject at the outset to qualification as respects some notable books. The list of Union brigade histories, for example, may contain no single volume better than Caldwell's charming story of Gregg's South Carolinians; but Mr. Commager most surely is correct in saying that Charles E. Davis's account of the Thirteenth Massachusetts is definitely the most interesting regimental history on either side.

If there is general, or average superiority in Southern memoirs and personal narratives, this doubtless is due to a number of circumstances that raise no questions of rival "cultures." Nearly always there is glamor to a "lost cause." Cromwell's body on the Tyburn gallows, "Bonnie Prince Charlie" in exile, and Bonaparte dying of cancer at Longwood never fail to arouse sympathy the Puritan Revolution, the Jacobite cause and Napoleonic imperialism cannot stir. It manifestly has been so with the South which had, in addition, a most unusual number of picturesque leaders. These men possessed the "color" and the peculiarities that inspire the *causerie de bivouac* the Little Corporal said every general should provide if he wished to be successful. Lee had a magnificence that awed his soldiers, who seldom cheered him; when Stonewall Jackson came in sight, riding awkwardly on a poor horse, the rebel yell nearly always would be raised. He fired the imagination of his troops as Lee never did until the *post-bellum* years. Albert Sidney Johnston, Forrest, Morgan, "Jeb" Stuart—these, too, were men to arouse enthusiasms that echoed in the memoirs of their followers. The North had soldiers and seamen of like appeal, but somehow the memory of nearly all these leaders was forgotten in the changes of population incident to the Westward movement and to expanded immigration. Static Southern society had longer memory.

Besides this, the South chanced to produce early a "war book" that set a standard which perhaps was considered representative, though actually it could not be maintained. This was Lieutenant General Richard Taylor's *Destruction and Reconstruction*, parts of which appeared in *The North American Review* in January-April 1878, the year before the memoirs were published in book form. Anyone reading that superb narrative would get an exalted conception of the literary skill of Southern military writers, a conception not borne out by later works of other authors. This is not derogatory because Taylor's book remains to this day the most exciting narrative of its kind by an American commander. It would be difficult to find anywhere a better told story of a military movement than Taylor's account of "Stonewall" Jackson's Valley Campaign of 1862 (Vol. I p. 150ff).

If these and other circumstances bear out Mr. Commager's statement regarding the excellence of some Confederate narratives, fair play requires a Southerner to put the emphasis on that word *narratives*. There certainly is not a like superiority in the poetry. Thomas De Leon, from whom Mr. Commager takes several diverting episodes, remarked in his *Four Years in Rebel Capitals* that he had accumulated 1,900 wartime poems of the South, and later added greatly to his list: "There were battle odes, hymns, calls to arms, paeans and dirges and prayers for peace—many of them good, few of them great; and the vast majority, alas! wretchedly poor."

De Leon could have carried his scrutiny of Southern literature twenty years further and would have found few Confederate poems besides those of the Catholic priest, Father Abram Joseph Ryan, that voiced impressively the full emotion of the Southern people. Frequently Theodore O'Hara's "The Bivouac of the Dead" is put forward with Father Ryan's "Conquered Banner," but O'Hara wrote in 1847 of the Kentuckians killed in the Battle of Buena Vista. It is a singular fact that John R. Thompson's verses on the Confederacy, though written, as it were, to the pulsing of the guns on the Richmond defenses, seldom reached the level of his best work. Simms, Hayne, Lanier, Timrod, Randall—none of these wrote of "the war" as their admirers might have expected. No theme seemed to elicit their finest utterance, not even "Marse Robert" himself. Lee remains the demigod of the South and has there a place even Washington does not hold, but where may be found a poem on Lee that anyone would wish to make a permanent part of one's mental acquisition? In contrast, Lowell outdid himself in the "Harvard Commemoration Ode"; Whitman's "O Captain! My Captain!" and his "When Lilacs Last in the Dooryard Bloomed" are among the author's most successful works; and as Mr. Commager says, the North produced the "one great battle hymn of our literature."

Perhaps the most remarkable feature of the 400 and more articles reproduced in this notable collection is the humor that runs through nearly all of them and particularly through those of Southern origin. Doubtless there was an Erich Remarque somewhere on the Rappahannock front; letters written home by Billy Yank and Johnny Reb contained the usual number of complaints and requests; but when the column was in motion, there were more jests than oaths on the lips of the soldiers. Laughter was the medicine for most of the ills visible to the men next in line, though fear and rebellious wrath and homesickness might be gnawing at the heart.

Good cheer was not unnatural in the Union Regiments after July 1863, but its persistence until the autumn of 1864 in most of the Southern forces, and particularly in the Army of Northern Virginia, is a phenomenon of morale. The same thing may be said of the attitude of the men toward the manifest inferiority of Southern military equipment. The graycoats laughed at their wagons and their harness, their tatters and their gaping shoes. Again and again this stirs one who opens these volumes at random and reads the first paragraph on which the eye falls: were these men mocking death as a foe long outwitted, or were they assuming a heroism they did not possess? Were they valiant or merely pretending? It scarcely seemed to matter where some of them were or what they were doing: they laughed their way from Manassas to Appomattox and even through the hospitals. Except for the military prisons, the Confederates, for instance, could have had few places of darker tragedy, written in tears and anguish, than Chimborazo Hospital in Richmond, where as many as 7,000 soldiers sometimes suffered together; yet it was life there that Mrs. Phoebe Pember described in some of the most humorous writing of the war.

These Confederate soldiers and nurses and citizens of beleaguered towns had one inspiration that twentieth-century America has not credited to them—the vigorous Revolutionary tradition. The men who fought at Gettysburg were as close in time to the turning point of that earlier struggle, the Trenton-Princeton campaign of 1777, as readers of 1950 are to the *dies irae* described by Colonel Frank Haskell in his famous account of the repulse of Pickett's charge. Many men in the ranks, North and South, had seen old soldiers of the Continental Army; thousands had heard stories of the sacrifices of 1777 and of the hunger and nakedness at Valley Forge. From its very nature, freedom was born in travail. Ignorant men sensed this vaguely, if at all; the literate reread William Gordon and Washington Irving and steeled themselves to like hardship. To some of the commanders, and above all to Lee, there daily was an inspiring analogy between the struggle of the Confederacy and that of Revolutionary America under the generalship of Lee's great hero, Washington. Many another Southern soldier told himself the road was no more stony than the one that had carried his father and his grandfather at last to Yorktown. If independence was to be the reward, patience, good cheer and the tonic of laughter would bring it all the sooner.

Those Confederates believed they were as good judges of humor as, say, of horses; and both they and their adversaries in blue regarded themselves as strategists or, at least, as competent critics of strategy. Quick to perceive the aim of the marches they were called upon to make, they discussed by every campfire and on every riverbank the shrewdness or the blunders of the men who led them. After the manner of youth in every land and of every era, they made heroes of the officers they admired and they denounced the martinets, but, in time, most of them learned from their discussion and, considering the paucity of their information, came to broad strategical conclusions their seniors would not have been ashamed to own.

Many of the diarists and letter writers were observant, too, and not infrequently recorded important fact no officer set down in any report. If some of these writers let their vanity adorn their tale, the majority were of honest mind. One somewhat renowned *post-bellum* lecturer who should have been an invaluable witness, progressively lost the truth of his narrative as he made it more and more dramatic and egocentric, but he did not have many fellow offenders outside the ranks of those known and branded prevaricators who bored their comrades of the U.C.V. or the G.A.R. as they told how "they won" the battle or the war. On the other hand, Mr. Commager quotes in these pages several veterans who wrote long after the conflict, without access to records, and yet were so astonishingly accurate that any psychologist, chancing on their memoirs, will wish he might have studied in person the mentality of the authors.

These men and women had no literary inhibitions other than those of a decency that is to be respected both for itself and for the contrasts it suggests with certain later writing on war and warriors. If, incidentally, the restraint and modesty of most of the soldiers' letters of the eighteen-sixties were Victorian, then so much the better for Victorianism. This apart, every man felt free to write of anything—and considered himself as competent as free—with the result that the source materials of the conflict are opulently numerous and almost bewilderingly democratic. Private Casler may dispute in a footnote the pronouncements of the learned Dr. Dabney on the strategy of "Old Jack"; the testimony of a boy who saw Grant once only may be preferred to that of a corps commander who conferred so often with "Unconditional Surrender" that, in retrospect, he confused the details of the various interviews.

Historically, then, it may be hoped that one result of the appearance of this book will be the use of other authorities than the few, such as "Rebel War Clerk" Jones and Mrs. Chesnut, for example, who have been overworked and, on some subjects, have been uncritically cited. The student will find that new witnesses have been made available, and that stirring tales have been assembled and prefaced sagely by an editor whose knowledge of the literature of 1861-65 is unexcelled. Henry Steele Commager has the admiration as well as the personal affection of all students who appreciate the catholicity of his scholarship and the penetrating justice of his judgment. Had members of his profession been asked by the publishers to name the individual best equipped to present "a history of the Civil War in the words of those who fought it," their choice would have been the man who flawlessly has rendered here that welcome service to the American people.

Douglas Southall Freeman

Westbourne,
Richmond, Virginia,
August 14, 1950.

INTRODUCTION

WE have fought five major wars in the last century or so, and three since Appomattox, but of them all it is the Civil War that has left the strongest impression on our minds, our imagination, and our hearts. It is the Civil War songs that we sing—who does not know "Marching Through Georgia" or "Tramp, Tramp, Tramp" or "Dixie"?—and that war gave us the one great battle hymn of our literature. It furnished our best war poetry, both at the time and since; no other war has produced anything as good as "Drum Taps" or the "Harvard Commemoration Ode," nor has any other been celebrated by an epic poem comparable to Stephen Benét's *John Brown's Body*. It has inspired more, and better, novels than any other of our wars and it excites even Hollywood to rise above mediocrity. It has furnished our standards of patriotism, of gallantry, and of fortitude; it has given us our most cherished military heroes—Lee and Jackson, Grant and Sherman, Sheridan and "Beauty" Stuart, and a host of others, and it has given us, too, our greatest national hero and our greatest sectional one, Lincoln and Lee. No other chapter in our history has contributed so much to our traditions and our folklore. The very words—whether they are Civil War or War between the States—conjure up for us a hundred images: Jackson standing like a stone wall; U. S. Grant becoming Unconditional Surrender Grant; Lee astride Traveller, "It is well war is so terrible, or we should get too fond of it"; Barbara Frietchie waving her country's flag; A. P. Hill breaking through the wheat fields at Antietam; Thomas standing like a rock at Chickamauga; Pickett's men streaming up the long slope of Cemetery Ridge; Farragut lashed to the mast at Mobile Bay, "Damn the torpedoes, full steam ahead"; the Army of the Cumberland scrambling up the rugged heights of Missionary Ridge; Hood's Texans forcing Lee to the rear before they would close the gap at Spotsylvania; Sheridan dashing down the Winchester Pike; Lincoln pardoning the sleeping sentinels, reading Artemus Ward to his Cabinet, dedicating the battlefield of Gettysburg; Grant and Lee at Appomattox Court House.

It was, in many respects, a curious war, one in which amenities were preserved. It could not begin until high-ranking officers of the army and navy had been permitted to resign and help organize a rebellion. Southerners tolerated outspoken Unionists, like Petigru or Botts; Northerners permitted Vallandigham to campaign openly against the war, and at the crisis of the conflict almost two million of them voted for a party that had formally pronounced the war a failure. Journalists seemed to circulate at will, and Northern papers had correspondents in the South while Confederates got much of their information about Federal army movements from the Northern newspapers. There was an immense amount of trading back and forth, some of it authorized or at least tolerated by the governments, and Sherman could say that Cincinnati furnished more supplies to the Confederacy than did Charleston.

Officers had been trained in the same schools and fought in the same armies and most of them knew one another or knew of one another; Mrs. Pickett tells us that when her baby was born Grant's staff celebrated with bonfires. There was a great deal of fraternization—a word which did not have the ugly connotations it achieved after World War II—both among soldiers and civilians. Pickets exchanged tobacco, food, and news; if Yankee officers did not marry Southern beauties as often as novelists imagined, there was at least some basis for the literary emphasis on romance. Confederates cheered Meagher's Irish Brigade as it charged up Marye's Heights, and the Yankees almost outdid the Confederates in admiration for Jackson and Pelham. There were plenty of atrocity stories, but few atrocities. There was a good deal of pillaging and vandalism—as in all wars—but little of that systematic destruction we know from two world wars. On the whole, civilians were safe; there were crimes against property but few against persons, and women everywhere were respected. When Butler affronted the ladies of New Orleans he was transferred to another command, and Sherman engaged in a wordy correspondence with the mayor of Atlanta seeking to justify what he thought a military necessity. Whether Sherman burned Columbia is still a matter of controversy; the interesting thing is that there should be a controversy at all. Both peoples subscribed to the same moral values and observed the same standards of conduct. Both displayed that "decent respect to the opinions of mankind" to which Jefferson had appealed three quarters of a century earlier. Both were convinced that the cause for which they fought was just—and their descendants still are.

Nor did the war come to an end, psychologically or emotionally, with Appomattox. Politicians nourished its issues; patriotic organizations cherished its memories; scholars refought its battles with unflagging enthusiasm. No other war has started so many controversies and for no other do they flourish so vigorously. Every step in the conflict, every major political decision, every campaign, almost every battle, has its own proud set of controversies, and of all the military figures only Lee stands above argument and debate. Was the election of Lincoln a threat to the South, and was secession justified? Was secession a revolutionary or a constitutional act, and was the war a rebellion or an international conflict? Was the choice of Davis a mistake, and did Davis interfere improperly in military affairs? Should the Confederacy have burned its cotton, or exported it? Was the blockade a success, and if so at what point? Should Britain have recognized the Confederacy, or did she go too far toward the assistance of the South as it was? Who was responsible for the attack on Fort Sumter, Lincoln or Beauregard, and was the call for 75,000 men an act of aggression? Was Jackson late at Seven Days? Was Grant surprised at Shiloh? Did the radicals sabotage McClellan's Peninsular campaign? Who was responsible for the disaster of Second Bull Run and was Fitz John Porter a marplot or a scapegoat? Should Lee have persisted in his offensive of the autumn of 1862 even after the discovery of the Lost Order? Should McClellan have renewed battle after Antietam? Why did Pemberton fail to link up with Johnston outside Vicksburg and why did Johnston fail to relieve

Pemberton? Would Gettysburg have been different had Jackson been there, or had Longstreet seized Little Round Top on the morning of the second day, or had Pickett been properly supported on the third? Who was responsible for the Confederate failure at Stones River and who for the debacle of Missionary Ridge, and why did Davis keep Bragg in command so long? Could Johnston have saved Atlanta, and did Hood lose it? Was Hood's Tennessee campaign strategically sound but tactically mismanaged, or was it the other way around? Was Lee deceived during those critical June days when Grant flung his army across the James? And why did the Federals fail to break through the thin lines of Petersburg? Who burned Columbia, and was Sherman's theory of war justified? What really happened at Five Forks, and would the outcome have been different had Pickett been more alert? What explains the failure to have supplies at Amelia Court House and could Lee have made good his escape and linked up with Johnston had the supplies been there? Could the Confederacy ever have won the war, or was defeat foredoomed; if defeat was not foredoomed what caused it? These and a thousand other questions are still avidly debated by a generation that has already forgotten the controversies of the Spanish War and the First World War.

Nor is it by chance that the cause lost on the battlefield should be celebrated in story and in history, or that the whole people, victors and vanquished alike, should exalt its heroism and cherish its leaders. Lee is only less of a hero than Lincoln, and the Federal Army boasts no figure so glamorous as Stonewall Jackson. Novelists have been kinder to the Confederacy than to the Union, and so, too, in our own day, the moving pictures and the radio. There is no literary monument to any Union general comparable to those erected to Lee and Jackson, and for a generation Northern historians found themselves apologizing for Appomattox. Southerners everywhere accept the verdict of the war, and even are thankful for it, but there are none so lacking in filiopietism that they would change a line of history.

From the point of view of the student of military history, too, the Civil War is inexhaustibly interesting, and it is no wonder that English, French, and German strategists and historians have assiduously studied its battles and campaigns. It was, in a sense, the last of the old wars and the first of the new. It had many of the characteristics of earlier wars—the chivalry that animated officers and men, and the mutual esteem in which the combatants held each other, for example; the old-fashioned weapons and tactics such as sabers and cavalry charges; the woeful lack of discipline; the pitiful inadequacy of medical and hospital services, of what we would now call service of supply, of any provision for welfare and morale; the almost total absence of any proper Intelligence service or adequate staff work, and the primitive state of maps; the casual and amateur air that pervaded it all. But it was, too, in many and interesting respects, a modern war, one that anticipated the "total" wars of the twentieth century. It was the first in which the whole nation was involved, and it is probable that a larger proportion of the population, North as well as South, was actually in uniform than in any previous war of modern history. It was the first in which there was an even partial control of the economy—this largely in the South rather than in the more fortunate North. It was the first in which a large-scale blockade was a really effective if not indeed a decisive weapon. It was the first in which the railroad and the telegraph played a major role. It involved almost every known form of warfare: large-scale battles, guerrilla fighting, trench warfare, sieges and investments, bold forays into enemy country and large-scale invasions, amphibious warfare along coastal and inland waters, blockade, privateering, surface and sub-surface naval war, the war of propaganda and of nerves. It produced in Lee one of the supreme military geniuses of history, in Farragut one of the great naval captains; in Grant a major strategist; in Sherman, Hancock, Jackson, A. P. Hill, and Joseph E. Johnston captains whose tactics are still worthy of study; in Thomas a master of artillery; in Forrest and Stuart, Buford, Sheridan and Wilson, cavalry leaders whose exploits have rarely been surpassed.

Every war dramatizes the ordinary and accentuates the characteristic; more than any other in which we have ever been engaged the Civil War brought out in sharp relief those qualities that we think of as distinctively American. The American was practical, experimental, inventive, intelligent, self-reliant, opportunistic, energetic, careless, undisciplined, amateurish, equalitarian, sentimental, humorous, generous and moral. He believed that the civil was superior to the military even in war, and that privates were as good as officers, that it was wrong to begin a war or to fight in a cause that was not just, that a war should be fought according to rules, and that moral standards should obtain in war as in peace. All these qualities and principles were carried over from the civil to the military arena.

Thus the war discovered a people wholly unprepared, and never willing to prepare, either materially or psychologically. Neither side ever really organized for war; neither ever used the whole of its resources—though the South came far closer to this than the North; neither accepted the iron discipline which modern war imposes. The war required the subordination of the individual to the mass, of the particular to the general interest, and of the local to the central government; but both Federals and Confederates indulged their individualism in the army and out, rejected military standards and discipline, selected officers for almost any but military reasons, pursued local and state interest at the expense of the national. The war required organization and efficiency, but both sides conducted the war with monumental inefficiency—witness the shambles of conscription, or of the procurement of ordnance or of finances. The war required the husbanding of resources, but both sides wasted their resources, human and material—witness the medical services, or desertion, or the indulgence of business as usual, especially in the North.

The Americans were an educated, informed, self-reliant and resourceful people, and the Civil War armies undoubtedly boasted the highest level of intelligence of any armies in modern history up to that time. It took foreigners to remark this quality, however; Americans themselves took it for granted. Everyone, as both Dicey and Trollope remarked in wonder, read newspapers, followed political debates, and had opinions on the war, slavery, politics, and everything else; almost everyone—as an editor knows—kept a diary or a journal. Resourcefulness was almost their most striking quality. This resourcefulness appeared in Grant, who kept at it until he had found the road to Vicksburg; it appeared in Lee, who was able to adjust his plans to his shifting opponents, and to count on the understanding and co-operation of his lieutenants; it appeared in the engineers, who built dams and bridges, laid railroad tracks—or tore them up—solved problems of transport and supply that appeared insoluble; it appeared in the privates of both armies, who improvised breastworks or camp shelters, foraged for food and supplies, chose their own officers, voted in the field, provided their own newspapers, theatricals, and religious services, and often fought their own battles with such weapons as they could piece together. It appeared, too, in civilians, especially in the South, who managed somehow to improvise most of the weapons of war and the essentials of domestic economy, to make do with such labor and such materials as they had, and to hold society together through four years of strife and want.

Thus the conduct of the war confounded both the critics and the prophets. It was thought a people as unmilitary as the Americans could not fight a long war, or would not—but they did. It was thought that an agricultural South could not produce the matériel of war, but no single Southern defeat could be ascribed to lack of arms or equipment. It was supposed that neither side could finance a major war, but both managed somehow, and though Confederate finances were a shambles the North emerged from the conflict richer than she had entered it. To blockade thousands of miles of coast line, to invade an area of continental dimensions—these had never been done successfully in modern times, but the Union did them. Curiously, Europe was not convinced; the same basic errors of judgment that plagued England and France during the Civil War reappeared in Germany in 1917 and in Germany, Italy, and France in 1940.

The Americans were a good-natured people, easygoing, careless, and kindly, and in a curious sense these qualities carried over even into war. Lincoln set the tone here, for the North—Lincoln, who somehow managed to mitigate the wrath of war and his own melancholy with his humor, and who never referred to the Confederates as rebels; and Lee for the South, Lee, who always called the enemy "those people." Relations between the two armies were, somehow, good-natured: the very names the combatants had for each other, Johnny Reb and Billy Yank, testified to this. Only occasionally were relations between these enemies who so deeply respected each other exacerbated by official policy or by the prejudices of an officer. The soldiers themselves—boys for the most part, for it was a boys' war—were high-spirited and amiable, and endured endless discomforts and privations with good humor. Their good humor emerged in their songs—"Goober Peas," "Mister, Here's Your Mule," "Grafted into the Army," "We are the Boys of Potomac's Ranks"—their stories, their campfire jokes, so naïve and innocent for the most part; it spilled over into their letters home and into the diaries and journals they so assiduously kept. There was bitterness enough in the war, especially for the South and for the women of the South, but probably no other great civil war was attended by so little bitterness and no other recorded so many acts of kindness and civility between enemies; certainly no other was so magnanimously concluded. Read over, for example, that moving account of the surrender at Appomattox by Joshua Chamberlain:

Before us in proud humiliation stood the embodiment of manhood: men whom neither toils and sufferings, nor the fact of death, nor disaster, nor hopelessness could bend from their resolve; standing before us now, thin, worn, and famished, but erect, and with eyes looking level into ours, waking memories that bound us together as no other bond;—was not such manhood to be welcomed back into a Union so tested and assured? . . . How could we help falling on our knees, all of us together, and praying God to pity and forgive us all!

The Americans were a moral people and carried their ordinary moral standards over into the conduct of war. They thought aggressive warfare wrong and the war could not get under way until Beauregard had fired on Fort Sumter; Southerners insisted that the firing was self-defense against Yankee aggression. Every war is barbarous, but—Sherman, Hunter, and Sheridan to the contrary notwithstanding—there was less barbarism in the Civil than in most other wars. Both peoples, as Lincoln observed, read the same Bible and prayed to the same God; both armies were devout; leaders on both sides managed to convince themselves that they stood at Armageddon and battled for the Lord. When the end came there was no vengeance and no bloodshed; this was probably the only instance in modern history where rebellion was crushed without punishing its leaders.

Above all, the generation that fought the war had that quality which Emerson ascribed pre-eminently to the English—character. It is an elusive word, as almost all great words are elusive—truth, beauty, courage, loyalty, honor—but we know well enough what it means and know it when we see it. The men in blue and in gray who marched thirty miles a day through the blistering heat of the Bayou Teche, went without food for days on end, shivered through rain and snow in the mountains of Virginia and Tennessee, braved the terrors of hospital and prison, charged to almost certain death on the crest of Cemetery Ridge, closed the gap at the Bloody Angle, ran the batteries of Vicksburg and braved the torpedoes of Mobile Bay, threw away their lives on the hills outside Franklin for a cause they held dear—these men had character. They knew what they were fighting for, as well as men ever know this, and they fought with a tenacity and a courage rarely equaled in history. So, too, their leaders, civil and military. It is, in last analysis, grandeur of character that assures immortality to Lincoln as to Lee, and it is character, too, we admire in Grant and Jackson, Sherman and Longstreet, the brave Reynolds and the gallant Pelham, and a thousand others. Winston Churchill tells us, in his account of Pearl Harbor, that there were some in

England who feared the consequences of that fateful blow and doubted the ability of Americans to stand up to the test of modern war. "But I had studied the American Civil War," he says, "fought out to the last desperate inch," and "I went to bed and slept the sleep of the saved and thankful."

But it is a veteran of the war itself who paid the finest tribute to his comrades in blue and in gray. "Through our great good fortune," said Justice Oliver Wendell Holmes—and he spoke for his whole generation—

in our youth our hearts were touched with fire. It was given us to learn at the outset that life is a profound and passionate thing. While we are permitted to scorn nothing but indifference, and do not pretend to undervalue the worldly rewards of ambition, we have seen with our own eyes, beyond and above the gold fields, the snowy heights of honor, and it is for us to bear the report to those who come after us.

What I have tried to do in these volumes is very simple, but the execution of the task has been far from simple. I have tried to present a well-rounded—I cannot call it complete—history of the Civil War in the words of those who fought it. From the four hundred and fifty-odd narratives which are presented here there will emerge, I hope, a picture of the war that is authentic, coherent, and interesting. All depends, to be sure, on the selection and the editing of the material, and it is relevant therefore to say something about the principles that have governed that selection and about editorial practices.

Only those who have worked in the rich fields of Civil War history know how apparently inexhaustible the material is, and how unorganized. Only the Puritan Revolution and the French Revolutionary and Napoleonic wars boast a comparable literature, and even here the literature is not really comparable. For the American Civil War affected the whole population and, as Edward Dicey remarked in astonishment, it was a highly literate population. Almost everyone could write, and almost everyone, it seems, did. Surely no other chapter of modern history has been so faithfully or so elaborately recorded by ordinary men and women; in the American Civil War Everyman was, indeed, his own historian. A disproportionate body of the available material is, to be sure, from officers or from statesmen; these were the more articulate members of the population and those who could better arrange for the publication of what they wanted to say. But to a remarkable degree the privates kept records, and so too did the folks back home. Their reminiscences, recollections, and journals are to be found not in the handsomely published volumes from the great publishing houses, but in the pages of regimental histories, of state, local, and patriotic historical societies, of magazines that printed letters from veterans or from their families. The richness of this literature is the delight and the despair of every student.

The choice of available material is, in short, fabulously wide. For every episode, every battle, every experience of camp life or discipline or prison, every social practice, there are a dozen first-rate accounts, and for some there are many more. During the twelve years in which I have been collecting material for this book I have tried to read all of these that I could lay my hands on; I do not know how many diaries, journals, letters, autobiographies, biographies, battle and campaign histories, regimental histories, volumes of learned societies, of historical societies, of magazines like the *Confederate Veteran* or the old *Century* I have read; that the selection here presented represents only a small fraction of the whole will surprise no one familiar with the field.

My point of departure has not, however, been literature but history. My concern has been the particular battle or campaign, the particular military or social institution, and I have worked out from these to the available literature, selecting not primarily what was interesting for its own sake, or dramatic or eloquent, but what illuminated the subject and the problem. I do not mean to imply that I have been immune to the purely literary appeal, or to the appeal of drama or of personality. Needless to say it is not for authenticity alone that I have preferred Haskell's to a score of other accounts of Pickett's charge, or Chamberlain's to a dozen others of the surrender at Appomattox.

I have tried to cover the whole war; not only the military, which has attracted disproportionate attention, and the naval, but the economic, social, political, and diplomatic as well. The war was not all fighting; it was public opinion, it was the draft, it was prison and hospital, it was ordnance and supplies, it was politics and elections, it was religion, and even play. Approximately half the material in these volumes records the actual fighting; another half is devoted to the other aspects of the war. I have tried to hold even the balance between Union and Confederate, the East and the West, the military and the civil, and to give some representation to women and to foreign observers. I cannot suppose that I have wholly succeeded in all this, for the available material has not always lent itself to a balanced picture. As every student knows, good battle accounts are voluminous but accounts of Intelligence or ordnance or supply are meager, and there are at least two capital descriptions of fighting for every one of politics or diplomacy or even of social conditions. Nor is the balance between the material available from officer and private really even. Almost every leading officer wrote his reminiscences or at least contributed them to the *Battles and Leaders* series or to one of the meetings of the state Loyal Legion or of the Confederate Veterans, and the temptation to draw on these magisterial accounts has been irresistible. Nor do I feel unduly apologetic about drawing on Grant and Sherman, Longstreet and Hood and others; think what we would give for the war memoirs of R. E. Lee!

Even in the matter of proper representation from Federal and Confederate participants and from the East and the West I have not been entirely a free agent. There are considerably more Union than Confederate narratives— quite naturally, considering the relative numbers involved and the mechanics and economy of publishing. On the whole, however—and I know this is a very dangerous thing to say—the Confederate narratives seem to be of a higher literary quality than the Federal, and this somewhat redresses the quantitative balance. Again, the literature on the fighting in the East, especially in Northern Virginia, is far more voluminous and more interesting than that on the fighting in the West; the reasons for this are not wholly clear, but the fact will not, I think, be disputed by any student of the war and it is one to which an editor must accommodate himself as best he can.

Two types of source material have been deliberately neglected, or discriminated against: official reports and newspapers. I have not, to be sure, been consistent here; the reader will find, in these pages, samples of both. Official reports are invaluable to the historian, but they are for the most part altogether too detailed, too technical, and too dull for use in a book of this character. As for newspaper accounts some of them, like those by "Bull Run" Russell or George Townsend, are indispensable, but most of them, again, are too verbose and detailed for our purposes. Scholars will note, and doubtless deplore, the omission of one other body of source material: I refer to manuscripts. I have examined a good many Civil War manuscripts, but, with the single exception of the Ramseur letters, which I could not resist, I have not used manuscript material in these volumes. A carefully edited documentary source book of the Civil War is badly needed, and so, too, a newspaper history of the war, while any number of volumes can be quarried from the vast mines of manuscript sources. But these are formidable tasks, and each one would have called for another decade of intensive work.

There are, of course, many gaps in these volumes, and these will doubtless pain some readers. Those whose grandfathers were wounded at Perryville will object, quite properly, that that battle is neglected; others whose forebears fought at Fort Pillow will wonder why the massacre is not included; students of economic or social history will doubtless feel that these important subjects have been slighted, while military historians, alive to the importance in our own day of Intelligence or logistics, will feel that the fighting war has been overemphasized. In extenuation I can only plead the obvious. Some of the gaps in these volumes are dictated by considerations of space, others by availability of material. I could not put in everything; I could not even put in everything that was important. As with most books of this kind a good deal more was left out, in the final selection, than was put in, and this with the usual heartburnings. That is part of the story. The other part is that many of the things that interest us most did not appear to interest the generation that fought the war—or that read about it. There are descriptions enough of food and cooking, but no systematic account of the services of supply. There must be a hundred narratives of prison life and prison escape for every one of the organization and administration of prisons. If there is any good analysis of what we now call Intelligence, outside voluminous official correspondence, I do not know it.

Again and again I have had to make choices which were painful to me, however they may affect the reader. Should I attempt to cover the whole of the diplomatic history of the war, or be content with relations with Britain? To have covered the whole—to have included the diplomatic relations of both belligerents with France and Mexico and the Vatican, for example—would have resulted in a fragmentary picture. I decided, I think rightly, to concentrate on that country whose policy was, after all, decisive. Again, what of politics, North and South; what of the westward movement and railroad building that went on during the war; what of the life of the mind and the spirit? I consoled myself that these things were either marginal to the war itself, or were adequately covered in the voluminous histories and source books already available such as McPherson's *Political History of the Great Rebellion* or Frank Moore's *Rebellion Record*.

I have tried in every case to get actual participants and observers to contribute to this co-operative history. Most of the contributors were participants in the physical sense; they experienced what Oliver Wendell Holmes called "the crush of Arctic ice." Others, and among them some of the most sagacious, were "behind the lines": poets who interpreted the significance of the war; diplomats who pleaded their country's cause abroad; women who lived "the lives which women have lead since Troy fell"; surgeons who treated the wounded and chaplains who comforted the dying. All these were participants even though they may not have held a musket, and all have something to tell us of the war.

It would be naïve for me, or for the reader, to suppose that the accounts here reproduced are in every case authentic, or that even the most authentic are wholly reliable. Most of those who claimed to be participants undoubtedly were so, but it would strain our imagination to suppose that all of our reporters actually witnessed everything they described. As every student of evidence knows, people do not always see what they think they see and they do not remember what they saw. There are doubtless many instances where soldiers, writing fifteen or twenty years after the event, deluded themselves, as well as their readers. They embroidered on their original stories; they incorporated into their accounts not only what they had experienced but what they had heard or read elsewhere; they went back and consulted official records and doctored their manuscripts. Soldiers whose companies did not actually get into a battle appear, in written recollections, in the thick of it; hangers-on, who have entertained their friends with the gossip of the capital for years, remember through the haze of time that they themselves directed great affairs of state.

All this is a commonplace of historical criticism, and there is no wholly effective safeguard against it. Diaries, journals, and letters are obviously to be preferred to later recollections, but there is no guarantee that diaries and letters conform to the strictest standards of accuracy and objectivity, or that they come to us untouched by the editorial pen, while many volumes of reminiscences, otherwise suspect for age, are based on diaries and letters and have claims on our confidence. Official reports are doubtless more reliable than merely personal accounts, but even official reports were often written months after the event and colored by imagination or wishful thinking, and there is no sound reason for supposing that the average officer, writing an official report, really knew the whole of what he was writing about.

We must keep in mind, too, that the Civil War was a far more casual affair than more recent wars. There was no proper organization for keeping records or for writing history. Even the most elementary facts are in dispute. It is no exaggeration to say that the statistical picture is a chaos. We do not know the numbers of those who fought on either side, or of those who took part in particular battles, or of casualties, and Confederate figures in these fields are mostly guesswork. Take so simple a matter as executions. Our literature tells us of innumerable executions. But Phisterer, author of a statistical handbook of the war, gives us three widely varying official figures, and historians who have gone into the matter accept none of them. Or take the matter of desertion. Both Ella Lonn and Fred Shannon have dealt with this at length, but about the best they can do for us is to give broad estimates. For what was desertion, after all? Were those who failed to register for conscription deserters, or those who having registered failed to show up? Were bounty jumpers deserters, and how often should one of them be counted? Were those who went home to visit their wives or to help get in the crops, and later returned to the army, deserters? Or what shall we say of the blockade? Was it ever really effective? How many blockade-runners were there, and how many of them got through the blockade? With the most elementary facts of the war in this state of confusion it is perhaps excessive to strain overmuch at discrepancies in accounts of the conduct of a company or a regiment in a particular battle.

Something should be said about the principles governing the reproduction of source material in these volumes. There has been no tinkering with the text except in three very minor details. First, in some instances where paragraphs seemed intolerably long, they have been broken up. Second, while I have faithfully indicated all omissions within any excerpt I have not thought it necessary to put the customary dots at the beginning and end of excerpts: these can usually be taken for granted. Third, in deference to modern usage I have capitalized the word Negro wherever it appears. Aside from these insignificant modifications the text appears here as it appears in the original source to which credit is given in the bibliography.

That authors themselves, or editors—often devoted wives or daughters— have sometimes tinkered with the text is, however, painfully clear. There is no protection against this, and nothing to be done about it short of going back to the original manuscript where that is available; ordinarily it is not available. And this leads me to a more important matter. Not only have I not presumed to correct spelling or punctuation, I have not attempted to correct factual statements or misstatements. To have done so would have involved both me and the reader in a wilderness of controversy. There are, after all, hundreds of histories that attempt to set the facts straight. Careful readers will therefore note many glaring errors in these accounts. Almost every soldier, for example, consistently exaggerated enemy strength, and enemy losses, and two accounts of the same battle will confidently submit wholly inconsistent statistical information. The reader must keep in mind that our contributors are not writing as scholarly historians. They are giving their story from their own point of view—a point of view at once circumscribed and biased. They are not only limited in their knowledge; they are often ignorant, prejudiced, and vain. Sometimes they are on the defensive; sometimes they are repeating rumor and gossip; sometimes they are yielding to the temptation of the purple passage; sometimes they are trying to make a good impression on the folks back home, or on posterity. The reader is warned: they are not always to be trusted. But there are some consolations and some safeguards. As we give both Federal and Confederate accounts the errors often cancel out. The vainglorious give themselves away, and so too the ignorant and the timid, while those who write with an eye on the verdict of history proclaim that fact in every line.

An enterprise of this nature, stretching over more than a decade, naturally incurs a great many debts and obligations. I could not have completed this work without the help of the staff of the Columbia University Library, who endured with patience and good humor continuous raids upon their collections and who co-operated generously in making their Civil War collection one of the best in the country. I am indebted, too, to libraries and librarians elsewhere: the Library of Congress, the New York Public Library, the libraries of Harvard University, the University of Virginia, the University of North Carolina, New York University, the University of California, to name but a few. To my graduate students who have helped in the arduous work of tracking down elusive books, transcribing and photostating, I am deeply indebted, and especially to Mrs. Elizabeth Kelley Bauer, Mr. Wilson Smith, and Mr. Leonard Levy. The editorial and production departments of The Bobbs-Merrill Company have co-operated far beyond the call of duty, and I owe a great deal to the sagacious judgment of Mr. Laurance Chambers, the astute editorial eye of Miss Judith Henley, the imaginative co-operation of Mr. Walter Hurley. To the many publishers, historical societies, university presses, and private individuals who have so generously given me permission to reproduce material in their control I am deeply grateful. To my wife, who magnanimously permitted the Yankees to win an occasional victory in these pages, my debt is, of course, beyond expression.

HENRY STEELE COMMAGER

Williamsville, Vermont
August, 1950

TABLE OF CONTENTS

LIST OF ILLUSTRATIONS

MAPS

THE BLUE AND THE GRAY

I

Darkening Clouds

With *the deeper causes of the Civil War we are not concerned, nor with the question which has commanded so much speculation, whether the war was a repressible or an irrepressible conflict. What is certain is that the leaders of the Deep South had convinced themselves, by December 1860, that separation was essential to the preservation of the "peculiar institution," and to the social and economic prosperity of their section. Whether these views fairly represented majority opinion, even in the Deep South, we do not and cannot know; all we can say is that there were substantial elements in every Southern state which did not subscribe to them and even larger elements which opposed secession. Unionist sentiment was particularly strong in the border states—Maryland, Virginia, Kentucky, Tennessee, and Missouri, and in North Carolina which had never been so deeply committed to slavery or the plantation system as other Southern states.*

The political machinery of most Southern states was in the hands of the secessionists; this was particularly the case in South Carolina, least democratic of states in its political organization. With the triumph of the Republicans in the November elections—a triumph which was far from giving that party a complete control of the government however—Southern hotheads decided to act, and South Carolina led the way. There were frantic efforts at compromise, North and South, but all foundered. One reason for their failure was the unwillingness or inability of Lincoln to accept any compromise which extended the area open to slavery; another was the conviction of Southern extremists that separation was inevitable and that compromise, on no matter what terms, would leave the South in a relatively weaker position for the future. So while Buchanan vacillated and the North marked time, the Deep South seceded and organized as an independent nation. With the secession of Virginia, in April, the capital was moved to Richmond and a permanent government established.

Meantime Lincoln, too, had organized his Cabinet—a Cabinet of all factions rather than all talents—and in his Inaugural Address appealed to "my countrymen, one and all" to sink their differences in a common patriotism. The appeal was in vain.

1. ABRAHAM LINCOLN IS NOMINATED IN THE WIGWAM

It was the nomination and subsequent election of the "Black Republican," Lincoln, that precipitated secession and, in the end, war. Lincoln actually

1

represented no immediate threat to the South, but many leading Southerners were convinced that Republican control of the Presidency and of Congress would, in the end, doom the "peculiar institution" of slavery and that separation was "now or never."

The story of Lincoln's nomination is here told by Murat Halstead, one of the most brilliant journalists of the day and long editor of the Cincinnati Commercial.

THIRD day [May 18, 1860].—After adjournment on Thursday (the second day) there were few men in Chicago who believed it possible to prevent the nomination of Seward. His friends had played their game to admiration and had been victorious on every preliminary skirmish. When the platform had been adopted, inclusive of the Declaration of Independence, they felt themselves already exalted upon the pinnacle of victory. They rejoiced exceedingly, and full of confidence, cried in triumphant tones, "Call the roll of states." But it was otherwise ordered. The opponents of Mr. Seward left the wigwam that evening thoroughly disheartened. Greeley was, as has been widely reported, absolutely "terrified." The nomination of Seward in defiance of his influence would have been a cruel blow. He gave up the ship. . . .

The New Yorkers were exultant. Their bands were playing and the champagne flowing at their headquarters as after a victory.

But there was much done after midnight and before the convention assembled on Friday morning. There were hundreds of Pennsylvanians, Indianians, and Illinoisians who never closed their eyes that night. I saw Henry S. Lane at one o'clock, pale and haggard, with cane under his arm, walking as if for a wager, from one caucus room to another, at the Tremont House. He had been toiling with desperation to bring the Indiana delegation to go as a unit for Lincoln. And then in connection with others, he had been operating to bring the Vermonters and Virginians to the point of deserting Seward.

The Seward men generally abounded in confidence Friday morning. The air was full of rumors of the caucusing the night before, but the opposition of the doubtful states to Seward was an old story; and after the distress of Pennsylvania, Indiana and Company on the subject of Seward's availability had been so freely and ineffectually expressed from the start, it was not imagined their protests would suddenly become effective. The Sewardites marched as usual from their headquarters at the Richmond House after their magnificent band, which was brilliantly uniformed—epaulets shining on their shoulders and white and scarlet feathers waving from their caps—marched under the orders of recognized leaders, in a style that would have done credit to many volunteer military companies. They were about a thousand strong, and protracting their march a little too far, were not all able to get into the wigwam. This was their first misfortune. They were not where they could scream with the best effect in responding to the mention of the name of William H. Seward.

When the convention was called to order, breathless attention was given the proceedings. There was not a space a foot square in the wigwam un-occupied. There were tens of thousands still outside, and torrents of men had rushed in at the three broad doors until not another one could squeeze in.

Everybody was now impatient to begin the work. Mr. Evarts of New York nominated Mr. Seward. Mr. Judd of Illinois nominated Mr. Lincoln.

Everybody felt that the fight was between them and yelled accordingly.

The applause when Mr. Evarts named Seward was enthusiastic. When Mr. Judd named Lincoln, the response was prodigious, rising and raging far beyond the Seward shriek. Presently, upon Caleb B. Smith seconding the nomination of Lincoln, the response was absolutely terrific. It now became the Seward men to make another effort, and when Blair of Michigan sec-onded his nomination,

> At once there rose so wild a yell,
> Within that dark and narrow dell;
> As all the fiends from heaven that fell
> Had pealed the banner cry of hell.

The effect was startling. Hundreds of persons stopped their ears in pain. The shouting was absolutely frantic, shrill and wild. No Comanches, no panthers, ever struck a higher note or gave screams with more infernal in-tensity. Looking from the stage over the vast amphitheater, nothing was to be seen below but thousands of hats—a black, mighty swarm of hats—flying with the velocity of hornets over a mass of human heads, most of the mouths of which were open. Above, all around the galleries, hats and handkerchiefs were flying in the tempest together. The wonder of the thing was that the Seward outside pressure should, so far from New York, be so powerful.

Now the Lincoln men had to try it again, and as Mr. Delano of Ohio on behalf "of a portion of the delegation of that state" seconded the nomination of Lincoln, the uproar was beyond description. Imagine all the hogs ever slaughtered in Cincinnati giving their death squeals together, a score of big steam whistles going (steam at a hundred and sixty pounds per inch), and you conceive something of the same nature. I thought the Seward yell could not be surpassed, but the Lincoln boys were clearly ahead and, feeling their vic-tory, as there was a lull in the storm, took deep breaths all round and gave a concentrated shriek that was positively awful, and accompanied it with stamping that made every plank and pillar in the building quiver.

Henry S. Lane of Indiana leaped upon a table, and swinging hat and cane, performed like an acrobat. The presumption is he shrieked with the rest, as his mouth was desperately wide open; but no one will ever be able to testify that he has positive knowledge of the fact that he made a particle of noise. His individual voice was lost in the aggregate hurricane.

The New York, Michigan, and Wisconsin delegations sat together and were in this tempest very quiet. Many of their faces whitened as the Lincoln *yawp* swelled into a wild hosanna of victory.

The convention now proceeded to business. The most significant vote was that of Virginia, which had been expected solid for Seward, and which now gave him but eight and gave Lincoln fourteen. The New Yorkers looked significantly at each other as this was announced. Then Indiana gave her twenty-six votes for Lincoln. This solid vote was a startler. The division of the first vote caused a fall in Seward stock. It was seen that Lincoln, Cameron, and Bates had the strength to defeat Seward, and it was known that the greater part of the Chase vote would go for Lincoln.

The convention proceeded to a second ballot. Every man was fiercely enlisted in the struggle. The partisans of the various candidates were strung up to such a pitch of excitement as to render them incapable of patience, and the cries of "Call the roll" were fairly hissed through their teeth. The first gain for Lincoln was in New Hampshire. The Chase and the Frémont vote from that state were given him. His next gain was the whole vote of Vermont. This was a blighting blow upon the Seward interest. The New Yorkers started as if an Orsini bomb had exploded. And presently the Cameron vote of Pennsylvania was thrown for Lincoln, increasing his strength forty-four votes. The fate of the day was now determined. New York saw "checkmate" next move and sullenly proceeded with the game, assuming unconsciousness of her inevitable doom. On this ballot Lincoln gained seventy-nine votes. Seward had one hundred and eighty-four and a half votes, Lincoln one hundred and eighty-one. . . .

While this [the third] ballot was taken amid excitement that tested the nerves, the fatal defection from Seward in New England still further appeared, four votes going over from Seward to Lincoln in Massachusetts. The latter received four additional votes from Pennsylvania and fifteen additional votes from Ohio. It was whispered about: "Lincoln's the coming man—will be nominated this ballot." When the roll of states and territories had been called, I had ceased to give attention to any votes but those for Lincoln and had his vote added up as it was given. The number of votes necessary to a choice were two hundred and thirty-three, and I saw under my pencil as the Lincoln column was completed the figures 231½—one vote and a half to give him the nomination. In a moment the fact was whispered about. A hundred pencils had told the same story. The news went over the house wonderfully, and there was a pause. There are always men anxious to distinguish themselves on such occasions. There is nothing that politicians like better than a crisis. I looked up to see who would be the man to give the decisive vote. In about ten ticks of a watch, Cartter of Ohio was up. I had imagined Ohio would be slippery enough for the crisis. And sure enough! Every eye was on Cartter, and everybody who understood the matter at all knew what he was about to do. He said: "I rise (eh), Mr. Chairman (eh), to announce the change of four votes of Ohio from Mr. Chase to Mr. Lincoln." The deed was done. There was a moment's silence. The nerves of the thousands, which through the hours of suspense had been subjected to terrible tension, relaxed, and as deep breaths of relief were taken, there was a noise in the wigwam like the rush of a great wind in the van of a storm—and in another breath, the storm was there. There were thousands cheering with the energy of insanity.

A man who had been on the roof and was engaged in communicating the results of the ballotings to the mighty mass of outsiders now demanded, by gestures at the skylight over the stage, to know what had happened. One of the secretaries, with a tally sheet in his hands, shouted: "Fire the salute! Abe Lincoln is nominated!"

The city was wild with delight. The "Old Abe" men formed processions and bore rails through the streets. Torrents of liquor were poured down the hoarse throats of the multitude. A hundred guns were fired from the top of the Tremont House.

I left the city on the night train on the Fort Wayne and Chicago road. The train consisted of eleven cars, every seat full and people standing in the aisles and corners. I never before saw a company of persons so prostrated by continued excitement. The Lincoln men were not able to respond to the cheers which went up along the road for "Old Abe." They had not only done their duty in that respect, but exhausted their capacity. At every station where there was a village, until after two o'clock, there were tar barrels burning, drums beating, boys carrying rails, and guns, great and small, banging away. The weary passengers were allowed no rest, but plagued by the thundering jar of cannon, the clamor of drums, the glare of bonfires, and the whooping of the boys, who were delighted with the idea of a candidate for the Presidency who thirty years ago split rails on the Sangamon River—classic stream now and forevermore—and whose neighbors named him "honest."

—HALSTEAD, *Caucuses of 1860*

2. "FIRST GALLANT SOUTH CAROLINA NOBLY MADE THE STAND"

Immediately upon the election of Lincoln the legislature of South Carolina called a convention to meet on December 17 to consider the question of secession. The convention met first at Columbia, then adjourned to Charleston, where, on December 20, it voted unanimously for secession, issuing at the same time a Declaration of Causes which emphasized above all the threat to slavery. By February 1861, six other states had joined South Carolina—Mississippi, Florida, Alabama, Georgia, Louisiana, and Texas—and delegates from these states shortly met at Montgomery, Alabama, to organize the Confederate States of America, draw up a Constitution, and name Jefferson Davis of Mississippi as provisional President.

A. SOUTH CAROLINA ORDINANCE OF SECESSION
December 20, 1860

AN *Ordinance to Dissolve the Union between the State of South Carolina and other States united with her under the compact entitled the Constitution of the United States of America:*

We, the people of the State of South Carolina, in Convention assembled, do declare and ordain, and it is hereby declared and ordained, that the ordinance adopted by us in Convention, on the 23d day of May, in the year of our Lord 1788, whereby the Constitution of the United States of America was ratified, and also all Acts and parts of Acts of the General Assembly of this State ratifying the amendments of the said Constitution, are hereby repealed, and that the union now subsisting between South Carolina and other States under the name of the United States of America is hereby dissolved.

B. South Carolina Declaration of Causes of Secession
December 24, 1860

The people of the State of South Carolina in Convention assembled, on the 2d day of April, A.D. 1852, declared that the frequent violations of the Constitution of the United States by the Federal Government, and its encroachments upon the reserved rights of the States, fully justified this State in their withdrawal from the Federal Union; but in deference to the opinions and wishes of the other Slaveholding States, she forbore at that time to exercise this right. Since that time these encroachments have continued to increase, and further forbearance ceases to be a virtue.

And now the State of South Carolina having resumed her separate and equal place among nations, deems it due to herself, to the remaining United States of America, and to the nations of the world, that she should declare the immediate causes which have led to this act. . . .

We affirm that these ends for which this Government was instituted have been defeated, and the Government itself has been destructive of them by the action of the nonslaveholding States. Those States have assumed the right of deciding upon the propriety of our domestic institutions; and have denied the rights of property established in fifteen of the States and recognized by the Constitution; they have denounced as sinful the institution of Slavery; they have permitted the open establishment among them of societies, whose avowed object is to disturb the peace of and eloin the property of the citizens of other States. They have encouraged and assisted thousands of our slaves to leave their homes; and those who remain, have been incited by emissaries, books, and pictures, to servile insurrection.

For twenty-five years this agitation has been steadily increasing, until it has now secured to its aid the power of the common Government. Observing the *forms* of the Constitution, a sectional party has found within that article establishing the Executive Department, the means of subverting the Constitution itself. A geographical line has been drawn across the Union, and all the States north of that line have united in the election of a man to the high office of President of the United States whose opinions and purposes are hostile to Slavery. He is to be intrusted with the administration of the common Government, because he has declared that "Government cannot endure permanently half slave, half free," and that the public mind must rest in the belief that Slavery is in the course of ultimate extinction.

This sectional combination for the subversion of the Constitution has been aided, in some of the States, by elevating to citizenship persons who, by the supreme law of the land, are incapable of becoming citizens; and their votes have been used to inaugurate a new policy, hostile to the South, and destructive of its peace and safety.

On the 4th of March next this party will take possession of the Government. It has announced that the South shall be excluded from the common territory, that the Judicial tribunal shall be made sectional, and that a war must be waged against Slavery until it shall cease throughout the United States.

The guarantees of the Constitution will then no longer exist; the equal rights of the States will be lost. The Slaveholding States will no longer have the power of self-government, or self-protection, and the Federal Government will have become their enemy.

Sectional interest and animosity will deepen the irritation; and all hope of remedy is rendered vain, by the fact that the public opinion at the North has invested a great political error with the sanctions of a more erroneous religious belief.

We, therefore, the people of South Carolina, by our delegates in Convention assembled, appealing to the Supreme Judge of the world for the rectitude of our intentions, have solemnly declared that the Union heretofore existing between this State and the other States of North America is dissolved, and that the State of South Carolina has resumed her position among the nations of the world, as a separate and independent state, with full power to levy war, conclude peace, contract alliances, establish commerce, and to do all other acts and things which independent States may of right do.

—MOORE, ed., *The Rebellion Record*

3. "SHE HAS LEFT US IN PASSION AND PRIDE"

Although Oliver Wendell Holmes published his first volume of poems in 1836 he devoted himself, for the next twenty years, almost entirely to medicine, serving as professor of anatomy and dean of the Harvard Medical School. With the founding of the Atlantic Monthly *in 1857 he came into his own as essayist and poet. To this magazine he contributed* The Autocrat of the Breakfast Table *and* The Professor at the Breakfast Table, *and in it appeared many of his best-known poems. It was to the* Atlantic, *too, that he contributed his famous "My Hunt after the Captain"—the story of his search for his son, wounded at Antietam.*

This poem is notable chiefly for its expression in poetry of what Lincoln said in his First Inaugural Address.

Brother Jonathan's Lament for Sister Caroline

She has gone,—she has left us in passion and pride,—
Our stormy-browed sister, so long at our side!
She has torn her own star from our firmament's glow,
And turned on her brother the face of a foe!

O Caroline, Caroline, child of the sun,
We can never forget that our hearts have been one,—
Our foreheads both sprinkled in Liberty's name,
From the fountain of blood with the finger of flame!

You were always too ready to fire at a touch;
But we said, "She is hasty,—she does not mean much."
We have scowled, when you uttered some turbulent threat;
But Friendship still whispered, "Forgive and forget!"

Has our love all died out? Have its altars grown cold?
Has the curse come at last which the fathers foretold?
Then Nature must teach us the strength of the chain
That her petulant children would sever in vain.

They may fight till the buzzards are gorged with their spoil,
Till the harvest grows black as it rots in the soil,
Till the wolves and the catamounts troop from their caves,
And the shark tracks the pirate, the lord of the waves:

In vain is the strife! When its fury is past,
Their fortunes must flow in one channel at last,
As the torrents that rush from the mountains of snow
Roll mingled in peace through the valleys below.

Our Union is river, lake, ocean, and sky:
Man breaks not the medal, when God cuts the die!
Though darkened with sulphur, though cloven with steel,
The blue arch will brighten, the waters will heal!

O Caroline, Caroline, child of the sun,
There are battles with Fate that can never be won!
The star-flowering banner must never be furled,
For its blossoms of light are the hope of the world!

Go, then, our rash sister! afar and aloof,
Run wild in the sunshine away from our roof;
But when your heart aches and your feet have grown sore,
Remember the pathway that leads to our door!
                                                —HOLMES, *Poems*
March 25, 1861

4. LINCOLN REFUSES TO COMPROMISE ON SLAVERY

*Secession brought frantic efforts to find some compromise which might
restore the Union and avoid the danger of a brothers' war. The most prominent of these proposals was the Crittenden Compromise which provided for
the extension of the Missouri Compromise line of 36°-30′ westward to Cali-*

fornia—a proposal which would have opened new territory in the West to slavery. It was on this issue that Lincoln, who was otherwise conciliatory, refused to yield. E. B. Washburne was a representative from the Galena district of Illinois, a friend of both Lincoln and Grant, and one of four brothers who were in Congress—the others all spelled their name without the final "e." James T. Hale was a representative from Pennsylvania. Seward, Lincoln's principal rival for the Republican nomination, had already accepted Lincoln's offer to make him Secretary of State.

A. LETTER TO E. B. WASHBURNE
(Private and Confidential)

Springfield, Ill., December 13, 1860

Hon. E. B. Washburne.

My Dear Sir:—Yours of the 10th is received. Prevent, as far as possible, any of our friends from demoralizing themselves and our cause by entertaining propositions for compromise of any sort on "slavery extension." There is no possible compromise upon it but which puts us under again, and leaves all our work to do over again. Whether it be a Missouri line or Eli Thayer's popular sovereignty, it is all the same. Let either be done, and immediately filibustering and extending slavery recommences. On that point hold firm, as with a chain of steel.

Yours as ever,

A. LINCOLN.

B. LETTER TO JAMES T. HALE
(Confidential)

Springfield, Illinois, January 11, 1861

My Dear Sir: Yours of the 6th is received. I answer it only because I fear you would misconstrue my silence. What is our present condition? We have just carried an election on principles fairly stated to the people. Now we are told in advance the Government shall be broken up unless we surrender to those we have beaten, before we take the offices. In this they are either attempting to play upon us or they are in dead earnest. Either way, if we surrender, it is the end of us and of the Government. They will repeat the experiment upon us *ad libitum*. A year will not pass till we shall have to take Cuba as a condition upon which they will stay in the Union. They now have the Constitution under which we have lived over seventy years, and acts of Congress of their own framing, with no prospect of their being changed; and they can never have a more shallow pretext for breaking up the Government, or extorting a compromise, than now. There is in my judgment but one compromise which would really settle the slavery question, and that would be a prohibition against acquiring any more territory.

C. LETTER TO W. H. SEWARD
(Private and Confidential)

Springfield, Illinois, February 1, 1861

My Dear Sir: . . . I say now . . . as I have all the while said, that on the territorial question—that is, the question of extending slavery under the national auspices—I am inflexible. I am for no compromise which assists or permits the extension of the institution on soil owned by the nation. And any trick by which the nation is to acquire territory, and then allow some local authority to spread slavery over it, is as obnoxious as any other. I take it that to effect some such result as this, and to put us again on the highroad to a slave empire, is the object of all these proposed compromises. I am against it. As to fugitive slaves, District of Columbia, slave trade among the slave States, and whatever springs of necessity from the fact that the institution is amongst us, I care but little, so that what is done be comely and not altogether outrageous. Nor do I care much about New Mexico, if further extension were hedged against.

—Complete Works of Abraham Lincoln

5. LINCOLN WRITES HIS INAUGURAL ADDRESS

This account of Lincoln's preparation for his Inauguration is given us by his law partner and friend, William Henry Herndon. It was in 1844 that Herndon joined Lincoln's office; when Lincoln went to Washington he asked Herndon to keep the old sign, Lincoln & Herndon, until he returned. After Lincoln's death Herndon devoted himself to collecting materials for a biography of his great friend. Some of these were sold to Ward Lamon and others were made available to other biographers. As an old man Herndon produced, in association with Jesse Weik, Herndon's Lincoln. The biography was notable for its frankness about Lincoln's early life and his marriage, and for its support to the Ann Rutledge story.

LATE in January Mr. Lincoln informed me that he was ready to begin the preparation of his inaugural address. He had, aside from his law books and the few gilded volumes that ornamented the centre-table in his parlor at home, comparatively no library. He never seemed to care to own or collect books. On the other hand I had a very respectable collection, and was adding to it every day. To my library Lincoln very frequently had access. When, therefore, he began on his inaugural speech he told me what works he intended to consult. I looked for a long list, but when he went over it I was greatly surprised. He asked me to furnish him with Henry Clay's great speech delivered in 1850; Andrew Jackson's proclamation against Nullification; and a copy of the Constitution. He afterwards called for Webster's reply to Hayne, a speech which he read when he lived at New Salem, and which he always regarded as the grandest specimen of American oratory.

With these few "volumes," and no further sources of reference, he locked himself up in a room upstairs over a store across the street from the State House, and there, cut off from all communication and intrusion, he prepared the address. Though composed amid the unromantic surroundings of a dingy, dusty, and neglected back room, the speech has become a memorable document. . . .

Early in February the last item of preparation for the journey to Washington had been made. Mr. Lincoln had disposed of his household goods and furniture to a neighbor, had rented his house; and as these constituted all the property he owned in Illinois there was no further occasion for concern on that score. In the afternoon of his last day in Springfield he came down to our office to examine some papers and confer with me about certain legal matters in which he still felt some interest. On several previous occasions he had told me he was coming over to the office "to have a long talk with me," as he expressed it. We ran over the books and arranged for the completion of all unsettled and unfinished matters. In some cases he had certain requests to make—certain lines of procedure he wished me to observe. After these things were all disposed of he crossed to the opposite side of the room and threw himself down on the old office sofa, which, after many years of service, had been moved against the wall for support.

He lay for some moments, his face towards the ceiling, without either of us speaking. Presently he inquired, "Billy,"—he always called me by that name,—"how long have we been together?" "Over sixteen years," I answered. "We've never had a cross word during all that time, have we?" to which I returned a vehement, "No, indeed we have not." He then recalled some incidents of his early practice and took great pleasure in delineating the ludicrous features of many a lawsuit on the circuit. It was at this last interview in Springfield that he told me of the efforts that had been made by other lawyers to supplant me in the partnership with him. He insisted that such men were weak creatures, who, to use his own language, "hoped to secure a law practice by hanging to his coattail."

I never saw him in a more cheerful mood. He gathered a bundle of books and papers he wished to take with him and started to go; but before leaving he made the strange request that the sign-board which swung on its rusty hinges at the foot of the stairway should remain. "Let it hang there undisturbed," he said, with a significant lowering of his voice. "Give our clients to understand that the election of a President makes no change in the firm of Lincoln and Herndon. If I live I'm coming back some time, and then we'll go right on practicing law as if nothing had ever happened." He lingered for a moment as if to take a last look at the old quarters, and then passed through the door into the narrow hallway.

I accompanied him downstairs. On the way he spoke of the unpleasant features surrounding the Presidential office. "I am sick of office-holding already," he complained, "and I shudder when I think of the tasks that are still ahead." He said the sorrow of parting from his old associates was deeper than most persons would imagine, but it was more marked in his case because of the feeling which had become irrepressible that he would never return alive. I argued against the thought, characterizing it as an illusory notion not in harmony or keeping with the popular ideal of a President. "But it is in keeping with my philosophy," was his quick retort.

Our conversation was frequently broken in upon by the interruptions of passers-by, who, each in succession, seemed desirous of claiming his attention. At length he broke away from them all. Grasping my hand warmly and with a fervent "Good-bye," he disappeared down the street, and never came back to the office again.

—WEIK, *Herndon's Lincoln*

6. LINCOLN IS INAUGURATED

On February 11 Lincoln left Springfield for Washington, planning to make a number of speeches en route. Because of threats of assassination, which his friends took seriously, the last stage of the trip, from Philadelphia to Washington, was made in complete secrecy.

Three descriptions are here given of the Inauguration—one from Herndon; another, written on the day itself, from young Wilder Dwight, member of a distinguished Massachusetts family and major of the 2nd Massachusetts Infantry; and the third from the mysterious Public Man whose identity—if indeed he ever existed—is still a secret. Frank Maloy Anderson, the most careful student of the "Public Man," concludes that the "Diary" itself was a fabrication, and that the author of the fabrication was probably Samuel Ward. Herndon's book was not published until a decade after the appearance, in the North American Review, *of the "Diary of a Public Man," and it may have been from this "Diary" that Herndon took his story of Douglas holding Lincoln's hat at the Inauguration. Whether the story is true or not, it belongs to the folklore of our history.*

A. HERNDON DESCRIBES THE INAUGURATION

HAVING at last reached his destination in safety, Mr. Lincoln spent the few days preceding his inauguration at Willard's Hotel, receiving an uninterrupted stream of visitors and friends. In the few unoccupied moments allotted him, he was carefully revising his inaugural address. On the morning of the 4th of March he rode from his hotel with Mr. Buchanan in an open barouche to the Capitol. There, slightly pale and nervous, he was introduced to the assembled multitude by his own friend Edward D. Baker, and in a fervid and impressive manner delivered his address. At its conclusion the customary oath was administered by the venerable Chief Justice Taney, and he was now clothed with all the powers and privileges of Chief Magistrate of the nation. He accompanied Mr. Buchanan to the White House and here the historic bachelor of Lancaster bade him farewell, bespeaking for him a peaceful, prosperous, and successful administration.

One who witnessed the impressive scene left the following graphic description of the inauguration and its principal incidents: "Near noon I found myself a member of the motley crowd gathered about the side entrance to Willard's Hotel. Soon an open barouche drove up, and the only occupant stepped out. A large, heavy, awkward-moving man, far advanced in years, short and thin gray hair, full face, plentifully seamed and wrinkled, head curiously inclined to the left shoulder, a low-crowned, broad-brimmed silk hat, an immense white cravat like a poultice, thrusting the old-fashioned standing collar up to the ears, dressed in black throughout, with swallow-tail coat not of the newest style. It was President Buchanan, calling to take his successor to the Capitol. In a few minutes he reappeared, with Mr. Lincoln on his arm; the two took seats side-by-side, and the carriage rolled away, followed by a rather disorderly and certainly not very imposing procession.

"I had ample time to walk to the Capitol, and no difficulty in securing a place where everything could be seen and heard to the best advantage. The attendance at the inauguration was, they told me, unusually small, many being kept away by anticipated disturbance, as it had been rumored—truly, too—that General Scott himself was fearful of an outbreak, and had made all possible military preparations to meet the emergency. A square platform had been built out from the steps to the eastern portico, with benches for distinguished spectators on three sides. Douglas, the only one I recognized, sat at the extreme end of the seat on the right of the narrow passage leading from the steps.

"There was no delay, and the gaunt form of the President-elect was soon visible, slowly making his way to the front. To me, at least, he was completely metamorphosed—partly by his own fault, and partly through the efforts of injudicious friends and ambitious tailors. He was raising (to gratify a very young lady, it is said) a crop of whiskers, of the blacking-brush variety, coarse, stiff, and ungraceful; and in so doing spoiled, or at least seriously impaired, a face which, though never handsome, had in its original state a peculiar power and pathos. On the present occasion the whiskers were reinforced by brand-new clothes from top to toe; black dresscoat, instead of the usual frock, black cloth or satin vest, black pantaloons, and a glossy hat evidently just out of the box. To cap the climax of novelty, he carried a huge ebony cane, with a gold head the size of an egg. In these, to him, strange habiliments, he looked so miserably uncomfortable that I could not help pitying him.

"Reaching the platform, his discomfort was visibly increased by not knowing what to do with hat and cane; and so he stood there, the target for ten thousand eyes, holding cane in one hand and hat in the other, the very picture of helpless embarrassment. After some hesitation he pushed the cane into a corner of the railing, but could not find a place for the hat except on the floor, where I could see he did not like to risk it. Douglas, who fully took in the situation, came to the rescue of his old friend and rival, and held the precious hat until the owner needed it again; a service which, if predicted two years before, would probably have astonished him.

"The oath of office was administered by Chief Justice Taney, whose black robes, attenuated figure, and cadaverous countenance reminded me of a galvanized corpse. Then the President came forward, and read his inaugural address in a clear and distinct voice. It was attentively listened to by all, but the closest listener was Douglas, who leaned forward as if to catch every word, nodding his head emphatically at those passages which most pleased him. There was some applause, not very much nor very enthusiastic.

"I must not forget to mention the presence of a Mephistopheles in the person of Senator Wigfall, of Texas, who stood with folded arms leaning against the doorway of the Capitol, looking down upon the crowd and the ceremony with a contemptuous air, which sufficiently indicated his opinion of the whole performance. To him the Southern Confederacy was already an accomplished fact. He lived to see it the saddest of fictions."

—WEIK, Herndon's Lincoln

B. WILDER DWIGHT SEES LINCOLN INAUGURATED

Washington, March 4, 1861

Dear Father,—

This morning broke badly, but at noon the sky cleared. I remained quietly at Willard's, and was present when Mr. Buchanan came to receive the President elect, and saw the interview, which was a formal one; then I saw Lincoln and Buchanan take their carriage, and, by back streets, reached the Capitol grounds, and got a good place.

Soon Lincoln and Judge Taney, followed by Buchanan and the other judges, etc. appeared. The band played Hail Columbia. The crowd was immense. The Capitol steps were covered with uniforms, etc. Baker, of Oregon, for the Committee of Arrangements, announced that Mr. Lincoln would speak; and when Abraham rose and came forward and rang out the words, 'Fellow-citizens of the *United* States,' he loomed and grew and was ugly no longer. I was not very near, but heard him perfectly. The address you will read, and like, I hope. Its effect was very good. An immense concourse—thousands—stood uncovered and silent, except occasional applause; the voice clear and ringing; the manner very good, often impressive, and even solemn; the words I think to the point, direct and clear. The scene itself was of its own kind. And I must say its effect upon me was far greater than I had supposed.

When the address closed and the cheering subsided, Taney rose, and, almost as tall as Lincoln, he administered the oath, Lincoln repeating it; and as the words, 'preserve, protect and defend the Constitution' came ringing out, he bent and kissed the book; and for one, I breathed freer and gladder than for months. The man looked a man, and acted a man and a President. So much for the inauguration.

—DWIGHT, The Life and Letters of Wilder Dwight

C. The Public Man Attends the Inauguration

Washington, March 4th.—I am sure we must attribute to the mischievous influence of the Blairs the deplorable display of perfectly unnecessary, and worse than unnecessary, military force which marred the inauguration to-day, and jarred so scandalously upon the tone of the inaugural. Nothing could have been more ill-advised or more ostentatious than the way in which the troops were thrust everywhere upon the public attention, even to the roofs of the houses on Pennsylvania Avenue, on which little squads of sharp-shooters were absurdly stationed. I never expected to experience such a sense of mortification and shame in my own country as I felt to-day, in entering the Capitol through hedges of marines armed to the teeth. ——, of Massachusetts, who felt as I did—indeed, I have yet to find a man who did not—recalled to me, as we sat in the Senate-chamber, the story of old Josiah Quincy, the President of Harvard College, who, having occasion to visit the Boston court-house during one of the fugitive-slave excitements in that city, found the way barred by an iron chain. The sentinels on duty recognized him, and stooped to raise the chain, that he might pass in, but the old man indignantly refused, and turned away, declaring that he would never pass into a Massachusetts court-house by the favor of armed men or under a chain.

It is really amazing that General Scott should have consented to preside over such a pestilent and foolish parade of force at this time, and I can only attribute his doing so to the agitation in which he is kept by the constant pressure upon him from Virginia, of which I heard only too much to-day from ——, who returned yesterday from Richmond. Fortunately, all passed off well, but it is appalling to think of the mischief which might have been done by a single evil-disposed person to-day. A blank cartridge fired from a window on Pennsylvania Avenue might have disconcerted all our hopes, and thrown the whole country into inextricable confusion.

That nothing of the sort was done, or even so much as attempted, is the most conclusive evidence that could be asked of the groundlessness of the rumors and old women's tales on the strength of which General Scott has been led into this great mistake. Even without this the atmosphere of the day would have been depressing enough. It has been one of our disagreeable, clear, windy, Washington spring days. The arrangements within the Capitol were awkward, and very ill attended to. No one was at his ease. Neither Mr. Buchanan nor Mr. Lincoln appeared to advantage. Poor Chief-Justice Taney could hardly speak plainly, in his uncontrollable agitation.

I must, however, except Senator Douglas, whose conduct can not be over-praised. I saw him for a moment in the morning, when he told me that he meant to put himself as prominently forward in the ceremonies as he properly could, and to leave no doubt on any one's mind of his determination to stand by the new Administration in the performance of its first great duty to maintain the Union. I watched him carefully. He made his way not without difficulty—for there was literally no sort of order in the arrangements—

to the front of the throng directly beside Mr. Lincoln, when he prepared to read the address. A miserable little rickety table had been provided for the President, on which he could hardly find room for his hat, and Senator Douglas, reaching forward, took it with a smile and held it during the delivery of the address. It was a trifling act, but a symbolical one, and not to be forgotten, and it attracted much attention all around me.

Mr. Lincoln was pale and very nervous, and did not read his address very well, which is not much to be wondered at under all the circumstances. His spectacles troubled him, his position was crowded and uncomfortable, and, in short, nothing had been done which ought to have been done to render the performance of this great duty either dignified in its effect or, physically speaking, easy for the President.

The great crowd in the grounds behaved very well, but manifested little or no enthusiasm, and at one point in the speech Mr. Lincoln was thrown completely off his balance for a moment by a crash not far in front of him among the people, followed by something which for an instant looked like a struggle. I was not undisturbed myself, nor were those who were immediately about me; but it appeared directly that nothing more serious had happened than the fall from a breaking bough of a spectator who had clambered up into one of the trees.

Mr. Lincoln's agitation was remarked, and I have no doubt must have been caused by the impressions which the alarmists have been trying so sedulously to make on his mind, and which the exaggerated preparations of General Scott to-day are but too likely to have deepened.

—RICE, ed., "The Diary of a Public Man"

7. "WE ARE NOT ENEMIES BUT FRIENDS"

In his eloquent and moving Inaugural Address, Lincoln insisted that the Union is perpetual and secession unconstitutional and void, and asserted that the government was determined to maintain its authority. At the same time he argued the physical impossibility of separation and urged the Southern people to return to their old place in the American household. The moving final paragraph was probably Seward's contribution.

THAT there are persons in one section or another who seek to destroy the Union at all events and are glad of any pretext to do it, I will neither affirm nor deny; but if there be such, I need address no word to them. To those, however, who really love the Union may I not speak?

Before entering upon so grave a matter as the destruction of our national fabric, with all its benefits, its memories, and its hopes, would it not be wise to ascertain precisely why we do it? Will you hazard so desperate a step while there is any possibility that any portion of the ills you fly from have no real existence? Will you, while the certain ills you fly to are greater than all the real ones you fly from—will you risk the commission of so fearful a mistake? . . .

Physically speaking, we cannot separate. We cannot remove our respective sections from each other, nor build an impassable wall between them. A husband and wife may be divorced and go out of the presence and beyond the reach of each other, but the different parts of our country cannot do this. They cannot but remain face to face, and intercourse, either amicable or hostile, must continue between them. Is it possible, then, to make that intercourse more advantageous or more satisfactory after separation than before? Can aliens make treaties easier than friends can make laws? Can treaties be more faithfully enforced between aliens than laws can among friends? Suppose you go to war, you cannot fight always; and when, after much loss on both sides, and no gain on either, you cease fighting, the identical old questions as to terms of intercourse are again upon you.

This country, with its institutions, belongs to the people who inhabit it. Whenever they shall grow weary of the existing government, they can exercise their constitutional right of amending it or their revolutionary right to dismember or overthrow it. . . .

Why should there not be a patient confidence in the ultimate justice of the people? Is there any better or equal hope in the world? In our present differences is either party without faith of being in the right? If the Almighty Ruler of nations, with His eternal truth and justice, be on your side of the North, or on yours of the South, that truth and that justice will surely prevail by the judgment of this great tribunal of the American people.

By the frame of the government under which we live, this same people have wisely given their public servants but little power for mischief; and have, with equal wisdom, provided for the return of that little to their own hands at very short intervals. While the people retain their virtue and vigilance, no administration, by any extreme of wickedness or folly, can very seriously injure the government in the short space of four years.

My countrymen, one and all, think calmly and well upon this whole subject. Nothing valuable can be lost by taking time. If there be an object to hurry any of you in hot haste to a step which you would never take deliberately, that object will be frustrated by taking time; but no good object can be frustrated by it. Such of you as are now dissatisfied still have the old Constitution unimpaired, and, on the sensitive point, the laws of your own framing under it, while the new administration will have no immediate power, if it would, to change either. If it were admitted that you who are dissatisfied hold the right side in the dispute, there still is no single good reason for precipitate action. Intelligence, patriotism, Christianity, and a firm reliance on Him who has never yet forsaken this favored land, are still competent to adjust in the best way all our present difficulty.

In your hands, my dissatisfied fellow countrymen, and not in mine, is the momentous issue of civil war. The government will not assail you. You can have no conflict without being yourselves the aggressors. You have no oath registered in heaven to destroy the government, while I shall have the most solemn one to "preserve, protect, and defend" it.

I am loath to close. We are not enemies, but friends. We must not be enemies. Though passion may have strained, it must not break, our bonds of affection. The mystic cords of memory, stretching from every battlefield and patriot grave to every living heart and hearthstone all over this broad land, will yet swell the chorus of the Union when again touched, as surely they will be, by the better angels of our nature.

—LINCOLN, "First Inaugural Address"

8. MR. LINCOLN HAMMERS OUT A CABINET

Because Lincoln was the first President elected by the Republican party, he faced peculiar difficulties in making up his Cabinet. It seemed wise to unite the party by giving places to as many of the principal Republican leaders as possible, whether their views agreed with his or not. He therefore selected two former Democrats, Salmon P. Chase of Ohio and Gideon Welles of Connecticut, and three former Whigs, the radical antislavery leader, William H. Seward of New York, a moderate Missourian, Edward Bates, and Caleb Smith of Indiana. The weakest appointment, as time proved, was a practical politician whose political affiliations had been varied—Simon Cameron of Pennsylvania.

Thurlow Weed, who here describes Lincoln's troubles, was editor of the Albany Evening Journal *and a political boss who, Henry Adams thought, was a "model of political management and patient address."*

M R. LINCOLN remarked, smiling, that he supposed I had had some experience in cabinet-making; that he had a job on hand, and as he had never learned that trade, he was disposed to avail himself of the suggestions of friends. Taking up his figure, I replied that though never a boss cabinetmaker, I had as a journeyman been occasionally consulted about state cabinets, and that although President Taylor once talked with me about reforming his cabinet, I had never been concerned in or presumed to meddle with the formation of an original Federal cabinet, and that he was the first President elect I had ever seen. The question thus opened became the subject of conversation at intervals during that and the following day. I say at intervals, because many hours were consumed in talking of the public men connected with former administrations, interspersed, illustrated, and seasoned pleasantly with Mr. Lincoln's stories, anecdotes, etc. And here I feel called upon to vindicate Mr. Lincoln, as far as my opportunities and observation go, from the frequent imputation of telling indelicate and ribald stories. I saw much of him during his whole presidential term, with familiar friends and alone, when he talked without restraint, but I never heard him use a profane or indecent word or tell a story that might not be repeated in the presence of ladies.

Mr. Lincoln observed that the making of a cabinet, now that he had it to do, was by no means as easy as he had supposed; that he had, even before the result of the election was known, assuming the probability of success, fixed upon the two leading members of his cabinet, but that in looking about for suitable men to fill the other departments, he had been much embarrassed, partly from his want of acquaintance with the prominent men of the day, and partly, he believed, that while the population of the country had immensely increased, really great men were scarcer than they used to be. He then inquired whether I had any suggestions of a general character affecting the selection of a cabinet to make. I replied that, along with the question of ability, integrity, and experience, he ought, in the selection of his cabinet, to find men whose firmness and courage fitted them for the revolutionary ordeal which was about to test the strength of our government, and that in my judgment it was desirable that at least two members of his cabinet should be selected from slave-holding States. He inquired whether, in the emergency which I so much feared, they could be trusted, adding that he did not quite like to hear Southern journals and Southern speakers insisting that there must be no "coercion"; that while he had no disposition to coerce anybody, yet after he had taken an oath to execute the laws, he should not care to see them violated. I remarked that there were Union men in Maryland, Virginia, North Carolina, and Tennessee, for whose loyalty, under the most trying circumstances and in any event, I would vouch. "Would you rely on such men if their states should secede?" "Yes, sir; the men whom I have in my mind can always be relied on." "Well," said Mr. Lincoln, "let us have the names of your white crows, such ones as you think fit for the cabinet." I then named Henry Winter Davis, of Maryland; John M. Botts, of Virginia; John A. Gilmer, of North Carolina; and Bailey Peyton, of Tennessee.

As the conversation progressed, Mr. Lincoln remarked that he intended to invite Governor Seward to take the State and Governor Chase the Treasury Department, remarking that, aside from their long experience in public affairs and their eminent fitness, they were prominently before the people and the convention as competitors for the Presidency, each having higher claims than his own for the place which he was to occupy. On naming Gideon Welles as the gentleman he thought of as the representative of New England in the cabinet, I remarked that I thought he could find several New England gentlemen whose selection for a place in his cabinet would be more acceptable to the people of New England. "But," said Mr. Lincoln, "we must remember that the Republican party is constituted of two elements, and that we must have men of Democratic as well as of Whig antecedents in the cabinet."

Acquiescing in this view, the subject was passed over. And then Mr. Lincoln remarked that Judge Blair had been suggested. I inquired, "What Judge Blair?" and was answered, "Judge Montgomery Blair." "Has he been suggested by any one except his father, Francis P. Blair, Sr.?" "Your question," said Mr. Lincoln, "reminds me of a story," and he proceeded with infinite humor to tell a story, which I would repeat if I did not fear that its spirit and effect would be lost. I finally remarked that if we were legislating on the question, I should move to strike out the name of Montgomery Blair and insert that of Henry Winter Davis. Mr. Lincoln laughingly replied, "Davis has been posting you up on this question. He came from Maryland

and has got Davis on the brain. Maryland must, I think, be like New Hampshire, a good state to move from." And then he told a story of a witness in a neighboring county, who, on being asked his age, replied, "Sixty." Being satisfied that he was much older, the judge repeated the question, and on receiving the same answer, admonished the witness, saying that the court knew him to be much older than sixty. "Oh," said the witness, "you're thinking about that fifteen year that I lived down on the eastern shore of Maryland; that was so much lost time, and don't count." This story, I perceived, was thrown in to give the conversation a new direction. It was very evident that the selection of Montgomery Blair was a fixed fact, and although I subsequently ascertained the reasons and influences that controlled the selection of other members of the cabinet, I never did find out how Mr. Blair got there.

—The Autobiography of Thurlow Weed

9. SEWARD TRIES TO TAKE CHARGE OF THE LINCOLN ADMINISTRATION

Like William Pitt, a century earlier, Seward was convinced that only he could save his country. As Gideon Welles observed, "Seward liked to be called premier." His "Thoughts for the President's Consideration" were intended to establish his dominance over Lincoln. Seward's proposal to substitute a series of foreign wars for a domestic one revealed, however, a lack of judgment that has never been satisfactorily explained. Lincoln's reply was a masterly rebuke, but one which did not alienate the self-confident secretary. It made clear, however, that Lincoln was going to run his own administration.

A. MEMORANDUM FROM SECRETARY SEWARD
APRIL 1, 1861

Some Thoughts for the President's Consideration

First. We are at the end of a month's administration, and yet without a policy either domestic or foreign.

Second. This, however, is not culpable, and it has even been unavoidable. The presence of the Senate, with the need to meet applications for patronage, have prevented attention to other and more grave matters.

Third. But further delay to adopt and prosecute our policies for both domestic and foreign affairs would not only bring scandal on the administration, but danger upon the country.

Fourth. To do this we must dismiss the applicants for office. But how? I suggest that we make the local appointments forthwith, leaving foreign or general ones for ulterior and occasional action.

Fifth. The policy at home. I am aware that my views are singular, and perhaps not sufficiently explained. My system is built upon this idea as a ruling one, namely, that we must

CHANGE THE QUESTION BEFORE THE PUBLIC FROM ONE UPON SLAVERY, OR
ABOUT SLAVERY, for a question upon UNION OR DISUNION:

In other words, from what would be regarded as a party question, to one
of patriotism or union.

The occupation or evacuation of Fort Sumter, although not in fact a
slavery or a party question, is so regarded. Witness the temper manifested
by the Republicans in the free States, and even by the Union men in the
South.

I would therefore terminate it as a safe means for changing the issue. I
deem it fortunate that the last administration created the necessity.

For the rest, I would simultaneously defend and reinforce all the ports in
the gulf, and have the navy recalled from foreign stations to be prepared for a
blockade. Put the island of Key West under martial law.

This will raise distinctly the question of union or disunion. I would maintain every fort and possession in the South.

FOR FOREIGN NATIONS

I would demand explanations from Spain and France, categorically, at
once.

I would seek explanations from Great Britain and Russia, and send agents
into Canada, Mexico, and Central America to rouse a vigorous continental
spirit of independence on this continent against European intervention.

And, if satisfactory explanations are not received from Spain and France,

Would convene Congress and declare war against them.

But whatever policy we adopt, there must be an energetic prosecution of
it.

For this purpose it must be somebody's business to pursue and direct it
incessantly.

Either the President must do it himself, and be all the while active in it, or

Devolve it on some member of his cabinet. Once adopted, debates on it
must end, and all agree and abide.

It is not in my especial province;

But I neither seek to evade nor assume responsibility.

B. REPLY TO SECRETARY SEWARD'S MEMORANDUM

Executive Mansion, April 1, 1861

My dear Sir: Since parting with you I have been considering your paper
dated this day, and entitled "Some Thoughts for the President's Consideration." The first proposition in it is, *"First,* We are at the end of a month's
administration, and yet without a policy either domestic or foreign."

At the beginning of that month, in the inaugural, I said: "The power
confided to me will be used to hold, occupy, and possess the property and
places belonging to the government, and to collect the duties and imposts."
This had your distinct approval at the time; and, taken in connection with the
order I immediately gave General Scott, directing him to employ every

means in his power to strengthen and hold the forts, comprises the exact domestic policy you now urge, with the single exception that it does not propose to abandon Fort Sumter.

Again, I do not perceive how the reinforcement of Fort Sumter would be done on a slavery or a party issue, while that of Fort Pickens would be on a more national and patriotic one.

The news received yesterday in regard to St. Domingo certainly brings a new item within the range of our foreign policy; but up to that time we have been preparing circulars and instructions to ministers and the like, all in perfect harmony, without even a suggestion that we had no foreign policy.

Upon your closing propositions—that "whatever policy we adopt, there must be an energetic prosecution of it.

"For this purpose it must be somebody's business to pursue and direct it incessantly.

"Either the President must do it himself, and be all the while active in it, or

"Devolve it on some member of his cabinet. Once adopted, debates on it must end, and all agree and abide"—I remark that if this must be done, I must do it. When a general line of policy is adopted, I apprehend there is no danger of its being changed without good reason, or continuing to be a subject of unnecessary debate; still, upon points arising in its progress I wish, and suppose I am entitled to have, the advice of all the cabinet.

Your obedient servant,

A. LINCOLN.

—*Complete Works of Abraham Lincoln*

10. THE CONFEDERACY ORGANIZES AT MONTGOMERY

On February 4, 1861, a convention, with representatives from six Southern states, met at Montgomery, Alabama, to organize the government of the Confederacy. This convention drew up a Constitution, chose a provisional President and Vice-President, and acted as a legislature pending the election of a regular Congress.

Thomas Cooper DeLeon, who here describes the political atmosphere of the temporary capital, was a litterateur of some prominence in his day who served in the Confederate Army throughout the war; his brother, David C. DeLeon, was Surgeon General of the Confederacy.

MONTGOMERY, like Rome, sits on seven hills. The city is picturesque in perch upon bold, high bluffs, which, on the city side, cut sheer down to the Alabama river; here, seemingly scarce more than a biscuit-toss across. From the opposite bank spread great flat stretches of marsh and meadow land, while on the other side, behind the town, the formation swells and undulates with gentle rise. As in most southern inland towns, its one great artery, Main street, runs from the river bluffs to the Capitol, perched on a high hill a full mile away. This street, wide and sandy, was in the cradle days badly paved, but rather closely built up.

Nor was the Capitol a peculiarly stately pile, either in size or architectural effect. Still it dominated the lesser structures, as it stared down the street with quite a Roman rigor. The staff upon its dome bore the flag of the new nation, run up there shortly after the Congress met by the hands of a noted daughter of Virginia. Miss Letitia Tyler was not only a representative of proud Old Dominion blood, but was also granddaughter of the ex-President of the United States, whose eldest son, Robert, lived in the new Capital. All Montgomery had flocked to Capitol Hill in holiday attire; bells rang and cannon boomed, and the throng—including all members of the government—stood bareheaded as the fair Virginian threw that flag to the breeze. Then a poet-priest—who later added the sword to the quill—spoke a solemn benediction on the people, their flag and their cause; and a shout went up from every throat that told they meant to honor and strive for it; if need be, to die for it. . . .

On the whole, the effect of Montgomery upon the newly arrived was rather pleasing, with a something rather provincial, quite in keeping with its location inland. Streets, various in length, uncertain in direction and impractical as to pavement, ran into Main street at many points; and most of them were closely built with pretty houses, all of them surrounded by gardens and many by handsome grounds. Equidistant from the end of Main street and from each other, stood, in these cradle days, the two hotels of which the Capital could boast. Montgomery Hall, of bitter memory—like the much-sung "Raven of Zurich," for uncleanliness of nest and length of bill—had been the resort of country merchants, horse and cattle-men; but now the Solon of the hour dwelt therein, with the possible hero of many a field. The Exchange—of rather more pretentions and vastly more comfort—was at that time in the hands of a northern firm, who "could keep a hotel." The latter was political headquarters—the President, the Cabinet and a swarm of the possible great residing there.

Montgomery was Washington over again; only on a smaller scale, and with the avidity and agility in pursuit of the spoils somewhat enhanced by the freshness of scent.

"The President is at this house?" I queried of the ex-member of Congress next me at dinner. "But he does not appear, I suppose?"

"Oh, yes; he's waiting here till his house is made ready. But he doesn't have a private table; takes his meals like an everyday mortal, at the ladies' ordinary."

He had scarcely spoken when Mr. Davis entered by a side door and took his seat, with only an occasional stare of earnest, but not disrespectful, curiosity from the more recent arrivals.

Even in the few weeks since I had seen him there was a great change. He looked worn and thinner; and the set expression of the somewhat stern features gave a grim hardness not natural to their lines. With scarcely a glance around, he returned the general salutations, sat down absently and was soon absorbed in conversation with General Cooper, who had recently resigned the adjutant-generalship of the United States army and accepted a similar post and a brigadier's commission from Mr. Davis. . . .

Little ceremony, or form, hedged the incubating government; and perfect simplicity marked every detail about Mr. Davis. His office, for the moment, was one of the parlors of the hotel. Members of the Cabinet and high officials came in and out without ceremony, to ask questions and receive very brief replies; or for whispered consultation with the President's private secretary, whose desk was in the same room. Casual visitors were simply announced by an usher, and were received whenever business did not prevent. Mr. Davis' manner was unvarying in its quiet and courtesy, drawing out all that one had to tell, and indicating by brief answer, or criticism, that he had extracted the pith from it. At that moment he was the very idol of the people; the grand embodiment to them of their grand cause; and they gave him their hands unquestioning, to applaud any move soever he might make. And equally unthinking as this popular manisfestation of early hero-worship was the clamor that later floated into Richmond on every wind, blaming the government—and especially its head—for every untoward detail of the facile descent to destruction.

A better acquaintance with the Confederate Capital impressed one still more with its likeness to Washington toward the end of the session; but many features of that likeness were salient ones, which had marred and debased the older city. The government just organizing, endless places of profit, of trust, or of honor, were to be filled; and for each and every one of them was a rush of justling and almost rapid claimants. The skeleton of the regular army had just been articulated by Congress, but the bare bones would soon have swelled to more than Falstaffian proportions, had one in every twenty of the ardent aspirants been applied as matter and muscle. The first "gazette" was watched for with straining eyes, and naturally would follow aching hearts; for disappointment here first sowed the dragon's teeth that were to spring into armed opponents of the unappreciative power.

The whole country was new. Everything was to be done—to be made; and who was so capable for both, in their own conceit, as that swarm of worn-out lobbymen and contractors who, having thoroughly exploited "the old concern," now gathered to gorge upon the new. And by the hundred flocked hither those unclean birds, blinking bleared eyes at any chance bit, whetting foul bills to peck at carrion from the departmental sewer. Busy and active at all hours, the lobby of the exchange, when the crowd and the noise rose to the flood at night, smacked no little of pandemonium. Every knot of men had its grievance; every flag in the pavement was a rostrum. Slowness of organization, the weakness of Congress, secession of the border states, personnel of the Cabinet and especially the latest army appointments—these and kindred subjects were canvassed with heat equaled only by ignorance. Men from every section of the South defended their own people in highest of keys and no little temper; startling measures for public safety were offered and state secrets openly discussed in this curbstone congress; while a rank growth of newspaper correspondents, with "the very latest," swelled the hum into a veritable Babel. And the most incomprehensible of all was the diametric opposition of men from the same neighborhood, in their views of the same subject. Often it would be a vital one, of doctrine, or of policy; and yet these neighbors would antagonize more bitterly than would men from opposite parts of the confederation.

—DeLeon, *Four Years in Rebel Capitals*

11. A WAR CLERK DESCRIBES DAVIS AND HIS CABINET

Some of the appointments to the Confederate Cabinet posts excited a good deal of surprise; even more astonishment was excited by the failure of Davis to invite to his official family men like Robert Barnwell Rhett of South Carolina and William L. Yancey of Alabama—men who for more than a decade had been leaders in the secession movement.

John Beauchamp Jones, who has been called the "Confederate Pepys," was an author and journalist of some note who obtained a position as clerk in the War Department in order to keep "a diary of the transactions of the government."

May 17th, 1861.—Was introduced to the President today. He was overwhelmed with papers and retained a number in his left hand, probably of more importance than the rest. He received me with urbanity, and while he read the papers I had given him, as I had never seen him before, I endeavored to scrutinize his features, as one would naturally do, for the purpose of forming a vague estimate of the character and capabilities of the man destined to perform the leading part in a revolution which must occupy a large space in the world's history. His stature is tall, nearly six feet; his frame is very slight and seemingly frail, but when he throws back his shoulders he is as straight as an Indian chief. The features of his face are distinctly marked with character, and no one gazing at his profile would doubt for a moment that he beheld more than an ordinary man. His face is handsome, and [on] his thin lip often basks a pleasant smile. There is nothing sinister or repulsive in his manners or appearance, and if there are no special indications of great grasp of intellectual power on his forehead and on his sharply-defined nose and chin, neither is there any evidence of weakness or that he could be easily moved from any settled purpose. I think he has a clear perception of matters demanding his cognizance, and a nice discrimination of details. As a politician he attaches the utmost importance to *consistency*—and here I differ with him. I think that to be consistent as a politician is to change with the circumstances of the case. When Calhoun and Webster first met in Congress, the first advocated a protective tariff and the last opposed it. This was told me by Mr. Webster himself, in 1842, when he was Secretary of State; and it was confirmed by Mr. Calhoun in 1844, then Secretary of State himself. Statesmen are the physicians of the public weal, and what doctor hesitates to vary his remedies with the new phases of disease?

When the President had completed the reading of my papers, and during the perusal I observed him make several emphatic nods, he asked me what I wanted. I told him I wanted employment with my pen, perhaps only temporary employment. I thought the correspondence of the Secretary of War would increase in volume, and another assistant besides Major Tyler would be required in his office. He smiled and shook his head, saying that such work would be only temporary indeed; which I construed to mean that even he did not then suppose the war to assume colossal proportions.

May 20th.—Mr. Walker, the Secretary of War, is some forty-seven or -eight years of age, tall, thin, and a little bent, not by age, but by study and bad health. He was a successful lawyer and, having never been in governmental employment, is fast working himself down. He has not yet learned how to avoid unnecessary labor, being a man of the finest sensibilities, and exacting with the utmost nicety all due deference to the dignity of his official position. He stands somewhat on ceremony with his brother officials and accords and exacts the etiquette natural to a sensitive gentleman who has never been broken on the wheel of office. I predict for him a short career. The only hope for his continuance in office is unconditional submission to the President, who, being once Secretary of War of the United States, is familiar with all the wheels of the department. But soon, if I err not, the President will be too much absorbed in the fluctuations of momentous campaigns to give much of his attention to any one of the departments. Nevertheless Mr. Walker, if he be an apt scholar, may learn much before that day; and Congress may simplify his duties by enacting a uniform mode of filling the offices in the field. The applications now give the greatest trouble, and the disappointed class give rise to many vexations.

May 21st.—Being in the same room with the Secretary and seen by all his visitors, I am necessarily making many new acquaintances; and quite a number recognize me by my books which they have read. Among this class is Mr. Benjamin, the Minister of Justice. . . . Mr. Benjamin is of course a Jew, of French lineage, born I believe in Louisiana, a lawyer and politician. His age may be sixty, and yet one might suppose him to be less than forty. His hair and eyes are black, his forehead capacious, his face round and as intellectual as one of that shape can be; and Mr. Benjamin is certainly a man of intellect, education, and extensive reading, combined with natural abilities of a tolerably high order. Upon his lip there seems to bask an eternal smile; but if it be studied, it is not a smile—yet it bears no unpleasing aspect.

May 22nd.—Today I had, in our office, a specimen of Mr. Memminger's oratory. He was pleading for an installment of the claims of South Carolina on the Confederacy; and Mr. Walker, always hesitating, argued the other side, merely for delay. Both are fine speakers, with most distinct enunciation and musical voices. The demand was audited and paid, amounting to, I believe, several hundred thousand dollars.

And I heard and saw Mr. Toombs today, the Secretary of State. He is a portly gentleman, but with the pale face of the student and the marks of a deep thinker. To gaze at him in repose, the casual spectator would suppose, from his neglect of dress, that he was a planter in moderate circumstances

and of course not gifted with extraordinary powers of intellect; but let him open his mouth, and the delusion vanishes. At the time alluded to he was surrounded by the rest of the cabinet, in our office, and the topic was the policy of the war. He was for taking the initiative and carrying the war into the enemy's country. And as he warmed with the subject, the man seemed to vanish, and the genius alone was visible. . . . These little discussions were of frequent occurrence; and it soon became apparent that the Secretary of War was destined to be the most important man among the cabinet ministers. His position afforded the best prospect of future distinction—always provided he should be equal to the position and his administration attended with success. I felt convinced that Toombs would not be long chafing in the cabinet but that he would seize the first opportunity to repair to the field.
—JONES, *A Rebel War Clerk's Diary at the Confederate States Capital*

12. A STATE AGENT CALLS ON THE CONFEDERATE LEADERS

One of the best descriptions of Confederate leaders comes from the graceful pen of John Peyton, agent from North Carolina to England. Born and educated in Virginia, Peyton had lived for some time in Illinois and was unalterably opposed to secession, which he regarded as not only unwise but unconstitutional. When Virginia seceded, however, he went with his state, raising a regiment largely at his own expense. Kept from active military service by poor health, he served his country in England, and after the war stayed on in the Island of Guernsey for many years.

I CALLED at the Navy Department the morning after my arrival. I found the Honourable Stephen R. Mallory, Secretary of State for the Admiralty, occupying a small room in the second storey of a brick building, north of the capitol square, a house which in former times had been used for some purpose in connection with the Fire Companies of Richmond. He was a short, fat man, with a solid neck, a big head, much strong grizzled hair, a leaden eye, and a heavy countenance. His arms, legs, and neck were very short, and his clothes tightly fitting—so tight, indeed, that, to use an American phrase in a literal sense, which is commonly used metaphorically to express a different idea, he seemed "too big for his breeches." His ideas seemed to be confused, and the right word never to be had at the right moment. What he did say was commonplace. In the first five minutes of my conversation, I found myself forgetting my business, while I wondered what could be Mr. Mallory's peculiar fitness for his position—what secret faculty he possessed for creating an armament and piloting it through the storms of a civil war. . . .

As I passed out of the office of the Secretary of the Navy, expressing a hope that he might enjoy his repast, and digest it satisfactorily, which I doubted, from the character of the provisions then in the Richmond market, I encountered in the hall a lean, yellow, care-worn man, his back bent forward almost into a hump, his chest bowed inward, one shoulder higher than the other, small arms and wasted legs, hands, and fingers long and bony—dress loose and wrinkled, and of shabby gray—looking damp and mouldy. His face was bony and emaciated, withered and twitching, his scanty hair fell on his shoulders in disorder. His chin was smooth and beardless, his breath short, while his restless eyes blazed with excitement. His voice, as he addressed such acquaintances as he met, was sharp, shrill, and squeaky, and his whole appearance faded, anxious, disappointed, extraordinary—so much so that he passed no one who did not turn and take a second gaze. I thought I had never seen so singular an object, and inquired of my nearest neighbor what apparition it was. Imagine my surprise when I was informed that it was Mr. Alexander H. Stephens, the eloquent Georgian orator, the Conservative statesman and energetic Vice-President of the Confederate States. . . .

During the week I had given myself to remain in Richmond I determined to ascertain as much as possible of the views and the policy of the Confederate leaders, and accordingly called from time to time, during leisure hours, upon the President and the members of the cabinet, several of whom I had for years known.

I generally saw Mr. Davis in his office in the United States Custom House, situated not far from the War and Navy departments, on the west side of the capitol square. In this building he occupied a small room, as an office for the transaction of public business and the reception of friends, before the door of which office paced a single sentinel in the gray Confederate uniform. Mr. Davis was thin, gaunt, sallow, terribly worn by the cares and anxieties of his position, but in as high spirits as even Mr. Mallory, as to the prospects of the future.

In person Mr. Davis is tall and slender—what is termed in American parlance "a raw-boned man"—with a small, fine head, blue eyes, one of which is defective, in consequence of a wound he received at the battle of Buena Vista, an aquiline contour, high narrow forehead, leonine cast of mouth, deeply marked by high spirit, strong sense, and no small experience of grim care. He had an easy, dignified manner. . . .

Mr. Davis always impressed me as a man of abilities, but engaged in an enterprise, the foundation of an empire, far too arduous for any energies he possessed; as a man by no means stamped by nature with power and genius, such as his situation and the great crisis demanded. His whole manner and bearing was that of one almost stunned by what was passing before his astonished vision, and incapable of safely controlling and directing the vessel of state, amidst the winds and waves of the tempest. He did not appear to be guiding his conduct by the sober deductions of cool reason, but to be acting without any of that far-seeing sagacity which conciliates enemies and retains friends. . . .

In a back room on the ground floor of an old red brick building, formerly used as the office of an auctioneer, and situated on the same street with the United States Custom House, the Secretary of State, R. M. T. Hunter, was generally found dreaming the day away, in the absence of official duties to occupy his time. Over the front door was a small board inscribed "State Department." I occasionally dropped in to see "Run Mad Tom," as he was called in earlier days, on account of his extreme radical views on the subject of State rights.

However mad he may have been once, he was decidedly sober and soporific then, tame rather than wild, and he illustrated how impossible it is to prevent what is "bred in the bone" from "coming out in the flesh." He was now, as when younger, the most uncompromising of Secessionists, and, as Pitt said on a memorable occasion to Horace Walpole, "ignorant in spite of experience." He professed to see nothing to weaken the force of his sanguine views as to Southern success, in the determination of the Federal Government to maintain the Union at every hazard; nothing in Negro slavery, but its Divine origin and its incalculable blessings for white and black, and nothing better for the South than to labour for its indefinite extension and perpetuity. The logic of passing events did not disturb his dreams, and he indulged in that kind of delusion which professed to believe the success of the South already secured, though the North was giving daily evidences of a determination to bring every energy of its richer, more highly developed country and greater population to bear upon the contest. . . .

Very near the offices of Mr. Mallory were those of Judah P. Benjamin, the acting Secretary of War, who was a short, stout, jaunty gentleman, with a sparkling black eye and a jovial Judaical physiognomy. He was not handsome, but his appearance was prepossessing, and his manners were natural. He was frank and open, with what might be termed a careless flow of spirits. He said a great many witty and pleasant things, and seemed in a short time to appreciate the characters of those with whom he associated. He was a distinguished jurist and statesman, and it was not difficult for even a casual acquaintance to trace in him the characteristics of both professions. He was long one of the leading lawyers of New Orleans, and at the commencement of the civil war, or rather the secession of South Carolina, was, as he had been for several years previous, a United States senator from Louisiana. He was regarded by many as the ablest of the President's cabinet council, and was one of the few persons connected with the Government, who had believed from the first that Secession would lead to a long and bloody war.

—PEYTON, *The American Crisis*

II

The Conflict Precipitated

WHY *did the Montgomery government permit the bombardment of Fort Sumter? It is almost a principle of American history that the "other side" must strike the first blow, and that Americans must fight only in defense of their nation and their principles. That was why Polk was so concerned to prove that "American blood had been shed on American soil." Yet at Sumter the South struck the first blow, thus forfeiting, in some part at least, the moral advantage of being the defender rather than the aggressor. From the Confederate point of view, to be sure, the North had already taken the offensive by the occupation of Sumter and by the effort to reprovision it, but this point of view was a bit astigmatic. Clearly the attack on the old flag would arouse and unite the North as would nothing else, and clearly, too, it would precipitate war.*

There was, however, one consideration that the Confederates could not afford to overlook. Two days before the bombardment of Sumter Roger Pryor, of Virginia, had put the matter succinctly. "I tell you, gentlemen, what will put Virginia in the Southern Confederacy in less than an hour by Shrewsbury clock—strike a blow." His timing was a bit off, but his argument was sound. Only by striking a blow could the Confederacy be sure of bringing in Virginia—and other wavering states.

Once the war was on, North and South rallied to their causes and their flags. At first unity seemed to obtain, on both sides; only after it became clear that the war would not be over in three months did dissatisfaction appear. There was, in fact, little real unity on either side, and far less real enthusiasm for war than patriotic orators pretended, or than some historians have recorded. Large segments of opinion in the North were opposed to holding the Union together by coercion. Large segments in the South still cherished the old Union and looked upon the war as a slaveholders' fight. Antiwar and disunion sentiment was to be found almost everywhere in the North, but more strongly in the Middle West than in New England; antiwar and Unionist sentiment in the South was controlled largely by geography: the western counties of Virginia seceded from the state and joined the Union, Maryland, Kentucky and Missouri stayed in the Union, and eastern Tennessee was predominantly Unionist in sentiment.

We shall see, later, something of the consequences of antiwar and Copperhead sentiment in the North, of Unionism and State rights in the South. An appreciation of the importance of these attitudes should not, however, blind us to the fact that the majority, in both sections, believed passionately in and fought loyally for their cause.

1. MRS. CHESNUT WATCHES THE ATTACK ON FORT SUMTER

When South Carolina seceded, Major Robert Anderson, commanding the Federal forces in Charleston, secretly moved his garrison from Fort Moultrie to Fort Sumter. The question whether his little force should be withdrawn or supported agitated the closing weeks of the Buchanan and the opening weeks of the Lincoln administration. While the fate of Fort Sumter was being discussed, the Confederacy took over all but four of the forts, arsenals, and military posts in the South.) *Against the advice of some members of his Cabinet, Lincoln finally decided not to reinforce but to provision the fort, and this decision precipitated the crisis, and the war. On April 11 General Beauregard, who was in command of Confederate forces in Charleston, acting on somewhat ambiguous instructions from Montgomery, demanded an immediate surrender of the fort; when this was refused Confederate batteries opened fire on the Stars and Stripes at dawn of the twelfth, and the war was on.*

Mary Boykin Chesnut, whose Diary gives us a lively account of life in the Confederacy, was the wife of ex-Senator Chesnut of South Carolina. She tells us here* of the excitement in Charleston when Sumter was attacked.

April 8th, 1861.—Allen Green came up to speak to me at dinner in all his soldier's toggery. It sent a shiver through me. Tried to read Margaret Fuller Ossoli, but could not. The air too full of war news, and we are all so restless.

Went to see Miss Pinckney, one of the last of the old-world Pinckneys. Governor Manning walked in, bowed gravely, and seated himself by me. Again he bowed low in mock-heroic style and with a grand wave of his hand said, "Madam, your country is invaded." When I had breath to speak I asked, "What does he mean?" He meant this: There are six men-of-war outside the bar. Talbot and Chew have come to say that hostilities are to begin. Governor Pickens and Beauregard are holding a council of war. Mr. Chesnut then came in and confirmed the story. Wigfall next entered in boisterous spirits and said, "There was a sound of revelry by night." In any stir of confusion my heart is apt to beat so painfully. Now the agony was so stifling I could hardly see or hear. The men went off almost immediately. And I crept silently to my room, where I sat down to a good cry.

Mrs. Wigfall came in, and we had it out on the subject of civil war. We solaced ourselves with dwelling on all its known horrors, and then we added what we had a right to expect with Yankees in front and Negroes in the rear. "The slaveowners must expect a servile insurrection, of course," said Mrs. Wigfall, to make sure that we were unhappy enough. Suddenly loud

---

* From: *A Diary from Dixie* by Mary B. Chesnut. Copyright, 1905, D. Appleton & Company. Reprinted by permission of the publishers, Appleton-Century-Crofts, Inc.

shouting was heard. We ran out. Cannon after cannon roared. We met Mrs. Allen Green in the passageway, with blanched cheeks and streaming eyes. Governor Means rushed out of his room in his dressing gown and begged us to be calm. "Governor Pickens," said he, "has ordered, in the plenitude of his wisdom, seven cannon to be fired as a signal to the Seventh Regiment. Anderson will hear as well as the Seventh Regiment. Now you go back and be quiet; fighting in the streets has not begun yet."

So we retired. Doctor Gibbes calls Mrs. Allen Green, Dame Placid. There was no placidity today, with cannon bursting and Allen on the island. No sleep for anybody last night. The streets were alive with soldiers, men shouting, marching, singing. Wigfall, the stormy petrel, is in his glory, the only thoroughly happy person I see. Today things seem to have settled down a little. One can but hope still. Lincoln or Seward has made such silly advances and then far sillier drawings back. There may be a chance for peace after all. Things are happening so fast. My husband has been made an aide-de-camp to General Beauregard.

Three hours ago we were quickly packing to go home. The convention has adjourned. Now he tells me the attack on Fort Sumter may begin tonight; depends upon Anderson and the fleet outside. . . .

Mrs. Hayne called. She had, she said, but one feeling—pity for those who are not here. Jack Preston, Willie Alston, "the take-life-easys," as they are called, with John Green, "the big brave," have gone down to the islands—volunteered as privates. Seven hundred men were sent over. Ammunition wagons were rumbling along the streets all night. Anderson is burning blue lights, signs and signals for the fleet outside, I suppose.

Today at dinner there was no allusion to things as they stand in Charleston harbor. There was an undercurrent of intense excitement. There could not have been a more brilliant circle. In addition to our usual quartet, Judge Withers, Langdon Cheves, and Trescott, our two ex-governors dined with us, Means and Manning. These men all talked so delightfully. For once in my life I listened. That over, business began in earnest. Governor Means has rummaged a sword and red sash from somewhere and brought it for Colonel Chesnut, who had gone to demand the surrender of Fort Sumter. And now, patience—we must wait.

Why did that green goose Anderson go into Fort Sumter? Then everything began to go wrong. Now they have intercepted a letter from him, urging them to let him surrender. He paints the horrors likely to ensue if they will not. He ought to have thought of all that before he put his head in the hole.

12th.—Anderson will not capitulate. Yesterday's was the merriest, maddest dinner we have had yet. Men were audaciously wise and witty. We had an unspoken foreboding that it was to be our last pleasant meeting. Mr. Miles dined with us today. Mrs. Henry King rushed in saying: "The news, I come for the latest news! All the men of the King family are on the island," of which fact she seemed proud.

While she was here our peace negotiator or envoy came in—that is, Mr.

Chesnut returned. His interview with Colonel Anderson had been deeply interesting, but Mr. Chesnut was not inclined to be communicative. He wanted his dinner. He felt for Anderson and had telegraphed to President Davis for instructions—what answer to give Anderson, etc. He has now gone back to Fort Sumter with additional instructions. When they were about to leave the wharf, A. H. Boykin sprang into the boat in great excitement. He thought himself ill-used, with a likelihood of fighting and he to be left behind!

I do not pretend to go to sleep. How can I? If Anderson does not accept terms at four, the orders are he shall be fired upon. I count four, St. Michael's bells chime out, and I begin to hope. At half past four the heavy booming of a cannon. I sprang out of bed, and on my knees prostrate I prayed as I never prayed before.

There was a sound of stir all over the house, pattering of feet in the corridors. All seemed hurrying one way. I put on my double gown and a shawl and went too. It was to the housetop. The shells were bursting. In the dark I heard a man say, "Waste of ammunition." I knew my husband was rowing a boat somewhere in that dark bay. If Anderson was obstinate, Colonel Chesnut was to order the fort on one side to open fire. Certainly fire had begun. The regular roar of the cannon, there it was. And who could tell what each volley accomplished of death and destruction?

The women were wild there on the housetop. Prayers came from the women and imprecations from the men. And then a shell would light up the scene. Tonight they say the forces are to attempt to land. We watched up there, and everybody wondered that Fort Sumter did not fire a shot. . . .

We hear nothing, can listen to nothing; boom, boom, goes the cannon all the time. The nervous strain is awful, alone in this darkened room. "Richmond and Washington ablaze," say the papers—blazing with excitement. Why not? To us these last days' events seem frightfully great. We were all women on that iron balcony. Men are only seen at a distance now. Stark Means was leaning over and looking with tearful eyes, when an unknown creature asked, "Why did he take his hat off?" Mrs. Means stood straight up and said, "He did that in honor of his mother; he saw me." She is a proud mother and at the same time most unhappy. Her lovely daughter Emma is dying in there, before her eyes, of consumption. At that moment I am sure Mrs. Means had a spasm of the heart.

13th.—Nobody has been hurt after all. How gay we were last night! Reaction after the dread of all the slaughter we thought those dreadful cannon were making. Not even a battery the worse for wear. Fort Sumter has been on fire. Anderson has not yet silenced any of our guns. So the aides, still with swords and red sashes by way of uniform, tell us. But the sound of those guns makes regular meals impossible. None of us goes to table. Tea trays pervade the corridors, going everywhere. Some of the anxious hearts lie on their beds and moan in solitary misery. Mrs. Wigfall and I solace ourselves with tea in my room. These women have all a satisfying faith. "God is on our side," they say. When we are shut in Mrs. Wigfall and I ask, "Why?" "Of course, He hates the Yankees," we are told, "You'll think that well of Him."

Not by one word or look can we detect any change in the demeanor of these Negro servants. Lawrence sits at our door, sleepy and respectful, and profoundly indifferent. So are they all, but they carry it too far. You could not tell that they even heard the awful roar going on in the bay, though it has been dinning in their ears night and day. People talk before them as if they were chairs and tables. They make no sign. Are they stolidly stupid? or wiser than we are; silent and strong, biding their time? . . .

15th.—I did not know that one could live such days of excitement. Some one called: "Come out! There is a crowd coming." A mob it was, indeed, but it was headed by Colonels Chesnut and Manning. The crowd was shouting and showing these two as messengers of good news. They were escorted to Beauregard's headquarters. For Sumter had surrendered! Those upon the housetops shouted to us, "The fort is on fire." That had been the story once or twice before.

When we had calmed down, Colonel Chesnut, who had taken it all quietly enough, if anything more unruffled than usual in his serenity, told us how the surrender came about. Wigfall was with them on Morris Island when they saw the fire in the fort; he jumped in a little boat and, with his handkerchief as a white flag, rowed over. Wigfall went in through a porthole. When Colonel Chesnut arrived shortly after and was received at the regular entrance, Colonel Anderson told him he had need to pick his way warily, for the place was all mined. As far as I can make out the fort surrendered to Wigfall. But it is all confusion. Our flag is flying there. Fire engines have been sent for to put out the fire. Everybody tells you half of something and then rushes off to tell something else or to hear the last news.

In the afternoon Mrs. Preston, Mrs. Joe Heyward, and I drove out around the battery. We were in an open carriage. What a changed scene—the very liveliest crowd I think I ever saw, everybody talking at once. All glasses were still turned on the grim old fort.

—CHESNUT, *A Diary from Dixie*

2. ABNER DOUBLEDAY DEFENDS FORT SUMTER

A New Yorker by birth and a West Point graduate who had fought in the Mexican War, Captain Abner Doubleday was second in command at Fort Sumter when it was captured by the Confederates in 1861. He served gallantly throughout the rest of the war, fighting at Antietam, at Fredericksburg, at Chancellorsville, and at Gettysburg, and rose to the rank of major general. His other claim to fame is as the "father" of baseball.

ABOUT 4 A.M. on the 12th I was awakened by some one groping about my room in the dark and calling out my name. It proved to be Anderson, who came to announce to me that he had just received a dispatch from Beauregard, dated 3:20 A.M., to the effect that he should open fire upon us in an hour. Finding it was determined not to return the fire until after breakfast, I remained in bed. As we had no lights, we could in fact do nothing before that time except to wander around in the darkness and fire without an accurate view of the enemy's works.

As soon as the outline of our fort could be distinguished, the enemy carried out their program. It had been arranged, as a special compliment to the venerable Edmund Ruffin, who might almost be called the father of secession, that he should fire the first shot against us from the Stevens battery on Cummings Point. Almost immediately afterward a ball from Cummings Point lodged in the magazine wall and by the sound seemed to bury itself in the masonry about a foot from my head, in very unpleasant proximity to my right ear. This is the one that probably came with Mr. Ruffin's compliments. In a moment the firing burst forth in one continuous roar, and large patches of both the exterior and interior masonry began to crumble and fall in all directions. The place where I was had been used for the manufacture of cartridges, and there was still a good deal of powder there, some packed and some loose. A shell soon struck near the ventilator, and a puff of dense smoke entered the room, giving me a strong impression that there would be an immediate explosion. Fortunately, no sparks had penetrated inside.

Nineteen batteries were now hammering at us, and the balls and shells from the ten-inch columbiads, accompanied by shells from the thirteen-inch mortars which constantly bombarded us, made us feel as if the war had commenced in earnest.

When it was broad daylight, I went down to breakfast. I found the officers already assembled at one of the long tables in the mess hall. Our party were calm and even somewhat merry. We had retained one colored man to wait on us. He was a spruce-looking mulatto from Charleston, very active and efficient on ordinary occasions, but now completely demoralized by the thunder of the guns and crashing of the shot around us. He leaned back against the wall, almost white with fear, his eyes closed, and his whole expression one of perfect despair. Our meal was not very sumptuous. It consisted of pork and water, but Doctor Crawford triumphantly brought forth a little farina which he had found in a corner of the hospital.

When this frugal repast was over, my company was told off in three details for firing purposes, to be relieved afterward by Seymour's company. As I was the ranking officer, I took the first detachment and marched them to the casemates which looked out upon the powerful ironclad battery of Cummings Point.

In aiming the first gun fired against the rebellion I had no feeling of self-reproach, for I fully believed that the contest was inevitable and was not of our seeking. . . .

Our firing now became regular and was answered from the rebel guns which encircled us on the four sides of the pentagon upon which the fort was built. The other side faced the open sea. Showers of balls from ten-inch columbiads and forty-two-pounders and shells from thirteen-inch mortars poured into the fort in one incessant stream, causing great flakes of masonry to fall in all directions. When the immense mortar shells, after sailing high in the air, came down in a vertical direction and buried themselves in the parade ground, their explosion shook the fort like an earthquake. . . .

The firing continued all day without any special incident of importance and without our making much impression on the enemy's works. They had a great advantage over us as their fire was concentrated on the fort which was in the center of the circle, while ours was diffused over the circumference. Their missiles were exceedingly destructive to the upper exposed portion of the work, but no essential injury was done to the lower casemates which sheltered us. . . .

From 4 to 6:30 A.M. [April 13] the enemy's fire was very spirited. From 7 to 8 A.M. a rainstorm came on, and there was a lull in the cannonading. About 8 A.M. the officers' quarters were ignited by one of Ripley's incendiary shells or by shot heated in the furnaces at Fort Moultrie. The fire was put out, but at 10 A.M. a mortar shell passed through the roof and lodged in the flooring of the second story, where it burst and started the flames afresh. This too was extinguished, but the hot shot soon followed each other so rapidly that it was impossible for us to contend with them any longer. It became evident that the entire block, being built with wooden partitions, floors, and roofing, must be consumed, and that the magazine, containing three hundred barrels of powder, would be endangered; for even after closing the metallic door sparks might penetrate through the ventilator. The floor was covered with loose powder where a detail of men had been at work manufacturing cartridge bags out of old shirts, woolen blankets, etc.

While the officers exerted themselves with axes to tear down and cut away all the woodwork in the vicinity, the soldiers were rolling barrels of powder out to more sheltered spots and were covering them with wet blankets. The labor was accelerated by the shells which were bursting around us, for Ripley had redoubled his activity at the first signs of a conflagration. We only succeeded in getting out some ninety-six barrels of powder, and then we were obliged to close the massive copper door and await the result. A shot soon after passed through the intervening shield, struck the door, and bent the lock in such a way that it could not be opened again. We were thus cut off from our supply of ammunition but still had some piled up in the vicinity of the guns. Anderson officially reported only four barrels and three cartridges as on hand when we left.

By 11 A.M. the conflagration was terrible and disastrous. One fifth of the fort was on fire, and the wind drove the smoke in dense masses into the angle where we had all taken refuge. It seemed impossible to escape suffocation. Some lay down close to the ground, with handkerchiefs over their mouths, and others posted themselves near the embrasures, where the smoke was somewhat lessened by the draught of air. Every one suffered severely. I crawled out of one of these openings and sat on the outer edge, but Ripley made it lively for me there with his case shot which spattered all around. Had not a slight change of wind taken place, the result might have been fatal to most of us.

Our firing having ceased and the enemy being very jubilant, I thought it would be as well to show them that we were not all dead yet, and ordered the gunners to fire a few rounds more. I heard afterward that the enemy loudly cheered Anderson for his persistency under such adverse circumstances.

The scene at this time was really terrific. The roaring and crackling of the flames, the dense masses of whirling smoke, the bursting of the enemy's shells and our own which were exploding in the burning rooms, the crashing of the shot, and the sound of masonry falling in every direction, made the fort a pandemonium. When at last nothing was left of the building but the blackened walls and smoldering embers, it became painfully evident that an immense amount of damage had been done. There was a tower at each angle of the fort. One of these, containing great quantities of shells upon which we had relied, was almost completely shattered by successive explosions. The massive wooden gates studded with iron nails were burned, and the wall built behind them was now a mere heap of debris, so that the main entrance was wide open for an assaulting party. The sally ports were in a similar condition, and the numerous windows on the gorge side which had been planked up had now become all open entrances.

About 12:48 P.M. the end of the flagstaff was shot down and the flag fell. . . .

About 2 P.M. Senator Wigfall, in company with W. Gourdin Young, of

Charleston, unexpectedly made his appearance at one of the embrasures, having crossed over from Morris Island in a small boat rowed by Negroes. He had seen the flag come down, and supposed that we had surrendered in consequence of the burning of the quarters. An artilleryman serving his gun was very much astonished to see a man's face at the entrance and asked him what he was doing there. Wigfall replied that he wished to see Major Anderson. The man, however, refused to allow him to enter until he had surrendered himself as a prisoner and given up his sword. . . . Wigfall, in Beauregard's name, offered Anderson his own terms, which were the evacuation of the fort, with permission to salute our flag and to march out with the honors of war with our arms and private baggage, leaving all other war material behind. As soon as this matter was arranged, Wigfall returned to Cummings Point.

All of the preliminaries having been duly adjusted, it was decided that the evacuation should take place the next morning. Our arrangements were few and simple, but the rebels made extensive preparations for the event in order to give it the greatest éclat and gain from it as much prestige as possible. The population of the surrounding country poured into Charleston in vast multitudes to witness the humiliation of the United States flag. We slept soundly that night for the first time, after all the fatigue and excitement of the two preceding days.

The next morning, Sunday, the 14th, we were up early, packing our baggage in readiness to go on board the transport. The time having arrived, I made preparations, by order of Major Anderson, to fire a national salute to the flag. . . .

The salute being over, the Confederate troops marched in to occupy the fort. The Palmetto Guard, Captain Cuthbert's company, detailed by Colonel De Saussure, and Captain Hollinquist's Company B, of the regulars, detailed by Colonel Ripley, constituted the new garrison under Ripley. Anderson directed me to form the men on the parade ground, assume command, and march them on board the transport. I told him I should prefer to leave the fort with the flag flying and the drums beating "Yankee Doodle," and he authorized me to do so. As soon as our tattered flag came down and the silken banner made by the ladies of Charleston was run up, tremendous shouts of applause were heard from the vast multitude of spectators; and all the vessels and steamers, with one accord, made for the fort.

—DOUBLEDAY, *Reminiscences of Forts Sumter and Moultrie*

3. MAJOR ANDERSON SURRENDERS FORT SUMTER

It was characteristic of the confusion of loyalties at the time that Major Anderson, who defended Fort Sumter heroically for thirty-four hours, was by birth a Kentuckian, of Virginia ancestry, and married to a Georgia girl. Doubleday asserts that he had been given command in Charleston harbor by Buchanan's Secretary of War Floyd precisely for this reason—that Floyd thought he would co-operate with the Confederacy. Anderson proved, how-

*ever, loyal to the Union. He was subsequently promoted to brigadier general
and was temporarily in charge of Union forces in Kentucky.*

Steamship Baltic, off Sandy Hook, April 18 (1861)—10:30 A.M.—via New
York—Having defended Fort Sumter for thirty-four hours, until the quarters
were entirely burned, the main gates destroyed by fire, the gorge walls
seriously injured, the magazine surrounded by flames, and its door closed
from the effects of heat, four barrels and three cartridges of powder only
being available, and no provisions remaining but pork, I accepted terms of
evacuation offered by General Beauregard, being the same offered by him
on the 11th instant, prior to the commencement of hostilities, and marched
out of the fort Sunday afternoon, the 14th instant, with colors flying and
drums beating, bringing away company and private property, and saluting
my flag with fifty guns.

> ROBERT ANDERSON
> Major, First Artillery, Commanding.
> —"Reports of Major Anderson . . ."

4. "THE HEATHER IS ON FIRE"

*Before the attack on Fort Sumter there had been a strong current of
opinion in the North which urged that the "erring sisters" be allowed to
"depart in peace." When Beauregard fired on the flag the whole North was
aroused and, for the moment, appeared to be unified in its determination to
put down rebellion.*

*The four excerpts given here describe the response of the North as seen
and interpreted by an Indiana farm boy, a Boston scholar, a Philadelphia
lawyer, and a New York girl.*

A. AN INDIANA FARM BOY HEARS THE NEWS

April, 1861

Father and I were husking out some corn. We could not finish before
it wintered up. When William Cory came across the field (he had been
down after the Mail) he was excited and said, "Jonathan the Rebs have
fired upon and taken Fort Sumpter." Father got white and couldn't say a
word.

William said, "The President will soon fix them. He has called for
75,000 men and is going to blocade their ports, and just as soon as those
fellows find out that the North means business they will get down off thier
high horse."

Father said little. We did not finish the corn and drove to the barn.
Father left me to unload and put out the team and went to the house. After
I had finished I went in to dinner. Mother said, "What is the matter with
Father?" He had gone right upstairs. I told her what we had heard. She
went to him. After a while they came down. Father looked ten years older.

We sat down to the table. Grandma wanted to know what was the trouble. Father told her and she began to cry. "Oh my poor children in the South! Now they will suffer! God knows how they will suffer! I knew it would come! Jonathan I told you it would come!"

"They can come here and stay," said Father.

"No they will not do that. There is thier home. There they will stay. Oh to think that I should have lived to see the day when Brother should rise against Brother."

She and Mother were crying and I lit out for the barn. I do hate to see women cry.

We had another meeting at the school house last night; we are raising money to take care of the families of those who enlist. A good many gave money, others subscribed. The Hulper boys have enlisted and Steve Lampman and some others. I said I would go but they laughed at me and said they wanted men not boys for this job; that it would all be over soon; that those fellows down South are big bluffers and would rather talk than fight. I am not so sure about that. I know the Hale boys would fight with thier fists at any rate and I believe they would fight with guns too if needs be. I remember how Charlie would get on our Dick and ride on a galop across our south field cutting mullin heads with his wooden sword playing they were Indians or Mexicans (his Father was in the Mexican War), and he looked fine. To be sure there was no danger but I feel pretty certain he could fight. May be it won't be such a picnic as some say it will. There has been a fight down in Virginia at Big Bethel. Al Beechers Nephew was in it and wrote to his Uncle and he read the letter in his store. I could not make out which side whipped but from the papers I think the Rebels had the best of it. Mother had a letter from the Hales. Charlie and his Father are in thier army and Dayton wanted to go but was too young. I wonder if I were in our army and they should meet me would they shoot me. I suppose they would.

—Winther, ed., *Journal of Theodore Upson*

B. "There Never Was Anything Like It"

To Sir Edmund Head.

Boston, April 21, 1861

My dear Head,—I sent you by yesterday's express a parcel, about which the two papers I enclose will give you all the information you will need. The Danish books, I think, will be all you will want for some time.

But there are other things to talk about now. The heather is on fire. I never before knew what a popular excitement can be. Holiday enthusiasm I have seen often enough, and anxious crowds I remember during the war of 1812-15, but never anything like this. Indeed, here at the North, at least, there never was anything like it; for if the feeling were as deep and stern in 1775, it was by no means so intelligent or unanimous; and the masses to be moved were as a handful compared to our dense population now.

The whole people, in fact, has come to a perception that the question is, whether we shall have anarchy or no. The sovereign—for the people is the only sovereign in this country—has begun to exercise his sovereign functions. Business is susbstantially suspended. Men think, wisely or unwisely, of the state of affairs, and not of much else. The whole population, men, women, and children, seem to be in the streets with Union favors and flags; walking about uneasily, because their anxiety and nervous excitement will not permit them to stay at home, where all ordinary occupation has become unsavory. Public meetings are held everywhere, in the small towns and villages as much as in the cities; considerable sums of money are voted to sustain the movement and take care of the families of those who are mustered into service; and still larger sums are given by individuals. Nobody holds back. Civil war is freely accepted everywhere; by some with alacrity, as the only means of settling a controversy based on long-cherished hatreds; by others as something sent as a judgment from Heaven, like a flood or an earthquake; by all as inevitable, by all as the least of the evils among which we are permitted to choose, anarchy being the obvious, and perhaps the only alternative.

Here in Boston the people are constantly gathering about the State House—which you know is in front of my windows—and about Faneuil Hall, where the troops chiefly assemble or halt on their way through town. When soldiers march by there is grave shouting; nothing like the common cheering. There is an earnestness such as I never witnessed before in any popular movement.

—TICKNOR AND HILLARD, eds., *Life, Letters, and Journals of George Ticknor*

C. "THERE IS BUT ONE THOUGHT—THE STARS AND STRIPES"

Horace Binney to Sir J. T. Coleridge.

Philadelphia, 27 May, 1861

. . . The assault upon Fort Sumter started us all to our feet, as one man; all political division ceased among us from that very moment. Private relations with the South have been put aside, no doubt with great regret. There is among us but one thought, one object, one end, one symbol,—the Stars and Stripes. We are to a great degree at present, and will shortly be throughout, an armed nation. We have the whole naval power of the country. We have nearly all its money at command. We know that we shall be both degraded and ruined unless this government is maintained; and we are not so much embittered at this time (as we hope we shall continue) as to be unable to make the combat as respectable in point of humanity as war between public belligerents can be.

Most of the seceded slave States are much divided. Eastern Tennessee, Northern Alabama, Western Virginia, are wholly in favour of the Union. Kentucky has expressly refused to go out. Tennessee is still balancing; Missouri cannot go. Maryland, now that her mob has been suppressed, speaks and acts the language of Union, and she is encouraged to it by the presence of Pennsylvania forces in Baltimore and overhanging her western counties, which at the same time are known to be faithful, thoroughly Union. It is the slave-selling and slave-working parts of the South that have alone desired to break away,—by no means all of these, nor any considerable part of them but through delusion, venality, or terror. How can the North and West withhold their effort to suppress the terror which has enchained so many? It is their sacred duty under the Constitution. We have, therefore, both duty and right to confirm us in the effort. It will, I have no doubt whatever, be strenuously made. We have no reason to doubt, from either the purposes we entertain, or the motives which actuate us, or the means we shall apply, that God will help us.

Some of the writers for the English press have but an imperfect knowledge of the necessities of the free States when they argue that the slave States should be allowed to depart and make another nation. We are large enough, they say,—and that is true enough, though nothing to the purpose. The North and West cannot conquer them. That also may be true, and yet nothing to the purpose. They will conquer the North and West and destroy the Union, if they can bring about what these writers recommend. Consider, Louisiana and Florida were purchased to make the union of the West with the Atlantic States possible. They hold the Gulf of Mexico and the river Mississippi under their control, if they are left as they claim to be. Texas bounds us and turns us in to the South on the western side of the Gulf. Our intercourse with the Pacific States, all faithful to the Union, lies over the Isthmus of Darien. How can any part of the West continue in union with the North, or the Pacific be united to the Atlantic States, if an independent power holds this control?

The question for negotiation is, Which shall be the master of the gates of entrance and exit to the North and West? Was such a question ever settled by negotiation? The States on the Mississippi and the Gulf must be in union with the North and West, or be commanded by them, or the West must fly from the North. This is an old question. I heard it argued in 1797, when we had Spain to deal with in regard to these waters; and not a man South or North but held the opinion I express. It was from our weakness then that we did not conquer them; and to this single end—of maintaining our Union—we bought them afterwards, which was better; but their importance to the Union of North and West is just what it was. Great Britain knew what their value to the Union was, when her forces endeavoured to seize New Orleans in 1815.

In fine, my dear sir, I do not say we can conquer. I do say that mere conquest would be an absurdity in our relations if we could achieve it; for the Southern States would become Territories again, if anything, and go into the old connection, to go into revolt a second time. But we may subdue the revolutionary violence which has got the upper hand; we may hearten the friends of the Union in those parts to vindicate their own rights in the Union; and if we cannot do this, we may detach Louisiana, Florida, and the river portions of Mississippi, and Arkansas. If we do not, then I admit our dream of union and our national existence in its present form is gone. And such a shame, dishonour, degradation, in the sight of all the world! God forbid that we should live to see it! Three hundred and fifty thousand masters of slaves—not more—breaking down the power and hopes of twenty millions of freemen, for the most part the descendants of Englishmen! You recollect Cowley's burst, in regard to Cromwell's usurpation:

> "Come the eleventh plague, rather than this should be,
> Come sink us rather in the sea.
> * * * * * * *
> In all the chains we ever bore,
> We griev'd, we sigh'd, we wept, we never blush'd before."

This has been a long ramble, my dear sir. I have no time to make it shorter, for I am deep in a commission to provide for the poor families of the mechanics who have become volunteers.

—BINNEY, *The Life of Horace Binney*

D. "ONE GREAT EAGLE SCREAM"

Jane Stuart Woolsey to a Friend in Paris.

8 Brevoort Place, Friday, May 10, 1861

I am sure you will like to hear what we are all about in these times of terrible excitement, though it seems almost impertinent to write just now. Everything is either too big or too little to put in a letter. . . . So it will be best perhaps not to try to give you any of my own "views" except, indeed, such views of war as one may get out of a parlor window. Not, in passing, that I haven't any! We all have views now, men, women and little boys,

> "Children with drums
> Strapped round them by the fond paternal ass,
> Peripatetics with a blade of grass
> Betwixt their thumbs,"—

from the modestly patriotic citizen who wears a postage stamp on his hat to the woman who walks in Broadway in that fearful object of contemplation, a "Union bonnet," composed of alternate layers of red, white and blue, with streaming ribbons "of the first." We all have our views of the war question and our plans of the coming campaign. An acquaintance the other day took her little child on some charitable errand through a dingy alley into a dirty, noisy, squalid tenement house. "Mamma," said he, "isn't this South Carolina?"

Inside the parlor windows the atmosphere has been very fluffy, since Sumter, with lint-making and the tearing of endless lengths of flannel and cotton bandages and cutting out of innumerable garments. How long it is since Sumter! I suppose it is because so much intense emotion has been crowded into the last two or three weeks, that the "time before Sumter" seems to belong to some dim antiquity. It seems as if we never were alive till now; never had a country till now. How could we ever have laughed at Fourth-of-Julys? Outside the parlor windows the city is gay and brilliant with excited crowds, the incessant movement and music of marching regiments and all the thousands of flags, big and little, which suddenly came fluttering out of every window and door and leaped from every church tower, house-top, staff and ship-mast. It seemed as if everyone had in mind to try and make some amends to it for those late grievous and bitter insults. You have heard how the enthusiasm has been deepening and widening from that time.

A friend asked an Ohio man the other day how the West was taking it. "The West?" he said, "the West is all one great Eagle-scream!" A New England man told us that at Concord the bells were rung and the President's call read aloud on the village common. On the day but one after that reading, the Concord Regiment was marching into Fanueil Hall. Somebody in Washington asked a Massachusetts soldier: "How many more men of your state are coming?" "All of us," was the answer. One of the wounded Lowell men crawled into a machine shop in Baltimore. An "anti-Gorilla" citizen, seeing how young he was, asked, "What brought you here fighting, so far away from your home, my poor boy?" "It was the stars and stripes," the dying voice said. Hundreds of such stories are told. Everybody knows one. You read many of them in the papers. In our own little circle of friends one mother has sent away an idolized son; another, two; another, four. One boy, just getting over diphtheria, jumps out of bed and buckles his knapsack on. One throws up his passage to Europe and takes up his "enfield." One sweet young wife is packing a regulation valise for her husband today, and doesn't let him see her cry. Another young wife is looking fearfully for news from Harper's Ferry, where her husband is ordered. He told me a month ago, *before Sumter*, that no Northman could be found to fight against the South. One or two of our soldier friends are surgeons or officers, but most of them are in the ranks, and think no work too hard or too mean, so it is for The Flag. Captain Schuyler Hamilton was an aid of General Scott's in Mexico, and saw service there, but he shouldered his musket and marched as a private with the Seventh. They wanted an officer when he got down there, and took him out of the ranks, but it was all the same to him; and so on, indefinitely.

The color is all taken out of the "Italian Question." Garibaldi indeed! "Deliverer of Italy!" Every mother's son of us is a "Deliverer." We women regretfully "sit at home at ease" and only appease ourselves by doing the little we can with sewing machines and patent bandage-rollers. Georgy, Miss Sarah Woolsey and half a dozen other friends earnestly wish to join the Nurse Corps, but are under the required age. The rules are stringent, no doubt wisely so, and society just now presents the unprecedented spectacle of many women trying to make it believed that they are over thirty!

The Vermont boys passed through this morning, with the "strength of the hills" in their marching and the green sprigs in their button-holes. The other day I saw some companies they told me were from Maine. They looked like it—sun-browned swingers of great axes, horn-handed "breakers of the glebe," used to wintering in the woods and getting frost-bitten and having their feet chopped off and conveying huge fleets of logs down spring-tide rivers in the snow and in the floods.—The sound of the drum is never out of our ears.

Never fancy that we are fearful or gloomy. We think we feel thoroughly that war is dreadful, especially war with the excitement off and the chill on, but there are so many worse things than gun-shot wounds! And among the worst is a hateful and hollow peace with such a crew as the "Montgomery mutineers." There was a dark time just after the Baltimore murders, when communication with Washington was cut off and the people in power seemed to be doing nothing to re-establish it. It cleared up, however, in a few days, and now we don't feel that the "social fabric"—I believe that is what it is called—is "falling to pieces" at all, but that it is getting gloriously mended. So, "Republicanism will wash"—*is* washed already in the water and the fire of this fresh baptism, "clothed in white samite, mystic, wonderful," and has a new name, which is *Patriotism*.

—BACON AND HOWLAND, eds., *Letters of a Family During the War*

5. "THE SPIRIT OF VIRGINIA CANNOT BE CRUSHED"

Virginia, where the tradition of nationalism was strong, hesitated to join the seceding states, but the attack on Fort Sumter and Lincoln's proclamation calling for 75,000 troops—together with geographical necessity—finally drew her into the Confederacy. On April 17, 1861, a convention voted for secession, 103 to 46, and this vote was ratified a month later by a popular vote of 96,750 to 32,134. Most of the minority vote came from the western counties, which shortly seceded and established the state of West Virginia.

The hopes and fears of Virginians are well illustrated by former President Tyler who, as President of the Peace Convention, labored for compromise but who, like Lee, went with his state when the die was cast. Mrs. Tyler, his second wife, was from New York.

John Tyler to Mrs. Tyler.

Richmond, April 17 [18], 1861

Well, my dearest one, Virginia has severed her connection with the Northern hive of abolitionists, and takes her stand as a sovereign and independent State. By a large vote she decided on yesterday, at about three o'clock, to resume the powers she had granted to the Federal government, and to stand before the world clothed in the full vestments of sovereignty. The die is thus cast, and her future in the hands of the god of battle. The contest into which we enter is one full of peril, but there is a spirit abroad in Virginia which cannot be crushed until the life of the last man is trampled out. The numbers opposed to us are immense; but twelve thousand Grecians conquered the whole power of Xerxes at Marathon, and our fathers, a mere handful, overcame the enormous power of Great Britain.

The North seems to be thoroughly united against us. The *Herald* and the *Express* both give way and rally the hosts against us. Things have gone to that point in Philadelphia that no one is safe in the expression of a Southern sentiment. . . . At Washington a system of martial law must have been established. The report is that persons are not permitted to pass through the city to the South. . . .

Two expeditions are on foot—the one directed against the Navy Yard at Gosport, the other Harper's Ferry. Several ships are up the river at the Navy Yard, and immense supplies of guns and powder; but there is no competent leader, and they have delayed it so long that the government has now a very strong force there. The hope is that Pickens will send two thousand men to aid in capturing it. From Harper's Ferry nothing is heard. The city is full of all sorts of rumors. To-morrow night is now fixed for the great procession; flags are raised all about town.

Your devoted,

J. Tyler.

Mrs. John Tyler to her mother.

Richmond, June 16, 1861

I rejoice in an opportunity to write you through the kindness of a gentleman who has some means of communication with Baltimore. The convention met again on the 12th, and I accompanied the President up. Shall return home on Tuesday. In the meantime the children left behind are in good hands. Mrs. R. Tyler and family of four children are at Sherwood. Gardie is with me here enjoying the military excitement, and Julia is at Mrs. Pegram's. All are well.

You have heard of the battle in the vicinity of Hampton and Bethel (that is around the location of Bethel church). The fight on the Southern side was more wonderful than the taking of Sumter—only 1,100 troops (eleven hundred) were there, eight hundred of whom were engaged against a force of Northern troops amounting to four or five thousand; but *one* killed and four slightly wounded on the Southern side; loss larger on the other. How can it be otherwise than that? The hand of Providence should assist this holy Southern cause. The Northern papers give garbled accounts, but *this* is the true statement. Hampton and vicinity have suffered all sorts of depredations from Lincoln's army—inoffensive people, and their private residences have been disturbed in every possible way; but the Villa I hear has been treated with more respect as yet.

More and more we have the *realization* of war; from day to day the people, the entire people, are making up their minds to it, until every family of high and low degree are seeing their male members don the soldier's dress and shoulder their musket to go forth for the protection of their invaded firesides. It makes the heart beat and the eyes fill to witness such noble resolution and bravery on the part of all, but in particular on the part of those who, bred in ease and luxury, still cheerfully accept every and any hardship that comes with a soldier's life, whether as officers or in the ranks, for the latter are thick with accomplished gentlemen, than permit the unresisted invasion of their dearest rights. The men have become heroes—*all*, from youths of seventeen to those far advanced in years; but one common feeling swells their bosoms, deep indignation against those who should have been their best friends, and not their worst enemies. An unlawful war has been waged against them, and if the possession of every warrior trait will enable them to "conquer a peace," there will soon be one for us. Every way I turn I see an acquaintance and friend, either in the flannel shirt of a private, or in the braided jacket of the zouave, or the plumed cap of the cavalry officer. It is women and children only that are not in arms *all ready* for a moment's notice. A large body of noble, brave Marylanders have found it impossible to *wait*, and have resigned with a feeling of relief their homes to *fight* side by side with their Southern brethren. By all sorts of stratagems they are slipping over fully armed, and joining their companions without delay.

Subjugate or *bring to terms* such a people! Little do you *dream* at the North of what stuff they are made. Why, even Gardie and Alex, mourn that they cannot at once be of them; they are *fired up* with enthusiasm for what they consider such a sacred cause as the defense of their soil from the wicked and cruel invader. It is a thrilling, melting sight to see the entrances into the city of troops by the trains from all parts of the Southern country, coming as they appear to feel, to the *rescue of old Virginia*. The fatigue of travel makes no impression upon them, and they joyfully march off to their encampments, apparently congratulating themselves they are so near the scene of action. "Still they come."

At church to-day Gen. Davis was introduced to me. He mentioned that Mrs. D. and himself would be to see me to-morrow. He is a splendid man, fine manners, and the bearing of one good and great. Gen. Lee called upon us after church; rather grayer than when I last met him, some years ago, but still the elegant officer, looking animated and full of vigor. He spoke very calmly and indifferently of the desecration of his home at Arlington, and the flight of his invalid wife. She has moved out of the way of the enemy twice, and now she says *they will have to take her*—she will move no more. The General laughed, as he repeated what she said, but added, as her health was much affected by rheumatism, it was quite a trial to her to be deprived of her home.

And now adieu, dear Mamma. Continue perfectly at ease about me. All I ask is, take care of yourself, and don't get sick.

Your affectionate daughter,

JULIA.

—TYLER, *Letters and Times of the Tylers*

6. "I AM FILLED WITH HORROR AT THE CONDITION OF OUR COUNTRY"

Nowhere in the Confederacy was Union sentiment stronger than in North Carolina, which was the last state to secede. The despair of Southern Union-

ists, faced as they were with hostility from both sides, can be read in the correspondence of Jonathan Worth, later governor of his state.

Jonathan Worth to Dr. C. W. Woolen.

Asheboro, May 17, 1861

I am filled with horror at the condition of our country. According to my notions of Government, there is much that is wrong on both sides. The Abolitionists of the Free States ought not to have agitated the slavery question at all, even conceding that their feeling is right. It only tends to make the treatment of slaves more vigorous and to encourage bitterness between the two sections. When it was seized upon as a party question it was easy to see it must soon become sectional. . . .

I have always regarded the dissolution of the Union as the greatest misfortune which could befall the whole nation and the whole human race. Hence I have abhorred the agitation of the slavery question as tending to this result. Acting on that conviction I have used all the efforts in my power to stay what I regarded as the madness of both sections, and in the immediate sphere of my influence have impressed my views upon others. My immediate constituents sustained me with greater unanimity than did the constituents of any other representative. I was the first public man in the State to call on the people to vote down the Convention on the 28th Feb., on the ground that the calling of it would tend to a dissolution of the Union. Everybody attributed to me a larger share of the credit or discredit of defeating the call of a Convention than to any other man in the State. I regarded the result in N. C. and Tenn. as arresting the march of madness. Union men had gained strength up to the proclamation of Lincoln. If he had withdrawn the garrison of Fort Sumter on the principle of a military necessity and in obedience in what seemed to be the will of Congress in refusing to pass the force bill, this State and Tenn. and the other slave States which had not passed the ordinance of Secession, would have stood up for the Union. In the feverish state of the popular mind, if he be a man of good sense, he knew he would crush the Union men in the Slave States by the policy he adopted. All of us who had stood by the Union, felt that he had abandoned us and surrendered us to the tender mercies of Democracy & the Devil. He must have known that he was letting loose on us a torrent to which we could oppose no resistance.

It may be said, theoretically, that this should not have been the effect. Statesmen should have common sense. All sensible men knew it would be the effect. We are still at a loss to determine whether he is an old goose, as well as each of his advisers, thinking to preserve the Union by his course, or whether he became apprehensive that the Union men were about to gain strength enough in the South to stay Secession and he desired to drive us all into rebellion, in order to make a crusade against slavery and desolate our section. In the former case he is a fool: in the latter—a devil. He could have adopted no policy so effectual to destroy the Union. Since the issue of that great proclamation, it is unsafe for a Union man in even N. C. to own he is for the Union. The feeling is to resist to the death. Union men feel that just as they had got so they could stand on their legs, Lincoln had heartlessly turned them over to the mercy of their enemies. We feel that his co-operation with the Secessionists left us no alternative but to take arms against our neighbors, or to defend ourself against his aggression.

I am still a Union man, but for military resistance to Lincoln, believing that Lincoln and his cabinet have acted on their mistaken impression that their policy was the best for the preservation of the Union, and that they do not intend to proclaim servile insurrection. If the latter is the design the South can be conquered only by extermination. If his purpose be, as he says, to respect property and discountenance rebellion or insurrection among our servile population, and our people become satisfied of this, many of our people will not willingly take arms.

I see no hope of any good and stable government except in the United government we are pulling down. It can not be united by war. If peace be immediately made, it will soon re-unite, with an anti-secession clause.

Write me again soon. The Quakers here will not believe your statements as to your Quakers volunteering and the floating of the Stars and Stripes over a Quaker Church.

—HAMILTON, ed., *The Correspondence of Jonathan Worth*

7. A NORTHERN DEMOCRAT URGES PEACEFUL SEPARATION

Peace sentiment was to be found in the North as well as in the South; many whose loyalty to the Union was beyond question were nevertheless in favor of letting the seceding states go in peace. Much of the antiwar sentiment, however, was inspired by distaste for Lincoln and for "black Republicanism." The attitude here expressed took extreme form in copperheadism, or in the activities of such organizations as the Knights of the Golden Circle.

John L. O'Sullivan was a distinguished lawyer, editor and journalist who is credited with the authorship of the phrase "manifest destiny"; he had been appointed Minister to Portugal by President Pierce and after his term ran out lingered on in Lisbon, Paris and London. Tilden was a leading Northern Democrat and, in 1876, candidate for the Presidency.

J. L. O'Sullivan to S. J. Tilden.

Lisbon, May 6, 1861

My Dear Tilden,—The heart-breaking news has just reached us here, first of the attack and capture of Sumter, for which the signal was so madly and so wickedly given by the administration (dominated, evidently, by the war portion of that party) in its despatch of reinforcements; and, secondly, of Lincoln's declaration of war by his proclamation for 75,000 volunteers for the recapture of all the Southern forts, that is, for the invasion of the South— an act followed of course, by secession of Virginia, and soon to be followed,

I have no doubt, by that of all or nearly all the border States. Also the telegraph tells of a Massachusetts regiment resisted in an (insane) attempt to force a passage through Baltimore. Gracious God, that we should have lived to see such things! You can better judge, than I could describe, my affliction. At first it drew from me convulsions of tears. . . .

What doom is sufficient for the mad authors of all this! By that I mean, for 9/10 of the crime, the ultra portion of the Republican party. The papers say that there is a common enthusiasm of all parties at the North for the support of the admn. I may stand alone, but I do not share this. I am extremely anxious to hear from you. Do write me your views. I chafe terribly under the impossibilities which alone prevent my hastening home. Not only have I not the means, but I cannot leave my debts here, when a short, prolonged stay will probably assure me the means of paying them. Then I shall come, to do my best in the fight at home for *peaceful* separation if reunion has become indeed impossible.

What will New York do? I trust devoutly that if any troops march from our State southward they may consist only of Republicans. My hope now is that the North will at last realize the mad horror of the whole thing, and that a cloud of witnesses will arise to protest against its being carried further. Thus far the country has drifted along, both sides standing obstinate to the consistency of their opposite *theories*. But surely all should now agree to pause and hold back! But the Republican leaders, I fear, will now move heaven and hell to push and drag the North to sustain them in the position to which they have brought things. And I fear much from the fighting character of our people. I dread the next news. If Maryland goes with Virginia, there will probably be dreadful fighting for the possession of Washington, unless the wise and patriotic like you can stop it.

We are exemplifying the fable of the dispute between the head and the tail of the snake for the right to lead. The Democratic party is the natural and the only possible government of our Democratic confederation. It alone has ever understood the idea of State rights. The tail has taken its turn of leadership and you see to what a pass it has brought the country.

Were it not for the immediate question of fighting to grow out of the question of the possession of Washington, I should say it were best that the border States should now all go at once, so as to make the North feel the absurdity of further prosecution of war. But reunion is now, I fear, scarcely to be hoped for!

Ever yours,

J. L. O'SULLIVAN.

—BIGELOW, ed., *Letters and Literary Memorials of Samuel J. Tilden*

8. "THE RACE OF PHILIP SIDNEYS IS NOT EXTINCT"

From his diplomatic post in Vienna the historian Motley watched with mounting anxiety the progress of the war. This letter to his old friend Dr. Holmes suggests something of the pride of the Boston aristocracy whose sons fought for the Union as the aristocrats of Virginia and South Carolina fought for independence.

The Wendell Holmes who had been wounded at Ball's Bluff was the later Justice of the U. S. Supreme Court, who said, "The generation that carried on the war has been set apart by its experience. Through our great good fortune our hearts were touched with fire."

John Lothrop Motley to Dr. O. W. Holmes.

Vienna, November 14th, 1861

My Dear Holmes,—Your letter of October 8th awaited me here. I need not tell you with what delight I read it, and with what gratitude I found you so faithful to the promises which we exchanged on board the *Europa*. . . . As soon as I read your letter I sat down to reply, but I had scarcely written two lines when I received the first telegram of the Ball's Bluff affair. I instantly remembered what you had told me—that Wendell "was on the right of the advance on the Upper Potomac, the post of honour and danger," and it was of course impossible for me to write to you till I had learned more, and you may easily conceive our intense anxiety. The bare brutal telegram announcing a disaster arrives always four days before any details can possibly be brought. Well, after the four days came my London paper; but, as ill-luck would have it, my American ones had not begun to arrive. At last, day before yesterday, I got a New York *Evening Post*, which contained Frank Palfrey's telegram. Then our hearts were saddened enough by reading, "Willie Putnam, killed; Lee, Revere, and George Perry, captured;" but they were relieved of an immense anxiety by the words, "O. W. Holmes, jun., slightly wounded."

Poor Mrs. Putnam! I wish you would tell Lowell (for to the mother or father I do not dare to write) to express the deep sympathy which I feel for their bereavement, that there were many tears shed in our little household in this distant place for the fate of his gallant, gentle-hearted, brave-spirited nephew. I did not know him much—not at all as grown man; but the name of Willie Putnam was a familiar sound to us six years ago on the banks of the Arno, for we had the pleasure of passing a winter in Florence at the same time with the Putnams, and I knew that that studious youth promised to be all which his name and his blood and the influences under which he was growing up entitled him to become. We often talked of American politics—I mean his father and mother and ourselves—and I believe that we thoroughly sympathized in our views and hopes. Alas, they could not then foresee that that fair-haired boy was after so short a time destined to lay down his young life on the Potomac, in one of the opening struggles for freedom and law with the accursed institution of slavery! Well, it is a beautiful death—the most beautiful that man can die. Young as he was, he had gained name and fame, and his image can never be associated in the memory of the hearts which mourn for him except with ideas of honor, beauty, and purity of manhood.

After we had read the New York newspaper, the next day came a batch of Boston dailies and a letter from my dear little Mary. I seized it with avidity and began to read it aloud, and before I had finished the first page it dropped from my hand and we all three burst into floods of tears. Mary wrote that Harry Higginson, of the 2nd, had visited the camp of the 20th, and that Wendell Holmes was shot through the lungs and not likely to re-cover. It seemed too cruel, just as we had been informed that he was but slightly wounded. After the paroxysm was over, I picked up the letter and read a rather important concluding phrase of Mary's statement, viz., "But this, thank God, has proved to be a mistake." I think if you could have been clairvoyant, and looked in upon our dark little sitting-room of the Archduke Charles Hotel, fourth storey, at that moment, you could have had proof enough, if you needed any fresh ones, of the strong hold that you and yours have on all our affections. There are very many youths in that army of freedom whose career we watch with intense interest; but Wendell Holmes is ever in our thoughts side by side with those of our own name and blood.

I renounce all attempt to paint my anxiety about our affairs. I do not regret that Wendell is with the army. It is a noble and healthy symptom that brilliant, intellectual, poetical spirits like his spring to arms when a noble cause like ours inspires them. The race of Philip Sidneys is not yet extinct, and I honestly believe that as much genuine chivalry exists in our Free States at this moment as there is or ever was in any part of the world, from the Crusaders down. I did not say a word when I was at home to Lewis Stackpole about his plans—but I was very glad when he wrote to me that he had accepted a captaincy in Stevenson's regiment. I suppose by this time that they are in the field. . . .

Nobody on this side the Atlantic has the faintest conception of our affairs. Let me hear from time to time, as often as you can, how you are impressed by the current events, and give me details of such things as im-mediately interest you. Tell me all about Wendell. How does your wife stand her trials? Give my love to her and beg her to keep a brave heart. *Haec olim meminisse juvabit.* And how will those youths who stay at home "account themselves accursed they were not there," when the great work has been done, as done it will be! Of that I am as sure as that there is a God in heaven.

—CURTIS, ed., *The Correspondence of John Lothrop Motley*

9. A YOUNG POET EXPLAINS THE SIGNIFICANCE OF THE WAR

Edmund Clarence Stedman was working on the New York World *when the war broke out. He hastened at once to Washington, went to the front as a war correspondent, and reported the First Battle of Bull Run. He took some pride in the fact that he had been the first to use the army telegraph—in June 1861. Later Stedman worked in the Attorney General's office and subsequently made a minor fortune in a brokerage office and a minor reputa-tion as a poet.*

This letter was in answer to maternal arguments against the war. It is perhaps worth adding that, though Stedman was only twenty-seven when war came, he did not enlist in the army.

Edmund Clarence Stedman to his mother.

Oct. 16, 1861 (Near Baker's Camp, Poolesville, Md.)

Pardon me for saying that I have attentively studied your and Mary's echoes of the family oracle's views on the war question, and think you do not have the slightest appreciation of the real points at issue. You need not take my notions for anything more than they are worth, but I am going, contrary to my usual habit, to give you some reasons for what you call my "enthusiasm." Premise that I am angry with myself for doing so, since first what is the use? Why trouble one's self with writing and arguing when no bread-and-butter are to be gained thereby? Why should I care what you think about it? and second, is it possible in a few lines, to make the issue to your mind? I think not; yet will make a few statements . . . from which your own judgment may reason out the whole.

I have enlisted all my humble energies in this cause, then, for two reasons: First, one of selfishness—the necessity for personal shaking-up and *rejuvenating*—the old, *healthy* love *action* rising in me, as described in the first part of the "Flood Tide"; the credit and reputation to be derived, and the subsistence earned, by my present occupation—the love of adventure, etc. Second, one of principle. I am really surprised to find myself sometimes forgetting self, and feeling human love and heartthrobs and patriotism. I think the War right and noble. For the first time the hackneyed stars-and-stripes have to me a significance. With the half-million noble and more simple-hearted men who are fighting for their country, I think that the "individual lessens and the cause is more and more." For eight years I have cared *nothing* for politics—have been disgusted with American life and doings. Now, for the first time, I am proud of my country and my grand heroic brethren. The greatness of the crisis, the Homeric grandeur of the contest, surrounds and elevates us all. See what it is:

1. *A complete revolution and renovation of all the customs and constitution of Americans North and South. A.* One million of the late emasculate Americans are put under magnificent hygienic training. Strong men and noble will henceforth inherit the land. *B.* The base passions attendant upon scheming and money-grubbing are laid aside for simple, chivalric, national love and hate, and henceforth the sentimental and poetic will fuse with the intellectual to dignify and elevate our race. The pride, pomp and *circumstance* of glorious war, and the big contests, *do* make ambition, virtue; and all *here, on the spot, see* that even bloodshed doeth its own good work. Men, that we once despised as small politicians, loafers, traders and what-not, are having all the good and heroic in them developed—are brightly transformed amid these altered scenes and nobler motives. *C.* Thousands of men of real talent, *born soldiers,* for whom in this country there has been no use hitherto, and who have consequently been "black sheep," gamblers, vagabonds, and

loafers, are now finding their legitimate calling—shooting back into their natural spheres. Suppose, there was no such thing as literature—what would fellows like myself do but be vagabonds and proletarians? Just so with your late fillibusters.

2. *The War is a duty on the part of the North.* It is not waged by abolitionists, it is *not* the result of abolitionism. We are not sure but that slavery is a very good thing in the Cotton states. In other latitudes I see for myself that it is good enough for the Negroes, but ruinous to the whites. There is a theory, that the Virginia and Kentucky gentry own slaves; this is false: I have seen for myself that the *niggars own the gentry.* Now I wish to make you and Mary understand that, although we see that this War will probably settle the slavery question, and possibly forever limit slavery to the Cotton States, *yet we are not fighting the Negro's cause.* Slavery has been the cause of the war in no sense other than that it has added another distinctness to the line betwixt North and South which climate and race had already drawn. The real cause of the War is a bitter and criminal hatred, entertained by the South against the North, and based on other than slave interests.

For fifty years the *character* of Southerners has become daily more domineering, insolent, irrational, haughty, scornful of justice. They have so long cracked their whips over Negroes that they now assume a certain inherent right to crack them over *white men;* assume the positive rights of a superior race; and have taken advantage of the North's desire for quiet and peace to impose upon us without stint. For years the tone of their actions and speeches, in Congress and society has expressed this sentiment and determination. Even Southern students at College, when I was at Yale, adopted the same tactics. One hundred of them—poor scholars, but blustering with rum and bowie knives—lorded it over four hundred studious New Englanders, simply because the latter *were* studious and desired to attain the objects aimed at in a collegiate course. At length the thing became degrading, and we arose one day and kicked them all out.

For fifty years the same plan has been practised on a larger scale in our national affairs. The South, assisted by Northern merchants whom it has governed, has been true enough to the Union, so long as every election gave *it* the power, and as foreign missions, army and navy commissions, presidencies, etc. were held in its own hands. But the census of 1850 shewed that the enterprising and industrious North was getting the balance of power. Then the South began to rebel and would have seceded had not the Clay compromise taken away *its sole pretext.* Now the census of 1860, and the Lincoln election have revived *both the desire and* the pretext, and it *has* seceded. . . .

3. *Right, power, and noble sentiments being on our side, it is our duty to carry on the War.* The South took active part in last Fall's election, thereby pledging itself to acquiesce in the result, and now *breaks* its pledge. The South has attacked the North; the South commenced the War; the South proceeded from domineering in Congress to actual hostilities, and I say that the North ignored the necessity of fighting for a period that became

almost degrading. You would perhaps like to have Northerners turn themselves into spittoons at once. Why, I was so indignant at the *too* long-suffering of the North that I seriously thought of disowning my own country and going to Canada or England to live. Tell your husband that if the Union is to be shattered at the will of a minority, we might as well give up the idea of nationality at once, disown patriotism and let all go to pieces. That nation is noblest which is the most sensitive about its own integrity, and will shed the most blood for a *principle*, and noble nations make noble individual men.

For such reasons I think the War of 1861 a benefit to both North and South, a duty on the part of the North, and please God, it shall be pushed to the true end. For one I have no objection to let the South go, and hope they will; but the dignity of right must first be sustained, and the injury to the republic avenged, and *they must ask to go in the proper way*. They might easily have effected a peaceful separation, by petition and vote, years ago. But that course would not have elevated Davis and the other ambitious men, now deluding their brave but senseless followers. And if we should now make peace, without proving our determination, power and heroism, we should forever hereafter be the world's laughing stock and the white slaves of our Southern neighbors.

You have lived so long away, and remained as it were, stationary in knowledge, of our affairs, that the whole character of America has whirled ten years by you and become transformed into necessities and emotions that you fail to comprehend.

Now don't say anything more against the War without first reading over this letter and seeing if I have now answered it.

—STEDMAN AND GOULD, *Life and Letters of Edmund Clarence Stedman*

10. THE SUPREME COURT UPHOLDS THE CONSTITUTION

Was the rebellion a war? Could the President proclaim a blockade, raise troops, and exercise, generally, war powers, without a recognition of a state of war by the Congress? These questions were not entirely in the realm of speculation. Alleging that only Congress could declare war, that there had been no such declaration or even recognition of war by Congress, that a blockade is an instrument of war, and that the Presidential proclamation of the blockade was therefore illegal, a group of owners of ships seized as prizes for trying to run the blockade sued for recovery of their property.

Justice Grier, in his decision in the so-called Prize Cases, recognized the existence of a state of war, sustained the blockade, and denounced the illegality of secession. But it was a close thing. Astonishing as it seems, today, four judges dissented.

Mr. Justice Grier:

Let us inquire whether, at the time this blockade was instituted, a state of war existed which would justify a resort to these means of subduing the hostile force.

War has been well defined to be, "That state in which a nation prosecutes its right by force."

The parties belligerent in a public war are independent nations. But it is not necessary, to constitute war, that both parties should be acknowledged as independent nations or sovereign States. A war may exist where one of the belligerents claims sovereign rights as against the other.

Insurrection against a government may or may not culminate in an organized rebellion, but a civil war always begins by insurrection against the lawful authority of the government. A civil war is never solemnly declared; it becomes such by its accidents—the number, power, and organization of the persons who originate and carry it on. When the party in rebellion occupy and hold in a hostile manner a certain portion of territory; have declared their independence; have cast off their allegiance; have organized armies; have commenced hostilities against their former Sovereign, the world acknowledges them as belligerents, and the contest a war. They claim to be in arms to establish their liberty and independence, in order to become a sovereign State, while the sovereign party treats them as insurgents and rebels who owe allegiance, and who should be punished with death for their treason. . . .

As a civil war is never publicly proclaimed, *eo nomine* against insurgents, its actual existence is a fact in our domestic history which the court is bound to notice and to know. . . .

This greatest of civil wars was not gradually developed by popular commotion, tumultuous assemblies, or local unorganized insurrections. However long may have been its previous conception, it nevertheless sprung forth suddenly from the parent brain, a Minerva in the full panoply of war. The President was bound to meet it in the shape it presented itself, without waiting for Congress to baptize it with a name; and no name given to it by him or them could change the fact.

It is not the less a civil war, with belligerent parties in hostile array, because it may be called an "insurrection" by one side, and the insurgents be considered as rebels or traitors. It is not necessary that the independence of the revolted province or State be acknowledged in order to constitute it a party belligerent in a war according to the law of nations. Foreign nations acknowledge it as war by a declaration of neutrality. The condition of neutrality cannot exist unless there be two belligerent parties. . . .

After such an official recognition by the sovereign, a citizen of a foreign State is estopped to deny the existence of a war, with all its consequences, as regards neutrals. They cannot ask a court to affect a technical ignorance of the existence of a war, which all the world acknowledges to be the greatest civil war known in the history of the human race, and thus cripple the arm of the government and paralyze its power by subtile definitions and ingenious sophisms.

The law of nations is also called the law of nature; it is founded on the common consent as well as the common sense of the world. It contains no such anomalous doctrine as that which this court are now for the first time desired to pronounce, to wit: That insurgents who have risen in rebellion

Frank Leslie's Illustrated Newspaper

Lincoln's First Inauguration

Harper's Weekly

The House Tops in Charleston During the Bombardment
of Fort Sumter

against their sovereign, expelled her courts, established a revolutionary government, organized armies, and commenced hostilities, are not enemies because they are traitors; and a war levied on the government by traitors, in order to dismember and destroy it, is not a war because it is an "insurrection."

—*Prize Cases,* 67 United States Supreme Court Reports 635 (1863)

III

The Gathering of the Hosts

LOOKING *back on four years of war Lincoln said, in his memorable Second Inaugural Address, "Neither party expected for the war the magnitude or the duration which it has already attained. . . . Each looked for an easier triumph, and a result less fundamental and astounding."*

Certainly neither side was prepared for a long war or even for a hard one. Northerners could hardly believe that the South would actually fight; Southerners deluded themselves that Yankee traders and workingmen were unwilling to fight. The North had a regular army of some 16,000, but with secession many of these resigned to go with their states; the South had no army, though as early as February 28 the President had been authorized to accept such state troops as were offered.

The firing on Fort Sumter inspired widespread enthusiasm in the South; in the North it inspired not so much enthusiasm as sober loyalty to the flag and the Union. Everywhere, North and South, boys and men rallied to the colors; everywhere great crowds assembled to see the new recruits march off to some near-by camp, proud of their improvised uniforms, happily unaware of what lay ahead.

> *North and South they assembled, one cry and the other cry.*
> *And both are ghosts to us now, old drums hung up on a wall,*
> *But they were the first hot wave of youth too-ready to die,*
> *And they went to war with an air, as if they went to a ball.*
>
> *Dress-uniform boys who rubbed their buttons brighter than gold,*
> *And gave them to girls for flowers and raspberry-lemonade,*
> *Unused to the sick fatigue, the route-march made in the cold,*
> *The stink of the fever camps, the tarnish rotting the blade.*

By act of March 8, 1861, the Confederate Congress created an army of seven regiments with enlistments for from three to five years. Two months later the President was authorized to accept the services of all volunteers who presented themselves. For the most part, however, the Confederacy raised its army through the states; some states even provided for conscription, on their own. As volunteering proved inadequate, the Confederate government

---

* From *John Brown's Body* in *The Selected Works of Stephen Vincent Benét*, published by Rinehart and Company, Inc. Copyright 1927, 1928 by Stephen Vincent Benét.

adopted conscription; an act of April 16, 1862, made all men between the ages of 18 and 35 subject to draft, and these age limits were later broadened to embrace all between 17 and 50.

On April 15, 1861, Lincoln called for 75,000 three-months volunteers, assigning quotas to each state and Territory. The method of raising companies was left pretty much to the states and localities. The initiative was usually taken by local leaders who undertook to recruit companies—and get themselves elected to captaincies or lieutenancies. When an appropriate number of volunteers had been pledged (many deserted to other companies), the governor of the state would enroll the company in the state militia and assume appropriate expenses. Such matters as providing uniforms, arms, equipment, even provisions, were handled haphazardly; sometimes these things were provided by rich men who raised the companies, sometimes by community effort, but usually by the states.

The first call for troops proved inadequate and on May 3 the President called for an additional 500,000; actually 700,000 were raised under this call. Thereafter came a series of calls for varying numbers and for varying periods of service. Altogether the states were required to raise 2,763,670 troops, and furnished 2,772,408, but this figure includes re-enlistments. Perhaps two thirds of these actually served in the army.

This is as good a place as any to deal with the vexatious question of numbers in the Union and Confederate armies. Let it be said at once that the statistics for the Union armies are confusing and unreliable, and that there are no satisfactory statistics whatever for the Confederate armies. A number of considerations enter into even the most elementary computations. There is, for example, the problem of differing periods of service. In both armies service varied from three months to three years, or the duration of the war: obviously a soldier in for four years counts more than one in for three or six months. There is the difficult question of desertion, or failure to report (which was technical desertion); this ran as high as ten per cent in both armies. There is the problem of re-enlistment, and of bounty jumping. There is the problem of the wounded and the sick; these were in the army, but were of course ineffectives.

Frederick Phisterer, statistician of the Union armies, gives a total of 2,772,408 furnished by the states and Territories, or credited to them; reducing this to a three-years-service standard he arrives at the figure 2,320,272. Thomas Livermore, whose Numbers and Losses *is perhaps more reliable, estimates total enlistments of 2,898,304 of whom some 230,000 failed to serve, for one reason or another. Reducing this figure to a three-years-service equivalent—and taking into account desertion—he gives a total of 1,556,678 for the Union armies. Estimates of the numbers in the Confederate Army run all the way from a low of 600,000 to a high of 1,500,000. Livermore's estimate of the number equivalent to three-years service is 1,082,119—perhaps as good as any.*

Far more illuminating are the numbers actually on the rolls at any one time: this gives a much truer index of relative numbers. The simplest thing

*here is to reproduce the table which Livermore worked out from the Official
Records:*

	UNION	CONFEDERATE
July 1861	186,751	112,040
Jan. 1862	575,917	351,418
Mar. 1862	637,126	401,395
Jan. 1863	918,121	446,622
Jan. 1864	860,737	481,180
Jan. 1865	959,460	445,203

*Two conclusions emerge from these figures. First that a relatively much
higher proportion of Southern than Northern men served in the army. Second that, given the requirements of offensive warfare, of invasion, and of
maintaining long lines of communication, the North had far less effective
numerical superiority than the bare figures would suggest.*

1. "OUR PEOPLE ARE ALL UNITED"

*A member of a great Huguenot family of South Carolina, Henry William
Ravenel is remembered for his career as one of the leading American botanists
and for his charming and illuminating* Journal, *from which this account of
the impact of the war is taken.*

[April 18, 1861] . . . This morning Mr. Cornish called to see us. One of
the remarkable features of the times is that men of all classes & conditions, of
all occupations & professions are of one mind. We have students of Divinity
& ministers of the Gospel in the ranks with musket on their shoulders doing
battle for their country. Some have gone as chaplains & followed their companies into camp. All give us their prayers & cheer us onward with words of
approval. The ablest vindication of our institution of domestic slavery has
only lately been published in New York from the pen of Dr. Seabury, a distinguished minister of the Prot. Epis. Church. The war feeling has been
nourished & stimulated at the North by the intense hatred of disappointed
politicans & mad fanatics, who would consummate their hellish purposes upon
us through a sea of blood if possible. The collision which has just taken place,
from their determined purpose to hold a fort in our waters & thus subject us
to a humiliating position, will probably raise a fury of excitement & bring
over many to their side, who think their Govt. should be sustained in war,
right or wrong;—but we have great numbers of staunch friends, who will be
heard in time, as soon as the first paroxysm is over. Old memories of former
party attachments, personal intercourse with Southerners, connections by
friendships & blood, & above all, self interest will bring about a reaction &
sober second thought will give them time for consideration, & to mature a
public feeling there, which even those who are thirsting for our blood, will
have to respect. . . .

Th. 25. . . . The New York Herald speaks of raising 500000 men & speedily conquering a peace. Easier said than done. We can do the same if necessary & fighting for our liberty & our homes, we have no doubt of the issue. All good men should ardently desire a return of peace, but it must be upon terms honorable to us & our rights. I fear the Northern people have an impression that we are unable to cope with them, from inferiority in numbers, want of necessary means; & that our slave population is an element of weakness. It may be necessary therefore that they should be disabused of such impressions, & learn to appreciate & understand us better. If we *must* pass through the terrible ordeal of War to teach them this lesson, so be it. It may be best in the end. We put our trust in the God of battles & the impartial Dispenser of Justice, & are willing to abide the issue. Our people are all united & stand up as one man in defence of their country. Our Negroes are contented & loyal. The old & the infirm who have not yet gone out to battle are ready to take their places in the ranks when their services are needed. Our women & children all enthusiastic for the common defence, 'Can such a population be subjugated?' . . .

M. 29. . . . We have never sought to assail the Northern people in any way—we have only asked to be let alone. We have been satisfied, in the sight of God & of our approving conscience, that our institutions were sanctioned by justice & religion, that mutual benefits were secured to both races inhabiting our Southern states—that our very existence as a people was staked upon its preservation;—& that it has the sanction of natural, as well as revealed religion. They have refused to permit us to remain in peace with them, & now that we have decided as a last effort of self preservation to establish a governt. for ourselves, they insolently threaten us with subjugation. We have desired to separate from them in peace, & have offered to negotiate on friendly terms the manner of separation. They have rejected all our overtures & have answered us with insult & defiance. They appeal to arms. We will meet them, putting our trust in Him who is the father of us all & in whose hands are the destinies of his people.

—CHILDS, ed., *The Private Journal of Henry William Ravenel*

2. SOUTHERN LADIES SEND THEIR MEN OFF TO WAR

Here is an unpretentious recollection of the impact of secession and war on a Georgia community. The enthusiasm of the women of the South for the war was remarked by countless contemporaries and has served as a theme for countless novels and stories. What Mrs. Ward says of the situation in Rome might have been said with equal truth about almost every other Southern community—"if the Southern men had not been willing to go I reckon they would have been made to go by the women."

Mrs. Ward was a Georgia matron of twenty when the war came; these recollections were given verbally to a Congressional committee investigating labor relations in the South. Douglas Freeman calls them "one of the most remarkable of all the women's commentaries on the war."

WELL, it was pretty hard for any one in private life, especially for a lady, to realize or appreciate the imminent danger that existed up to the very breaking out of the war, up to the time that the troops were ordered out. Discussions about the state of the country and about the condition of public affairs and the causes for war were frequent, of course, and I think I may safely say that in those discussions the women of the South without exception all took the secession side. There were a great many men in the Southern homes that were disposed to be more conservative and to regret the threatened disruption of the Union, but the ladies were all enthusiastically in favor of secession. Their idea was to let war come if it must, but to have the matter precipitated and get through with it, because this feeling of apprehension and this political wrangling had been continued for many years previous, and we felt that we in the South were strong in our own resources, and in fact we knew very little of the resources of the North compared with those of the South. My mother was a Northern woman and she always regarded the threat of war with the greatest apprehension and fear, because, as she said, she knew more about the resources of the North than others did, more than I did, for instance, or the other people of my age. But the women of the South generally were altogether in favor of secession and of the war, if there had to be a war, and if the Southern men had not been willing to go I reckon they would have been made to go by the women.

The day that Georgia was declared out of the Union was a day of the wildest excitement in Rome. There was no order or prearrangement about it at all, but the people met each other and shook hands and exchanged congratulations over it and manifested the utmost enthusiasm. Of course a great many of the older and wiser heads looked on with a great deal of foreboding at these rejoicings and evidences of delight, but the general feeling was one of excitement and joy.

Then we began preparing our soldiers for the war. The ladies were all summoned to public places, to halls and lecture-rooms, and sometimes to churches, and everybody who had sewing-machines was invited to send them; they were never demanded because the mere suggestion was all-sufficient. The sewing-machines were sent to these places and ladies that were known to be experts in cutting out garments were engaged in that part of the work, and every lady in town was turned into a seamstress and worked as hard as anybody could work; and the ladies not only worked themselves but they brought colored seamstresses to these places, and these halls and public places would be just filled with busy women all day long.

But even while we were doing all these things in this enthusiastic manner, of course there was a great deal of the pathetic manifested in connection with this enthusiasm, because we knew that the war meant the separation of our soldiers from their friends and families and the possibility of their not coming back. Still, while we spoke of these things we really did not think that there was going to be actual war. We had an idea that when our soldiers got upon the ground and showed, unmistakably that they were really ready and willing to fight—an idea that then, by some sort of hocus-pocus, we didn't know what, the whole trouble would be declared at an end. Of course we were not fully conscious of that feeling at the time, but that the feeling existed was beyond doubt from the great disappointment that showed itself afterwards when things turned out differently. We got our soldiers ready for the field, and the Governor of Georgia called out the troops and they were ordered out, five companies from Floyd County and three from Rome. They were ordered to Virginia under the command of General Joseph E. Johnston. The young men carried dress suits with them and any quantity of fine linen. . . .

Every soldier, nearly, had a servant with him, and a whole lot of spoons and forks, so as to live comfortably and elegantly in camp, and finally to make a splurge in Washington when they should arrive there, which they expected would be very soon indeed. That is really the way they went off; and their sweethearts gave them embroidered slippers and pin-cushions and needle-books, and all sorts of such little et ceteras, and they finally got off, after having a very eloquent discourse preached to them at the Presbyterian church, by the Presbyterian minister, Rev. John A. Jones. I remember his text very well. It was, "Be strong and quit yourselves like men." I don't know that I have had occasion to think of that sermon for years, but although this occurred more than twenty years ago, I remember it very distinctly at this moment. Then the choir played music of the most mournful character—"Farewell," and "Good Bye," and all that, and there was just one convulsive sob from one end of the church to the other, for the congregation was composed of the mothers and wives and sisters and daughters of the soldiers who were marching away.

The captain of the Light Guards, the most prominent company, a company composed of the *élite* of the town, had been married on the Thursday evening before this night of which I am speaking. He was a young Virginian. His wife came of very patriotic parents, and was a very brave woman herself. She came into the church that day with her husband, and walked up the aisle with him. She had on a brown traveling-dress, and a broad scarf crossed on her dress, and, I think, on it was inscribed, "The Rome Light Guards," and there was a pistol on one side and a dagger on the other. This lady went to the war with her husband, and staid there through the whole struggle, and never came home until the war was over.

—Testimony of Mrs. Mary A. Ward

3. TWO ENGLISH VISITORS DESCRIBE THE CONFEDERATE ARMY

How remarkable the American volunteer armies really were has never been appreciated by Americans themselves. It is foreigners who note the difference between American and European armies. The American Civil War attracted a large number of foreign observers, and most of them seemed to find their way into the Confederacy. A substantial number of them went home to write articles about their experiences.

*Here we have two English views of the Confederate armies and soldiers.
As neither of them is signed, it is difficult to know just when these visitors
got their glimpse of the Confederacy, but it was clearly in 1861 and 1862.*

A. "The Personnel of the Army Is Very Varied"

THE appearance which a regiment presents on parade is remarkable to
the eye of a European. Many are composed of companies who have
uniforms of different colours; but in these cases there is always some distinc-
tive badge by which their particular corps can be easily told. This defect,
consequent upon the companies being raised in different neighbourhoods, is
being quickly remedied, and we saw numerous regiments which had lately
arrived, whose dress was all that the Horse Guards could desire.

The *personnel* of the army is very varied. For instance, in the Louisiana
regiments are seen the bronzed and fiery-eyed French creoles mingled with
many Irish and native Americans from New Orleans. The Alabamans, proud
of their gallant 4th, their flying artillery, and other regiments, may be known
by their strong frames, gay manners, and devil-may-care air. The South
Carolinians, sallow in complexion, tall in stature, seldom need the Palmetto
to tell the stranger the State from which they come; but in all regiments it
is easy to perceive differences in manner and bearing, indicative of the various
classes of which the army is composed.

Numbers of wealthy planters serve as privates side by side with the professional man, the shopkeeper, the clerk, the labourer; and all go through the
ordinary fatigue duties incident to camp-life. We saw a poor Negro servant
actually shedding tears because his master, on being told off to dig a trench
round a battery, would not allow him "to lend a hand."

" 'Twill nebber do, massa," he said; "I go 'tarnal mad wid dem darn'd
Yankees."

One day we heard a lad boasting to one of a different regiment of the
number of gentlemen in his company who had thousands of dollars at their
command. The latter replied, "Oh, of course they fight; but we have some
in ours who have not got a cent!" The Washington artillery, comprising
many batteries is composed of the best blood in New Orleans. The gunners,
dressed in light-blue uniforms, are all men of independent means. General
Beauregard's son, for instance, left his father's staff, and entered as a private.
The drivers are regularly enlisted into the army, and paid by the regiment; so
here is a force which does not cost the country a single farthing. Their
efficiency is undoubted, and the execution which they did at Bull's Run has
led to their material augmentation, and the formation of others on similar
principles. From the same city comes a very different regiment, called the
New Orleans "Zouaves," dressed in red caps, blue braided jackets, and
trousers striped with light grey and red. These men look like pirates—bearded,
fierce-looking fellows. . . . As they marched past the General with a long
swinging step, singing a wild martial air, we thought they were as formidable
a body of men as we should care to see.

The drill of the army is the same as the French, the step even quicker than the Zouaves, and a good deal longer than that of the English infantry. Movements are executed with considerable precision, and as rapidly as in English light-infantry battalions.

From the reports we had heard in the North, we expected to find ragged and half-clad regiments; instead of which we failed, during many rides through the various camps, to see one man who was not clad in serviceable attire. It was expected that winter clothing would be served out before the 1st of November, and that dress would then become more uniform.

But the point to which the chief attention of officers and men is directed is the arms. Besides the Enfield rifle, most of the privates in the army carry at least one revolver and a bowie-knife: these are invariably kept bright and in good condition; and the early training which all Southerners undergo in shooting squirrels as soon as they are able to handle a gun, gives them a facility of using their weapons and a correctness of aim that renders their fire unusually formidable.

—Anonymous, "A Month with the 'Rebels'"

B. "The High Standards of Intelligence"

The Confederate soldier at first sight certainly presented a somewhat uncouth and even sorry appearance: about his person any kind of coat, or more commonly nothing beyond shirt and pantaloons; on his head, as the case might be, a cap, a straw hat, a slouch hat, or no hat at all. A closer scrutiny, however, showed that essentials were well provided. Besides his musket and cartridge-box, every man had a canteen, most men a blanket and a haversack. A more suitable equipment for summer service in Virginia could hardly have been devised.

What gives peculiar interest to the Confederate soldier's dress is the individual history which attaches to each separate article. From the blanket he sleeps on to the cartridge he shoots with, almost everything has been appropriated from the enemy at one time or another. This rifle was exchanged for the old flint-lock on the field of Manassas; that canteen was taken at Shiloh; the grey mare yonder, with M'Clellan's saddle, was captured in the cavalry charge at Williamsburg; these boots were taken out of the Yankee stores at Winchester. The Negro who is following with the saucepan and the extra blanket, being wiser than his master, has consulted comfort rather than prejudice, and prevailed upon himself to wear a Yankee uniform, in consideration that the former proprietor was a full colonel.

Entire batteries pass down the road, with "U. S." in prominent white letters on the caissons. It is no exaggeration to say that a great part of the Confederate army has been equipped at the expense of the United States. Flint-locks and fowling-pieces have been exchanged for good Minie rifles. There was, however, still so great a want of small-arms, that a considerable part of the army were armed with smooth-bore of home manufacture, loaded with a ball and three buckshot. This deficiency has, perhaps, not been altogether a disadvantage, inasmuch as the necessity of getting to close quarters, in order to put themselves on an equality with their opponents, has in no small degree produced among the Confederates that habit of closing with the enemy which has proved so inconvenient to the Northern troops. It seems inconceivable until witnessed, that the same men who have been marching, or rather carelessly lounging, along the road in loose and slovenly array, should, at the sound of the first shell that whistles overhead, form up at the words of their officers, with ease and rapidity, into a line so close and compact, that the sight of it would give joy to a martinet's heart. The soldiers of the Southern army were scrambled together in a few months, and the greater part of them never have gone through any regular course of drill, and are, therefore, wanting in the smartness and precision which distinguish good troops in Europe. Men take off their hats instead of saluting; orders are given in a loose conversational tone, and the gunner in a battery will suggest an opinion to the captain. But though, for these reasons, the troops might not be presentable on parade, a year's hard service has rendered them efficient for the field.

The very high standard of individual intelligence, moreover, supplies the want of order in a great measure. Things which, in other armies, if not done on strict rule, would be altogether neglected, somehow "get themselves done" in this volunteer army. . . .

The great strength and power of the Southern army lies in the individual resolution of the men. Every private feels a determination, not only to carry his regiment through the fight, but to see his country through the war. Boys of fifteen may be seen by the side of grey-haired men. Men who could not obtain arms have been known to fall in with the rear rank, and go into action on the chance of picking up a musket on the first opportunity. It has been described how, at the commencement of the war, all the wealthiest men crowded into the ranks: there has been time for the first enthusiasm to wear away, and yet there are no signs of any flinching from the contest. Scores of names could be mentioned of men who, after having served out their first term of enlistment (twelve months), spent a week with their relations, and then returned to volunteer for three years or for the war. Indeed, no man who shrank from the war could ever again venture to address a lady.

Such was the condition and such the material of the army under General Lee, who, after having for weeks awaited an onward move to Richmond on the part of the Federal army, was now about to take the initiative.

—Anonymous, "Ten Days in Richmond"

4. THE NORTH BUILDS A VAST ARMY OVERNIGHT

The United States was notoriously unprepared for war, and the temper of the people—in the North even more than in the South—was pacific. Many foreign critics doubted that a nation without military traditions or a military caste could organize for war. Edward Dicey, a liberal English journalist and scholar, spent six months in the United States in the midst of the Civil

War and, after his return, hastened to publish a book giving his countrymen
a better appreciation of the Union cause. Another Englishman, the novelist
Anthony Trollope, who visited the United States during these years, was
similarly impressed by the might of the North.

SURELY no nation in the world has gone through such a baptism of war
as the people of the United States underwent in one short year's time.
With the men of the Revolution the memories of the revolutionary wars had
died out. Two generations had passed away to whom war was little more
than a name. The Mexican campaign was rather a military demonstration
than an actual war, and the sixteen years which had elapsed since its termination form a long period in the life of a nation whose whole existence has
not completed its first century. Twenty months ago there were not more
than 12,000 soldiers in a country of 31,000,000. A soldier was as rare an object
throughout America as in one of our country hamlets. I recollect a Northern
lady telling me that, till within a year before, she could not recall the name
of a single person whom she had ever known in the army, and that now she
had sixty friends and relatives who were serving in the war; and her case was
by no means an uncommon one.

Once in four years, on the fourth of March, two or three thousand troops
were collected in Washington to add to the pomp of the Presidential inauguration; and this was the one military pageant the country had to boast
of. Almost in a day this state of things passed away. Our English critics
were so fond of repeating what the North could not do—how it could not
fight, nor raise money, nor conquer the South—that they omitted to mention what the North *had* done. There was no need to go farther than my
windows at Washington to see the immensity of the war. It was curious to
me to watch the troops as they came marching past. Whether they were
regulars or volunteers, it was hard for the unprofessional critic to discern;
for all were clad alike, in the same dull, grey-blue overcoats, and most of
the few regular regiments were filled with such raw recruits that the difference between volunteer and regular was not a marked one.

Of course it was easy enough to pick faults in the aspect of such troops.
As each regiment marched, or rather waded through the dense slush and mud
which covered the roads, you could observe many inaccuracies of military
attire. One man would have his trousers rolled up almost to his knees; another would wear them tucked inside his boots; and a third would appear
with one leg of his trousers hanging down, and the other gathered tightly
up. It was not unfrequent, too, to see an officer with his epaulettes sewed on
to a common plain frock-coat. Then there was a slouching gait about the
men, not soldierlike to English eyes. They used to turn their heads round
when on parade, with an indifference to rule which would drive an old drill-
sergeant out of his senses. There was an absence, also, of precision in the
march. The men kept in step; but I always was at a loss to discover how
they ever managed to do so. The system of march, it is true, was copied
rather from the French than the English or Austrian fashion; but still it was

something very different from the orderly disorder of a Zouave march. That all these, and a score of similar irregularities, are faults, no one—an American least of all—would deny. But there are two sides to the picture.

One thing is certain, that there is no physical degeneracy about a race which could produce such regiments as those which formed the army of the Potomac. Men of high stature and burly frames were rare, except in the Kentucky troops; but, on the other hand, small, stunted men were almost unknown. I have seen the armies of most European countries; and I have no hesitation in saying that, as far as the average raw material of the rank and file is concerned, the American army is the finest.

The officers are, undoubtedly, the weak point of the system. They have not the military air, the self-possession which long habit of command alone can give; while the footing of equality on which they inevitably stand with the volunteer privates, deprives them of the esprit de corps belonging to a ruling class. Still they are active, energetic, and constantly with their troops.

Wonderfully well equipped too, at this period of the war, were both officers and men. Their clothing was substantial and fitted easily, their arms were good, and the military arrangements were as perfect as money alone could make them.

It was remarkable to me how rapidly the new recruits fell into the habits of military service. I have seen a Pennsylvanian regiment, raised chiefly from the mechanics of Philadelphia, which, six weeks after its formation, was, in my eyes, equal to the average of our best-trained volunteer corps, as far as marching and drill-exercise went. Indeed, I often asked myself what it was that made the Northern volunteer troops look, as a rule, so much more soldier-like than our own. I suppose the reason is, that across the Atlantic there was actual war, and that at home there was at most only a parade. I have no doubt that, in the event of civil war or invasion, England would raise a million volunteers as rapidly as America has done—more rapidly she could not; and that, when fighting had once begun, there would only be too much of grim earnestness about our soldiering; but it is not want of patriotism to say that the American volunteers looked to me more business-like than our own. At the scene of war itself there was no playing at soldiering. No gaudy uniforms or crack companies, no distinction of classes. From every part of the North; from the ports of New York and Boston; from the homesteads of New England; from the mines of Pennsylvania and the factories of Pittsburgh; from the shores of the great lakes; from the Mississippi valley; and from the far-away Texan prairies, these men had come to fight for the Union. It is idle to talk of their being attracted by the pay alone. Large as it is, the pay of thirteen dollars a month is only two dollars more than the ordinary pay of privates in the Federal army during peace times. Thirteen shillings a week is poor pay for a labouring man in America, even with board, especially during this war, when the wages of unskilled labour amounted to from twenty to thirty shillings a week. . . .

The bulk of the native volunteers consisted of men who had given up good situations in order to enlist, and who had families to support at home;

and for such men the additional pay was not an adequate inducement to incur the dangers and hardships of war. Of course, wherever there is an army, the scum of the population will always be gathered together; but the average morale and character of the couple of hundred thousand troops collected round Washington was extremely good. There was very little outward drunkenness, and less brawling about the streets than if half a dozen English militia regiments had been quartered there. The number of papers purchased daily by the common soldiers, and the amount of letters which they sent through the military post, was astonishing to a foreigner, though less strange when you considered that every man in that army, with the exception of a few recent immigrants, could both read and write. The ministers, also, of the different sects, who went out on the Sundays to preach to the troops, found no difficulty in obtaining large and attentive audiences.

—DICEY, *Six Months in the Federal States*

5. NORTHERN BOYS JOIN THE RANKS

We have here four brief accounts of the process of recruiting companies. Warren Goss of the 2nd Massachusetts Artillery contributes the first; he fought through most of the campaigns in the East, was twice captured and exchanged, and lived to write a number of lively books on the war.

Josiah Favill, who got himself a commission as a lieutenant, rose to be brevet colonel before the end of the war; his diary is one of the better accounts of the war in the East.

Sergeant—later Captain—John Adams enlisted in the 1st Battalion of Rifles, part of the 19th Massachusetts Infantry; his major, Ben: Perley Poore, was a famous journalist and historian whose experience in the war was of the briefest.

The fourth, and the most realistic of them all, is from the pen of Michael Fitch, of the 6th (later the 21st) Wisconsin Volunteers; Fitch was brevetted out as a colonel at the end of the war.

A. WARREN GOSS ENLISTS IN THE UNION ARMY

BEFORE the war had really begun I enlisted. I had read the papers, and attended flag-raisings, and heard orators declaim of "undying devotion to the Union." One speaker to whom I listened declared that "human life must be cheapened," but I never learned that he helped on the work experimentally. When men by the hundred walked soberly and deliberately to the front and signed the enlistment papers, he didn't show any inclination that way. As I came out of the hall with conflicting emotions, feeling as though I should have to go finally or forfeit my birthright as an American citizen, one of the orators who stood at the door, glowing with enthusiasm and patriotism, and shaking hands effusively with those who enlisted, said to me:

"Did you enlist?"

"No," I said, "Did you?"

"No; they won't take me. I have got a lame leg and a widowed mother to take care of."

Another enthusiast I remember, who was eager to enlist—others. He declared the family of no man who went to the front should suffer. After the war he was prominent among those in our town who at town meeting voted to refund the money to such as had expended it to procure substitutes during the war. He has, morever, been fierce and uncompromising toward the ex-Confederates since the war closed, and I have heard him repeatedly express the wish that all the civil and general officers of the late Confederacy might be court-martialled and shot.

I was young, but not unobserving, and did not believe, from the first, in a sixty days' war; nor did I consider ten dollars a month and the promised glory, large pay for the services of an able-bodied young man. Enlistment scenes are usually pictured as entirely heroic, but truth compels me to acknowledge that my feelings were mixed. At this moment I cannot repress a smile of amusement and pity for that young recruit—myself.

It was the news that the Sixth Massachusetts Regiment had been mobbed by roughs on their passage through Baltimore which gave me the war fever. When I read Governor Andrews' pathetic telegram to have the hero martyrs "preserved in ice and tenderly sent forward," somehow, though I felt the pathos of it, I could not reconcile myself to the ice. Ice in connection with patriotism did not give me agreeable impressions of the war, and when I came to think of it, the stoning of the heroic "sixth" didn't suit me; it detracted from my desire to die a soldier's death. I lay awake all night thinking it over, with the "ice" and "brickbats" before my mind. However, the fever culminated that night, and I resolved to enlist.

"Cold chills" ran up and down my back as I got out of bed after the sleepless night, and shaved, preparatory to other desperate deeds of valor. I was twenty years of age, and when anything unusual was to be done, like fighting or courting, I shaved. With a nervous tremor convulsing my whole system, and my heart thumping like muffled drum-beats, I stood before the door of the recruiting office and, before turning the knob to enter, read and re-read the advertisement for recruits posted thereon, until I knew all its peculiarities. The promised chances for "travel and promotion" seemed good, and I thought I might have made a mistake in considering war so serious after all. "Chances for travel." I must confess now, after four years of soldiering, that the "chances for travel" were no myth. But "promotion" was a little uncertain and slow.

I was in no hurry to open the door. Though determined to enlist I was half inclined to put it off awhile; I had a fluctuation of desires; I was faint-hearted and brave; I wanted to enlist,—and yet—— Here I turned the knob, and was relieved. I had been more prompt, with all my hesitation, than the officer in his duty; he wasn't in.

Finally he came and said: "What do you want, my boy?"

"I want to enlist," I responded, blushing deeply with upwelling patriotism and bashfulness. Then the surgeon came to strip and examine me. In justice to myself, it must be stated that I signed the rolls without a tremor. It is common to the most of humanity, I believe, that when confronted with actual danger, men have less fear than in its contemplation.

My first uniform was a bad fit; my trousers were too long by three or four inches; the flannel shirt was coarse and unpleasant, too large at the neck and too short elsewhere. The forage cap was an ungainly bag with pasteboard top and leather visor; the blouse was the only part which seemed decent; while the overcoat made me feel like a little nib of corn amid a preponderance of husk. Nothing except "Virginia mud" ever took down my ideas of military pomp quite so low.

After enlisting I didn't seem of so much consequence as I expected. There was not so much excitement on account of my military appearance as I deemed justly my due. I was taught my facings, and at the time I thought the drill-master needlessly fussy about shouldering, ordering, and presenting arms. At this time men were often drilled in company and regimental evolutions long before they learned the manual of arms, because of the difficulty of obtaining muskets. These we obtained at an early day, but we would willingly have resigned them after carrying them for a few hours. The musket, after an hour's drill, seemed heavier and less ornamental than it had looked to be. The first day I went out to drill, getting tired of doing the same things over and over, I said to the drill-sergeant: "Let's stop this fooling and go over to the grocery."

His only reply was addressed to the corporal: "Corporal, take this man out and drill him like hell."; and the corporal did. I found that suggestions were not as well appreciated in the army as in private life, and that no wisdom was equal to a drill-master's. "Right face," "Left wheel," and "Right, oblique, march."

It takes a raw recruit some time to learn that he is not to think or suggest, but obey. Some never do learn. I acquired it at last, in humility and mud, but it was tough. Yet I doubt if my patriotism, during my first three weeks' drill, was quite knee high. Drilling looks easy to a spectator, but it isn't. . . . After a time I cut down my uniform so that I could see out of it, and conquered the drill sufficiently to see through it. Then the word came: On to Washington! . . .

We bad adieu to our friends with heavy hearts, for lightly as I may seem to treat the subject, it was no light thing for a boy of twenty to start out for three years into the unknown dangers of a civil war. Our mothers—God bless them!—had brought us something good to eat,—pies, cakes, doughnuts, and jellies. . . . Our young ladies, (sisters, of course) brought an invention, generally made of leather or cloth, containing needles, pins, thread, buttons, and scissors, so that nearly every recruit had an embryo tailor's shop—with the goose outside. One old lady, in the innocence of her heart, brought her son an umbrella. We did not see anything particularly laughable about it at the time, but our old drill-sergeant did.

—Goss, *Recollections of a Private*

B. Lieutenant Favill Raises a Company and Gets a Commission

As soon as I was mustered out of service with the Seventy-first regiment I lost no time in seeking for a commission, fully determined to return to the field, but not as a private soldier. I soon found that commissions were to be obtained only by securing a certain number of men to enlist, and so after applying to various organizations in every state of formation, all with the same results, in connection with an ex-Danish officer, Julius Ericcson, living in Brooklyn, I set to work to raise the requisite number of men to secure the prize.

New York and Brooklyn were transformed into immense recruiting camps. In all the public squares and parks hundreds of tents were erected, covered with flags and immense colored bills, on which the advantage of the various branches of the service were fully stated. There were bands of music and scores of public speakers, all engaged by patriotic citizens, to stimulate the military ardor of the other fellow, and get him to enlist for three years.

We soon found a great change had come over the spirit of the people since the departure of the military regiments in April. Then, everybody wanted to go; now, apparently, most people wanted to stay at home. We put up a wall tent in the New York City Hall Park, and another at the junction of the Atlantic and Flatbush Avenues, Brooklyn, in an open lot. The captain and I took turns in attendance in New York, while John Ericcson, the captain's eldest son, who was to go out as orderly sergeant, was put in charge of the Brooklyn tent. We got some immense posters printed, and among other inducements offered by our company was the experience of the future officers, one gained in a foreign service, the other on the field of Bull Run. Notwithstanding these seeming advantages, our best efforts, and the prodigious enthusiasm of the times, recruiting proved very slow. I coaxed one man into enlisting, through my knowledge of the Crimean War, one Stuart, a fine six-foot Englishman who had served in the Crimean War and had been a soldier in the British army almost all his life. He took hold with a will, and we put him in charge of the tent as second sergeant.

As the recruiting proved so slow at home, it was decided to send me, at the expense of the State, to Oswego, N. Y., and there I promptly repaired; advertised in both the daily papers, setting forth the advantages of a metropolitan regiment. While there I enjoyed the brief distinction of being the only man in town who had been at Bull Run, and in consequence, was feted and honored as an exceptional personage.

With the assistance of a young man named Hamilton, native there, I actually obtained some twenty-nine or thirty men, and was just upon the point of starting with them to New York, when they deserted in a body, and went over to one of the local organizations. Disgusted, I returned immediately, and in a few days afterwards went to Poughkeepsie, and remained there for two weeks, but succeeded in getting only about half a dozen men, mostly from Wappingers Falls. I was taken, while in that place, with a severe attack of fever and ague and was almost shaken to pieces.

Considering the ground no longer profitable I returned home, and found we had already got more than the number required by the State, to muster us into its service, with a captain and first lieutenant; and so, on the 23rd of September, 1861, we marched our company of recruits to the state arsenal on Elm Street, where they were stripped naked, examined by a surgeon, and all of them passed as able bodied men. Then the mustering officer called the roll, and every man in succession stepped one pace to the front, took the oath of allegiance to the State, and swore to serve as a soldier for three years, or during the war. Immediately afterwards, in compliance with the state law a very perfunctory election of officers took place, in the presence of the mustering officer; and Julius Ericcson was declared duly elected captain and I the first lieutenant of the new company. The muster roll was made out, signed by the mustering officer, and we were at last in the service of the State; legally held for duty, and under pay. Before leaving the arsenal, the company was furnished with uniforms, underclothing, haversacks, canteens, and blankets, and at once divested themselves of their citizen garb, and emerged from the arsenal, looking something like real soldiers.

—FAVILL, *The Diary of a Young Officer*

C. RECRUITING A BATTALION OF "SAVAGES"

It was my good fortune to enlist April 19th, 1861, in Company A, 1st Battalion of Rifles. The old battalion was commanded by Major Ben: Perley Poore, and was called "The Savages." Our uniform was dark green, trimmed with light green, and I was the greenest thing in the whole outfit. We were armed with Windsor rifles, with sabre bayonets; our drill, as I remember it, was running around the old Town Hall in West Newbury, yelling like devils, and firing at an imaginary foe. We drilled in these tactics some three months, and were then ordered to Lynnfield, forming a part of the 19th Massachusetts Infantry, and when placed under an experienced drill-master, found that it would have been better not to have drilled at all. Before being mustered into the service of the United States, we elected the members of the company, and were, therefore, picked men.

One day while in camp at Lynnfield, an Irishman came into the company street. He looked the company over carefully, then went to the captain's tent. Taking off his hat, he said: "Captain, I am an Irishman, born in the old country, but an adopted citizen of the United States. The prosperity of this country is my prosperity, its life is in danger and I feel that I ought to enlist to save it. Will you take me in your company?"

After dress parade, his name was proposed and he was elected. We soon found we had made no mistake. Mike was a true son of Erin, and was at once a favorite with the men. One night at Camp Benton, Mike was on guard. It had rained hard and he was wet to the skin. His post was at Headquarters, in front of the colonel's tent. In the morning Colonel Hincks came out. Mike saw him and said: "Pardon me, Colonel, but I would like to speak a word with you." "What is it?" said the colonel. "Well," said Mike, "I wish you believed as you did before the war." "Don't I?" said the colonel. "I think not," said Mike. "You used to run a paper, and your motto was 'Put none but Americans on guard;' and here I am, an Irishman, wet to the skin, while the Americans are sleeping in their tents." Colonel Hincks had, before the war, edited a "Know-nothing" paper, and the motto was, "Put none but Americans on guard." . . .

Another man who joined the company at Lynnfield was Benjamin F. Falls. He had been a sailor and said that having sailed under the old flag for years, he would like a job to follow it on land. He was a grand old man, and was soon called "Uncle Ben." He brought his palm needle and thread with him, and was in constant demand as a tent mender. Colonel Hincks had known Uncle Ben in Lynn, and would often send for him to repair his tent. Ben would send the orderly back to know if it was a wet job or a dry one. If wet, he would take Mike with him to hold the tent, and they would return from their work in a happy condition.

Our company was made up of young men from the country, and was sometimes called "Merritt's Sabbath School children," on account of their goodness, but at Harper's Ferry, as is often the case, these good men fell. Captain Merritt as provost marshal, captured six barrels and a ten gallon keg of whiskey. The keg was lost in transit and could not be accounted for. We were quartered in a deserted house, and the captain came to inform me (I being at the time first sergeant) that we were to march to Bolivar Heights to join the regiment. He soon saw that the missing keg must have been found, for the men were in every stage of intoxication, from the moderate drinker to the gutter drunkard. As we were going through the rooms, we met Uncle Ben perfectly sober. The captain, feeling sad that the company had gone wrong, said,—"Ben, I am sorry." Ben said,—"It is not my fault, Captain. I have been on guard and have not found the stuff, but as soon as I do, will catch up and be just as drunk as the best of them."

At the battle of White Oak Swamp, a shot struck Ben's musket as he was going into the fight at right shoulder shift. It took the lock off, and all thought Ben severely wounded. In a few minutes, we were again moving forward and up came Ben with another gun. "Wasn't you wounded, Ben?" said the captain. "No, only winged, I am all right now."

—ADAMS, "Sunshine and Shadows of Army Life"

D. "WE THOUGHT THE REBELLION WOULD BE OVER BEFORE OUR CHANCE WOULD COME"

The region in northwestern Wisconsin, bounded on the west and north-west by the Mississippi and the St. Croix rivers, and contiguous thereto, in 1861 was sparsely settled. There was no railroad. Transportation was made either by steamboat on the water or by horses on the land. These factors made the raising of a volunteer company for service, an arduous task. When

Mr. Lincoln made the first call for seventy-five thousand volunteers, the quota of Wisconsin was one regiment. At least, only one regiment of three months' men left the state under that call. That regiment, I believe, was largely made up of militia companies that had been previously organized and equipped. Yet active recruiting commenced at once all over the state in the latter part of April, 1861. I presume every company that was recruited in any part of the state at that time, made effort to get into that three months' regiment. The sentiment then was quite universal that three months would close the war. Hence, whoever failed to become a part of the first regiment would see no service and receive no military glory.

A mass meeting was held at once in our town, Prescott, Pierce County. Several addresses were made. Patriotism was effervescent, and thirty young men signed the roll of the Prescott Guards. We at once notified the Governor that we would like to be a part of the troops about to be called. But at that time, as we were informed, enough companies had been offered to fill four regiments. As only one regiment was called for three months, our little squad out on the northwestern border had very little show. This did not discourage this little patriotic band. They began drilling every day, studied the tactics, erected a liberty pole mounted by a bayonet, pointing south, with the stars and stripes floating from its top. The fiery spirit of '76, as we understood it, was thoroughly aroused. By April 30th, a full company was enlisted.

Daniel J. Dill, a prominent merchant who had military tastes and who afterwards became captain of the company, went up the river to Hastings, Minnesota, and down the river to various towns, in pursuit of recruits. Rollin P. Converse and myself took a pair of horses and a buggy and started into the back country. That ride across the prairie and through the woods for several days, was novel and exceedingly interesting. We visited, not only the towns, but every farm. At one town, I think River Falls, we met recruiting officers from Hudson, the county seat of the adjoining county of St. Croix, on the same errand. We held a joint meeting at night at which several addresses were made.

We found western pioneer hospitality everywhere. Every rugged backwoodsman, whether American, German or Norwegian, was full of patriotism. Indignation at the firing on Fort Sumter was genuine and universal. The roads, especially through the woods, were in a wretched condition. It rained, and the mud was frightful. One evening in a lonely spot in the primeval forest, a singletree of the buggy broke. But there stood, by the side of the road, a sturdy pioneer with an axe on his shoulder. In five minutes he had cut a hickory withe, twisted it into a pliable rope, tied it around the broken tree in the most skilful manner, and sent us on our way rejoicing, with a buggy stronger than it was before. Wherever we stopped over night the host would refuse pay for our entertainment. The mother and daughters would look after our comfort, even drying our apparel when wet with rain. Everywhere we were bidden Godspeed in our patriotic efforts.

How many recruits we procured on this trip, I have now forgotten. But some walked to Prescott for miles to enlist. The muster rolls of the company show that almost every township in Pierce County was represented among its members. There were no better soldiers in the army than many of these backwoods farmer boys. A number of them never returned. We had some enlistments from far up the St. Croix River among the lumbermen and loggers. Captain Dill was successful in getting recruits from Hastings, Menominee and other towns. A. C. Ellis, a bright-eyed boy with curly black hair brought quite a number from Menominee.

Before the first of May, between ninety and one hundred had taken the oath of service and allegiance to the United States. I administered the oath to each one who signed the enlistment. D. J. Dill was elected captain. Two alleged Mexican war veterans were made lieutenants. I was appointed first sergeant. The Governor was notified that we were ready for service. But, not only the first, but the second, third, fourth and fifth regiments of volunteer infantry were organized at Madison without our company being assigned. There was great uncertainty for some time after this about being called into service. The men went back to their homes, and some of them enlisted in other companies. We thought the rebellion would be over before our chance would come. However, by May 10th, we were informed that we were the sixth company in the sixth regiment.

—FITCH, *Echoes of the Civil War*

6. THE REVEREND JAMES T. AYERS RECRUITS NEGRO SOLDIERS IN TENNESSEE

Although many Northern Negroes offered to enlist in the Union ranks, President Lincoln was at first opposed to using them as soldiers. Several Union officers—Butler and Hunter for example—attempted to use "contrabands" for semimilitary purposes, but were repudiated by the administration. In October 1861 came a modification of this no-Negro policy, and the next year General Hunter raised a Negro regiment in South Carolina, only to disband it when Congress refused to provide pay or maintenance. With Congressional authorization for Negro recruiting in July 1862, a number of Negro regiments were raised. The next year saw a vast expansion of Negro recruiting. Altogether a total of 186,000 Negroes fought in the Union Army, of which over 100,000 were recruited in Confederate territory. Negro troops were, however, consistently discriminated against, both in pay and promotions.

James T. Ayers was a Methodist minister from Illinois who was assigned to Federal recruiting headquarters at Nashville—one of 237 Federal agents. After the war he enlisted as chaplain with the 104th Regiment of Colored Troops.

Huntsville May 6th 64.

Just been to Dinner. Eat harty, had Salit　　　Asparagrass, turnip top greens, good fryed ham　　　Corn and wheat bread and buttermilk for Dinner. I am Boarding with or Rather hiring them to Board me now 2 black women and am Living fine for A soaldier. My health Never better than now, but what of all this. Oh I am So loansome way down here. Soaldiers nearly all gon no one to Associate with, nothing to do but Eat and grow fat, set at my window and watch the Rebs, as they geather in groups at the Corners to plot Deviltry and Hatch Secession and for those geatherings Bully Corner Acrosst the Street North of my office is the most fruitful. They rally here soon in the morning and a Crowd there mostly all day. Once and a while I pitch in among them and try to Raise A dust but they have give me over Long since for A hard Job boath Men and women. A few days since I came in Contact with three women. I had just took one of there nigger men and he had deserted me and Missus had him hid. This happened in Trianna A Little vilage on the Tennessee River 14 miles from here. I went to Missus house and was searching for Cuffy and out comes Missus Russeling in Silk and Curls with two other women, Ladys I suppose they call them-selves and says Missus "What on earth, sir, are you hunting here? Is Any thing missing?"

"Yes mam my nigger man. Just a few minutes since Run in at this gate and is missing, and I am hunting for him. Have you seen him?"

"Why no sir, your nigger man who is he?"

"Why, mam, he is one I just now presst up at the incampment for to make A soldier of."

"What is his name, Mister," says she.

"Sam he calls himself."

"I dont know anything of him" said she.

"Dont you live here, mam" said I.

"Yes sir" was the Reply.

"Well, mam, not five minutes ago this niger Come in at that gate, and he cant get out of here only at the same place without being helped for I have stood in sight of the gate ever since he entered. He told me he wanted to get his coat and would come Strait back. I waited but he haint Come." This Lot was fenced in with Boards Eight or nine foot high nailed on end-wise A kind of nigger Jail or pen with several Houses in and one verry fine House where this woman Stayed. "Well," said I "aint this fellow your nigger?" The niger had toald me his missus Lived there as we Came from incampment.

"Well I gess he is Likely."

"And do you say, mam, you haint seen him within the Last Five minutes?"

"Why dear me I told you once I had not seen him."

"Well now look here, mam, I always want to be kind to Ladys, but you must Excuse me when I tell you you Could not help seeing him and you did see him and have him now hid Away." Thare was A black Boy with me that belonged to the Capt thare he had sent with me. Said I "Joe stand at this gate and watch while I search. I am bound to have this fellow dead or Alive."

Said the oald lady, "what did you say you wanted him for, A soaldier?"

"Yes mam."

"Why he wont make A soaldier" says she.

"Well," said I, "thats my business not yours."

"Well do you not think it is wicket to take our Slaves from us?"

"No mam."

"Why I am A widow woman and have no one else to Chop and hawl wood and see to my affairs but this nigger."

"Why dont you keep [*him*] at home then?"

"Why dear me I do," says she.

"You do, why, Mam, the Colonel out yonder toald me he had been sneaking Round the camps for two months past stealing hard tacks and sow belly, for himself and you, till he was tired of him, and hoped I would take him Away, and now you say you keep him at home. Come tell me whare he is. I am determined to have him."

"Do you take them whether they are willing or not?"

"Not generally, but in cases Like this I do, whare they are Loafing round stealing for themselves and there masters two."

"Well do you think slaverry is wrong?" says she.

"I dont think it is write," said I.

"Well the Bible is full of slaverry."

"Oh yes Mam and so is it full of war and blood shed. Do you think war and bloodshead is write mam?"

"No sir."

"Well I dont think so Either so thare we Agree."

"May I not ask Aint you A minister?"

"Sometimes pass for one, Mam."

"I thought so."

Now up steps Paul pry or who Ever she was and Rather Likely at that had she not been Reb. Say she "and you are A minister then are you?"

"They say so, yes mam."

"Well do you sir feel you are doing write in the sight of God and man to Come here Among us peacible citizens and take our slaves Away? They are our money, beside this one you are after now belongs to this widowed Lady. What on Earth will she do if you take him Away?"

"Send and get her son home out of the Rebel Army. He is there now plotting with others how to Cut the throats of yanks as you Call us." This was A Jolter and choked my Little fair faiced new comer for A while but she Rallyed Again.

"Well if you are a preacher I suppose you believe the bible."

"Well, yes, mam, I profess to, to some extent At least."

"Well, sir, I am prepaired to show you Clearly and plainly that slaverry is A bible doctrine. Why sir from first of Genesis to Last of Revelation the Bible is full of slaverry, and the best of men owned slaves, why Abraham Isaac Jacob and all the oald fathers and christians owned there slaves."

"Oh, yes mam, we will not fall out here by no means but Dear woman did you Ever for one Moment Reflect that the verry same Bible gives A historical Account all Along through as much or more Even, how men used to have wives. Why Solomon had three hundred, and not satisfyed with them took seven hundred concubines. David had several wives and was still Dissatisfyed, kiled Uriah and took his wife. And now, siss," says I, "in all good Continence how would you like the thousand wife sistom Revived? Would you like to be one of seven hundred Concubines all the darlings of one man or even the two hundred and 99th Lovely darling who was called wife of one man or would you be willing some one should kill your man Just for the sake of putting you Among his herd of wives. I guess not, you would say give me My Uriah, Ill be satisfyed. I think it is wrong men should have so many wives. Well thease are Historical Accounts of former usages and Customs Among the People which the Bible from some cause keeps silent only in Davids Case who the Bible says was sorely punished. And now Ladys I have A good way to go yet this afternoon. Sorry I haint the time to Discuss this subject longer. Hope Ill see you again and have more Leisure   will be pleased to talk with you. You seem like women of inteligence and are disposed to treat me Courteously for which I thank you Ladys. I am Aware of the prejudices you southerners have in favour of the institution of slavery and am prepared on my part to mak Allowances in that direction."

"Well," said the oald Lady, "I Really like to hear you talk. You talk Reasonable and Jentlemanly. You must call Again."

"Thank you," said I.

"Well now," said this Little bewitching yong Blue Eyed fairskined widow tidy Enough for one to eat, "you will Leave Aunts nigger wont you?" Well I leave you to guess whether I did or know. I made A Low Bow with A promise to call Again hoped, they might enjoy happyer days when this war was over and so I left fully intending if ever convenient to Call Again and see them Blue eyes that wore by that little Angel widow. When I had Rode Awhile why said I "that Little woman has Caused me to forget my nigger. Well let him go," so I joged on Humming Away some oald tune to kill time.

   And this is only one Case. Those cases for some two months or more ware nearly of every day occurrence and sometimes two or three times A day only the Blue eyed widow seldom do I meet her Eaquals anywhere. She is A Splendid Little Piece of Humanity in Shape of A Female, and gained her Point, and saved the nigger. God bless the Little widow, them Blue Eyes that Little plump Rosy Cheek   them Delicate Lilly white hands that Lady Like Smile   that well Seasoned Christian Like spirit. Man would be A monster Could he Deny such an Angel as this. So my Cannon being Spiked I Rode off, threatening A return at A Convenient season.

Jas. T. Ayers.

—Franklin, ed., *The Diary of James T. Ayers*

7. BALTIMORE MOBS ATTACK THE SIXTH MASSACHUSETTS

Massachusetts, which had been preparing since January, was the first state to respond to the President's call to arms. On April 16 the state militia began

*to muster at Boston, and on the following day the famous 6th Massachusetts
started its historic trip to Washington. There was no through railroad connection to the capital at that time; the 6th, which reached Baltimore on the
morning of April 19 had to ride on horsecars, or walk, from the Philadelphia,
Wilmington and Baltimore Railroad station to the Baltimore and Ohio Railroad station. Seven companies managed to get through on horse cars; then
a mob of Southern sympathizers erected street barricades to block the passage of the remaining four. The militia fought its way through, but at the
cost of four killed and 36 wounded; the mob casualties are unknown.*

*"The excitement is fearful," the Governor of Maryland wired the Presi-
dent. "Send no more troops here." To avoid a repetition of the riot the
Maryland authorities burned down the railroad bridges connecting Baltimore
with Philadelphia and Harrisburg.*

*This Baltimore fracas excited, among other things, "Maryland! My Mary-
land!"*

EARLY on the morning of April 19th, 1861, a train of thirty-five cars left
the Broad and Washington avenue depot, Philadelphia, having on board
twelve hundred troops from Boston, Lowell, and Acton, Massachusetts, and
known as the Sixth Massachusetts Regiment, under the command of Colonel
Edward F. Jones, a gallant soldier and courteous gentleman; and a regiment,
one thousand strong, from Philadelphia, under the command of Colonel William F. Small. Nothing was known in Baltimore of their departure from
Philadelphia, but about eleven o'clock it became noised abroad that a large
force of Federal soldiers had arrived at President street depot. This depot
is in the southeastern portion of the city, and is connected with the Baltimore
and Ohio depot, which is situated in the southwestern section, by a line of
rail along Pratt street—a leading thoroughfare—and some minor streets. It was
necessary for the troops, on disembarking at President street depot, either to
march to the Baltimore and Ohio depot or to be drawn thither in the cars by
horses. The news of the arrival of the troops spread like wildfire, and in a
comparatively short time an immense crowd gathered on Pratt street, with
the intention of preventing the passage of the troops. While waiting for the
appearance of the soldiers the crowd kept itself up to the requisite pitch of
indignation and enthusiasm by "groaning" for Lincoln, Hicks, and the Federal Government, and by cheering Jefferson Davis and the Southern Confederacy.

The first intimation had by the city authorities that the troops were about
to enter the city was received by Mayor Brown about ten o'clock. Mr. Brown
at once repaired to the office of the Police Commissioners, but found that the
Marshal of Police had already gone to Camden station, where he had concentrated his men by request of the railroad authorities. The Mayor at once
followed him to Camden station, and on arriving there found him posted
with his men prepared to put down any attack. Unfortunately the mob had
gathered not at Camden station but on Pratt street, at a point a short distance
west of the depot where the troops were disembarking. Pratt street is a nar-

row thoroughfare, and easily capable of defense. The strategical position of the mob was excellent as they proceeded to fortify it.

About half-past eleven o'clock a car drawn by horses was seen approaching, and was greeted by the mob with cheers for the South. The car, and eight others which followed, were, however, permitted to pass without any molestation, except the usual taunts and gibes at the occupants. A trivial accident, which happened to the tenth car, let loose all the elements of disorder in the mob, and precipitated the fatal conflict. As this car neared Commerce street the brake was accidentally thrown out of gear, and the car stopped. The crowd took advantage of the mishap at once, and began to attack the occupants with stones. Windows were broken, and a few of the soldiers were hurt, but not seriously. Finally the driver of the car became frightened, lost his head, and, having attached his team to the other end of the car, started to haul it back to the depot. The mob followed the car, stoning it all the while, but the driver having urged the horses to a run, succeeded in distancing them. A large portion of the mob, however, followed it into the depot.

The section of the mob which remained at the bridge on Pratt street then, under the advice of their leaders, many of whom, as I have said, were well known citizens of Baltimore, began to build a barricade, Paris fashion. They commenced by digging up the paving stones and the railroad track for a distance of some fifty yards. The stones were piled up with the iron rails, the bridges over the gutters were torn up, and eight large anchors which were found on the wharf near by were placed on the barricade. A car loaded with sand attempted to pass, but was seized by the rioters, who backed it up to the barricade, and emptied the sand on the pile of stones and anchors. A large number of Negroes were working on the wharves at the time. These were ordered to quit work, which they did with alacrity, and were directed by the rioters to assist them on the barricade. . . .

In the meantime, the commander of the Massachusetts troops, finding that the cars would not be permitted to pass through, decided to disembark his men and force a passage on foot through the mob. When this determination was announced, some confederates of the Pratt street rioters at once communicated the news to them. It was also rumored that the troops had decided to go by a different route to Camden station. A portion of the rioters at once started to head them off, while the main body maintained its position on Pratt street. A large crowd assembled at the depot during the disembarkation of the troops, and here several exciting, but not very sanguinary, encounters occurred between Unionists and secessionists in the crowd. As the troops descended from the cars they were hooted, jeered, and twitted. They succeeded, however, in forcing their way to the footway, which extends for several hundred yards along the outer edge of the depot, where they formed in double file and awaited the orders of their officers.

At this point a man appeared bearing a Confederate flag at the head of about one hundred rioters. His appearance was the signal for wild cheering. A rush for the flag was made by several Northern sympathizers in the crowd, and the flag-staff was broken. One of these men was caught by the flag-bearer who, with his companions, throttled, and would have killed him, but for the interference of the police, who succeeded in bearing him away. The shreds of the flag were caught up and tied to the flag-staff. On being raised again they were saluted with an outburst of cheering.

The men surrounding the flag then began to taunt the troops, and declared that they would be forced to march behind it to the Camden depot. Colonel Jones gave the order to march, and the troops started. The men surrounding the flag, however, planted themselves directly in front of the soldiers and refused to yield an inch. The troops wheeled about, but found themselves surrounded on all sides, and were unable to move in any direction. Several of the soldiers were hustled away from their comrades, and would have been roughly used by the crowd but for the police, who succeeded, with great difficulty, in rescuing them. The troops again endeavored to force a passage, and this time, with the assistance of the police, they succeeded. As they started, however, the Confederate flag was borne to the front, and they were compelled to march for several squares behind this flag. Too much praise cannot be given to the commander or men for their admirable self-control during this trying episode.

The presence of the Confederate flag was the immediate cause of the sanguinary street fight and loss of life which followed. Several Northern sympathizers in the mob, exasperated at the triumph of the flag-bearer and his friends, made another dash for the flag, but were defeated and pursued. Some of them took refuge in the ranks of the soldiers. This exasperated the citizens against the soldiers, and a savage attack upon the latter was made with stones and other missiles. One of the soldiers, William Patch, was struck in the back with a large paving-stone, and fell to the ground. His musket was seized, and the poor wretch was brutally beaten by the rioters before the police could rescue him. When Patch was seen to fall Colonel Jones gave the order "double quick" to his men, and the whole column started off at a run, ducking and dipping to avoid the stones. At this the crowd set up a yell of derision and started after them full tilt. Two soldiers were knocked down, while running, but managed to make their escape—one of them with the assistance of the police.

While the foregoing events were transpiring in and near President street depot, an immense concourse of people had gathered at the barricade. When the troops appeared in full run a great shout was raised, and the head of the column was greeted with a shower of paving-stones. The troops faltered, and finally, in the face of a second shower of stones, came to a dead halt. The patience of their commander was at last exhausted. He cried out in a voice, which was heard even above the yells of the mob, "Fire!" The soldiers leveled their pieces and the mob seemed to pause, as if to take breath. The soldiers fired. A young man, named F. X. Ward, now a well-known lawyer of this city, fell pierced by a ball. A hoarse yell of fear and rage went up from the mob, but it did not give way. The troops fired again and again, and the crowd wavering, they rushed upon them with fixed bayonets and forced a passage over the barricade.

A scene of bloody confusion followed. As the troops retreated, firing, the rioters rushed upon them only to be repulsed by the line of bayonets. Some of the rioters fought like madmen. Finally, the mob, exasperated by their failure to prevent the passage of the troops, made a desperate rush upon them, and one young man, who was in the front rank of the rioters, was forced close upon the soldiery. One of the soldiers raised his gun, took deliberate aim at the rioter and fired. The cap exploded, but the gun failed to go off. The rioter rushed forward, seized the gun, wrested it by an almost super-human effort from the soldier's grasp, and plunged the bayonet through the man's shoulder.

During the firing a number of the rioters fell, killed and wounded. At the intersection of Charles and Pratt streets, Andrew Robbins, a soldier from Stoneham, Massachusetts, was shot in the neck by a rioter. He was carried into a drug store near by, and was protected from the mob. At Howard street a strong force of rioters from Camden station met the troops and refused to yield. The soldiers fired again and the mob gave way. The soldiers again started at the double quick and reached Camden station without further trouble. Thirteen cars were drawn out, and the soldiers left the depot amid the hisses and groans of the multitude.

One of the most remarkable features of the riot was the persistency and courage with which the mob hung on to the troops, in spite of the continued firing. Another remarkable feature was the extraordinary coolness and for-bearance of the troops.

—Frederic Emory, "The Baltimore Riots"

8. HOW THE SEVENTH REGIMENT GOT FROM NEW YORK TO WASHINGTON

Because the Maryland authorities had burned the railroad bridges leading from Philadelphia to Baltimore, the New York 7th and the Massachusetts 8th were transported by water up Chesapeake Bay to Annapolis, whence they marched to Annapolis Junction and then entrained for the capital.

The story of this famous march can be read in Theodore Winthrop's article in the Atlantic Monthly *for June 1861; it is told here by the gifted poet, dramatist and journalist Fitz-James O'Brien who was decorated for gallantry in action at Bloomery Gap and paid with his life for his devotion to the Union.*

The Capitol, Washington, Saturday, April 27, 1861

We are here. Those three words sum up as much as Napier's "Peccavi," when he took Scinde, and we all feel somewhat as Mr. Caesar Augustus must have felt when he had crossed the Rubicon.

It is almost unnecessary for me to detail to you the events of the day on which we left New York. . . .

At 3 o'clock, P.M., we mustered at the Armory, against which there beat a surge of human beings like waves against a rock. Within, all was commotion.

Fitting of belts, wild lamentations over uniforms expected but not arrived. Hearty exchanges of comradeships between members of different companies, who felt that they were about to depart on a mission which might end in death. Here and there flickered Spring bonnets, which inclosed charming faces, as the calyx enfolds the flower; and, let me tell you, that on the faces of many of those dear blossoms there hung drops of mournful dew. At last the regiment was formed in companies, and we marched. Was there ever such an ovation? . . .

The faces of the buildings were so thick with people, that it seemed as if an army of black ants were marching, after their resistless fashion, through the city, and had scaled the houses. Handkerchiefs fluttered in the air like myriads of white butterflies. An avenue of brave, honest faces smiled upon us as we passed, and sent a sunshine into our hearts that lives there still. In a prominent position stood Major Anderson, who saluted us, and was welcomed as such a man should be welcomed. And so on to the ferry.

Swift through New Jersey—against which no sneer be uttered evermore. All along the track shouting crowds, hoarse and valorous, sent to us, as we passed, their hopes and wishes. When we stopped at the different stations, rough hands came in through the windows, apparently unconnected with any one in particular until you shook them, and then the subtle magnetic thrill told that there were bold hearts beating at the end. This continued until night closed, and, indeed, until after midnight. . . .

Our arrival at Philadelphia took place at 4 o'clock. We slept in the cars, awaiting orders from our Colonel, but at daylight hunger—and it may be thirst—becoming imperious, we sallied out, and roamed about the cheerless neighborhood that surrounds the depot. Close by there was a small wooden shanty—let us say an Irish palace—which was presently filled by arid soldiers. The prog in the larder of this sumptuous residence was, I regret to say, limited. I did not even see the traditional pig about, although heaven knows he would have been appropriate enough.

Finding that we were likely to remain for some time in the city—although under the impression that we were to go straight through to Baltimore—we wandered away from the Desert of the Depot and descended on civilized quarters. The superintendent of the Deaf and Dumb Asylum was a man for the emergency. He provided a handsome breakfast for all such members of the Seventh as chose to partake of it, and we commanded beefsteak on our fingers, and ordered tea by sign-manual. Great numbers of our regiment, being luxurious dogs, went down to the Continental and Girard hotels, where they campaigned on marble floors, and bivouacked on velvet couches. They are such delicate fellows, the Seventh Regiment! Further on you will see what those delicate hands have done. . . .

There was one peculiar difference that I noticed existing between the Massachusetts regiments that we met in Philadelphia and our men. The Massachusetts men—to whom all honor be given for the splendid manner in which they afterwards acted in a most trying situation—presented a singular moral contrast to the members of the Seventh. They were earnest, grim, determined. Badly equipped, haggard, unshorn, they yet had a manhood in their look that hardships could not kill. They were evidently thinking all the time of the contest into which they were about to enter. Their gray, eager eyes seemed to be looking for the heights of Virginia. With us, it was somewhat different. Our men were gay and careless, confident of being at any moment capable of performing, and more than performing, their duty. They looked battle in the face with a smile, and were ready to hobnob with an enemy and kill him afterwards. The one was courage in the rough; the other was courage burnished. The steel was the same in both, but the last was a little more polished.

On April 20, at 4:20 P.M., we left the Philadelphia dock, on board the steamer *Boston*. The regiment was in entire ignorance of its destination. Some said we were going back to New York, at which suggestion there was a howl of indignation. Others presumed that we were going to steam up the Potomac—a course which was not much approved of, inasmuch that we were cooped up in a kind of river steamer that a shot from the fort at Alexandria might sink at any moment. We, however—to make use of a familiar expression—"went it blind," and the faces did not smile the less because our object was unknown. . . .

I regret to say that all was not rose-colored. The steamer that the Colonel chartered had to get ready at three or four hours' notice, he having changed his plans, in consequence of the tearing up of the rails around Baltimore. The result was that she was imperfectly provisioned. As the appetites of the men began to develop, the resources of the vessel began to appear. In the first place, she was far too small to accommodate a thousand men, and we were obliged to sleep in all sorts of impossible attitudes. There is an ingenious device known to carpenters as "dove-tailing," and we were so thick that we had positively to dove-tail, only that there was very little of the dove about it; for when perambulating soldiers stepped on the faces and stomachs of the sleepers, as they lay on the deck, the greeting that they received had but little flavor of the olive branch.

Notwithstanding that we found very soon that the commissariat was in a bad way, the men were as jolly as sandboys. I never saw a more good-humored set of men in my life. Fellows who would at Delmonico's have sent back a *turban de volaille aux truffes* because the truffles were tough, here cheerfully took their places in file between decks, tin plates and tin cups in hand, in order to get an insufficient piece of beef and a vision of coffee. But it was all merrily done. The scant fare was seasoned with hilarity; and here I say to those people in New York who have sneered at the Seventh Regiment as being dandies, and guilty of the unpardonable crimes of cleanliness and kid gloves, that they would cease to scoff and remain to bless, had they beheld the square, honest, genial way in which these military Brummells roughed it. . . .

On the afternoon of the 22d we landed at the Annapolis dock. . . . For the first time in his life your correspondent was put to work to roll flour-barrels. He was entrusted with the honorable and onerous duty of transporting stores from the steamer to the dock. Later still he descended to the position of mess servant, when, in company with gentlemen well known in Broadway for immaculate kids, he had the honor of attending on his company with buckets of cooked meat and crackers. The only difference between him and Co. and the ordinary waiter being, that the former were civil. . . .

We were quartered in the buildings belonging to the Naval School at Annapolis. I had a bunking-place in what is there called a fort, which is a rickety structure, that a lucifer match would set on fire, but furnished with imposing guns. I suppose it was merely built to practice the cadets, because as a defence it is worthless. The same evening boats were sent off from the yard, and towards nightfall the Massachusetts men landed, fagged, hungry, thirsty, but indomitable. At an early hour there was a universal snore through the Naval School of Annapolis. . . .

On the morning of the 24th of April we started on what afterwards proved to be one of the hardest marches on record. The Secessionists of Annapolis and the surrounding district had threatened to cut us off in our march, and even went so far as to say that they would attack our quarters. This, of course, was the drunken Southern ebullition. A civilian told me that he met in the streets of Annapolis two cavalry soldiers who came to cut our throats without delay, but as each brave warrior was endeavoring to hold the other up, my friend did not apprehend much danger.

A curious revulsion of feeling took place at Annapolis, and indeed all through Maryland, after our arrival.

The admirable good conduct which characterizes the regiment, the open liberality which it displays in all pecuniary transactions, and the courteous demeanor which it exhibits to all classes, took the narrow-minded population of this excessively wretched town by surprise. They were prepared for pillage. They thought we were going to sack the place. They found, instead, that we were prepared and willing to pay liberal prices for everything, and that even patriotic presentations were steadily refused. While we were in the Navy School, of course all sorts of rumors as to our operations were floating about. It surprised me that no one suggested that we were to go off in a balloon; however, all surmises were put to an end by our receiving orders, the evening of the 23d, to assemble in marching order next morning. The dawn saw us up. Knapsacks, with our blankets and overcoats strapped on them, were piled on the green. A brief and insufficient breakfast was taken, our canteens filled with vinegar and water, cartridges distributed to each man, and after mustering and loading, we started on our first march through a hostile country. . . .

The tracks had been torn up between Annapolis and the Junction, and here it was that the wonderful qualities of the Massachusetts Eighth Regiment came out. The locomotives had been taken to pieces by the inhabitants, in order to prevent our travel. In steps a Massachusetts volunteer, looks at the piecemeal engine, takes up a flange, and says coolly, "I made this engine, and I can put it together again." Engineers were wanted when the engine was ready. Nineteen stepped out of the ranks. The rails were torn up. Practical railroad makers out of the regiment laid them again, and all this, mind you, without care or food. These brave boys, I say, were starving while they were doing this good work. What their Colonel was doing, I can't say. As we marched along the track that they had laid, they greeted us with ranks of smiling but hungry faces. One boy told me, with a laugh on his young lips, that he had not eaten any thing for thirty hours. There was not, thank God, a haversack in our regiment that was not emptied into the hands of these ill-treated heroes, nor a flask that was not at their disposal. I am glad to pay them tribute here, and mentally doff my cap. . . .

After marching about eight miles, during which time several men caved in from exhaustion, and one young gentleman was sunstruck and sent back to New York, we halted, and instantly, with the Divine instinct which characterizes the hungry soldier, proceeded to forage. The worst of it was there was no foraging to be done. The only house within reach was inhabited by a lethargic person, who, like most Southern men, had no idea of gaining money by labor. We offered him extravagant prices to get us fresh water, and it was with the utmost reluctance we could get him to obtain us a few pailfuls. Over the mantel-piece of his miserable shanty I saw—a curious coincidence—the portrait of Col. Duryea, of our regiment.

After a brief rest of about an hour, we again commenced our march; a march which lasted until the next morning—a march than which in history, nothing but those marches in which defeated troops have fled from the enemy, can equal. Our Colonel, it seems, determined to march by railroad, in preference to the common road, inasmuch as he had obtained such secret information as led him to suppose that we were waited for on the latter route. Events justified his judgment. There were cavalry troops posted in defiles to cut us off. They could not have done it, of course, but they could have harassed us severely. As we went along the railroad we threw out skirmishing parties from the Second and Sixth companies, to keep the road clear.

I know not if I can describe that night's march. I have dim recollections of deep cuts through which we passed, gloomy and treacherous-looking, with the moon shining full on our muskets, while the banks were wrapped in shade, and each moment expecting to see the flash and hear the crack of the rifle of the Southern guerilla. The tree frogs and lizards made a mournful music as we passed. The soil on which we travelled was soft and heavy. The sleepers lying at intervals across the track made the march terribly fatiguing. On all sides dark, lonely pine woods stretched away, and high over the hooting of owls or the plaintive petition of the whip-poor-will rose the bass commands of Halt! Forward, march!—and when we came to a ticklish spot, the word would run from the head of the column along the line, "Holes," "Bridge, pass it along," &c.

As the night wore on the monotony of the march became oppressive. Owing to our having to explore every inch of the way, we did not make more than a mile or a mile and a half an hour. We ran out of stimulants, and almost out of water. Most of us had not slept for four nights, and as the night advanced our march was almost a stagger. This was not so much fatigue as want of excitement. Our fellows were spoiling for a fight, and when a dropping shot was heard in the distance, it was wonderful to see how the languid legs straightened, and the column braced itself for action. If we had had even the smallest kind of a skirmish the men would have been able to walk to Washington. As it was, we went sleepily on. I myself fell asleep walking in the ranks. Numbers, I find, followed my example; but never before was there shown such indomitable pluck and perseverance as the Seventh showed in the march of twenty miles. The country that we passed through seemed to have been entirely deserted. The inhabitants, who were going to kill us when they thought we daren't come through, now vamosed their respective ranches, and we saw them not. Houses were empty. The population retired into the interior, burying their money, and carrying their families along with them. They, it seems, were under the impression that we came to ravage and pillage, and they fled as the Gauls must have fled when Attila and his Huns came down on them from the North. As we did at Annapolis, we did in Maryland State. We left an impression that cannot be forgotten. Every thing was paid for. No discourtesy was offered to any inhabitant, and the sobriety of the regiment should be an example to others.

I have now to finish without bringing our journey up to here. But let that rest for my next letter. I wish, however, before I conclude, to state that nothing could have been more effective or energetic than the movements of the Engineer Corps, to whom we were indebted for the rebuilding of a bridge in an incredibly short space of time.

—O'Brien, in the *New York Times*

9. FRANK WILKESON GOES SOUTH WITH BLACKGUARDS, THIEVES, AND BOUNTY JUMPERS

Joining the army and entraining for the battle front was not all a matter of cheers and flag-waving. As the going got tougher and the government resorted increasingly to bounties, a regular system of bounty jumping sprang up, and the army had to take drastic measures to see to it that men who enlisted for bounties actually stayed in the army.

Frank Wilkeson, who found himself in the bad company which he here describes so graphically, was a Buffalo boy who later became lieutenant in the 4th United States Artillery and, after the war, worked on the staffs of the New York Sun *and the* New York Times.

THE war fever seized me in 1863. All the summer and fall I had fretted and burned to be off. That winter, and before I was sixteen years old, I ran away from my father's high-lying Hudson River valley farm. I went to Albany and enlisted in the Eleventh New York Battery, then at the front in Virginia, and was promptly sent out to the penitentiary building.

There, to my utter astonishment, I found eight hundred or one thousand ruffians, closely guarded by heavy lines of sentinels, who paced to and fro,

Thomas Nast

March of New York 7th Regiment Down Broadway

A. J. Volck

The Battle in the Streets of Baltimore, April 19, 1861

day and night, rifle in hand, to keep them from running away. When I entered the barracks these recruits gathered around me and asked, "How much bounty did you get?" "How many times have you jumped the bounty?" I answered that I had not bargained for any bounty, that I had never jumped a bounty, and that I had enlisted to go to the front and fight. I was instantly assailed with abuse. Irreclaimable blackguards, thieves, and ruffians gathered in a boisterous circle around me and called me foul names. I was robbed while in these barracks of all I possessed—a pipe, a piece of tobacco, and a knife.

I remained in this nasty prison for a month. I became thoroughly acquainted with my comrades. A recruit's social standing in the barracks was determined by the acts of villainy he had performed, supplemented by the number of times he had jumped the bounty. The social standing of a hard-faced, crafty pick-pocket, who had jumped the bounty in say half a dozen cities, was assured. He shamelessly boasted of his rascally agility. Less active bounty-jumpers looked up to him as to a leader. He commanded their profound respect. When he talked, men gathered around him in crowds and listened attentively to words of wisdom concerning bounty-jumping that dropped from his tobacco-stained lips. His right to occupy the most desirable bunk, or to stand at the head of the column when we prepared to march to the kitchen for our rations, was undisputed.

If there was a man in all that shameless crew who had enlisted from patriotic motives, I did not see him. There was not a man of them who was not eager to run away. Not a man who did not quake when he thought of the front. Almost to a man they were bullies and cowards, and almost to a man they belonged to the criminal classes. . . .

On my urgent solicitation Major Van Rensselaer promised to ship me with the first detachment of recruits going to the front. One cold afternoon, directly after the ice had gone out of the Hudson River, we were ordered out of the barracks. We were formed into ranks, and stood in a long, curved line 1,000 rascals strong. We were counted, as was the daily custom, to see if any of the patriots had escaped. Then, after telling us to step four paces to the front as our names were called, the names of the men who were to form the detachment were shouted by a sergeant, and we stepped to the front, one after another, until 600 of us stood in ranks. We were marched to the barracks, and told to pack our knapsacks as we were to march at once.

The 400 recruits who had not been selected were carefully guarded on the ground, so as to prevent their mingling with us. If that had happened, some of the recruits who had been chosen would have failed to appear at the proper time. The idea was that if we were kept separate, all the men in the barracks, all outside of the men grouped under guard, would have to go. Before I left the barracks I saw the guards roughly haul straw-littered, dust-coated men out of mattresses, which they had cut open and crawled into to hide. Other men were jerked out of the water-closets. Still others were drawn by the feet from beneath bunks. One man, who had burrowed into the contents of a water-tight swill-box, which stood in the hall and into which we threw our waste food and coffee slops, was fished out, covered with coffee grounds and bits of bread and shreds of meat, and kicked down stairs and out of the building. Ever after I thought of that soldier as the hero of the swill-tub.

Cuffed, prodded with bayonets, and heartily cursed, we fell into line in front of the barracks. An officer stepped in front of us and said in a loud voice that any man who attempted to escape would be shot. A double line of guards quickly took their proper positions around us. We were faced to the right and marched through a room, where the men were paid their bounties. Some men received $500, others less; but I heard of no man who received less than $400. I got nothing.

As the men passed through the room they were formed into column by fours. When all the recruits had been paid, and the column formed, we started to march into Albany, guarded by a double line of sentinels. Long before we arrived at State Street three recruits attempted to escape. They dropped their knapsacks and fled wildly. Crack! crack! crack! a dozen rifles rang out, and what had been three men swiftly running were three bloody corpses. The dead patriots lay by the roadside as we marched by. We marched down State Street, turned to the right at Broadway, and marched down that street to the steamboat landing.

Previous to my enlistment I had imagined that the population of Albany would line the sidewalks to see the defenders of the nation march proudly by, bound for the front, and that we would be cheered, and would unbend sufficiently to accept floral offerings from beautiful maidens. How was it? No exultant cheers arose from the column. The people who saw us did not cheer. The faces of the recruits plainly expressed the profound disgust they felt at the disastrous outcome of what had promised to be a remunerative financial enterprise. Small boys derided us. Mud balls were thrown at us. One small lad, who was greatly excited by the unwonted spectacle, rushed to a street corner, and after placing his hands to his mouth, yelled to a distant and loved comrade: "Hi, Johnnie, come see de bounty-jumpers!" He was promptly joined by an exasperating, red-headed, sharp-tongued little wretch, whom I desired to destroy long before we arrived at the steamboat landing. Men and women openly laughed at us. Fingers, indicative of derision, were pointed at us. Yes, a large portion of the populace of Albany gathered together to see us; but they were mostly young males, called gutter-snipes. They jeered us, and were exceedingly loth to leave us. It was as though the congress of American wonders were parading in the streets preparatory to aërial flights under tented canvas.

Once on the steamboat; we were herded on the lower deck, where freight is usually carried, like cattle. No one dared to take off his knapsack for fear it would be stolen. Armed sentinels stood at the openings in the vessel's sides out of which gangplanks were thrust. Others were stationed in the bows; others in the dark, narrow passage-ways where the shaft turns; still others were on the decks. We were hemmed in by a wall of glistening steel. "Stand back, stand back, damn you!" was the only remark the alert-eyed, stern-faced sentinels uttered, and the necessity of obeying that command was impressed on us by menacing bayonets. Whiskey, guard-eluding whiskey, got in. Bottles, flasks, canteens, full of whiskey, circulated freely among us, and many men got drunk. There was an orgie on the North River steamer that night, but comparatively a decent one.

In spite of the almost certain death sure to ensue if a man attempted to escape, two men jumped overboard. I saw one of these take off his knapsack, loosen his overcoat and then sit down on his knapsack. He drew a whiskey flask from an inner pocket and repeatedly stimulated his courage. He watched the guards who stood by the opening in the vessel's side intently. At last they turned their heads for an instant. The man sprang to his feet, dropped his overcoat and ran to the opening and jumped far out into the cold waters of the river. Above us, in front of us, at our sides, behind us, wherever guards were stationed, there rifles cracked. But it was exceeding dark on the water, and I believe that the deserter escaped safely. Early in the morning, before it was light, I again heard firing. I was told that another recruit had jumped overboard and had been killed.

—WILKESON, *Recollections of a Private Soldier*

10. SUPPLYING THE CONFEDERACY WITH ARMS AND AMMUNITION

The industrial development of the South was in its infancy at the time of secession, and the Confederacy experienced greatest difficulty in supplying itself with the munitions for modern warfare. Edward P. Alexander, from whose entrancing Memoirs *this passage is taken, had been an instructor at West Point where he perfected the system of military signals used by both armies during the war. President Davis appointed him Chief of Ordnance of the Army of Northern Virginia, and he served later as chief artillerist in Longstreet's corps.*

ON the day after Bull Run I was appointed Chief of Ordnance of Beauregard's corps, and within a few days Johnston extended my office over the whole army, which, about this period, took the name ever afterwards used,—"The Army of Northern Virginia." The enemy, about the same time, adopted their equally well-known title, "The Army of the Potomac."

My new duties largely absorbed my time, but I remained in charge of the signal service, the work being now confined to sending instructed parties to all parts of the Confederacy where they might be of use. During the fall a "Department of Signals" was organized in Richmond, and the charge of it, with the rank of colonel, was offered me, but declined, as I was unwilling to leave the field. As head of a department I was soon made Major, and, later, Lieutenant-Colonel of Artillery. Col. William Norris of Baltimore became Chief Signal Officer.

Briefly, my duties embraced the supply of arms and ammunition to all troops in the field,—infantry, artillery, and cavalry. I organized the department, with an ordnance officer or sergeant in every regiment, from whom I received weekly statements showing the arms and ammunition on hand in cartridge boxes and regimental wagons. Reserve storehouses were provided at the nearest railroad points, and reserve trains for brigades and divisions, to run between the storehouses and the troops. For emergency, under my own control was held a train of ammunition and battery wagons equipped with tools and expert mechanics for all sorts of repairs from a broken mainspring to a spiked fieldpiece. I was fortunate in securing for superintendent of this train, Maj. George Duffy, an expert from Alexandria, who became an institution in the army, and remained with it throughout the war.

In its early stages we had great trouble with the endless variety of arms and calibres in use, scarcely ten per cent of them being the muzzle-loading rifle musket, calibre .58, which was then the regulation arm for United States infantry. There were several breech-loading small-arms manufactured at the North, but none had secured the approval of the United States Ordnance Department, although many of them would have made more formidable weapons than any muzzle-loaders.

The old idea was still widely entertained that, because the percentage of hits is always small, the fire of infantry should not be rapid, lest the men waste too much ammunition. After a year or two some of the best breech-loaders got admission among cavalry regiments, and common sense and experience gradually forced a recognition of the value of a heavy fire. By 1864, the Spencer breech-loading carbine had been adopted as the regulation arm for the Federal cavalry, and by the fall of that year brigades of infantry began to appear with it. . . .

There is reason to believe that had the Federal infantry been armed from the first with even the breech-loaders available in 1861 the war would have been terminated within a year.

The old smooth-bore musket, calibre .69, made up the bulk of the Confederate armament at the beginning, some of the guns, even all through 1862, being old flint-locks. But every effort was made to replace them by rifled muskets captured in battle, brought through the blockade from Europe, or manufactured at a few small arsenals which we gradually fitted up. Not until after the battle of Gettysburg was the whole army in Virginia equipped with the rifled musket. In 1864 we captured some Spencer breech-loaders, but we could never use them for lack of proper cartridges.

Our artillery equipment at the beginning was even more inadequate than our small-arms. Our guns were principally smooth-bore 6-Prs. and 12-Prs. howitzers, and their ammunition was afflicted with very unreliable fuses. Our arsenals soon began to manufacture rifled guns, but they always lacked the copper and brass, and the mechanical skill necessary to turn out first-class ammunition. Gradually we captured Federal guns to supply most of our needs, but we were handicapped by our own ammunition until the close of the war.

No department of our government deserves more credit than our Ordnance Bureau in Richmond under Gen. Josiah Gorgas, for its success in supplying the enormous amount of ordnance material consumed during the war. Although always economical of ammunition, yet we never lost any action from the lack of it. We were, however, finally very near the end of our resources, in the supply of one indispensable article. To make percussion caps nitric acid, mercury, and copper were required. Our Nitre and Mining Bureau had learned to make saltpetre from caves, and the earth under old barns and smoke houses, and from all kinds of nitrogenous waste material. From the saltpetre our chemists could make nitric acid. Our quicksilver came from Mexico, but after the fall of Vicksburg we were cut off from it, and about the same time our supply of sheet copper was exhausted. The chemists found out a mixture of chlorate of potash and sulphuret of antimony which they could use in place of fulminate of mercury; and we collected all the turpentine and apple-brandy stills in the country and sent them to Richmond to be cut up and rerolled into copper strips.

From this copper and the above chemical mixture all the caps were made which we used during the last year of the war, but at its close the copper stills were exhausted. It is hard to imagine what we would then have done had not the surrender at Appomattox relieved the quandary.

—ALEXANDER, *Military Memoirs of a Confederate*

11. HOW THE ARMY OF NORTHERN VIRGINIA GOT ITS ORDNANCE

Almost wholly without industries, and cut off from Europe by the block-ade, the Confederacy had to get its arms and equipment as best it could. Some ordnance was seized when the Confederate states seceded; some was imported before the blockade became effective; some was smuggled in from the North; substantial quantities were captured from the enemy or "gleaned" on the battlefield.

Colonel William Allan, from whose reminiscences this excerpt is taken, was Chief of Ordnance of the Second Army Corps and author of an invalu-able history of the campaign in the Shenandoah Valley and of the Army of Northern Virginia.

THE troops at this time [1863] were armed in a heterogeneous fashion. Many of the men had smooth bore muskets, calibre .69. Others had rifled muskets, calibre .54; and others still had Springfield muskets, calibre .58. There were some other arms, as, for instance, some Belgian rifles, calibre .70, but the three kinds I have mentioned were the principal kinds in the hands of the infantry in January, 1863. We were all anxious to replace the smooth bores with rifles, and especially with calibre .58, which was the model the Confederate as well as the Federal Government had adopted. The battlefields of the preceding summer had enabled many commands to exchange their smooth bores for Springfield muskets, but as nine-tenths of the arms in the Confederacy at the beginning of the war had been smooth bore muskets, it required time and patience to effect a complete re-arming. This was finally done in the Second corps at Chancellorsville, but in the winter of 1862-'63, there was often found in the same brigade the three kinds of arms above enumerated, and the same wagon often carried the three kinds of ammunition required. During this winter it was found difficult to obtain arms as fast as we needed them for the new men, and of course we were very glad to take what the department could furnish. Between the first of January and the first of May, General Jackson's corps grew from about twenty-three thousand muskets to thirty-three thousand. These ten thousand arms we obtained from Richmond in small quantities, and they were of different calibres, but the corps was fully armed when it went to Chancellorsville. After that battle the men all had muskets, calibre .58, and henceforth but one sort of ammunition was needed.

Our artillery armament was even more heterogeneous. Six-pounder guns, howitzers, some Napoleons, three-inch rifles, ten-pounder Parrotts, and a few twenty-pounder Parrotts were in our corps, besides, probably, some other odd pieces. I remember a Blakely gun or two and a Whitworth, the latter used both at Chancellorsville and Gettysburg. Our batteries had been greatly improved by a number of guns captured from the enemy. We especially valued the three-inch rifles, which became the favorite field piece. During the winter of 1862-'63, the artillery was first thoroughly organized under General Pendleton as chief. Batteries were detached from brigades, and were organized into battalions, containing four batteries, usually of four guns each. A number of these battalions were assigned to each corps under the chief of artillery of that corps, while a number of others constituted the general reserve, of which General Pendleton took immediate oversight. All that our supplies admitted was done to thoroughly equip these batteries during the winter, and they were ready for action when the campaign opened. A train of wagons was organized to carry the reserve ammunition for the artillery, and this was placed in charge of the artillery ordnance officer of the corps, and, besides this, there was a reserve train for the army under the direct orders of the chief ordnance officer of the army. . . .

Gleaning the battlefields was one of the important duties of the field ordnance officers. They were directed to save everything which could be made of use. Of course they took care of the good arms and good ammunition, but they had to preserve no less carefully all damaged arms, gun barrels, wasted ammunition, of which the lead was the valuable consideration, bayonets, cartridge-boxes, &c. After Chancellorsville and the gathering which had been done during the battle, an ordnance officer of the Second corps was sent to the field with power to call upon a neighboring brigade for as large details as he wished, and he spent a week in gathering the débris of the battle and sending it to Guiney's Station or Hamilton's Crossing, whence it was shipped to Richmond. My recollection is that over twenty thousand stand of damaged arms were sent in this way to the arsenal, besides a considerable quantity of lead, &c. After the first day at Gettysburg the battlefield was gleaned, and such material as we had transportation for sent back. . . .

In the winter of 1864 it was impossible to obtain an adequate quantity of horseshoes and nails from the ordnance department. The cavalry, which had been with General Early during that fall, had seen severe service, and it was absolutely necessary, in reference to the future, to procure in some way a supply of horseshoes and nails during the winter. We had to depend upon ourselves. I determined to establish, if possible, twenty forges in Waynesboro', Augusta county, Virginia, and have blacksmiths detailed from the army to make shoes and nails. We sent through the country and got such blacksmith tools as we were able to find. I think I got some, too, from Richmond, from the ordnance department. There was no difficulty in getting good blacksmiths out of the army. A number of men were put to work, and horseshoes and nails began to accumulate. We soon ran out of iron, however, and found that the department at Richmond could not fully supply our wants. There was a fine lot of iron at Columbia furnace, near Mount Jackson, which was at this time in the debatable ground between the two armies. This iron was of fine quality, suitable for casting cannon as well as any other purpose. The commander of the arsenal informed me that if I could manage to get this to Richmond he would give me back in bars as much as I needed for horseshoes and nails. Trains of wagons were sent after it from Staunton, and these trains were protected by cavalry, which General Early sent for the purpose, and they returned in safety with the iron, which was promptly shipped to Richmond.

From this time forward our forges were fully supplied, and I think when Sheridan overhauled and dispersed our forces at Waynesboro', at the beginning of March, 1865, we had manufactured some twenty thousand pounds of horseshoes and nails. They were loaded upon the cars, which were gotten through the tunnel, but were captured by some of Sheridan's people at or near Greenwood depot.

—ALLAN, "Reminiscences of Field Ordnance Service"

12. THE TREDEGAR IRON WORKS SERVE THE CONFEDERATE ARMIES

Aside from the foundries at Selma, Alabama, the Tredegar Iron Works was almost the only source for the supply of Confederate arms; it was the existence of these works outside Richmond which imperatively demanded the defense of Richmond and influenced the choice of that city as permanent capital of the Confederacy. During the war the Tredegar works expanded to include rolling mills, machine shops, forges, coal mines, sawmills, and even a blockade-runner, employed some 2,500 men, and produced some 1,100 cannon for the Confederacy.

We have met Thomas Cooper DeLeon before.

GAMBLE'S hill, a pretty but steep slope, cuts the river west of the bridge. Rising above its curves, from the Capitol view-point, are the slate-roofed Tredegar Works; their tall chimneys puffing endless black smoke against the sunshine, which reflects it, a livid green, upon the white foam of the rapids.

So potent a factor in the aggressive power of the Confederacy was this foundry that it overtopped the regular government agencies. When the war began, this was the only rolling-mill of great capacity, of which the South could boast; the only one, indeed, capable of casting heavy guns. Almost the first decisive act of Virginia was to prevent, by seizure, the delivery to United States officers of some guns cast for them by the Tredegar Works; and, from that day, there were no more earnest and energetic workers for the cause of southern independence than the firm of Jos. R. Anderson & Co.

It was said, at this time that the firm was in financial straits. But it thrived so well on government patronage—spite of sundry boards to consider if army and navy work was not paid for at ruinously low rates—that it greatly increased in size; added to its utility by importations of costly machinery, through the blockade; stood loss of one-third of its buildings, by fire; used a ship of its own for importation; and, at the close of the struggle, was in better condition than at the commencement. The senior partner was, for a time, in the field at head of his brigade; but affairs were so well managed, in the interval, by the Messrs. Tanner—father and son, who were partners with General Anderson—that his absence was not appreciable in the work.

It was at the Tredegar Works that the famous "Brooke gun"—a rifled 7-inch—was cast, tested and perfected. Here the plates for the iron-clads, in almost all southern waters, were rolled or made ready for use. Here heavy ordnance for the forts was cast, together with shells and shot; and here the torpedoes—sometimes so effective, and usually so useless—were contrived and made. Indeed, the Tredegar Works so greatly aided the Confederacy, that the lengthening of the war may be, in large measure, attributed to their capacity, and to the able zeal with which they were managed.

So great and effective an agent could not fail to receive, from the Richmond government, every aid in obtainance of supplies, labor and transportation. "The Works" had mines, mills and pork packeries in various sections of the South; thus obtaining coal and metals, as well as food—at reduced rates, within reach of their wages—for an army of employés. So great was the necessary number of these—whites, skilled in labor—that even closest conscription left the junior of the firm a full battalion of infantry. This, drilled and equipped from his own shops, Major Tanner led in person, when raids or other straits made their soldiering paramount to other occupation. And—even when greatest scarcity of provisions came—the agents of "the Works" proceeded with those of the commissary of the Confederacy, *pari passu.*

An odd incident, coming to mind just here, will point the general estimate of the importance of the Tredegar Works. A special train was crossing the bridge, en route for Petersburg, at a time when transportation was rare. A huge Negro, blacker than the soot upon his face, sat placidly on the platform of the rear car.

"What are you doing here?" was asked by the officer in charge.

"Rid'n' t' Petesbug," was the placid reply.

"Have you paid your fare?"

"Don' got non t' pay, boss. Rides onner pass, I does!"

"Work for the government?"—this rather impatiently.

Ebo rolled his eyes, with expression of deep disgust, as he responded grandly:

"No—*sah!* Fur t'uther consarn!"

—DeLeon, *Four Years in Rebel Capitals*

13. SECRETARY BENJAMIN RECALLS THE MISTAKES OF THE CONFEDERATE CONGRESS

The Confederate government was no more ready for war than was the Union government, and confusion and mismanagement attended the beginnings of that conflict on both sides. More serious even than incompetence and shortsightedness, as events were to prove, was that jealousy between state and federal governments to which Secretary Benjamin here refers.

Benjamin himself, whom we have already met in the pages of Jones's Diary *and Peyton's visit to Richmond, was successively Attorney General, Secretary of War, and Secretary of State of the Confederacy, and probably the ablest and most trusted of President Davis' advisers. This letter was written after the war to Charles Marshall, an aide-de-camp of Lee.*

AS soon as war became certain, every possible effort was made by the President and his advisers to induce Congress to raise an army enlisted "for the war." The fatal effects of enlistments for short terms, shown by the history of the War of Independence against England, were invoked as furnishing a lesson for our guidance. It was all in vain. The people as we were informed by the members would not volunteer for the war, but they would rise in mass as volunteers for twelve months. We did not wish them to rise in mass nor in great numbers for any such short term, for the reason that *we could not arm them*, and their term of service would expire before we could equip them. I speak from memory as to numbers, but only a moderate force was raised (all that we could provide with arms) for twelve months service, and thus a *provisional* army was formed, but the fatal effect of the short term of service, combined with the painful deficiency of supplies, were felt long before the end of the year. While the Northern States after the Battle of Manassas were vigorously engaged in preparing for an overwhelming descent upon Virginia, our own army was falling to pieces. . . .

The representatives of the people could not be persuaded to pass measures unpalatable to the people; and the unthinking multitude upon whose *voluntary* enlistments Congress forced us to depend were unable to foresee or appreciate the dangers of the policy against which we protested. It was only the imminent danger of being left without *any* army by the return home in mass of the first levy of twelve-month volunteers that drove Congress into passing a law for enlistments for the war, and in order to induce the soldiers under arms to re-enlist we were driven to the fatal expedient of granting them not only bounties but furloughs to return from Virginia to their homes in the far South, and if our actual condition had been at all suspected by the enemy they might have marched through Virginia with but the faintest show of resistance.

As to supplies of munitions I will give a single instance of the straits to which we were reduced. I was Secretary of War *ad interim* for a few months, during which Roanoke Island, commanded by General Wise, fell into the hands of the enemy. The report of that General shows that the capture was due in great measure to the persistent disregard by the Secretary of War of his urgent demands for munitions and supplies. Congress appointed a committee to investigate the conduct of the Secretary. I consulted the President whether it was best for the country that I should submit to unmerited censure or reveal to a Congressional Committee our poverty and my utter inability to supply the requisitions of General Wise, and thus run the risk that the fact should become known to some of the spies of the enemy of whose activity we were well assured. It was thought best for the public service that I should suffer the blame in silence and a report of censure on me was accordingly made by the Committee of Congress.

The *dearth* even of powder was so great that during the descent of the enemy on Roanoke, General Wise having sent me a despatch that he was in instant need of ammunition, I ordered by telegraph General Huger at Norfolk to send an immediate supply; this was done but accompanied by a despatch from General Huger protesting against this exhausting of his small store, and saying that it was insufficient to defend Norfolk for a day. General Lee was therefore ordered to send a part of his very scanty supply to Norfolk, General Lee being in his turn aided by a small cargo of powder which had just run into one of the inlets on the coast of Florida.

Another terrible source of trouble, disorganisation and inefficiency was the incurable jealousy in many states of the General Government. Each State has its own mode of appointing officers, generally by election. Until disaster forced Congress to pass the Conscription law, all that we could do was to get laws passed calling for certain quotas of troops from the states, and in order to prevent attempts made to create officers of higher rank than the Confederate officers, who would thus have been placed under the orders of raw militia generals, we resorted to the expedient of refusing to receive any higher organisation than a regiment. But the troops being State troops officered by the State officers, the army was constantly scandalized by electioneering to replace regimental officers, and Confederate Commanders were without means of enforcing discipline and efficiency except through the cumbrous and most objectionable expedient of Courts Martial. Another fatal defect was that we had no power to consolidate regiments, battalions, and companies. If a company was reduced to five men or a regiment to fifty, we had no power to remedy this. The message of the President of the 12th of August, 1862, showed the fatal effects of our military system, and a perusal of that message will shed a flood of light on the actual position of things and the hopeless helplessness to which the Executive was reduced by the legislation of Congress, and the restrictions imposed on his power to act efficiently for military success by the jealousy of Congress and the States. When I look back on it all, I am lost in amazement that the struggle could have been so prolonged, and one of the main, if not the main source of strength and encouragement to the Executive was the genius, ability, constancy, fidelity, and firmness of General Lee.

—Sir Frederick Maurice, ed., *An Aide-de-Camp of Lee*

14. NORTHERN ORDNANCE

The North, with its highly developed arms industries, and with easy access to Britain, had no difficulty supplying its armies with whatever weapons were needed, yet the supply of small arms did not meet requirements until the war was a year old. Altogether some four million muskets were issued to Union soldiers, but less than eight thousand cannon.

The Comte de Paris, from whose compendious history of the Civil War this extract is taken, served, with his brother the Duc de Chartres, on McClellan's staff, fighting at Yorktown and Gaines' Mill.

THE task of supplying the Federal troops with arms and ammunition, which devolved upon the ordnance department, was the most difficult of all. In fact, both the government armories and private manufactories were insufficient to meet the demand, and it required time to establish additional ones. The wonderful machines by which the most complicated rifles now in use throughout Europe are constructed almost without the aid of man are of American invention, and have given a well-deserved reputation to the expansion rifles manufactured at the government armory in Springfield. But this establishment had only capacity for producing from ten to twelve thousand yearly, and the supply could not be increased except by constructing new machines. The private workshops were equally insufficient; the Federal factory at Harper's Ferry had been destroyed by fire, and the dépôts were empty. It was important, however, to supply the most pressing of all the wants of the soldier, that of having a weapon in his hands.

During the first year of the war the ordnance department succeeded in furnishing the various armies in the field, not counting what was left at the dépôts, one million two hundred and seventy-six thousand six hundred and eighty-six portable firearms (muskets, carbines, and pistols), one thousand nine hundred and twenty-six field- or siege-guns, twelve hundred pieces for batteries in position, and two hundred and fourteen million cartridges for small-arms and for cannon. But it was obliged to apply to Europe for muskets and ammunition; this was the only war commodity that America procured in considerable quantities from the Old World, and it was this supply which proved to be the most defective. Agents without either experience or credit, and sometimes unscrupulous, bought in every part of Europe, on account of the Federal government, all the muskets they could pick up, without any regard to their quality or price. The English and Belgian manufactories not being able to satisfy their demands fast enough, they procured from the little German states all their old-fashioned arms, which those states hastened to get rid of at a price which enabled them to replace them with needle-guns. In short, the refuse of all Europe passed into the hands of the American volunteers.

A portion of the muskets being unfit for use, the few that were serviceable had to be kept for the soldiers doing guard duty in each company. The calibres were all mixed up; conical balls were issued for the large German smooth-bore muskets, while the old American cartridge, containing one ball and four buckshot, was given to those who had the good fortune to possess a minie rifle. The defective armament of the infantry would have been sufficient to delay the opening of the campaign for several months. In order to remedy this it was found necessary, in the first instance, to classify the calibres of the muskets by regiments, then gradually to throw aside the most worthless. After a while the American factories, both national and private, were able to furnish a sufficient quantity of new arms to justify this process.

While willing to encourage private enterprise to a great extent, the Federal government determined to control it; and in order to avoid being at its mercy, it largely extended its own establishments. Thus, in 1862, the Springfield manufactory delivered two hundred thousand rifles, while in the year 1863, during which there were manufactured two hundred and fifty thousand there, the importation of arms from Europe by the Northern States ceased altogether. The rifle which bore the name of the Federal manufactory had the advantage of not requiring heavy charges, of giving a great precision of aim at a distance of from six to seven hundred metres, and of being easily loaded and managed. It was therefore introduced throughout the army as fast as the ordnance department was able to meet the demands that were made for that arm from every quarter.

But, at the same time, a great number of new inventions were tried upon a scale which enabled the authorities to test their merits. Some were even adopted by whole regiments of cavalry; and the practice of breech-loading, which was common to all the systems, contributed greatly to their efficiency in the numerous engagements in which those regiments had to fight on foot. With the exception of this mode of loading, they differed greatly in their construction; it would be impossible for us to describe all, for there were no less than eleven of the first class. We shall only mention two belonging to the class called repeating-rifles—that is to say, arms which fire a certain number of shots without being reloaded. The Colt rifle is a long-barrelled revolver with five or six chambers, and the ball is forced into seven grooves forming a spiral which grows more and more contracted. This heavy weapon was formidable in practiced hands, but it required considerable time to reload it. The second was the Spencer rifle, an excellent arm, the use of which became more and more extended in the Federal army. The butt is pierced, in the direction of the length, by a tube containing seven cartridges, which are deposited successively, after each fire, in the chamber, replacing in turn those which, when discharged, are thrown out by a very simple mechanism. This magazine, entirely protected, is very easily recharged. Many extraordinary instances have been cited of successful personal defence due to the rapidity with which this arm can be fired, and some Federal regiments of infantry which made a trial of it were highly pleased with the result. Most of these rifles were of two models—one for the use of the infantry, the other, lighter and shorter, for the cavalry.

The *matériel* of the artillery, which had to be created, was as extensive as the armament of the infantry, and its construction was also new to American manufactories. Nevertheless, the great workshops for smelting iron and steel were so rapidly transformed into cannon foundries that the ordnance department was not obliged to depend on Europe for a supply.

At the time when the war broke out none of the systems of rifle cannon invented a few years before had ever been adopted, or even seriously experimented upon, by the officers of the regular army. But the latter, while adhering to the brass smooth-bore cannon, had studied these different inventions, and did not conceal their preference for the rifled system, by which the ball, like the minie bullet, inserted through the mouth of the cannon, is driven into the grooves under the pressure of the gases which propel it forward. The impression obtained from these inquiries in common was never forgotten by the officers who were placed in positions of command in the two hostile armies; and notwithstanding the diversity of details, the guns of those two armies always bore a strong family resemblance. But nothing could limit the fertility of inventors stimulated by the war.

—COMTE DE PARIS, *History of the Civil War in America*

IV

Bull Run and the Peninsular Campaign

AFTER the attack on Fort Sumter and the secession of Virginia, both sides marked time. Neither was eager to assume the offensive, and neither was prepared to do so.

Conscious that it could never hope to muster the numerical or material strength of the North, the Confederacy preferred to exploit the great advantages of defensive operations and of interior lines of communication. Nor was there, from the larger political or diplomatic point of view, anything to be gained by invading the North. The Confederacy was merely asking to be let alone. It wanted to go its way in peace; if the North would not permit this it was prepared to fight. But it rested its hopes of victory not in conquest of the North but in wearing down the Northern will to fight, and in foreign intervention.

The North, on the other hand, could not escape the offensive. Its military task was to invade and conquer the South. This required an altogether more elaborate military organization than it was possible to create in a few months. It meant not only a large army—one necessarily much larger than the Confederate—but a permanent one; three-months militiamen would be worse than useless for an invasion. It meant building up immense quantities of war matériel, developing and maintaining long lines of communication, imposing a blockade on the South, wresting major ports and rivers from Southern control. It meant, in short, a military effort on a scale unprecedented in modern history.

General Scott's original plan was to make the major offensive down the Mississippi—a plan which had much to commend it. Circumstances, however—the proximity of the two capitals to each other, and of the first armies that were organized—dictated that Virginia should be the first and for long the major theater of the war. It is important therefore that we get clearly in mind the geography of that theater in so far as it controlled military operations.

Just a hundred miles separated the two capitals, Washington and Richmond. Between them lay four great rivers—the James, the York, the Rappahannock, and the Potomac—and many lesser streams such as the Chickahominy, the North and South Anna, and Bull Run. The ground between these two cities, and particularly from the Rappahannock to the James, was low, swampy, covered with woods and underbrush; the roads were deep in mud in winter and spring. To the west lay a series of hills and mountains, notably the Blue Ridge and the Shenandoah. The great Valley

*between these ranges ran northeast and southwest. Its mouth came out on
the Potomac, that is to say on the Baltimore and Ohio Railroad and the
Chesapeake and Ohio Canal—just fifty miles from Washington, and opened
up into the rich Maryland and Pennsylvania country just across the Potomac.
Thus the Confederates could use the Valley for striking into the heart of
the North, cutting communications with Washington, and threatening that
city. But to the Federals the Valley was of little value. If they succeeded in
fighting their way up it to Staunton they were as far from Richmond as
ever.*

*Thus while Washington was vulnerable to attack from both south and
west, an attack on Richmond presented formidable difficulties. There were
two possible approaches to Richmond: the direct approach by land, southward through Fredericksburg; the approach by sea to the Peninsula and up
the Peninsula to the capital city. There was a variation on these, or a combination of them, that Grant finally used: a movement southward by land,
across the James, and to Petersburg, and an attack on the rear of the city.*

*During May both governments tried to organize armies chiefly for de-
fensive purposes. By the beginning of June Davis had one army of about
22,000 men under Beauregard at Manassas Junction, an important railroad
center some 25 miles southwest of Washington; and a smaller force of about
11,000 under Joseph E. Johnston at Winchester, in the Valley. General
Scott, the aged veteran of the War of 1812 and the Mexican War, had
assembled a force of some 35,000, under McDowell, in and around Centerville, Virginia, and a force of about 12,000 under the veteran General Patterson at Harpers Ferry. Here at once we see the advantages that the
Confederacy enjoyed in its interior lines. Johnston and Beauregard were
only a few hours apart, by rail; Patterson and McDowell were days apart.*

*Scott had no intention of launching an offensive with his three-months
militia, but public opinion called loudly for action. On June 24, McDowell
submitted his plan for an offensive; it was approved and early in July he
began to move on Beauregard. Meantime, however, everything depended on
Patterson holding Johnston in the Valley. This he failed to do, with results
that were disastrous for the Union cause. The result was the defeat at First
Bull Run.*

*That story and its sequel are told in the following accounts. The direct
overland approach having failed, McClellan tried the approach by sea and up
the Peninsula. That, too, failed, but whether through the incompetence of
the Federal commander, or the interference in his plans by the administration, or the genius of Lee will ever remain a subject of debate.*

1. A CONFEDERATE DOCTOR DESCRIBES
THE VICTORY AT FIRST BULL RUN

*The first major engagement of the war came when public opinion forced
an advance on Richmond before the raw Union army was ready for fighting. Union troops, under McDowell, outnumbered the Confederates under*

*Beauregard, but the success of the Union advance depended on the ability of
General Patterson to prevent the Confederate General J. E. Johnston from
bringing a force of some 9,000 men from the Shenandoah Valley. In this
Patterson failed, and on July 20 the vanguard of Johnston's forces began to
arrive at Manassas Junction. Before dawn on Sunday, July 21, 1861, Mc-
Dowell attacked and by three o'clock that afternoon seemed to have carried
the day. Then additional Confederate reinforcements threw themselves on
the weary Federals and drove them back across the Bull Run. Soon the reverse became a disorderly retreat. Bull Run—or First Manassas as it is known
in the South—proved a costly victory, for it created a sense of overconfidence
in the South while it spurred the North on to more determined efforts.*

Richmond, July 23, 1861

Dear Harleston: I have seen the great and glorious battle of Manassas,
which brought a nation into existence, and the scene was grand and impressive beyond the power of language. We foresaw the action several days
ahead—the enemy were known to be advancing in immense masses from
Arlington towards Fairfax, and the master stroke was at once made, to order
Johnston down from Winchester, by forced marches, before Patterson could
get down on the other side. Johnston's troops marched all twenty-six miles,
then crowded into the railroad, came down in successive trains, without
sleeping or eating, (15,000,) and arrived, many of them, while the battle was
raging.

I got to Manassas the morning of the day previous to the fight; and knowing well both Generals Beauregard and Johnston, and their staff officers, I
went immediately to headquarters. . . . General Beauregard determined to
attack them in several columns at once the next morning, so as to cut them
up before Patterson could arrive—but our scouts came early in the morning, informing the generals that the enemy had been in motion since two
hours before day, which settled the question as to their intention to make
the attack. Beauregard, who had studied the whole ground around—knew
every hill, ravine, and pathway—had made all the necessary arrangements
and planned the battle. Not knowing at what point of a semicircle of ten
miles around Manassas the enemy would attack, his forces had to be scattered
in such a way as to guard all points, prevent a flank movement on either side,
and guard his intrenchments and supplies in the centre.

We got up in the morning at daylight, took a cup of coffee and remained quietly laughing and talking at head-quarters, while the scouts were
passing in and out bringing news from the enemy. At a quarter past six in
the still, bright morning, we heard the first deep-toned sound of cannon on
the centre of our line, about three miles off. We waited till nine for further
information, and at nine the generals ordered to horse, and away we dashed
to the hill overlooking the point at which cannon, like minute guns, had continued slowly to fire. The enemy could not see any of our troops, but were
firing at the dust kicked up along the road, which they saw above the low
trees. We were for some time at the point they were firing at, and some

twenty or thirty balls of their rifled cannons whizzed through the air above us, and I felt very forcibly the remark of Cuddy to his mother Mause, that "a straggling bullet has nae discretion" and might take my head off as well as that of anybody else.

The firing at this point kept up slowly from a quarter past six till eleven, when we heard a gun fire on the extreme left of the semicircle, and we were then satisfied that the firing in front was a mere feint. In a few minutes the cannon firing came in rapid succession, as if one battery was answering another. The generals then ordered "to horse" again, and away we rode to the seat of battle, about three miles off. When we arrived on the top of a hill, in an old field, we could get glimpses of the fight through the woods. The cannons were roaring and the musketry sounded like a large bundle of fire crackers, and the constant roaring of the big guns, the sharp sound of rifled cannons, Minié rifles and muskets, with the bursting of shells, made one feel that death was doing his work with fearful rapidity.

The enemy had concentrated all his forces on this one point while ours were scattered around a half circle of ten miles, and the few regiments who received the first onset were most terribly cut up. It was far greater odds than human nature could stand, the regiments were torn to pieces, driven back, and so overwhelmed by numbers that I feared the day was lost. At this stage of the game the enemy was telegraphing to Washington that the battle had been won, and secession was about to be crushed. My heart failed me as I saw load after load of our poor wounded and dying soldiers brought and strewed on the ground, along the ravine where I was at work. Dr. Fanthray, who belonged to General Johnston's staff, and myself were just getting fully to work, when an old surgeon, whom I do not know, came to us and said the enemy were carrying every thing before them, and ordered us to fall back to another point with the wounded, as they were turning our flank, and the battle would soon be upon us. Accordingly the wounded were taken up and we fell back, but after following the ambulances for a mile, we found that they were to be taken all the way to Manassas—about four miles— where there were hospitals and surgeons to receive them, and we returned to our position near the battle.

At this juncture I saw our reinforcements pouring in with the rapidity and eagerness of a fox chase, and was satisfied that they would drive every thing before them. No one can imagine such a grand, glorious picture as these patriots presented, rushing to the field through the masses of wounded bodies which strewed the roadside as they passed along. For half a mile behind me the road passed down a gradual slope, and through an old field, as I looked back, I could see a regiment of infantry coming in a trot, with their bright muskets glittering in the sun; then would come a battery of artillery, each gun carriage crowded with men and drawn by four horses in full gallop. Next came troops of cavalry, dashing with the speed of Murat; after these followed, with almost equal speed, wagons loaded with ammunition, &c., screaming all the while, "push ahead boys," "pitch into the d—d Yankees," "drive them into the Potomac."

This kept up from about mid-day till dark, and I felt as if the Alps them-selves could not withstand such a rush. The cannon and small-arms were roaring like a thunder storm as they rushed to the battle-field. One regiment, which had been driven back by overwhelming numbers, was now supported and I soon perceived that the firing was getting further off, as I had expected, and I knew that the "pet lambs" now could only be saved by their superior heels. About this time, too, the last of General Johnston's command arrived on the cars, opposite the battle-ground, to the number of some three or four thousand, and although they had been two nights without sleep, they jumped from the cars and cut across to the field.

By this time we had collected about 15,000 against their 35,000, and, from all accounts, no red fox ever made tracks, so fast as did these cowardly wretches. They were all fresh and better accoutred in every respect than our men, one half or more of whom had to make forced marches to get at them. They had selected their position coolly and deliberately in the morn-ing, while ours were scattered over ten miles and had to run through the mid-day sunshine. If our men had been equally fresh they would have gone straight into their intrenchments at Arlington.

But I will not speculate on the future and weary you with details which really will reach you through print long before this.

—Letter of Dr. J. C. Nott

2. "BULL RUN RUSSELL" REPORTS THE ROUT OF THE FEDERALS

The English journalist William Howard Russell arrived in America in 1861 with a great and merited reputation as war correspondent, and soon began sending the London Times *shrewd and outspoken accounts of Ameri-can men and affairs. His description of the Federal demoralization after First Bull Run aroused a good deal of criticism, but all the evidence shows that it was by no means exaggerated.*

July 20th, 1861.—The great battle which is to arrest rebellion or to make it a power in the land is no longer distant or doubtful. McDowell has com-pleted his reconnaissance of the country in front of the enemy, and General Scott anticipates that he will be in possession of Manassas tomorrow night....

Some senators and many congressmen have already gone to join Mc-Dowell's army or to follow in its wake in the hope of seeing the Lord deliver the Philistines into his hands.... Every carriage, gig, wagon, and hack has been engaged by people going out to see the fight. The price is enhanced by mysterious communications respecting the horrible slaughter in the skirmishes at Bull Run. The French cooks and hotelkeepers, by some occult process of reasoning, have arrived at the conclusion that they must treble the prices of their wines and of the hampers of provisions which the Washington people are ordering to comfort themselves at their bloody Derby....

It was a strange scene before us. From the hill a densely wooded country,

THE FIRST BATTLE OF BULL RUN

dotted at intervals with green fields and cleared lands, spread five or six miles in front, bounded by a line of blue and purple ridges, terminating abruptly in escarpments toward the left front and swelling gradually towards the right into the lower spines of an offshoot from the Blue Ridge Mountains. On our left the view was circumscribed by a forest which clothed the side of the ridge on which we stood and covered its shoulder far down into the plain. A gap in the nearest chain of the hills in our front was pointed out by the by-standers as the Pass of Manassas by which the railway from the West is carried into the plain, and still nearer at hand before us is the junction of that rail with the line from Alexandria and with the railway leading south-ward to Richmond. The intervening space was not a dead level; undulating lines of forest marked the course of the streams which intersected it and gave by their variety of color and shading an additional charm to the landscape which, inclosed in a framework of blue and purple hills, softened into violet in the extreme distance, presented one of the most agreeable displays of simple pastoral woodland scenery that could be conceived.

But the sounds which came upon the breeze and the sights which met our eyes were in terrible variance with the tranquil character of the land-scape. The woods far and near echoed to the roar of cannon, and thin, frayed lines of blue smoke marked the spots whence came the muttering sound of rolling musketry; the white puffs of smoke burst high above the treetops, and the gunners' rings from shell and howitzer marked the fire of the artillery.

Clouds of dust shifted and moved through the forest, and through the wavering mists of light blue smoke and the thicker masses which rose com-mingling from the feet of men and the mouths of cannon, I could see the gleam of arms and the twinkling of bayonets.

On the hill beside me there was a crowd of civilians on horseback and in all sorts of vehicles, with a few of the fairer, if not gentler, sex. A few officers and some soldiers, who had straggled from the regiments in reserve, moved about among the spectators and pretended to explain the movements of the troops below, of which they were profoundly ignorant. . . .

The spectators were all excited, and a lady with an opera glass who was near me was quite beside herself when an unusually heavy discharge roused the current of her blood—"That is splendid. Oh, my! Is not that first-rate? I guess we will be in Richmond this time tomorrow." These, mingled with coarser exclamations, burst from the politicians who had come out to see the triumph of the Union arms. . . .

Loud cheers suddenly burst from the spectators as a man dressed in the uniform of an officer, whom I had seen riding violently across the plain in an open space below, galloped along the front, waving his cap and shouting at the top of his voice. He was brought up, by the press of people round his horse, close to where I stood. "We've whipped them on all points," he cried. "We have taken all their batteries. They are retreating as fast as they can, and we are after them." Such cheers as rent the welkin! The congressmen shook hands with each other and cried out: "Bully for us! Bravo! Didn't I tell you so?" The Germans uttered their martial cheers, and the Irish hur-rahed wildly. At this moment my horse was brought up the hill and I mounted and turned toward the road to the front. . . .

I had ridden between three and a half and four miles, as well as I could judge, when I was obliged to turn for the third and fourth time into the road by a considerable stream which was spanned by a bridge, toward which I was threading my way, when my attention was attracted by loud shouts in advance and I perceived several wagons coming from the direction of the battlefield, the drivers of which were endeavoring to force their horses past the ammunition carts going in the contrary direction near the bridge; a thick cloud of dust rose behind them, and running by the side of the waggons were a number of men in uniform whom I supposed to be the guard. My first impression was that the waggons were returning for fresh supplies of am-munition. But every moment the crowd increased; drivers and men cried out with the most vehement gestures: "Turn back! Turn back! We are whipped." They seized the heads of the horses and swore at the opposing drivers. Emerging from the crowd, a breathless man in the uniform of an officer, with an empty scabbard dangling by his side, was cut off by getting between my horse and a cart for a moment. "What is the matter, sir? What is all this about?" "Why, it means we are pretty badly whipped, that's the truth," he gasped, and continued.

By this time the confusion had been communicating itself through the line of waggons toward the rear, and the drivers endeavored to turn round their vehicles in the narrow road, which caused the usual amount of impre-cations from the men and plunging and kicking from the horses.

The crowd from the front continually increased, the heat, the uproar, and the dust were beyond description, and these were augmented when some cavalry soldiers, flourishing their sabers and preceded by an officer, who cried out, "Make way there—make way there for the General," attempted to force a covered waggon, in which was seated a man with a bloody hand-kerchief round his head, through the press.

I had succeeded in getting across the bridge, with great difficulty, before the waggon came up, and I saw the crowd on the road was still gathering thicker and thicker. Again I asked an officer, who was on foot with his sword under his arm, "What is all this for?" "We are whipped, sir. We are all in retreat. You are all to go back." "Can you tell me where I can find General McDowell?" "No! nor can any one else. . . ."

In a few seconds a crowd of men rushed out of the wood down toward the guns, and the artillerymen near me seized the trail of a piece and were wheeling it round to fire when an officer or sergeant called out: "Stop! stop! They are our own men"; and in two or three minutes the whole battalion came sweeping past the guns at the double and in the utmost disorder. Some of the artillerymen dragged the horses out of the tumbrils, and for a moment the confusion was so great I could not understand what had taken place; but a soldier whom I stopped said, "We are pursued by their cavalry; they have cut us all to pieces."

Murat himself would not have dared to move a squadron on such ground. However, it could not be doubted that something serious was taking place; and at that moment a shell burst in front of the house, scattering the soldiers near it, which was followed by another that bounded along the road; and in a few minutes more out came another regiment from the wood, almost as broken as the first. The scene on the road had now assumed an aspect which has not a parallel in any description I have ever read. Infantry soldiers on mules and draft horses with the harness clinging to their heels, as much frightened as their riders; Negro servants on their masters' chargers; ambulances crowded with unwounded soldiers; waggons swarming with men who threw out the contents in the road to make room, grinding through a shouting, screaming mass of men on foot who were literally yelling with rage at every halt and shrieking out: "Here are the cavalry! Will you get on?" This portion of the force was evidently in discord.

There was nothing left for it but to go with the current one could not stem. I turned round my horse. . . . I was unwillingly approaching Centerville in the midst of heat, dust, confusion, imprecations inconceivable. On arriving at the place where a small rivulet crossed the road the throng increased still more. The ground over which I had passed going out was now covered with arms, clothing of all kinds, accouterments thrown off and left to be trampled in the dust under the hoofs of men and horses. The runaways ran alongside the waggons, striving to force themselves in among the occupants, who resisted tooth and nail. The drivers spurred and whipped and urged the horses to the utmost of their bent. I felt an inclination to laugh which was overcome by disgust and by that vague sense of something extraordinary taking place which is experienced when a man sees a number of people acting as if driven by some unknown terror. As I rode in the crowd, with men clinging to the stirrup leathers or holding on by anything they could lay hands on, so that I had some apprehension of being pulled off, I spoke to the men and asked them over and over again not to be in such a hurry. "There's no enemy to pursue you. All the cavalry in the world could not get at you." But I might as well have talked to the stones. . . .

It never occurred to me that this was a grand debacle. All along I believed the mass of the army was not broken and that all I saw around was the result of confusion created in a crude organization by a forced retreat, and knowing the reserves were at Centerville and beyond, I said to myself, "Let us see how this will be when we get to the hill." . . .

I was trotting quietly down the hill road beyond Centerville when suddenly the guns on the other side or from a battery very near opened fire, and a fresh outburst of artillery sounded through the woods. In an instant the mass of vehicles and retreating soldiers, teamsters, and civilians, as if agonized by an electric shock, quivered throughout the tortuous line. With dreadful shouts and cursings the drivers lashed their maddened horses and, leaping from the carts, left them to their fate and ran on foot. Artillerymen and foot soldiers and Negroes, mounted on gun horses with the chain traces and loose trappings trailing in the dust, spurred and flogged their steeds down the road or by the side paths. The firing continued and seemed to approach the hill, and at every report the agitated body of horsemen and waggons was seized, as it were, with a fresh convulsion.

Once more the dreaded cry: "The cavalry! cavalry are coming!" rang through the crowd, and looking back to Centerville, I perceived coming down the hill, between me and the sky, a number of mounted men who might at a hasty glance be taken for horsemen in the act of sabering the fugitives. In reality they were soldiers and civilians, with, I regret to say, some officers among them, who were whipping and striking their horses with sticks or whatever else they could lay hands on. I called out to the men who were frantic with terror beside me, "They are not cavalry at all; they're your own men"—but they did not heed me. A fellow who was shouting out, "Run! run!" as loud as he could beside me, seemed to take delight in creating alarm; and as he was perfectly collected as far as I could judge, I said: "What on earth are you running for? What are you afraid of?" He was in the roadside below me and, at once turning on me and exclaiming, "I'm not afraid of you," presented his piece and pulled the trigger so instantaneously that had it gone off I could not have swerved from the ball. As the scoundrel deliberately drew up to examine the nipple, I judged it best not to give him another chance and spurred on through the crowd, where any man could have shot as many as he pleased without interruption. The only conclusion I came to was that he was mad or drunken. When I was passing by the line of the bivouacs a battalion of men came tumbling down the bank from the field into the road with fixed bayonets, and as some fell in the road and others tumbled on top of them, there must have been a few ingloriously wounded.

22d.—I awoke from a deep sleep this morning about six o'clock. The rain was falling in torrents and beat with a dull, thudding sound on the leads outside my window; but louder than all came a strange sound as if of the tread of men, a confused tramp and splashing and a murmuring of voices. I got up and ran to the front room, the windows of which looked on the street, and there, to my intense surprise, I saw a steady stream of men covered with mud, soaked through with rain, who were pouring irregularly, without any semblance of order, up Pennsylvania Avenue toward the Capitol. A dense stream of vapor rose from the multitude, but looking closely at the men, I perceived they belonged to different regiments, New Yorkers, Michiganders, Rhode Islanders, Massachusetters, Minnesotans, mingled pellmell together. Many of them were without knapsacks, crossbelts, and firelocks. Some had neither greatcoats nor shoes; others were covered with blankets. Hastily putting on my clothes, I ran downstairs and asked an officer who was passing by, a pale young man who looked exhausted to death and who had lost his sword, for the empty sheath dangled at his side, where the men were coming from. "Where from? Well, sir, I guess we're all coming out of Virginny as far as we can, and pretty well whipped too." "What! the whole army, sir?" "That's more than I know. They may stay that like. I know I'm going home. I've had enough of fighting to last my lifetime."

The news seemed incredible. But there before my eyes were the jaded, dispirited, broken remnants of regiments passing onward, where and for what I knew not, and it was evident enough that the mass of the grand army of the Potomac was placing that river between it and the enemy as rapidly as possible. "Is there any pursuit?" I asked of several men. Some were too surly to reply; others said, "They're coming as fast as they can after us"; others, "I guess they've stopped it now—the rain is too much for them." A few said they did not know and looked as if they did not care. . . .

The rain has abated a little, and the pavements are densely packed with men in uniforms, some with, others without, arms, on whom the shopkeepers are looking with evident alarm. They seem to be in possession of all the spirit houses. Now and then shots are heard down the street or in the distance, and cries and shouting, as if a scuffle or a difficulty were occurring. Willard's is turned into a barrack for officers and presents such a scene in the hall as could only be witnessed in a city occupied by a demoralized army. There is no provost guard, no patrol, no authority visible in the streets. General Scott is quite overwhelmed by the affair and is unable to stir. General McDowell has not yet arrived. The Secretary of War knows not what to do, Mr. Lincoln is equally helpless, and Mr. Seward, who retains some calmness, is, notwithstanding his military rank and militia experience, without resource or expedient. There are a good many troops hanging on about the camps and forts on the other side of the river, it is said; but they are thoroughly disorganized and will run away if the enemy comes in sight without a shot, and then the capital must fall at once. Why Beauregard does not come I know not, nor can I well guess. I have been expecting every hour since noon to hear his cannon. Here is a golden opportunity. If the Confederates do not grasp that which will never come again on such terms, it stamps them with mediocrity.

—RUSSELL, *My Diary North and South*

3. HOW THE WOMEN TOOK THE NEWS OF BULL RUN

The fortitude and gallantry of the women of the South is a thrice-told tale. It was they, in the words of Stephen Benét,

> *That mended the broken gentlemen*
> *And sent them out to the war again . . .*
> *Made courage from terror and bread from bran*
> *And propped the South on a swansdown fan. . . .**

Susan Blackford, whose letter is reproduced here,† was the wife of Charles Minor Blackford of the 2nd Virginia Cavalry, and sister-in-law to Colonel W. W. Blackford, whose War Years with Jeb Stuart *is one of the minor classics of the war.*

---

* From *John Brown's Body* in *The Selected Works of Stephen Vincent Benét*, published by Rinehart and Company, Inc. Copyright 1927, 1928 by Stephen Vincent Benét.
† Reprinted from *Letters from Lee's Army* by Susan Lee Blackford; copyright 1947 by Charles Scribner's Sons; used by permission of the publishers.

[July 1861. From Lynchburg]

The sound of the cannon were distinctly heard on the hills of Lynchburg, and we well knew that a great battle was being fought from early morn until sunset, and that not only the fate of our country and our homes was at stake, but that each boom which stirred the air might be fraught with the dying sigh of those we loved best. Mrs. Robert C. Saunders, whose husband was in the battle, stood all day on one of the hills near her home in Campbell and listened in agony to every gun. Other ladies whom I knew did the same thing near Pedlar Mills in Amherst County. Mrs. Saunders was all of one hundred and seventy miles from the battlefield. A large number of people came into town Sunday evening from the surrounding country to hear the news of the result, and many stayed long enough to hear sad tidings the next day of those for whom their hearts beat with such nervous strain; amongst the latter was Mrs. Winston Radford, of Bedford, whose husband was killed by a shell from a battery of the enemy commanded by a Captain Arnald.

The next day the rain poured in torrents. Mrs. Robert C. Saunders came up from her home to Father Blackford's to hear tidings of her husband. We could hear nothing Sunday night except that a great battle had been fought. I remained at Father's with Betty Colston and the children waiting and trembling, at one time on my knees praying for my husband's safety and at another trying to prepare myself for the worse news should it come.

This Monday morning was a time of terrible strain on us all. Father and Mother Blackford were very nervous, and he could not go down to his business, but walked about trying to take comfort from every circumstance mentioned. He had prayers in which we all joined. He and Mother had three sons in the battle, and Mrs. Saunders and myself our respective husbands. Old Dr. Thomas Blackford came up and sat with us. He, too, had one or more sons in the fight and was very nervous. My dear little children seemed to understand the trouble which cast its dark shadow over us all and little Nannie clung to me and whispered words of hope in my ear. Father at last went down town to hear what could be heard, while we waited with growing impatience and terror for his return.

At last we heard his footsteps on the front porch, and our hearts stopped beating, but the hurried way in which he opened the front door and the elasticity of his step announced the good news to my eager ear. With one bound we rushed to meet him, and sent out a shout of grateful joy when he caught his breath enough to say, with choking voice, "All safe"! We all gathered around Mother's bed where she was lying, some of us sobbing for joy, while Father offered up thanks to God for having spared our loved ones.

The telegrams which came were from my husband to me, which was the first which had come through, and one from Eugene and William which soon followed. Mr. Blackford's also told that none of his men were hurt, and my first impulse was to rush out and tell the wives and mothers of his men. It was such a happy day! I never shall forget it.

—BLACKFORD, ed., *Letters from Lee's Army*

4. STONEWALL JACKSON CREDITS GOD WITH
THE VICTORY

*First Bull Run gave the Confederacy one of its greatest heroes. When on
the morning of that battle the bluecoats were driving the Confederates back
across the Warrenton turnpike, Thomas J. Jackson's brigade stood firm.
"Look at Jackson," cried General Bee to his troops. "There he stands like a
stonewall." Courage was common enough in the Confederate command;
Jackson was soon to reveal other military qualities of a high order. His letter
to his wife, written two days after the battle, shows that devoutness which
was just as characteristic of the man as was courage.*

Manassas, July 23d [1861]

My Precious Pet,—Yesterday we fought a great battle and gained a great
victory, for which all the glory is due to *God alone.* Although under a
heavy fire for several continuous hours, I received only one wound, the
breaking of the longest finger of my left hand; but the doctor says the finger
can be saved. It was broken about midway between the hand and knuckle,
the ball passing on the side next the forefinger. Had it struck the centre, I
should have lost the finger. My horse was wounded, but not killed. Your
coat got an ugly wound near the hip, but my servant, who is very handy, has
so far repaired it that it doesn't show very much. My preservation was entirely due, as was the glorious victory, to our God, to whom be all the
honor, praise and glory. The battle was the hardest that I have ever been in,
but not near so hot in its fire. I commanded the centre more particularly,
though one of my regiments extended to the right for some distance. There
were other commanders on my right and left. Whilst great credit is due to
other parts of our gallant army, God made my brigade more instrumental
than any other in repulsing the main attack. This is for your information
only—say nothing about it. Let others speak praise, not myself.
—M. Jackson, *Life and Letters of General Thomas J. Jackson*

5. "THE CAPTURE OF WASHINGTON SEEMS INEVITABLE"

*After Bull Run the Confederates could have advanced on Washington;
had they moved promptly they could probably have taken the city. But
political and diplomatic considerations suggested that such an offensive
would be inadvisable. The people of Washington, however, were for a time
a-tremble for their safety.*

*Edwin M. Stanton—who had the jitters easily—had been Attorney General
under Buchanan and was shortly to be appointed Secretary of War by Lincoln.*

Washington, July 26, 1861

Dear Sir: ... The dreadful disaster of Sunday can scarcely be mentioned.
The imbecility of this Administration culminated in that catastrophe—an

irretrievable misfortune and national disgrace never to be forgotten are to be added to the ruin of all peaceful pursuits and national bankruptcy as the result of Lincoln's "running the machine" for five months. You perceive that Bennett is for a change of the Cabinet, and proposes for one of the new Cabinet Mr. Holt. . . . It is not unlikely that some change in the War and Navy Departments may take place, but none beyond these two departments until Jefferson Davis turns out the whole concern.

The capture of Washington seems now to be inevitable—during the whole of Monday and Tuesday it might have been taken without any resistance. The rout, overthrow, and utter demoralization of the whole army is complete. Even now I doubt whether any serious opposition to the entrance of the Confederate forces could be offered. While Lincoln, Scott, and the Cabinet are disputing who is to blame, the city is unguarded and the enemy at hand. General McClellan reached here last evening. But, if he had the ability of Caesar, Alexander, or Napoleon, what can he accomplish? Will not Scott's jealousy, Cabinet intrigues, Republican interference, thwart him at every step? While hoping for the best, I can not shut my eyes against the dangers that beset the Government, and especially this city. It is certain that Davis was in the field on Sunday, and the Secessionists here assert that he headed in person the last victorious charge. General Dix is in Baltimore. After three weeks' neglect and insult he was sent there. The warm debate between Douglas's friend Richardson and Kentucky Burnett has attracted some interest, but has been attended with no bellicose result.

Since this note was commenced, the morning paper has come in, and I see that McClellan did *not* arrive last night, as I was informed he had. General Lee was after him, but will have to wait awhile before they can meet.

Yours truly,
Edwin M. Stanton.

His Excellency, James Buchanan

—Rice, ed., "A Page of Political Correspondence"

6. THE YANKEES SUFFER DISASTER AT BALL'S BLUFF

After Bull Run, McClellan was appointed commander of all land forces around Washington and, in a short time, replaced the aged Scott as commander in chief of the United States Army. Meantime, as the Union soldiers drilled and the Confederates strengthened their position, all was quiet along the Potomac. On October 21, however, General Stone crossed the river at Leesburg, just above Washington, to attack what he thought was a handful of defenders. The Confederates got wind of the attack and turned it into a rout. Colonel Baker, Senator from Oregon and Lincoln's friend, was killed; young Lieutenant Oliver Wendell Holmes was badly wounded. The disaster at Ball's Bluff led to the creation of the ill-omened Congressional Committee on the Conduct of the War.

Randolph Abbott Shotwell, from whose autobiography this account is taken, was a Virginia-born boy of seventeen studying in Pennsylvania when the war broke out. He promptly headed south, joined the first regiment he found—the 8th Virginia—and fought through the war until his capture at Cold Harbor. After the war he was long prominent in North Carolina politics and journalism.

Oct. 21, '61—General Evans decided to advance and meet McCall, taking post at the "burned bridge" over Goose Creek, three miles southeast of Leesburg. This stream, notwithstanding its euphonious title, is no duck-pond outlet; but, with its wooded bluffs, forms quite a good line of defense against an enemy approaching from the east. . . . During the afternoon a scouting party returned with information that General McCall's corps, after marching up as far as Dranesville, had then, like the king of France, "marched down again." So the morning's flurry was a false alarm. But hold!—here is a dispatch, captured on a Federal courier, which bears the address "To General Stone, in Leesburg." Other intimations reveal the whole plot. Meantime, Gen. Stone, watching from the Maryland heights, rubs his hands in glee on seeing Evans' four regiments filing down the turnpike towards Dranesville. Orders were hastily issued for Colonel Devens to cross into Virginia and push forward to Leesburg; while other troops are to follow as fast as they can cross the Potomac.

Colonel Devens, with five companies, landed upon Harrison's Island shortly after midnight; and while a portion of the command were transporting the boats across the island, the remainder were employed in digging rifle pits to command the passage. . . . Opposite the island, the Virginia shore rises abruptly; in many places directly from the water's edge, in cliffs or bluffs, now historic as "Ball's Bluff." These cliffs, while favorable to the secrecy of the Federal advance, in the end proved a source of fearful disaster. . . .

Colonel Devens drew up his battalion along the brow of Ball's Bluff about 2:30 A.M. on the morning of October 21st, and began to advance in skirmish order toward Leesburg. The citizens of that town had retired early, fatigued by the excitements of the day, and blissfully unconscious of impending peril. All the troops were miles away, except one company of Mississippians, under Captain Duff, which had been left as a camp-guard. Morning brought a startling apparition to these men, as they rubbed their eyes, and yawned for breakfast. Over the green-clad hills toward the northeast, within musket-shot of town, came a long line of blue-coated skirmishers, their polished musket-barrels gleaming in the sunlight, and the "red, white, and blue" fluttering in vivid contrast with the dark foliage of the cedar copse. It was Devens' battalion, advancing from the Potomac! But Captain Duff was no "duffer"; he speedily trotted his men to the nearest fence in the path of the invaders and opened a scorching fire, killing six and wounding twenty before he lost a man, owing to the advantage of shelter and his defensive attitude.

Colonel Devens, seeing a section of artillery coming into town, fell back a short distance into a skirt of timber, to await instructions and reinforcements. He was now joined by Colonel Lee, with four companies; but about the same time two strong companies of Mississippians came to the rescue of Captain Duff, taking Devens on the flank and compelling him to retire nearer Ball's Bluff. Meanwhile General Stone, with the Nineteenth Massachusetts and other troops, had crossed the Potomac at Edwards' ferry, just above the mouth of Goose Creek; his apparent design being to seize the bridge over the turnpike one mile above and oppose Evans' return from Dranesville. Finding, however, the Thirteenth Mississippi, a strong regiment (which he supposed a full brigade), confronting him at the ferry, he hastened to send the main body of his army to cross at Harrison's, two and a half miles above. This column, which he styled "the right wing," was now given into command of Colonel E. D. Baker. It was composed of the Fifteenth and Twentieth Massachusetts, the First California, the "Tammany" (New York) Regiment, and some "unattached" companies, with four mountain howitzers and one 6-pound rifled-gun. Intelligence of these proceedings reached General Evans at an early hour, and Colonel Eppa Hunton with the Eighth Virginia, was sent at a rapid trot three miles across the fields to drive back Devens.

Colonel Hunton, having deployed his men along a little ridge, advanced and engaged the Federals a few minutes after 1:00 P.M. Sharp musketry firing ensued and continued during the next two hours. Here was the fatal mistake of the day on the Federal side. In the long-range duello the Confederates had all the advantage. So thin was their line that nearly every man could have the shelter of a tree or stump; whereas their own shots could hardly miss the dense line of blue coats. The Virginians and Mississippians being accustomed to the rifle, most of them old hunters, rarely missed their man. Climbing into the tops of trees, creeping through the tall grass, or concealed in the gullies, they plied their weapons with murderous havoc especially among the Federal officers. It was very poor management to allow this to go on. Had Baker ordered a couple of regiments to sweep the woods he would have cleared his path of all those death-stinging hornets and marched into Leesburg. The Federal position at this time was upon the plateau of the bluff, some 700 yards in front of the river, where there was a cleared field of ten or twelve acres, with a shallow ravine or hollow, running through the middle of it. The artillery was planted to sweep this clearing in front, while the flanks were measurably protected by a series of steep little hills and rocky ravines, overgrown with scrubby, stunted pines.

By 4:00 P.M. the last of the Federal troops had crossed and were drawn up in horseshoe shape, with the point of the shoe fronting the ten-acred cleared lot, 600 yards from the bluff. But the loss in officers had greatly crippled the effectiveness of the force. Lieutenant-Colonel Wistar, of the First California, had been killed, and his regiment much shattered. Furthermore, the Confederates had been reinforced by the remainder of the Seventeenth Mississippi, perhaps 600 muskets, and the Eighteenth Mississippi was within one mile, advancing rapidly. *Per contra* the Virginia regiment had exhausted its ammunition, and no one knew where the wagon trains could be found; war was a new business at that date. Men could be seen crawling about, searching the boxes of the dead or borrowing cartridges of their comrades—to get one more shot. Colonel Hunton dispatched his adjutant to say to General Evans: "My powder is out; what shall I do?" "Fix bayonets and run 'em into the river!" quoth "Old Shanks" (his regular army *sobriquet*) who had just taken a liquid reinforcement, equivalent to 10,000 men. It was time for some decisive measure, for Colonel Baker had ordered his right wing to advance and flank the little ridge whence came the rebel bullets.

Fortunately for the Confederates, at the moment this movement began, there was heard the pattering footsteps and jingling canteens of the Eighteenth Mississippi double quicking through the brush, then a wild, terror striking yell; then the simultaneous crash of 1,000 muskets, each hurling its leaden contents along the Federal left and centre! The effect was electric. The roar of this sudden, blinding, raking volley was like the crack of doom to the already demoralized Federals, most of whom were under fire for the first time! A strange report ran along the lines that General Joe Johnston, with 10,000 fresh men, had just arrived. Colonel Baker, himself, remarked to an aide that he had seen Johnston, mounted on a white horse, riding in advance. Baker, Colonel Cogswell, Major Harvey and others were at the time working the small howitzers, which had been crippled several times, being plainly exposed to the fire of the concealed sharp-shooters. The rifled six-pounder could not be used.

Seeing that the crisis was come—as the Confederates were assuming the offensive and closing upon him from three sides, with the river at his back—Colonel Baker turned to the bayonet as the last hope. Calling to the nearest battalions, he shouted, ordered, and entreated them to advance, to charge! His voice, ringing above the murderous crack of the rifle, could be heard even in the Confederate ranks, urging his men to charge and save the day for themselves. Thus incited they began to move, but in a wavering irresolution—a sure precursor of failure. Baker ran forward and at once received a stinging wound. But without pausing he gallantly rushed onward and was at the head of his men, when a beardless youth emptied five barrels of his revolver into him, at twenty paces. Four of the balls took effect, the first passing through his brain!

At this moment the hostile lines were within stone's throw, and both advancing. The Federals, seeing the fall of their leader, halted. Some soldiers seized Baker's body and ran with it rearward. This started the rest, and a general retreat took place, though several brave fellows moved so slowly that hand-to-hand fights raged along the whole line during the next ten minutes. Many of the Southerners also stopped at the cannon, which they wheeled around and endeavored to fire upon their late owners, but could not succeed. Subsequently one of the guns was found to have the ball put in before the powder—a very good reason for its refusal to explode. The temporary failure to pursue enabled Colonel Cogswell—now in command—to rally a portion of the survivors on the brow of a bluff, but he himself bleeding from a wound; Colonel Devens was in like condition; all regimental order was lost, and the huddling of the men on the hill rendered the Confederate fire, which was rapidly closing in on all sides, so much the more fatal. Suddenly the Seventeenth Mississippi closed in on the flank with a terrific volley and ended the battle.

Then ensued an awful spectacle! A kind of shiver ran through the huddled mass upon the brow of the cliff; it gave way; rushed a few steps; then, in one wild, panic-stricken herd, rolled, leaped, tumbled over the precipice! The descent is nearly perpendicular, with ragged, jutting crags, and a water laved base. Screams of pain and terror filled the air. Men seemed suddenly bereft of reason; they leaped over the bluff with muskets still in their clutch, threw themselves into the river without divesting themselves of their heavy accoutrements, hence went to the bottom like lead. Others sprang down upon the heads and bayonets of those below. A gray-haired private of the First California was found with his head mashed between two rocks by the heavy boots of a ponderous "Tammany" man, who had broken his own neck by the fall! The side of the bluff was worn smooth by the number sliding down.

From the beginning of the battle a steady stream of wounded men had been trickling down the zig-zag path leading to the narrow beach, whence the boats were to convey them to the Island. As it happened, the two larger bateaux were just starting with an overload when the torrent of terror-stricken fugitives rolled down the bluffs—upon them. Both boats were instantly submerged, and their cargoes of helpless human beings (crippled by wounds) were swept away to unknown graves! The whole surface of the river seemed filled with heads, struggling, screaming, fighting, dying! Man clutched at man, and the strong, who might have escaped, were dragged down by the weaker. Voices that strove to shout for help were stifled by the turbid, sullen waters of the swollen river and died away in gurgles. It is strange how persons about to drown turn to their fellows for strength; they may be in mid-ocean, with no hope for any, yet will they grasp one another and sink in pairs. Captain Otter, of the First California, (an apposite name for a swimmer,) was found a few days later with two men of his company clutching his neckband. Had he attempted to save them, or had they seized him and dragged him down? One officer was found with $126 in gold in his pocket; it had cost his life.

—SHOTWELL, "Three Years in Battle"

7. McCLELLAN OPENS THE PENINSULAR CAMPAIGN

George B. McClellan is doubtless the most controversial military figure of the Civil War. We meet him first as he embarks on the campaign that is to reduce Richmond, destroy Johnston's army, and end the war; we shall meet him again. With an army almost twice as strong as Johnston's, he was reluctant to take the offensive, and while the North clamored for action, he stayed in and around Washington. Finally on January 27, 1862, President Lincoln issued War Order No. 1 positively ordering an advance on or before February 22, but McClellan ignored this as well as subsequent orders. Early in March McClellan decided to shift his army to Urbana, on the south bank of the Rappahannock, but when Johnston moved his forces south of the Rappahannock this shift of base became pointless. On March 17 McClellan embarked his army for Fortress Monroe, and on April 4 began a snaillike advance up the Peninsula toward Yorktown, investing the ground as he went. Johnston withdrew from Yorktown to Williamsburg, and there, on May 5, the blue and the gray locked in battle. Although McClellan claimed a victory, his losses were 50 per cent higher than Johnston's. This letter to his wife reveals his characteristic self-confidence and vanity.

Williamsburg, May 6, 1862—

I telegraphed you this morning that we had gained a battle. Every hour its importance is proved to be greater. On Sunday I sent Stoneman in pursuit with the cavalry and four batteries of horse-artillery. He was supported by the divisions of Hooker, Smith, Couch, Casey, and Kearny, most of which arrived on the ground only yesterday. Unfortunately I did not go with the advance myself, being obliged to remain to get Franklin and Sedgwick started up the river for West Point. Yesterday I received pressing messages from Smith and others begging me to go to the front. I started with half a dozen aides and some fifteen orderlies, and found things in a bad state. Hancock was engaged with a vastly inferior force some two miles from any support. Hooker fought nearly all day without assistance, and the mass of the troops were crowded together where they were useless. I found everybody discouraged, officers and men; our troops in wrong positions, on the wrong side of the woods; no system, no co-operation, no orders given, roads blocked up.

As soon as I came upon the field the men cheered like fiends, and I saw at once that I could save the day. I immediately reinforced Hancock and arranged to support Hooker, advanced the whole line across the woods, filled up the gaps, and got everything in hand for whatever might occur. The result was that the enemy saw that he was gone if he remained in his position, and scampered during the night. His works were very strong, but his loss was very heavy. The roads are in such condition that it is impossible to pursue except with a few cavalry.

It is with the utmost difficulty that I can feed the men, many of whom have had nothing to eat for twenty-four hours and more. I had no dinner yesterday, no supper; a cracker for breakfast, and no dinner yet. I have no baggage; was out in the rain all day and until late at night; slept in my clothes and boots, and could not even wash my face and hands. I, however, expect my ambulance up pretty soon, when I hope for better things. I have been through the hospitals, where are many of our own men and of the rebels. One Virginian sent for me this morning and told me that I was the only general from whom they expected any humanity. I corrected this mistake.

This is a beautiful little town; several very old houses and churches, pretty gardens. I have taken possession of a very fine house which Joe Johnston occupied as his headquarters. It has a lovely flower-garden and conservatory. If you were here I should be much inclined to spend some weeks here.

THE PENINSULAR CAMPAIGN

G. W. was one of the whipped community, also Joe Johnston, Cadmus Wilcox, A. P. Hill, D. H. Hill, Longstreet, Jeb Stuart, Early (badly wounded); and many others that we know. We have all their wounded; eight guns so far. In short, we have given them a tremendous thrashing, and I am not at all ashamed of the conduct of the Army of the Potomac.

—Letter to his wife, in *McClellan's Own Story*

8. GENERAL WOOL TAKES NORFOLK

Johnston's withdrawal from Yorktown exposed Norfolk to capture, and on May 9 the Confederates blew up the crippled Merrimac *and abandoned the city which they had held since the beginning of the war. General Wool who "captured" Norfolk had been a major in the War of 1812 and a general in the Mexican War, and was 77 at the outbreak of the Civil War. The happily named Egbert Ludovicus Viele was a brigadier general of volunteers; after the war he projected a plan for subways for New York City and served as commissioner of parks.*

NO time was lost on the following morning in re-embarking the troops for the purpose of marching on Norfolk by the rear. At the last moment General Wool, with much emotion begged the Secretary (Chase) to allow him to command the troops. The Secretary had decided to relieve him of the command of the expedition on account of his advanced age, but finally reversed his decision with the remark that he could not inflict sorrow upon gray hairs. . . .

Starting at once to the front with our escort, we had not gone very far before it became evident that a great deal of confusion existed in the command—in fact, that there was no organization, and an utter absence of definite instructions or orders of any kind. Overtaking a regiment that was scattered along the road—most of the men lying down wherever any shade could be found, as the day was intensely warm—Mr. Chase inquired of the colonel to whose command he belonged and what his orders were. He replied that he had no idea who was his commander, that some said Weber and some said Mansfield. He had received no orders except that when he landed he was told to take a certain road, and he thought he would wait to see what was to be done next. Overtaking another regiment a mile or two beyond, the Secretary received the same answers. Going on still farther, we came upon General Mansfield and his staff, who had dismounted in the shade near a spring of cool water. Farther still, another straggling regiment was found; yet no one had any orders or instructions. Suddenly the booming of cannon was heard immediately in front, and as no artillery had been landed by us, it was evident that the firing proceeded from the enemy. Straggling soldiers now came running toward us with exaggerated rumors of the enemy being in force, burning the bridges, and contesting with artillery the passage of the streams that crossed the road. The ridiculousness of the situation would have been amusing if it had not been for the serious aspect that it was gradually assuming. Two regiments of cavalry had been embarked and two batteries of artillery; yet not a horse or a gun had been sent to the front. Four regiments of infantry were marching along, uncertain what road to take and unassigned to any brigade; two brigadier generals and their staffs, without orders and without commands, were sitting by the roadside waiting for something to turn up. This was the situation with the enemy firing in front.

Secretary Chase took it all in at a glance and rose at once to the necessities of the occasion. Tearing some leaves from his memorandum book, he directed me to send one of our escort back to General Wool with a written requisition for artillery and cavalry. This brought the general to the front with two pieces of artillery and some mounted troops. As he rode up, Mr. Chase expressed to him in very strong language his astonishment at the condition of things. General Wool replied by saying that he presumed General Mansfield had felt some delicacy in assuming command over General Weber and that General Weber had hesitated to act while General Mansfield was so near.

"Talk of delicacy," exclaimed the Secretary, "with the enemy firing in front! What absurdity! Let General Mansfield go to the rear and bring up reinforcements, and that will settle all questions of delicacy." This brought about a prolonged discussion between Generals Wool and Mansfield, which was carried on at a short distance from the rear under the shade of a large sycamore tree. Losing all patience, the Secretary exclaimed, "Two cackling hens!" and turning to me with a voice and manner that would have become Wellington or Soult, he said: "Sir! I order you in the name of the President of the United States to take command of these troops and march them upon Norfolk."

An infantry regiment was deployed at double-quick as skirmishers in advance, and the other regiments were soon moving rapidly down the Norfolk road. They had proceeded some distance before General Wool was aware of the movement. He was not long in overtaking us, however, and on his demand for an explanation from me Mr. Chase assumed the responsibility, after which we proceeded harmoniously toward our destination. At the extreme limits of the city and before the formidable line of intrenched works was reached, a large deputation headed by the mayor and municipal councils made its appearance with a flag of truce and performed a most skillful ruse to gain time for the Confederates to secure their retreat from the city. The mayor, with all the formality of a medieval warden, appeared with a bunch of rusty keys and a formidable roll of papers which he proceeded to read with the utmost deliberation previous to delivering the "keys of the city." The reading of the documents—which embraced a large portion of the history of Virginia, the causes that led to the war, the peculiar position of the good citizens of Norfolk, and in short a little of everything that could have the remotest bearing upon the subject and exhaust the longest possible space of time in reading—was protracted until nearly dark.

In the meantime the Confederates were hurrying with their artillery and stores over the ferry to Portsmouth, cutting the water pipes and flooding the public buildings, setting fire to the navy yard, and having their own way generally, while our General was listening in the most innocent and complacent manner to the long rigmarole so ingeniously prepared by the mayor and skillfully interlarded with fulsome personal eulogium upon himself. . . .

And now another well-devised plan presented itself in the shape of a number of carriages which the mayor particularly desired should be used by the officers in taking possession of the city, the troops in the meanwhile to remain where they were. Falling readily into this second little trap, the General accepted and we were driven to the city hall, where some more rusty keys were produced and more formal speeches were made. A collection of several thousand people, some of them in butternut and gray, assembled in front of the building. While the General and mayor were going through their high formalities, Mr. Chase asked for a pen and a piece of paper and wrote an order assigning the command of the city to myself as military governor, which General Wool signed at his direction. Then, bidding me goodbye, he took the General by the arm and departed, leaving me the solitary occupant of the city hall, without a soldier within two miles and with not even an aide-de-camp to assist me. Fortunately an enterprising newspaper correspondent had followed the carriages on foot, and him I appointed an aide and dispatched for the troops. By the time the troops arrived the moon had risen, and by its light they were placed in position. A regiment dispatched to the navy yard was too late to rescue it from almost complete destruction, but it cut off the *Merrimac* from any supplies from either side of the river.

It was long after midnight before the final disposition of troops was made, and this had hardly been accomplished when, with a shock that shook the city and with an ominous sound that could not be mistaken, the magazine of the *Merrimac* was exploded, the vessel having been cut off from supplies and deserted by the crew; and thus this most formidable engine of destruction that had so long been a terror not only to Hampton Roads but to the Atlantic coast went to her doom.

—Viele, "A Trip with Lincoln, Chase and Stanton"

9. THE ARMY OF THE POTOMAC MARCHES TO MEET McCLELLAN

By the end of May McClellan had worked his way slowly and painfully up the Peninsula, and was within sight—and sound—of Richmond. The Federals outnumbered the Confederates probably by a ratio of five to three, but as new regiments and companies swarmed in to the defense of the beleaguered capital the opposing forces became more nearly equal. At this time the Confederate army north of Richmond was called the Army of the Potomac; this is not to be confused with the Federal army of the same name.

Sallie Putnam, from whose delightful reminiscences of Richmond during the war this excerpt is taken, was one of the Virginia gentry who stayed on in the city throughout the war.

THE day of the passage of the Army of the Potomac through Richmond will long be remembered by those who were in the city. It was known that they were on their way to the Peninsula, and for days they had been expected to march through the streets of the capital. The greatest interest and excitement prevailed. The morning was bright and beautiful in the early spring, balmy with the odors of the violet and the hyacinth, and the flaunting narcissus, the jonquil, and myriads of spring flowers threw on their parti-colored garments to welcome the army of veterans as they passed.

From an early hour until the sun went down in the West the steady tramp of the soldier was heard on the streets. Continuous cheers went up from thousands of voices; from every window fair heads were thrust, fair hands waved snowy handkerchiefs, and bright eyes beamed "Welcome!" Bands of spirit-stirring music discoursed the favorite airs,—Dixie's Land, My Maryland, the Bonny Blue Flag, and other popular tunes—and as the last regiments were passing we heard the strains of "Good-Bye," and tears were allowed to flow, and tender hearts ached as they listened to the significant tune. Soldiers left the ranks to grasp the hands of friends in passing, to receive some grateful refreshment, a small bouquet, or a whispered congratulation. Officers on horseback raised their hats, and some of the more gallant ventured to waft kisses to the fair ones at the doors and windows. We shall never forget the appearance of General Longstreet, the sturdy fighter, the obstinate warrior, as he dashed down Main Street surrounded by his splendid staff.

Through other streets poured our cavalry, under their gallant chieftain, the pink of Southern chivalry,—the gay, rollicking, yet bold, daring and venturous "Jeb." Stuart. As we saw him then, sitting easily on his saddle, as though he was born to it, he seemed every inch the cavalier. His stout yet lithe figure, his graceful bearing, his broad, well-formed chest and shoulders, on which was gracefully poised his splendid head, his bright, beaming countenance, lighted up with a smile as pleasant as a woman's, his dark red hair and flowing beard, with his lower limbs encased in heavy cavalry boots, made up the *tout ensemble* of this brave son of Maryland. His genial temperament made him the idol and companion of the most humble of his men, and his deeds of daring and heroic courage made him respected as their leader.

As they swept through our streets on that beautiful morning, with their horses in good order, their own spirits buoyant and cheerful, many of them wearing in their caps bouquets of the golden daffodils of early spring, cheered on by the ringing sounds of the bugle, we thought never to see them pass again with worn-out horses and weary, listless spirits, as they spurred on their broken-down steeds; but so it was. . . .

—[SALLIE PUTNAM], *Richmond during the War*

10. R. E. LEE TAKES COMMAND

After First Bull Run Joseph E. Johnston was assigned to command the Confederate armies in northern Virginia, and in July 1861 appointed gen-

*eral—fourth in rank in the whole Confederacy. When McClellan got himself
entangled in the swamps of the Chickahominy, Johnston moved out to meet
him. The Battle of Seven Pines, or Fair Oaks, which came on May 31 and
June 1, was, in Freeman's phrase, "a battle of strange errors." Badly fought
on both sides, it was at best indecisive. Though Confederate losses ran to
almost eight thousand, and Union to less than six thousand, the Confederates
claimed a victory. General Johnston was severely wounded on the battle-
field and Davis turned to Lee—who then held the ambiguous position of
"general in charge of military operations under the direction of the President" and assigned him the command. That very day he baptized the army
by the name it was to make immortal, "The Army of Northern Virginia."*

*General Evander M. Law, who tells us here how Lee appeared when he
took command during the Battle of Seven Pines, was a South Carolinian who
was teaching at an Alabama military academy when the war broke out. He
raised a company from his own school and took it to Virginia. He served all
through the war in the East until wounded at Cold Harbor.*

DURING the months of April, May, and the early part of June, while
Jackson in the Valley was conducting a series of the most brilliant operations of the war, successively defeating Milroy, Banks, Shields, and Fremont,
and while McDowell was oscillating like an eccentric pendulum between the
Rappahannock and the Valley, General McClellan's army had been transferred by water to the lower Peninsula, and was moving upon Richmond
from the southeast. His advance was met by General Magruder, who, with
his small command of eleven thousand men, took up a short and strong defensive line extending from Yorktown on his left to the James River on his
right, a portion of his front being covered by the Warwick River.

In the meantime General Johnston was rapidly transferring his army from
Centreville and the posts on the lower Potomac, where it had wintered, to
unite with Magruder on the lines at Yorktown. Johnston held the line established by Magruder until the 4th of May, when he evacuated Yorktown and
slowly retired up the Peninsula. McClellan followed promptly, and coming
up with the Confederate rear on the 6th, the battle of Williamsburg was
fought. Another smaller affair occurred on the 7th at Eltham's Landing, at
the head of York River, where a portion of Whiting's division attacked and
drove back to the river a Federal force under General Franklin, which had
been pushed up by water to fall upon the flank of the Confederate army as it
retired. The Federal advance was thenceforward much more cautious, and
it was not until the 24th of May that McClellan's army was in position along
the east bank of the Chickahominy and the struggle for Richmond itself
began.

The Federal army, holding the line of the Chickahominy from Mechanicsville to Bottom's bridge, at once commenced the construction of military
bridges between those points, and before the end of May McClellan's left
wing was advanced by throwing the two corps of Heintzelman and Keyes
across the river. The latter took position and entrenched on a line running

BATTLEFIELDS OF THE SEVEN DAYS

in front of "Seven Pines" on the Williamsburg road, with its right extending across the York River Railroad in front of Fair Oaks station. Heintzelman was placed in supporting distance in the rear, near Savage's station. Mc-Clellan's outposts were now within five miles of Richmond. Almost near enough to realize President Lincoln's suggestion, when he inquired by telegraph on May 26th, "Can you get near enough to throw shells into the city?" This amiable desire was not destined to be gratified, for during the afternoon and night of the 30th of May a heavy rain-storm occurred, flooding the low grounds of the Chickahominy and threatening the destruction of the military bridges constructed by the Federal army. The two wings were to a certain extent isolated, and General Johnston took advantage of this condition of affairs to attack Keyes' corps near Seven Pines on the 31st of May. This corps was assailed by D. H. Hill's division and thoroughly routed. Heintzelman came to its support, but by this time the divisions of Longstreet and G. W. Smith had united in the attack with D. H. Hill, and this corps fared little better than that of Keyes. By the most strenuous exertions Sumner's Federal corps was thrown across the almost ruined bridges, during the afternoon and night of the 31st, and this timely reinforcement, together with the intervention of night, saved the left wing of McClellan's army from destruction.

The tardy movements of some of the Confederate commanders on the extreme right delayed the attack several hours beyond the time when it should have been made, and this delay was fatal to the complete success of General Johnston's plans. While G. W. Smith's division, to which I was attached, was warmly engaged near the junction of the "Nine Mile" road and the York River Railroad, General Johnston rode up and gave me an order as to the movements of my command. Night was rapidly approaching, and he seemed anxious to urge forward the attack with all possible speed so as to clear the field of the enemy before night. He was moving with the troops and personally directing the advance, when he received a severe wound in the shoulder and was compelled to relinquish the command. The Confederates had been checked on their left wing by the arrival of Sumner's corps, and the fighting ceased just after dark. It was renewed on our right wing on the morning of the 1st of June without advantage to either side, and by 2 o'clock P.M. the battle was over, without having accomplished the purpose for which it was fought.

General G. W. Smith, an officer of acknowledged ability, succeeded General Johnston in command of the Confederate army on the night of the 31st of May. But during the afternoon of the next day, June 1st, he in turn relinquished the command to General Lee, under orders from President Davis. Our right wing was at once withdrawn from its advanced position, and Smith's division on the left followed the next day. As I was standing near the Nine Mile road a day or two after the battle, General Lee passed along the road accompanied by two staff officers. I had never seen him before, and he was pointed out by some one near me. I observed the new commander of the "Army of Northern Virginia" very closely and with a great deal of interest. General Johnston was universally beloved and pos-

sessed the unbounded confidence of the army, and the commander who succeeded him must be "every inch a man" and a soldier to fill his place in their
confidence and affection. General Lee had up to this time accomplished
nothing to warrant the belief in his future greatness as a commander. He
had made an unsuccessful campaign in Western Virginia the year before,
and since that time had been on duty first at Charleston and then in Richmond. There was naturally a great deal of speculation among the soldiers
as to how he would "pan out." The general tone, however, was one of confidence, which was invariably strengthened by a sight of the man himself.
Calm, dignified, and commanding in his bearing, a countenance strikingly
benevolent and self-possessed, a clear, honest eye that could look friend or
enemy in the face; clean-shaven, except a closely-trimmed mustache which
gave a touch of firmness to the well-shaped mouth; simply and neatly dressed
in the uniform of his rank, felt hat, and top boots reaching to the knee; sitting
his horse as if his home was in the saddle; such was Robert E. Lee as he appeared when he assumed command of the army of "Northern Virginia" in
the early days of June, 1862, never to relinquish it for a day, until its colors
were furled for ever at Appomattox.

—LAW, "The Fight for Richmond"

11. "BEAUTY" STUART RIDES AROUND McCLELLAN'S ARMY

*Although heavily outnumbered Lee planned to seize the offensive and
destroy McClellan's army or drive it off the Peninsula. In preparation for the
offensive he sent J. E. B. (Beauty) Stuart out to reconnoiter the Federal
position, especially between the Chickahominy and the Totopotomy. Stuart
set out on June 12 with some 1,000 cavalrymen, made the called-for reconnaissance, and then, instead of turning back, decided to ride 150 miles around
McClellan's whole army.*

*This account of the last part of the ride is by the famous Virginia novelist
and historian who fought all through the war with Stuart, John Esten Cooke.*

THE gayest portion of the raid now began. From this moment it was
neck or nothing, do or die. We had one chance of escape against ten of
capture or destruction.

Stuart had decided upon his course with that rapidity, good judgment,
and decision, which were the real secrets of his splendid efficiency as a leader
of cavalry, in which capacity I believe that he has never been surpassed, either
in the late war or any other. He was now in the very heart of the enemy's
citadel, with their enormous masses upon every side. He had driven in their
advanced force, passed within sight of the white tents of General McClellan's
headquarters, burned their camps, and ascertained all that he wished. How
was he to return? He could not cross the Pamunkey, and make a circuit
back; he had no pontoons. He could not return over the route by which
he had advanced. As events afterward showed, the alarm had been given,
and an overpowering force of infantry, cavalry, and artillery had been rapidly

moved in that direction to intercept the daring raider. Capture stared him in the face, on both of these routes—across the Pamunkey, or back as he came; he must find some other loophole of escape.

Such was the dangerous posture of affairs, and such was the important problem which Stuart decided in five minutes. He determined to make the complete circuit of McClellan's army; and crossing the Chickahominy below Long Bridge, re-enter the Confederate lines from Charles City. If on his way he encountered cavalry he intended to fight it; if a heavy force of infantry barred his way he would elude, or cut a path through it; if driven to the wall and debarred from escape he did not mean to surrender. A few days afterward I said to him:

"That was a tight place at the river, General. If the enemy had come down on us, you would have been compelled to have surrendered."

"No," was his reply; "one other course was left."

"What was that?"

"To *die game.*"

And I know that such was his intention. When a commander means to die game rather than surrender he is a dangerous adversary. . . .

Everywhere the ride was crowded with incident. The scouting and flanking parties constantly picked up stragglers, and overhauled unsuspecting wagons filled with the most tempting stores. In this manner a wagon, stocked with champagne and every variety of wines, belonging to a General of the Federal army, fell a prey to the thirsty gray-backs. Still they pressed on. Every moment an attack was expected in front or rear. Colonel Will. T. Martin commanded the latter. "Tell Colonel Martin," Stuart said to me, "to have his artillery ready, and look out for an attack at any moment." I had delivered the message and was riding to the front again, when suddenly a loud cry arose of "Yankees in the rear!" Every sabre flashed, fours were formed, the men wheeled about, when all at once a stunning roar of laughter ran along the line; it was a *canard.* The column moved up again with its flanking parties well out. The men composing the latter were, many of them, from the region, and for the first time for months saw their mothers and sisters. These went quite wild at sight of their sons and brothers. . . .

The column was now skirting the Pamunkey, and a detachment hurried off to seize and burn two or three transports lying in the river. Soon a dense cloud rose from them, the flames soared up, and the column pushed on. Everywhere were seen the traces of flight—for the alarm of "hornets in the hive" was given. Wagons had turned over, and were abandoned—from others the excellent army stores had been hastily thrown. This writer got a fine red blanket, and an excellent pair of cavalry pantaloons, for which he still owes the United States. Other things lay about in tempting array, but we were approaching Tunstall's, where the column would doubtless make a charge; and to load down a weary horse was injudicious. The advance guard was now in sight of the railroad. There was no question about the affair before us. The column must cut through, whatever force guarded the railroad; to reach the lower Chickahominy the guard here must be overpowered. Now was the time to use the artillery, and every effort was made to hurry it forward. But alas! it had got into a tremendous mudhole, and the wheels were buried to the axle. The horses were lashed, and jumped, almost breaking the traces; the drivers swore; the harness cracked—but the guns did not move.

"Gat! Lieutenant," said a sergeant of Dutch origin to the brave Lieutenant McGregor, "it can't be done. But just put that keg on the gun, Lieutenant," pointing, as he spoke, to a keg of whiskey in an ambulance, the spoil of the Federal camp, "and tell the men they can have it if they pull through!"

McGregor laughed, and the keg was quickly perched on the gun. Then took place an exhibition of herculean muscularity which would have delighted Guy Livingston. With eyes fixed ardently upon the keg, the powerful cannoneers waded into the mudhole up to their knees, seized the wheels of gun and caisson loaded down with ammunition, and just simply lifted the whole out, and put them on firm ground. The piece whirled on—the keg had been dismounted—the cannoneers revelled in the spoils they had earned.

Tunstall's was now nearly in sight, and that good fellow Captain Frayser, afterward Stuart's signal officer, came back and reported one or two companies of infantry at the railroad. Their commander had politely beckoned to him as he reconnoitred, exclaiming in wheedling accents, full of Teutonic blandishment, "Koom yay!" But this cordial invitation was disregarded; Frayser galloped back and reported, and the ringing voice of Stuart ordered "Form platoons! draw sabre! charge!" At the word the sabres flashed, a thundering shout arose, and sweeping on in column of platoons, the gray people fell upon their blue adversaries, gobbling them up, almost without a shot. . . .

The men swarmed upon the railroad. Quick axes were applied to the telegraph poles, which crashed down, and Redmond Burke went in command of a detachment to burn a small bridge on the railroad near. Suddenly in the midst of the tumult was heard the shrill whistle of a train coming from the direction of the Chickahominy. Stuart quickly drew up his men in a line on the side of the road, and he had no sooner done so than the train came slowly round a wooded bend, and bore down. When within two hundred yards it was ordered to halt, but the command was not obeyed. The engineer crowded on all steam; the train rushed on, and then a thundering volley was opened upon the "flats" containing officers and men. The engineer was shot by Captain Farley, of Stuart's staff, and a number of the soldiers were wounded. The rest threw themselves upon their faces; the train rushed headlong by like some frightened monster bent upon escape, and in an instant it had disappeared.

Stuart then reflected for a single moment. The question was, should he go back and attack the White House, where enormous stores were piled up? It was tempting, and he afterwards told me he could scarcely resist it. But a considerable force of infantry was posted there; the firing had doubtless given them the alarm; and the attempt was too hazardous. The best thing for that gray column was to set their faces toward home, and "keep moving," well closed up both day and night, for the lower Chickahominy. Beyond the railroad appeared a world of wagons, loaded with grain and coffee— standing in the road abandoned. Quick work was made of them. They were all set on fire, and their contents destroyed. From the horse-trough of one I rescued a small volume bearing on the fly-leaf the name of a young lady of Williamsburg. I think it was a volume of poems—poetic wagon-drivers!

These wagons were only the "vaunt couriers"—the advance guard—of the main body. In a field beyond the stream thirty acres were covered with them. They were all burned. The roar of the soaring flames was like the sound of a forest on fire. How they roared and crackled! The sky over-head, when night had descended, was bloody-looking in the glare. . . .

Pushing on by large hospitals which were not interfered with, we reached at midnight the three or four houses known as Talleysville; and here a halt was ordered to rest men and horses, and permit the artillery to come up. This pause was fatal to a sutler's store from which the owners had fled. It was remorselessly ransacked and the edibles consumed. This historian ate in succession figs, beef-tongue, pickle, candy, tomato catsup, preserves, lemons, cakes, sausages, molasses, crackers, and canned meats. In presence of these attractive commodities, the spirits of many rose. Those who in the morning had made me laugh by saying, "General Stuart is going to get his command destroyed—this movement is mad," now regarded Stuart as the first of men; the raid was a feat of splendour and judicious daring which could not fail in terminating successfully. Such is the difference in the views of the military machine, unfed and fed. . . .

The column . . . began to move on the road to Forge Bridge. The high-way lay before us, white in the unclouded splendour of the moon. The critical moment was yet to come. Our safety was to turn apparently on a throw of the dice, rattled in the hand of Chance. The exhaustion of the march now began to tell on the men. Whole companies went to sleep in the saddle, and Stuart himself was no exception. He had thrown one knee over the pommel of his saddle, folded his arms, dropped the bridle, and—chin on breast, his plumed hat drooping over his forehead—was sound asleep. His sure-footed horse moved steadily, but the form of the General tottered from side to side, and for miles I held him erect by the arm. The column thus moved on during the remainder of the night, the wary advance guard en-countering no enemies and giving no alarm. At the first streak of dawn the Chickahominy was in sight, and Stuart was spurring forward *to the ford.*

It was impassable! The heavy rains had so swollen the waters that the crossing was utterly impracticable! Here we were within a few miles of McClellan's army, with an enraged enemy rushing on our track to make us rue the day we had "circumvented" them, and inflicted on them such injury and insult; here we were with a swollen and impassable stream directly in our front—the angry waters roaring around the half-submerged trunks of the trees—and expecting every instant to hear the crack of carbines from the rear-guard indicating the enemy's approach! The "situation" was not pleasing. I certainly thought that the enemy would be upon us in about an hour, and death or capture would be the sure alternative. This view was general. I found that cool and resolute officer, Colonel William H. F. Lee, on the river's bank. He had just attempted to swim the river, and nearly drowned his horse among the tangled roots and snags. I said to him:

"What do you think of the situation, Colonel?"

"Well, Captain," was the reply, in the speaker's habitual tone of cheerful courtesy, "I think we are caught."

The men evidently shared this sentiment. The scene upon the river's bank was curious. The men lay about in every attitude, half-overcome with sleep, but holding their bridles, and ready to mount at the first alarm. Others sat their horses asleep, with drooping shoulders. Some gnawed crackers; others ate figs, or smoked, or yawned. Things looked "blue," and the colour was figuratively spread over every countenance. When this writer assumed a gay expression of countenance, laughed, and told the men it was "all right," they looked at him as sane men regard a lunatic! The general conviction evidently was that "all right" was the very last phrase by which to describe the situation.

There was only one man who never desponded, or bated one "jot or tittle of the heart of hope." That was Stuart. . . . He said a few words to Colonel Lee, found the ford impassable, and then ordering his column to move on, galloped down the stream to a spot where an old bridge had formerly stood. Reaching this point, a strong rear-guard was thrown out, the artillery placed in position, and Stuart set to work vigorously to rebuild the bridge, determined to bring out his guns or die trying.

The bridge had been destroyed, but the stone abutments remained some thirty or forty feet only apart, for the river here ran deep and narrow between steep banks. Between these stone sentinels, facing each other, was an "aching void" which it was necessary to fill. Stuart gave his personal superintendence to the work, he and his staff labouring with the men. A skiff was procured; this was affixed by a rope to a tree, in the mid-current just above the abutments, and thus a movable pier was secured in the middle of the stream. An old barn was then hastily torn to pieces and robbed of its timbers; these were stretched down to the boat, and up to the opposite abutment, and a foot-bridge was thus ready. Large numbers of the men immediately unsaddled their horses, took their equipments over, and then returning, drove or rode their horses into the stream, and swam them over. In this manner a considerable number crossed; but the process was much too slow. There, besides, was the artillery, which Stuart had no intention of leaving. A regular bridge must be built without a moment's delay, and to this work Stuart now applied himself with ardour.

Heavier blows resounded from the old barn; huge timbers approached, borne on brawny shoulders, and descending into the boat anchored in the middle of the stream, the men lifted them across. They were just long enough; the ends rested on the abutments, and immediately thick planks were hurried forward and laid crosswise, forming a secure footway for the cavalry and artillery horses. Standing in the boat beneath, Stuart worked with the men, and as the planks thundered down, and the bridge steadily advanced, the gay voice of the General was heard humming a song. He was singing carelessly, although at every instant an overpowering force of the enemy was looked for, and a heavy attack upon the disordered cavalry.

At last the bridge was finished; the artillery crossed amid hurrahs from the men, and then Stuart slowly moved his cavalry across the shaky footway. . . . The hoofs clattered on the hasty structure, the head of the column was turned toward the ford beyond, the last squadron had just passed, and the bridge was being destroyed, when shots resounded on the opposite bank of the stream, and Colonel Rush thundered down with his "lancers" to the bank. He was exactly ten minutes too late. Stuart was over with his artillery, and the swollen stream barred the way, even if Colonel Rush thought it prudent to "knock up against" the one thousand five hundred crack cavalry of Stuart. His men banged away at Colonel Lee, and a parting salute whizzed through the trees as the gray column slowly disappeared. . . .

—COOKE, *Wearing of the Gray*

12. PRESIDENT DAVIS VISITS THE BATTLEFIELD AT MECHANICSVILLE

With the information which Stuart was able to bring him, with large reinforcements from Georgia and the Carolinas, and with the aid of Jackson, who had just concluded his whirlwind campaign in the Valley, Lee was now prepared to initiate his campaign against the Federals. Summoning Jackson from the Valley, Lee planned to concentrate most of his forces north of the Chickahominy and roll up the Union flank. Jackson was unaccountably late, but the attack came off, almost as planned, on June 26—the first of the famous Seven Days battles.

President Davis, who could never forget that he had been colonel of the Mississippi Riflemen and Secretary of War, fancied himself as a military leader and tended constantly to intervene in the military conduct of the war. His visits to the battlefields—one of which is here described by the famous social leader Constance Harrison—were wholly in character, as was General Lee's courteous but firm handling of the situation.

DURING all this time President Davis was a familiar and picturesque figure on the streets, walking through the Capitol square from his residence to the executive office in the morning, not to return until late in the afternoon, or riding just before nightfall to visit one or another of the encampments near the city. He was tall, erect, slender, and of a dignified and soldierly bearing, with clear-cut and high-bred features, and of a demeanor of stately courtesy to all. He was clad always in Confederate gray cloth, and wore a soft felt hat with wide brim. Afoot, his step was brisk and firm; in the saddle he rode admirably and with a martial aspect.

His early life had been spent in the Military Academy at West Point and upon the then north-western frontier in the Black Hawk War, and he afterward greatly distinguished himself at Monterey and Buena Vista in Mexico; at the time when we knew him, everything in his appearance and manner was suggestive of such a training. He was reported to feel quite out of place in the office of President, with executive and administrative duties, in the midst of such a war; General Lee always spoke of him as the best of military advisers; his own inclination was to be with the army, and at the first tidings of sound of a gun, anywhere within reach of Richmond, he was in the saddle and off for the spot—to the dismay of his staff-officers, who were expected to act as an escort on such occasions, and who never knew at what hour of the night or of the next day they should get back to bed or to a meal.

The stories we were told of his adventures on such excursions were many, and sometimes amusing. For instance, when General Lee had crossed the Chickahominy, President Davis, with several staff-officers, overtook the column, and, with the Secretary of War and a few other non-combatants, forded the river just as the battle of Mechanicsville began. General Lee, surrounded by members of his own staff and other officers, was found a few hundred yards north of the bridge, in the middle of the broad road, mounted and busily engaged in directing the attack then about to be made by a brigade sweeping in the line over the fields to the east of the road and toward Ellerson's Mill, where in a few minutes a hot engagement commenced. Shot, from the enemy's guns out of sight, went whizzing overhead in quick succession, striking every moment nearer the group of horsemen in the road as the gunners improved their range.

General Lee observed the President's approach, and was evidently annoyed at what he considered a foolhardy expedition of needless exposure of the head of the Government, whose duties were elsewhere. He turned his back for a moment, until Colonel Chilton had been dispatched at a gallop with the last direction to the commander of the attacking brigade; then, facing the cavalcade and looking like the god of war indignant, he exchanged with the President a salute, with the most frigid reserve of anything like welcome or cordiality.

In an instant, and without allowance of opportunity for a word from the President, the general, looking not at him but at the assemblage at large, asked in a tone of irritation: "Who are all this army of people, and what are they doing here?"

No one moved or spoke, but all eyes were upon the President; everybody perfectly understood that this was only an order for him to retire to a place of safety, and the roar of the guns, the rattling fire of musketry, and the bustle of a battle in progress, with troops continually arriving across the bridge to go into action, went on. The President twisted in his saddle, quite taken aback at such a greeting—the general regarding him now with glances of growing severity. After a painful pause the President said, deprecatingly: "It is not my army, General."

"It certainly is not *my* army, Mr. President," was the prompt reply, "and this is no place for it"—in an accent of command.

Such a rebuff was a stunner to Mr. Davis, who, however, soon regained his serenity and answered: "Well, General, if I withdraw, perhaps they will follow," and, raising his hat in another cold salute, he turned his horse's head to ride slowly toward the bridge—seeing, as he turned, a man killed immediately before him by a shot from a gun which at that moment got the range of the road. The President's own staff-officers followed him, as did various others; but he presently drew rein in a stream, where the high bank and the bushes concealed him from General Lee's repelling observation, and there remained while the battle raged. The Secretary of War had also made a show of withdrawing, but improved the opportunity afforded by rather a deep ditch on the roadside to attempt to conceal himself and his horse there for a time from General Lee, who at that moment was more to be dreaded than the enemy's guns.

—Harrison, "Richmond Scenes in '62"

13. THE FIGHTING AT GAINES' MILL

After his initial attack at Mechanicsville, Lee struck eastward to Gaines' Mill, in the second of the Seven Days battles. Although McClellan's forces greatly outnumbered Lee's, so faulty were the Union general's tactics that Lee was able to throw some 57,000 troops against scarcely half that number under the unfortunate Fitz-John Porter. Porter put up a magnificent resistance, but by sundown of June 27 the Federal ranks were broken and the Federals retreated across the Chickahominy.

The two selections here given describe the fighting as seen by the ordinary soldier of both armies. J. B. Polley, the author of the first selection, was a private in the 4th Texas Regiment of Hood's Texas Brigade. His vivacious letters to his "charming Nellie"—whom he did not meet personally until the close of the war—are entertaining, but not wholly reliable. Oliver Norton, who answered Lincoln's first call for volunteers, fought through the entire war, first as a private in the 83rd Regiment, Pennsylvania Volunteers, then as a first lieutenant of the 80th United States Colored Troops. He participated in as many as 26 battles and skirmishes. He here describes how he was wounded three times within a few moments.

A. Hood's Texans Capture a Battery at Gaines' Mill

Camp Near Richmond, July 12, 1862

Friday morning, June 27, we again advanced. The Yankees fell back until they reached a strong, almost impregnable position on the ground in the vicinity of Gaines' Mill. They occupied a ridge overlooking the Chickahominy and between us and that stream, their artillery being massed behind three lines of breastworks so constructed along the side of the ridge next to us that firing from one could be done over the heads of the troops in the other. All the force of the enemy on our side of the Chickahominy was concentrated to check the advance of Jackson. The Confederates began their assaults on this position about noon, but were constantly beaten back. Brigade after brigade had been ordered to charge. They had charged and met repulse before Whiting's division—which consists, you know, of Law's brigade and ours—reached the scene of action at 4 o'clock in the evening.

Said General Whiting to General Hood, pointing to a battery that was doing tremendous execution in the Confederate rank, "That battery ought to be taken, General."

"Then why has it not been done?" asked Hood.

"Because the position is too strong," answered Whiting. "My brigade is composed of veterans, but they can do nothing with it."

"I have a regiment that will capture it," said Hood; and, galloping to the Fourth Texas, dismounted and called it to attention. Then marching it by the flank to an open field, he gave the orders to bring it into line of battle, and shouted, "Forward!"

Shot and shell began to come thick and fast as, surmounting the rise of the hill, we arrived in plain view of the Yankees, and half way across the field men began to drop, wounded or dead, from the ranks. We passed over two regiments—said to have been Virginians—who, protected by a depression of the ground, were lying down, apparently afraid either to advance or retreat. At the crest of the hill Hood shouted rapidly the orders, "Fix bayonets! Make ready! Aim! Fire! Charge!" The timber between us and the enemy hid them from view, but we pulled triggers nevertheless, and rushed down the hill into and across the branch, at the Yankees in the first line of breastworks. They waited not for the onset, but fled like a flock of sheep, carrying with them their supports in the second and third lines. Reaching the road which ran along the summit of the hill beyond the branch, and looking to our left, we could see large bodies of the enemy in full retreat, but they were so far behind us that, mistaken for our own troops, not a shot was fired at them. . . .

The regiment had more work to do, and gallantly did it. Hood formed the remnant of the command in an old apple orchard while exposed to a terrific fire from the batteries, and once more gave the order to charge. Lieutenant-Colonel Warwick sprang to the front, shouting, "Wait, General, until I get ahead of them," and fifty yards farther fell mortally wounded. The Fourth rushed down into a ravine and up the steep bank to find that instead of one battery, there were three so disposed as to attack from the front and on the flank. The enemy made no stand at the first, but supporting the second were eight companies of the Second United States Cavalry—among them the very company in which Hood had served as a lieutenant. A squadron of this command charged upon the Fourth, but more than half of it were killed and wounded, and the balance forced to retire in disorder. This was the last organized resistance, the third battery being easily captured and the enemy driven a mile beyond it. Then night came on and human slaughter ceased. . . .

After the fighting I was surprised to learn how little of it I had really seen and participated in. It is only the General, who stands back in the rear and directs the movements of an army, who is able to take note of all that occurs. We privates look only to our immediate front, right, and left, and are not permitted to stand on eminences which overlook the whole field of battle. Therefore you must bear in mind that much of what I relate comes from the lips of others. Caesar could say, "*Veni, vidi, vici*," but the privates of his army had to speak in the first person plural, and say, "*We* came, *we* saw, *we* conquered."

General Hood kept the promise made to us when he was promoted to be brigadier-general, and commanded the Fourth in its first fight. He exposed himself most recklessly, but was not harmed. The Veteran said to me yesterday. "I tell you what, Joe, I got mighty nervous and shaky while we were forming in the apple orchard to make that last desperate charge on the batteries. But when I looked behind me and saw old Hood resting on one foot, his arm raised above his head, his hand grasping the limb of a tree, looking as unconcerned as if we were on dress parade, I just determined that if he could stand it, I would."

—POLLEY, *A Soldier's Letters to Charming Nellie*

B. OLIVER NORTON FIGHTS LIKE A MADMAN AT GAINES' MILL

Camp near James River, July 4, 1862

Dear Friends at Home:—

I sent a few words to you yesterday just to relieve your suspense, and to-day I will write a little more, though, in the present condition of my mind and body, worn out by fatigue and exposure, you cannot expect much but a disconnected letter. The papers will have told you of the strategic movement of McClellan's army, its causes and its complete success. All that remains for me to write, and all that I can be expected to know is where the Eighty-third went and what it did.

The fight on the right began on Thursday, the 26th of June, and we took all on our backs and went out that afternoon but did no fighting. Friday morning at daylight we fell back to a position on a stream near Gaines' Mill. The rebels soon followed, feeling their way along, and at about 2 o'clock the fighting became general along the whole line. Our brigade formed the left flank of the line and lay nearest the river. The Eighty-third was posted in a deep gully, wooded, and with the stream I mentioned running in front of us. We built a little breastwork of logs and had a good position. On the hill behind us the Forty-fourth and Twelfth New York and the Sixteenth Michigan were posted. When the rebels made the first attack, we could not fire a shot, the hill concealing them from us, and so we lay still while the bullets of two opposing lines whistled over our heads. They were repulsed, but only to pour in new troops with greater vigor than before.

Suddenly I saw two men on the bank in front of us gesticulating violently and pointing to our rear, but the roar of battle drowned their voices. The order was given to face about. We did so and tried to form in line, but while the line was forming, a bullet laid low the head, the stay, the trust of our regiment—our brave colonel, and before we knew what had happened the major shared his fate. We were then without a field officer, but the boys bore up bravely. They rallied round the flag and we advanced up the hill to find ourselves alone. It appears that the enemy broke through our lines off on our right, and word was sent to us on the left to fall back. Those in the rear of us received the order but the aide sent to us was shot before he reached us and so we got no orders. Henry and Denison were shot about the same time as the colonel. I left them together under a tree.

I returned to the fight, and our boys were dropping on all sides of me. I was blazing away at the rascals not ten rods off when a ball struck my gun just above the lower band as I was capping it, and cut it in two. The ball flew in pieces and part went by my head to the right and three pieces struck just below my left collar bone. The deepest one was not over half an inch, and stopping to open my coat I pulled them out and snatched a gun from Ames in Company H as he fell dead. Before I had fired this at all a ball clipped off a piece of the stock, and an instant after, another struck the seam of my canteen and entered my left groin. I pulled it out, and, more maddened than ever, I rushed in again. A few minutes after, another ball took six inches off the muzzle of this gun. I snatched another from a wounded man under a tree, and, as I was loading kneeling by the side of the road, a ball cut my rammer in two as I was turning it over my head. Another gun was easier got than a rammer so I threw that away and picked up a fourth one. Here in the road a buckshot struck me in the left eyebrow, making the third slight scratch I received in the action. It exceeded all I ever dreamed of, it was almost a miracle.

Then came the retreat across the river; rebels on three sides of us left no choice but to run or be killed or be taken prisoners. We left our all in the hollow by the creek and crossed the river to Smith's division. The bridge was torn up and when I came to the river I threw my cartridge box on my shoulder and waded through. It was a little more than waist deep. I stayed that night with some Sherman boys in Elder Drake's company in the Forty-ninth New York.

Sunday night we lay in a cornfield in the rain, without tent or blanket. Monday we went down on the James river, lying behind batteries to support them. Tuesday the same—six days exposed to a constant fire of shot and shell, till almost night, when we went to the front and engaged in another fierce conflict with the enemy. Going on to the field, I picked up a tent and slung it across my shoulder. The folds of that stopped a ball that would have passed through me. I picked it out, put it in my pocket, and, after firing sixty rounds of my own and a number of a wounded comrade's cartridges, I came off the field unhurt, and ready, but not anxious, for another fight.

—Norton, *Army Letters*

14. THE END OF SEVEN DAYS

Lee's success at Gaines' Mill forced McClellan to shift his base from White House on the Pamunkey to Harrison's Landing on the James—a shift which he made with great skill. As soon as Lee discovered that his opponent was heading for the James, he set his troops the task of turning the retreat into a rout. In this he was, however, unsuccessful. The Confederate attacks at Savage's Station and Frayser's Farm, on June 29 and 30, were unco-ordinated and without strategic value. During the night of the twenty-ninth Mc-Clellan retreated across the White Oak Swamp, a swampy tributary of the Chickahominy. Longstreet and A. P. Hill attacked him there, on the thirtieth, but Jackson failed to get into the fight; once more it was inconclusive and the Federals managed to get away to the heights of Malvern Hill.

The final attack at Malvern Hill, on July 1, was likewise a failure—again chiefly because of Lee's failure to bring all his available troops into battle. While Confederate losses in the Seven Days campaign were heavier than the Union, the campaign must be accounted a Confederate success because it achieved its object of relieving pressure on Richmond and persuaded the administration to abandon the Peninsula.

Thomas Livermore, from whose fascinating wartime reminiscences these excerpts are taken, was a boy of seventeen when the war broke out, studying at Lombard College, Illinois. He hurried east to get into the fighting, found the 1st New Hampshire Infantry encamped in Maryland, and enlisted; he ended the war as colonel of the 18th New Hampshire Volunteers.

A. The Federals Are Forced Back at White Oak Swamp

THE sun rose and darted his fiery rays upon us, and as most of us had eaten, we stuck our rifles up by the bayonets, fastened our blankets in the locks, and lay down in their shade to shun the scorching rays, and sleep. The dust of the barren plain was a sweet couch, and the stifling heat which enveloped us could not prevent profound sleep. A few, perhaps, bestirred themselves to complete the breakfasts which had been begun at our first halt when we had crossed the bridge, but there seemed to be a soothing quiet around us, and we could praise the economy of Nature which made the pleasure of sleep so intense as to requite us almost for our labors and deprivations before. What I thought or dreamed of I do not know, but suddenly, whatever visions of peace hovered around me were dispelled by the thunders of artillery, the shriek of shells, and the horrid humming of their fragments. Hell seemed to have opened upon us. In a twinkling every man was on his feet, the blankets were slung over our shoulders, and the men were in their places, shrinking under the storm, perhaps, but steady and prepared for action. The rebels had planted a large number of cannon on the other side of the swamp, and having pointed them at the host which lay on the plain had fired them all at once.

And what a scene it was! As far as the eye could see the tired troops were springing to arms; batteries were whirling into position or hurrying out of reach with horses on the gallop; wagons drawn by teams of frightened mules, driven by frantic drivers, rattled away to the woods; the teams of six mules which belonged to a pontoon train which were surprised watering at the swamp, fled up the hill and away, leaving their boats; stragglers and non-combatants of all kinds fled in all directions from the fire; while the air was filled with clouds of dust and wreaths of smoke which spread out from the fierce clouds, breathing fire of bursting shells, and the ear was dimmed with explosions, shouts, and a storm of other noises.

The —— New York Volunteers was said to have run away when the first shell burst in front of it, and —— battery, also of New York, I think, disgraced itself in like manner. But the rest of the troops quickly formed lines of battle, and when we in a very few minutes had reached our position and lain down in line with our faces to the enemy, order had come out of chaos. Near us, in front and rear and right, the troops of our own division lay in parallel lines; on other parts of the plain Smith's division and Naglee's brigade were in similar order, and a few rods in front the welcome sight of Hazzard's battery of our corps, firing with rapidity at the enemy, greeted our eyes. The enemy's fire was unremitting, and from noon until nearly dark we endured the slow torture of seeing our comrades killed, mangled, and torn around us, while we could not fire a shot, as our business was to lie and wait to repel attacks and protect our batteries. With every discharge of the enemy's guns, the shells would scream over our heads and bury themselves in the woods beyond, burst over us and deal death in the ranks, or ricochet over the plain, killing whenever they struck a line.

The —— New York Volunteers in changing position either attempted to escape to the rear or mistook its colonel's orders and retreated right down toward us. General Caldwell, who was near, galloped to our rear and cried out, "5th New Hampshire, rise up!" and we rose, leveled our bayonets, and received the —— at their points. This was a decisive barrier to further retreating, and after a little confusion they went back and behaved themselves. We were pleased to have rebuked this cowardice, but were sorry for Colonel ——, who was a brave man.

The shot hit some of our men and scattered their vitals and brains upon the ground, and we hugged the earth to escape this horrible fate, but nothing could save a few who fell victims there. I saw a shot strike in the 2d Delaware, a new regiment with us, which threw a man's head perhaps twenty feet into the air, and the bleeding trunk fell over toward us. The men seemed paralyzed for a moment, but presently gathered up the poor fellow's body in a blanket and carried it away. I do not know that I have ever feared artillery as I did then, and I can recollect very well how close I lay to the ground while the messengers of death, each one seemingly coming right into us, whistled over us. . . .

I had just reached my place, when the order was given to rise up and face about. A cannon shot came quicker than the wind through my company, and close by me. Tibbetts fell and Nichols fell. We reached the line designated with a few hasty steps, and resumed our line with faces to the front. Nichols got up, and came back to the captain and said, "Captain, I am wounded and want to go to the rear." The poor fellow held up one arm with the other hand, for it dangled only by a strip of flesh. Some men went forward and hastily gathered up Tibbetts in a blanket and bore him away; the shot had gone through his body. We felt a little safer now. Hazzard's battery withdrew, cut to pieces, and with Captain Hazzard mortally wounded; and for a short time it seemed as if the rebels would fire unmolested, but Pettit galloped up with his battery of 10-pounder Parrotts and went into action, and then iron *did* fly, and the rebels had their hands full. Captain Keller sat up on a knapsack in front of us and gave warning when the shells were coming, and perhaps saved lives by it; anyhow it was a brave thing to do.

It was not a long time before we perceived that Captain Pettit's fire was getting too hot for the rebels, and they only fired at intervals; and at last Pettit would hold up until they fired, when he would fire his whole battery at them, and as his shells went screaming over the tops of the trees to where the smoke was seen, our hearts bounded, for we perceived that their range was almost perfect; the rebels grew timid, and finally toward night they ceased firing, and we felt grateful to Pettit for it.

Once during the afternoon we saw a battery heavily engaged on our side close to the swamp on the right, and I think that we heard in that direction the rattle of musketry, perhaps where the rebels were attempting a crossing. The portion of the pontoon train which was left on the plain was set fire to in the afternoon, and the smoke and flames added to the infernal aspect of affairs. If ever stillness and rest were appreciated, I think it was on the verge of that evening, and even the dusty plain must have assumed a lovely hue when it was no longer disturbed by ricocheting shot.

—Livermore, *Days and Events*

B. Captain Livermore Fights at Malvern Hill

This was the morning of July 1, and we were on Malvern Hill. The army had retreated during the day before and that night, and on this morning were placed in position to meet the advancing enemy again, and I have an indistinct recollection of seeing General McClellan on the field that morning, but he went on board a gunboat soon after and stayed until late in the day. The sun rose as hot as ever and again prostrated some of the men.

Presently a battery appeared in our front and opened fire on us at the distance of perhaps three quarters of a mile. As we lay directly on the crest of the hill, we presented a fair mark and our quarters were decidedly uncomfortable.

Ammunition was sent to us, and I was ordered to distribute it. As I was performing the work, or about that time, a cannon shot took off the foot of a man lying near by, and I was glad when I could lie down again.

The slow hours dragged along until the middle of the afternoon, when the battle opened in earnest on our left far down in front. Cannon and muskets roared and rattled, the blue smoke made the air heavy, and cheers and yells made the heavens ring. We did not remain long in suspense; an order came to move, and setting our faces to the fighting ground, we shook from our feet the dust of that ground where we were fired at without the privilege of a return fire. We moved down the hill, in front of the woods, and into a road, and marched toward the left flank. On our right was a wheatfield and beyond it another field. Through this last one, as we passed it, the shot came whirling over and through our ranks, spending their force in the woods, where they cracked and crashed through limbs, trunks, and foliage. Our men in the line of battle cheered and cheered again, and our hearts bounded to think that we had met with a success. A color sergeant, with his colors all torn, came by us and reported victory. We filed into the field on our right and moved forward. But I must not omit to mention that while we marched by the flank a shot crashed through the ranks of the 61st New York which led us. Captain —— fell and cried out in mortal agony, "One man! two men! three men! carry me off the field!" The pitying men sprang forward and raised him up gently to find that the shot had only taken off his coat-tail.

As I have said, we formed line on our right and moved forward. At this time Colonel Barlow, of the 61st New York, was with General Caldwell, and seemed to be maneuvering the brigade for him and in a very cool manner. We moved forward, and as we neared the fight could see our men crouching behind the fences and hedges, firing with a will. The rest of the brigade moved away from us, where I knew not, and we halted behind what was, I think, West's house by the Quaker road. Here we lay down for a few minutes in peace, but very soon a rebel battery close in front opened on us with fury. Some of our officers had got into an outbuilding just in front of us for shelter, but a shell came right in among them and they left. General Howe, a fine-looking man, whose command was near by, rode up and ordered Captain Sturtevant to move over to the right and support one of our batteries. In order to do this the quickest way, we had to move directly in front of the rebel battery within not more than four hundred yards, over an open plain with no obstacle between us.

The general rode away, and Captain Sturtevant, who was honest and brave, but a little wanting in decision, got up and, beginning scratching his leg, said, "There! I am ordered to go and support that battery. If I go clear out of range I shall be too long, and if I go across we shall go right into the fire of the rebels; I don't know what to do!"

Perhaps my boldness arose from having been placed in command of "I" Company that day, its officers being absent; but whatever might be the cause, I said to him, "Well, Captain, we might just as well go across under fire as to lie here, for we shall get killed here; so let us go!"

"That's so," said he; "rise up, men! Forward, march!"—and away we went on the double-quick; and then how the rebel battery did pepper us!

Shells flew all around us, and the wonder was that more were not hurt. I turned my head to the left and saw the battery and the gunners, springing to their work amid the smoke. I saw one pull the string, saw the flash of the piece, heard the roar, and the whiz of the shell, heard it burst, heard the humming of the fragments, and wondered if I was to be hit, and quicker than a flash something stung my leg on the calf, and I limped out of the ranks, a wounded man. My first impulse was to go to the rear, but the plain for a quarter of a mile was dotted with dust raised by the flying pieces and ricocheting shot, and I concluded that if I could, 't were better to stay at the front than to be killed going to the rear. So I stooped down, opened the ragged hole in my trousers leg, and saw no blood, but the form of a piece of shell two or three inches long, printed in a cruel bruise on my leg; then I limped to the regiment, which had halted and lain down. I took my place, and was so vexed with pain that I swore at a Frenchman in my company roundly for being out of his place, and then commenced behaving myself. The same shell wounded two or three others, I believe.

We lay just behind the crest of a gentle slope and in front of some trees. In front of us first came the open field and then some woods. The rebel battery had been silenced somehow, but sharpshooters in the farther woods shot at us with uncomfortable precision. The battery on our left threw shell into the woods and I imagine made hot quarters for the sharpshooters. In the course of an hour my leg had swelled badly, and my lameness was such that I could hardly step otherwise than on my toes. It was a matter of honor and pride with me to stay with the regiment as long as I could, but Captain Sturtevant and Captain Cross both urged me to go to the hospital, for (they said) we were liable to move on the enemy at any moment, and as I seemed to grow lamer, I might be in such a plight that I should give out in a bad place and lose my life or be taken prisoner. The force of these arguments was evident, and at length I hobbled away. I passed some of the Third Corps in a field where the wheat was stacked in many piles, and reached the road on which we had marched down, and then climbed the hill and searched for the hospital. I met a good-looking Negro man in my wanderings, and with an eye to business engaged him as a servant, his former employer, a captain in our army, having been killed that day, he said.

At length I found a building which looked like a church, in the darkness which had now settled on the field, around which great numbers of our wounded lay among the trees, groaning and complaining bitterly, and it was a scene of utter misery. I groped around carefully among the prostrate men, who were agonized if any one stepped too close to them, and sat down by a tree. Beside me a groaning man proved to be Second Lieutenant Lawrence, of our regiment, who dolefully informed me that he was very badly wounded in the ankle, but who really, as I learned afterwards, had nothing but a contusion. He was the color sergeant who was promoted to second lieutenant at Camp California, and never rejoined the regiment for duty. How it transpired I do not recollect, but I found our own regimental hospital wagon in the woods, and got my leg bound up, and then lay down in company with some of our men to sleep.

—LIVERMORE, *Days and Events*

15. RICHARD AUCHMUTY REVIEWS THE PENINSULAR CAMPAIGN

A member of one of the most distinguished of New York families, Richard Auchmuty was practicing architecture in New York, in the office of the famous Renwick, when the war broke out. He was commissioned a captain in the V Corps of the Army of the Potomac, and fought gallantly through all the campaigns in Virginia to Gettysburg. Invalided out he took work in the War Department, and participated in the defense of Washington at the time of Early's raid in 1864. After the war Auchmuty devoted himself to architecture and philanthropy.

Harrison's Landing, James River, Saturday, July 5, 1862
My Dear Mother,—

I sincerely thank God that I have passed unhurt through the horrors of the last ten days. I am, of course, worn out with fatigue, but am otherwise well.

I see by the *Times* of the 4th, that you are still but slightly informed of what has been going on here. The correspondents mostly wrote from the steamboats on the Pamunkey.

The army is too immense for one person to have a clear idea of what is going on all along the line. I will confine myself to the right wing, which was supposed to be sufficient to protect the rear.

McClellan undoubtedly meant to swing the army around until it rested on the James; but the fate of war had, in the end, more to do with it than he. On Thursday [June 26], about five o'clock, while enjoying a dinner of lamb and green peas, an order came to send a brigade to assist McCall near Mechanicsville. Butterfield's brigade was on an expedition to the rear, Martindale's somewhere else, and Griffin's (he had taken command that day of the Second) alone remained. We went with them about four miles, and got in a very heavy cannonading, the rebels having crossed the Chickahominy at that point. This lasted until about 9 P.M. The cannonading was the loudest I have heard, batteries being planted for nearly a mile; and after dark it became more terrible than by day. The Fourth Michigan came to close quarters with the Fourteenth Louisiana and Sixty-sixth Virginia, losing fifty men. The rest of our division suffered but slightly. At eight o'clock Morrell left me with Weedon and went to look after Martindale. I lay on one of the gun-carriages and got a nap of two hours.

At 2 A.M., an order came to fall back to our old camp near Gaines' Mills (Camp New Bridge); I went after Griffin, and by daylight we were on our way back, the rebels shelling the road. At Gaines' Mills we had breakfast, and heard that our camp was to be abandoned for a better position. Most of the supplies had been sent over the Chickahominy during the night; those remaining were burned.

At 9 A.M., on Friday, the 27th, we crossed the mill-dam and broke down the bridge, the rebel scouts coming in sight. The men were posted in order of battle, and lay down to rest. The sun was extremely hot. Morrell's division was posted along a wooded ravine, with an open field rising behind them. In the ravine ran a creek, draining the mill-dam. I did not see the position of the right of the line. Behind us, in reserve, was McCall's division.

About twelve, the artillery commenced, and the skirmishers, who were in a field beyond the ravine, returned. Musketry began on the right, and gradually worked down to us. About one o'clock hell itself seemed to break loose on our division. First Martindale's, then Griffin's, and then Butterfield's brigades, caught a storm of shot, shell, and musketry, which made the trees wave like a hurricane. The enemy would bring a large number of guns to bear on one point, and then advance a whole brigade on one of our regiments. Three times they did this, each attack lasting about half an hour. After each attack, reënforcements went in, but our men still formed the front line. At six came the fourth attack, more fearful than any. The right wing had gradually fallen back, until our line was thus:

Suddenly a rush of men, horses, and guns passed over the field, the line was broken, the battle was lost. A line was attempted further back, but it broke at once and all moved towards the bridge. A line of fresh troops being formed near the bridge, the men halted, and the officers tried to collect the regiments, or even the brigades, together. Darkness coming on, the firing ceased, and the men were sent over the bridge in good order. The last passed about 6 A.M., destroying it after them.

I got a cup of coffee, and slept on the ground for two or three hours at daylight. At one o'clock we were told to move to Savage Station, about three miles, but marched eight miles to White Oak Swamp. There we had a beautiful camp and a good night's rest. We were around the house of a Mr. Brilton. The next morning McClellan and his staff took breakfast with us. Everything looked so pretty and peaceful there, that I left my horse that had been shot at Gaines' Mills with him, but the next day the whole army swept over his place and destroyed everything. The rear guard was attacked, a fight took place, and his house was burned to the ground.

That day (Sunday) we were posted ready for an attack, and at night commenced to make for the James River. The night was an awful one, as dark as pitch, with constant alarms that the cavalry were upon us, when all would be confusion. To add to our troubles, it was found that our corps had gone by the wrong road, which made it 10 A.M. before we reached the James.

We lay down in a wheat field till one o'clock (on Monday), when heavy firing began, and we were sent to the front. The enemy shelled us from the woods without doing much harm. In the meantime McCall and Heintzelman suffered terribly and fell back to our line.

We were encamped at a lovely place—an old picturesque brick house, surrounded by splendid white oak trees, on a terrace as fine as Hyde Park, overlooking the river. This terrace, instead of following the river, came abruptly around at right angles to it, overlooking the fields and woods, which were humming and crashing under the shells from the gunboats. Towards the enemy the ground sloped gradually down, rising again in wooded hills, first occupied by Heintzelmann and now by the enemy.

The men slept that night in order of battle. I got about an hour, on the floor of the old house. At daybreak things were gotten ready, and at 8 A.M. the enemy opened. The day was clear and cool. The Second Brigade was posted around two sides of the front. At 5 P.M. the enemy advanced in great force on the Fourteenth New York and Sixty-second Pennsylvania, and much the same scene as at Gaines' Mills was gone through, excepting that the men stood like heroes.

At 6.30 things looked very black. Then up came Porter, who took command in person, with Meagher's Irish brigade. As they passed to the front, Colonel Cass, of the Ninth Massachusetts, was being brought back, his jaw shattered by a ball. As they recognized a fellow-countryman, they gave a yell that drowned the noise of the guns. They moved to the front, and Porter sent for a battery of thirty-two-pounders, something very unusual in a field fight. This turned the enemy back. They said they lay down trembling with fright as the immense shells roared through the woods. At nine the firing ceased on our side, the rebels having stopped about an hour before.

We had repulsed their attack, and remained masters of the field, but, great God! what a field it was. To the surprise of all came the order to retreat. The troops could not stand another such attack, no reënforcements having come.

I took part of the Second Brigade with me, and after showing them the way, went back for our light wagon, which I got in a battery, and rushed through, riding in it myself. This retreat was a regular stampede, each man going off on his own hook, guns in the road at full gallop, teams on one side in the fields, infantry on the other in the woods. At daybreak came rain in torrents, and the ground was ankle deep in mud. This was Wednesday. I found shelter in a quartermaster's tent, and lay down to rest.

Your affectionate son,

R. T. A.

—E. S. A., ed., *Letters of Richard Tylden Auchmuty*

V

Stonewall Jackson and the Valley Campaign

JACKSON'S *Valley campaign has long been regarded as one of the most brilliant in the history of modern warfare; perhaps no other in American warfare, unless it is Lee's campaign at Second Manassas or Grant's below Vicksburg, has been so assiduously studied abroad. The grand strategy of the Valley campaign was Lee's and, to some extent, Joe Johnston's; but the tactics were Jackson's—and the resolute spirit that gave them meaning. The strategy of the Valley campaign was essentially simple, though the campaign itself is one of the most confusing, in detail, in the history of the war. That strategy was to prevent McDowell from joining McClellan on the Peninsula, to frighten Washington into scattering its effective forces on offensive-defensive operations, and to defend Richmond from the west. All these purposes it attained.*

After his brilliant performance at Bull Run Jackson had been made a major general and assigned command in the Shenandoah Valley. Only a familiarity with the geography of the Valley will make clear the details of the campaign, and that requires a careful study of the map. It is sufficient to note here that the Valley between the Blue Ridge and the Shenandoah mountains was divided by the Massanutten range, thus making in effect two valleys—the Luray to the east and the Shenandoah to the west. At the head, or southern end, of the Valley was Staunton, connected by railroad with Richmond; midway down the Valley was Strasburg on the Manassas Gap Railroad which also connected with Richmond; at the mouth, or northern end, was Harpers Ferry. Jackson knew the Valley intimately, had a small and mobile force, and interior lines of communication. The Valley campaign, as he conducted it, was a military chess game; his objective not so much to defeat the enemy as to distract, confuse, check, and eventually checkmate them.

Altogether, even with the forces of Ewell and Edward Johnson that were added to his command, Jackson had only some 18,000 men. Against these were Frémont, in the west with 15,000, and Banks, at Winchester with over 20,000, while McDowell on the Rappahannock stood ready to send reinforcements if needed. Jackson knew that he could not defeat all these forces, but he hoped to prevent them from combining, and to hold them in the Valley while Johnston and Lee dealt with McClellan.

In March 1862 Banks advanced from Harpers Ferry to Winchester. Jackson fell back, to Strasburg and then to Mount Jackson on the western edge of the Massanuttens. Supposing that he had driven Jackson from the Valley Banks prepared to move east to McDowell. This was what Jackson had to prevent. First he sent his cavalry leader Ashby to strike Shields at Winchester; then he himself moved down to Kernstown to join in the attack. Banks brought up his full forces, repulsed Jackson, and threw him back to Mount Jackson. It was a defeat, but it served its purpose. Banks was back in the Valley in full strength; McDowell was held on the Rappahannock ready to go to his aid. Moving swiftly up the Valley Jackson crossed over westward at Staunton, surprised and defeated Frémont at the Battle of McDowell, then hurried back down the Valley and burst on the astonished Banks at Front Royal (May 23). Banks retreated to Winchester where Jackson struck and scattered his forces. Panic-stricken, Washington detached 20,000 from McDowell's command and hurried them to the Valley.

Jackson meantime doubled on his tracks and retired up the Valley to Port Republic. His plan was to hold Frémont at Cross Keys with Ewell's division while he dealt with Shields. The plan worked out, and with the twin battles of Cross Keys and Port Republic the Valley campaign came to an end. A week later Jackson was on his way east to join Lee in the Peninsular campaign. In three months he had immobilized a good part of the Union army, defeated Milroy, Banks, Shields and Frémont, and proved the value of the Valley as a threat to Washington and the North.

1. STONEWALL JACKSON BREAKS THE SABBATH

"An iron sabre vowed to an iron Lord," Stephen Vincent Benét calls Jackson, and the phrase suggests something of that Covenanter quality which Jackson, more than any other Civil War general, indubitably had. Both of his wives were daughters of Presbyterian ministers, and he himself was so devout that he would neither march nor fight on the Sabbath if he could avoid it. He regarded himself as an instrument of the Lord, and to the Lord he gave credit for every victory.

His letters to his wife are filled with pious admonitions and with protestations of devotion and humility.

April 11th [1862]. I am very much concerned at having no letter this week, but my trust is in the Almighty. How precious is the consolation flowing from the Christian's assurance that "all things work together for good to them that love God!" ... God gave us a glorious victory in the Southwest (at Shiloh), but the loss of the great Albert Sidney Johnston is to be mourned. I do not remember having ever felt so sad at the death of a man whom I had never seen. . . .

Although I was repulsed in the attempt to recover Winchester, yet the enemy's loss appears to have been three times that of ours. In addition to this, the great object which required me to follow up the enemy, as he fell back from Strasburg, seems to have been accomplished very thoroughly. I am well satisfied with the result. Congress has passed a vote of thanks, and General Johnston has issued a very gratifying order upon the subject, one which will have a fine effect upon my command. The great object to be acquired by the battle demanded time to make known its accomplishments. Time has shown that while the field is in possession of the enemy, the most essential fruits of the battle are ours. For this and all of our Heavenly Father's blessings, I wish I could be ten thousand times more thankful. Should any report be published, my views and object in fighting and its fruits will then become known.

You appear much concerned at my attacking *on Sunday*. I was greatly concerned, too; but I felt it my duty to do it, in consideration of the ruinous effects that might result from postponing the battle until morning. So far as I can see, my course was a wise one; the best that I could do under the circumstances, though very distasteful to my feelings; and I hope and pray to our Heavenly Father that I may never again be circumstanced as on that day. I believed that so far as our troops were concerned, necessity and mercy both called for the battle.

I do hope the war will soon be over, and that I shall never again have to take the field. Arms is a profession that, if its principles are adhered to for success, requires an officer to do what he fears may be wrong, and yet, according to military experience, must be done, if success is to be attained. And this fact of its being necessary to success, and being accompanied with success, and that a departure from it is accompanied with disaster, suggests that it must be right. Had I fought the battle on Monday instead of Sunday, I fear our cause would have suffered; whereas, as things turned out, I consider our cause gained much from the engagement.

—M. Jackson, *Life and Letters of General Thomas J. Jackson*

2. DICK TAYLOR CAMPAIGNS WITH JACKSON IN THE VALLEY

Richard Taylor, from whose recollections this and the following selection are taken, was the son of President Zachary Taylor, and a Louisiana planter and politician of wealth and prominence. Commissioned colonel of the 9th Louisiana Infantry, Taylor fought through the whole of the war—in the Valley, at Seven Days, on the Red River, and in Hood's Tennessee campaign, rising to the rank of lieutenant general. He was a man of unusual intellectual attainments—he had studied at Edinburgh and Paris as well as at Harvard and Yale—and his volume of reminiscences is one of the most enchanting of all Civil War books. His account of the Valley campaign during May and June of 1862 tells the story in sufficient detail.

EWELL'S division reached the western base of Swift Run Gap on a lovely spring evening, April 30, 1862, and in crossing the Blue Ridge seemed to have left winter and its rigors behind. Jackson, whom we moved to join, had suddenly that morning marched toward McDowell, some eighty miles west, where, after uniting with a force under General Edward Johnson, he defeated the Federal general Milroy. Some days later he as suddenly returned. Meanwhile we were ordered to remain in camp on the Shenandoah near Conrad's store, at which place a bridge spanned the stream.

The great Valley of Virginia was before us in all its beauty. Fields of wheat spread far and wide, interspersed with woodlands, bright in their robes of tender green. Wherever appropriate sites existed, quaint old mills, with turning wheels, were busily grinding the previous year's harvest; and grove and eminence showed comfortable homesteads. The soft vernal influence shed a languid grace over the scene. The theatre of war in this region was from Staunton to the Potomac, one hundred and twenty miles, with an average width of some twenty-five miles; and the Blue Ridge and Alleghanies bounded it east and west. Drained by the Shenandoah with its numerous affluents, the surface was nowhere flat, but a succession of graceful swells, occasionally rising into abrupt hills. . . . Frequent passes or gaps in the mountains, through which wagon roads had been constructed, afforded easy access from east and west; and pikes were excellent, though unmetaled roads became heavy after rains.

But the glory of the Valley is Massanutten. Rising abruptly from the plain near Harrisonburg, twenty-five miles north of Staunton, this lovely mountain extends fifty miles, and as suddenly ends near Strasburg. Parallel with the Blue Ridge, and of equal height, its sharp peaks have a bolder and more picturesque aspect, while the abruptness of its slopes gives the appearance of greater altitude. Midway of Massanutten, a gap with good road affords communication between Newmarket and Luray. The eastern or Luray valley, much narrower than the one west of Massanutten, is drained by the east branch of the Shenandoah, which is joined at Front Royal, near the northern end of the mountain, by its western affluent, whence the united waters flow north, at the base of the Blue Ridge, to meet the Potomac at Harper's Ferry.

The inhabitants of this favored region were worthy of their inheritance. The north and south were peopled by scions of old colonial families, and the proud names of the "Old Dominion" abounded. In the central counties of Rockingham and Shenandoah were many descendants of German Settlers. These were thrifty, substantial Farmers, and, like their kinsmen of Pennsylvania, expressed their opulence in huge barns and fat cattle. The devotion of all to the Southern cause was wonderful. Jackson, a Valley man by reason of his residence at Lexington, south of Staunton, was their hero and idol. The women sent husbands, sons, lovers, to battle as cheerfully as to marriage feasts. No oppression, no destitution could abate their zeal. Upon a march I was accosted by two elderly sisters, who told me they had secreted a large quantity of bacon in a well on their estate, hard by. Federals had been in possession of the country, and, fearing the indiscretion of their slaves, they had done the work at night with their own hands, and now desired to *give* the meat to their people. Wives and daughters of millers, whose husbands and brothers were in arms, worked the mills night and day to furnish flour

THE VALLEY OF VIRGINIA

152

Illustrated London News

The Stampede from Bull Run

Malvern Hill

to their soldiers. To the last, women would go distances to carry the modicum of food between themselves and starvation to a suffering Confederate....

While in camp near Conrad's store, the 7th Louisiana, Colonel Hays, a crack regiment, on picket down stream, had a spirited affair, in which the enemy was driven with the loss of a score of prisoners. Shortly after, for convenience of supplies, I was directed to cross the river and camp some miles to the southwest. The command was in superb condition, and a four-gun battery from Bedford county, Virginia, Captain Bowyer, had recently been added to it. The four regiments, 6th, 7th, 8th, and 9th Louisiana, would average above eight hundred bayonets.... The 6th, Colonel Seymour, recruited in New Orleans, was composed of Irishmen, stout, hardy fellows, turbulent in camp and requiring a strong hand, but responding to kindness and justice, and ready to follow their officers to the death. The 9th, Colonel Stafford, was from North Louisiana. Planters or sons of planters, many of them men of fortune, soldiering was a hard task to which they only became reconciled by reflecting that it was "niddering" in gentlemen to assume voluntarily the discharge of duties and then shirk. The 8th, Colonel Kelly, was from the Attakapas— "Acadians," the race of which Longfellow sings in "Evangeline." A home-loving, simple people, few spoke English, fewer still had ever before moved ten miles from their natal *cabanas;* and the war to them was "a liberal education," as was the society of the lady of quality to honest Dick Steele. They had all the light gayety of the Gaul, and, after the manner of their ancestors, were born cooks. A capital regimental band accompanied them, and whenever weather and ground permitted, even after long marches, they would waltz and "polk" in couples with as much zest as if their arms encircled the supple waists of the Célestines and Mélazies of their native Teche. The Valley soldiers were largely of the Presbyterian faith, and of a solemn, pious demeanor, and looked askant at the caperings of my Creoles, holding them to be "devices and snares." ...

At nightfall of the second day in this camp, an order came from General Jackson to join him at Newmarket, twenty odd miles north; and it was stated that my division commander, Ewell, had been apprised of the order. Our position was near a pike leading south of west to Harrisonburg, whence, to gain Newmarket, the great Valley pike ran due north.... Early dawn saw us in motion, with lovely weather, a fairish road, and men in high health and spirits.

Later in the day a mounted officer was dispatched to report our approach and select a camp, which proved to be beyond Jackson's forces, then lying in the fields on both sides of the pike. Over three thousand strong, neat in fresh clothing of gray with white gaiters, bands playing at the head of their regiments, not a straggler, but every man in his place, stepping jauntily as on parade, though it had marched twenty miles and more, in open column with arms at "right shoulder shift," and rays of the declining sun flaming on polished bayonets, the brigade moved down the broad, smooth pike, and wheeled on to its camping ground. Jackson's men, by thousands, had gathered on either side of the road to see us pass. Indeed, it was a martial sight, and no man with a spark of sacred fire in his heart but would have striven hard to prove worthy of such a command.

After attending to necessary camp details, I sought Jackson, whom I had never met. . . . The mounted officer who had been sent on in advance pointed out a figure perched on the topmost rail of a fence overlooking the road and field, and said it was Jackson. Approaching, I saluted and declared my name and rank, then waited for a response. Before this came I had time to see a pair of cavalry boots covering feet of gigantic size, a mangy cap with visor drawn low, a heavy, dark beard, and weary eyes—eyes I afterward saw filled with intense but never brilliant light. A low, gentle voice inquired the road and distance marched that day.

"Keazletown road, six and twenty miles."

"You seem to have no stragglers."

"Never allow straggling."

"You must teach my people; they straggle badly." A bow in reply. Just then my creoles started their band and a waltz. After a contemplative suck at a lemon, "Thoughtless fellows for serious work" came forth. I expressed a hope that the work would not be less well done because of the gayety. A return to the lemon gave me the opportunity to retire. Where Jackson got his lemons "no fellow could find out," but he was rarely without one. To have lived twelve miles from that fruit would have disturbed him as much as it did the witty Dean.

Quite late that night General Jackson came to my camp fire, where he stayed some hours. He said we would move at dawn, asked a few questions about the marching of my men, which seemed to have impressed him, and then remained silent. If silence be golden, he was a "bonanza." He sucked lemons, ate hard-tack, and drank water, and praying and fighting appeared to be his idea of the "whole duty of man."

In the gray of the morning, as I was forming my column on the pike, Jackson appeared and gave the route—north—which, from the situation of its camp, put my brigade in advance of the army. After moving a short distance in this direction, the head of the column was turned to the east and took the road over Massanutten gap to Luray. Scarce a word was spoken on the march, as Jackson rode with me. From time to time a courier would gallop up, report, and return toward Luray. An ungraceful horseman, mounted on a sorry chestnut with a shambling gait, his huge feet with out-turned toes thrust into his stirrups, and such parts of his countenance as the low visor of his shocking cap failed to conceal wearing a wooden look, our new commander was not prepossessing. That night we crossed the east branch of the Shenandoah by a bridge, and camped on the stream, near Luray. Here, after three long marches, we were but a short distance below Conrad's store, a point we had left several days before. I began to think that Jackson was an unconscious poet, and, as an ardent lover of nature, desired to give strangers an opportunity to admire the beauties of his Valley. It seemed hard lines to be wandering like sentimental travelers about the country, instead of gaining "kudos" on the Peninsula.

Off the next morning, my command still in advance, and Jackson riding with me. The road led north between the east bank of the river and the western base of the Blue Ridge. Rain had fallen and softened it, so as to delay the wagon trains in rear. Past midday we reached a wood extending from the mountain to the river, when a mounted officer from the rear called Jackson's attention, who rode back with him. A moment later, there rushed out of the wood to meet us a young, rather well-looking woman, afterward widely known as Belle Boyd. Breathless with speed and agitation, some time elapsed before she found her voice. Then, with much volubility, she said we were near Front Royal, beyond the wood; that the town was filled with Federals, whose camp was on the west side of the river, where they had guns in position to cover the wagon bridge, but none bearing on the railway bridge below the former; that they believed Jackson to be west of Massanutten, near Harrisonburg; that General Banks, the Federal commander, was at Winchester, twenty miles northwest of Front Royal, where he was slowly concentrating his widely scattered forces to meet Jackson's advance, which was expected some days later.

All this she told with the precision of a staff officer making a report, and it was true to the letter. Jackson was possessed of these facts before he left Newmarket, and based his movements upon them; but, as he never told anything, it was news to me, and gave me an idea of the strategic value of Massanutten—pointed out, indeed by Washington before the Revolution. There also dawned on me quite another view of our leader than the one from which I had been regarding him for two days past.

Convinced of the correctness of the woman's statements, I hurried forward at "a double," hoping to surprise the enemy's idlers in the town, or swarm over the wagon bridge with them and secure it. Doubtless this was rash, but I felt immensely "cocky" about my brigade, and believed that it would prove equal to any demand. Before we had cleared the wood Jackson came galloping from the rear, followed by a company of horse. He ordered me to deploy my leading regiment as skirmishers on both sides of the road and continue the advance, then passed on. We speedily came in sight of Front Royal, but the enemy had taken the alarm, and his men were scurrying over the bridge to their camp, where troops could be seen forming.

The situation of the village is surpassingly beautiful. It lies near the east bank of the Shenandoah, which just below unites all its waters, and looks directly on the northern peaks of Massanutten. The Blue Ridge, with Manassas Gap, through which passes the railway, overhangs it on the east; distant Alleghany bounds the horizon to the west; and down the Shenandoah, the eye ranges over a fertile, well-farmed country. Two bridges spanned the river—a wagon bridge above, a railway bridge some yards lower. A good pike led to Winchester, twenty miles, and another followed the river north, whence many cross-roads united with the Valley pike near Winchester. The river, swollen by rain, was deep and turbulent, with a strong current. The Federals were posted on the west bank, here somewhat higher than the opposite, and a short distance above the junction of waters, with batteries bearing more especially on the upper bridge.

Under instructions, my brigade was drawn up in line, a little retired from the river, but overlooking it—the Federals and their guns in full view. So far, not a shot had been fired. I rode down to the river's brink to get a better look at the enemy through a field-glass, when my horse, heated by the march, stepped into the water to drink. Instantly a brisk fire was opened on me, bullets striking all around and raising a little shower-bath. Like many a foolish fellow, I found it easier to get into than out of a difficulty. I had not yet led my command into action, and, remembering that one must "strut" one's little part to the best advantage, sat my horse with all the composure I could muster. A provident camel, on the eve of a desert journey, would not have laid in a greater supply of water than did my thoughtless beast. At last he raised his head, looked placidly around, turned, and walked up the bank.

This little incident was not without value, for my men welcomed me with a cheer; upon which, as if in response, the enemy's guns opened, and, having the range, inflicted some loss on my line. We had no guns to reply, and, in advance as has been mentioned, had outmarched the troops behind us. Motionless as a statue, Jackson sat his horse some few yards away, and seemed lost in thought. Perhaps the circumstances mentioned some pages back had obscured his star; but if so, a few short hours swept away the cloud, and it blazed, Sirius-like, over the land. I approached him with the suggestion that the railway bridge might be passed by stepping on the cross-ties, as the enemy's guns bore less directly on it than on the upper bridge. He nodded approval.

The 8th regiment was on the right of my line, near at hand; and dismounting, Colonel Kelly led it across under a sharp musketry fire. Several men fell to disappear in the dark water beneath; but the movement continued with great rapidity, considering the difficulty of walking on ties, and Kelly with his leading files gained the opposite shore. Thereupon the enemy fired combustibles previously placed near the center of the wagon bridge. The loss of this structure would have seriously delayed us, as the railway bridge was not floored, and I looked at Jackson, who, near by, was watching Kelly's progress. Again he nodded, and my command rushed at the bridge. Concealed by the cloud of smoke, the suddenness of the movement saved us from much loss; but it was rather a near thing. My horse and clothing were scorched, and many men burned their hands severely while throwing brands into the river. We were soon over, and the enemy in full flight to Winchester, with loss of camp, guns, and prisoners.

Just as I emerged from flames and smoke, Jackson was by my side. How he got there was a mystery, as the bridge was thronged with my men going at full speed; but smoke and fire had decidedly freshened up his costume. . . .

Late in the night Jackson came out of the darkness and seated himself by my camp fire. He mentioned that I would move with him in the morning, then relapsed into silence. I fancied he looked at me kindly, and interpreted it into an approval of the conduct of the brigade. The events of the day, anticipations of the morrow, . . . drove away sleep, and I watched Jackson. For hours he sat silent and motionless, with eyes fixed on the fire. I took up the idea that he was inwardly praying, and he remained through the night.

Off in the morning, Jackson leading the way, my brigade, a small body of horse, and a section of the Rockbridge (Virginia) artillery forming the column. Major Wheat, with his battalion of "Tigers," was directed to keep close to the guns. Sturdy marchers, they trotted along with the horse and artillery at Jackson's heels, and after several hours were some distance in advance of the brigade, with which I remained.

A volley in front, followed by wild cheers, stirred us up to a "double," and we speedily came upon a moving spectacle. Jackson had struck the Valley pike at Middletown, twelve miles south of Winchester, along which a large body of Federal horse, with many wagons, was hastening north. He had attacked at once with his handful of men, overwhelmed resistance, and captured prisoners and wagons. The gentle Tigers were looting right merrily, diving in and out of wagons with the activity of rabbits in a warren; but this occupation was abandoned on my approach, and in a moment they were in line, looking as solemn and virtuous as deacons at a funeral. Prisoners and spoil were promptly secured. . . .

At dusk we overtook Jackson, pushing the enemy with his little mounted force, himself in advance of all. I rode with him, and we kept on through the darkness. There was not resistance enough to deploy infantry. A flash, a report, and a whistling bullet from some covert met us, but there were few casualties. I quite remember thinking at the time that Jackson was invulnerable, and that persons near him shared that quality. An officer, riding hard, overtook us, who proved to be the chief quartermaster of the army. He reported the wagon trains far behind, impeded by a bad road in Luray Valley.

"The ammunition wagons?" sternly.

"All right, sir. They were in advance, and I doubled teams on them and brought them through."

"Ah!" in a tone of relief.

To give countenance to this quartermaster, if such can be given of a dark night, I remarked jocosely: "Never mind the wagons. There are quantities of store in Winchester, and the General has invited me to breakfast there to-morrow."

Jackson, who had no more capacity for jests than a Scotchman, took this seriously, and reached out to touch me on the arm. In fact, he was of Scotch-Irish descent, and his unconsciousness of jokes was *de race*. Without physical wants himself, he forgot that others were differently constituted, and paid little heed to commissariat; but woe to the man who failed to bring up ammunition! In advance, his trains were left far behind. In retreat, he would fight for a wheelbarrow.

Some time after midnight, by roads more direct from Front Royal, other troops came on the pike, and I halted my jaded people by the roadside, where they built fires and took a turn at their haversacks.

Moving with the first light of morning, we came to Kernstown, three miles from Winchester, and the place of Jackson's fight with Shields. Here heavy and sustained firing, artillery and small arms, was heard. A staff officer approached at full speed to summon me to Jackson's presence and move up my command. A gallop of a mile or more brought me to him. Winchester was in sight, a mile to the north. To the east Ewell with a large part of the army was fighting briskly and driving the enemy on to the town. On the west a high ridge, overlooking the country to the south and southeast, was occupied by a heavy mass of Federals with guns in position. Jackson was on the pike, and near him were several regiments lying down for shelter, as the fire from the ridge was heavy and searching. A Virginian battery, Rockbridge artillery, was fighting at a great disadvantage, and already much cut up. Poetic authority asserts that "Old Virginny never tires," and the conduct of this battery justified the assertion of the muses. With scarce a leg or wheel for man and horse, gun or caisson, to stand on, it continued to hammer away at the crushing fire above.

Jackson, impassive as ever, pointed to the ridge and said, "You must carry it." I replied that my command would be up by the time I could inspect the ground, and rode to the left for that purpose. A small stream, Abraham's creek, flowed from the west through the little vale at the southern base of the ridge, the ascent of which was steep, though nowhere abrupt. At one point a broad, shallow, trough-like depression broke the surface, which was further interrupted by some low copse, outcropping stone, and two fences. On the summit the Federal lines were posted behind a stone wall, along a road coming west from the pike. Worn somewhat into the soil, this road served as a countersink and strengthened the position. Further west, there was a break in the ridge, which was occupied by a body of horse, the extreme right of the enemy's line.

There was scarce time to mark these features before the head of my column appeared, when it was filed to the left, close to the base of the ridge, for protection from the plunging fire. Meanwhile, the Rockbridge battery held on manfully and engaged the enemy's attention. Riding on the flank of my column, between it and the hostile line, I saw Jackson beside me. This was not the place for the commander of the army, and I ventured to tell him so; but he paid no attention to the remark. We reached the shallow depression spoken of, where the enemy could depress his guns, and his fire became close and fatal. Many men fell, and the whistling of shot and shell occasioned much ducking of heads in the column. This annoyed me no little, as it was but child's play to the work immediately in hand. Always an admirer of delightful "Uncle Toby," I had contracted the most villainous habit of his beloved army in Flanders, and, forgetting Jackson's presence, ripped out, "What the h— are you dodging for? If there is any more of it, you will be halted under this fire for an hour."

The sharp tones of a familiar voice produced the desired effect, and the men looked as if they had swallowed ramrods; but I shall never forget the reproachful surprise expressed in Jackson's face. He placed his hand on my shoulder, said in a gentle voice, "I am afraid you are a wicked fellow," turned, and rode back to the pike.

The proper ground gained, the column faced to the front and began the ascent. At the moment the sun rose over the Blue Ridge, without cloud or mist to obscure his rays. It was a lovely Sabbath morning, the 25th of May, 1862. The clear, pure atmosphere brought the Blue Ridge and Alleghany and Massanutten almost overhead. Even the cloud of murderous smoke from the guns above made beautiful spirals in the air, and the broad fields of luxuriant wheat glistened with dew. . . .

As we mounted we came in full view of both armies, whose efforts in other quarters had been slackened to await the result of our movement. I felt an anxiety amounting to pain for the brigade to acquit itself handsomely; and this feeling was shared by every man in it. About half way up, the enemy's horse from his right charged; and to meet it, I directed Lieutenant-Colonel Nicholls, whose regiment, the 8th, was on the left, to withhold slightly his two flank companies. By one volley, which emptied some saddles, Nicholls drove off the horse, but was soon after severely wounded. Progress was not stayed by this incident. Closing the many gaps made by the fierce fire, steadied the rather by it, and preserving an alignment that would have been creditable on parade, the brigade, with cadenced step and eyes on the foe, swept grandly over copse and ledge and fence, to crown the heights from which the enemy had melted away. Loud cheers went up from our army, prolonged to the east, where warm-hearted Ewell cheered himself hoarse, and led forward his men with renewed energy. In truth, it was a gallant feat of arms, worthy of the pen of him who immortalized the charge of the "Buffs" at Albuera.

Breaking into column, we pursued closely. Jackson came up and grasped my hand, worth a thousand words from another, and we were soon in the streets of Winchester, a quaint old town of some five thousand inhabitants. There was a little fighting in the streets, but the people were all abroad— certainly all the women and babies. They were frantic with delight, only regretting that so many "Yankees" had escaped, and seriously impeded our movements.

A buxom, comely dame of some five and thirty summers, with bright eyes and tight ankles, and conscious of these advantages, was especially demonstrative, exclaiming, "Oh! you are too late—too late!"

Whereupon, a tall creole from the Teche sprang from the ranks of the 8th regiment, just passing, clasped her in his arms, and imprinted a sounding kiss on her ripe lips, with "*Madame! je n'arrive jamais trop tard.*" A loud laugh followed, and the dame, with a rosy face but merry twinkle in her eye, escaped.

—Taylor, *Destruction and Reconstruction*

3. TAYLOR'S IRISHMEN CAPTURE A BATTERY AT PORT REPUBLIC

The climax of the Valley campaign came on June 8 and 9 with the battles of Cross Keys on the north and Port Republic on the south bank of the Shenandoah. Confronted by two armies—one under Frémont, the other under

Shields—Jackson, instead of retreating, struck each of them separately. At Cross Keys, on June 8, Ewell checked Frémont while on the following day Ewell and Taylor broke the strongly entrenched Union line at Port Republic, and forced the enemy back to Conrad's Store, some five miles down the river. It was, as Jackson said, a "delightful excitement."

EWELL, in immediate charge at Cross Keys, was ready early in the morning of the 8th, when Fremont attacked. The ground was undulating, with much wood, and no extended view could be had. In my front the attack, if such it could be called, was feeble in the extreme—an affair of skirmishers, in which the enemy yielded to the slightest pressure.

A staff officer of Jackson's, in hot haste, came with orders from his chief to march my brigade double-quick to Port Republic. Elzey's brigade, in second line to the rear, was asked to take my place and relieve my skirmishers; then, advising the staff officer to notify Ewell, whom he had not seen, we started on the run, for such a message from Jackson meant business. Two of the intervening miles were quickly passed, when another officer appeared with orders to halt.

In half an hour, during which the sound of battle at Cross Keys thickened, Jackson came. . . . He had passed the night in the village, with his staff and escort. Up as usual at dawn, he started alone to recross the bridge, leaving his people to follow. The bridge was a few yards below the last house in the village, and some mist overhung the river. Under cover of this a small body of horse, with one gun, from Shields's forces, had reached the east end of the bridge and trained the gun on it. Jackson was within an ace of capture. As he spurred across, the gun was fired on him, but without effect, and the sound brought up staff and escort, when the horse retired north. This incident occasioned the order to me. After relating it (all save his own danger), Jackson passed on to Ewell. Thither I followed, to remain in reserve until the general forward movement in the afternoon, by which Fremont was driven back with loss of prisoners. We did not persist far, as Shields's force was near upon us.

From Ewell I learned that there had been some pretty fighting in the morning, though less than might have been expected from Fremont's numbers. I know not if the presence of this commander had a benumbing influence on his troops, but certainly his advanced cavalry and infantry had proved bold and enterprising.

In the evening we moved to the river and camped. Winder's and other brigades crossed the bridge, and during the night Ewell, with most of the army, drew near, leaving Trimble's brigade and the horse at Cross Keys. No one apprehended another advance by Fremont. The following morning, Sunday, June 9, my command passed the bridge, moved several hundred yards down the road, and halted. Our trains had gone east over the Blue Ridge. The sun appeared above the mountain while the men were quietly breakfasting. Suddenly, from below, was heard the din of battle, loud and sustained, artillery and small arms. The men sprang into ranks, formed column, and marched, and I galloped forward a short mile to see the following scene:

From the mountain, clothed to its base with undergrowth and timber, a level—clear, open, and smooth—extended to the river. This plain was some thousand yards in width. Half a mile north, a gorge, through which flowed a small stream, cut the mountain at a right angle. The northern shoulder of this gorge projected farther into the plain than the southern, and on an elevated plateau of the shoulder were placed six guns, sweeping every inch of the plain to the south. Federal lines, their right touching the river, were advancing steadily, with banners flying and arms gleaming in the sun. A gallant show, they came on. Winder's and another brigade, with a battery, opposed them. This small force was suffering cruelly, and its skirmishers were driven in on their thin supporting line. As my Irishmen predicted, "Shields's boys were after fighting." Below, Ewell was hurrying his men over the bridge, but it looked as if we should be doubled up on him ere he could cross and develop much strength.

Jackson was on the road, a little in advance of his line, where the fire was hottest, with reins on his horse's neck, seemingly in prayer. Attracted by my approach, he said, in his usual voice, "Delightful excitement." I replied that it was pleasant to learn he was enjoying himself, but thought he might have an indigestion of such fun if the six-gun battery was not silenced. He summoned a young officer from his staff, and pointed up the mountain.

The head of my approaching column was turned short up the slope, and speedily came to a path running parallel with the river. We took this path, the guide leading the way. From him I learned that the plateau occupied by the battery had been used for a charcoal kiln, and the path we were follow-ing, made by the burners in hauling wood, came upon the gorge opposite the battery. Moving briskly, we reached the hither side a few yards from the guns. Infantry was posted near, and riflemen were in the undergrowth on the slope above. Our approach, masked by timber, was unexpected. The battery was firing rapidly, enabled from elevation to fire over the advancing lines. The head of my column began to deploy under cover for attack, when the sounds of battle to our rear appeared to recede, and a loud Federal cheer was heard, proving Jackson to be hard pressed.

It was rather an anxious moment, demanding instant action. Leaving a staff officer to direct my rear regiment—the 7th, Colonel Hays—to form in the wood as a reserve, I ordered the attack, though the deployment was not completed, and our rapid march by a narrow path had occasioned some disorder. With a rush and shout the gorge was passed and we were in the battery. Surprise had aided us, but the enemy's infantry rallied in a moment and drove us out. We returned, to be driven a second time. The riflemen on the slope worried us no little, and two companies of the 9th regiment were sent up the gorge to gain ground above and dislodge them, which was accomplished. The fighting in and around the battery was hand to hand, and many fell from bayonet wounds. Even the artillerymen used their rammers in a way not laid down in the Manual, and died at their guns. As Conan said to the devil, " 'Twas claw for claw." I called for Hays, but he, the promptest of men, and his splendid regiment, could not be found. Something unexpected had occurred, but there was no time for speculation. With a desperate rally, in which I believe the drummer-boys shared, we carried the battery for the third time, and held it.

Infantry and riflemen had been driven off, and we began to feel a little comfortable, when the enemy, arrested in his advance by our attack, appeared. He had countermarched, and, with left near the river, came into full view of our situation. Wheeling to the right, with colors advanced, like a solid wall he marched straight upon us. There seemed nothing left but to set our backs to the mountain and die hard. At the instant, crashing through the underwood, came Ewell, outriding staff and escort. He produced the effect of a reenforcement, and was welcomed with cheers. The line before us halted and threw forward skirmishers. A moment later, a shell came shrieking along it, loud Confederate cheers reached our delighted ears, and Jackson, freed from his toils, rushed up like a whirlwind, the enemy in rapid retreat. We turned the captured guns on them as they passed, Ewell serving as a gunner.

Though rapid, the retreat never became a rout. Fortune had refused her smiles, but Shields's brave "boys" preserved their organization and were formidable to the last; and had Shields himself, with his whole command, been on the field, we should have had tough work indeed.

Jackson came up, with intense light in his eyes, grasped my hand, and said the brigade should have the captured battery. I thought the men would go mad with cheering, especially the Irishmen. A huge fellow, with one eye closed and half his whiskers burned by powder, was riding cock-horse on a gun, and, catching my attention, yelled out, "We told you to bet on your boys."

—TAYLOR, *Destruction and Reconstruction*

4. GENERAL LAW DESCRIBES JACKSON AT SEVEN DAYS

As soon as Jackson had achieved the purpose of the Valley campaign— holding strong Federal forces in the Valley and preventing the reinforcement of McClellan—he hastened to join Lee to take part in the battles that were to drive McClellan from Richmond.

General Law, who here gives us a vivid picture of "Stonewall" at the height of his popularity, we have met before.

HERE, too, I saw General Jackson for the first time since I had seen him in the heat of the fight at the battle of Manassas. He passed our division on the march, and for a time no one seemed to know who he was. As soon as he was recognized, however, a general shout was raised for "Old Stonewall," which continued as long as he was in sight. He was mounted on a very ordinary sorrel horse, whose appearance indicated rather short rations. His uniform was well-worn, faded, and covered with the yellow dust which was plentiful along the line of march. His cap, originally blue, but now faded and dusty, was of the style then known as the "Beauregard," the crown falling forward upon the visor which nearly touched the point of his nose. He certainly needed the new uniform presented to him shortly afterward by the ladies of Richmond. An ordinary saber with an iron scabbard completed his equipment. He was not a graceful rider, and sat his horse carelessly. He looked neither to the right nor to the left, but straight forward, as if that was the one direction in which he cared to think or move. The square and massive lower jaw, covered with a short, thick beard, the firm, set lips, and the preoccupied expression of his whole face were forcibly suggestive of his *nom de guerre*, "Stonewall," in their firmness as well as inscrutability.

A few days later, June 26th, as we were approaching McClellan's lines in rear of Mechanicsville, I went to report to General Whiting the result of a *reconnoissance* that had been ordered on our left flank as we advanced. I found him at the edge of the field near the road, in company with General Jackson. Jackson was leaning carelessly against a fence which separated the field from the adjacent woods. They were both perfectly silent, not a word passing between them, and, so far as I could judge from their attitudes, had been so from the time I came in sight. When I had made my report, Jackson asked a question or two and again relapsed into silence, which was unbroken by a word until I left them. But this plain, silent soldier, as he appeared on the march, was not always the same. At the first sounds of approaching battle, his whole appearance changed; his movements became quick and energetic; his eyes seemed to gleam with a fierce joy, and every muscle became tense with the fire that burned within. And when he led a regiment or a brigade to the charge, which he sometimes did, he became the very incarnation of battle. He was "a man of iron and fire," enthusiastically admired by his men, almost invariably successful in his undertakings, and one of the very few Confederate commanders who knew how to improve a victory.

—LAW, "The Fight for Richmond"

5. COLONEL WOLSELEY VISITS STONEWALL JACKSON

Fresh from campaigns in the Crimea, India and China, Colonel Garnet Wolseley—later Lord Wolseley—was ordered to Canada as quartermaster general in December 1861. In August of the next year he applied for leave of absence and, without the approval of his superiors, made his way into the Confederate States and visited scenes of recent battles, and the headquarters of Lee and Jackson. Already favorable to the Confederate cause, his enthusiasm was confirmed by what he saw. His account of his month's visit to Confederate Headquarters, which appeared anonymously in Blackwood's Magazine, *aroused widespread interest in Britain and America.*

UPON leaving, we drove to Bunker's Hill, six miles nearer Martinsburg, at which place Stonewall Jackson, now of world-wide celebrity, had his headquarters. With him we spent a most pleasant hour, and were agreeably surprised to find him very affable, having been led to expect that he was silent and almost morose. Dressed in his grey uniform, he looks the hero that he is; and his thin compressed lips and calm glance, which meets yours unflinchingly, give evidence of that firmness and decision of character for which he is so famous. He has a broad open forehead, from which the hair is well brushed back; a shapely nose, straight, and rather long; thin colourless cheeks, with only a very small allowance of whisker; a cleanly-shaven upper lip and chin; and a pair of fine greyish-blue eyes, rather sunken, with overhanging brows, which intensify the keenness of his gaze, but without imparting any fierceness to it. Such are the general characteristics of his face; and I have only to add, that a smile seems always lurking about his mouth when he speaks; and that though his voice partakes slightly of that harshness which Europeans unjustly attribute to *all* Americans, there is much unmistakable cordiality in his manner: and to us he talked most affectionately of England, and of his brief but enjoyable sojourn there.

The religious element seems strongly developed in him; and though his conversation is perfectly free from all puritanical cant, it is evident that he is a person who never loses sight of the fact that there is an omnipresent Deity ever presiding over the minutest occurrences of life, as well as over the most important.

Altogether, as one of his soldiers said to me in talking of him, "he is a glorious fellow!" and, after I left him, I felt that I had at last solved the mystery of Stonewall Bridge, and discovered why it was that it had accomplished such almost miraculous feats. With such a leader men would go anywhere, and face any amount of difficulties; and for myself, I believe that, inspired by the presence of such a man, I should be perfectly insensible to fatigue, and reckon upon success as a moral certainty.

Whilst General Lee is regarded in the light of infallible Jove, a man to be reverenced, Jackson is loved and adored with all that childlike and trustful affection which the ancients are said to have lavished upon the particular deity presiding over their affairs. The feeling of the soldiers for General Lee resembles that which Wellington's troops entertained for him—namely, a fixed and unshakable faith in all he did, and a calm confidence of victory when serving under him. But Jackson, like Napoleon, is idolised with that intense fervour which, consisting of mingled personal attachment and devoted loyalty, causes them to meet death for his sake, and bless him when dying.

—[WOLSELEY], "A Month's Visit to Confederate Headquarters"

6. STONEWALL JACKSON GETS A NEW UNIFORM

Heros von Borcke, who gives us this delightful anecdote of Jackson and his new uniform, was one of the most picturesque figures in the Confederate Army. A Prussian nobleman and professional soldier, he obtained leave of absence from the staff of the Prince of Prussia, ran the blockade, and was promptly made Stuart's chief of staff. Gigantic in stature, lusty, gay, reckless, yet withal a good soldier, he was known in the South as "Major Bandbox." Stuart wanted Von Borcke to succeed to his own command, but instead the Confederacy sent him, in 1864, on a futile mission to England. His Memoirs of the Confederate War *are hard to beat for color and excitement. This episode occurred in September 1862.*

FROM a long rest, after the dissipations of the past night, I was roused about noon by General Stuart, with orders to ride, upon some little matters of duty, to the camp of General Jackson. I was also honoured with the pleasing mission of presenting to old Stonewall, as a slight token of Stuart's high regard, a new and very "stunning" uniform coat, which had just arrived from the hands of a Richmond tailor. The garment, neatly wrapped up, was borne on the pommel of his saddle by one of our couriers who accompanied me; and starting at once I reached the simple tent of our great general just in time for dinner. I found him in his old weather-stained coat, from which all the buttons had been clipped long since by the fair hands of patriotic ladies, and which, from exposure to sun and rain and powder-smoke, and by reason of many rents and patches, was in a very unseemly condition.

When I had despatched more important matters, I produced General Stuart's present, in all its magnificence of gilt buttons and sheeny facings and gold lace, and I was heartily amused at the modest confusion with which the hero of many battles regarded the fine uniform from many points of view, scarcely daring to touch it, and at the quiet way in which, at last, he folded it up carefully, and deposited it in his portmanteau, saying to me, "Give Stuart my best thanks my dear Major—the coat is much too handsome for me, but I shall take the best care of it, and shall prize it highly as a souvenir. And now let us have some dinner." But I protested energetically against this summary disposition of the matter of the coat, deeming my mission, indeed, but half executed, and remarked that Stuart would certainly ask me how the uniform fitted its owner, and that I should, therefore, take it as a personal favour if he would put it on.

To this he readily assented with a smile, and having donned the garment, he escorted me outside the tent to the table where dinner had been served in the open air. The whole of the Staff were in a perfect ecstasy at their chief's brilliant appearance, and the old Negro servant, who was bearing the roast-turkey from the fire to the board, stopped in mid-career with a most bewildered expression, and gazed in wonderment at his master as if he had been transfigured before him. Meanwhile, the rumour of the change ran like electricity through the neighboring camps, and the soldiers came running by hundreds to the spot, desirous of seeing their beloved Stonewall in his new attire; and the first wearing of a fresh robe by Louis XIV., at whose morning toilet all the world was accustomed to assemble, never created half the sensation at Versailles, that was made in the woods of Virginia by the investment of Jackson in this new regulation uniform.

—VON BORCKE, *Memoirs of the Confederate War for Independence*

7. HENRY KYD DOUGLAS REMEMBERS STONEWALL JACKSON

Henry Kyd Douglas, whose reminiscences give us the liveliest and fullest picture of Jackson that we have from any contemporary, was practicing law in St. Louis when the war broke out. Hastening home he enlisted as a private in the 2nd Virginia Regiment—part of the Stonewall Brigade. He was later aide-de-camp to Jackson, and fought with him until his death at Chancellorsville. Douglas rose to be brigadier general—the youngest in either army, it is said—and his brigade fired the last shot and was the last to surrender at Appomattox.

IN face and figure Jackson was not striking. Above the average height, with a frame angular, muscular, and fleshless, he was, in all his movements from riding a horse to handling a pen, the most awkward man in the army. His expression was thoughtful, and, as a result I fancy of his long ill health, was generally clouded with an air of fatigue. His eye was small, blue, and in repose as gentle as a young girl's. With high, broad, forehead, small sharp nose, thin, pallid lips generally tightly shut, deep-set eyes, dark, rusty beard, he was certainly not a handsome man. His face in tent or parlor, softened by his sweet smile, was as different from itself on the battlefield as a little lake in summer noon differs from the same lake when frozen. Walking or riding the General was ungainly: his main object was to get over the ground. He rode boldly and well, but not with grace or ease; and "Little Sorrel" was as little like a Pegasus as he was like an Apollo. He was not a man of style. General Lee, on horseback or off, was the handsomest man I ever saw. It was said of Wade Hampton that he looked as knightly when mounted as if he had stepped out from an old canvas, horse and all. John C. Breckinridge was a model of manly beauty, John B. Gordon, a picture for the sculptor, and Joe Johnston looked every inch a soldier. None of these things could be said of Jackson.

The enemy believed he never slept. In fact he slept a great deal. Give him five minutes to rest, he could sleep three of them. Whenever he had nothing else to do he went to sleep, especially in church. He could sleep in any position, in a chair, under fire, or on horseback. Being a silent man, he gave to sleep many moments which other men gave to conversation. And yet he was never caught "napping."

He was quiet, not morose. He often smiled, rarely laughed. He never told a joke but rather liked to hear one, now and then. He did not live apart from his personal staff, although they were nearly all young; he liked to have them about, especially at table. He encouraged the liveliness of their conversation at meals, although he took little part in it. His own words seemed to embarrass him, unless he could follow his language by action. As he never told his plans, he never discussed them. He didn't offer advice to his superiors, nor ask it of his subordinates. Reticent and self-reliant he believed "he walks with speed who walks alone." The officer next in command often and very justly complained of this risky reticence; but Jackson is reported to have said, "If my coat knew what I intended to do, I'd take it off and throw it away." Such reticence at times was neither judicious nor defensible; but luck saved him from evil consequences. . . .

On the battlefield where Longstreet's doughty men were confronting a stubborn foe and A. P. Hill, as usual, was doing his share of the fighting, soldiers heard the cannonade and were encouraged in their hot work. Soon came to them a sharper and more earnest clamor, and there was such a rattle and roar of musketry as I never heard before or after. A staff officer dashed along Longstreet's wearied lines, crying out, "Stonewall's at them!" and was answered with yell after yell of joy, which added a strange sound to the din of battle. The battle was on in earnest; skirmishing died away and was succeeded by the crash of line meeting line.

General Jackson mounted his gaunt sorrel (not "Little Sorrel") and leaving his position moved more to the front. At that moment someone handed him a lemon—a fruit of which he was specially fond. Immediately a small piece was bitten out of it and slowly and unsparingly he began to extract its flavor and its juice. From that moment until darkness ended the battle, that lemon scarcely left his lips except to be used as a baton to emphasize an order. He listened to Yankee shout or Rebel yell, to the sound of musketry advancing or receding, to all the signs of promise or apprehension, but he never for an instant lost his interest in that lemon and even spoke of its excellence. His face, nevertheless, was calm and granite-like. His blue eye was restful and cold, except when now and then it gave, for a moment, an ominous flash. His right hand lay open and flat on his thigh, but now and then was raised into the air as was his habit—a gesture which the troops learned to believe was as significant as the extended arm of Aaron. But the lemon was not abandoned.

The moment came when it was taken from his mouth with an impatient jerk. A wild yell came from the battlefield which attracted his attention. Pendleton came up and said it was from the Stonewall Brigade, for he had just seen Winder taking them in. He drew the lemon away abruptly and said, "We shall soon have good news from that charge. Yes, they are driving the enemy!" and he lifted up his yellow banner, as if in triumph. When I last saw that lemon, it was torn open and exhausted and thrown away, but the day was over and the battle was won. . . .

The 6th of July [1862] was a very warm day. The General had returned from his morning ride to the front and was trying to make himself comfortable. Headquarters were in bivouac. He seated himself at the foot of a large tree to take a nap—he could always go to sleep when he had nothing else to do. After a very short rest he aroused himself and asked me if I had a novel. I did not have one, nor did any of the staff, as all books had been left in the vicinity of Mechanicsville with the wagons. He said he had not read a novel for a long time before the war. Hugh McGuire, a clerk at Headquarters, afterwards Captain in T. L. Rosser's Cavalry Brigade, handed me a yellow-back novel of the sensational type, saying he had picked it up on the battle-field. It looked like literary trash, and it was—sensational and full of wood cuts. I handed it to the General, who looked at it with a smile, seated him-self again at the foot of the tree, and began to read it. He gave his whole attention to it, as if it was a duty not to give it up, and waded on through it. Now and then his features would relax and smile, but he did not take his eyes from the book. He did not speak a word but kept on until he had finished it; fortunately, it was a small paper volume of large print. He then returned it with thanks, saying it had been a long time since he had read a novel and it would be a long time until he read another. This was the only book not strictly military or religious that I ever saw him attempt to read in the army.

On the 8th of July [1862] the Army of Northern Virginia began to move back to the vicinity of Richmond. When Jackson's command started he and his staff remained behind until some time after the rest of the army had gone. It was after dark when he started and about midnight when he reached his Headquarters. He was riding along at ten or eleven o'clock with his drowsy staff, nodding on "Little Sorrel," as was his custom, and trusting to that intelligent beast not to give him a fall. More than once did we see his head nod and drop on his breast and his body sway a little to one side or the other, expecting to see him get a tumble; but he never got it. On this occa-sion our sleepy cavalcade at different times passed small squads of soldiers in fence corners before blazing fires, roasting green corn and eating it. Passing one of these, our staggering leader was observed by one of those thirsty stragglers, who was evidently delighted at the sight of a drunken cavalry-man. Perhaps encouraged with the hope of a drink ahead, the ragged Reb jumped up from his fire and, brandishing a roasting-ear in his hand, sprang into the road and to the head of the General's horse, with, "Hello! I say, old fellow, where the devil did you get your licker?"

The General suddenly woke up and said, "Dr. McGuire, did you speak to me? Captain Pendleton, did you? Somebody did," and reined up his horse.

The soldier got a look at him and took in the situation; he saw whom he had thus spoken to. "Good God! it's Old Jack!" he cried, and with several bounds and a flying leap he had cleared the road, was over the fence, and disappeared in the dark.

As soon as the staff could recover from their laughter, McGuire explained the situation to the General, who was much amused. He immediately rode up to the fence, dismounted, and took half an hour's nap. Then he roused himself, said he felt better, and we went on to Headquarters. . . .

Under orders from General Leee, General Jackson left his camp at Richmond for Gordonsville about the 14th of July. General John Pope, Commander of the Army of Virginia, was gathering his forces for an ad-vance from the vicinity of Washington. He had settled himself "in the saddle" and from that contracted Headquarters had fulminated his cele-brated proclamation in the shape of a general order, for which he was afterward ridiculed by the pen and punished by the sword. Believing that Jackson was not likely to be scared by so much military fustian, General Lee sent him to look after his advancing Hannibal. The General went on in advance and we were soon far ahead of troops and wagon trains on the road to Ashland.

About sundown of the first day, we were driven temporarily into a blacksmith shop for shelter from a rain storm, and from there sent out to seek shelter for the night. We found it in a most hospitable house where a plentiful supper, good rooms, and pleasant beds were made doubly enjoyable by the easy and sincere hospitality of host and hostess. The next morning we were in Ashland early and had sundry invitations to breakfast. The General seemed in excellent humor and unusually talkative. While waiting for breakfast he sat in the parlor, amused himself and others as well by his attempts to be playful with a prattling little girl who was running about the room, and then again listened with most respectful attention to a young lady who was at the piano, giving us such songs and instrumental music as she thought to our taste. Now the General had the least possible knowledge of music and, as was said of him, he had so little of it in his soul, that he was necessarily "fit for treason, strategy and spoils." Still it was a matter of amazement to his staff, when he said with much politeness to the young lady, "Miss ——, won't you play a piece of music they call 'Dixie'? I heard it a few days ago and it was, I thought, very beautiful."

The young lady was nonplussed and answered, "Why, General, I just sang it a few minutes ago—it is about our oldest war song."

"Ah, indeed, I didn't know it."

He had heard it a thousand times. Perhaps he thought he would startle the young lady with his knowledge of music; if so, he succeeded. . . .

One night, after the middle of it, General Stuart came riding into our Headquarters, accompanied by his artillery pet, Captain John Pelham, the "boy Major," as he was afterwards called, or "the gallant Pelham," as General Lee named him at Fredericksburg. . . . Everyone had gone to rest. Stuart went directly to General Jackson's tent; Pelham came into mine. The General was asleep and the cavalry chief threw himself down by his side, taking off nothing but his sabre. As the night became chilly, so did he, and unconsciously he began to take possession of blankets and got between the sheets. There he discovered himself in the early morn in the full panoply of war, and he got out of it. After a while, when a lot of us were standing by a blazing log-fire before the General's tent, he came out for his ablutions.

"Good morning, General Jackson," said Stuart, "how are you?"

Old Jack passed his hands through his thin and uncombed hair and then in tones as nearly comic as he could muster he said, "General Stuart, I'm always glad to see you here. You might select better hours sometimes, but I'm always glad to have you. But, General"—as he stooped and rubbed himself along the legs—"you must not get into my bed with your boots and spurs on and ride me around like a cavalry horse all night!"

—Douglas, *I Rode with Stonewall*

VI

Second Bull Run and Antietam

THE *Peninsular campaign was indecisive. Lee had saved Richmond, but at heavy cost, and McClellan was at Harrison's Landing preparing to renew the contest. But Lincoln and Halleck, who in July had been appointed Military Adviser to the President, had different plans. They had lost confidence in McClellan and wanted to try a different commander; they decided that the scattered armies in Virginia ought to be consolidated into one great fighting force. First the armies of the Valley were consolidated under John Pope, who had won a somewhat dubious reputation in the West; then Burnside was ordered north from Fortress Monroe to Falmouth; finally McClellan was directed to bring his great army to Alexandria and unite with Pope.*

There was only one serious flaw in this plan: it ignored Lee and the Army of Northern Virginia. While the Union commanders were carrying through these complicated operations, Lee determined to strike. His forces were so small that he could not hope to contest with a united Federal army, but he could strike the scattered armies singly. And for this he had the great advantage of interior lines of communication.

Leaving only a few brigades to protect Richmond Lee started his army toward the Valley. There was a sharp fight at Cedar Mountain near Culpeper Court House, where Jackson inflicted heavy losses on the hapless Banks. Then while Pope was trying to concentrate his forces along the Rapidan, Jackson swung around his rear and on August 26 destroyed Pope's headquarters and supply depots at Manassas Junction. Pope fatuously supposed that he had Jackson in a trap and hurried to close it. Jackson marched west to Groveton and invited the attack of Pope's forces. On August 29 Pope finally caught up with Stonewall and all day long wore out his army in desperate assaults on Jackson's iron lines. Meanwhile Longstreet was hurrying up the valley between the Blue Ridge and the Bull Run Mountains. On the twenty-ninth he turned east, forced Thoroughfare Gap—which Pope had left practically undefended—and the next day struck Pope's left flank, rolled it up, and sent the whole army reeling toward Bull Run.

The battle ended in a cloud of recriminations, and no wonder. Porter's corps had stood idle the whole afternoon of the twenty-ninth; Banks's 6,500 men had taken no part in the fight; McClellan, at near-by Alexandria, had failed to get any part of his large army to Pope in time to do any good. Porter was later made the scapegoat for all this tragedy of errors, but the real failure was Pope's and McClellan's.

On August 3 Pope withdrew to the defenses of Washington, and two days later McClellan supplanted him as commander of the Army of the

Potomac. Lee now determined to carry the war to the North. He knew that his army was in no condition to wage an aggressive campaign, but he hoped that an invasion of the North might be effected without any major battle and that it might accomplish many things. He hoped to cut the B. & O. and possibly the Pennsylvania Railroad, thus temporarily isolating Washington; to reprovision his troops—many of them without shoes; to relieve pressure on Virginia; to bring foreign recognition.

In the first week of September, then, Lee's butternuts were splashing across the fords of the Potomac onto the shores of Maryland. "Virginia shall not call in vain," James Randall had written in the song that every Southerner was singing, but it did: Lee lost more soldiers by straggling and desertion than he gained. His ultimate objective was probably Harrisburg and he planned originally to move his army north between the Catoctin and South Mountains into Pennsylvania. To make sure of his communications he detached half his force under Jackson to take Harpers Ferry. Thus by September 13 his meager force—some 50,000 at most—was badly scattered.

At this juncture fate intervened. Lee's famous Order 191 detailing the entire plan of the campaign fell into McClellan's hands. That general moved with what was for him admirable rapidity. He was convinced that Lee had an army of 120,000 men, so he observed his customary caution, but at least he did go forward. The first clashes came on September 14 at South Mountain and Crampton's Gap. Both were Federal victories, but they did not come in time to save Harpers Ferry, which fell on the morning of the fifteenth, the Confederates bagging 11,000 prisoners and an immense body of equipment.

With his rear safe Lee moved back to Sharpsburg, entrenching his army along the little Antietam creek, his flanks resting on two bends of the Potomac. He had only 18,000 men, McClellan was hot on his trail with 70,000, and prudence would have dictated a retreat. But McClellan did not attack, and the next day Jackson came up, raising Lee's forces to about 40,000: A. P. Hill was still at Harpers Ferry. The great battle came the next day and was, perhaps, the most hotly contested of the whole war. All day long the mighty hosts in blue hurled themselves on the thin gray lines, first on Jackson on the left; then on Hill at the center; then on Longstreet on the right. Again and again it seemed as if the Confederates would be overwhelmed and destroyed, but each time they managed to hang on and to inflict such losses that the final blow was suspended. When night fell McClellan still had not used his reserves, Lee had held his lines, and the battle could fairly be called a draw. Federal losses in killed and wounded were 14,000, Confederate over 11,000.

1. "WHO COULD NOT CONQUER WITH SUCH TROOPS AS THESE?"

Reinforced by A. P. Hill's division, Jackson started toward the Valley on August 7. On the ninth he reached Cedar Mountain, south of Culpeper, and there ran into Banks. Banks attacked, won some initial success, and was then thrown back and overwhelmed by superior numbers. Finding the whole of Pope's army in front of him, on the Rapidan line, Jackson fell back toward Gordonsville. After some maneuvering for position, Lee decided to send Jackson around Pope's army, and it is one phase of this great swinging movement that Robert Dabney here describes.

A distinguished clergyman and college professor, Dabney was a major on Jackson's staff and later wrote a biography of his idolized hero.

WHILE the enemy was thus deluded with the belief that the race up the Rappahannock was ended, and that he now had nothing more to do than to hold its northern bank at this place, General Jackson was preparing, under the instructions of the Commander-in-Chief, for the most adventurous and brilliant of his exploits. This was no less than to separate himself from the support of the remainder of the army, pass around Pope to the westward, and place his *corps* between him and Washington City, at Manassa's Junction. To effect this, the Rappahannock must be passed on the upper part of its course, and two forced marches made through the western quarters of the county of Fauquier, which lie between the Blue Ridge and the subsidiary range of the Bull Run Mountains. Having made a hasty and imperfect issue of rations, Jackson disembarrassed himself of all his trains, save the ambulances and the carriages for the ammunition, and left Jeffersonton early on the morning of August 25th. Marching first westward, he crossed the two branches of the Rappahannock, passed the hamlet of Orlean, and paused at night, after a march of twenty-five miles, near Salem, a village upon the Manassa's Gap Railroad. His troops had been constantly marching and fighting since the 20th; many of them had no rations, and subsisted upon the green corn gathered along the route; yet their indomitable enthusiasm and devotion knew no flagging. As the weary column approached the end of the day's march, they found Jackson, who had ridden forward, dismounted, and standing upon a great stone by the road-side.

His sun-burned cap was lifted from his brow, and he was gazing toward the west, where the splendid August sun was about to kiss the distant crest of the Blue Ridge, which stretched far away, bathed in azure and gold; and his blue eye, beaming with martial pride, returned the rays of the evening with almost equal brightness. His men burst forth into their accustomed cheers, forgetting all their fatigue at his inspiring presence; but, deprecating the tribute by a gesture, he sent an officer to request that there should be no cheering, inasmuch as it might betray their presence to the enemy. They at once repressed their applause, and passed the word down the column to their comrades: "No cheering, boys; the General requests it." But as they passed him, their eyes and gestures, eloquent with suppressed affection, silently declared what their lips were forbidden to utter. Jackson turned to his Staff, his face beaming with delight, and said: "Who could not conquer, with such troops as these?" . . .

On the morning of the 26th, he turned eastward, and passing through the

Bull Run Mountains, at Thoroughfare Gap, proceeded to Bristoe Station, on the Orange Railroad, by another equally arduous march. At Gainsville, he was joined by Stuart, with his cavalry, who now assumed the duty of guarding his right flank, and watching the main army of Pope, about Warrenton. As the Confederates approached Bristoe Station, about sunset, the roar of a railroad train proceeding eastward, was heard, and dispositions were made to arrest it, by placing the brigade of Hays, under Colonel Forno, across the track. The first train broke through the obstructions placed before it, and escaped. Two others which followed it were captured, but were found to contain nothing.

The *corps* of Jackson, had now marched fifty miles in two days. The whole army of Pope was interposed between it and its friends. They had no supplies whatever, save those which they might capture from the enemy. But they were between that enemy and his capital, and were cheered by the hope of inflicting a vital blow upon him before he escaped. This movement would be pronounced wrong, if judged by a formal and common-place application of the maxims of the military art. But it is the very prerogative of true genius to know how to modify the application of those rules according to circumstances. It might have been objected, that such a division of the Confederate army into two parts, subjected it to the risk of being beaten in detail; that while the Federal commander detained and amused one by a detachment, he would turn upon the other with the chief weight of his forces, and crush it into fragments. Had Pope been a Jackson, this danger would have been real; but because Pope was but Pope, and General Lee had a Jackson to execute the bold conception, and a Stuart to mask his movement during its progress, the risk was too small to forbid the attempt. The promptitude of General Stuart in seizing the only signal station whence the line of march could possibly be perceived, and the secrecy and rapidity of General Jackson in pursuing it, with the energy of his action when he had reached his goal, ensured the success of the movement.

—DABNEY, *Life and Campaigns of Lt. Gen. Thomas J. Jackson*

2. JACKSON OUTSMARTS AND OUTFIGHTS POPE AT MANASSAS

Jackson's plans worked out to perfection. While Pope's forces were scattered over a wide area between the Catharpin and the Cedar Run rivers, Jackson circled around through Thoroughfare Gap, captured Pope's headquarters at Manassas Junction, swung northward to Groveton and westward to Gainesville. Pope ordered his forces to concentrate at Manassas, then set out in pursuit of the elusive Jackson, wearying his men with marches and countermarches and his commanders with orders that were confusing and contradictory. On August 29 Pope's army finally converged on Jackson between Groveton and Sudley Springs and exhausted itself in savage piecemeal attacks on Stonewall's line. Meantime Longstreet was swinging through Thoroughfare Gap ready to pounce on Pope's flank.

The "rebel lieutenant" of this narrative is John Hampden Chamberlayne, a young graduate of the University of Virginia who fought through the whole war to Petersburg, then made his way west hoping to find an army that would continue the fighting.

Frederick City, Md., Saturday, Sept. 6 [1862]

My Dear Mother:

I am brimful of matter as an egg of meat. Let me try to outline our progress since my last letter—date not remembered—from Raccoon Ford—you bearing in mind that I am in A. P. Hill's division, in Jackson's corps—that corps consisting of Jackson's own division, Ewell's and Hill's. You will not think me egotistical for speaking of this corps and of the corps of Hill's division, for of them I know most, and in truth their share was, to me at least, the most memorable in the almost incredible campaign of the last fortnight.

Crossing Raccoon Ford, Jackson in front—remember, Jackson, so used, includes Hill, Ewell, and the Stonewall division—General Lee, without much opposition, reached Rappahannock River, a few miles above Rappahannock station, where a part of Longstreet's troops had a sharp fight. On Friday Evening, August twenty-second, Jackson bivouacked in Culpeper, opposite Warrenton Springs, and the same evening threw over two of Ewell's brigades. The river rose and destroyed the bridge. Saturday the bridge was rebuilt, and that night the two brigades, after some sharp fighting, were withdrawn.

On Monday morning the enemy appeared in heavy force, and the batteries of Hill's division were put in position and shelled their infantry. They retired the infantry, and bringing up a large number of batteries, threw a storm of shot and shell at us—we not replying. They must have exploded several thousand rounds, and in all, so well sheltered were we, our killed did not reach twenty. That evening Jackson's whole force moved up to Jefferson, in Culpeper County, Longstreet close to him. The enemy was completely deceived, and concluded that we had given the thing up.

Now comes the great wonder. Starting up the bank of the river on Monday, the twenty-fifth, we marched through Amosville, in Rappahannock County—still further up, crossed the Rappahannock within ten miles of the Blue Ridge, marched across open fields, by strange country paths and comfortable homesteads, by a little town in Fauquier, called Orleans, on and on, as if we would never cease—to Salem, on the Manassas Gap Railroad, reaching there after midnight. Up again by day-dawn, and still on, along the Manassas Gap road, meeting crowds—all welcoming, cheering, staring with blank amazement. So all day Tuesday, through White Plains, Haymarket, Thoroughfare Gap, in Bull Run Mountains, Gainesville, to Bristow station, on the Orange and Alexandria Railroad—making the difference from Amosville to Bristow (between forty-five and fifty miles) within the forty-eight hours. We burned up at Bristow two or three railway-trains, and moved up to Manassas Junction on Wednesday, taking our prisoners with us. Ewell's division brought up the rear, fighting all the way a force Pope had sent up from Warrenton, supposing us a cavalry party.

Upon reaching Manassas Junction, we met a brigade—the First New-Jersey—which had been sent from Alexandria on the same supposition. They were fools enough to send a flag demanding our surrender at once. Of course we scattered the brigade, killing and wounding many, and among them the Brigadier-General (Taylor,) who has since died. At the Junction was a large dépôt of stores, five or six pieces of artillery, two trains containing probably two hundred large cars loaded down with many millions of quarter-master and commissary stores. Beside these, there were very large sutlers' dépôts, full of every thing; in short, there was collected there, in the space of a square mile, an amount and variety of property such as I had never conceived of, (I speak soberly.) 'Twas a curious sight to see our ragged and famished men helping themselves to every imaginable article of luxury or necessity, whether of clothing, food, or what not. For my part, I got a tooth-brush, a box of candles, a quantity of lobster salad, a barrel of coffee, and other things which I forget. But I must hurry on, for I have not time to tell the hundredth part, and the scene utterly beggars description.

A part of us hunted that New-Jersey brigade like scattered partridges over the hills just to the right of the battle-field of the eighteenth of July, 1861, while the rest were partly plundering, partly fighting the forces coming on us from Warrenton. Our men had been living on roasted corn since crossing the Rappahannock, and we had brought no wagons, so we could carry little away of the riches before us. But the men could eat for one meal at least. So they were marched up, and as much of every thing eatable served out as they could carry. To see a starving man eating lobster-salad and drinking Rhine wine, barefooted and in tatters, was curious; the whole thing was incredible.

Our situation now was very critical. We were between Alexandria and Warrenton—between the hosts of McClellan and Pope with over eighteen thousand jaded men, for the corps had not more than that. At nightfall, fire was set to the dépôt, storehouses, the loaded trains, several, empty trains, sutlers' houses, restaurants, every thing. As the magnificent conflagration began to subside, the Stonewall or First division of Jackson's corps moved off toward the battlefield of Manassas, the other two divisions to Centreville, six miles distant.

As day broke, we came in sight of Centreville, rested a few hours, and toward evening the rear-guard of the corps crossed Bull Run at Stone Bridge—the scene of the great slaughter of last year—closely pursued by the enemy. A part of the force came up the Warrenton turnpike, and in a furious action of two hours—the last two daylight hours of Thursday, August twenty-eighth—disputed the possession of a ridge running from Sudley Church Ford to the Warrenton turnpike. We drove them off, and on Friday morning we held the ridge, in front of which runs an incomplete railroad-cut and embankment. Now, we had made a circuit from the Gap in Bull Run Mountains around to the Junction and Centerville, breaking up the railroad and destroying their stores, and returned to within six miles of the Gap, through which Longstreet must come. The enemy disputed his passage and delayed him till late in the day, and, meanwhile, they threw against our corps, all day long, vast masses of troops—Sigel's, Banks's, and Pope's own division. We got out of ammunition; we collected more from cartridge-boxes of fallen friend and foe; that gave out, and we charged with never-failing yell and steel. All day long they threw their masses on us; all day they fell back shattered and shrieking. When the sun went down, their dead were heaped in front of the incomplete railway, and we sighed with relief, for Longstreet could be seen coming into position on our right. The crisis was over; Longstreet never failed yet; but the sun went down so slowly. . . .

I am proud to have borne my humble part in these great operations—to have helped, even so little, to consummate the grand plan, whose history will be a text-book to all young soldiers, and whose magnificent success places Lee at the side of the greatest captains, Hannibal, Caesar, Eugene, Napoleon. I hope you have preserved my letters in which I have spoken of my faith in Lee. He and his round-table of generals are worthy the immortality of Napoleon and his Marshals. He moves his agencies like a god—secret, complicated, vast, resistless, complete.

—[CHAMBERLAYNE], "Narrative by a Rebel Lieutenant"

3. POPE WASTES HIS STRENGTH ON JACKSON

Had Pope been able to employ all of his available forces, or had he employed what he had properly, he might have driven Jackson from the field on August 29, or overwhelmed him. But Porter's corps, near Bristoe, failed for some reason to get into the fight; Sigel, Reynolds, Heintzelman and Reno attacked separately, McDowell came late. The result was a repulse for the Federals. Pope should have realized that Longstreet was coming up on his flank, and retired to some defensive position where he could have awaited help from McClellan. Instead he elected to renew the battle on the following day.

This account of the fighting on the twenty-ninth is from the pen of David Strother, a Virginia littérateur who went with the Union, served on the staffs of Banks, McClellan, Pope and Hunter, and ended the war with a brigadier generalship. While his account is in diary form, there is some doubt that it was actually written up from day to day, and some of his statements are probably inaccurate.

August 29, Friday.—Clear and warm. At three o'clock this morning I was aroused by Colonel Ruggles in person to carry written orders to General Fitz-John Porter, supposed to be lying at Manassas Junction, or alternatively at Bristoe. . . . Porter's orders are to move his Corps on Centreville without delay.

I started with an orderly. It was pitchy dark—so dark that I couldn't see my horse's ears—and I presently found I had wandered from the road. The orderly knew nothing, or was stupid from sleepiness, so that in endeavoring to retrieve I found myself entangled in thickets, and then wandering through the half-decayed villages of log-huts built by the rebels during their first occupation. As I got out of one of these desolate encampments I fell into another, and began to suspect I was wandering in circles, which frequently happens to people bewildered or benighted. I at length dismounted, and feeling the road got out into the open plain, where the still smouldering fires of the recent destruction served to guide me. I found no troops here, and it was broad daylight when I reached Porter's quarters at Bristoe. Entering his tent I found the handsome General lying on his cot, covered with a blanket of imitation leopard skin.

At his request I lit a candle and read the message, then handed it to him. While he coolly read it over I noted the time by his watch, which marked five o'clock and twenty minutes precisely. He then proceeded to dress himself, and continued to question me in regard to the location of the different commands and the general situation. As I was but imperfectly informed myself I could only give vague and general replies to his queries. We believed Jackson separated from the main army of Lee by a day's march at least; and General Pope desired to throw all his disposable force upon him and crush him before Lee came up. The troops were immediately ordered to cook breakfast and prepare for the march.

Meanwhile the head-quarters breakfast had been served, and I sat down with the Staff officers to partake. The General, who was busy writing dispatches on the corner of the same table, looked up and asked, How do you spell "chaos?" I spelled the word letter by letter c-h-a-o-s. He thanked me, and observed, smiling, that, by a singular lapse of memory, he often forgot the spelling of the most familiar words. . . .

I immediately took leave and started back to general head-quarters. The road was now lined with wagons, stragglers, and droves of cattle, all moving northward. From time to time at long intervals the cannon sounded, but no heavy firing yet. Arrived at Bull Run I found our camp broken up; but meeting with Lieutenant-Colonel Myers I was informed that the enemy had developed in great force near Centreville, and I must seek the General in that direction. Riding rapidly forward I found the General and Staff grouped around a house on the heights of Centreville, observing a fight which was going on some five or six miles distant in the direction of the old Bull Run battlefield. The fight was evidently thickening and extending, as could be seen by the white cumulus clouds hanging over the batteries, and the long lines of thinner smoke rising above the tree-tops.

We could furthermore see the moving dust-clouds, indicating the march of supporting columns all converging toward the centre of action. The line of the Bull Run Mountains was visible beyond and from Thoroughfare Gap, which appeared to the right of the battle-cloud. We could see the dust and reciprocal artillery-fire of our retreating and the enemy's advancing forces. Between eleven and twelve o'clock I was standing with Colonel Beckwith and commenting on these movements, when I learned that this was probably Longstreet's command forcing back Ricketts's Division from the Gap, which he had attempted to hold. I was afterward informed it was an artillery duel between the cavalry forces of Stuart and Buford. . . .

As we approached the field the pounding of the guns was tremendous, but as we were ascending the last hill that rose between us and the magnificent drama, and just beginning to snuff the sulphurous breath of battle, a Staff officer from Sigel (I think) rode up to General Pope and reported that the ammunition was failing. Immediately the General turned to me: "Captain, ride back to Centreville and hurry up all the ammunition you can find there!" I felt for a moment disgusted and mutinous, but I could not dispute the importance of my mission, so I sullenly drew rein and galloped back over the hot and dusty road. Amidst the vast accumulation of vehicles and baggage-trains at Centreville I should have had great difficulty in finding the wagons I was in search of, had I not fortunately fallen in with Lieutenant-Colonel Myers, of M'Dowell's Corps, who seemed to be always on hand in an emergency. With his assistance in a marvelously short time I got between twenty-five and thirty wagons started in the proper direction: and then, by his invitation, stopped to swallow a cup of coffee and a hasty lunch. Observing a considerable body of well-equipped troops lying here apparently idle, I expressed astonishment, and inquired the cause of it. The answer was expressed evasively, but with some bitterness: "There are officers here to-day who would be doing themselves far more credit by marching to the battle-field than by lying idle and exciting disaffection by doubts, sneering criticism, and open abuse of the Commander-in-Chief."

I followed my wagons until I had got them clear of Centreville and in a full trot down the turnpike; I then dug spurs into my mare's flanks, and in the shortest time possible returned to the great centre of interest. I found the General and Staff grouped around a large pine-tree which stood solitary on the crest of an open hill, overlooking our whole line of battle. The summit immediately in our front was occupied by a line of batteries, some thirty or forty pieces, blazing and fuming like furnaces. Behind these a fine brigade of Reno's command lay resting on their arms. To their right stood Heintzelman, with the divisions of Hooker and Kearney, whose musketry kept up a continuous roar. Supporting the left of this line of guns was Sigel, also sharply engaged with small-arms. On an open bluff still further to the left, and on the opposite side of the valley traversed by the Warrenton turnpike, lay Schenck's Division, which had been a good deal cut up, and was not actively engaged at this moment. The dry grass which covered the hill he occupied had taken fire, and was burning rapidly, occasionally obscuring that portion of the field with its smoke. Beyond him, on the extreme left of our line, General Reynolds, with the Pennsylvania Reserves, lay masked from the enemy by a wood. The enemy's position can only be known by the smoke of his guns, for all his troops and batteries are concealed by the wood. He occupies strong lines on a plateau and along an unfinished railroad embankment, which is equal to a regularly intrenched line. He fights stubbornly, and has thus far resisted all our efforts to dislodge him. The General relies on the advance of M'Dowell and Porter to crush him, and we are in momentary expectation of hearing their guns. The shot and shells of the enemy directed at the batteries in our front render this position rather uncomfortable, as they are continually screeching over our heads, or plowing the gravelly surface with an ugly rasping whir, that makes one's flesh creep. . . .

Our efforts to carry the wood in front having thus far failed, I was sent to General Reno with orders that he should throw forward the division lying in reserve to support the attack of Heintzelman's troops. The order was promptly and gallantly executed, the troops moving in beautiful order and with admirable spirit. I accompanied the advance until they passed our guns beyond the summit, and remained there admiring until the troops, moving down a fine open slope, reached the edge of the wood. The enemy was pelting away industriously from his wooded strong-hold, and the air was lively with singing bullets. For half an hour or more the roar of musketry was unceasing. At length Reno in person reported to the General, and stated that he had failed to carry the wood. Simultaneously with his return our position was so sharply raked with shot and shell that the General withdrew a short distance to the right, establishing himself on the verge of a wood. . . .

It was now about four o'clock when General Phil Kearney came in and received orders to attack and carry the disputed position at all hazards. He rode off promising to do so. While he was forming his troops for the advance it was thought necessary to pound the position with artillery. Reno, who was riding beside the Commanding General, remarked, "The wood is filled with the wounded of both armies." The Commander replied, "And yet the safety of this army and the nation demands their sacrifice, and the lives of thousands yet unwounded." After a moment's hesitation the necessity of the order was acquiesced in, and forty guns were opened upon the fatal wood. The artillerymen worked with a fiendish activity, and the sulphurous clouds which hung over the field were tinged with a hot coppery hue by the rays of the declining sun. Meanwhile Kearney had gone in, and the incessant roar of musketry resembled the noise of a cataract.

An hour later Kearney again appeared, and informed the General that the coveted position was carried. I stood beside him as he gave in his report, and while elated with the tidings he communicated, admired the man as the finest specimen of the fighting soldier I had ever seen. With his small head surmounted by the regulation forage-cap, his thin face with its energetic beck, his colorless eyes, glaring as it were with a white heat, his erect figure with the empty coat-sleeve pinned across his breast, down to the very point of his sabre, whose ragged leathern scabbard stuck out like a gaff, he looked the game-cock all over. His very voice had the resolute guttural cluck which characterizes that gallant fowl. . . .

Meanwhile M'Dowell in person arrived on the field, and reported the approach of his command. It is a relief to see him here, although it is too late for him to accomplish any thing decisive. While exchanging greetings with me M'Dowell looked toward the west, where the radiance of a rich golden sunset was breaking through the grim battle-clouds, illuminating the mingled glories and horrors of the hard-fought field. "Look," said he, "what a dramatic and magnificent picture! How tame are all Vernet's boasted battle-pieces in comparison with such a scene as this! Indeed, if an artist could successfully represent that effect it would be criticised as unreal and extravagant."

I warmed toward a man who amidst the dangers and responsibilities of the occasion could mark its passing beauties and sublimities. At this point the two Generals, with their aids and escort, rode to the front to inspect the situation. . . . The battery was still working rapidly, and the enemy fighting back with equal spirit, when one of the guns burst, throwing off a heavy fragment of the muzzle, which described an arc immediately over the heads of the line of officers and fell with a thud, just clearing the last man and horse; two feet lower and it would have swept off the whole party. I had remarked since we came over that the ammunition used seemed miserably and dangerously defective; nearly all the shells bursting prematurely, and several so close to the muzzles of the pieces as to endanger the artillerymen. . . .

We remained on this hill until after sunset, when the firing gradually ceased. When it became quite dark there was a beautiful pyrotechnical display about a mile distant on our left, and near the Warrenton turnpike, occasioned by a collision of King's Division of M'Dowell's Corps with the enemy's right. The sparkling lines of musketry shone in the darkness like fire-flies in a meadow, while the more brilliant flashes of artillery might have been mistaken for swamp meteors. This show continued for an hour, the advancing and receding fires indicating distinctly the surging of the battle tide; and all this time not the slightest sound either of small-arms or artillery was perceptible. It seemed at length that the fire of the enemy's line began to extend and thicken, while ours wavered and fell back, but still continued the contest. Between eight and nine o'clock it ceased entirely, and we returned to our head-quarters station, where we picketed our horses and prepared to pass the night beside a camp-fire.

—Strother, "Personal Recollections of the War"

4. GENERAL GREGG EXHORTS HIS MEN
TO DIE IN THEIR TRACKS

Perhaps the hottest fighting of the twenty-ninth came on the extreme left of the Confederate line where Gregg's South Carolinians held a little knoll commanding the Sudley Springs road. If the Federals succeeded in overrunning this point they could turn Jackson's flank and roll him up in defeat. All afternoon Kearny hurled his men against Gregg's thin line; when Hill inquired whether he could hold out he made the famous answer that his ammunition was almost gone but he could hold with the bayonet.

Edward McCrady, who tells the story of Gregg's brigade, was a lieuten-

ant colonel of the 1st South Carolina Volunteers who later distinguished him-
self as the historian of his state.

TEN hours of actual conflict had exhausted all the romance of the battle.
It was business; it was work, wearisome work, in the face of death we
were doing. Our feet were worn and weary, and our arms were nerveless.
Our ears were deadened with the continuous roar of the battle, and our eyes
were dimmed with the smoke. Ah! we too needed rest. The rest Schurz's
men were having yonder, over the hill in their rear. But Kearney was pitiless.
It mattered not to him that we were tired, and that our ammunition was gone.
On, on he came, pouring into us his deadly volleys, and then the rush. Our
men fell fast around us. The Thirteenth and the First after having held our
position all day, at last were pushed back. The enemy pressed on, crossed the
cut, and slowly but steadily compelled us, step by step, to yield the long
coveted position—the position, on the extreme left, a little in advance of Hill's
line, with which, early in the morning, our brigade had been entrusted, and
which we had maintained all day. But we would not give it up without a
desperate struggle. Now again the same hand to hand fight we had with
Grover, we renewed with Kearney—we were not, however, entirely without
help. General Branch came to our assistance with one of his regiments, and,
literally, with coat off, personally took part in the affray. With his aid we
made a stand on the top of the knoll, and there, over the bodies of our dead
and wounded comrades, we struggled on. On our left, too, the Rifles were
still contending for the cornfield, and there that gallant soldier, Colonel J.
Foster Marshall, and his Lieutenant-Colonel, D. A. Leadbetter, were both
killed, with many other good men of that devoted regiment, but the enemy
attacking them was again repulsed, and those who had pressed the rest of us
back to the top of the hill, now hesitated and commenced to yield. We
pressed them in our turn. They broke and fell back in disorder.

I recollect that as they did so, they left a mule which, notwithstanding all
the turmoil, was quietly cropping a green blade, here and there, in the blood-
stained grass around him. His singular appearance attracted our attention
even in that terrible moment, and I was looking at him, wondering, when
some one exclaimed, "Why, he has a mountain howitzer behind him!" Sure
enough, there it was. Amidst the roar of musketry and the din of arms we
had not noticed this instrument of destruction which, in a few yards of us,
had been mowing down our men with canister. Probably it was one of the
same that Sigel had sent to Krzyzanowski and which Gordon tells us were
"happily placed" in his skirmish line in the first attack in the morning.

But Stevens, who was supporting Kearney, was on hand to make one
more last effort of the day. We heard the cheers of his men as he ordered
them in—telling us that our work was not yet done.

It was at this time that an officer rode up to Gregg, with a message from
General Hill, asking if he could hold the position any longer; and then was
his famous reply, that his ammunition was exhausted, but "he thought he
could still hold his position with the bayonet."

And this was absolutely true. The ammunition we had carried into action had been expended for some time; and it was one of the cruelties of our position, that before the Infirmary corps were allowed to help a wounded man, before his wound was looked at, he must be stripped of his accoutrements, and his ammunition distributed among his comrades. This economy, and the ammunition we got from the dead and wounded of our assailants, had enabled us to carry on the fight.

I have always wished that the scene which followed General Gregg's message could be painted by some great artist able to do it justice. Having sent word to Hill that he had no ammunition, but would hold the position with the bayonet, General Gregg drew up the remnants of his five regiments, now reduced to a mere handful in two lines, the Twelfth, Thirteenth and Fourteenth in one line, in front, under Lieutenant-Colonel Simpson, of the Fourteenth, and the First and Rifles under my command, as a second line, behind the First. All the other field officers, except Lieutenant-Colonel Jones, of the Twelfth, had by this time been killed or wounded. We were upon the top of the hill, the point to which we had been driven back by Kearney, some two or three hundred yards from the railroad excavation. Here General Gregg formed us to await the assault of the enemy, whose cheers we heard as they were ordered forward.

I can see him now, as with his drawn sword, that old Revolutionary scimitar we all knew so well, he walked up and down the line, and hear him as he appealed to us to stand by him and die there. "Let us die here, my men, let us die here." And I do not think that I exaggerate when I say that our little band responded to his appeal, and were ready to die, at bay, there if necessary.

The moment was, indeed, a trying one—a trying one to men who had shown themselves no cowards that day. We could hear the enemy advancing, and had not a round with which to greet them, but must wait the onslaught with only our bayonets. On they came. They had nearly reached the railroad, and were about to cross to the charge when a shout behind paralyzed us with dread. Was all the glorious fight we had made that livelong day to end in our capture by an unseen movement to our rear? Terror stricken we turned, when lo! there were our friends coming to our assistance, and not the enemy to our attack. Field, with his Virginians, and Pender, with his North Carolinians, relieved by Early and Forno, of Ewell's division, came rushing up, comparatively fresh for the work, and cheering us as they advanced on either side of our little band, waited not the assault, as we were doing perforce, but with a wild Confederate yell, rushed upon Stevens as he was in the confusion of crossing to our attack. The Federals halted, turned and fled, our friends crossing the railroad and pursuing them.

—McCRADY, "Gregg's Brigade in the Second Battle of Manassas"

5. LONGSTREET OVERWHELMS POPE AT MANASSAS

Both Jackson and Pope were exhausted on the evening of the twenty-ninth. Jackson, however, knew that Longstreet was at hand; Pope merely hoped that Franklin and Sumner were on the way from Alexandria. But Pope had deluded himself that Jackson was whipped and in full retreat, he had finally brought up Porter's corps, and he refused to credit the information that Longstreet was through Thoroughfare Gap and on the battlefield. He therefore determined to renew the fight the next day. Later he gave a somewhat different explanation. "I felt it my duty," he said, "notwithstanding the desperate condition of my command from great fatigue, from want of provisions and forage, and from the small hope I had of any effective assistance from Alexandria, to hold my position at all hazards and under all privations." The battle was renewed early on the afternoon of the thirtieth, Porter assaulting Jackson furiously. Just when this fighting was at its height Longstreet, whose forces were stretched out at almost a right angle to Jackson's, moved forward with his whole line and overwhelmed Porter and Reynolds.

The story is told here by Alexander Hunter, a private in the 17th Virginia—part of Hood's division. That division had made an initial thrust at the Federal lines on the night of the twenty-ninth, and on the thirtieth it led the attack.

T HE rapid pounding of the artillery caused us to hurry through the morning meal, almost before the sun rose above the hill, and we pushed for Thoroughfare Gap to rejoin the regiment. We knew by instinct that there would be a battle that day; for there was blood upon the moon. . . . Never had life seemed more worth living than on a morning such as this; never existence sweeter; never Death so loath the dying.

Long streams of soldiers were wending their way to the front. The troops seemed everywhere; they filled the railroad track as far as the eye could reach; they emerged from the narrow gap in the mountain and spread out over the fields and meadows; they wound along the base of the hills, and marched in a steady tramp over the dusty highways; following a dozen different routes, but each face turned directly or obliquely northward. Ordnance wagons were being pushed rapidly ahead; batteries were taking position, staff officers were riding at a gallop, as if seconds and minutes were golden. In short, all fighting material was pushing to the van and all the peacefully inclined were valiantly seeking the rear. By a law as fixed as that which bound the Stoics, as unalterable as those which govern the affinities of the chemical world, this separation of the two types ever occurred on the eve of battle. An instant sifting of wheat from the tares took place quietly but surely in every company, and the mass of men so lately mingled became as incapable of mixture as oil and water.

The great receding tide at full ebb sank back toward the Gap; the mighty army of the backsliders whom naught could hinder, non-combatants, camp darkies, shirking soldiers playing possum, and camp followers. Warm work was expected and all this genus, like war-horses, "sniffed danger from afar." . . .

It was this crowd belonging to the wagon-train or detailed for work such as blacksmithing, using every artifice to avoid the marching and fighting, which hung on the army like barnacles on a staunch ship's bottom, impeding its course and weighting it down. It was the impedimenta that flocked to the battle-field as soon as the shot and shell ceased firing, and despoiled and stripped friend and foe alike, dead or wounded, it mattered not, though they never killed or illtreated the injured or maimed.

Reaching the Gap we found that the brigade had passed through. Fol-

SECOND BATTLE OF BULL RUN
POSITION OF TROOPS
AT SUNSET,
AUG. 29. 1862.

UNION   CONFEDERATE
Troops
Cavalry
Skirmishers
Scale of   ½   1 One Mile

A. J. Volck

Prayer in Stonewall Jackson's Camp

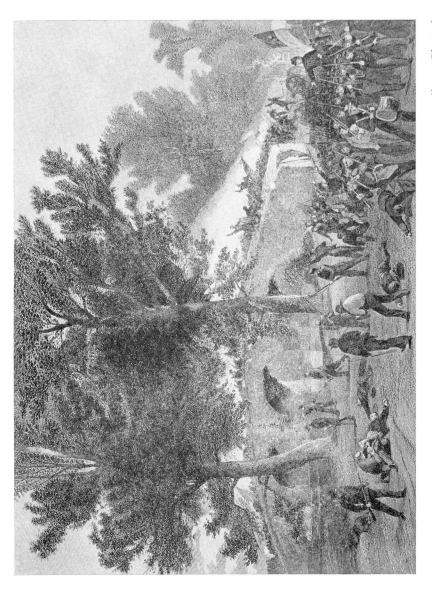

Alonzo Chappel

The Fight at Burnside's Bridge, Antietam

lowing hard upon the track, our little squad after an hour's march caught up and took its place in rank.

The men were in a fearful humor, grumbling at their luck and cursing the commissary. They had ample cause; not a single ration had been issued to the troops for several days and the soldiers were savage from hunger. . . .

The forenoon had passed and the sound of hostile cannon was breaking the silence in our front while a battle was being fought on our left. . . .

"Fall in!" the officers shouted, and the men sprang to their feet, the line was dressed, and the brigade headed to the front to take position. On the way we were halted, and every soldier was compelled to strip for the fight by discarding his blanket,—if he had one, which was not often—oilcloth or overcoat. All these were deposited in a large pile, and guards set over them, looking very much as if we did not intend to retreat. Cartridge-boxes were filled with forty rounds, and in our haversacks we carried twenty more, making sixty rounds per man.

Soon the crack of the skirmisher's rifles were heard, then the artillery opened, and the purple-colored smoke drifted like mist from lowland marshes, across the valley.

"Forward! Guide to the colors! March!"

Across that level plateau the First Brigade moved, the flower of Virginia in its ranks, the warm blood rushing in its veins as it did in warrior ancestors centuries ago. It was a glorious and magnificent display, the line keeping perfect time, the colors showing red against the azure sky. There was no cheering, only the rattling of the equipments and the steady footfalls of the men who trod the earth with regular beat. As the brigade swept across the plain it was stopped by a high Virginia snake fence; hundreds of willing hands caught the rails, tossed them aside, and then instinctively touching each other's elbows, the ranks were dressed as if by magic.

The first shell now shrieked over us. Another burst not ten feet from the ground directly over the heads of our forces. The long chain kept intact, though close to the spot where the explosion occurred; the links vibrated and oscillated for a moment, then grew firm again and pressed onward.

How the shells rained upon us now; a Yankee six-gun battery, on a hill about half a mile off, turned its undivided attention upon us and essayed to shatter the advancing line. It did knock a gap here and there, but the break was mended almost as soon as broken, and the living wall kept on. Shells were bursting everywhere, until it seemed as if we were walking on torpedoes. They crackled, split and exploded all around, throwing dirt and ejecting little spirts of smoke that for a moment dimmed the sky.

Colonel Marye dismounted, drew his sword from the scabbard, and looking the beau ideal of a splendid soldier, placed himself at the head of his men. He stopped for a moment and pointed his sword with an eloquent and vivid gesture toward the battery on the hill. A cheer answered him, and the line instinctively quickened its pace. Though the shells were tearing through the ranks, the men did not falter. One man's resonant voice was sounding above the din, exercising a magical influence; one man's figure strode on in front

and where he led, his men kept close behind. We followed unwaveringly
our colonel over the hill, down the declivity, up the slope, straight across
the plain toward the battery, with even ranks, though the balls were tearing
a way through flesh and blood. The brigade stretched out for several hundred yards, forming, as they marched, a bow with concave toward the enemy. The Seventeenth was on the right of the line, and the other regiments
dressed by our colors as we bore right oblique toward the battery, which
was now hidden by a volleying fume that settled upon the crest.

Still the advance was not stayed nor the ranks broken. We neared the
Chinn House, when suddenly a long line of the enemy rose from behind an
old stone wall and poured straight in our breasts a withering volley at point-
blank distance. It was so unexpected, this attack, that it struck the long line
of men like an electric shock. Many were falling killed or wounded, and
but for the intrepid coolness of its colonel, the Seventeenth would have retired from the field in disorder. His clear, ringing voice was heard, and the
wavering line reformed. A rattling volley answered the foe, and for a minute or two the contest was fiercely waged. Then the colonel fell with his
knee frightfully shattered by a Minie-ball. Once down, the calm, reassuring
tones heard no longer, the line broke. Now individual bravery made up for
the disaster. The officers surged ahead with their swords waving in the air,
cheering on the men, who kept close to their heels, loading and firing as they
ran. The line of blue was not fifty yards distant and every man took a sure,
close aim before his finger pressed the trigger. It was a decisive fight of about
ten minutes, and both sides stood up gamely to their work. Our foes were a
Western regiment from Ohio, who gave and received and asked no odds.
The left of our brigade having struck the enemy's right and doubled it up,
now sent one volley into their flank.

In a moment the blue line quivered and then went to pieces. Officers and
men broke for the rear, one regimental colors captured by Jim Coleman, of
the Seventeenth. In a few moments there were none left except the dead
and wounded.

There was hardly a breathing spell, only time indeed to take a full draught
from the canteen, transfer the cartridges from the haversacks to the cartridge-
box, and the enemy was upon us with a fresh line.

We were now loading and firing at the swiftly approaching enemy, who
were about two hundred yards distant, advancing straight towards us and
shouting with their steady hurrah, so different from the Rebel yell. It was a
trying moment and proved the metal of the individual man. Some ran, or
white with fear cowered behind the Chinn House, while others hid in a long
gulley near by; others yet stood in an irregular form and loaded and fired,
unmindful of the dust and noise of the hurtling shell and screaming shot. . . .

The brigade was scattered everywhere now. For an hour they had fired
as fast as the cartridges could be rammed home. When the Union troops
came up to retake the Chinn House, our men began to give ground. On
came the Yankees in splendid style, with the Stars and Stripes waving and
their line capitally dressed. It was a perfect advance, and some of us forgot

to fire our muskets while watching them. In their front line was a little drummer beating a *pas de charge*, the only time we ever heard the inspiriting sound on the battle-field. The dauntless little fellow was handling his sticks lustily, too, for the roll of the drum was heard above the noise of the guns.

It was high time to be leaving, we thought, and now our men were turning to fire one good shot before heeling it to the rear, when right behind us there came with a rush and a vim a fresh Rebel brigade aiming straight for the Yankees. They ran over us and we joined their lines. Not a shot was fired by them in response to the fusilade of musketry that was raining lead all around. Every man with his head bent sideways and down, like people breasting a hailstorm, for soldiers always charge so, and the Gray and the Blue met with a mighty shock. A tremendous sheet of flame burst from our line; the weaker side went to the ground in a flash, and with a wild yell the Gray swept on toward the six-gun battery that had been sending forth a stream of death for the past hour. We could only see the flashes of light through the dense smoke.

The line stopped a moment at the foot of the hill to allow itself to catch up. It was late in the evening and the battle was raging in all its deadliest fury. On our right, on our left, in the front, in the rear, from all directions came the warring sound of cannon and musketry. We could see nothing but smoke, breathe nothing except the fumes of burning powder, feel nothing save the earth jarred by the concussion of the guns, hear nothing but the dire, tremendous clamor and blare of sound swelling up into a vast volume of fire. How hot it was! The clothes damp with perspiration, the canteens empty, throats parched with thirst, faces blackened by powder, the men mad with excitement.

The left of the line came up and then some one asked:

"Whose brigade is this?"

"Hood's," was the answer.

Then burst a ringing cry, "Forward, Texans!"

The line sprang like a tightly-bent bow suddenly loosened, and rushed up the hill in a wild, eager dash—a frenzied, maddening onset up the hill through the smoke, nearer and nearer to the guns.

When about a hundred yards from them the dense veil lifted, floated upward and softly aside, and discovered to us that the battery had ceased firing. We could see the muzzles of the guns, their sullen black mouths pointing at us, and behind them the gunners, while from the center of the battery was a flag that lay drooping upon its staff. It was for a second only, like the rising of the curtain for a moment on a hideous tableau, only to be dropped as the eye took in the scene in all its horrors, yet it impressed itself, that vivid picture, brief as it was, upon mind, heart and brain.

At once came a noise like a thunder shock, that seemed as if an earthquake had riven the place. The ground trembled with the concussion. The appalling sound was heard of iron grapeshot tearing its way through space and through bodies of bone, flesh and blood.

Mercifully for us, but not intended by our foes, the guns were elevated

too high, or it would have been simply annihilation; for when those six
guns poured their volley into the charging lines they were loaded to the
muzzle with grape, and the distance was only about pistol shot. Of course
the execution was fearful, and for a second the line was stupefied and nearly
senseless from the blow. The ground was covered with victims and the
screams of the wounded rose high above the din and were awful to hear.

The advance was not stayed long.

"Forward, boys! Don't stop now! Forward, Texans!" and with a cry
from every throat the Southerners kept on, officers and men together without form or order, the swiftest runners ahead, the slowest behind, 'tis true,
but struggling desperately to better their time. Up! Still up! until we reached
the crest! As the Yankees pulled the lanyards of the loaded pieces our men
were among them. A terrific shock. A lane of dead in front. Those standing
before the muzzles were blown to pieces like captured Sepoy rebels. I had
my hand on the wheel of one cannon just as it fired, and I fell like one dead,
from the concussion. There was a frenzied struggle in the semi-darkness
around the guns, so violent and tempestuous, so mad and brain-reeling that
to recall it is like fixing the memory of a horrible, blood-curdling dream.
Every one was wild with uncontrollable delirium.

Then the mists dissolved and the panting, gasping soldiers could see the
picture as it was. The battery had been captured by the Texans and every
man at the pieces taken prisoner. Many were killed by a volley that we had
poured into them when only a few paces distant, and a large proportion
wounded. The few who escaped unhurt stood in a group, so blackened with
powder that they ceased to look like white men. These soldiers had nobly
worked their guns and had nothing to be ashamed of. All that men could do
they had done. . . .

Just as the day was drawing to a close a mighty yell arose, a cry from
twice ten thousand throats, as the Rebel reserves, fresh from the rear, rushed
resistlessly to the front. Never did mortal eyes behold a grander sight; not
even when MacDonald put his columns in motion at Wagram or Ney charged
the Russian center at Borodino.

It was an extended line, reaching as far as the eye could see, crescent in
form, and composed of many thousand men. It was, in fact, a greater part
of Longstreet's corps. The onset was thrilling in the extreme, as the men
swept grandly forward, the little battle-flags with the Southern cross in the
center fluttering saucily and jauntily aloft, while the setting sun made of
each bayonet and musket-barrel a literal gleam of fire that ran along the
chain of steel in a scintillating flame. As they swept over the plain they took
up all the scattered fighting material, and nothing was left but the wounded
which had sifted through, and the dead.

Then ensued the death struggle, a last fearful grappling in mortal combat.
The enemy threw forward all their reserves to meet the shock, and for the
space of fifteen minutes the commotion was terrible. Bursts of sound surpassed everything that was ever heard or could be conceived. The baleful
flashes of the cannon, darting out against the dusky horizon, played on the

surface of the evening clouds like sharp, vivid lightning. Long lines of musketry vomited through the plain their furious volleys of pestilential lead, sweeping scores of brave soldiers into the valley of the Shadow of Death. . . .

At last the enemy staggered, wavered, broke and fled in utter rout. Where Longstreet was dealing his heavy blows, they were throwing away their knapsacks and rushing madly for the rear. Only one final stand was made by a brigade in the woods close by; but as the long gray line closed in on each flank they threw down their arms and surrendered with but few exceptions; those few, as they ran, turned and fired.

On the hill, which had been occupied by the Washington Artillery of eighteen guns in the earlier part of the day, the eye took in a dim and fast-fading yet extended view of the whole surrounding country. A vast panorama stretched out on an open plain with patches of wood here and there on its surface, and with but two or three hills in the whole range of sight to break the expanded level. It was unutterably grand. Jackson could be seen swinging his left on his right as a pivot, and Longstreet with his entire corps in the reverse method. The whole Yankee army was in retreat, and certainly nothing but darkness prevented it from becoming *une affaire flambée.*

—Hunter, *Johnny Reb and Billy Yank*

6. STEVENS AND KEARNY ARE KILLED AT CHANTILLY

After his defeat at Bull Run Pope withdrew to Centreville, some twenty miles from Washington, where he was joined by the corps of Franklin and Sumner. Stuart swung northward, and down the Little River Turnpike, to cut his communications, and Jackson hurried on after Stuart. To meet this threat Pope sent two brigades of infantry under General Isaac Stevens toward the threatened turnpike. The opponents met at the little village of Chantilly; just as Jackson was forcing the outnumbered Federals back, Kearny arrived with his division and succeeded in stemming the enemy advance until darkness fell. The delay was purchased at a high price: both Stevens and Kearny were killed.

General Stevens had been colonel of the mutinous 79th New York; it is gratifying to find that regiment fighting so courageously at Chantilly. Kearny was one of the most romantic figures in the Union Army, and one of its most promising officers. Distinguished in appearance and in family, and distinguished, too, by his great wealth, he had early dedicated himself to a military career. He had seen service on the frontier, in Algiers, lost an arm in the Mexican War, and fought with the French army in Italy. On the outbreak of the war he was appointed brigadier general of the 1st New Jersey Brigade. His superiors admired him, his men loved him, and his death was a serious blow to the Union cause.

EARLY on the morning of September 1, a beautiful morning, Jackson moved slowly forward on the Little-River turnpike, reaching Chantilly about noon, while Longstreet was pressing forward to join him. Owing, probably, both to the extreme weariness of his troops and a desire to have Longstreet within close supporting distance, Jackson's three divisions moved from Chantilly up the turnpike slowly and well in hand. . . . The infantry moved in two columns, one on each side of the road, with the artillery in the road.

The Union army, at a terrible disadvantage in the broken-down condition of its cavalry, was unaware of the strength of the Confederate movement until nearly noon of Monday, September 1. . . .

It is probable that General Pope was informed of Jackson's flanking movement by stragglers from the late battle-field, or by some fortunate accident. . . .

At 12 o'clock Gen. Pope ordered McDowell to hasten with his corps to Fairfax Court-House, take command of the two brigades there, and occupy Germantown with his whole force, so *as to cover the turnpike from Centreville to Alexandria* (in other words, keep open his line of retreat). . . .

McDowell acted with great vigor; and, at once putting his troops in motion, hastened towards Fairfax Court-House. Fortunately meeting Gen. Patrick's brigade, . . . and who, after observations from the hill-tops, seeing no signs of the enemy, were on the return march to Centreville, Gen. McDowell at once diverted them into the old intrenchments across the Little-River turnpike near Germantown. This brigade was posted with two guns bearing upon the turnpike before 4 o'clock in the afternoon, just in time, in conjunction with some of Buford's cavalry and Gen. Ricketts's (Second) division of the Third Corps, to receive and repulse Stuart's cavalry. . . .

To aid in securing time to get his army to the new position near Fairfax Court-House, Gen. Pope, early in the afternoon, sent Reno's command . . . (which was then under Gen. Stevens's command, as Gen. Reno, commander of the Second Division and the ranking officer, was sick and off active duty) to march at once across the fields to the Little-River turnpike, take a position across it, and hold in check a Confederate force said to be advancing by that road towards Fairfax Court-House. These men were under orders to accompany Gen. Stevens as guides on the march, and did so. As they rode with Capt. Stevens, in advance of the division, they informed him that, while foraging down the Little-River pike that morning, they had seen a large body of Confederate infantry moving east, had ridden back at once and informed Gen. Pope, and had then been directed by him to guide Gen. Stevens to a point on the turnpike some distance in advance of the place where they had noticed the head of the Confederate column.

Getting his command under arms with all possible haste Gen. Stevens moved rapidly towards the indicated point, his division (the First) having the lead, followed shortly by the Second Brigade of the Second (Reno's) Division. . . .

Meanwhile, Stevens's approach having been noticed, Jackson was hurrying Branch's and Brockenbrough's brigades into position to strike him.

Gen. Stevens, who was watching the development of affairs from a wooded knoll near the old railroad, as his skirmishers began to come in set to work to throw his division of six regiments into a column of attack. . . .

General Stevens had formed his men for the attack with great rapidity, and his column was ready to move as soon as his skirmishers had come in. At about half-past 4 o'clock he gave the order to advance, first sending Capt. Belcher, provost-marshal on the division staff, back to the Warrenton pike, to report that his division was engaged with a heavy force of the enemy, and must have support, with orders to give the message to Gen. Pope, if he could find him at once, if not, to every corps and division commander that he could find until support was furnished.

Dismounting from his horse the General had taken post in the centre of the charging column, and, to aid in holding the men to their work and driving the charge home with all possible vigor, had assigned a member of his staff to each of his regiments; his Adjutant-General (his son, Capt. Hazard Stevens) being assigned to the Seventy-ninth New York, of which regiment the General had formerly been Colonel. The column moved forward across the open land, with the left skirting through the cornfield, some hundreds of yards, steadily and in silence, without a shot being fired, until they came to within 75 yards of a rail fence on the edge of the woods bordering the fields; then, from Branch's brigade of five North Carolina and Brocken-brough's of three Virginia regiments, a terrific fire of musketry was opened from the cover of the fence, and the Seventy-ninth and Twenty-eighth, suffering terribly, came to a halt.

To be checked there in the open ground was to be lost; the colors of the Seventy-ninth were down, and the column wavered. Passing by his son, who had fallen wounded in the hip and arm, Gen. Stevens seized the flag of the Seventy-ninth, and ran in front of the column, shouting, "Follow me, my Highlanders!" The wavering column moved on again with resistless force; surging up to the fence, they threw it over and gained the edge of the woods, breaking Branch's brigade, and forcing back Brockenbrough; but Gen. Stevens, their devoted leader, was now lying dead upon the broken fence, a rebel bullet through his brain, with the colors of his Highlanders still held firmly in his grasp. . . .

The rain had now ceased, and, although it could hardly have been later than half-past 6 o'clock in the evening, the atmosphere was thick, and the sky still so heavily overcast, that night coming on prematurely made it impossible to distinguish any object clearly more than a few rods away. As the shattered Twenty-first Massachusetts regiment emerged from the woods, Gen. Kearny, who had just arrived upon the field, and was searching for troops to cover Birney's right flank, rode full upon us, and in fierce haste ordered the regiment to move on the run to take post on Birney's right, the position of whose line was indicated only by the flashes of their muskets.

When Gen. Kearny came upon us there was hardly a musket in our line that could be fired, as our disastrous fight in the woods had occurred in the midst of the terrific thunder-storm which had soon rendered the guns unserviceable. The officer in command of the regiment at the time begged the General to allow them a few moments to draw the wet charges from the guns, but was refused, with a hot sneer at our cowardice, and the threat that unless the regiment moved instantly, as ordered, he would turn a battery upon us, emphasizing his threat by riding from us directly towards Randolph's battery, posted a few rods in our rear, and which was then firing with solid shot (its only ammunition) into the woods across the cornfield. The General, fearful for Birney's right, and perhaps, also, somewhat unduly excited by the reply provoked by his imputation upon the valor of the regiment, at once sent an officer from the battery to us, with his compliments, coupled with the assurance that it would play upon us unless the order given was instantly obeyed.

Luckily two of our companies, which had been detached in the woods to cover our flanks, had escaped the ambuscade into which the others had fallen, and had now joined us with serviceable guns, and the regiment, about two hundred strong, moved across the open ground towards the cornfield and the front of Birney's right, deploying a thin skirmish line to cover our right and front as we advanced.

As our skirmishers came up to the rail fence of the cornfield they were fired on by Thomas's skirmishers, whose brigade, with two of Pender's regiments, was in the cornfield and coming from the woods, well on Birney's right. Crossing the line of the fence we soon halted in the corn, under a dropping fire from the enemy.

Gen. Kearny was following us up closely, and as we came to a halt fiercely tried to force us forward, saying that we were firing on our own men, and that there were no rebels near us. We had the proof in two prisoners—an officer and private of a Georgia regiment—brought in by our skirmishers, beside the warning cries of "Surrender!" coming both from our right and front; but, unfortunately, Kearny's judgment seemed unable to appreciate the existence of the peril which his military instinct had caused him to guard against. Lieut. Walcott, of the brigade staff, took our prisoners to him, saying, "General, if you don't believe there are rebels in the corn, here are two prisoners from the Forty-ninth Georgia, just taken in our front."

Crying out fiercely, "—— —— you and your prisoners!" the General, entirely alone, apparently in uncontrollable rage at our disregard of his peremptory orders to advance, forced his horse through the deep, sticky mud of the cornfield past the left of the regiment, passing within a few feet of where I was standing. I watched him moving in the murky twilight through the corn, and, when less than twenty yards away, saw his horse suddenly rear and turn, and half-a-dozen muskets flash around him: so died the intrepid soldier, Gen. Philip Kearny!

—General Charles F. Walcott, "The Battle of Chantilly"

7. "LITTLE MAC" IS REAPPOINTED TO COMMAND

Pretty clearly neither the army nor public opinion would tolerate Pope after the fiasco of Second Bull Run. On September 5 Lincoln relieved him of command and, over vigorous opposition from his Cabinet, reappointed McClellan to command of the now reunited Army of the Potomac.

McClellan is the most controversial military figure of the Civil War and, after ninety years, the controversy still rages. Lee was supposed to have characterized him as the ablest of his opponents, but it is highly doubtful that he ever did so, and if he did the characterization was palpable nonsense. That McClellan was an able organizer, a close student of war, and beloved by his troops, few will deny. On the other hand his timidity, vacillation, procrastination and sensitiveness, his persecution mania, his arrogance toward Lincoln, and his monumental egotism, suggest a psychopathic personality. To an almost total want of real military ability he united a vaulting ambition; discredited on the field of battle he sought compensation in politics, and his career is a standing warning against the mixture of the military and the civil.

The three following selections present varying views of McClellan. The first is from the acid but honest pen of Gideon Welles; the second from General Sherman; and the third the same Norton whose account of the Seven Days fighting we have already read. It is important to note the dates of the observations. Welles wrote just after Pope's debacle and just before McClellan was reappointed to command; Sherman two years after McClellan's final dismissal; Norton at the height of McClellan's popularity.

A. "To Fight Is Not His Forte"

September 3, 1862

McClellan is an intelligent engineer and officer, but not a commander to lead a great army in the field. To attack or advance with energy and power is not in him; to fight is not his forte. I sometimes fear his heart is not earnest in the cause; yet I do not entertain the thought that he is unfaithful. The study of military operations interests and amuses him. It flatters him to have on his staff French princes and men of wealth and position; he likes show, parade, and power. Wishes to outgeneral the Rebels, but not to kill and destroy them. In a conversation which I had with him in May last at Cumberland on the Pamunkey, he said he desired of all things to capture Charleston; he would demolish and annihilate the city. He detested, he said, both South Carolina and Massachusetts, and should rejoice to see both States extinguished. Both were and always had been ultra and mischievous, and he could not tell which he hated most. These were the remarks of the General-in-Chief at the head of our armies then in the field, and when as large a proportion of his troops were from Massachusetts as from any State in the Union. . . .

I cannot relieve my mind from the belief that to him, in a great degree, and to his example, influence, and conduct, are to be attributed some portion of our late reverses, more than to any other person on either side. His reluctance to move or to have others move, his inactivity, his detention of Franklin, his omission to send forward supplies unless Pope would send a cavalry escort from the battle-field, and the tone of his conversation and dispatches, all show a moody state of feeling. The slight upon him and the generals associated with him, in the selection of Pope, was injudicious, impolitic, wrong perhaps, but is no justification for their withholding one tithe of strength in a great emergency, where the lives of their countrymen and the welfare of the country were in danger. The soldiers whom McClellan has commanded are doubtless attached to him. They have been trained to it, and he has kindly cared for them while under him. With partiality for him they have imbibed his prejudices, and some of the officers have, I fear, a spirit more factious and personal than patriotic.

—*Diary of Gideon Welles*

B. General Sherman Explains Why He Cannot Like McClellan

To his wife.*

Gaylesville, Ala., October 27, 1864

You ask my opinion of McClellan. I have been much amused at similar inquiries of John and others in answer to a news paragraph that I pledged ninety-nine votes of the hundred to McClellan. Of course this is the invention of some knave. I never said such thing. I will vote for nobody, because I am not entitled to vote. Of the two, with the inferences to be drawn at home and abroad, I would prefer Lincoln, though I know that McClellan, Vallandigham or even Jeff Davis if President of the U. S. would prosecute the war, and no one with more vigor than the latter.

But at the time the howl was raised against McClellan I knew it was in a measure unjust, for he was charged with delinquencies that the American people are chargeable for. Thus, how unjust to blame me for any misfortune now when all the authorities and people are conspiring to break up the Army till the election is over. Our armies vanish before our eyes and it is useless to complain because the election is more important than the war. Our armies are merely paper armies. I have 40,000 Cavalry on paper but less than 5,000 in fact. A like measure runs through the whole, and so it was with McClellan. He had to fight partly with figures.

Still I admit he never manifested the simple courage and manliness of Grant, and he had too much staff, too many toadies, and looked too much to No. 1. When I was in Kentucky he would not heed my counsels, and never wrote me once, but since I have gained some notoriety at Atlanta and the papers announced, as usually falsely, that I was for him, he has written me twice and that has depreciated him more in my estimation than all else. He cannot be elected. Mr. Lincoln will be, but I hope it will be done quick, that voters may come to their regiments and not give the Rebels the advantage they know so well to take.

I believe McClellan to be an honest man as to money, of good habits, decent, and of far more than average intelligence, and therefore I never have joined in the hue and cry against him. In revolutions men fall and rise. Long before this war is over, much as you hear me praised now, you may hear me

* Reprinted from *Home Letters of General Sherman* edited by M. A. De Wolfe Howe; copyright 1909 by Charles Scribner's Sons, 1937 by M. A. De Wolfe Howe; used by permission of the publishers.

cursed and insulted. Read history, read Coriolanus, and you will see the true measure of popular applause. Grant, Sheridan and I are now the popular favorites, but neither of us will survive this war. Some other must rise greater than either of us, and he has not yet manifested himself.

—Howe, ed., *Home Letters of General Sherman*

C. "Little Mac's A-Coming"

Harrison's Landing, James River, Va., Sunday, July 13, 1862

Dear Brother and Sister:—

We had a review by moonlight a few nights ago. "Old Abe" was down here to see the army, and he did not get round to us till 9 o'clock at night, but it was beautiful moonlight, and as he went galloping past, riding beside "Little Mac," everyone could tell him by his "stovepipe hat" and his un-military acknowledgment of the cheers which everywhere greeted him. His riding I can compare to nothing else than a pair of tongs on a chair back, but notwithstanding his grotesque appearance, he has the respect of the army.

But the man in the army is "Little Mac." No general could ask for greater love and more unbounded confidence than he receives from his men, and the confidence is mutual. He feels that he has an army he can depend on to do all that the same number of men can do anywhere. He is everywhere among "his boys," as he calls them, and everywhere he is received with the most unbounded enthusiasm.

He was here yesterday about noon. The boys were getting dinner or lounging about under the trees, smoking, reading or writing, when we heard a roar of distant cheers away down the road a mile or more. "Little Mac's a-coming" was on every tongue. "Turn out the guard—General McClellan," called the sentry on the road. The guard paraded and the men flocked to the roadside. He came riding along on his "Dan Webster," by the way as splen-did a horse as you ever saw. He rode slowly, looking as jovial and hearty as if he could not be more happy. Up go the caps, and three rousing cheers that make the old woods ring, greet the beloved leader of the Army of the Potomac. He raises his cap in graceful acknowledgement of the compliment, and so he passes along. Those cheers always give notice of his approach. He speaks an occasional encouraging word, and the men return to their occupa-tions more and more devoted to the flag and their leader.

But what have they to say to the men who have been using their influence to prevent his being reinforced, to secure his defeat, and in some way to so prolong the war as to make the abolition of slavery a military necessity? Curses loud and deep are heaped on such men. Old Greeley would not live twenty-four hours if he should come here among the army. I used to be something of an abolitionist myself, but I've got so lately that I don't believe it is policy to sacrifice everything to the nigger. Such a policy as Greeley advocates, of letting this army be defeated for the purpose of making the people see that slavery must be abolished before we could end the war, I tell you is "played out." Ten thousand men have been sacrificed to that idea now, and the remainder demand that some other policy be adopted henceforth.

We want that three hundred thousand men raised and sent down here immediately. We want them drafted if they won't volunteer. We want the men who have property to furnish the government with the means to carry on the war. We want such a force sent here that the whole thing can be finished up by fall. We've been fooling about this thing long enough, and now we want a change. No more playing at cross purposes by jealous generals, no more incompetent or traitorous officials. The army demands and the people demand such a vigorous prosecution of the war as shall give some hope of ending it some time or other. McClellan must be reinforced sufficiently to enable him to do something more than keep at bay three times his force. That will never conquer the South. We must take the offensive and destroy their army and take their capital. When this is done, the clouds will begin to break.

—NORTON, *Army Letters*

8. McCLELLAN "SAVES HIS COUNTRY" TWICE

But let McClellan speak for himself. We give here excerpts from his letters to his wife. These letters, it will be seen, begin with the Peninsular campaign and carry through the Antietam campaign to McClellan's dismissal from the command of the Army of the Potomac. As they are valuable primarily for their reflection of McClellan's character rather than for their analysis of military operations, we print them as a unit even though this violates chronolgy.

April 8, 1862, 8 A.M.—

I have raised an awful row about McDowell's corps. The President very coolly telegraphed me yesterday that he thought I had better break the enemy's lines at once. I was much tempted to reply that he had better come and do it himself.

April 11, 1862—

Don't worry about the wretches; they have done nearly their worst, and can't do much more. I am sure that I will win in the end, in spite of all their rascality. History will present a sad record of these traitors who are willing to sacrifice the country and its army for personal spite and personal aims. The people will soon understand the whole matter.

May 12, 1862, Monday P.M.—

I hope that the result in front of Richmond will cause still greater satisfaction to the country. I still hope that the God who has been so good to me will continue to smile upon our cause, and enable me to bring this war to a speedy close, so that I may at last have the rest I want so much. . . . I do need rest. You know I have had but little in my life. But the will of God be done! What is given me to do I will try to do with all my might. . . .

I think one more battle here will finish the work. I expect a great one, but feel that confidence in my men and that trust in God which makes me very sanguine as to the result. They will fight me in front of Richmond, I am confident. Defeat there is certain destruction to them, and I think will prove the ruin of their wretched cause. They are concentrating everything for the last death-struggle. My government, alas! is not giving me any aid. But I will do the best I can with what I have, and trust to God's mercy and the courage of my men for the result. . . .

We march in the morning to Cumberland, gradually drawing nearer to Richmond.

July 17, 1862, A.M.—

You do not feel one bit more bitterly towards those people than I do. I do not say much about it, but I fear they have done all that cowardice and folly can do to ruin our poor country, and the blind people seem not to see it. It makes my blood boil when I think of it. I cannot resign so long as the fate of the Army of the Potomac is entrusted to my care. I owe a great duty to this noble set of men, and that is the only feeling that retains me. I fear that my day of usefulness to the country is past—at least under this adminis- tration. I hope and trust that God will watch over, guide, and protect me. I accept most resignedly all He has brought upon me. Perhaps I have really brought it on myself; for while striving conscientiously to do my best, it may well be that I have made great mistakes that my vanity does not permit me to perceive. When I see so much self-blindness around me I cannot ar- rogate to myself greater clearness of vision and self-examination.

I *did* have a terrible time during that week [the Seven Days], for I stood alone, without any one to help me. I felt that on me rested everything, and I felt how weak a thing poor, mortal, erring man is! I felt it sincerely, and shall never, I trust, forget the lesson; it will last me to my dying days. . . . I am very well now, perfectly well, and ready for any amount of fatigue that can be imagined.

July 18, 1862, 9:00 P.M.—

I am inclined now to think that the President will make Halleck com- mander of the army, and that the first pretext will be seized to supersede me in command of this army. Their game seems to be to withhold reinforce- ments, and then to relieve me for not advancing, well knowing that I have not the means to do so. If they supersede me in the command of the Army of the Potomac I will resign my commission at once. If they appoint Halleck commanding general I will remain in command of this army as long as they will allow me to, provided the army is in danger and likely to play an active part. I cannot remain as a subordinate in the army I once commanded any longer than the interests of my own Army of the Potomac require. I owe no gratitude to any but my own soldiers here; none to the government or to the country. I have done my best for the country; I expect nothing in return; they are my debtors, not I theirs. . . .

If things come to pass as I anticipate I shall leave the service with a sad heart for my country, but a light one for myself. But one thing keeps me at my work—love for my country and my army. Surely no general had ever better cause to love his men than I have to love mine.

July 20, 1862, P.M.—

Which despatch of mine to Stanton do you allude to? The telegraphic one in which I told him that if I saved the army I owed no thanks to any one in Washington, and that he had done his best to sacrifice my army? It was pretty frank and quite true. Of course they will never forgive me for that. I knew it when I wrote it; but as I thought it possible that it might be the last I ever wrote, it seemed better to have it exactly true. The President, of course, has not replied to my letter, and never will. His reply may be, however, to avail himself of the first opportunity to cut my head off. I see it reported in this evening's paper that Halleck is to be the new general-in-chief. Now let them take the next step and relieve me, and I shall once more be a free man. . . .

Later.—I believe it is now certain that Halleck is commander-in-chief. . . . I am content. I have not disgraced my name, nor will my child be ashamed of her father. Thank God for that! I shall try to get something to do which will make you comfortable; and it will be most pleasant and in the best taste for me that we should lead hereafter a rather quiet and retired life. It will not do to parade the tattered remnants of my departed honors to the gaze of the world. Let us try to live for each other and our child, and to prepare for the great change that sooner or later must overtake us all.

I have had enough of earthly honors and place. I believe I can give up all and retire to privacy once more, a better man than when we gave up our dear little home with wild ideas of serving the country. I feel that I have paid all that I owe her. I am sick and weary of all this business. I am tired of serving fools. God help my country! He alone can save it. It is grating to have to serve under the orders of a man whom I know by experience to be my inferior. But so let it be. God's will be done! All will turn out for the best. My trust is in God, and I cheerfully submit to His will.

August 10, 1862, 4 P.M.—

The absurdity of Halleck's course in ordering the army away from here is that it cannot possibly reach Washington in time to do any good, but will necessarily be too late. I am sorry to say that I am forced to the conclusion that H. is very dull and very incompetent. Alas, poor country! I hope to be ready tomorrow afternoon to move forward in the direction of Richmond. I will try to catch or thrash Longstreet, and then, if the chance offers, follow in to Richmond while they are lamming away at Pope. It is in some respects a desperate step, but it is the best I can do for the nation just now, and I would rather even be defeated than retreat without an effort to relieve Washington in the only way at all possible. If I fail, why well and good. I will fall back. If I win I shall have saved my country, and will then gracefully retire to private life. . . .

I half apprehend that they will be too quick for me in Washington, and relieve me before I have the chance of making the dash. If so, well and good. I am satisfied that the dolts in Washington are bent on my destruction, if it is possible for them to accomplish it.

August 22, 1862, 10 A.M. (Fort Monroe)—

I think they are all pretty well scared in Washington, and probably with good reason. I am confident that the disposition to be made of me will depend entirely upon the state of their nerves in Washington. If they feel safe there I will, no doubt, be shelved; perhaps placed in command here *vice* Gen. Dix. I don't care what they do; would not object to being kept here for a while, because I could soon get things in such condition that I could have you here with me. . . .

Their sending for me to go to Washington only indicates a temporary alarm. If they are at all reassured you will see that they will soon get rid of me. I shall be only too happy to get back to quiet life again; for I am truly and heartily sick of the troubles I have had, and am not fond of being a target for the abuse and slander of all the rascals in the country. Well, we will continue to trust in God and feel certain that all is for the best. It is often difficult to understand the ways of Providence; but I have faith enough to believe that nothing is done without some great purpose.

September 2, 1862, 12:30 P.M.—

I was surprised this morning, when at breakfast, by a visit from the President and Halleck, in which the former expressed the opinion that the troubles now impending could be overcome better by me than by any one else. Pope is ordered to fall back upon Washington, and, as he re-enters, everything is to come under my command again! A terrible and thankless task. Yet I will do my best, with God's blessing, to perform it. God knows I need His help. I am too busy to write any more now. Pray that God will help me in the great task now imposed upon me. I assume it reluctantly, with a full knowledge of all its difficulties and of the immensity of the responsibility. I only consent to take it for my country's sake and with the humble hope that God has called me to it; how I pray that He may support me! . . . Don't be worried; my conscience is clear, and I trust in God.

September 5, 1862, 11 A.M.—

Again I have been called upon to save the country. The case is desperate, but with God's help I will try unselfishly to do my best, and, if He wills it, accomplish the salvation of the nation. My men are true and will stand by me till the last. I still hope for success, and will leave nothing undone to gain it. . . . How weary I am of this struggle against adversity! But one thing sustains me—that is, my trust in God. I know that the interests at stake are so great as to justify His interference; not for me, but for the innocent thousands, millions rather, who have been plunged in misery by no fault of theirs. It is probable that our communications will be cut off in a day or two, but don't be worried. You may rest assured that I am doing all I can for my country, and that no shame shall rest upon you, wilfully brought upon you by me. . . . My hands are full, so is my heart.

September 8, 1862, camp near Rockville—

You don't know what a task has been imposed upon me! I have been obliged to do the best I could with the broken and discouraged fragments of two armies defeated by no fault of mine. Nothing but a desire to do my duty could have induced me to accept the command under such circumstances. Not feeling at all sure that I could do anything, I felt that under the circumstances no one else *could* save the country, and I have not shrunk from the terrible task.

McDowell's own men would have killed him had he made his appearance among them; even his staff did not dare to go among his men. I can afford to forgive and forget him. I saw Pope and McDowell for a few moments at Upton's Hill when I rode out to meet the troops and assume command. I have not seen them since; I hope never to lay eyes on them again. Between them they are responsible for the lives of many of my best and bravest men. They have done all they could (unintentionally, I hope) to ruin and destroy the country. I can never forgive them that. Pope has been foolish enough to try to throw the blame of his defeat on the Army of the Potomac. He would have been wiser to have accepted his defeat without complaint.

I will probably move some four or five miles further to the front tomorrow, as I have ordered the whole army forward. I expect to fight a great battle and to do my best at it. I do not think secesh will catch me very badly.

September 20, 1862, 9 A.M., camp near Sharpsburg—

The battle of Wednesday *was* a terrible one. I presume the loss will prove not less than 10,000 on each side. Our victory was complete, and the disorganized rebel army has rapidly returned to Virginia, its dreams of "invading Pennsylvania" dissipated for ever. I feel some little pride in having, with a beaten and demoralized army, defeated Lee so utterly and saved the North so completely. Well, one of these days history will, I trust, do me justice in deciding that it was not my fault that the campaign of the Peninsula was not successful. . . .

Since I left Washington, Stanton has again asserted that *I*, not Pope, lost the battle of Manassas No. 2! . . . I am tired of fighting such disadvantages, and feel that it is now time for the country to come to my help and remove these difficulties from my path. If my countrymen will not open their eyes and assist themselves they must pardon me if I decline longer to pursue the thankless avocation of serving them.

September 20, 1862, 9 P.M., camp near Sharpsburg—

I feel that I have done all that can be asked in twice saving the country. If I continue in its service I have at least the right to demand a guarantee that I shall not be interfered with. I know I cannot have that assurance so long as Stanton continues in the position of Secretary of War and Halleck as general-in-chief. . . . I can retire from the service for sufficient reasons without leaving any stain upon my reputation. I feel now that this last short campaign is a sufficient legacy for our child, so far as honor is concerned. . . .

You should see my soldiers *now!* You never saw anything like their enthusiasm. It surpasses anything you ever imagined. . . . My tent is filled quite to overflowing with trophies in the way of captured secesh battle-flags. We have more than have been taken in all battles put together, and all sorts of inscriptions on them.

November 7, 1862, 11:30 P.M. (camp near Rectorton)—

Another interruption—this time more important. It was in the shape of Burnside, accompanied by Gen. Buckingham, the secretary's adjutant-general. They brought with them the order relieving me from the command of the Army of the Potomac, and assigning Burnside to the command. No cause is given. I am ordered to turn over the command immediately and repair to Trenton, N. J., and on my arrival there to report by telegraph for further orders. . . .

Of course I was much surprised; but as I read the order in the presence of Gen. Buckingham I am sure that not the slightest expression of feeling was visible on my face, which he watched closely. . . .

They have made a great mistake. Alas for my poor country! I know in my inmost heart she never had a truer servant. I have informally turned over the command to Burnside, but shall go to-morrow to Warrenton with him, and perhaps remain a day or two there in order to give him all the information in my power. . . .

Do not be at all worried—I am not. I have done the best I could for my country; to the last I have done my duty as I understand it. That I must have made many mistakes I cannot deny. I do not see any great blunders; but no one can judge of himself. Our consolation must be that we have tried to do what was right; if we have failed it was not our fault.

—Letters of McClellan to his wife, in *McClellan's Own Story*

9. McCLELLAN FINDS THE LOST ORDER

Almost before Pope had carried out his retirement to Washington, Lee had started his army northward into Maryland. There were large strategic, and even political, purposes in this campaign, but there were practical purposes too—a chance to get food for soldiers and forage for animals. McClellan learned almost at once of Lee's advance, but did not know what his ultimate objectives would be. When news came that Lee was across the Potomac McClellan edged ahead to head him off, reaching Frederick, Maryland, on the twelfth. The next day he had the great good fortune to learn the whole of Lee's plans.

Mystery still surrounds the loss of Special Order 191. That it was picked up at Frederick, Maryland, by Private Mitchell of the 27th Indiana on September 13 and delivered promptly to McClellan's headquarters is clear, but who was responsible for its loss is not known. Lee learned that the Order was

*in McClellan's hands sometime the next day. To what extent the disclosure of
his plans forced Lee to change them is not wholly clear. According to
Colonel Allan, historian of the Army of Northern Virginia, Lee said in 1868
that "had the Lost Dispatch not been lost . . . I would have had all my troops
reconcentrated on Md. side, stragglers up, men rested, and intended then to
attack McClellan hoping the best results from state of my troops and those
of the enemy."*

O N the 13th an order fell into my hands, issued by General Lee, which
fully disclosed his plans, and I immediately gave orders for a rapid and
vigorous forward movement.

The following is a copy of the order referred to:

"SPECIAL ORDERS No. 191.

"Headquarters Army of Northern Virginia,

"September 9, 1862.

"The army will resume its march to-morrow, taking the Hagerstown
road. General Jackson's command will form the advance, and, after passing
Middletown, with such portions as he may select, take the route towards
Sharpsburg, cross the Potomac at the most convenient point, and, by Friday
night, take possession of the Baltimore and Ohio railroad, capture such of
the enemy as may be at Martinsburg, and intercept such as may attempt to
escape from Harper's Ferry.

"General Longstreet's command will pursue the same road as far as Boonsboro', where it will halt with the reserve, supply and baggage trains of the
army.

"General McLaws, with his own division and that of General R. H. Anderson, will follow General Longstreet; on reaching Middletown, he will
take the route to Harper's Ferry, and, by Friday morning, possess himself
of the Maryland heights, and endeavor to capture the enemy at Harper's
Ferry and vicinity.

"General Walker, with his division, after accomplishing the object in
which he is now engaged, will cross the Potomac at Cheek's ford, ascend its
right bank to Lovettsville, take possession of Loudon heights, if practicable,
by Friday morning; Keys's ford on his left, and the road between the end of
the mountain and the Potomac on his right. He will, as far as practicable,
co-operate with General McLaws and General Jackson in intercepting the
retreat of the enemy.

"General D. H. Hill's division will form the rear guard of the army, pursuing the road taken by the main body. The reserve artillery, ordnance and
supply trains, &c., will precede General Hill.

"General Stuart will detach a squadron of cavalry to accompany the
commands of Generals Longstreet and McLaws, and, with the main body of
the cavalry, will cover the route of the army, and bring up all stragglers that
may have been left behind.

"The commands of Generals Jackson, McLaws, and Walker, after accomplishing the objects for which they have been detached, will join the main body of the army at Boonsboro' or Hagerstown.

"Each regiment on the march will habitually carry its axes in the regimental ordnance wagons, for use of the men at their encampments, to procure wood, &c.

"By command of General R. E. Lee.

"R. H. Chilton,

"Assistant Adjutant General."

—*Letter of the Secretary of War*

10. McCLELLAN FORCES TURNER'S GAP AND CRAMPTON'S GAP

As the Lost Order tells, Lee divided his little army, sending Jackson with some 25,000 men to seize Harpers Ferry. Alive to the danger of being cut off from Jackson, now that McClellan knew his plans, Lee turned westward toward Sharpsburg, leaving only token forces to hold back the Federals. Moving with unwonted celerity McClellan pushed after the Confederates. The armies were separated by two low-lying ranges, South Mountain and Elk's Ridge; the easiest roads through these were at Turner's Gap and Crampton's Gap. The Confederates put up a stiff resistance at both places, but were brushed aside.

Here is David Strother, whom we have already met at Manassas, telling how these fights looked from McClellan's headquarters. His comments on Maryland's reaction to the invasion are especially perspicacious.

September 13, Saturday.—Fair and pleasant. Making an early start we entered Frederick City about ten o'clock A.M., and were welcomed with a spontaneous ovation that stirred every soul to its depths. The whole city was fluttering with national flags; while the streets through which we passed, from the sidewalks to the house-tops, shone with happy human faces. It seemed as if the whole population had turned out, wild with joy. Handkerchiefs fluttered and flowers showered upon the moving troops; and when the Commander and Staff appeared the crowd became so demonstrative that we were forcibly brought to a halt. The officers of the Staff received their due share of the floral honors, but the General and horse were absolutely covered with wreaths and bouquets; while old men, women, and children crowded around, anxious to touch his hand, or by some word or act to testify their enthusiasm for the leader of the National power.

As soon as the General could release himself from this pleasing but rather embarrassing position he rode to Burnside's head-quarters on the Baltimore turnpike, and then dismounting entered the General's tent. While waiting outside I fell into conversation with a cavalry officer, who narrated the following incident of the occupation which took place on yesterday: Our advanced cavalry met that of the enemy in the streets and drove them through the town. Being reinforced the enemy returned, driving our men back as rapidly as they had advanced. Meanwhile a section of artillery had been un-limbered and posted to support the cavalry, the guns charged with canister and the gunners with the lanyards taut, ready to open at command. As our squadrons rushed back in disordered flight a stupid trooper rode between the gunner and the piece, thus drawing the friction primer and discharging the gun full in the faces of our men, killing two outright and wounding half a dozen. Our infantry having arrived in the mean time, the rebels abandoned the town, retiring westward by the Hagerstown road. While the Commander tarried with General Burnside I rode into the city again, accompanied by some young Staff officers, and hoping to meet some former acquaintance among the citizens. . . .

Lee entered Maryland evidently indulging in the belief that the State would rise and welcome the Southern army. His proclamation was plausibly framed to engage the good-will of the inhabitants, and the conduct of his troops as constrainedly regular as was possible under the circumstances. The observation of a few days was sufficient to disenchant him. In the districts which he visited the mass of the population was of undoubted and un-compromising loyalty. Yet the open defiance and hatred of this class was not so discouraging as the coldness and even terror with which the Maryland secessionists regarded their ragged and needy liberators. In truth, the spirit of rebellion which had boiled over scalding hot in April, 1861, had by this time simmered down to a tepid sentimentalism which manifested itself in weak social snobbery, silly songs, intriguing, speculating, and blockade-run-ning. There were, indeed, some more daring spirits left, who, in spite of the Federal martial law, would on occasions drink themselves drunk to the suc-cess of "the good cause," and hurrah for Jeff Davis at the risk of a night in the guard-house. But that living, practical faith which is willing to undergo hard knocks for opinion's sake, and take pay in Confederate promises, is totally lacking in Maryland. In brief, except a few young Hotspurs attracted by the love of adventure, and a few cock-eyed politicians who have com-promised themselves unwittingly, rebel Maryland seems to prefer the side-board to the field, and from all accounts Lee will lose two by desertion where he gains one by recruiting. . . .

September 14, Sunday.—Pleasant. On rising this morning I heard cannon sounding to the westward, and evidently nearer to us than Harper's Ferry. I also observed our columns moving in the same direction, and winding over the Catoctin Ridge, which divides Frederick from the Middletown Valley. We were presently in the saddle; and on arriving at the summit of the moun-tain with one accord drew rein to admire the scene which presented itself. The Valley of the Catoctin, which lay beneath us like a map unrolled, is one of the most fertile and best improved districts in Maryland. As far as the eye can reach, north and southward, it is dotted with handsome farm-houses, and pretty thriving villages, and checkered with cultivated fields and scraps of woodland, enlivened by silvery streams and traversed by fine public roads. The western horizon is limited by a mountain range which rises abruptly to the height of a thousand feet. This ridge, about four miles distant, is a continuation of the Great Blue Ridge of Virginia, here called the South Mountain, and within sight is crossed by two great highways—the national turnpike passing over Turner's Gap immediately in front of us, and a less important road passing at Crampton's Gap opposite Burkittsville, about five miles to the southward and leading directly to Maryland Heights and Harper's Ferry. From both these passes we could hear the sullen booming of the guns, and see the white wreaths of smoke rolling up the blue face of the mountain. Across the lovely valley, by every road and pathway, our columns of horse, foot, and artillery were moving, all centring toward the defiant batteries.

Comprehending the beauty and thrilling interest of the scene at a glance, the Commander rode rapidly forward to Middletown, where he stopped at Burnside's quarters, located in an orchard at the eastern end of the village. . . .

About two o'clock P.M. it was ascertained that the passage of South Mountain would cost us a battle; and following the Commander through Middletown we rode forward about two miles, and ascending a spur of the mountain took a position between two of our batteries. From this point we had as comprehensive a view of the position as could be conveniently obtained. The windings of the main turnpike through cleared fields were visible from the valley to the summit; but the flanking roads and positions to the right and left of the turnpike were a good deal obscured by forest which covered the ridge continuously. By both these flanking roads our columns were already ascending to the attack—that on the left commanded by Reno, while Hooker led the forces on the right. At the same time Gibbon's Brigade was advanced on the national turnpike in the centre to amuse the enemy with a feint attack. Generals Cox and Wilcox with their brigades had already made a lodgment on the left summit, and the continuous peals of musketry from that quarter showed that they were stoutly resisted. Sturgis was ordered forward to support them; and as his glittering column was seen ascending the steep road Reno, who had been riding with McClellan, started forward, saying, "I must see to this matter in person."

There is nothing like the master's eye "when work is to be done," and for an hour after Reno's departure the redoubled roar of musketry proved the truth of the proverb. In time the sounds waxed fainter and fainter, the line of white smoke disappeared over the crest, and then news came that the position was carried and the enemy retreating.

Simultaneously with this action the column under Hooker, supported by Meade, was seen crawling up the rocky and difficult ascent on the right. Slowly trailing across the open ground, now entering a piece of wood, and again emerging on the upper side, winding over spurs and up ravines, the march resembled the course of a black serpent with glittering scales stealing upon its prey.

At length we had a glimpse of Hooker's command in some open ground on the summit, moving in column of companies, and heading in toward the Gap. They presently disappeared in the wood, and then came the distant muttering of musketry, which continued with little intermission until after dark, and always approaching the Gap. As Hooker moved in from the exterior position on the right, we could discern a dense and continuous column of the enemy moving to meet him by a road diverging from the National turnpike at the Summit House. This we ascertained was Longstreet's reinforcing column, and it seemed a heavy one; but after a short time it was seen retiring by the same route. All the while the batteries posted on the different eminences were unremitting in their activity, but so broken and densely wooded was the field that comparatively little artillery was used, and that probably with but little effect.

From the position of the Staff we also had a good view of Franklin's operations at Burkittsville and Crampton's Gap, between three and four miles distant, and as matters in our immediate proximity seemed to promise a fortunate conclusion, we found leisure at intervals to turn our glasses in that direction. From the summit the enemy's guns were working industriously, no batteries replying from our side, but the line of musketry smoke was evidently advancing up the ascent, and that indicated a victory there.

About sunset it was understood that both our flanking columns had established themselves solidly in positions commanding the main pass. The enemy had contested the ground with the greatest obstinacy, making repeated and determined efforts to recover what they had lost, but all in vain. As they still maintained a defiant attitude, Gibbon was ordered to advance on the centre, and carry the main road. This he did in gallant style, deploying his lines on either side of the turnpike, and moving a section of artillery on the road. His advance was difficult and slow, as the enemy had greatly the advantage of position, and disputed every step with bitter tenacity. This fight took place after dark, and the General-in-Chief, riding to an adjacent knoll, continued to overlook the sparkling combat until after nine o'clock. About that time the fires died away, Gibbon having advanced apparently about half-way up the mountain. . . .

General McClellan occupied a room in which was a table, two or three chairs, and a couple of tallow-candles, without other furniture or embellishment. Here, surrounded by the officers of his Staff and the chiefs of the army, he discussed the events of the day. We had carried all our points, and inflicted heavy loss on the enemy, capturing between one and two thousand prisoners. . . .

It seems that we have spent the day manœuvring and studying the ground. I don't like the delay. We should have attacked on sight, Monday evening, or this morning at all risks. We might then have got Lee at a disadvantage. But while we take time to concentrate he will do the same or escape. If he is here to-morrow it will be because he feels quite confident of his game. We are entirely too methodical.

—STROTHER, "Personal Recollections of the War"

11. THE BLOODIEST DAY OF THE WAR

With the loss of the passes through South Mountain and the major part of his army still tied down at Harpers Ferry, Lee decided to recross the

Potomac and stand on the defensive. Then on September 15 he got word
that Harpers Ferry had fallen and that Jackson was on his way. Lee decided
to go ahead with his original plan; by the night of the fifteenth he had three
of his divisions in place along the Antietam, and next day Jackson came up
and took place alongside them. That day, too, McClellan brought up his
mighty host—twice the force that Lee commanded—but did not offer battle.

A word about the terrain and the disposition of the contending forces.
Sharpsburg stands in a great bend in the Potomac; the little Antietam flows
below the town, winding through woods, orchards and fields of grain. Lee
ranged his divisions between the Antietam and the town, Jackson on the
left, D. H. Hill at the center, Longstreet on the right, Walker's division in
reserve. It was, strategically, about as bad a position as an army could take.
Both flanks were vulnerable, and if McClellan could roll up the right flank
he would interpose his army between Lee and Virginia. McClellan's forces
straddled the Antietam, Hooker, Sumner and Franklin on the right, across
the stream, and Burnside on the left, east of the stream, with Porter in reserve.

The battle itself was a piecemeal affair, fought not by armies or even by
corps, but by divisions and brigades. At no time did McClellan launch a
concerted assault on the Confederate line or use his reserves; instead he wasted
his superior strength in a series of fragmentary attacks. While there was some
fighting all along the line most of the day, there were in fact three major
and separate battles: first, Hooker's attack on the Confederate left; second,
Sumner's drive on the Confederate center; third, Burnside's struggle to get
across the river and his assault on the Confederate right. All three were
partially successful, none was followed through to that complete success
which would have destroyed Lee's army and might have spelled the end of
the Confederacy.

Antietam was not a decisive battle—but it might have been. A signal
victory by Lee would not have altered the military situation, for the Con-
federate commander could not have followed up victory. But a victory by
McClellan would have cut Lee off from his base, or destroyed him and ex-
posed Richmond to imminent capture. McClellan, to be sure, claimed a
victory but, as the historian Major Steele observes, "it is hard to say which
should reflect least credit upon the Union commander, not to have defeated
Lee's army, or not to have destroyed it if he defeated it. Truth to tell, Mc-
Clellan did neither."

We begin our story of the battle with a general view—a sort of head-
quarters view—by Colonel Strother, who had the confidence of McClellan.

September 17, Wednesday. . . . At Newcomer's I found the Commander-
in-Chief, surrounded by a number of subordinate generals, planning and receiving orders. Thus far the great argument had been opened and conducted
solely by those stately and bombastic orators—the cannon. The dispute presently assumed a closer and more conversational tone as the angry chattering
of the musketry prevailed. About half past seven o'clock this had swelled to
an ominous roar, accompanied by repeated and triumphant cheers. The Gen-

eral-in-Chief, followed by all his attendants, hurried to a bluff just behind the house, whence they had a splendid view of Hooker's advance driving the enemy before them in rapid and disordered flight.

Horses were forthwith ordered, and we rode rapidly across to a commanding knoll on the eastern side of the Sharpsburg turnpike, about the centre of our line of battle, and nearly opposite the town of Sharpsburg, whose locality was indicated by the belfry of a small church which peered above the opposite hill. This was the same point from which the General reconnoitred the enemy on Monday afternoon, and afforded the most comprehensive view of the field that could be had from any single point.

Our order of battle, as detailed to me by McClellan on yesterday afternoon, was as follows: Our right wing under Sumner was established across the Antietam, and would swing round, closing in upon the enemy's left and forcing it back upon the centre, thus cutting off the roads to Hagerstown and Williamsport. Our left, under Burnside, was ordered to force the passage of the Antietam at a stone bridge a mile below the central turnpike, and driving the enemy's right back on Sharpsburg, would bar his retreat toward Antietam Ford on the Potomac and Harper's Ferry, thus (to use the General's own words) pinching him up in a vice. Our centre was refused, and lay behind the stream ready to act as circumstances might require. . . .

The enemy's lines, occupying the ridge which conceals Sharpsburg from us, and thence westward along the Hagerstown pike and the wood behind the Dunker church, are only indicated by the smoke of his guns and an occasional horseman showing himself over the summit to reconnoitre. Meanwhile Sumner had crossed and taken full possession of the position in front of the Dunker church, driving the enemy back into the wood. Several brigades, which I understood to be Richardson's Division, advanced to a position still nearer the centre, confronting the enemy between the Dunker church and the town. To meet them the enemy's lines moved out into the open ground and opened fire, when a portion of our troops broke in confusion and ran down the road toward the central bridge. In a few moments, however, they were rallied, and returned to their positions, showing great steadiness for the rest of the day. The rebel line also stood as straight and firm as a stone-wall, although under a heavy fire both of artillery and musketry. I saw the shells strike them frequently, and when there appeared symptoms of wavering I could see the officers collaring the men and forcing them back to their places.

Our troops fought splendidly, and made several advances at a run, but the force seemed entirely too light and too much isolated to effect any decisive purpose. They did their part, however, and gave their *vis-à-vis* full occupation. A portion of Sumner's advance had pushed forward nearly to the line of fence in front of the Dunker church; but they seemed to be so cut up and reduced in numbers that they took shelter behind a slope in the field, and only kept up a light skirmishing against the wood.

During these operations the clamor of the artillery along the whole line of battle (several miles in extent) was incessant. We could hear the distant muttering of musketry from the flanks, but Sumner's movement had evidently come to a stand. This produced a lull in the battle within our sight, and I had leisure to remark upon the head-quarters group immediately about me. In the midst was a small redan built of fence-rails, behind which sat General Fitz John Porter, who, with a telescope resting on the top rail, studied the field with unremitting attention, scarcely leaving his post during the whole day. His observations he communicated to the commander by nods, signs, or in words so low-toned and brief that the nearest by-standers had but little benefit from them. When not engaged with Porter, McClellan stood in a soldierly attitude intently watching the battle and smoking with the utmost apparent calmness; conversing with surrounding officers and giving his orders in the most quiet under-tones. General Marcy, his Chief of Staff, was always near him, and through him orders were usually given to the aides-de-camp to be transmitted to distant points of the field. Several foreign officers of the French, Prussian, and Sardinian service were present. Every thing was as quiet and punctilious as a drawing-room ceremony.

While the activity of the infantry within sight seemed to have been temporarily suspended, the thunder of between two and three hundred pieces of artillery still kept up the continuity of the battle. The shells had set fire to several barns, which were in full blaze, while at intervals I recognized from among the enemy's guns the sudden spring of that tall mushroom-shaped cloud which indicates the explosion of a caisson or ammunition-wagon, showing that our artillery was doing good work.

Franklin's Corps having arrived on the field he is ordered to fill a gap between Sumner and Hooker, occasioned by the rapid advance of the latter doubling back the enemy's left. Shortly after this order was sent I observed a sudden movement from the line of wood behind the Dunker church, and in a moment, as it appeared, the whole field in front was covered with masses of the enemy, formed in columns of grand divisions, advancing at a run, with arms at right shoulder shift, and yelling like demons. I could see the heads of four columns, which seemed to be composed of a brigade each; but the extreme left of the movement was masked by a wood and the smoke of a burning farm-house. The attack was evidently made to recover the wood and position from which they had been driven by Hooker at the commencement of the fight.

The rush of this fiery avalanche swept away the feeble remnant of Sumner's command as the flame of a torch scatters the swarms of blue flies from the shambles. As these, in their disordered and more rapid flight, unmasked the front of the rebel advance there was a swell in the chorus of the battle so vast and voluminous that it seemed as if heaven and earth vibrated with the stunning roar. Cannon and musketry mingled in a tonic outpouring that exceeded in grandeur all sounds I ever heard, except, perhaps, Niagara. The check of pulsation produced by this sudden apparition was relieved by an officer, who whispered: "That's Franklin. Hear him!"

The rebel columns had swept on, disappearing entirely in the dust raised by their own movement through the trampled field, the rolling smoke of the burning houses, and the sulphurous cloud which rose like a snowy mountain over the assailed position. We could distinctly see Sumner's débris rallying behind the wood, forming in line, and returning to the combat. Higher and higher rolled the white clouds, steady and unbroken; the roar of ordnance continued for twenty minutes or more, when, emerging from the smoke, flying in the wildest disorder, thinned and scattered, we saw the enemy returning to the wood from which he had advanced. Shot and shell followed with vengeful rapidity, and anon our ordered lines were seen sweeping over the disputed field to resume their position in front of the Dunker church. As the smoke and dust disappeared I was astonished to observe our troops moving along the front and passing over what appeared to be a long, heavy column of the enemy without paying it any attention whatever. I borrowed a glass from an officer, and discovered this to be actually a column of the enemy's dead and wounded lying along a hollow road—afterward known as Bloody Lane. Among the prostrate mass I could easily distinguish the movements of those endeavoring to crawl away from the ground; hands waving as if calling for assistance, and others struggling as if in the agonies of death.

I was standing beside General McClellan during the progress and conclusion of this attack. The studied calmness of his manner scarcely concealed the underlying excitement, and when it was over he exclaimed: "By George, this is a magnificent field, and if we win this fight it will cover all our errors and misfortunes forever!"

"General," I said, "fortune favors the bold; hurl all our power upon them at once, and we will make a glorious finish of the campaign and the war."

"Colonel," said he, "ride forward to Pleasonton and tell him to throw a couple of squadrons forward on the Sharpsburg road, as far as they can go, to find out what is there."

I surmise, from this order, the General had suspected the enemy's line immediately in front of our centre was weak. I rode down the turnpike, leaving Porterstown to the left, and near the central bridge found General Pleasonton, to whom I delivered the message. He responded promptly by throwing forward two horse-batteries, which took position across the Antietam on either side of the turnpike.

Thus far we had heard nothing and seen no results from Burnside's wing. The General was impatient, and frequently asked: "What is Burnside about? Why do we not hear from him?" During the morning he sent several messengers to hasten his movements; but we only heard vaguely that he had not yet effected a crossing and could not carry the bridge.

Meanwhile the news from the right showed that matters were taking an unfavorable turn there. Hooker was wounded and withdrawn from the field. Mansfield was killed, and a number of other valuable general officers *hors de combat*. Our right wing seemed to have spent its aggressive power, and held its ground because the enemy was equally incapable of aggression.

About one o'clock we had news that Burnside had carried the bridge; but there seemed to be a lull in the battle along the whole line from right to left. An aid was wanted to carry another urgent message to Burnside. General

Marcy asked me if I was ready for the service. I promptly led up my mare, but the General observing that she was sweltering from my recent ride, called Colonel Key, whose horse was fresh, and asked him to ride over to General Burnside's position and ascertain what was the cause of the delay. I was extremely anxious to see what was going on there, and begged to be permitted to carry the message, but Key would not yield. He returned with the information that Burnside had effected a crossing and thought he could hold the bridge.

The Commander-in-Chief replied, "He should be able to do that with five thousand men; if he can do no more I must take the remainder of his troops and use them elsewhere in the field." . . .

As the afternoon wore away, and while the Commanding General was absent, the fires of death were rekindled along the whole line. Since the over-whelming repulse by Franklin of the enemy's powerful attacking column he seemed to have yielded the contested ground on the right, and to have fallen back to a more sheltered line between the Dunker church and the town. Yet, though his infantry was less demonstrative, his artillery appeared to be stronger and more active than during the forenoon. About this time we witnessed one of the handsomest exhibitions of gallantry which occurred during the day. A battery of ours was seen entering the field in the vicinity of Richardson's Division; moving at a walk and taking position, apparently in advance of our line, it opened fire at short range, and maintained its ground for half an hour under the concentrated fire of at least forty guns of the enemy. As they moved in with the utmost deliberation I saw a number of shells strike and overthrow men and horses, and during the combat the bat-tery sometimes appeared covered with the smoke and dust of the enemy's bursting shells. Unable to sustain the unequal contest they at length with-drew to shelter, and then we saw parties returning to the ground to bring off the wounded in blankets and to remove the limbers of two guns the horses of which had been killed. This, I afterward ascertained, was Graham's Bat-tery United States Artillery, and I was further informed by Lieutenant Elder, who commanded a section in the action, that in half an hour they lost eleven men and seventeen horses. The affair was observed from head-quarters with the greatest interest, and elicited the warmest commendation, especially from the foreign officers on the ground.

At length, about four o'clock in the afternoon, the cumulating thunder on the left announced that Burnside's advance had at last commenced (three hours too late). The advance was distinctly visible from our position, and the movement of the dark columns, with arms and banners glittering in the sun, following the double line of skirmishers, dashing forward at a trot, load-ing and firing alternately as they moved, was one of the most brilliant and exciting exhibitions of the day. As this splendid advance seemed to be carry-ing every thing before it our attention was withdrawn to the right by the appearance of large bodies of the enemy with glittering arms and banners moving up the Hagerstown road toward the Dunker church with the ap-parent intention of renewing the attack in that direction. In a short time, however, this menacing cloud was dispelled by the concentrated fire of forty-two guns which Franklin had in position.

Meanwhile Burnside's attack had carried the height overlooking Sharpsburg on the left, having driven the enemy and captured the guns; but a counter attack on his troops, exhausted with their victory, sent them streaming down the hill again, and the last rays of the setting sun shone upon the bayonets of the enemy crowning the hill from which ours had just been driven. At this crisis the General, followed by his whole retinue, rode forward to a bluff nearer the scene of action. It was nearly dark when we reached the point, yet the sullen boom of an occasional gun, and the sparkling lines of musketry on a line about midway between Sharpsburg and the Antietam, showed that ours still held on to a portion of the field they had wrested from the enemy. About this time Burnside's messenger, asking for reinforcements, arrived. It was too late to repair errors or initiate any new movement, and they were not sent.

By eight o'clock the wailing cries of the wounded and the glare of the burning buildings alone interrupted the silence and darkness which reigned over the field of the great battle. The General then led us back to the headquarters camp, established in the rear of Keedysville, where, forgetting the events of the day for the time, we supped heartily and slept profoundly.

—Strother, "Personal Recollections of the War"

12. HOOKER HAMMERS THE CONFEDERATE LEFT—IN VAIN

The Federal attack was launched at sunrise as Doubleday and Ricketts, of Hooker's corps, moved with great élan on Jackson's line stretching at almost a right angle from the Dunker Church through the West Woods toward the Potomac. Stuart opened with artillery; Jackson moved Lawton's Georgians into a field of corn, head-high; and the lines held. Hooker sent in reserves, and Jackson called on Hood to go to the rescue. The fighting raged for an hour; then Hood sent his famous message, "Tell General Jackson unless I get reinforcements I must be forced back, but I am going on while I can." Reinforcements came—from Early and finally from McLaws, who had come up just that morning. But the Federal attack, too, was reinforced. Mansfield's corps—now under Williams—entered the battle, drove the Confederates back through the savage cornfield, and captured the Dunker Church. A counterattack by McLaws recaptured it. By nine o'clock both sides were exhausted, and the fighting on the left died down. When a brother officer asked Hood, "Where is your division?" he answered, "Dead on the field."

Those who actually participated in fighting of this kind could give only their own experience and that of their company or regiment. Here are a Federal and a Confederate account of the fighting through the cornfield and for the Dunker Church. Major Rufus R. Dawes was with the 6th Wisconsin; James Graham a captain in the 27th North Carolina—one of the regiments that was rushed to the rescue of Hood. A third item, from Longstreet himself, fills out the story that Graham has to tell.

A. Wisconsin Boys Are Slaughtered in the Cornfield

OUR lines on the left now came sweeping forward through the corn and the open fields beyond. I ordered my men up to join in the advance, and commanded: "Forward—guide left—march!" We swung away from the turnpike, and I sent the sergeant-major to Captain Kellogg, commanding the companies on the turnpike, with this order: "If it is practicable, move forward the right companies, aligning with the left wing." Captain Kellogg said: "Please give Major Dawes my compliments, and say it is impracticable; the fire is murderous."

As we were getting separated, I directed Sergeant Huntington to tell Captain Kellogg that he could get cover in the corn, and to join us, if possible. Huntington was struck by a bullet, but delivered the order. Kellogg ordered his men up, but so many were shot that he ordered them down again at once. While this took place on the turnpike, our companies were marching forward through the thick corn, on the right of a long line of battle. Closely following was a second line. At the front edge of the cornfield was a low Virginia rail fence. Before the corn were open fields, beyond which was a strip of woods surrounding a little church, the Dunkard church. As we appeared at the edge of the corn, a long line of men in butternut and gray rose up from the ground. Simultaneously, the hostile battle lines opened a tremendous fire upon each other. Men, I can not say fell; they were knocked out of the ranks by dozens. But we jumped over the fence, and pushed on, loading, firing, and shouting as we advanced. There was, on the part of the men, great hysterical excitement, eagerness to go forward, and a reckless disregard of life, of every thing but victory. Captain Kellogg brought his companies up abreast of us on the turnpike.

The Fourteenth Brooklyn Regiment, red legged Zouaves, came into our line, closing the awful gaps. Now is the pinch. Men and officers of New York and Wisconsin are fused into a common mass, in the frantic struggle to shoot fast. Every body tears cartridges, loads, passes guns, or shoots. Men are falling in their places or running back into the corn. The soldier who is shooting is furious in his energy. The soldier who is shot looks around for help with an imploring agony of death on his face. After a few rods of advance, the line stopped and, by common impulse, fell back to the edge of the corn and lay down on the ground behind the low rail fence.

Another line of our men came up through the corn. We all joined together, jumped over the fence, and again pushed out into the open field. There is a rattling fusilade and loud cheers. "Forward" is the word. The men are loading and firing with demoniacal fury and shouting and laughing hysterically, and the whole field before us is covered with rebels fleeing for life, into the woods. Great numbers of them are shot while climbing over the high post and rail fences along the turnpike. We push on over the open fields half way to the little church. The powder is bad, and the guns have become very dirty. It takes hard pounding to get the bullets down, and our

ANTIETAM

firing is becoming slow. A long and steady line of rebel gray, unbroken by the fugitives who fly before us, comes sweeping down through the woods around the church. They raise the yell and fire. It is like a scythe running through our line. "Now, save, who can." It is a race for life that each man runs for the cornfield. A sharp cut, as of a switch, stings the calf of my leg as I run. Back to the corn, and back through the corn, the headlong flight continues.

At the bottom of the hill, I took the blue color of the state of Wisconsin, and waving it, called a rally of Wisconsin men. Two hundred men gathered around the flag of the Badger state. Across the turnpike just in front of the haystacks, two guns of Battery "B," 4th U. S. artillery were in action. The pursuing rebels were upon them. General John Gibbon, our brigade commander, who in regular service was captain of this battery, grimed and black with powder smoke in himself sighting these guns of his old battery, comes running to me, "Here, major, move your men over, we must save these guns."

I commanded "Right face, forward march," and started ahead with the colors in my hand into the open field, the men following. As I entered the field, a report as of a thunderclap in my ear fairly stunned me. This was Gibbon's last shot at the advancing rebels. The cannon was double charged with canister. The rails of the fence flew high in the air.

A line of union blue charged swiftly forward from our right across the field in front of the battery, and into the corn-field. They drove back the rebels who were firing upon us. It was our own gallant 19th Indiana, and here fell dead their leader, Lieutenant Colonel A. F. Bachman; but the youngest captain in their line, William W. Dudley, stepped forward and led on the charge.

I gathered my men on the turnpike, reorganized them, and reported to General Doubleday, who was himself there. He ordered me to move back to the next woods in the rear, to remain and await instruction. Bullets, shot, and shell, fired by the enemy in the corn-field, were still flying thickly around us, striking the trees in this woods, and cutting off the limbs. I placed my men under the best shelter I could find, and here we figured up, as nearly as we could, our dreadful losses in the battle. Three hundred and fourteen officers and men had marched with us into battle. There had been killed and wounded, one hundred and fifty-two. Company "C" under Captain Hooe, thirty-five men, was not in the fight in front of the corn-field. That company was on skirmish duty farther to our right. In this service they lost two men. Of two hundred and eighty men who were at the corn-field and turnpike, one hundred and fifty were killed or wounded. This was the most dreadful slaughter to which our regiment was subjected in the war. We were joined in the woods by Captain Ely, who reported to me, as the senior officer present, with the colors and eighteen men of the second Wisconsin. They represented what remained for duty of that gallant regiment.

—DAWES, *Service with the Sixth Wisconsin Volunteers*

B. McLAWS TO THE RESCUE OF HOOD

Before day on the morning of 17 September, 1862, we were moved and placed in line of battle on the extreme right of the Confederate lines, our left resting upon the yard of a man whose name I did not learn, who, to prevent our getting water, broke off his pump-handle and destroyed his pump, so that we were compelled to fill our canteens from a mud hole in his stable lot or do without water. Most of us filled from this mud-hole, and I can testify that, while not as fresh and sweet as some I have seen, yet in the heat and strife of that day its filth was almost forgotten and it served very well to quench thirst. We remained in this position till about 8:30 o'clock A.M., when we were ordered to the left centre. After double-quicking one and a half or two miles we were placed in line about one mile to the left of the town of Sharpsburg.

The Twenty-seventh North Carolina infantry, Colonel John R. Cooke, and the Third Arkansas, Captain Ready commanding, were detached from the rest of the division and fought as a little brigade by themselves under the command of Colonel Cooke of the Twenty-seventh North Carolina; Colquitt's Georgia Brigade being some 500 yards to our right, and the rest of our division about the same distance to our left. Forming in a corn field we advanced under a heavy fire of grape and canister at a quick step, up a little rise, and halted at a rail fence, our right considerably advanced. Captain Greenough's battery, attached to General Kershaw's Brigade was placed on our left, but was soon withdrawn. After holding this position for half an hour or more our front was changed; the left retiring about ten steps and the right thrown back considerably, so as to be upon a line with the other troops.

In the meantime we had suffered heavily and, I think inflicted equally as much damage upon the enemy. The Yankees getting possession of a piece of woods upon our left, Companies F, K, and G, the three left companies of the Twenty-seventh, were directed to center their fire upon that point; and right well did they do their work, as it appeared upon an examination of the field next day that the enemy were piled two or three deep in some places. About 1 o'clock P.M., the enemy having retired behind the hill upon which they were posted, and none appearing within range in our front, Colonel Cooke ordered us to fall back some twenty steps in the corn field and lie down, so as to draw them on; he in the meantime, regardless of personal danger from sharpshooters, remained at the fence beside a small hickory tree.

After remaining there some twenty minutes the enemy attempted to sneak up a section of artillery to the little woods on our left. Colonel Cooke, watching the movement, ordered the four left companies of the Twenty-seventh North Carolina up to the fence and directed them to fire upon this artillery. At the first fire, before they had gotten into position, nearly every horse and more than half the men fell, and the infantry line which had moved up to support them showed evident signs of wavering. Colonel Cooke seeing this, and having received orders to charge if opportunity offered, ordered a charge. Without waiting a second word of command both regiments leaped the fence and "went at them" and soon we had captured these guns and had the troops in front of us in full retreat. A battery posted near a little brick church upon a hill (the Dunkard church, so often referred to in accounts of this battle, which was situated on the "Hagerstown Pike" and just to our left and front), was playing sad havoc with us, but thinking that would be taken by the troops upon our left, who we supposed were charging with us, we still pursued the flying foe. Numbers of them surrendered to us and they were ordered to the rear. Two or three hundred took shelter behind a lot of haystacks, and fastening white handkerchiefs to their muskets and bayonets, held them out offering to surrender.

We pushed on, and soon wheeling to the right drove down their line, giving them an enfilade fire, and succeeded in breaking six regiments, which fled in confusion. Only one Federal regiment, that I saw, left the field in anything like good order. After pushing on in this way, we found ourselves opposed by a body of the enemy behind a stone wall in a corn field. Stopping to contend with these we found that we were almost out of ammunition; the cartridges which we had captured on the field, and of these there was a large quantity, not fitting our guns.

Colonel Cooke, learning this fact, and seeing that we were not supported in our charge, ordered us to fall back to our original position. This, of course, was done at double-quick. As we returned we experienced the perfidy of those who had previously surrendered to us and whom we had not taken time to disarm. They, seeing that we were not supported, attempted to form a line in our rear and in a few minutes would have done so. As it was, we had to pass between two fires, a part of the troops having been thrown back to oppose our movement on their flank and these supposed prisoners having formed on the other side. A bloody lane indeed it proved to us. Many a brave man lost his life in that retreat. At some points the lines were not sixty yards distant on either side of us. Arriving at our original position both regiments halted and were soon reformed.

In this retreat we were very materially aided and protected by Cobb's Brigade, then commanded by Colonel William MacRae, of the Fifteenth North Carolina Regiment. . . .

As soon as the regiments could reform behind their rail fence, they opened fire with the few cartridges they had left and soon checked the advance of the enemy who did not come beyond the line which they had occupied in the morning. In a short while all our ammunition was exhausted. Colonel Cooke sent courier after courier for ammunition, but still none was sent. Four or five times during the afternoon General Longstreet sent couriers telling Colonel Cooke to hold the position at all hazards, that "it was the key to the whole line." Colonel Cooke's reply was always, "Tell General Longstreet to send me some ammunition. I have not a cartridge in my command, but will hold my position at the point of the bayonet."

The rail fence, which was our only protection, was riddled with bullets and torn with shot and shell and our men were falling fast, but still the Twenty-seventh North Carolina and the Third Arkansas flinched not. Imbued with the courage of their commander, they stood firm to their post.

For about two hours and a half they held the position literally without a cartridge. . . . Between 4 and 5 o'clock in the afternoon we were relieved (I think by the Third North Carolina and a Louisiana regiment), and were moved about a mile to the rear to get ammunition and fresh water. After resting about half an hour we were marched again to the front and placed in position just behind and in support of the troops who had relieved us. Here we were subjected to a severe shelling, but had no chance to return the fire. The day had been a long one, but the evening seemed longer; the sun seemed almost to go backwards, and it appeared as if night would never come. As soon as it became dark we were moved to the left, rejoined our division, and with them bivouacked upon the battlefield.

The regiment entered the battle with 325 officers and men and lost in killed and wounded 203, about 63 per cent. One company (G) went in 30 strong and had but five left at the end of the day. Another (Company E), with an average company and a full complement of officers, lost its Captain, First Lieutenant and Second Lieutenant killed, and two-thirds of its men killed or wounded.

—Graham, "Twenty Seventh Regiment"

C. Longstreet Turns a Battery on the Federals

We were under the crest of a hill occupying a position that ought to have been held by from four to six brigades. The only troops there were Cooke's regiment of North Carolina infantry, and they were without a cartridge. As I rode along the line with my staff I saw two pieces of the Washington Artillery (Miller's battery), but there were not enough men to man them. The gunners had been either killed or wounded. This was a fearful situation for the Confederate center. I put my staff-officers to the guns while I held their horses. It was easy to see that if the Federals broke through our line there, the Confederate army would be cut in two and probably destroyed, for we were already badly whipped and were only holding our ground by sheer force of desperation. Cooke sent me word that his ammunition was out. I replied that he must hold his position as long as he had a man left. He responded that he would show his colors as long as there was a man alive to hold them up. We loaded up our little guns with canister and sent a rattle of hail into the Federals as they came up over the crest of the hill.

That little battery shot harder and faster, with a sort of human energy, as though it realized that it was to hold the thousands of Federals at bay or the battle was lost. So warm was the reception we gave them that they dodged back behind the crest of the hill. We sought to make them believe we had many batteries before them. As the Federals would come up they would see the colors of the North Carolina regiment waving placidly and then would receive a shower of canister. We made it lively while it lasted. In the meantime General Chilton, General Lee's chief of staff, made his way to me and asked, "Where are the troops you are holding your line with?" I pointed to my two pieces and to Cooke's regiment, and replied, "There they are; but that regiment hasn't a cartridge."

Chilton's eyes popped as though they would come out of his head; he struck spurs to his horse and away he went to General Lee. I suppose he made some remarkable report, although I did not see General Lee again until night. After a little a shot came across the Federal front, plowing the ground in a parallel line. Another and another, each nearer and nearer their line. This enfilade fire, so distressing to soldiers, was from a battery on D. H. Hill's line, and it soon beat back the attacking column.

Meanwhile, R. H. Anderson and Hood came to our support and gave us more confidence. It was a little while only until another assault was made against D. H. Hill, and extending far over toward our left, where McLaws and Walker were supporting Jackson. In this desperate effort the lines seemed to swing back and forth for many minutes, but at last they settled down to their respective positions, the Confederates holding with a desperation which seemed to say, "We are here to die."

—LONGSTREET, "The Invasion of Maryland"

13. THE DESPERATE FIGHTING ALONG BLOODY LANE

The second part of the battle came at the Confederate center, and almost by accident. About nine in the morning Sumner's corps had moved out to support Hooker. French's division went astray, and struck at the Confederate line as it curved eastward from the Dunker Church. Here D. H. Hill stood behind a sunken lane that was that day to be rebaptized "bloody." French was shortly joined by Richardson's division. Outnumbered, Hill put up a savage resistance. "The combat that took place," writes the historian Ropes, "was beyond question one of the most sanguinary and desperate in the whole war." When the Federals succeeded in enfilading the lane, the Confederates withdrew, leaving a yawning hole between the left and the center. It was a crucial moment for the Confederacy; General Alexander later wrote that "Lee's army was ruined and the end of the Confederacy was in sight." Now was the moment for McClellan to hurl in his reserves— Franklin's VI Corps, which had scarcely seen action, and Porter's V. McClellan did nothing. The attack ebbed away, the Confederates rallied, and the line held.

We have included two accounts of this fight at the center. The first is from Thomas Livermore of the 18th New Hampshire; we have met him before and he needs no further introduction. The second is by the famous John B. Gordon, who rose to be lieutenant general by the end of the war and was subsequently Senator from Georgia and commander in chief of the Confederate Veterans.

A. THOMAS LIVERMORE PUTS ON HIS WAR PAINT

THE events of a battle in which the troops maneuver a good deal are almost always confused in one's memory, and I am not exactly certain of the order in which I place events, nor of the duration of the various struggles here, but they are related as now pictured on my mind. I believe that while we fired by file a little before we advanced across the road, yet that we did not meet with great opposition here, probably because the Irish regiment we relieved had done considerable toward using up the line we first dealt with. At any rate, we swept forward, and as we were advancing (either now or previously across the sward) I heard old General Richardson cry out, "Where's General ———?" I looked over my right shoulder and saw that gallant old fellow advancing on the right of our line, almost alone, afoot and with his bare sword in his hand, and his face was as black as a thunder cloud; and well it might be, for some of our own men, turning their heads toward him, cried out, "Behind the haystack!" and he roared out, "God damn the field officers!" I shall never cease to admire that magnificent fighting general who advanced with his front line, with his sword bare and ready for use, and his swarthy face, burning eye, and square jaw, though long since lifeless dust, are dear to me.

We swept on over the road into the cornfield, taking prisoner the broken remnants of the line which had opposed, now crouching in the corn before us, and down into a ravine, to the foot of the slope on which the rebel batteries stood, and not more than two hundred yards from them; all the time being pelted with canister from the battery in our front, which hurtled through and tore down even the slender cornstalks. . . . The rebels then attempted to send a line of battle down the slope to meet us under cover of the artillery fire, but by this time we had advanced beyond the range of the batteries on the right, and my impression is that either on account of the depth of the ravine we were in or because of the advancing rebel line being in the way, the pieces of the battery in our front were not depressed enough to hurt us, and we gave our undivided attention to this advancing line. We were fresh, and opened a withering, *literally* withering, fire on the rebels; for although they may have started in regular order, yet before they got to the foot of the slope there was no semblance of a line, and the individuals of what had been the line, either by reason of invincible bravery, or for the purpose of gaining shelter, ran forward scatteringly in the face of our fire, with heads down as if before a storm, to a fence which was a few yards in front of us, but did not form a line which annoyed us, that I recollect.

In my opinion here was a glorious chance to win the victory. We seemed to have penetrated to the right flank of the enemy, no infantry appeared to turn our left flank at this juncture, and no battery opened on our left front, and the line which the rebels sent down in our front was broken by a regiment of 300 men or less. Of course, I don't know what troops there were in reserve behind the rebel line at this point, but from all that I have learned I see no reason to doubt that if the prolongation of our line to the left, which we ended, had been continued by one division, we should have turned the right of the left wing of this rebel army.

But, however triumphant our advance had been, it seems that Colonel Cross found that he was not only in advance of the line on his right, but that there was an interval between his right and its left on the same alignment; so to avoid the catastrophe which such a position might bring upon us, he moved us to the right and rear until at length we found ourselves in the vicinity of the sunken road again with our line intact. The rebels followed this movement closely with an advance of a formidable line of battle, which we met with a rapid fire, but the rebels now attempted a maneuver, which was the very one I have suggested we might have accomplished, that is, the flanking of our left. We were very busily engaged in the corn when some one on the left detected this movement of the enemy around our left, which was concealed from the most of us by the corn. Colonel Cross convinced himself that this was the case when he in some way changed our front "to the left and rear" so as to confront the rebel line squarely. . . .

And then we filed to the left . . . and outflanking the rebel line in turn poured such a fire into it as to drive it off. As I was near the right of the line I did not see how much the rebels outflanked us, nor did I see how much we outflanked them, and was very busily occupied with the rebels in my own front.

At this time we were subjected to a most terrible fire of artillery, and I recollect one shell or case shot which burst in the middle of "G," the color company, and killed and wounded eight men and tore a great hole in one of our flags, and our regiment, already weakened, was fast losing men from its ranks. At this trying time the rebel infantry advanced for the third time against us, when the colonel moved us into the sunken road and there we planted ourselves for the last struggle.

On looking around me I found that we were in the old, sunken road mentioned several times before, and that the bed of it lay from one to three feet below the surface of the crest along which it ran. In this road there lay so many dead rebels that they formed a line which one might have walked upon as far as I could see, many of whom had been killed by the most horrible wounds of shot and shell, and they lay just as they had been killed apparently, amid the blood which was soaking the earth. It was on this ghastly flooring that we kneeled for the last struggle. The rebels advanced through the corn, firing, the artillery played upon us without mercy, and now we were harder pressed than ever before, with no help at hand from the reserves which we could see. The battle still raged on our right, and it seemed useless to expect aid from that quarter; this is retrospective, however, and I am not aware that we thought of or prayed for help.

As the rebel advance became apparent, we plied the line with musketry with all our power, and no doubt with terrible effect, but they still advanced. A color-bearer came forward within fifteen yards of our line, and with the utmost desperation waved a rebel flag in front of him. Our men fairly roared, "Shoot the man with the flag!" and he went down in a twinkling and the flag was not raised in sight again. As the fight grew furious, the colonel cried out, "Put on the war paint"; and looking around I saw the glorious man standing erect, with a red handkerchief, a conspicuous mark, tied around his bare head and the blood from some wounds on his forehead streaming over his face, which was blackened with powder. Taking the cue somehow we rubbed the torn end of the cartridges over our faces, streaking them with powder like a pack of Indians, and the colonel, to complete the similarity, cried out, "Give 'em the war whoop!" and all of us joined him in the Indian war whoop until it must have rung out above all the thunder of the ordnance. I have sometimes thought it helped to repel the enemy by alarming him to see this devilish-looking line of faces, and to hear the horrid whoop; and at any rate, it reanimated us and let him know we were unterrified.

Added to the inspiration of these devices, a stream of shouts, curses, and appeals to "Fire! Fire! Fire faster!" came from our mouths, and while with our first advance into the cornfield my contemplation of death in the abstract had given place to inflicting it in reality, at this time my spirits became fairly boisterous between firing, shouts, and the smell of powder smoke and all. The dead rebel whom I knelt on held in his hands a "Belgian rifle" (a poor enough arm, but worth something in a pinch like this), and although it was my duty to tend solely to my men's behavior, yet as they were each one of them doing their best, and the cap on this rifle denoted that it was loaded, I took it out of his hands, and discharged it at his living comrades, and liking the work I looked around for another piece to discharge, when Colonel Cross, who was omnipresent, omniscient, and omnipotent in the fight, cried out sharply, "Mr. Livermore, tend to your company!" and I quenched my aspirations and thenceforward watched my men. . . .

Among the incidents I remember on this day were these. I saw a private of the 61st New York, who was mounted for some reason, with a brilliant red shirt on, riding to and fro along the infantry line when the musketry was hottest, and he being the only mounted man in his vicinity was especially conspicuous, and I learned that he was doing his best to encourage the men. I was told, too, that a woman, who followed the Irish Brigade as laundress or nurse, went up with it, and standing with it in the fight, swung her bonnet around and cheered on the men; and that Colonel Barlow, of the 61st New York, tired of seeing his drummers shrink from their duty, tied them to his waist with his sash and led them under fire. A rebel in flying before our advance was killed as he was climbing over a fence and remained fixed upon it, and through mistake or rage our men had shot or bayoneted him many times.

—LIVERMORE, Days and Events

B. GENERAL GORDON IS WOUNDED FIVE TIMES AT ANTIETAM

Vigorously following up the success achieved at South Mountain, Mc-Clellan, on the 16th day of September, 1862, marshalled his veteran legions on the eastern hills bordering the Antietam. On the opposite slopes, near the picturesque village of Sharpsburg, stood the embattled lines of Lee. As these vast American Armies, the one clad in blue and the other in gray, stood contemplating each other from the adjacent hills, flaunting their defiant banners, they presented an array of martial splendor that was not equalled, perhaps, on any other field. It was in marked contrast with other battle-grounds. On the open plain, where stood these hostile hosts in long lines, listening in silence for the signal summoning them to battle, there were no breastworks, no abatis, no intervening woodlands, nor abrupt hills, nor hiding-places, nor impassable streams. The space over which the assaulting columns were to march, and on which was soon to occur the tremendous struggle, consisted of smooth and gentle undulations and a narrow valley covered with green grass and growing corn. From the position assigned me near the centre of Lee's lines, both armies and the entire field were in view. . . .

On the elevated points beyond the narrow valley the Union batteries were rolled into position, and the Confederate heavy guns unlimbered to answer them. For one or more seconds, and before the first sounds reached us, we saw the great volumes of white smoke rolling from the mouths of McClellan's artillery. The next second brought the roar of the heavy discharges and the loud explosions of hostile shells in the midst of our lines, inaugurating the great battle. The Confederate batteries promptly responded; and while the artillery of both armies thundered, McClellan's compact columns of infantry fell upon the left of Lee's lines with the crushing weight of a land-slide. The Confederate battle line was too weak to withstand the momentum of such a charge. Pressed back, but neither hopelessly broken nor dismayed, the Southern troops, enthused by Lee's presence, reformed their lines, and, with a shout as piercing as the blast of a thousand bugles, rushed in counter-charge upon the exulting Federals, hurled them back in confusion, and recovered all the ground that had been lost. Again and again, hour after hour, by charges and counter-charges, this portion of the field was lost and recovered, until the green corn that grew upon it looked as if it had been struck by a storm of bloody hail.

Up to this hour not a shot had been fired in my front. There was an ominous lull on the left. From sheer exhaustion, both sides, like battered and bleeding athletes, seemed willing to rest. General Lee took advantage of the respite and rode along his lines on the right and centre. He was accompanied by Division Commander General D. H. Hill. With that wonderful power which he possessed of divining the plans and purposes of his antagonist, General Lee had decided that the Union commander's next heavy blow would fall upon our centre, and those of us who held that important position were notified of this conclusion. We were cautioned to be prepared for a determined assault and urged to hold that centre at any sacrifice, as a break at that point would endanger his entire army. My troops held the most advanced position on this part of the field, and there was no supporting line behind us. It was evident, therefore, that my small force was to receive the first impact of the expected charge and to be subjected to the deadliest fire. To comfort General Lee and General Hill, and especially to make, if possible, my men still more resolute of purpose, I called aloud to these officers as they rode away: "These men are going to stay here, General, till the sun goes down or victory is won." Alas! many of the brave fellows are there now.

General Lee had scarcely reached his left before the predicted assault came. The day was clear and beautiful, with scarcely a cloud in the sky. The men in blue filed down the opposite slope, crossed the little stream (Antietam), and formed in my front, an assaulting column four lines deep. The front line came to a "charge bayonets," the other lines to a "right shoulder shift." The brave Union commander, superbly mounted, placed himself in front, while his band in rear cheered them with martial music. It was a thrilling spectacle. The entire force, I concluded, was composed of fresh troops from Washington or some camp of instruction. So far as I could see, every soldier wore white gaiters around his ankles. The banners above them had apparently never been discolored by the smoke and dust of battle. Their gleaming bayonets flashed like burnished silver in the sunlight. With the precision of step and perfect alignment of a holiday parade, this magnificent array moved to the charge, every step keeping time to the tap of the deep-sounding drum. As we stood looking upon that brilliant pageant, I thought, if I did not say, "What a pity to spoil with bullets such a scene of martial beauty!" But there was nothing else to do. . . .

My extraordinary escapes from wounds in all the previous battles had made a deep impression upon my comrades as well as upon my own mind. So many had fallen at my side, so often had balls and shells pierced and torn my clothing, grazing my body without drawing a drop of blood, that a sort of blind faith possessed my men that I was not to be killed in battle. This belief was evidenced by their constantly repeated expressions: "They can't hurt him." "He's as safe one place as another." "He's got a charmed life."

If I had allowed these expressions of my men to have any effect upon my mind the impression was quickly dissipated when the Sharpsburg storm came and the whizzing Miniés, one after another, began to pierce my body.

The first volley from the Union lines in my front sent a ball through the brain of the chivalric Colonel Tew, of North Carolina, to whom I was talking, and another ball through the calf of my right leg. On the right and the left my men were falling under the death-dealing crossfire like trees in a hurricane. The persistent Federals, who had lost so heavily from repeated repulses, seemed now determined to kill enough Confederates to make the debits and credits of the battle's balance-sheet more nearly even. Both sides stood in the open at short range and without the semblance of breastworks, and the firing was doing a deadly work. Higher up in the same leg I was again shot; but still no bone was broken. I was able to walk along the line and give encouragement to my resolute riflemen, who were firing with the coolness and steadiness of peace soldiers in target practice. When later in the day the third ball pierced my left arm, tearing asunder the tendons and mangling the flesh, they caught sight of the blood running down my fingers, and these devoted and big-hearted men, while still loading their guns, pleaded with me to leave them and go to the rear, pledging me that they would stay there and fight to the last. I could not consent to leave them in such a crisis. The surgeons were all busy at the field-hospitals in the rear, and there was no way, therefore, of stanching the blood, but I had a vigorous constitution, and this was doing me good service.

A fourth ball ripped through my shoulder, leaving its base and a wad of clothing in its track. I could still stand and walk, although the shocks and loss of blood had left but little of my normal strength. I remembered the pledge to the commander that we would stay there till the battle ended or night came. I looked at the sun. It moved very slowly; in fact, it seemed to stand still.

I thought I saw some wavering in my line, near the extreme right, and Private Vickers, of Alabama, volunteered to carry any orders I might wish to send. I directed him to go quickly and remind the men of the pledge to General Lee, and to say to them that I was still on the field and intended to stay there. He bounded away like an Olympic racer; but he had gone less than fifty yards when he fell, instantly killed by a ball through his head. I then attempted to go myself, although I was bloody and faint, and my legs did not bear me steadily. I had gone but a short distance when I was shot down by a fifth ball, which struck me squarely in the face, and passed out, barely missing the jugular vein. I fell forward and lay unconscious with my face in my cap; and it would seem that I might have been smothered by the blood running into my cap from this last wound but for the act of some Yankee, who, as if to save my life, had at a previous hour during the battle, shot a hole through the cap, which let the blood out.

I was borne on a litter to the rear, and recall nothing more till revived by stimulants at a late hour of the night.

—GORDON, *Reminiscences of the Civil War*

14. "THE WHOLE LANDSCAPE TURNS RED" AT ANTIETAM

The third, and what should have been the most important, battle came on the Confederate right. Burnside was massed east of the Antietam; a thin line of Confederates under Longstreet were ranged on the hills along the western side of the stream. The first efforts to get across what came to be known as Burnside's Bridge were repulsed by Toombs. Not until one o'clock was the bridge carried; not until almost four did Burnside finally launch a full-scale attack. It was irresistible. The Federals swept up the hill, pushed the butter-nuts back onto the Cemetery and into Sharpsburg, and threatened disaster to the whole Confederate army.

Then came one of the dramatic moments of the war. Jackson had left A. P. Hill at Harpers Ferry with about 2,500 men. Early on the seventeenth Hill had started for Sharpsburg, a 15-mile hike which involved fording the Potomac. Just as Burnside broke the Confederate line, Hill's men came up on the double-quick from Shepardstown, and sounding the rebel yell burst on the triumphant Federals, hurled them back down the hill, and saved the day. That was the end. The next day Lee stood his ground; then he slipped away, across the Potomac and into Virginia.

David Thompson, who here recalls the fighting across the Burnside Bridge, was a member of the 9th New York Volunteers.

ABOUT noon the battle began afresh. This must have been Franklin's men of the Sixth Corps, for the firing was nearer, and they came up behind the center. Suddenly a stir beginning far up on the right, and running like a wave along the line, brought the regiment to its feet. A silence fell on every one at once, for each felt that the momentous "now" had come. Just as we started I saw, with a little shock, a line-officer take out his watch to note the hour, as though the affair beyond the creek were a business appointment which he was going to keep.

When we reached the brow of the hill the fringe of trees along the creek screened the fighting entirely, and we were deployed as skirmishers under their cover. We sat there two hours. All that time the rest of the corps had been moving over the stone bridge and going into position on the other side of the creek. Then we were ordered over at a ford which had been found below the bridge, where the water was waist-deep. One man was shot in mid-stream. At the foot of the slope on the opposite side the line was formed and we moved up through the thin woods. Reaching the level we lay down behind a battery which seemed to have been disabled. There, if anywhere, I should have remembered that I was soaking wet from my waist down. So great was the excitement, however, that I have never been able to recall it. Here some of the men, going to the rear for water, discovered in the ashes of some hay-ricks which had been fired by our shells the charred remains of several Confederates. After long waiting it became noised along the line that we were to take a battery that was at work several hundred yards ahead on the top of a hill. This narrowed the field and brought us to consider the work before us more attentively.

Right across our front, two hundred feet or so away, ran a country road bordered on each side by a snake fence. Beyond this road stretched a plowed field several hundred feet in length, sloping up to the battery, which was hidden in a cornfield. A stone fence, breast-high, inclosed the field on the left, and behind it lay a regiment of Confederates, who would be directly on our flank if we should attempt the slope. The prospect was far from encouraging, but the order came to get ready for the attempt.

Our knapsacks were left on the ground behind us. At the word a rush was made for the fences. The line was so disordered by the time the second fence was passed that we hurried forward to a shallow undulation a few feet ahead, and lay down among the furrows to re-form, doing so by crawling up into line. A hundred feet or so ahead was a similar undulation to which we ran for a second shelter. The battery, which at first had not seemed to notice us, now, apprised of its danger, opened fire upon us. We were getting ready now for the charge proper, but were still lying on our faces. Lieutenant-Colonel Kimball was ramping up and down the line. The discreet regiment behind the fence was silent. Now and then a bullet from them cut the air over our heads, but generally they were reserving their fire for that better shot which they knew they would get in a few minutes. The battery, however, whose shots at first went over our heads, had depressed its guns so as to shave the surface of the ground. Its fire was beginning to tell. I remember looking behind and seeing an officer riding diagonally across the field—a most inviting target—instinctively bending his head down over his horse's neck, as though he were riding through driving rain. While my eye was on him I saw, between me and him, a rolled overcoat with its straps on bound into the air and fall among the furrows. One of the enemy's grape-shot had plowed a groove in the skull of a young fellow and had cut his overcoat from his shoulders. He never stirred from his position, but lay there face downward—a dreadful spectacle. A moment after, I heard a man cursing a comrade for lying on him heavily. He was cursing a dying man.

As the range grew better, the firing became more rapid, the situation desperate and exasperating to the last degree. Human nature was on the rack, and there burst forth from it the most vehement, terrible swearing I have ever heard. Certainly the joy of conflict was not ours that day. The suspense was only for a moment, however, for the order to charge came just after. Whether the regiment was thrown into disorder or not, I never knew. I only remember that as we rose and started all the fire that had been held back so long was loosed. In a second the air was full of the hiss of bullets and the hurtle of grape-shot. The mental strain was so great that I saw at that moment the singular effect mentioned, I think, in the life of Goethe on a similar occasion—the whole landscape for an instant turned slightly red. I see again, as I saw it then in a flash, a man just in front of me drop his musket and throw up his hands, stung into vigorous swearing by a bullet behind the ear. Many men fell going up the hill, but it seemed to be all over in a moment, and I found myself passing a hollow where a dozen wounded men lay—among them our sergeant-major, who was calling me to come down. He had caught sight of the blanket rolled across my back, and called me to unroll it and help to carry from the field one of our wounded lieutenants.

When I returned from obeying this summons the regiment (?) was not to be seen. It had gone in on the run, what there was left of it, and had disappeared in the corn-field about the battery. There was nothing to do but lie there and await developments. Nearly all the men in the hollow were wounded, one man—a recruit named Devlin, I think—frightfully so, his arm being cut short off. He lived a few minutes only. All were calling for water, of course, but none was to be had.

We lay there till dusk, perhaps an hour, when the fighting ceased. During that hour, while the bullets snipped the leaves from a young locust-tree growing at the edge of the hollow and powdered us with the fragments, we had time to speculate on many things—among others, on the impatience with which men clamor, in dull times, to be led into a fight. We heard all through the war that the army "was eager to be led against the enemy." It must have been so, for truthful correspondents said so, and editors confirmed it. But when you came to hunt for this particular itch, it was always the next regiment that had it. The truth is, when bullets are whacking against tree-trunks and solid shot are cracking skulls like egg-shells, the consuming passion in the breast of the average man is to get out of the way. Between the physical fear of going forward and the moral fear of turning back, there is a predicament of exceptional awkwardness from which a hidden hole in the ground would be a wonderfully welcome outlet.

Night fell, preventing further struggle. Of 600 men of the regiment who crossed the creek at 3 o'clock that afternoon, 45 were killed and 176 wounded. The Confederates held possession of that part of the field over which we had moved, and just after dusk they sent out detachments to collect arms and bring in prisoners. When they came to our hollow all the unwounded and slightly wounded there were marched to the rear—prisoners of the 15th Georgia. We slept on the ground that night without protection of any kind; for, with a recklessness quite common throughout the war, we had thrown away every incumbrance on going into the fight.

—THOMPSON, "With Burnside at Antietam"

VII

Fredericksburg and Chancellorsville

MᴄCʟᴇʟʟᴀɴ *had won a technical victory at Antietam, and Lincoln took advantage of it to issue his preliminary Emancipation Proclamation. But once again "Little Mac" had the slows. On October 6 Halleck ordered him "to cross the Potomac and give battle to the enemy," but McClellan procrastinated. While he delayed Stuart rode with impunity around his army. Finally, on November 2, McClellan succeeded in getting his army across the Potomac; five days later Lincoln relieved him from command and appointed General Ambrose Burnside—who gave his name to sideburns—to his place. A second-rate officer with little to recommend him, Burnside was ambitious to succeed where so many had failed. Noting that Lee's forces were widely scattered, he proposed to drive south through Fredericksburg to Richmond before Lee could collect an army to oppose him. Moving with laudable celerity Burnside concentrated his "Grand Divisions" at Falmouth, just north of Fredericksburg on the Rappahannock. But alas there were no pontoons, and while the army marked time Jackson joined Lee at Fredericksburg and the Confederates dug in.*

Properly defended, Fredericksburg was well-nigh impregnable, and with Lee in command of over 75,000 men and 306 guns there was no doubt that it would be properly defended. The town lay on a bend of the broad Rappahannock; behind it were a series of low-lying hills from Marye's Heights southward to Prospect Hill, along the base of which ran the tiny Massapomax River. It was along these heights that the Confederates were entrenched, Jackson commanding the left, on Marye's Heights, and Longstreet the right. In front of Marye's Heights ran a drainage ditch, and at the base of Marye's Hill—a knoll at the southern end of the Heights—was a sunken road with a stone retaining wall which offered almost perfect protection to infantry. It was against this position that Burnside hurled his army, in vain.

Fredericksburg ended in a bloody repulse. Burnside blamed his subordinates, and demanded that the President dismiss them or him. Lincoln dismissed him, and—somewhat reluctantly, as his letter reveals—appointed in his place "Fighting Joe" Hooker, whom Burnside had declared to be "unfit to hold an important commission during a crisis like the present." It was, perhaps, the one time when Burnside's judgment proved sound.

Hooker took command of an army that had been defeated but was far from demoralized, and that was far larger than Lee's; when Longstreet was sent south of the James to find provisions and forage for men and horses, Hooker outnumbered Lee by at least two to one.

Hooker's strategy was admirable. Leaving Sedgwick with 40,000 men at Fredericksburg, he planned to move up the Rappahannock, cross over through the Wilderness, catch Lee in a giant pincers movement, and overwhelm him. If Lee chose to stand and fight at Fredericksburg, Hooker could strike him from the rear; if he moved into the Wilderness to grapple with Hooker, Sedgwick could sweep down on Richmond. By the end of April Hooker had completed the reorganization and rebuilding of his army, and on the twenty-seventh his advance guard began fording the Rappahannock. By the thirtieth the whole army, except for a reserve corps, was across and prepared to move on Lee.

But once again, as we shall see, Lee outgeneraled and outfought his adversary, using on Hooker the strategy that Hooker had planned to use on him. Instead of being himself caught in a pincers, he caught Hooker in a pincers, rolled him up on both flanks, and pushed him back to the edge of the river; then he turned on the hapless Sedgwick and sent him, too, hurtling back across the river. It was a great victory, in some ways the most spectacular of Lee's career, but it was bought at a great price: Jackson.

1. LINCOLN URGES McCLELLAN TO ADVANCE

McClellan's conduct of the Antietam campaign seemed to vindicate his reappointment to the command of the armies. Once that battle was over, however, he fell back into his old habits of delay. On October 1 Lincoln went personally to view the situation and on his return to Washington formally ordered McClellan "to cross the Potomac and give battle to the enemy." Even this categorical demand was disregarded. The following letter, characteristically patient and reasonable, was sent a week later. McClellan met it with the plea that his cavalry was broken down—a reply which drew from Lincoln the memorable retort, "Will you pardon me for asking what the horses of your army have done since the battle of Antietam that fatigues anything?" Finally on October 26 McClellan got under way, but when he permitted Lee to interpose his army between Richmond and the Federal forces, Lincoln removed him.

Few generals, it is safe to say, ever did more to merit dismissal. The Democrats sought to make a martyr out of McClellan, nominating him for the Presidency in 1864 on a platform which called the war a failure and demanded a cessation of hostilities. McClellan repudiated this plank in the platform but accepted the nomination; fortunately for the Union he was defeated that November.

To General G. B. McClellan.

Executive Mansion, Washington, October 13, 1862

My Dear Sir:—You remember my speaking to you of what I called your over-cautiousness. Are you not over-cautious when you assume that you cannot do what the enemy is constantly doing? Should you not claim to be at least his equal in prowess, and act upon the claim?

As I understand, you telegraphed General Halleck that you cannot subsist your army at Winchester unless the railroad from Harper's Ferry to that point be put in working order. But the enemy does now subsist his army at Winchester, at a distance nearly twice as great from railroad transportation as you would have to do, without the railroad last named. He now wagons from Culpepper Court-House, which is just about twice as far as you would have to do from Harper's Ferry. He is certainly not more than half as well provided with wagons as you are. I certainly should be pleased for you to have the advantage of the railroad from Harper's Ferry to Winchester; but it wastes all the remainder of autumn to give it to you, and, in fact, ignores the question of *time*, which cannot and must not be ignored.

Again, one of the standard maxims of war, as you know, is "to operate upon the enemy's communications as much as possible, without exposing your own." You seem to act as if this applies *against* you, but cannot apply in your *favor*. Change positions with the enemy, and think you not he would break your communication with Richmond within the next twenty-four hours? You dread his going into Pennsylvania. But if he does so in full force, he gives up his communications to you absolutely, and you have nothing to do but to follow and ruin him; if he does so with less than full force, fall upon and beat what is left behind all the easier.

Exclusive of the water line, you are now nearer to Richmond than the enemy is, by the route that you *can* and he *must* take. Why can you not reach there before him, unless you admit that he is more than your equal on a march? His route is the arc of a circle, while yours is the chord. The roads are as good on yours as on his.

You know I desired, but did not order, you to cross the Potomac below instead of above the Shenandoah and Blue Ridge. My idea was, that this would at once menace the enemy's communications, which I would seize if he would permit. If he should move northward, I would follow him closely, holding his communications. If he should prevent our seizing his communications, and move toward Richmond, I would press closely to him, fight him if a favorable opportunity should present, and at least try to beat him to Richmond on the inside track. I say "try;" if we never try, we shall never succeed. If he makes a stand at Winchester, moving neither north or south, I would fight him there, on the idea that if we cannot beat him when he bears the wastage of coming to us, we never can when we bear the wastage of going to him. This proposition is a simple truth, and is too important to be lost sight of for a moment. In coming to us he tenders us an advantage which we should not waive. We should not so operate as to merely drive him away. As we must beat him somewhere or fail finally, we can do it, if at all, easier near to us than far away. If we cannot beat the enemy where he now is, we never can, he again being within the intrenchments of Richmond. . . .

It is all easy if our troops march as well as the enemy, and it is unmanly to say they cannot do it. This letter is in no sense an order.

Yours truly,

A. LINCOLN.

—War of the Rebellion . . . Official Records

2. A DAY OF REBEL RULE IN CHAMBERSBURG

While the President—and the nation—was waiting impatiently for Mc-Clellan to take up the pursuit of Lee after Antietam, the Confederates seized the initiative. On October 10 General Stuart, acting under instructions from Lee, began his second "ride around the army." Crossing the Potomac with some 1,800 cavalry he rode into Chambersburg, destroyed some stores, and, before any intercepting force could be organized, turned east to Cashtown and thence down the Emmitsburg road and across the Potomac to rejoin Lee. Aside from the destruction of stores the raid was of little value, but as the total cost to Stuart was one man wounded, it was doubtless worth while. The courtesy and restraint which characterized Confederate conduct was in accordance with Lee's specific orders.

Colonel McClure, who here describes rebel rule in Chambersburg, was owner and editor of the local newspaper and a power in the Republican party.

Chambersburgh, Pa., October ——, 1862

Our people were confounded with astonishment at the brilliant audacity of the rebels penetrating twenty miles in Gen. McClellan's rear; but, however reckless or well devised on their part, the fact and the rebels were both staring our people in the face. The rain was pouring down in torrents, and in a little time citizens were seen running to and fro with their muskets; but there was no organization, and no time to effect one. Col. Kennedy attempted to improvise mounted pickets for the several roads on which they might enter, but he had scarcely got his forces mounted until the clattering of hoofs was heard on the western pike, and in a few minutes the rebel advance was in the centre of the town. They stated that they bore a flag of truce, and wished to be taken to the commandant of the post. . . .

I went up town to meet the flag of truce, and found a clever-looking "butternut," dripping wet, without any mark of rank, bearing a dirty white cloth on a little stick. He politely stated that he sought the commander or authorities of the town, and in the name of the general commanding the confederate forces, he demanded the surrender of the village. He refused to give his name, or the name of the general commanding, and he could not state on what terms they would accept a surrender. As I had no command other than the scattered and bewildered home guards—all brave enough, but entirely without drill or organization—and about three hundred wounded men in hospitals, I acted with the citizens as one of them; and it did not require a protracted council to determine that we could not successfully

resist cavalry and artillery. So we concluded that the venerable village had
to be consigned over to rebel keeping. . . .

General Hampton . . . assured us that he would scrupulously protect
citizens—would allow no soldiers to enter public or private houses unless
under command of an officer upon legitimate business—that he would take
such private property as he needed for his government or troops, but that
he would allow no wanton destruction, and who would give receipts for the
same, if desired, so that claim might be made therefor against the United
States Government. All property belonging to or used by the United States,
he stated, he would use or destroy at his pleasure, and the wounded in hospitals would be paroled. . . .

The committee went through the form of a grave but brief consultation,
somewhat expedited, perhaps, by the rain, and we then solemnly and formally
surrendered the town upon the terms proposed. . . . So rebel rule began at
Chambersburgh. They marched in very orderly, and most of their force
started out different roads to procure horses, forage, and provisions.

I started in advance of them for my house, but not in time to save the
horses. I confidently expected to be overrun by them, and to find the place
one scene of desolation in the morning. I resolved, however, that things
should be done soberly, if possible, and I had just time to destroy all the
liquors about the house. As their pickets were all around me, I could not get
it off. A barrel of best old rye, which Senator Finney had sent me to prove
the superiority of the Crawford County article over that of Franklin, was
quietly rolled out of a cellar side-door, and a good-sized hole bored into it.
A keg of Oberholtzer's best, sent me several years ago, but never tapped,
followed Finney's testimonial to Crawford County distillation; and a couple
cases of Presbury's best Girard House importation had the necks of the
bottles taken off summarily, and the contents given to the angry storm. I
finished just in time, for they were soon out upon me in force, and every
horse in the barn—ten in all—was promptly equipped and mounted by a rebel
cavalryman. They passed on towards Shippensburgh, leaving a picket-force
on the road.

In an hour they returned with all the horses they could find, and dismounted to spend the night on the turnpike in front of my door. It was now
midnight, and I sat on the porch observing their movements. They had my
best corn-field beside them, and their horses fared well. In a little while, one
entered the yard, came up to me, and, after a profound bow, politely asked
for a few coals to start a fire. I supplied him, and informed him as blandly
as possible where he would find wood conveniently, as I had dim visions of
camp-fires made of my palings. I was thanked in return, and the mild-man-
nered villain proceeded at once to strip the fence and kindle fires. Soon after,
a squad came and asked permission to get some water. I piloted them to the
pump, and again received a profusion of thanks.

Communication having thus been opened between us, squads followed
each other closely for water, but each called and asked permission before
getting it, and promptly left the yard. I was somewhat bewildered at this

uniform courtesy, and supposed it but a prelude to a general movement upon every thing eatable in the morning. . . .

About one o'clock, half a dozen officers came to the door and asked to have some coffee made for them, offering to pay liberally for it in confederate scrip. After concluding a treaty with them on behalf of the colored servants, coffee was promised them, and they then asked for a little bread with it. They were wet and shivering, and seeing a bright, open wood-fire in the library, they asked permission to enter and warm themselves until their coffee should be ready, assuring me that under no circumstances should any thing in the house be disturbed by their men. I had no alternative but to accept them as my guests until it might please them to depart, and I did so with as good grace as possible.

Once seated around the fire, all reserve seemed to be forgotten on their part, and they opened a general conversation on politics, the war, the different battles, the merits of generals in both armies, etc. They spoke with entire freedom upon every subject but their movement into Chambersburgh. Most of them were men of more than ordinary intelligence and culture, and their demeanor was in all respects eminently courteous. I took a cup of coffee with them, and have seldom seen any thing more keenly relished. They said they had not tasted coffee for weeks before, and then they had paid from six dollars to ten dollars per pound for it. When they were through, they asked whether there was any coffee left, and finding that there was some, they proposed to bring some more officers and a few privates who were prostrated by exposure to get what was left. They were, of course, as welcome as those present, and on they came in squads of five or more, until every grain of browned coffee was exhausted. They then asked for tea, and that was served to some twenty more.

In the mean time, a subordinate officer had begged of me a little bread for himself and few men, and he was supplied in the kitchen. He was followed by others in turn, until nearly an hundred had been supplied with something to eat or drink. All, however, politely asked permission to enter the house, and behaved with entire propriety. They did not make a single rude or profane remark, even to the servants. In the mean time, the officers, who had first entered the house, had filled their pipes from the box of Killickinick on the mantel—after being assured that smoking was not offensive—and we had another hour of free talk on matters generally. When told that I was a decided Republican, they thanked me for being candid. . . .

At four o'clock in the morning the welcome blast of the bugle was heard, and they rose hurriedly to depart. Thanking me for the hospitality they had received, we parted mutually expressing the hope that should we ever meet again, it would be under more pleasant circumstances. In a few minutes, they were mounted and moved into Chambersburgh. About seven o'clock I went into town, and found that the First brigade, under General Hampton, had gone toward Gettysburg. Gen. Stuart sat on his horse in the centre of the town, surrounded by his staff, and his command was coming from the country in large squads, leading their old horses and riding the new ones they had found in the stables hereabouts. General Stuart is of medium size, has a keen eye, and wears immense sandy whiskers and moustache. His demeanor to our people was that of a humane soldier. In several instances his men commenced to take private property from stores, but they were arrested by General Stuart's provost-guard. In a single instance only, that I have heard of, did they enter a store by intimidating the proprietor. All our shops and stores were closed, and, with a very few exceptions, were not disturbed.

There were considerable Government stores here—some two hundred pairs of shoes, a few boxes of clothing, and a large quantity of ammunition captured recently from General Longstreet. It was stored in the warehouses of Wunderlich & Nead. About eleven o'clock their rear-guard was ready to leave, and they notified the citizens residing near the warehouses to remove their families, as they were going to burn all public property. The railroad station-house, machine-shops, round house, and the warehouses, filled with ammunition, were then fired, and the last of the rebels fled the town. In a little time a terrific explosion told that the flames had reached the powder, and for hours shells were exploding with great rapidity. The fire companies came out as soon as the rebels left, but could not save any of the buildings fired because of the shells. They saved all others, however.

So ended a day of rebel rule in Chambersburgh. They took some eight hundred horses from our people, and destroyed, perhaps, one hundred thousand dollars' worth of property for the Cumberland Valley Railroad Company, probably five thousand dollars for Wunderlich & Nead, and one hundred and fifty thousand dollars for the Government. Our people generally feel that, bad as they are, they are not so bad as they might be. . . .

Hoping that I shall never again be called upon to entertain a circle of rebels around my fireside, believe me, truly thine,

A. K. McClure.

—McClure, "The Invasion of Pennsylvania"

3. BURNSIDE BLUNDERS AT FREDERICKSBURG

We have here two accounts of Fredericksburg—a Confederate and a Union. Each tells its own story, and it is unnecessary to recapitulate that story here, but we may give something of the setting of the battle. It was on December 10 that Burnside began laying five pontoon bridges across the Rappahannock. Confederate sharpshooters interfered effectively with this undertaking and Burnside attempted to drive them out first by a heavy bombardment of the town itself, then by sending four companies of Federal sharpshooters across in boats to hold down the Confederate fire. By the twelfth two of the "Grand Divisions" were across the river—Sumner's in Fredericksburg itself and Franklin's to the south. On the morning of the thirteenth the attack began, all along the line.

The first account here is by one of the defenders, William Owen of the Washington Artillery of New Orleans. Few of those who have left us records had a more varied experience than this Louisianian who fought in the Virginia

*campaigns to 1863, then went west, took part in the Chickamauga-Chatta-
nooga campaign, and then returned east to fight in the Wilderness and at
Petersburg. The second account is taken from the* Cincinnati Commercial.

A. The Yankees Attack Marye's Heights

O N the night of the 10th of December [1862] we, of the New Orleans
Washington Artillery, sat up late in our camp on Marye's Heights, entertaining some visitors in an improvised theater, smoking our pipes, and
talking of home. A final punch having been brewed and disposed of, everybody crept under the blankets and was soon in the land of Nod.

In an hour or two we were aroused by the report of a heavy gun. I was
up in an instant, for if there should be another it would be the signal that
the enemy was preparing to cross the river. Mr. Florence, a civilian in the
bivouac, bounced as if he had a concealed spring under his blanket, and cried
out, "Wake up! wake up! what's that?"

The deep roar of the second gun was heard, and we knew what we had
to do. It was 4 o'clock. Our orders were that upon the firing of these signal
guns we should at once take our places in the redoubts prepared for us on
Marye's Hill, and await developments. "Boots and saddles" was sounded, and
the camp was instantly astir, and in the gray of the morning we were on the
Plank road leading up the hill. The positions reached, . . . without delay the
men made the redoubts as snug as possible, and finding the epaulements not
to their liking, went to work with pick and shovel throwing the dirt a little
higher, and fashioning embrasures to fire through. The engineers objected,
and said they were "ruining the works," but the cannoneers said, "We have
to fight here, not you; we will arrange them to suit ourselves." And General
Longstreet approvingly said, "If you save the finger of a man's hand, that
does some good." A dense fog covered the country, and we could not discern what was going on in the town.

The morning of the 12th was also foggy, and it was not until 2 P.M. that
it cleared off, and then we could see the Stafford Heights, across the river,
densely packed with troops. At 3 P.M. a heavy column moved down toward
one of the bridges near the gas-works, and we opened upon it, making some
splendid practice and apparently stirring them up prodigiously, for they soon
sought cooler localities. While our guns were firing, the enemy's long range
batteries on the Stafford Heights opened upon us, as much as to say, "What
are you about over there?" We paid no attention to their inquiry, as our guns
could not reach them.

At dawn the next morning, December 13th, in the fresh and nipping air,
I stepped upon the gallery overlooking the heights back of the little old-
fashioned town of Fredericksburg. Heavy fog and mist hid the whole plain
between the heights and the Rappahannock, but under cover of that fog and
within easy cannon-shot lay Burnside's army. Along the heights, to the right
and left of where I was standing, extending a length of nearly five miles, lay
Lee's army.

BATTLE
of
FREDERICKSBURG
Dec 10-16. 1862   1 mile

236

The bugles and the drum corps of the respective armies were now sounding reveille, and the troops were preparing for their early meal. All knew we should have a battle to-day and a great one, for the enemy had crossed the river in immense force, upon his pontoons during the night. On the Confederate side all was ready, and the shock was awaited with stubborn resolution. Last night we had spread our blankets upon the bare floor in the parlor of Marye's house, and now our breakfast was being prepared in its fire-place, and we were impatient to have it over. After hastily dispatching this light meal of bacon and corn-bread, the colonel, chief bugler, and I (the adjutant of the battalion) mounted our horses and rode out to inspect our lines . . . and found everything ready for instant action. . . .

At 12 o'clock the fog had cleared, and while we were sitting in Marye's yard smoking our pipes, after a lunch of hard crackers, a courier came to Colonel Walton, bearing a dispatch from General Longstreet for General Cobb, but, for our information as well, to be read and then given to him. It was as follows: "Should General Anderson, on your left, be compelled to fall back to the second line of heights, you must conform to his movements." Descending the hill into the sunken road, I made my way through the troops, to a little house where General Cobb had his headquarters, and handed him the dispatch. He read it carefully, and said, "Well! if they wait for me to fall back, they will wait a long time."

Hardly had he spoken, when a brisk skirmish fire was heard in front, toward the town, and looking over the stone-wall we saw our skirmishers falling back, firing as they came; at the same time the head of a Federal column was seen emerging from one of the streets of the town. They came on at the double-quick, with loud cries of "Hi! Hi! Hi!" which we could distinctly hear. Their arms were carried at "right shoulder shift," and their colors were aslant the shoulders of the color-sergeants. They crossed the canal at the bridge, and getting behind the bank to the low ground to deploy, were almost concealed from our sight. It was 12:30 p.m., and it was evident that we were now going to have it hot and heavy.

The enemy, having deployed, now showed himself above the crest of the ridge and advanced in columns of brigades, and at once our guns began their deadly work with shell and solid shot. How beautifully they came on! Their bright bayonets glistening in the sunlight made the line look like a huge serpent of blue and steel. The very force of their onset leveled the broad fences bounding the small fields and gardens that interspersed the plain. We could see our shells bursting in their ranks, making great gaps; but on they came, as though they would go straight through and over us. Now we gave them canister, and that staggered them. A few more paces onward and the Georgians in the road below us rose up, and, glancing an instant along their rifle barrels, let loose a storm of lead into the faces of the advance brigade. This was too much; the column hesitated, and then, turning, took refuge behind the bank.

But another line appeared from behind the crest and advanced gallantly, and again we opened our guns upon them, and through the smoke we could discern the red breeches of the "Zouaves," and hammered away at them especially. But this advance, like the preceding one, although passing the point reached by the first column, and doing and daring all that brave men could do, recoiled under our canister and the bullets of the infantry in the road, and fell back in great confusion. Spotting the fields in our front, we could detect little patches of blue—the dead and wounded of the Federal infantry who had fallen facing the very muzzles of our guns.

Cooke's brigade of Ransom's division was now placed in the sunken road with Cobb's men. At 2 P.M. other columns of the enemy left the crest and advanced to the attack; it appeared to us that there was no end of them. On they came in beautiful array and seemingly more determined to hold the plain than before; but our fire was murderous, and no troops on earth could stand the *feu d'enfer* we were giving them. In the foremost line we distinguished the green flag with the golden harp of old Ireland, and we knew it to be Meagher's Irish brigade. The gunners of the two rifle-pieces, Corporals Payne and Hardie, were directed to turn their guns against this column; but the gallant enemy pushed on beyond all former charges, and fought and left their dead within five and twenty paces of the sunken road.

Our position on the hill was now a hot one, and three regiments of Ransom's brigade were ordered up to reënforce the infantry in the road. We watched them as they came marching in line of battle from the rear, where they had been lying in reserve. They passed through our works and rushed down the hill with loud yells, and then stood shoulder to shoulder with the Georgians. The 25th North Carolina regiment, crossing Miller's guns, halted upon the crest of the hill, dressed its line, and fired a deadly volley at the enemy at close range, and then at the command "Forward!" dashed down the hill. It left dead men on Miller's redoubt, and he had to drag them away from the muzzles of his guns.

At this time General Cobb fell mortally wounded, and General Cooke was borne from the field, also wounded. Among other missiles a 3-inch rifle-ball came crashing through the works and fell at our feet. Kursheedt picked it up and said, "Boys, let's send this back to them again"; and into the gun it went, and was sped back into the dense ranks of the enemy.

General Kershaw now advanced from the rear with two regiments of his infantry, to reënforce the men in the sunken road, who were running short of ammunition, and to take command.

The sharp-shooters having got range of our embrasures, we began to suffer. Corporal Ruggles fell mortally wounded, and Perry, who seized the rammer as it fell from Ruggles's hand, received a bullet in the arm. Rodd was holding "vent," and away went his "crazy bone." In quick succession Everett, Rossiter, and Kursheedt were wounded. Falconer in passing in rear of the guns was struck behind the ear and fell dead. We were now so short-handed that every one was in the work, officers and men putting their shoulders to the wheels and running up the guns after each recoil. The frozen ground had given way and was all slush and mud. We were compelled to call upon the infantry to help us at the guns. Eshleman crossed over from the right to report his guns nearly out of ammunition; the other officers reported the same. They were reduced to a few solid shot only. It was now 5 o'clock, P.M., and there was a lull in the storm. The enemy did not seem inclined to renew his efforts, so our guns were withdrawn one by one, and the batteries of Woolfolk and Moody were substituted.

The little whitewashed brick-house to the right of the redoubt we were in was so battered with bullets during the four hours and a half engagement that at the close it was transformed to a bright brick-dust red. An old cast-iron stove lay against the house, and as the bullets would strike it it would give forth the sound of "bing! bing!" with different tones and variations. During the hottest of the firing old Mr. Florence, our non-combatant friend, was peering around the end of the house (in which, by the way, our wounded took refuge), looking out to see if his son, who was at the gun, was all right. A cannon-ball struck the top of the work, scattering dirt all over us and profusely down our necks, and, striking the end of the house, carried away a cart-load of bricks, just where Mr. Florence had been looking an instant before. We thought surely he had met his fate, but in a moment we were pleased to see his gray head "bob up serenely," determined to see "what was the gage of the battle."

After withdrawing from the hill the command was placed in bivouac, and the men threw themselves upon the ground to take a much-needed rest. We had been under the hottest fire men ever experienced for four hours and a half, and our loss had been three killed and twenty-four wounded. Among them was Sergeant John Wood, our leading spirit in camp theatricals, who was severely injured and never returned to duty. One gun was slightly disabled, and we had exhausted all of our canister, shell and case shot, and nearly every solid shot in our chests. At 5:30 another attack was made by the enemy, but it was easily repulsed, and the battle of Fredericksburg was over, and Burnside was baffled and defeated.

—Owen, "A Hot Day on Marye's Heights"

B. "Fredericksburg Was a Trap"

Falmouth, December 17, 1862

On Friday morning [Dec. 12, 1862] those of us not fully posted, and not conversant with all the mysteries of "strategy," expected a battle. But the morning passed quietly, the smoke veiling all distant objects from observation. Our troops were crossing into Fredericksburgh. . . . The town, in the afternoon, literally swarmed with troops. The enemy's batteries were ominously silent. If the rebel general had any particular objections to the presence of our troops in the town, why did he not open upon them from his batteries? What was to prevent the enemy from shelling the town, as we had done? I asked several military gentlemen the question, for the situation appeared to me to be one of the deepest peril. One said: "The enemy had not ammunition to spare." Another: "Oh! a bombardment don't amount to any thing any how." Another: "They don't care about bombing us, it is an inconsequential sort of business. We threw four thousand shells yesterday, and it amounted to nothing." Another: "They're afraid of our siege-guns on this side." Another: "General Lee thinks he will have a big thing on us about the bombardment of this town. He proposes to rouse the indignation of the civilized world, as they call it. You'll see he won't throw a shell into it. He is playing for the sympathies of Europe." Another thought the enemy were skedaddling, and spoke of the laugh that would be raised at Burnside's expense in that case. But I think a private soldier came nearer the mark than any one else. He said, with the usual expletives: "They want us to get in. Getting out won't be quite so smart and easy. You'll see if it will." . . .

At night I crossed into the town. . . . The streets were full of soldiers lounging and smoking about their fires, or wrapped in their blankets and sleeping, their muskets stacked, in numbers that indicated the immense mass of troops that occupied the place. The sky was clear, and thickly as the stars sparkled overhead the camp-fires blazed along the Rappahannock, lighting up the front of the shattered city, and gleaming far and wide to the north. Behind the dark and gloomy hills compassing the town on the enemy's side, there was a wide glare of many fires, like an aurora borealis, marking the presence of the rebel army of Virginia. Returning to the north side of the river, the roads were choked with batteries of field-artillery, and ammunition and supply-trains, rumbling and creaking forward. . . .

It was after eleven o'clock before the contest deepened into earnest, desperate battle. Then our columns were visible along the slope leading to the second terrace, and as they advanced, battery after battery of the rebels, quiet through all the bombardment, opened. It was evident that without artillery to support them, our troops would be overpowered by the withering cannonade of the enemy. I had been told the day before, by an officer who ought to have been well informed, that when the battle begun we would open a battery of heavy rifled guns upon the rebels, and make them glad to stop their artillery, and rely on musket and bayonet and the natural advantages of their position. I waited and watched for the opening of this battery, which was to astonish the rebels, with a sharp interest and anxiety that it would be impossible to express. Our long columns of noble fellows pushed on, and the weight of the enemy's artillery-fire continued every minute to increase.

Our batteries upon the left augmented their fire, and the guns of which I had been led to hope so much opened. I saw with horror that at least half the shells were bursting behind our own men, and that they were certainly killing more of them than the enemy. Gen. Burnside, I have since learned, sent orders to the battery to cease firing, and it did so. Then for dreadful hours the rebel artillerists had it all their own way. They had, at one time, seven batteries in full blast upon our devoted columns. Several of their guns were very heavy ones. One seven-inch rifle was heard loud and often over the roar of other arms in the engagement. I shall always have a profound remembrance of the keen, terrific report of that gun. Every shot made the hills quiver, and the number of times it spoke during the day was surprising. It seemed that the reports of that piece, like the movements of a pendulum, divided the time into periods—that the wicked emphasis of its utterances must be taken to note the passage of time and mark the progress of the fight.

It became perfectly apparent to all observers of any reasonable degree of intelligence, as the din of rebel artillery and the rage of the musketry increased, and as the big rebel rifle spoke through the gloom of the conflict, as appeared the very voice of doom, that the fortunes of the day on our side were desperate. It was manifestly absolutely impossible for our columns of unsupported infantry to carry the terrible heights. Our only hope then was in Franklin. It might be possible that he would do something grand on the left, break the enemy's line, turn his position, and come sweeping along the crest, from which the murderous artillery "volleyed and thundered." But it was drearily evident that Franklin's progress was slow. We could hear the grumbling of his guns, and see, in the distance, the battle-cloud that swelled from the combat, but alas, that cloud did not advance by perceptible degrees. The sound of the guns came no more distinctly. Clearly enough, there was hard work and slow progress on the left. . . .

While our artillery was silent, and that of the enemy was jarring the earth and filling the valley of the Rappahannock with crashing reverberations, our noble infantry maintained, for hours, a line of fire across the field, the smoke rolling from the play of their muskets in long fleecy clouds. Presently some batteries of our field-artillery got to work, and for a while the action did not look so one-sided. Flash answered flash, as gun responded to gun, but it was our field-guns to their siege-guns; and their batteries, with advantages of position and number of pieces, as well as weight of metal, and after a gallant contest our guns were silenced. It was impossible the result should be otherwise, as the converging fire of the enemy was plainly crushing. When the enemy charged upon our men they met their masters, and were invariably beaten back, terribly damaged. But their bellowing batteries, the smoke of which rushed from nearly every clump of pines—batteries opened out here and there, as occasion offered, as if the country were literally full of them— and the swarm of sharp-shooters, secure in rifle-pits and behind a stone wall, and in a sunken road, . . . were too much for the naked valor of our infantry. No troops in the world would have won a victory if placed in the position ours were. Few armies, however renowned, would have stood as well as ours did. It can hardly be in human nature for men to show more valor, or generals to manifest less judgment, than were perceptible on our side that day.

It was with a deep sense of relief that I saw the sun go down, and felt that in a little while darkness would put an end to the unequal combat. But for a time the fury of the fire on both sides redoubled as the discovery was made by the combatants that their day's work was about done. For half an hour, the din was awful, and the smoke drifted through the streets, as sometimes in a city, when there is a high wind and a great dust. There was severe fighting even after dark, and the sparkle of musketry made a fine display. Then the big rebel rifled cannon ceased to mark time, the sputter and crackle of small arms ceased on the centre, Franklin and Jackson's guns throbbed heavily a few times on the left; and all was still on the north side of the river, save the rumble of army-wagons, which are probably intimately connected with Bryant's "innumerable caravan, that moves for ever through the gate of death." . . .

It was not possible for any one who had witnessed the fight, and was candid with himself, to dispute the fact that we had had the worst of it. We had started out to take the enemy's batteries on the hills. That we had done no such thing was painfully apparent. . . . The city of Fredericksburgh was a trap, and we had plunged into it. The policy of permitting us to "occupy and possess" it under commanding batteries, was clear enough. The blunder stood revealed.

—Cincinnati Commercial

4. THE ASSAULT ON MARYE'S HILL

It was the attack on the Confederate left, on Marye's Hill, that proved most costly to the Union army. All through that deadly afternoon of December 13 Burnside hurled his men against the sunken road and the stone walls and the artillery of the Confederates, and when in the end darkness fell upon the battlefield Union losses had mounted to over 6,000.

Here are a Confederate and a Union account of the assaults on the Hill. The first is from the pen of the effervescent J. B. Polley, who fought with Hood's Texans—and whose figures are dramatic rather than accurate; the second by Corporal—later Captain—John McCrillis of the 5th New Hampshire Volunteers, one of the regiments that suffered most heavily in the attack on Marye's Hill.

A. The Irish Brigade Is Repulsed on Marye's Hill

Camp near Fredericksburg, Va., Dec. 20, 1862

At nine o'clock on the morning . . . the battle began in earnest. On the top of the hill, and close to the edge of the bluff, there was a battery, and behind the stone fence crouched Cobb's brigade of Georgians—one of the regiments being the gallant Eighteenth, which, when in our brigade, complimented us by its willingness to be known as the Third Texas. . . . To assault this position was a desperate undertaking. . . . Even Irish hearts had to be tempered for the ordeal, and to this end it was necessary not only to appeal to their love for "ould Ireland" but to imbue them with a supplemental fictitious courage. Only when a sprig of arbor vitae, stolen from the deserted yards of the town, was pinned upon their caps to remind them of the shamrock of their native Isle, their throats moistened liberally and their canteens filled with liquor, did they become ready to move forward as an initiatory forlorn hope. . . .

Between the last houses of the town proper and the stone fence stretched a piece of level open ground about two hundred yards wide. Entering this, the Federals halted a second or two to reform their lines; and then, some shouting "Erin go bragh," and others the Yankee huzzah, they rushed impetuously forward against a storm of grape and canister that, as long as the guns on the hilltop could be sufficiently depressed, tore great gaps in their ranks. But, wavering not, they closed together and rushed onward until within fifty yards of the stone fence, when in one grand, simultaneous burst of light, sound, and death, came the blinding flash, the deafening roar, the murderous destruction of two thousand well-aimed rifles, the wild, weird, blood-curdling Confederate yell, and two thousand Irishmen sank down wounded or dead, and a cowed and demoralized remnant sought safety in inglorious flight.

Seven assaults were made on the stone fence during the day, and five thousand men were sent to eternity before Burnside convinced himself that the position was impregnable. Only two regiments of our division were engaged in any undertaking that might be called a battle. These were the Fifty-seventh and Fifty-fourth North Carolina regiments composed of conscripts—young men under twenty and old men—all dressed in homespun, and presenting to the fastidious eyes of us veterans a very unsoldierly appearance. But we judged hastily. Ordered to drive the enemy back, they not only charged with surprising recklessness, but kept on charging until, to save them from certain capture, General Hood peremptorily recalled them. As they passed our brigade on their return, one old fellow halted, wiped the powder grime from his weather-beaten face with the sleeve of his coat, and wrathfully exclaimed, "Durn ole Hood, anyhow! He jes' didn't have no bus'ness ter stop us when we'uns was a-whippin' the durn blue-bellies ter h-ll an' back, an' eff we'uns hadder bin you Texicans, he'd never o' did it."

—POLLEY, *A Soldier's Letters to Charming Nellie*

B. THE 5TH NEW HAMPSHIRE TO THE RESCUE

On the 13th at 12:30 P.M., the order was given for the Second Corps to assault the rebel position. In less than thirty minutes French's Division was driven back, shattered and broken with a loss of about one-half its number killed and wounded. The brigades of Zook and Meagher advance and are broken, and lose more than one-half their men.

At this time, and during the operations of the Irish Brigade, General Hancock sat upon his horse in our immediate front, cool and collected. All at once his voice is heard above the cannon's roar. How well I remember the precise words; they have been ringing in my ears ever since: 'General Caldwell, you will forward your brigade at once; the Irish Brigade is suffering severely.' Then comes the quick and impetuous command of Colonel Cross: 'Attention! Every man is expected to do his duty to-day. If I fall never mind me. Fix bayonets! No man to fire a shot until he is inside the rebel lines. Shoulder arms! Trail arms! Forward, march!' Each man firmly grasps his musket, and the lines move forward into that rain of death, and the last march of many, this side of the eternal camping-ground, begins.

The artillery fire seemed to increase, shells bursting overhead and in the ranks, the solid shot crashing through that on-sweeping line of blue, opening large gaps which were quickly closed up again to have, the next moment, that crimson swath again cut through. Now we are in range of their infantry behind a stone wall, when a stream of fire and a shower of leaden hail causes the line to disappear like dew before a morning sun. 'Close in on the colors!' is the order heard above the din of battle. 'Steady! Forward!' rose in trumpet tones from lips that were the next moment hushed in death. The colors go down, only to be again upborne by some brave spirit who in his turn slept the sleep that knows no waking.

The line has now reached the brick house. Every man belonging to the color guard of the Fifth is dead or wounded. Colonel Cross is severely wounded; no man dares to leave the ranks to assist him. Major Sturtevant, Captains Perry, Murray and Moore, Lieutenants Ballou, Nettleton and Little are killed. Beyond the brick house extends a close board fence, parallel to the stone wall. We have now reached the fence, the point beyond which no previous line had been able to go. The dead and dying lay in a windrow along this fence. With the butts of our muskets we knocked the boards off in several places. Sergeant George S. Gove of Company K, with the colors, dashed on toward the rebel line.

At the fence all formation of the line of battle was lost. Beyond this point we saw no officers, neither did we receive any orders. At about twenty-five yards from the stone wall, Gove halted. I was the first man on his left; next on my left was Foss of Company E. Gove and Foss were the only two men standing. All the others, who were not shot down, fell down of their own accord. I asked them to lay down. Gove made no reply, while Foss said he would stand up until he was hit. Hardly had Foss said this before he was shot through the hip. At the same instant I heard Gove call my name. I looked, and he was down. I started to go to him when I was struck with a piece of shell in the left arm above the elbow, cutting a piece out of my overcoat, blouse and shirt, rendering my arm useless. I managed to get to Gove. He told me that he was shot through, and that I must save the colors and not mind anything about him. I rolled him over as carefully as I could, and gathered the tattered folds about the staff.

The fire of the enemy had slackened considerably. At this time there was no one in sight to my right or left, except the dead or wounded. Fixing my eye on an opening in the fence, I made a break for the rear, out to the brick house, where there were hundreds of men huddled. A shell dropped in their midst, killing and wounding a great many. I decided to go on to the rear. Arriving at the place where we came into line near the canal, I found a few of our own regiment and one officer. By his orders we fell back into the city.

Of the 5,500 men of Hancock's Division, 2,000 were killed and wounded. The Fifth went into action with 249 officers and men. Out of nineteen commissioned officers, seven were killed and ten wounded. Total loss, killed and wounded, 180.

—McCRILLIS in CHILD, *A History of the Fifth New Hampshire Volunteers*

5. THE GALLANT PELHAM AT FREDERICKSBURG

The Confederate artillery took a heavy toll of the Federals at Fredericksburg, and much of the credit for its performance went to "the gallant Pelham." This "boy major," as he was known, was one of the most romantic figures in the Army of Northern Virginia. Resigning from West Point in 1861 he entered the Confederate Army as a lieutenant, was assigned to the horse artillery, fought effectively in the Seven Days campaign, at Second Manassas and Antietam, and was promoted to a majority in 1862, at the age of twenty-one. Handsome, chivalrous, and courageous, he was one of the most widely admired officers in the army. Stuart named his daughter "Virginia Pelham," Lee characterized him as "the gallant Pelham" and recommended his promotion to a lieutenant colonelcy. When he was killed at Kelly's Ford, in March 1863, the whole South mourned.

This account is from the pen of the romantic novelist, John Esten Cooke.

HE was ever by the guns which were under the hottest fire; and, when the enemy shifted their fire to other portions of the field, he proceeded thither, riding at full speed, and directed the fresh batteries in person. His men will remember how cheering and inspiring was his presence with them—how his coolness steadied them in the most exciting moments—and his brave cheerful voice was the herald of success. "He was the bravest human being I ever saw in my life," said one of his officers whom I conversed with recently; and all who have seen him under fire will bear similar testimony. His coolness had something heroic in it. It never deserted him, or was affected by those chances of battle which excite the bravest. He saw guns shattered and dismounted, or men torn to pieces, without exhibiting any signs of emotion. His nature seemed strung and every muscle braced to a pitch which made him rock; and the ghastliest spectacle of blood and death left his soul unmoved—his stern will unbent.

That unbending will had been tested often, and never had failed him yet. At Manassas, Williamsburg, Cold Harbour, Groveton, Oxhill, Sharpsburg, Shepherdstown, Kearneysville, Aldie, Union, Upperville, Markham, Barbee's, Hazel River, and Fredericksburg—at these and many other places he fought his horse artillery, and handled it with heroic coolness. One day when I led him to speak of his career, he counted up something like a hundred actions which he had been in—and in every one he had borne a prominent part. Talk with the associates of the young leader in those hard-fought battles, and they will tell you a hundred instances of his dauntless courage. At Manassas he took position in a place so dangerous that an officer, who had followed him up to that moment, rode away with the declaration that "if Pelham was fool enough to stay there, *he was not.*"

But General Jackson thanked him, as he thanked him at Cold Harbour, when the brave young soldier came back covered with dust from fighting his Napoleon—the light of victory in his eyes. At Markham, while he was fighting the enemy in front, they made a circuit and charged him in the rear;

but he turned his guns about, and fought them as before, with his "Napoleon detachment" singing the loud, triumphant *Marseillaise*, as that same Napoleon gun, captured at Seven Pines, and used at Fredericksburg, drove them back. All that whole great movement was a marvel of hard fighting, however, and Pelham was the hero of the stout, close struggle. Any other chief of artillery might have sent his men in at Fredericksburg and elsewhere, leaving the direction of the guns to such officers as the brave Captain Henry; but this did not suit the young chieftain. He must go himself with the one gun sent forward, and beside that piece he remained until it was ordered back— directing his men to lie down, but sitting his own horse, and intent solely upon the movements and designs of the enemy, wholly careless of the "fire of hell" hurled against him. . . .

The work done by Pelham on the great day of Fredericksburg is a part of history now. All know how stubbornly he stood on that day—what laurels encircled his young brow when night at last came. This was the climax of his fame—the event with which his name will be inseparably connected. With one Napoleon gun, he opened the battle on the right, and instantly drew upon himself the fire, at close range, of three or four batteries in front, and a heavy enfilading fire from thirty-pound Parrots across the river. But this moved him little. That Napoleon gun was the same which he had used at the battle of Cold Harbour—it was taken from the enemy at Seven Pines—and, in the hands of the young officer, it had won a fame which must not be tarnished by defeat! Its grim voice must roar, however great the odds; its reverberating defiance must roll over the plain, until the bronze war-dog was silenced.

So it roared on steadily with Pelham beside it, blowing up caissons, and continuing to tear the enemy's ranks. General Lee was watching it from the hill above, and exclaimed, with eyes filled with admiration, "It is glorious to see such courage in one so young!" It was glorious indeed to see that one gun, placed in an important position, hold its ground with a firmness so unflinching. Not until his last round of ammunition was shot away did Pelham retire; and then only after a peremptory order sent to him. He afterwards took command of the entire artillery on the right, and fought it until night with a skill and courage which were admirable. He advanced his guns steadily, and at nightfall was thundering on the flank of the retreating enemy, who no longer replied. No answering roar came back from those batteries he had fought with his Napoleon so long; he had triumphed. That triumph was complete, and placed for ever upon record when the great Commander-in-Chief, whom he loved and admired so ardently, gave him the name in his report of "the gallant Pelham."

—Cooke, *Wearing of the Gray*

6. NIGHT ON THE FIELD OF FREDERICKSBURG

Here is a description of the dreadful night of December 13-14, from the pen of one of the most gifted of all the chroniclers of the war, General Joshua

L. Chamberlain, colonel of the 20th Maine Volunteers. A professor at Bow-
doin College, Chamberlain enlisted in 1862, received the Congressional Medal
of Honor for his defense of Little Round Top, was promoted to brevet major
general, was six times wounded, and was selected to receive the surrender of
the Confederates at Appomattox. Later he was four times governor of Maine,
and president of Bowdoin College. We shall meet him again—at Gettysburg
and at Appomattox.

THE desperate charge was over. We had not reached the enemy's fortifications, but only that fatal crest where we had seen five lines of battle
mount but to be cut to earth as by a sword-swoop of fire. We had that costly
honor which sometimes falls to the "reserve"—to go in when all is havoc and
confusion, through storm and slaughter, to cover the broken and depleted
ranks of comrades and take the battle from their hands. Thus we had replaced the gallant few still struggling on the crest, and received that withering fire, which nothing could withstand, by throwing ourselves flat in a slight
hollow of the ground, within pistol shot of the enemy's works; and, mingled
with the dead and dying that strewed the field, we returned the fire till it
reddened into night, and at last fell away through darkness into silence.

But out of that silence from the battle's crash and roar rose new sounds
more appalling still; rose or fell, you knew not which, or whether from the
earth or air; a strange ventriloquism, of which you could not locate the
source, a smothered moan that seemed to come from distances beyond reach
of the natural sense, a wail so far and deep and wide, as if a thousand discords
were flowing together into a key-note weird, unearthly, terrible to hear and
bear, yet startling with its nearness; the writhing concord broken by cries for
help, pierced by shrieks of paroxysm; some begging for a drop of water;
some calling on God for pity; and some on friendly hands to finish what the
enemy had so horribly begun; some with delirious, dreamy voices murmuring
loved names, as if the dearest were bending over them; some gathering their
last strength to fire a musket to call attention to them where they lay helpless
and deserted; and underneath, all the time, that deep bass note from closed
lips too hopeless or too heroic to articulate their agony.

Who could sleep, or who would? Our position was isolated and exposed.
Officers must be on the alert with their command. But the human took the
mastery of the official; sympathy of soldiership. Command could be devolved; but pity, not. So with a staff officer I sallied forth to see what we
could do where the helpers seemed so few. Taking some observations in
order not to lose the bearing of our own position, we guided our steps by
the most piteous of the cries. Our part was but little; to relieve a painful
posture; to give a cooling draught to fevered lips; to compress a severed
artery, as we had learned to do, though in bungling fashion; to apply a rude
bandage, which yet might prolong the life to saving; to take a token or farewell message for some stricken home; it was but little, yet it was an endless
task. We had moved towards the right and rear of our own position—the
part of the field immediately above the city. The farther we went the more

the need deepened, and the calls multiplied. Numbers half wakening from the lethargy of death, or of despair, by sounds of succor, begged us to take them quickly to a surgeon; and when we could not do that, imploring us to do the next most merciful service and give them quick dispatch out of their misery. Right glad were we when, after midnight, the shadowy ambulances came gliding along, and the kindly hospital stewards, with stretchers and soothing appliances, let us feel that we might return to our proper duty.

And now we were aware of other figures wandering, ghostlike, over the field. Some on errands like our own, drawn by compelling appeals; some seeking a lost comrade, with uncertain steps amidst the unknown, and ever and anon bending down to scan the pale visage closer, or, it may be, by the light of a brief match, whose blue, flickering flame scarcely can give the features a more recognizable or more human look; some man, desperately wounded, yet seeking, with faltering step, before his fast ebbing blood shall have left him too weak to move, some quiet or sheltered spot out of sound of the terrible appeals he could neither answer nor endure, or out of reach of the raging battle coming with the morning; one creeping, yet scarcely moving, from one lifeless form to another, if, perchance, he might find a swallow of water in the canteen still swung from the dead soldier's side; or another, as with just returning or just remaining consciousness, vainly striving to rise from a mangled heap, that he may not be buried with them while yet alive; or some man, yet sound of body, but pacing feverishly his ground because in such a bivouac his spirit could not sleep. And so we picked our way back, amidst the stark, upturned faces, to our little living line.

The night chill had now woven a misty veil over the field. Fortunately, a picket fence we had encountered in our charge from the town had compelled us to abandon our horses, and so had saved our lives on the crest; but our overcoats had been strapped to the saddles, and we missed them now. Most of the men, however, had their overcoats or blankets—we were glad of that. Except the few sentries along the front, the men had fallen asleep—the living with the dead. At last, outwearied and depressed with the desolate scene, my own strength sunk, and I moved two dead men a little and lay down between them, making a pillow of the breast of a third. The skirt of his overcoat drawn over my face helped also to shield me from the bleak winds. There was some comfort even in this companionship. But it was broken sleep. The deepening chill drove many forth to take the garments of those who could no longer need them, that they might keep themselves alive. More than once I was startled from my unrest by some one turning back the coat-skirt from my face, peering, half vampire-like, to my fancy, through the darkness, to discover if it too were of the silent and unresisting; turning away more disconcerted at my living word than if a voice had spoken from the dead.

Having held our places all the night, we had to keep to them all the more closely the next day, for it would be certain death to attempt to move away. As it was, it was only by making breastworks and barricades of the dead men that covered the field that we saved any alive. We did what we could

Edwin Forbes

A Cavalry Charge

A. C. Redwood

Cobb's and Kershaw's Troops Behind the Stone Wall at Fredericksburg

The Seat of the War in Virginia

to take a record of these men. A testament that had fallen from the breast pocket of the soldier who had been my pillow, I sent soon after to his home— he was not of my command—and it proved to be the only clue his parents ever had to his fate.

The next midnight, after thirty-six hours of this harrowing work, we were bidden to withdraw into the town for refreshment and rest. But neither rest nor motion was to be thought of till we had paid fitting honor to our dead. We laid them on the spot which they had won, on the sheltered edge of the crest, and committed their noble forms to the earth, and their story to their country's keeping.

> We buried them darkly, at dead of night,
> The sod with our bayonets turning.

Splinters of boards torn by shot and shell from the fences we had crossed served as headstones, each name hurriedly carved under brief match lights, anxiously hidden from the foe. It was a strange scene around that silent and shadowy sepulture. "We will give them a starlight burial," it was said; but heaven ordained a more sublime illumination. As we bore them in dark and sad procession, their own loved North took up the escort and lifting all her glorious lights led the triumphal march over the bridge that spans the worlds— an aurora borealis of marvelous majesty! fiery lances and banners of blood and flame, columns of pearly light, garlands and wreaths of gold, all pointing upward and beckoning on. Who would not pass on as they did, dead for their country's life, and lighted to burial by the meteor splendors of their native sky?   —CHAMBERLAIN, "Night on the Field of Fredericksburg"

7. LINCOLN APPOINTS HOOKER TO THE COMMAND OF THE ARMY

After Fredericksburg Burnside prepared an order dismissing Hooker and three other general officers, and relieving Franklin and four other officers from duty. This he laid before Lincoln with the choice of accepting it or dismissing him. Inevitably Lincoln relieved Burnside from command and— less inevitably—appointed Hooker to his place. A West Pointer, with experience in the Florida campaign and the Mexican War, Hooker had been appointed brigadier general of volunteers in 1861 and had fought in the Peninsular and the Antietam campaigns. Like Pope he was given to boasting. "My plans are perfect," he said shortly after his appointment to the top command. "May God have mercy on General Lee for I will have none." Lincoln, as this famous letter reveals, was not so sure.

Major-General Hooker:

General:

Executive Mansion, Washington, D. C.
January 26, 1863

I have placed you at the head of the Army of the Potomac. Of course I have done this upon what appears to me to be sufficient reasons, and yet I think it best for you to know that there are some things in regard to which I am not quite satisfied with you. I believe you to be a brave and skillful soldier, which, of course, I like. I also believe you do not mix politics with your profession, in which you are right. You have confidence in yourself, which is a valuable, if not an indispensable, quality. You are ambitious, which, within reasonable bounds, does good rather than harm; but I think that during General Burnside's command of the army you have taken counsel of your ambition, and thwarted him as much as you could, in which you did a great wrong to the country and to a most meritorious and honorable brother officer. I have heard, in such a way as to believe it, of your recently saying that both the Army and the Government needed a dictator. Of course, it was not for this, but in spite of it, that I have given you the command. Only those generals who gain successes can set up dictators. What I now ask of you is military success, and I will risk the dictatorship. The Government will support you to the utmost of its ability, which is neither more nor less than it has done or will do for all commanders. I much fear that the spirit which you have aided to infuse into the army, of criticizing their commander and withholding confidence from him, will now turn upon you. I shall assist you as far as I can to put it down. Neither you nor Napoleon, if he were alive again, could get any good out of an army while such a spirit prevails in it. And now beware of rashness. Beware of rashness, but with energy and sleepless vigilance go forward and give us victories.

Yours, very truly,

A. Lincoln.

—War of the Rebellion . . . Official Records

8. LEE WHIPS HOOKER AT CHANCELLORSVILLE

By the end of April Hooker had what he called "the finest army on the planet." Certainly it was the largest and best equipped that had ever been seen in America. Against Hooker's force of some 130,000 men Lee could muster less than 60,000, for Longstreet's corps was south of the James. No wonder Hooker was sure of victory. "The enemy must either ingloriously fly, or come out from behind his defenses and give us battle on our own ground where certain destruction awaits him," he said in an order to his troops. First he sent Stoneman off on a raid designed to disorganize Lee's communications and threaten Richmond. Then, leaving Sedgwick at Fredericksburg, he moved the rest of his vast army up the Rappahannock and Rapidan, crossed at Kelly's Ford, and on April 30 reached Chancellorsville in the heart of the Wilderness. He failed however to catch Lee by surprise and when Slocum's corps moved down the Plank Road toward Fredericksburg, the next day, it ran into the well-entrenched Confederates. Instead of joining battle Hooker mysteriously withdrew his forces to Chancellorsville, giving the initiative over to Lee, who promptly seized and exploited it.

We begin with a general account of the battle. Charles Morse here re-counts the errors of judgment that led to Federal defeat. A colonel of the 2nd Massachusetts Infantry, Morse fought in Virginia through the first two years of the war, then in Tennessee and the Carolinas.

Stafford C. H., May 7, 1863

I am going to give you without any introduction, a history of this last campaign against Richmond by the army under the great Joe Hooker. I believe I have seen it and judged it fairly.

On Monday, April 27th, our corps broke camp early in the morning and marched to Hartwood Church, ten miles; there it went into camp for the night. The Eleventh and Fifth Corps also came up there and camped in our vicinity; next morning, we all moved and camped that night near Kelly's Ford. A pontoon bridge was thrown across and the Eleventh was over before daylight Wednesday; the other corps followed rapidly and the advance began towards the Rapidan. The Eleventh and Twelfth marched on the road to Germana Ford, the Fifth on the road to Ely's Ford; all three of the corps were under command of General Slocum. I was detailed, the morning of the advance, as Aide to General Slocum, and another officer was made Acting Provost Marshal. All the companies of the Second Massachusetts were sent to the Regiment. We skirmished all the way to Germana Ford; there we met quite a determined resistance; our cavalry was drawn in and the Second Massachusetts and the Third Wisconsin sent forward to clear the way; they drove everything before them and, by their heavy fire, forced the rebels at the Ford to surrender (about one hundred officers and men). We lost in this skirmish about a dozen killed and wounded.

General Slocum now determined to cross the Rapidan, though there was no bridge and the ford was almost impassable. . . . At about noon [April 30], we arrived at Chancellorsville, and found the Fifth Corps already there. We had a small cavalry skirmish, . . . but besides that, nothing of importance occurred during that day; the troops were formed in line of battle, but were not attacked. Up to this time you see everything had gone well and success seemed certain.

Towards night [April 30], General Hooker arrived with his staff, and we heard of the crossing at the U. S. Ford of the Second, Third and First Corps. All the headquarters were in the vicinity of the Chancellor House, a large, fine brick mansion. General Hooker took supper with General Slocum; he didn't seem to be able to express his gratification at the success of General Slocum in bringing the three corps up so rapidly. Then, in the most ex-travagant, vehement terms, he went on to say how he had got the rebels, how he was going to crush them, annihilate them, etc.

The next morning at ten, the Fifth and Twelfth Corps advanced in order of battle on two parallel roads; we soon met the enemy and skirmished for about two miles, when they appeared in considerable force and the battle began. We were in a splendid position and were driving the enemy when an order came to General Slocum to retire his command to its former position. No one could believe that the order was genuine, but almost immediately, another of General Hooker's staff brought the same order again. Now, perhaps, you don't know that to retire an army in the face of an enemy when you are engaged is one of the most difficult operations in war; this we had to do. I carried the order to General Geary to retire his division in echelon by brigades, and stayed with him till the movement was nearly completed. It was a delicate job; each brigade would successively bear the brunt of the enemy's attack. Before the last brigades of the Fifth and Twelfth Corps were in position, the enemy made a furious attack on the Chancellor House; luckily we had considerable artillery concentrated there and they were driven back. The next attack was on our corps, but the enemy was severely repulsed. This about ended the fighting on Friday; we lost, I suppose, about five hundred men.

During the night, the men were kept at work digging trenches and throwing up breastworks of logs. Our headquarters were at Fairview, an open piece of ground rising into quite a crest in the centre. Skirmishing began at daylight next morning [May 2] and continued without much result to either side, till afternoon, when the enemy began to move, in large force, towards our right, opposite General Howard, Eleventh Corps. This corps was in a fine position in intrenchments, with almost open country in front of them, the right resting on Hunting Creek. At about four P.M. the Third Corps, General Sickles, was moved out to the right of the Twelfth and advanced towards Fredericksburgh. The order then came to General Slocum that the enemy were in full retreat, and to advance his whole line to capture all he could of prisoners, wagons, etc. Our right, General Williams' Division, advanced without much trouble, driving the enemy before it, but the Second Division had hardly got out of the trenches before it was attacked with great determination, yet it steadily retained its position.

At about five P.M. a tremendous and unceasing musketry fire began in the direction of the Eleventh Corps. As it was necessary to know what was going on there in order to regulate the movements of the Twelfth Corps, General Slocum and the rest of us rode for our lives towards this new scene of action. What was our surprise when we found that instead of a fight, it was a complete Bull Run rout. Men, horses, mules, rebel prisoners, wagons, guns, etc. etc. were coming down the road in terrible confusion, behind them an unceasing roar of musketry. We rode until we got into a mighty hot fire, and found that no one was attempting to make a stand, but every one running for his life. Then General Slocum dispatched me to General Hooker to explain the state of affairs, and three other staff officers to find General Williams and order him back to his trenches with all haste.

I found General Hooker sitting alone on his horse in front of the Chancellor House, and delivered my message; he merely said, "Very good, sir." I rode back and found the Eleventh Corps still surging up the road and still this terrible roar behind them. Up to this time, the rebels had received no check, but now troops began to march out on the plank road and form across it, and Captain Best, Chief of Artillery of our corps, had on his own responsibility gathered together all the batteries he could get hold of, had put them in position (forty-six guns in all) on Fairview, and had begun firing at the rate of about one hundred guns a minute, into the rebels. This, in my opinion, saved our army from destruction. . . .

The artillery men were hard at work all night, throwing up traverses to protect their guns, and about two in the morning we all lay down on the ground and slept until about four, when daylight [May 3] began to appear. Our right was now formed by the Third, Fifth and First Corps, about five hundred yards in the rear of our first position. The rebels began the attack as soon as there was light enough, from the left of our First Division to about the right of the Third Corps. General Birney's Division of the Third Corps was out in front of General Williams; his men behaved badly, and after a slight resistance, fell back into our lines, losing a battery.

The rebels now charged down our First Division, but were met with such a deadly fire that they were almost annihilated. Their second line was then sent in, but met the same fate, and their third and last line advanced. Our men now had fired more than forty rounds of cartridges and were getting exhausted. General Slocum sent almost every one of his staff officers to General Hooker, stating his position and begging for support; Hooker's answer was, "I can't make men or ammunition for General Slocum."

Meantime, Sickles' Corps was holding its own on the right of ours, but it was rapidly getting into the same condition as the Twelfth. The rebels were driven back every time they advanced, and we were taking large numbers of prisoners and colors. All this time while our infantry was fighting so gallantly in front, our battery of forty-six guns was firing incessantly. The rebels had used no artillery until they captured the battery from Birney, when they turned that on us, making terrible destruction in General Geary's line. General Meade, Fifth Corps, now went to Hooker and entreated that he might be allowed to throw his corps on the rebel flank, but General Hooker said, "No, he was wanted in his own position." On his own responsibility General Meade sent out one brigade, which passed out in the rear of the enemy's right, recaptured a battery, three hundred of our men who were prisoners, and four hundred of the rebels, and took them safely back to their corps.

It was now after seven o'clock. Our men had fired their sixty rounds of cartridges and were still holding their position; everything that brave men could do, these men had done, but now nothing was left but to order them to fall back and give up their position to the enemy. This was done in good order and they marched off under a heavy fire to the rear of our batteries. The rebels, seeing us retreating, rushed forward their artillery and began a fearful fire. I found I could be useful to Captain Best, commanding our artillery, so I stayed with him. I never before saw anything so fine as the attack on that battery; the air was full of missiles, solid shot, shells, and musket balls. I saw one solid shot kill three horses and a man, another took a leg off one of the captains of the batteries. Lieutenant Crosby of the Fourth Artillery was shot through the heart with a musket ball; he was a particular friend of Bob Shaw and myself; he lived just long enough to say to Captain Best, "Tell father I die happy."

The rebels came up to the attack in solid masses and got within three hundred yards, but they were slaughtered by the hundreds by the case-shot and canister, and were driven back to the woods. Still not an infantry man was sent to the support of the guns. More than half the horses were killed or wounded; one caisson had blown up, another had been knocked to pieces; in ten minutes more the guns would have been isolated. They, too, therefore, were ordered to retire, which they did without losing a gun. You see, now our centre was broken, everything was being retired to our second line, the rebel artillery was in position, their line of battle steadily advancing across our old ground. This fire of the batteries was concentrated on the Chancellor House, Hooker's original headquarters, and it was torn almost to pieces by solid shot and was finally set on fire by a shell.

The army was now put in position in the second line; the centre was on a rising piece of ground and protected by a battery of forty or fifty guns. . . . You can easily see that, if the enemy once forced our right or left, our communications would at once be cut and all possibility of retreat prevented. Late that night we lay down close beside the Rappahannock. By three o'clock next morning we were awakened by a heavy artillery fire and shells bursting over us. Our guns replied and kept at it for about an hour, when the enemy's batteries were silenced. We now mounted our horses and rode along the lines to look at our position; we found that it was a very strong one and capable of being made very much more so. . . .

I doubt if ever in the history of this war, another chance will be given us to fight the enemy with such odds in our favor as we had last Sunday, and that chance has been worse than lost to us. I don't believe any men ever fought better than our Twelfth Corps, especially the First Division; for two hours, they held their ground without any support, against the repeated assaults of the enemy; they fired their sixty rounds of cartridges and held their line with empty muskets until ordered to fall back. The old Second, of course, did splendidly, and lost heavily. . . . Our colors got thirty holes in them and the staff (the third one) was smashed to pieces.

—Morse, *Letters Written During the Civil War*

9. PLEASONTON STOPS THE CONFEDERATES AT HAZEL GROVE

Early on May 2 Lee sent Jackson with the bulk of the army along the Plank Road and through the Wilderness to Hooker's rear. Although Hooker was repeatedly warned of this movement, he fatuously insisted that the Confederates were retreating, and took no precautions. On the afternoon of the second Jackson swept out of the woods and fell on Howard's corps and on Sickles. Pleasonton hurried up his cavalry, collected scattered elements of infantry and artillery, and made a stand that may have saved the army from destruction.

General Pleasonton was a West Pointer with long military experience in the Mexican, Sioux and Seminole wars, who commanded the Union cavalry at Gettysburg and was later transferred to the Trans-Mississippi theater.

ON arriving at Hazel Grove, about one mile from Chancellorsville, I found that General Sickles was moving two of the divisions of the Third Corps in the direction of Catherine Furnace, and shortly after he became engaged there with a strong rear-guard. Hazel Grove was the highest ground in the neighborhood and was the key of our position, and I saw that if Lee's forces gained it the Army of the Potomac would be worsted.

General Sickles wanted some cavalry to protect his flanks, and I gave him the 6th New York. This left me with only the 8th and 17th Pennsylvania regiments and Martin's New York battery of horse artillery. I posted this command at the extreme west of the clearing, about two hundred yards from the woods in which the Eleventh Corps was encamped. This position at Hazel Grove was about a quarter of a mile in extent, running nearly northeast and south-west, but was in no place farther than two hundred yards from the woods, and on the south and east it sloped off into a marsh and a creek. It commanded the position of the army at Fairview and Chancellorsville and enfiladed our line. The moving out to the Furnace of the two divisions of the Third Corps left a gap of about a mile from Hazel Grove to the right of the Twelfth Corps. Shortly after General Sickles had been engaged at the Furnace, he sent me word that the enemy were giving way and cavalry could be used to advantage in pursuit. Before moving my command I rode out to the Furnace to comprehend the situation. It was no place for cavalry to operate, and as I could hear spattering shots going more and more toward the north-west, I was satisfied that the enemy were not retreating.

I hastened back to my command at Hazel Grove; when I reached it, the Eleventh Corps to our rear and our right was in full flight, panic-stricken beyond description. We faced about, having then the marsh behind us. It was an ugly marsh, about fifty yards wide, and in the stampede of the Eleventh Corps, beef cattle, ambulances, mules, artillery, wagons, and horses became stuck in the mud, and others coming on crushed them down, so that when the fight was over the pile of débris in the marsh was many feet high. I saw that something had to be done, and that very quickly, or the Army of the Potomac would receive a crushing defeat. The two cavalry regiments were in the saddle, and as I rode forward Major Keenan of the 8th Pennsylvania came out to meet me, when I ordered him to take the regiment, charge into the woods, which, as we had previously stood, were to our rear, and hold the enemy in check until I could get some guns into position. He replied, with a smile at the size of the task, that he would do it, and started off immediately. Thirty men, including Major Keenan, Captain Arrowsmith, and Adjutant Haddock, never came back.

I then directed Captain Martin to bring his guns into battery, load with double charges of canister, and aim them so that the shot would hit the ground half-way between the guns and the woods. I also stated that I would give the order to fire. Just then a handsome young lieutenant of the 4th U. S. Artillery, Frank B. Crosby (son of a distinguished lawyer of New York City), who was killed the next day, galloped up and said, "General, I have a battery of six guns; where shall I go? what shall I do?" I told him to place his battery in line on the right of Martin's battery, and gave him the same instructions I had given Martin as to how I wanted him to serve his guns. These 2 batteries gave me 12 guns, and to obtain more I then charged 3 squadrons of the 17th Pennsylvania Cavalry on the stragglers of the Eleventh Corps to clear the ground, and with the assistance of the rest of the regiment succeeded in placing 10 more pieces of artillery in line. The line was then ready for Stonewall Jackson's onset. It was dusk when his men swarmed out of the woods for a quarter of a mile in our front (our rear ten minutes before). They came on in line five and six deep, with but one flag—a Union flag dropped by the Eleventh Corps.

I suspected deception and was ready for it. They called out not to shoot, they were friends; at the same time they gave us a volley from at least five thousand muskets. As soon as I saw the flash I gave the command to fire, and the whole line of artillery was discharged at once. It fairly swept them from the earth; before they could recover themselves the line of artillery had been loaded and was ready for a second attack. After the second discharge, suspecting that they might play the trick of having their men lie down, draw the fire of the artillery, then jump up and charge before the pieces could be reloaded, I poured in the canister for about twenty minutes, and the affair was over. . . .

For half an hour General Jackson had the Army of the Potomac at his mercy. That he halted to re-form his troops in the woods, instead of forging ahead into the clearing, where he could reform his troops more rapidly, and where he could have seen that he was master of the situation, turned out to be one of those fatalities by which the most brilliant prospects are sacrificed. When he advanced upon the artillery at Hazel Grove Jackson had another opportunity to win, if his infantry had been properly handled. The fire of his infantry was so high it did no harm; they should have been ordered to fire so low as to disable the cannoneers at the guns. Had his infantry fire been as effective as that of our artillery, Jackson would have carried the position. The artillery fire was effective because I applied to it that principle of dynamics in which the angle of incidence is equal to the angle of reflection,— that is to say, if the muzzle of a gun is three feet from the ground and it is discharged so that the shot will strike the ground at a distance of one hundred yards, it will glance from the earth at the same angle at which it struck it, and in another one hundred yards will be three feet from the ground. I knew my first volley must be a crushing one, or Jackson, with his superior numbers, would charge across the short distance which separated us and capture the artillery before the guns could be reloaded.

—PLEASONTON, "The Successes and Failures of Chancellorsville"

10. CAPTAIN LIVERMORE HOLDS THE LINES AGAINST JACKSON

After the smart engagement at Hazel Grove Jackson circled around through the Wilderness to the rear of Hooker's army. Toward sundown he fell like a thunderbolt on Hooker's exposed right flank. The impact of his impetuous charge scattered the Federals and threatened, for the moment, to turn the whole flank. The XI Corps retreated in disorder, but elements from the corps of Reynolds, Couch and Sickles hurried to the rescue. "Through the surging rout of the XI Corps," writes John Bigelow, "these sterling organizations forged their way, unchecked and unshaken, towards the mass of yelling and firing assailants."

Livermore we already know as an officer—later colonel—of the 18th New Hampshire Volunteers and as the author of the invaluable study, Numbers and Losses of the Civil War.

NOW, at about sunset [May 2, 1863] there was a rattling of musketry all along our southern and western fronts, but nothing severe enough to cause us any anxiety. I think the fight on our right flank had dwindled to a skirmish and things did not to me look like hot work before next day. We were resting easily with our arms beside us or stacked, and I suppose about eating our evening rations. There seemed to us to have been nothing serious against us, and no one of us in the companies had reason to suppose we should be otherwise than successful, that I am aware of. We could see the situation of the troops on our right; saw the evidences of a large force of our men on the west and north fronts; knew that General Hooker was at the Chancellorsville house close by; and could see parties of the reserves who lay to the east of us; but further than this we were ignorant, at least I was, and I did not know that any rebels had been marching along our western front; did not know anything of the contact of the Twelfth Corps with the rear of his column; of Barlow's movements; of the position of the Eleventh Corps, nor in fact anything more than I saw, and I suppose the most of the army were just as ignorant.

While resting satisfied in this blissful state of ignorance, and facing the foe on the south with placidity and waiting his next advance, our astonished ears were greeted with a sudden outburst of the most tremendous musketry and cannonade directly in our rear on the north front, accompanied with all the yells and confused noises of a bloody engagement. We sprang to our feet and looked with anxious hearts across the plain to the north. The noise continued for some minutes, and then suddenly wagons, ambulances, men, artillery, and everything that makes an army, came rushing out of the woods on the north into the plain and across it and down the turnpike, and after a short interval a flying, confused, panic-stricken mass of soldiers in the direst confusion, to the number of thousands, running for life, and alas! our own men.

When this contest broke out, the presence of the enemy in an attacking force on our north front seemed so improbable that we offered ourselves every explanation but the right one. The most plausible story was that General Stoneman, who was known to have gone off in the enemy's rear, or some one else, had now come up in the rear of a body of the enemy and was driving them toward us. I was so elated with the news that I behaved quite extravagantly with cheering and "cutting up" generally, and the shells which came sailing over from the northwest high in the air, which we could distinguish by their burning fuses in the twilight now come, actually added to the delusion, since I thought with the rest that they were those of our forces advancing in the rear of the enemy. When the truth dawned upon my mind, I kept up my cheerfulness for the sake of appearances, that the men might not learn the truth, and there was need of every precaution, for in less time than it has taken to write this page, after the first group of soldiers appeared running out of the woods, the plain was swarming with them, flying with all speed, and in such bodies and so blindly terrified that neither natural obstacles nor the well-ordered array of lines arrested their flight; and some, escaping through the south front, actually ran clear to our skirmish line and through it to or toward the enemy on the south. The musketry kept crashing away in the woods as long as there were men to fire at, and the shells screamed through the air trailing fire like shooting stars clear over to the Chancellorsville house.

It was a trying time. No one could fail to see that our north front was broken, and it was uncertain how short a time would elapse before the victorious enemy might be upon our backs, and the flying Dutchmen, for they proved to be the Eleventh Corps, actually endangered our formation; but we made our men lie flat on the ground facing south and then each officer with drawn sword paced in rear of his company and drove back every Dutchman. Our men behaved admirably. Neither the dangers nor the panic affected them, but they lay calmly in their places, aided no doubt by their contempt for the Dutch who were running away. Some idea of the numbers who endangered us may be found when I say that about sixty Dutchmen were captured by my regiment. They were kept in our ranks and some were killed on the next day, I believe. One general came rushing over to Colonel Cross, who was lying down. The colonel arose and with infuriated looks and drawn saber rushed upon him. He fled to the shelter of a ditch, crying, "Sare, you do not know who I am! I am a Prigadier Gineral!" To which the colonel replied, "You are n't, you're a damned coward!"

At last the torrent of fugitives ceased, and astonishing to relate the enemy did not advance across the plain. But a tremendous artillery fire which had been opened by some batteries of ours on the north side of the plain had undoubtedly prevented his advancing farther. When order was secure, I stood a little back of my company, where I could see across the plain, and watched for developments on the north side. The firing had nearly ceased, and an ominous stillness prevailed. Peering through the not impenetrable darkness now lighted by the moon, I saw moving into position in the plain facing north two or three lines of troops numbering several thousand, whose dark bodies in serried ranks holding grim silence were exceedingly majestic. I had no doubt they were our own men of some other corps who were to restore our broken lines, and presently they moved forward slowly and in beautiful order apparently with a brigade front. Their advance was pursued in silence close up to the woods, when a sheet of flame like a most brilliant flash of lightning burst out from their front, followed instantly by the tremendous crash of a volley, and moving forward still they maintained their position, and in some measure, I do not know how far, restored our lines. This, I think, was Wood's division of the Third Corps.

The events of the few hours of this afternoon and evening are imprinted on my memory in a grand picture. I can now, and probably always shall be able to again bring before my eyes the dusty plain bounded by long lines of men on all sides; the smoke of musketry and batteries, whose thunders still reverberate in my ears; the gradual diminishing of the battle, and then the sudden rush of fugitives accompanied by the roar of muskets and cannon; the dire confusion of the panic; the curves of fire described in the sky by the shrieking shells; then darkness, the deliberate movements of the dark masses who constituted our attacking force, and the sheet of flame which burst out as they approached the woods; and can still hear the tumult of the battle.

—LIVERMORE, *Days and Events*

11. STUART AND ANDERSON LINK UP AT CHANCELLORSVILLE

The timely employment of artillery, the coming of darkness, and the death of Jackson combined to save the Federals on the second day. Early next morning Lee renewed the attack on both flanks, Stuart on the right, Anderson at the center, and McLaws on the left. Stuart quickly seized Hazel Grove and pushed on ahead to take Chancellorsville itself; at about noon his line linked up with Anderson's, and the Federals were hemmed in on three sides. Hooker had been injured that morning by a falling brick; perhaps that is why he failed to put in his reserves or to get Sedgwick's attack under way in time to afford any effective relief. Sedgwick had, to be sure, swept the thin Confederate line off Marye's Heights, but when Lee sent McLaws to Early's aid Sedgwick found himself encircled just as Hooker was encircled, and retired across the Rappahannock. The Federals, still twice as strong as Lee, stood their ground on May 4, but next day withdrew across the river.

Heros von Borcke, the jolly Prussian whom we have met before, here tells the story of the third day.

THE enemy, fully three times our number, occupied a piece of wood extending about two miles from our immediate front towards the plateau and open fields round Chancellorsville, a village consisting of only a few houses. The Federals had made good use of their time, having thrown up in the wood during the night three successive lines of breastworks, constructed of strong timber, and on the plateau itself, occupied by their reserves, had erected a regular line of redoubts, mounted by their numerous artillery, forty pieces of which were playing on the narrow plank-road. . . .

All our divisions now moving forward, the battle soon became general, and the musketry sounded in one continued roll along the lines. Nearly a hundred hostile guns opening fire at the same time, the forest seemed alive with shot, shell, and bullets, and the plank-road, upon which, as was before mentioned, the fire of forty pieces was concentrated, was soon enveloped in a cloud of smoke from the bursting of shells and the explosion of caissons. This road being our principal line of communication, and crowded therefore with ambulances, ammunition-trains, and artillery, the loss of life soon became fearful, and dead and dying men and animals were strewing every part of it. How General Stuart, and those few staff-officers with him who had to gallop to and fro so frequently through this *feu infernal*, escaped unhurt, seems to me quite miraculous. . . .

Stuart was all activity, and wherever the danger was greatest there was he to be found, urging the men forward, and animating them by the force of his example. The shower of missiles that hissed through the air passed round him unheeded; and in the midst of the hottest fire I heard him, to an old melody, hum the words, "Old Joe Hooker get out of the Wilderness."

After a raging conflict, protracted for several hours, during which the tide of battle ebbed and flowed on either side, we succeeded in taking the advanced works, and driving the enemy upon their third line of intrenchments, of a still stronger character than those before it. This partial success was only gained with a sad sacrifice of life, while countless numbers were seen limping and crawling to the rear. The woods had caught fire in several places from the explosion of shells—the flames spreading principally, however, over a space of several acres in extent where the ground was thickly covered with dry leaves; and here the conflagration progressed with the rapidity of a prairie-fire, and a large number of Confederate and Federal wounded thickly scattered in the vicinity, and too badly hurt to crawl out of the way, met a terrible death. The heartrending cries of the poor victims, as the flames advanced, entreating to be rescued from their impending fate—entreaties which it was impossible to heed in the crisis of the battle, and amidst duties on which the lives of many others depended—seem still in my ears.

Among the heart-sickening scenes of this terrible conflict which are still vivid in my memory, is one no lapse of time can ever efface, and in contemplating which I scarcely could check the tears from starting to my eyes. Riding to the front, I was hailed by a young soldier, whose boyish looks and merry songs on the march had frequently attracted my attention and excited my interest, and who was now leaning against a tree, the life-blood streaming down his side from a mortal wound, and his face white with the pallor of approaching death. "Major," said the poor lad, "I am dying, and I shall never see my regiment again; but I ask you to tell my comrades that the

Yankees have killed but not conquered me." When I passed the place again half an hour afterwards I found him a corpse. Such was the universal spirit of our men, and in this lay the secret of many of our wonderful achievements.

The enemy had in the meanwhile been strongly reinforced, and now poured forth from their third line of intrenchments a fire so terrible upon our advancing troops that the first two divisions staggered, and, after several unsuccessful efforts to press onward, fell back in considerable confusion. In vain was it that our officers used every effort to bring them forward once more; in vain even was it that Stuart, snatching the battle-flag of one of our brigades from the hands of the colour-bearer and waving it over his head, called on them as he rode forward to follow him. Nothing could induce them again to face that tempest of bullets, and that devastating hurricane of grape and canister vomited at close range from more than sixty pieces of artillery, and the advantages so dearly gained seemed about to be lost. At this critical moment, we suddenly heard the yell of Rodes's division behind us, and saw these gallant troops, led by their heroic general, charge over the front lines, and fall upon the enemy with such impetus that in a few minutes their works were taken, and they were driven in rapid flight from the woods to their redoubts on the hills of Chancellorsville.

A slight pause now intervened in the conflict, both sides, after the terrible work of the last few hours, being equally willing to draw breath awhile; and this gave us an opportunity to re-form our lines and close up our decimated ranks. The contest, meanwhile, was sustained by the artillery alone, which kept up a heavy cannonade; and the nature of the ground being now more favourable, most of our batteries had been brought into action, while from a hill on our extreme right, which had only been abandoned by the enemy after the charge of Rodes's division, twenty 12-pounder Napoleons played with a well-directed flank-fire upon the enemy's works, producing a terrible effect upon their dense masses.

About half-past ten we had news from General Lee, informing us that, having been pressing steadily forward the entire morning, he had now, with Anderson's and M'Laws's divisions, reached our right wing. I was at once despatched by Stuart to the Commander-in-Chief to report the state of affairs, and obtain his orders for further proceedings. I found him with our twenty-gun battery, looking as calm and dignified as ever, and perfectly regardless of the shells bursting round him, and the solid shot ploughing up the ground in all directions. General Lee expressed himself much satisfied with our operations, and intrusted me with orders for Stuart, directing a general attack with his whole force, which was to be supported by a charge of Anderson's division on the left flank of the enemy.

With renewed courage and confidence our three divisions now moved forward upon the enemy's strong position on the hills, encountering, as we emerged from the forest into the open opposite the plateau of Chancellorsville, such a storm of canister and bullets, that for a while it seemed an impossibility to take the heights in the face of it. Suddenly we heard to our right, piercing the roar and tumult of the battle, the yell of Anderson's men, whom we presently beheld hurled forward in a brilliant charge, sweeping everything before them. Short work was now made of the Federals, who, in a few minutes, were driven from their redoubts, which they abandoned in disorderly flight, leaving behind them cannons, small-arms, tents, and baggage in large quantities, besides a host of prisoners, of whom we took 360 in one redoubt.

A more magnificent spectacle can hardly be imagined than that which greeted me when I reached the crest of the plateau, and beheld on this side the long lines of our swiftly advancing troops stretching as far as the eye could reach, their red flags fluttering in the breeze, and their arms glittering in the morning sun; and farther on, dense and huddled masses of the Federals flying in utter rout towards the United States Ford, whilst high over our heads flew the shells which our artillery were dropping amidst the crowd of the retreating foe. The Chancellorsville House had caught fire, and was now enveloped in flames, so that it was with difficulty that we could save some portion of the Federal wounded lying there, to the number of several hundreds, the majority of whom perished. . . . The flight and pursuit took the direction of United States Ford, as far as about a mile beyond Chancellorsville, where another strong line of intrenchments offered their protection to the fugitives, and heavy reserves of fresh troops opposed our further advance.
—Von Borcke, *Memoirs of the Confederate War for Independence*

12. LEE LOSES HIS RIGHT ARM

Chancellorsville was a dearly bought victory; Confederate casualties were 13,156, of whom almost eleven thousand were killed and wounded. Irreparable was the loss of Stonewall Jackson, wounded by his own men. To Chaplain Lacy Lee said, "Give him my affectionate regards, and tell him to make haste and get well and come back to me as soon as he can. He has lost his left arm; but I have lost my right arm." But pneumonia and other complications set in and the mighty Stonewall "passed over the river."

The Reverend James Power Smith, who here describes the wounding of Jackson, was Jackson's aide-de-camp.

WHEN Jackson had reached the point where his line now crossed the turnpike, scarcely a mile west of Chancellorsville, and not half a mile from a line of Federal troops, he had found his front line unfit for the farther and vigorous advance he desired, by reason of the irregular character of the fighting, now right, now left, and because of the dense thickets, through which it was impossible to preserve alignment. Division commanders found it more and more difficult as the twilight deepened to hold their broken brigades in hand. Regretting the necessity of relieving the troops in front, General Jackson had ordered A. P. Hill's division, his third and reserve line, to be placed in front.

While this change was being effected, impatient and anxious, the general rode forward on the turnpike, followed by two or three of his staff and a number of couriers and signal sergeants. He passed the swampy depression and began the ascent of the hill toward Chancellorsville, when he came upon a line of the Federal infantry lying on their arms. Fired at by one or two muskets (two musket-balls from the enemy whistled over my head as I came to the front), he turned and came back toward his line, upon the side of the road to his left.

As he rode near to the Confederate troops, just placed in position and ignorant that he was in the front, the left company began firing to the front, and two of his party fell from their saddles dead—Captain Boswell, of the Engineers, and Sergeant Cunliffe, of the Signal Corps. Spurring his horse across the road to his right, he was met by a second volley from the right company of Pender's North Carolina brigade. Under this volley, when not two rods from the troops, the general received three balls at the same instant. One penetrated the palm of his right hand and was cut out that night from the back of his hand. A second passed around the wrist of the left arm and out through the left hand. A third ball passed through the left arm half-way from shoulder to elbow. The large bone of the upper arm was splintered to the elbow-joint, and the wound bled freely. His horse turned quickly from the fire, through the thick bushes which swept the cap from the general's head, and scratched his forehead, leaving drops of blood to stain his face.

As he lost his hold upon the bridle-rein, he reeled from the saddle, and was caught by the arms of Captain Wilbourn, of the Signal Corps. Laid upon the ground, there came at once to his succor General A. P. Hill and members of his staff. The writer reached his side a minute after, to find General Hill holding the head and shoulders of the wounded chief. Cutting open the coat-sleeve from wrist to shoulder, I found the wound in the upper arm, and with my handkerchief I bound the arm above the wound to stem the flow of blood. Couriers were sent for Dr. Hunter McGuire, the surgeon of the corps and the general's trusted friend, and for an ambulance. Being outside of our lines, it was urgent that he should be moved at once. With difficulty litter-bearers were brought from the line near by, and the general was placed upon the litter and carefully raised to the shoulder, I myself bearing one corner.

A moment after, artillery from the Federal side was opened upon us; great broadsides thundered over the woods; hissing shells searched the dark thickets through, and shrapnels swept the road along which we moved. Two or three steps farther, and the litter-bearer at my side was struck and fell, but, as the litter turned, Major Watkins Leigh, of Hill's staff, happily caught it. But the fright of the men was so great that we were obliged to lay the litter and its burden down upon the road. As the litter-bearers ran to the cover of the trees, I threw myself by the general's side and held him firmly to the ground as he attempted to rise. Over us swept the rapid fire of shot and shell—grape-shot striking fire upon the flinty rock of the road all around us, and sweeping from their feet horses and men of the artillery just moved to the front.

Soon the firing veered to the other side of the road, and I sprang to my feet, assisted the general to rise, passed my arm around him, and with the wounded man's weight thrown heavily upon me, we forsook the road. Entering the woods, he sank to the ground from exhaustion, but the litter was soon brought, and again rallying a few men, we essayed to carry him farther, when a second bearer fell at my side. This time, with none to assist, the litter careened, and the general fell to the ground, with a groan of deep pain. Greatly alarmed, I sprang to his head, and, lifting his head as a stray beam of moonlight came through clouds and leaves, he opened his eyes and wearily said: "Never mind me, Captain, never mind me." Raising him again to his feet, he was accosted by Brigadier-General Pender: "Oh, General, I hope you are not seriously wounded. I will have to retire my troops to re-form them, they are so much broken by this fire." But Jackson, rallying his strength, with firm voice said: "You must hold your ground, General Pender; you must hold your ground, sir!" and so uttered his last command on the field.

Again we resorted to the litter, and with difficulty bore it through the bush, and then under a hot fire along the road. Soon an ambulance was reached, and stopping to seek some stimulant at Chancellor's (Dowdall's Tavern), we were found by Dr. McGuire, who at once took charge of the wounded man. Passing back over the battle-field of the afternoon, we reached the Wilderness store, and then, in a field on the north, the field-hospital of our corps under Dr. Harvey Black. Here we found a tent prepared, and after midnight the left arm was amputated near the shoulder, and a ball taken from the right hand.

All night long it was mine to watch by the sufferer, and keep him warmly wrapped and undisturbed in his sleep. At 9 A.M., on the next day, when he aroused, cannon firing again filled the air, and all the Sunday through the fierce battle raged, General J. E. B. Stuart commanding the Confederates in Jackson's place. A dispatch was sent to the commanding general to announce formally his disability,—tidings General Lee had received during the the night with profound grief. There came back the following note:

"GENERAL: I have just received your note, informing me that you were wounded. I cannot express my regret at the occurrence. Could I have directed events, I should have chosen, for the good of the country, to have been disabled in your stead. I congratulate you upon the victory which is due to your skill and energy. Most truly yours, R. E. LEE, GENERAL."

When this dispatch was handed to me at the tent, and I read it aloud, General Jackson turned his face away and said, "General Lee is very kind, but he should give the praise to God."

The long day was passed with bright hopes for the wounded general, with tidings of success on the battle-field, with sad news of losses, and messages to and from other wounded officers brought to the same infirmary.

On Monday the general was carried in an ambulance, by way of Spotsylvania Court House, to most comfortable lodging at Chandler's, near Guinea's

Station, on the Richmond, Fredericksburg and Potomac railroad. And here, against our hopes, notwithstanding the skill and care of wise and watchful surgeons, attended day and night by wife and friends, amid the prayers and tears of all the Southern land, thinking not of himself, but of the cause he loved, and for the troops who had followed him so well and given him so great a name, our chief sank, day by day, with symptoms of pneumonia and some pains of pleurisy, until, at 3:15 P.M. on the quiet of the Sabbath afternoon, May 10th, 1863, he raised himself from his bed, saying, "No, no, let us pass over the river, and rest under the shade of the trees"; and, falling again to his pillow, he passed away, "over the river, where, in a land where warfare is not known or feared, he rests forever 'under the trees.'"

—SMITH, "Stonewall Jackson's Last Battle"

VIII

How the Soldiers Lived: Eastern Front

THE *Union and Confederate armies were haphazardly raised, badly organized, poorly trained, inadequately fed, clothed and housed, and almost wholly without comforts, sports, entertainments or proper medical care. Whether a regiment was well or badly trained, disciplined, and cared for depended largely on its officers, and to some extent on the initiative and enterprise of the men themselves. Regiments camped where they could, foraged for fuel and often for food, and depended on their own resources, on the sutlers, and on friends and relatives, for amusement and for luxuries. The Civil War armies were youthful, high-spirited, sentimental, and for the most part moral. They endured what seem to us wholly unnecessary hardships—heavy woolen clothing in the summertime, for example, or leaky tents or maggoty food—but they managed to enjoy themselves, indulged in rough sports and horseplay, fixed up their winter quarters with "all the comforts of home," sang romantic songs, enjoyed religious services and revivals, and generally acted like civilians on a picnic—when the enemy permitted!*

Most of these items tell their own story; few need explanatory introductions. The first 11 describe various aspects of camp life—clothing, housing, marching, work and play. The others deal more specifically with the everlasting problem of food, with religion, politics, red tape, corruption, and morale. Some of them are by men who for one reason or another distinguished themselves—in soldiering, in literature, in politics—or merely by writing a memorable memoir. Others are by men whom it has not been possible to rescue from obscurity. The notes will serve as introductions to the writers rather than to the subjects—which explain themselves.

1. THEODORE WINTHROP RECALLS A TYPICAL DAY AT CAMP CAMERON

Lawyer, novelist, and professional traveler, Theodore Winthrop is probably best remembered for his two volumes of sketches: The Canoe and the Saddle *and* Life in the Open Air; *his novels,* Cecil Dreeme *and* John Brent, *are universally unread. At the beginning of the war he enlisted in the 7th New York, and his account of its journey to Washington has already been mentioned. He was killed in a charge at the Battle of Great Bethel, June 1861.*

BOOM! I would rather not believe it; but it is—yes, it is—the morning gun, uttering its surly "Hullo!" to sunrise. Yes,—and, to confirm my suspicions, here rattle in the drums and pipe in the fifes, wooing us to get up, *get up,* with music too peremptory to be harmonious.

I rise up *sur mon séant* and glance about me. I, Private W., chance, by
reason of sundry chances, to be a member of a company recently largely
recruited and bestowed all together in a big marquee. As I lift myself up, I
see others lift themselves up on those straw bags we kindly call our mattresses. The tallest man of the regiment, Sergeant K., is on one side of me.
On the other side I am separated from two of the fattest men of the regiment
by Sergeant M., another excellent fellow, prime cook and prime forager.

We are all presently on our pins,—K. on those lengthy continuations of
his, and the two stout gentlemen on their stout supporters. The deep sleepers are pulled up from those abysses of slumber where they had been choking,
gurgling, strangling, death-rattling all night. There is for a moment a sound
of legs rushing into pantaloons and arms plunging into jackets.

Then, as the drums and fifes whine and clatter their last notes, at the flap
of our tent appears our orderly, and fierce in the morning sunshine gleams
his moustache,—one month's growth this blessed day. "Fall in, for roll-call!"
he cries, in a ringing voice. The orderly can speak sharp, if need be.

We obey. Not "Walk in!" "March in!" "Stand in!" is the order; but
"Fall in!" as sleepy men must. Then the orderly calls off our hundred. There
are several boyish voices which reply, several comic voices, a few mean
voices, and some so earnest and manly and alert that one says to himself,
"Those are the men for me, when work is to be done!" I read the character
of my comrades every morning in each fellow's monosyllable "Here!"

When the orderly is satisfied that not one of us has run away and accepted a Colonelcy from the Confederate States since last roll-call, he noti-
fies those unfortunates who are to be on guard for the next twenty-four
hours of the honor and responsibility placed upon their shoulders. Next he
tells us what are to be the drills of the day. Then, "Right face! Dismissed!
Break ranks! March!"

With ardor we instantly seize tin basins, soap, and towels, and invade a
lovely oak-grove at the rear and left of our camp. Here is a delicious spring
into which we have fitted a pump. The sylvan scene becomes peopled with
"National Guards Washing,"—a scene meriting the notice of Art as much
as any "Diana and her Nymphs." But we have no Poussin to paint us in the
dewy sunlit grove. Few of us, indeed, know how picturesque we are at all
times and seasons.

After this *beau idéal* of a morning toilet comes the ante-prandial drill.
Lieutenant W. arrives, and gives us a little appetizing exercise in "Carry
arms!" "Support arms!" "By the right flank, march!" "Double quick!"

Breakfast follows. My company messes somewhat helter-skelter in a big
tent. We have very tolerable rations. Sometimes luxuries appear of potted
meats and hermetical vegetables, sent us by the fond New-Yorkers. Each
little knot of fellows, too, cooks something savory. Our table-furniture is
not elegant, our plates are tin, there is no silver in our forks; but *à la guerre,
comme à la guerre*. Let the scrubs growl! Lucky fellows, if they suffer no
worse hardships than this!

By and by, after breakfast, come company drills, bayonet practice, battalion drills, and the heavy work of the day. Our handsome Colonel, on a nice black nag, manoeuvres his thousand men of the line-companies on the parade for two or three hours. Two thousand legs step off accurately together. Two thousand pipe-clayed cross-belts—whitened with infinite pains and waste of time, and offering a most inviting mark to a foe—restrain the beating bosoms of a thousand braves, as they—the braves, not the belts—go through the most intricate evolutions unerringly. Watching these battalion movements, Private W., perhaps, goes off and inscribes in his journal—"Any clever, prompt man, with a mechanical turn, an eye for distance, a notion of time, and a voice of command, can be a tactician. It is pure pedantry to claim that the manoeuvring of troops is difficult; it is not difficult, if the troops are quick and steady. But to be a general, with patience and purpose and initiative,—ah!" thinks Private W., "for that purpose you must have the man of genius; and in this war he already begins to appear out of Massachusetts and elsewhere."

Private W. avows without fear that about noon, at Camp Cameron, he takes a hearty dinner, and with satisfaction. Private W. has had his feasts in cot and chateau in Old World and New. It is the conviction of said private that nowhere and no-when has he expected his ration with more interest, and remembered it with more affection, than here.

In the middle hours of the day, it is in order to get a pass to go to Washington, or to visit some of the camps, which now, in the middle of May, begin to form a cordon around the city. . . . Our capital seems arranged by nature to be protected by fortified camps on the circuit of its hills. It may be made almost a Verona, if need be. Our brother regiments have posts nearly as charming as our own, in these fair groves and on these fair slopes on either side of us.

In the afternoon comes target practice, skirmishing-drill, more company- or recruit-drill, and at half past five our evening parade. Let me not forget tent-inspection, at four, by the officer of the day, when our band plays deliciously.

At evening parade all Washington appears. A regiment of ladies, rather indisposed to beauty, observe us. Sometimes the Dons arrive,—Secretaries of State, of War, of Navy,—or military Dons, bestriding prancing steeds, but bestriding them as if "'twas *not* their habit often of an afternoon." All which,—the bad teeth, pallid skins, and rustic toilets of the fair, and the very moderate horsemanship of the brave,—privates, standing at ease in the ranks, take note of, not cynically, but as men of the world.

Wondrous gymnasts are some of the Seventh, and after evening parade they often give exhibitions of their prowess to circles of admirers. Muscle has not gone out, nor nerve, nor activity, if these athletes are to be taken as the types or even as the leaders of the young city-bred men of our time. All the feats of strength and grace of the gymnasiums are to be seen here, and show to double advantage in the open air.

Then comes sweet evening. The moon rises. It seems always full moon at Camp Cameron. Every tent becomes a little illuminated pyramid. Cooking-fires burn bright along the alleys. The boys lark, sing, shout, do all these merry things that make the entertainment of volunteer service. The gentle moon looks on, mild and amused, the fairest lady of all that visit us.

At last when the songs have been sung and the hundred rumors of the day discussed, at ten the intrusive drums and scolding fifes get together and stir up a concert, always premature, called tattoo. The Seventh Regiment begins to peel for bed; at all events, Private W. does; for said W. takes, when he can, precious good care of his cuticle, and never yields to the lazy and unwholesome habit of soldiers,—sleeping in the clothes. At taps—half past ten—out go the lights. If they do not, presently comes the sentry's peremptory command to put them out. Then, and until the dawn of another day, a cordon of snorers inside of a cordon of sentries surrounds our national capital. The outer cordon sounds its "All's well"; and the inner cordon, slumbering, echoes it.

And that is the history of any day at Camp Cameron. It is monotonous, it is not monotonous, it is laborious, it is lazy, it is a bore, it is a lark, it is half war, half peace, and totally attractive, and not to be dispensed with from one's experience in the nineteenth century.

—WINTHROP, *Life in the Open Air, and Other Papers*

2. DAILY LIFE IN CAMP MILLINGTON

Lawrence Van Alstyne was a young Hudson Valley boy who enlisted in August 1862 in the 128th New York Volunteers—popularly called "Bostwick's Tigers." He trained for a short time at Camp Hudson, and then at Camp Millington, outside Baltimore, before sailing to the Gulf region. His account of daily life in the camp, in diary form, is one of the most authentic that has come down to us.

September 17, 1862. Maybe I have described our life here before, but as no one description can do it justice I am going to try again. We are in a field of 100 acres, as near as I can judge, on the side of a hill, near the top. The ground is newly seeded and wets up quickly, as such ground usually does. We sleep in pairs, and a blanket spread on the ground is our bed while another spread over us is our covering. A narrow strip of muslin, drawn over a pole about three feet from the ground, open at both ends, the wind and rain, if it does rain, beating in upon us, and water running under and about us; this, with all manner of bugs and creeping things crawling over us, and all the while great hungry mosquitoes biting every uncovered inch of us, is not an overdrawn picture of that part of a soldier's life, set apart for the rest and repose necessary to enable him to endure several hours of right down hard work at drill, in a hot sun with heavy woollen clothes on, every button of which must be tight-buttoned, and by the time the officers are tired watching us, we come back to camp wet through with perspiration and too tired to make another move.

Before morning our wet clothes chill us to the marrow of our bones, and why we live and apparently thrive under it, is something I cannot understand. But we do, and the next day are ready for more of it. Very few even take cold. It is part of the contract, and while we grumble and growl among ourselves, we don't really mean it, for we are learning what we will be glad to know at some future time.

Now I am about it, and nothing better to do, I will say something about our kitchen, dining room and cooking arrangements. Some get mad and cuss the cooks, and the whole war department, but that is usually when our stomachs are full. When we are hungry we swallow anything that comes and are thankful for it. The cook's house is simply a portion of the field we are in. A couple of crotches hold up a pole on which the camp kettles are hung, and under which a fire is built. Each company has one, and as far as I know they are all alike. The camp kettles are large sheet-iron pails, one larger than the other so one can be put inside the other when moving. If we have meat and potatoes, meat is put in one, and potatoes in the other. The one that gets cooked first is emptied into mess pans, which are large sheet-iron pans with flaring sides, so one can be packed in another. Then the coffee is put in the empty kettle and boiled. The bread is cut into thick slices, and the breakfast call sounds. We grab our plates and cups, and wait for no second invitation. We each get a piece of meat and a potato, a chunk of bread and a cup of coffee with a spoonful of brown sugar in it. Milk and butter we buy, or go without. We settle down, generally in groups, and the meal is soon over. Then we wash our dishes, and put them back in our haversacks. We make quick work of washing dishes. We save a piece of bread for the last, with which we wipe up everything, and then eat the dish rag. Dinner and breakfast are alike, only sometimes the meat and potatoes are cut up and cooked together, which makes a really delicious stew. Supper is the same, minus the meat and potatoes.

The cooks are men detailed from the ranks for that purpose. Every one smokes or chews tobacco here, so we find no fault because the cooks do both. Boxes or barrels are used as kitchen tables, and are used for seats between meals. The meat and bread are cut on them, and if a scrap is left on the table the flies go right at it and we have so many the less to crawl over us. They are never washed, but are sometimes scraped off and made to look real clean. I never yet saw the cooks wash their hands, but presume they do when they go to the brook for water.

—Van Alstyne, *Diary of an Enlisted Man*

3. ABNER SMALL PAINTS A PORTRAIT OF A PRIVATE IN THE ARMY OF THE POTOMAC

Abner Small, whose diary, The Road to Richmond, *is one of the best of Civil War sources, enlisted as a private in the 16th Maine Volunteers, fought through all the campaigns until 1864, was captured at Petersburg and imprisoned in Libby prison. He was later appointed historian of his regiment.*

PORTRAIT *of a private.*—The ideal picture of a soldier makes a veteran smile. Be a man never so much a man, his importance and conceit dwindle when he crawls into an unteaseled shirt, trousers too short and very baggy behind, coat too long at both ends, shoes with soles like firkin covers, and a cap as shapeless as a feed bag. Let me recall how our private looked to me in the army, in the ranks, a position he chose from pure patriotism. I can see him exactly as I saw him then. He is just in front of me trying to keep his balance and his temper, as he spews from a dry mouth the infernally fine soil of Virginia, and with his hands—he hasn't a handkerchief—wipes the streaks of dirty sweat that make furrows down his unshaven face. No friend of civilian days would recognize him in this most unattractive and disreputable-looking fellow, bowed under fifty-eight pounds of army essentials, and trying to suck a TD.

His suit is a model one, cut after the regulation pattern, fifty thousand at a time, and of just two sizes. If he is a small man, God pity him; and if he is a big man, God pity him still more; for he is an object of ridicule. His forage cap, with its leather visor, when dry curls up, when wet hangs down, and usually covers one or both ears. His army brogans, nothing can ever make shine or even black. Perhaps the coat of muddy blue can be buttoned in front, and it might be lapped and buttoned behind. The tailor never bushels army suits, and he doesn't crease trousers, although he is always generous in reënforcing them with the regulation patch.

The knapsack (which is cut to fit, in the engraving) is an unwieldy burden with its rough, coarse contents of flannel and sole leather and some-times twenty rounds of ammunition extra. Mixed in with these regulation essentials, like beatitudes, are photographs, cards, huswife, Testament, pens, ink, paper, and oftentimes stolen truck enough to load a mule. All this is crowned with a double wool blanket and half a shelter tent rolled in a rub-ber blanket. One shoulder and the hips support the "commissary depart-ment"—an odorous haversack, which often stinks with its mixture of bacon, pork, salt junk, sugar, coffee, tea, desiccated vegetables, rice, bits of yester-day's dinner, and old scraps husbanded with miserly care against a day of want sure to come.

Loaded down, in addition, with a canteen, full cartridge-box, belt, cross belt, and musket, and tramping twenty miles in a hurry on a hot day, our private was a soldier, but not just then a praiser of the soldier's life. I saw him multiplied by thousands. A photograph of any one of them, covered with yellow dust or mosaics of mud, would have served any relation, North or South, and ornamented a mantel, as a true picture of "Our Boy." . . .

Beans.—Long, weary marches were patiently endured if in the distant perspective could be seen the company bean-hole, and no well-disciplined New England regiment would be in camp thirty minutes without the re-quisite number. When we went into bivouac, every cook would have one dug and a fire over it before the companies broke to the rear and stacked arms. In the early morning I would hang around a particular hole, and ask Ben to just h'ist the cover and let me get a sniff for an appetizer; and how

Ben would roll his orbs, till only the whites were visible, and say, "Golly, Adjutant, dem yalla-eyes don' got dere kivers off yet; you'll just natchely have to wait a while!" But many's the time we would have to "git up and git," eating our beans half-cooked, and then would come an internal disturbance—not that infernal demon, dyspepsia, of civil life, but an almighty bellyache that would double a man up and send him into line at "Surgeon's Call."

Desiccated vegetables.—Too many beans with salt junk demanded an antiscorbutic, so the government advertised proposals for some kind of vegetable compound in portable form, and it came—tons of it—in sheets like pressed hops. I suppose it was healthful, for there was variety enough in its composition to satisfy any condition of stomach and bowels. What in Heaven's name it was composed of, none of us ever discovered. It was called simply "desiccated vegetables." Ben once brought in just before dinner a piece with a big horn button on it, and wanted to know "if dat 'ere was celery or cabbage?" I doubt our men have ever forgotten how a cook would break off a piece as large as a boot top, put it in a kettle of water, and stir it with the handle of a hospital broom. When the stuff was fully dissolved, the water would remind one of a dirty brook with all the dead leaves floating around promiscuously. Still, it was a substitute for food. We ate it, and we liked it, too.

—SMALL, *The Road to Richmond*

4. LIFE WITH THE THIRTEENTH MASSACHUSETTS

The 13th Massachusetts was organized in Boston shortly after the attack on Fort Sumter and, after brief training at Fort Independence, left for New York in July 1861. The story of the march southward to the fields of battle is told in these pages of diaries put together by the regimental historian, Charles E. Davis. The regiment fought in the Valley campaign, at Antietam, Chancellorsville, Gettysburg, and Petersburg. Davis himself was wounded and imprisoned at Manassas. It is no exaggeration to say that this is on the whole the most interesting of all the many regimental histories.

1861. Thursday, Aug. 1, Hagerstown: After tents were pitched some of the men turned in and went to sleep, though the novelty of the thing was too great for most of us, who straggled back into town. During the day one of the boys brought in a Virginia paper in which it was stated that one "Southerner could lick five Northern mudsills." It was not so very comforting to feel that we were to be killed off in blocks of five. Nothing was said to us on the 16th of July, the date of our muster-in, about this wholesale slaughter. There was a kind of airy confidence as well as contemptuousness about the statement that made our enlistment look a little less like a picnic than when we marched down Broadway. It was hard to realize that we had come so far from home merely to solve a problem in mathematics, yet so it seemed to the writer of that philippic.

Some time during the night an alarm was sounded by the beating of the "long roll," and we were ordered into line to drive the terrible foe, who was thought, even then, to be in our midst. Immediately everything was excitement and confusion. We can afford to laugh now, but then it was terribly serious, and no doubt we did some silly things; but it should be borne in mind that this was very early in the war. When it was discovered, as it shortly was, that all this excitement was caused by a pig who strolled into camp and was mistaken by the officer of the guard for the rebel army, many of us were imbued with a courage we hardly felt before. There was little sleep during the balance of the night, as the matter had to be discussed and talked about, as most things were in the rank and file of the Thirteenth, particularly when it related to the foolishness of an officer.

Although orders awaited us, on our arrival in Hagerstown, to march to Harper's Ferry, we were delayed on account of the bad condition of the roads from recent rains. This kind of consideration went out of fashion very soon after, we are sorry to say.

About sunset we struck tents and marched to Boonesboro', fourteen miles, arriving there at the witching hour of night when it is said church-yards yawn. We were led into an empty corral, lately occupied by mules, to bivouac for the night.

Ordinarily a mule-yard would not be considered a desirable place in which to spend the night, but it was midnight, and we were weary with marching, and worn out with excitement and loss of sleep. This was our fifth night from home. The first night was spent on a Sound steamer, the second on our way to Philadelphia, the third *en route* to Hagerstown, and the fourth in driving pigs out of camp, so that this old mule-yard, as far as we could see it, appeared the most delightful place in the world. At eighteen to twenty years of age little time is wasted in seeking sleep. It comes quickly and takes entire possession of your soul and body, and all we did was to drop in our tracks, making no inquiries about camp or picket guard, but let Morpheus lead us to the land of pleasant dreams. This being our first bivouac, occurrences made a deeper impression than at any time afterward. When reveille was sounded, and our eyes opened to the bright sunlight, we looked about to see where we were and who were near us. The bright red blankets of the regiment made the place look attractive. Many of the boys were still stretching themselves into activity, while others were examining their bed to account for sundry pains in the body from neglect to brush the stones aside when they laid down. How we all laughed when we saw where we were! Many and many a time while sitting round a camp fire have we recalled this night in the mule-yard.

Saturday, Aug. 3: A very hot day. Shortly after breakfast we left for Pleasant Valley, sixteen miles, where we arrived in the afternoon, and where we bivouacked for the night. A good many of the men were overcome by the heat, and didn't reach camp until after dark. The size of the knapsack was too heavy for men unused to carrying such a weight. It must be reduced, and there were no more Bibles. Just what to throw away it was difficult to decide, as many of the articles we carried were connected by association with those we held most dear. Some of the boys had dressing-cases among their luxuries. They hated to dispense with them, but it had to be done.

Among the articles provided us by the State were "havelocks," commonly used in hot countries by the English army. The havelock was named after Sir Henry Havelock, a distinguished English general. It is made of white linen, to be worn on the head as a protection from the rays of the sun. As it was made sufficiently large to cover the neck and shoulders, the effect, when properly adjusted, was to deprive the wearer of any air he might otherwise enjoy. An Englishman would melt in his boots before he would give up a custom enjoyed by his grandfather. Not so a Yankee. The motive which prompted the State to supply them was a good one, as was also the suggestion that prompted their immediate transfer to the plebeian uses of a dish-cloth or a coffee-strainer, which suggestion was universally adopted,—a dish-cloth or coffee-strainer being the only things in the world, apparently, we were unprovided with.

Friday, Aug. 23: While at Sandy Hook we received the hats and uniform coats issued to us by the State, and which were forwarded by express. The coat was much too heavy, with the thermometer in the eighties. It was made with long skirts, and when fitting the wearer was not a bad-appearing garment; but as very few of them did fit, our personal appearance was not improved. They were made large in front, to meet an abnormal expansion of chest. Until we grew to them, it was a handy place to stow some of the contents of our knapsack.

The hats were neither useful nor ornamental. They were made of black felt, high-crowned, with a wide rim turned up on one side, and fastened to the crown by a brass shield representing an eagle with extended wings, apparently screaming with holy horror at so base an employment. On the front of the crown was a brass bugle containing the figure 13. Now it so happened that the person who selected the sizes was under the impression that every man from Massachusetts had a head like Daniel Webster—a mistake that caused most of us much trouble, inasmuch as newspapers were in great demand to lessen the diameter of the crown. Those of us who failed to procure newspapers made use of our ears to prevent its falling on our shoulders. As will be seen later on, they mysteriously disappeared. . . .

September 13: A man in one of the Connecticut regiments was shot to-day for sleeping on guard. It was not pleasant to feel that a quiet nap, on picket, might be followed by death, so we swore off sleeping while on guard.

It was at Darnestown that we were first made acquainted with an article of food called "desiccated" vegetables. For the convenience of handling, it was made in to large, round cakes about two inches thick. When cooked, it tasted like herb tea. From the flow of language which followed, we suspected it contained powerful stimulating properties. It became universally known in the army as "desecrated" vegetables, and the aptness of this term would be appreciated by the dullest comprehension after one mouthful of the abominable compound. It is possible that the chaplain, who overheard some of the remarks, may have urged its discontinuance as a ration, inasmuch as we rarely, if ever, had it again.

[1862]. Wednesday, March 12: The rattle of drums and the sweet singing of birds announced that morn was here. The army was to move on Winchester at once, so we hastily cooked our coffee, and as quickly as possible ate our breakfast. There was no time to spare, as orders to "fall in" were heard in every direction. Orders were received for the Thirteenth to take the advance of the column as skirmishers. Winchester was four miles away, occupied by 25,000 troops under Stonewall Jackson, and well-fortified by earthworks. As soon as we were out of the woods the regiment was deployed as skirmishers, and marched in that order in quick time across fields, over fences and stone walls, fording brooks or creeks, preserving distances and line as well as we could under such disadvantages.

The sensations we experienced on this bright, beautiful morning are not likely to be forgotten. It was very warm, and the march a hard one, because the line was irregularly obstructed. That is to say, while one part would be marching on the smooth surface of the ground, another part might be climbing a fence or wading a brook. To keep the line tolerably straight under such exasperating circumstances was very trying and perspiring work. In addition to this we were, for the first time, in line of battle, and in plain sight of the rest of the division, who were watching our movements as they followed in close column.

Situated as we were, there was no opportunity for obeying, without disgrace, those instincts of discretion which are said to be the better part of valor, and which prompt human nature to seek safety in flight. Those of us who omitted to sneak away before the line was formed, but who afterward showed such ingenuity and skill in escaping the dangers of battle, found no chance open for skulking on this occasion. Yes! like other regiments, we had our percentage of men who dared to run away, that they might live to fight some other, far distant day.

We saw those dreaded earthworks a long time before we reached them, and wondered at the enemy's silence, but concluded they were reserving their fire until we should be close enough for the greatest execution. Whatever the boys felt, there was no faltering or wavering. Within a short distance of the earthworks we formed in close order, and with a yell and a rush we bounded over them to find, after all our fears and anticipations, they were empty. We were soon formed in line, and marched, in columns of companies, into town, being the first Union regiment that entered Winchester. We felt proud enough at our bloodless victory.

We had hardly entered the main street of the town when General Jackson and Colonel Ashby were discovered on horseback, in front of the Taylor House, waving an adieu with their hats. An order was immediately given to fire, but we were not quick enough to do them harm or retard their flight. This was a daring thing to do, though common enough with such men as Jackson and Ashby.

We marched down the main street, the band playing patriotic airs, while the people scanned our appearance to see what a Yankee looked like. Some who were prepared to scoff could get no farther than "How fat they are!"

After the companies were assigned to quarters the officers met at the Taylor House, and dined on the meal provided for Jackson and his staff.

Tuesday, July 22: In passing through towns and villages, and even on the high-roads, we naturally attracted a good deal of attention. We frequently noticed among the crowds so gathered, the scowling faces of women, who, upon learning we were from Massachusetts, saluted us as "Nigger-lovers," and other opprobrious epithets, while it occasionally happened that by grimaces only could they express the intensity of their feelings. . . .

The remarks we heard from the bystanders as we marched along often became by-words in the regiment. We were no exception to the generality of mankind, of liking to see a pretty face, even if it did belong to a woman of "secesh" sentiments. When the boys at the head of the column discovered a pretty girl, if she was on the right side of the road, *"guide right"* would be passed along the line; and *"guide left"* if on the left side of the road. By this ingenious device we were enabled to direct our eyes where we would receive the largest return for our admiration. . . .

Various were the devices adopted by the boys to relieve the monotony of weary marches. On these occasions, as conversation was allowed, stories were told, gossip repeated, discussions carried on, and criticisms made on the acts of public men, as well as on the merits of our commanders. An occasional silence would be broken by the starting of a familiar song, and very soon the whole regiment would join in the singing. Sometimes it would be a whistling chorus, when all would be whistling. Toward the end of a day, however, so tired we were all, that it was difficult to muster courage for these diversions, then our only reliance for music would be the band. When a temporary halt was granted, it was curious to see how quickly the boys would dump themselves over on their backs at the side of the road as soon as the word was given, looking like so many dead men. There was one thing we were thankful to the colonel for, and that was his freedom from nonsense on such occasions. No "right-facing," no "right-dressing," no "stacking arms," to waste valuable minutes, but "get all the rest you can, boys," and when the order was given to "forward," each man took his place in line without confusion or delay. . . .

It would often occur, when we were tired and dusty from a long day's march, "Old Festive" would ride by, when suddenly you would hear sung:

"Saw my leg off,
Saw my leg off,
Saw my leg off—
SHORT!!!"

There was another man in the regiment who contributed a large share of fun for the amusement of others, and that was the "Medicine man"—the man who honored the doctor's sight-drafts for salts, castor-oil, etc., delicacies intended for the sick, but greatly in demand by those who wished to rid themselves of unpleasant duties. He was the *basso profundo* of the glee club, and could gaze without a tremor at the misery of a man struggling with castor-oil, while at the same time encouraging him to show his gratitude at the generosity of the Government by drinking the last drop. "Down with it, my boy, the more you take the less I carry."

Saturday, Aug. 9: The last place to look for a stock company would be among a regiment of soldiers. After being deprived of camp kettles, mess pans, etc., each man was obliged to do his own cooking, as already stated, in his tin dipper, which held about a pint. Whether it was coffee, beans, pork, or anything depending on the services of a fire to make it palatable, it was accomplished by the aid of the dipper only. Therefore any utensil like a frying-pan was of incalculable service in preparing a meal. There were so few of these in the regiment, that only men of large means, men who could raise a dollar thirty days after a paymaster's visit, could afford such a luxury.

In one instance the difficulty was overcome by the formation of a joint-stock company, composed of five stockholders, each paying the sum of twenty cents toward the purchase of a frying-pan, which cost the sum of one dollar. The par value of each share was therefore twenty cents. It was understood that each stockholder should take his turn at carrying the frying-pan when on a march, which responsibility entitled him to its first use in halting for the night. While in camp, it passed from one to the other each day in order of turn. It was frequently loaned for a consideration, thereby affording means for an occasional dividend among the stockholders. The stock advanced in value until it reached as high as forty cents per share, so that a stockholder in the "Joint Stock Frying Pan Company" was looked upon as a man of consequence. Being treated with kindness and civility by his comrades, life assumed a roseate hue to the shareholders in this great company, in spite of their deprivations. It was flattering to hear one's self mentioned in terms of praise by some impecunious comrade who wished to occupy one side of it while you were cooking.

On this particular morning, when we started out, expecting shortly to be in a fight, the stock went rapidly down, until it could be bought for almost nothing. As the day progressed, however, there was a slight rise, though the market was not strong. When the order was given to leave knapsacks, it necessarily included this utensil, and so the "Joint Stock Frying Pan Company" was wiped out.

—DAVIS, *Three Years in the Army*

5. MINUTIAE OF SOLDIER LIFE IN THE ARMY OF NORTHERN VIRGINIA

To an extraordinary degree—or what to us now seems an extraordinary degree—the Civil War soldier, North and South, was on his own. He often supplied his own uniform and his own arms; often he had to depend upon his own ingenuity, or that of his company, for food. He depended almost wholly upon himself for entertainment. He was—like American soldiers in all wars—an individualist. He regarded all regulations with distaste, avoided regimentation, tried to live his own life as much as he could.

Of all the many accounts of life in the Confederate armies, that of Carlton McCarthy is the best—the best because the most detailed. McCarthy was a private in the famous Richmond Howitzers.

THE volunteer of 1861 made extensive preparations for the field. Boots, he thought, were an absolute necessity, and the heavier the soles and longer the tops the better. His pants were stuffed inside the tops of his boots, of course. A double-breasted coat, heavily wadded, with two rows of big brass buttons and a long skirt, was considered comfortable. A small stiff cap, with a narrow brim, took the place of the comfortable "felt," or the shining and towering tile worn in civil life.

Then over all was a huge overcoat, long and heavy, with a cape reaching nearly to the waist. On his back he strapped a knapsack containing a full stock of underwear, soap, towels, comb, brush, looking-glass, tooth-brush, paper and envelopes, pens, ink, pencils, blacking, photographs, smoking and chewing tobacco, pipes, twine string, and cotton strips for wounds and other emergencies, needles and thread, buttons, knife, fork, and spoon, and many other things as each man's idea of what he was to encounter varied. On the outside of the knapsack, solidly folded, were two great blankets and a rubber or oil-cloth. This knapsack, etc., weighed from fifteen to twenty-five pounds, sometimes more. All seemed to think it was impossible to have on too heavy clothes, or to have too many conveniences, and each had an idea that to be a good soldier he must be provided against every possible emergency.

In addition to the knapsack, each man had a haversack, more or less costly, some of cloth and some of fine morocco, and stored with provisions always, as though he expected any moment to receive orders to march across the Great Desert, and supply his own wants on the way. A canteen was considered indispensable, and at the outset it was thought prudent to keep it full of water. Many, expecting terrific hand-to-hand encounters, carried revolvers, and even bowie-knives. Merino shirts (and flannel) were thought to be the right thing, but experience demonstrated the contrary. Gloves were also thought to be very necessary and good things to have in winter time, the favorite style being buck gauntlets with long cuffs.

In addition to each man's private luggage, each mess, generally composed of from five to ten men, drawn together by similar tastes and associations, had *its* outfit, consisting of a large camp chest containing skillet, frying pan, coffee boiler, bucket for lard, coffee box, salt box, meal box, flour box, knives, forks, spoons, plates, cups, etc., etc. These chests were so large that eight or ten of them filled up an army wagon, and were so heavy that two strong men had all they could do to get one of them into the wagon. In addition to the chest each mess owned an axe, water bucket, and bread tray. Then the tents of each company, and little sheet-iron stoves, and stove pipe, and the trunks and valises of the company officers, made an immense pile of stuff, so that each company had a small wagon train of its own.

All thought money to be absolutely necessary, and for a while rations were disdained and the mess supplied with the best that could be bought with the mess fund. Quite a large number had a "boy" along to do the cooking and washing. Think of it! a Confederate soldier with a body servant all his own, to bring him a drink of water, black his boots, dust his clothes, cook his corn bread and bacon, and put wood on his fire. Never was there fonder admiration than these darkies displayed for their masters. Their chief delight and glory was to praise the courage and good looks of "Mahse Tom," and prophesy great things about his future. Many a ringing laugh and shout of fun originated in the queer remarks, shining countenance, and glistening teeth of this now forever departed character.

It is amusing to think of the follies of the early part of the war, as illustrated by the outfits of the volunteers. They were so heavily clad, and so burdened with all manner of things, that a march was torture, and the wagon trains were so immense in proportion to the number of troops, that it would have been impossible to guard them in an enemy's country. Subordinate officers thought themselves entitled to transportation for trunks, mattresses, and folding bedsteads, and the privates were as ridiculous in their demands.

Thus much by way of introduction. The change came rapidly, and stayed not until the transformation was complete. Nor was this change attributable alone to the orders of the general officers. The men soon learned the inconvenience and danger of so much luggage, and, as they became more experienced, they vied with each other in reducing themselves to light-marching trim.

Experience soon demonstrated that boots were not agreeable on a long march. They were heavy and irksome, and when the heels were worn a little one-sided, the wearer would find his ankle twisted nearly out of joint by every unevenness of the road. When thoroughly wet, it was a laborious undertaking to get them off, and worse to get them on in time to answer the morning roll-call. And so, good, strong brogues or brogans, with broad bottoms and big, flat heels, succeeded the boots, and were found much more comfortable and agreeable, easier put on and off, and altogether the more sensible.

A short-waisted and single-breasted jacket usurped the place of the long-tailed coat, and became universal. The enemy noticed this peculiarity, and called the Confederates gray jackets, which name was immediately transferred to those lively creatures which were the constant admirers and inseparable companions of the Boys in Gray and in Blue.

Caps were destined to hold out longer than some other uncomfortable things, but they finally yielded to the demands of comfort and common sense, and a good soft felt hat was worn instead. A man who has never been a soldier does not know, nor indeed can know, the amount of comfort there is in a good soft hat in camp, and how utterly useless is a "soldier hat" as they are generally made. Why the Prussians, with all their experience, wear

A. R. Waud

The Army of the Potomac on the Move, January 1863

General Stuart's Headquarters on the Rapidan

Commissary Department of the 6th Massachusetts

their heavy, unyielding helmets, and the French their little caps, is a mystery to a Confederate who has enjoyed the comfort of an old slouch.

Overcoats an inexperienced man would think an absolute necessity for men exposed to the rigors of a northern Virginia winter, but they grew scarcer and scarcer; they were found to be a great inconvenience. The men came to the conclusion that the trouble of carrying them on hot days outweighed the comfort of having them when the cold day arrived. Besides they found that life in the open air hardened them to such an extent that changes in the temperature were not felt to any degree. Some clung to their overcoats to the last, but the majority got tired lugging them around, and either discarded them altogether, or trusted to capturing one about the time it would be needed. Nearly every overcoat in the army in the latter years was one of Uncle Sam's captured from his boys.

The knapsack vanished early in the struggle. It was inconvenient to "change" the underwear too often, and the disposition not to change grew, as the knapsack was found to gall the back and shoulders, and weary the man before half the march was accomplished. The better way was to dress out and out, and wear that outfit until the enemy's knapsacks, or the folks at home supplied a change. Certainly it did not pay to carry around clean clothes while waiting for the time to use them.

Very little washing was done, as a matter of course. Clothes once given up were parted with forever. There were good reasons for this: cold water would not cleanse them or destroy the vermin, and hot water was not always to be had. One blanket to each man was found to be as much as could be carried, and amply sufficient for the severest weather. This was carried generally by rolling it lengthwise, with the rubber cloth outside, tying the ends of the roll together, and throwing the loop thus made over the left shoulder with the ends fastened together hanging under the right arm.

The haversack held its own to the last, and was found practical and useful. It very seldom, however, contained rations, but was used to carry all the articles generally carried in the knapsack; of course the stock was small. Somehow or other, many men managed to do without the haversack, and carried absolutely nothing but what they wore and had in their pockets.

The infantry threw away their heavy cap boxes and cartridge boxes, and carried their caps and cartridges in their pockets. Canteens were very useful at times, but they were as a general thing discarded. They were not much used to carry water, but were found useful when the men were driven to the necessity of foraging, for conveying buttermilk, cider, sorghum, etc., to camp. A good strong tin cup was found better than a canteen, as it was easier to fill at a well or spring, and was serviceable as a boiler for making coffee when the column halted for the night.

Revolvers were found to be about as useless and heavy lumber as a private soldier could carry, and early in the war were sent home to be used by the women and children in protecting themselves from insult and violence at the hands of the ruffians who prowled about the country shirking duty.

Strong cotton was adopted in place of flannel and merino, for two reasons: first, because easier to wash; and second, because the vermin did not propagate so rapidly in cotton as in wool. Common white cotton shirts and drawers proved the best that could be used by the private soldier.

Gloves to any but a mounted man were found useless, worse than useless. With the gloves on, it was impossible to handle an axe, buckle harness, load a musket, or handle a rammer at the piece. Wearing them was found to be simply a habit, and so, on the principle that the less luggage the less labor, *they* were discarded.

The camp-chest soon vanished. The brigadiers and major-generals, even, found them too troublesome, and soon they were left entirely to the quarter-masters and commissaries. One skillet and a couple of frying pans, a bag for flour or meal, another bag for salt, sugar, and coffee, divided by a knot tied between served the purpose as well. The skillet passed from mess to mess. Each mess generally owned a frying pan, but often one served a company. The oil-cloth was found to be as good as the wooden tray for making up the dough. The water bucket held its own to the last!

Tents were *rarely seen*. All the poetry about the *"tented field"* died. Two men slept together, each having a blanket and an oil-cloth; one oil-cloth went next to the ground. The two laid on this, covered themselves with two blankets, protected from the rain with the second oil-cloth on top, and slept very comfortably through rain, snow or hail, as it might be.

Very little money was seen in camp. The men did not expect, did not care for, or often get any pay, and they were not willing to deprive the old folks at home of their little supply, so they learned to do without any money.

When rations got short and were getting shorter, it became necessary to dismiss the darkey servants. Some, however, became company servants, instead of private institutions, and held out faithfully to the end, cooking the rations away in the rear, and at the risk of life carrying them to the line of battle to their "young mahsters."

Reduced to the minimum, the private soldier consisted of one man, one hat, one jacket, one shirt, one pair of pants, one pair of drawers, one pair of shoes, and one pair of socks. His baggage was one blanket, one rubber blanket, and one haversack. The haversack generally contained smoking tobacco and a pipe, and a small piece of soap, with temporary additions of apples, persimmons, blackberries, and such other commodities as he could pick up on the march.

The company property consisted of two or three skillets and frying pans, which were sometimes carried in the wagon, but oftener in the hands of the soldiers. The infantry-men generally preferred to stick the handle of the frying pan in the barrel of a musket, and so carry it.

The wagon trains were devoted entirely to the transportation of ammunition and commissary and quartermaster's stores, which had not been issued. Rations which had become company property, and the baggage of the men, when they had any, was carried by the men themselves. If, as was sometimes the case, three days' rations were issued at one time and the troops ordered to cook them, and be prepared to march, they did cook them, *and eat them if possible,* so as to avoid the labor of carrying them. It was not such an undertaking either, to eat three days' rations in one, as frequently none had been issued for more than a day, and when issued were cut down one half.

The infantry found out that bayonets were not of much use, and did not hesitate to throw them, with the scabbard, away.

The artillerymen, who started out with heavy sabres hanging to their belts, stuck them up in the mud as they marched, and left them for the ordnance officers to pick up and turn over to the cavalry.

The cavalrymen found sabres very tiresome when swung to the belt, and adopted the plan of fastening them to the saddle on the left side, with the hilt in front and in reach of the hand. Finally sabres got very scarce even among the cavalrymen, who relied more and more on their short rifles.

No soldiers ever marched with less to encumber them, and none marched faster or held out longer.

The courage and devotion of the men rose equal to every hardship and privation, and the very intensity of their sufferings became a source of merriment. Instead of growling and deserting, they laughed at their own bare feet, ragged clothes and pinched faces; and weak, hungry, cold, wet, worried with vermin and itch, dirty, with no hope of reward or rest, marched cheerfully to meet the well-fed and warmly clad hosts of the enemy.

—McCarthy, *Detailed Minutiae of Soldier Life in
the Army of Northern Virginia*

6. GETTING A HAIRCUT IN THE ARMY

Here is another example of what now would seem to be the primitive conditions of warfare in the sixties. There was no organized barber service; the soldiers arranged for their own haircuts and shaves—or went without. The popularity of beards actually antedated the Civil War by a year or two— witness Lincoln's growing a beard after his nomination—but the exigencies of wartime service helped make beards fashionable.

William Dame was a Maryland Confederate, a student of theology who entered the ministry after the war. His volume of memoirs is particularly valuable for its pictures of daily life in the army.

THERE was only one man in the Battery who could cut hair—Sergeant Van McCreery—and he had the only pair of scissors that could cut hair. So every aspirant to this fashionable cut tried to make interest with Van to fix him up; and Van, who was very good natured, would, as he had time and opportunity, accommodate the applicant, and trim him close.

Several of us had gone under the transforming hands of this tonsorial artist, when Bob McIntosh got his turn. Bob was a handsome boy with a luxuriant growth of hair. He had raven black, kinky hair that stuck up from his head in a bushy mass, and he hadn't had his hair cut for a good while, and it was very long and seemed longer than it was because it stuck out so from his head. Now, it was all to go, and a crowd of the boys gathered 'round to see the fun. The modus operandi was simple, but sufficient. The candidate sat on a stump with a towel tied 'round his neck, and he held up the corners making a receptacle to catch the hair as it was cut. Why this—I don't know; force of habit I reckon. . . .

Van stood behind Bob and began over his right ear. He took the hair off clean, as he went, working from right to left over his head; the crowd around—jeering the victim and making comments on his ever-changing appearance as the scissors progressed, making a clean sweep at every cut. We were thus making much noise with our fun at Bob's expense, until the shears had moved up to the top of his head, leaving the whole right half of the head as clean of hair as the palm of your hand, while the other half was still covered with this long, kinky, jet black hair, which in the absence of the departed locks looked twice as long as before—and Bob did present a spectacle that would make a dog laugh. It was just as funny as it could be.

Just at that moment, in the midst of all this hilarity, suddenly we heard a man yell out something as he came running down the hill from the guns. We could not hear what he said. The next moment, he burst excitedly into our midst, and shouted out, "For God's sake, men, get your guns. The Yankees are across the river and making for the guns. They will capture them before you get there, if you don't hurry up."

This was a bolt out of a clear sky—but we jumped to the call. Everybody instantly forgot everything else and raced for the guns. I saw McCreery running with the scissors in his hand; he forgot that he had them—but it was funny to see a soldier going to war with a pair of scissors! I found myself running beside Bob McIntosh, with his hat off, his head half shaved and that towel, still tied round his neck, streaming out behind him in the wind.

Just before we got to the guns, Bob suddenly halted and said, "Good Heavens, Billy, it has just come to me what a devil of a fix I am in with my head in this condition. I tell you now that if the Yankees get too close to the guns, I am going to run. If they got me, or found me dead, they would say that General Lee was bringing up the convicts from the Penitentiary in Richmond to fight them. I wouldn't be caught dead with my head looking like this. . . ."

In the meantime, the enemy guns across the river opened on us and the shells were flying about us in lively fashion. It was rather a sudden transition from peace to war, but we had been at this busines before; the sound of the shells was not unfamiliar—so we were not unduly disturbed. We quickly got the guns loaded, and opened on that Infantry, advancing up the hill. We worked rapidly, for the case was urgent, and we made it as lively for those fellows as we possibly could. In a few minutes a pretty neat little battle was making the welkin ring. . . .

The battle ceased, the picket line was restored along the river bank, and all was quiet again. Bob McIntosh was more put out by all this business than anybody else—it had interrupted his hair cut. When we first got the guns into action, everybody was too busy to notice Bob's head. After we got settled down to work, I caught sight of that half-shaved head and it was the funniest object you ever saw. Bob was No. 1 at his gun, which was next to mine, and had to swab and ram the gun. This necessitated his constantly turning from side to side, displaying first this, and then the other side of his head. One side was perfectly white and bare; the other side covered by a mop of kinky, jet black hair; but when you caught sight of his front elevation, the effect was indescribable. While Bob was unconsciously making this absurd exhibition, it was too much to stand, even in a fight. I said to the boys around my gun, "Look at Bob." They looked and they could hardly work the gun for laughing.

Of course, when the fight was over McCreery lost that pair of scissors, or *said* he did. There was not another pair in camp, so Bob had to go about with his head in that condition for about a week—and he wearied of life. One day in his desperation, he said he wanted to get some of that hair off his head so much that he would resort to any means. He had tried to cut some off with his knife. One of the boys, Hunter Dupuy, was standing by chopping on the level top of a stump with a hatchet. Hunter said, "All right, Bob, put your head on this stump and I'll chop off some of your hair." The blade was dull, and it only forced a quantity of the hair down into the wood, where it stuck, and held Bob's hair fast to the stump, besides pulling out a lot by the roots, and hurting Bob very much. He tried to pull loose and couldn't. Then he began to call Hunter all the names he could think of, and threatened what he was going to do to him when he got loose. Hunter, much hurt by such ungracious return for what he had done at Bob's request, said, "Why, Bob, you couldn't expect me to cut your hair with a hatchet without hurting some"—which semed reasonable. We made Bob promise to keep the peace, on pain of leaving him tied to the stump—then we cut him loose with our knives.

After some days, when we had had our fun, Van found the scissors and trimmed off the other side of his head to match—Bob was happy.

—DAME, *From the Rapidan to Richmond*

7. INVENTIONS AND GADGETS USED BY THE SOLDIERS

Civil War soldiers, like their successors in the First and Second World Wars, were endlessly resourceful. They had to be. Their resourcefulness appeared not only in such contrivances as those here described, but in the creation of new weapons and new techniques of warfare.

John D. Billings, whose Hardtack and Coffee *is one of the most entertaining of all Civil War books, was a member of the 10th Massachusetts battery of light artillery.*

ONE of the first products of their genius which I recall was a combination *knife-fork-and-spoon* arrangement, which was peddled through the state camping-grounds in great numbers and variety. Of course every man must have one. So much convenience in so small a compass must be taken advantage of. It was a sort of soldier's trinity, which they all thought that they understood and appreciated. But I doubt whether this invention, on the average, ever got beyond the first camp in active service.

I still have in my possession the remnants of a *water-filterer* in which I invested after enlistment. There was a metallic mouth-piece at one end of a small gutta-percha tube, which latter was about fifteen inches long. At the other end of the tube was a suction-chamber, an inch long by a half-inch in diameter, with the end perforated, and containing a piece of bocking as a filter. Midway of the tubing was an air-chamber. The tubing long since dried and crumbled away from the metal. It is possible that I used this instrument half a dozen times, though I do not recall a single instance, and on breaking camp just before the Gettysburg Campaign, I sent it, with some other effects, northward.

I remember another filterer, somewhat simpler. It consisted of the same kind of mouth-piece, with rubber tubing attached to a small conical piece of pumice stone, through which the water was filtered. Neither of these was ever of any practical value.

There was another invention that must have been sufficiently popular to have paid the manufacturer a fair rate on his investment, and that was the steel-armor enterprise. There were a good many men who were anxious to be heroes, but they were particular. They preferred to be *live* heroes. They were willing to go to war and fight as never man fought before, if they could only be insured against bodily harm. They were not willing to assume all the risks which an enlistment involved, without securing something in the shape of a drawback.

Well, the iron tailors saw and appreciated the situation and sufferings of this class of men, and came to the rescue with a vest of steel armor, worth, as I remember it, about a dozen dollars, and greaves. The latter, I think, did not find so ready a market as the vests, which were comparatively common. These ironclad warriors admitted that when panoplied for the fight their sensations were much as they might be if they were dressed up in an old-fashioned air-tight stove; still, with all the discomforts of this casing, they felt a little safer with it on than off in battle, and they reasoned that it was the right and duty of every man to adopt all honorable measures to assure his safety in the line of duty.

This seemed solid reasoning, surely; but, in spite of it all, a large number of these vests never saw Rebeldom. Their owners were subjected to such a storm of ridicule that they could not bear up under it. It was a stale yet common joke to remind them that in action these vests must be worn behind. Then, too, the ownership of one of them was taken as evidence of faint-heartedness. Of this the owner was often reminded; so that when it came to the packing of the knapsack for departure, the vest, taking as it did considerable space, and adding no small weight to his already too heavy burden, was in many cases left behind. The officers, whose opportunity to take baggage along was greater, clung to them longest; but I think that they were quite generally abandoned with the first important reduction made in the luggage. . . .

Then there were fancy patent-leather haversacks, with two or three compartments for the assortment of rations, which Uncle Sam was expected to furnish. But those who invested in them were somewhat disgusted at a little later stage of their service, when they were ordered to throw away all such "high-toned" trappings and adopt the regulation pattern of painted cloth. This was a bag about a foot square, with a broad strap for the shoulder, into which soldiers soon learned to bundle all their food and table furniture, which . . . after a day's hard march were always found in such a delightful hodge-podge. . . .

The Turkish fez, with pendent tassel, was seen on the heads of some soldiers. Zouave regiments wore them. They did very well to lie around camp in, and in a degree marked their owner as a somewhat conspicuous man among his fellows, but they were not tolerated on line; few of them ever survived the first three months' campaigning.

And this recalls the large number of the soldiers of '62 who did not wear the forage cap furnished by the government. They bought the "McClellan cap," so called, at the hatters' instead, which in most cases faded out in a month. This the government caps did not do, with all their awkward appearance. They may have been coarse and unfashionable to the eye, but the colors would stand. Nearly every man embellished his cap with the number or letter of his company and regiment and the appropriate emblem. For infantry this emblem is a bugle, for artillery two crossed cannons, and for cavalry two crossed sabres.

—BILLINGS, *Hardtack and Coffee*

8. SHOEMAKING AND TAILORING IN WINTER QUARTERS

Here is another account of the ingenuity of the American soldier. McHenry Howard, who gives us this fascinating insight into the domestic economy of a Southern army in winter quarters, was a Marylander who, at the outbreak of the war, hurried south and joined Johnston's army at Bull Run. Subsequently he fought through the whole war, serving as a staff officer to Jackson and Lee. He was taken by the Federals and held for a time on Johnson's Island in Lake Erie.

A NUMBER of shoemakers in the different regiments, seventeen I think, were encouraged to send home—and in some instances were given leave to go—for their tools, and were put to work repairing shoes, being exempted from guard and other routine camp duty, but ready to fall in with their commands on any call to arms. The shoe-shops were a separate camp of tents, near brigade headquarters and under our immediate supervision, guarded by sentinels, and no person was allowed to visit them or to carry his shoes to be mended without a pass and order from his company and regimental commanders, approved by the adjutant or inspector general. A careful estimate and report of the saving of the issue of shoes to our brigade during the winter was made to the higher authorities at one time, but I am afraid to say from memory what the saving was confidently stated to have been, certainly several hundred pairs; besides, the men's feet were kept in better condition by the correction of ill fitting shoes. On the march back from Gettysburg in the summer before, the "barefooted" men of the division—not literally that except in the case of some, but those whose shoes were worn out or whose feet were sore from wearing bad shoes or other causes—were organized into a separate command, under officers, to pick their way on the grassy roadside and by easy stages on each day's march. My recollection is that this barefooted and sorefooted command sometimes numbered a fourth of the division.

Having taken a sort of census of the whole brigade, we knew exactly where to look at any time for skilled workmen in different occupations. The 37th Virginia, from the mountains of the south-western part of the State, we found to furnish a greater proportion of mechanics—or at least men who were used to doing jobs of handywork—the other regiments being more largely composed of men from the farming class or from sections where there were regular artizans and stores convenient. Wheelwrights were detailed to put the ambulances (this under the zealous charge of Surgeon Henkel of that regiment, senior surgeon or medical director), and transportation generally in good order. I think log shelters were made for the horses and they were carefully looked after. General Steuart had also detailed, or meditated detailing, tinners to mend canteens, cups and other tinwork. Drummers or tanners were given a few days leave to go to their homes or places not far distant on condition of bringing back dog skins for drum heads, and although the animal's integument was tanned in a marvellously short time, it was found to answer very well.

The General was especially desirous of establishing "tailor shops" to patch and mend clothing, on a like scale with the shoe shops, or greater, and sent up urgent applications for waste odds and ends of cloth and thread at the government factories, but had received no response when the opening of the Spring campaign put a check to these and many other schemes.

In short, recognizing the straits that the Confederacy was now put to in the furnishing of supplies, we aimed to save and eke out issues in every possible way.

—Howard, *Recollections of a Maryland Confederate Soldier*

9. HOW THE SOLDIERS MARCHED

No hardships were harder than those of the march, if we are to trust the voluminous testimony of the foot soldiers. The roads were dusty in the summer, muddy in the winter; the soldier was dressed in heavy woolens, loaded down with fifty or sixty pounds of equipment, often without food for long stretches of the day. It is no wonder that straggling was almost

*universal, or that literally thousands of men fell out of line and got lost. It
is difficult to know whether the Confederate or the Federal soldiers suffered
most from marching. More Confederates than Federals were country bred,
and therefore more accustomed to cross-country hiking; on the other hand
the Confederacy was low on shoes, and there are any number of stories of
Southern soldiers marching barefoot, even in the winter months.*

*Joel Cook, who here describes some of the techniques of the seasoned
marcher, was a correspondent of the* Philadelphia Press *who was with Mc-
Clellan during the Peninsular campaign.*

IN the army of the Potomac there were two species of marching employed,—in "heavy marching-order," and in "light marching-order." The
former meant that the troops were to carry all they possessed with them; the
other was to march with only the musket, ammunition, haversack, and canteen, thus being in trim for working or fighting. Every order to march specified one or the other manner. For heavy marches, two or three hours' notice
were usually given, so that time might be had for preparation; light marches,
unless to picket, were generally to be commenced on the instant. Another
style of order, always implying light marching-order, was sometimes made.
This was "to be held in readiness to march at five minutes' notice." Such an
order as this was given when an engagement was in progress or anticipated,
and the soldiers stood in line behind their musket-stacks until the order was
rescinded or they were marched off in accordance with it.

In a heavy march to a new camp, the generals of division and brigade
would first arrange the order of the brigades and artillery on the line of
march, and next the order of the regiments of each brigade. This would all
be specified in the official order commanding the march, and every part of
the whole would be able to, and usually did, fall into its proper place in the
line, without confusion. The division general and staff preceded the division,
and each brigadier and staff rode at the head of his brigade. Artillery rolled
along in regular order—cannon, caisson, forge and ammunition wagon—to the
end of their line. A regiment marched in the following manner: first the
adjutant; then the pioneers; then the band and drum-corps; then the colonel
and lieutenant-colonel; then the regiment, each man with his knapsack, haversack, canteen, and arms; and, bringing up the rear, the major, chaplain, and
two surgeons, and, on foot, the hospital-knapsack-carrier. The colonel and
adjutant sometimes exchanged places, however.

When these marches commenced, the men would be in regular military
order, four abreast; but the first half-mile usually broke up all regularity.
The men before they had walked that distance would become dispersed all
over the road, some walking along the banks and others in the ditches: a
squad straggling along the centre would be all the orderly part of the regiment. Some ran down into gullies to search for water, and others started off
to see curiosities. Many on long marches became exhausted by fatigue, and
lay down under the trees to rest. In warm weather these marches—if prolonged to six or eight miles—were most trying. The suffering for water was

usually the greatest trouble,—men carrying such heavy burdens as the soldiers requiring a great deal, and good water in any quantity being rarely discovered. Several halts of an hour or half-hour each were made in these marches, to allow the men to unsling knapsacks and rest or search for water, and to give the stragglers time to come up. The wagon-trains of each regiment followed at the rear of the division in the same order as the regiments marched. Each regimental quartermaster and quartermaster-sergeant attended the teams of his regiment.

A march to battle would be made in light marching-order, the men four abreast, and generally on the double quick. The men were held under strict discipline during such marches. The march from the field, however, was far different. If a victory had been gained, the men would cheer and talk, and the officers imposed no restraint. If a defeat had been suffered, angry arguments about its cause would foreshadow the disaster long before they reached the camp. A march to picket was in light marching order, and at common or quick time, and, when the picket tour was approached, it was conducted with great care and quietness. Homeward it was the same.

A march to chop wood or build roads and bridges would also be in light marching-order, at common or quick time, and—if the place to which the troops were going was not a dangerous one—without arms. Upon reaching the scene of labor, the command was usually given to an officer of engineers, who, through their company officers, directed the movements of the men. The march back to camp was as the one from it.

The general conduct of the troops upon these marches was such as could scarcely be found fault with. The burdens carried in heavy marches, and the discipline exercised in light ones, usually kept them to the road,—though, of course, in the former some would stray and visit the deserted houses in the fields. The inmates of every Negro-hut were besought for "hoecakes;" and when the amazed woman would naturally say, "Why, bress de Lord! how can I gub one cake to all o' you?—dar, ye see dat I hab but one!"—some oily customer's reply would come, "Give it to me, aunty; I asked you first." Plaguing the Negroes for "hoecakes" was usually the greatest extent of lawlessness when the troops were marching. No rapine or wanton destruction disgraced the marches of the army of the Potomac.

—Cook, *The Siege of Richmond*

10. HARDTACK AND COFFEE

Here is the invaluable John Billings again, giving us what appears to be a wholly faithful account of eating—and not eating—in the Army of the Potomac.

I WILL now give a complete list of the rations served out to the rank and file, as I remember them. They were salt pork, fresh beef, salt beef, rarely ham or bacon, hard bread, soft bread, potatoes, an occasional onion, flour, beans, split pease, rice, dried apples, dried peaches, desiccated vegetables, coffee, tea, sugar, molasses, vinegar, candles, soap, pepper, and salt.

It is scarcely necessary to state that these were not all served out at one time. There was but one kind of meat served at once, and this . . . was usually pork. When it was hard bread, it wasn't *soft* bread or flour, and when it was pease or beans it wasn't rice.

Here is just what a single ration comprised, that is, what a soldier was entitled to have in one day. He should have had twelve ounces of pork or bacon, *or* one pound four ounces of salt or fresh beef; one pound six ounces of soft bread or flour, *or* one pound of hard bread, *or* one pound four ounces of corn meal. With every hundred such rations there should have been distributed one peck of beans or pease; ten pounds of rice or hominy; ten pounds of green coffee, *or* eight pounds of roasted and ground, *or* one pound eight ounces of tea; fifteen pounds of sugar; one pound four ounces of candles; four pounds of soap; two quarts of salt; four quarts of vinegar; four ounces of pepper; a half bushel of potatoes when practicable, and one quart of molasses. Desiccated potatoes or desiccated compressed vegetables might be substituted for the beans, pease, rice, hominy, or fresh potatoes. Vegetables, the dried fruits, pickles, and pickled cabbage were occasionally issued to prevent scurvy, but in small quantities.

But the ration thus indicated was a camp ration. Here is the *marching* ration: one pound of hard bread; three-fourths of a pound of salt pork, or one and one-fourth pounds of fresh meat; sugar, coffee, and salt. The beans, rice, soap, candles, etc., were not issued to the soldier when on the march, as he could not carry them; but, singularly enough, as it seems to me, unless the troops went into camp before the end of the month, where a regular depot of supplies might be established from which the other parts of the rations could be issued, they were *forfeited*, and *reverted to the government*— an injustice to the rank and file, who, through no fault of their own, were thus cut off from a part of their allowance at the time when they were giving most liberally of their strength and perhaps of their very heart's blood. . . .

I will speak of the rations more in detail, beginning with the hard bread, or, to use the name by which it was known in the Army of the Potomac, *Hardtack*. What was hardtack? It was a plain flour-and-water biscuit. Two which I have in my possession as mementos measure three and one-eighth by two and seven-eighths inches, and are nearly half an inch thick. Although these biscuits were furnished to organizations by weight, they were dealt out to the men by number, nine constituting a ration in some regiments, and ten in others; but there were usually enough for those who wanted more, as some men would not draw them. While hardtack was nutritious, yet a hungry man could eat his ten in a short time and still be hungry. . . .

For some weeks before the battle of Wilson's Creek, Mo., where the lamented Lyon fell, the First Iowa Regiment had been supplied with a very poor quality of hard bread (they were not then [1861] called hard*tack*). During this period of hardship to the regiment, so the story goes, one of its members was inspired to produce the following touching lamentation:—

> Let us close our game of poker,
> Take our tin cups in our hand,
> While we gather round the cook's tent door,
> Where dry mummies of hard crackers
> Are given to each man;
> O hard crackers, come again no more!

Chorus:
> 'Tis the song and sigh of the hungry,
> "Hard crackers, hard crackers, come again no more!
> Many days have you lingered upon our stomachs sore,
> O hard crackers, come again no more!"

> There's a hungry, thirsty soldier
> Who wears his life away,
> With torn clothes, whose better days are o'er;
> He is sighing now for whiskey,
> And, with throat as dry as hay,
> Sings, "Hard crackers, come again no more!"
>   Chorus.

> 'Tis the song that is uttered
> In camp by night and day,
> 'Tis the wail that is mingled with each snore,
> 'Tis the sighing of the soul
> For spring chickens far away,
> "O hard crackers, come again no more!"
>   Chorus.

When General Lyon heard the men singing these stanzas in their tents, he is said to have been moved by them to the extent of ordering the cook to serve up corn-meal mush, for a change, when the song received the following alteration:—

> But to groans and to murmurs
> There has come a sudden hush,
> Our frail forms are fainting at the door;
> We are starving now on horse-feed
> That the cooks call mush,
> O hard crackers, come again once more!

Chorus:
> It is the dying wail of the starving,
> Hard crackers, hard crackers, come again once more;
> You were old and very wormy, but we pass your failing o'er.
> O hard crackers, come again once more!

The name hardtack seems not to have been in general use among the men in the Western armies.

But I now pass to consider the other bread ration—the *loaf* or *soft bread*. Early in the war the ration of flour was served out to the men uncooked; but as the eighteen ounces allowed by the government more than met the needs of the troops, who at that time obtained much of their living from outside sources . . . it was allowed, as they innocently supposed, to be sold for the benefit of the Company Fund, already referred to. Some organizations drew, on the requisition, ovens, semi-cylindrical in form, which were properly set in stone, and in these regimental cooks or bakers baked bread for the regiment. But all of this was in the tentative period of the war. As rapidly as the needs of the troops pressed home to the government, they were met with such despatch and efficiency as circumstances would permit. For a time, in 1861, the vaults under the broad terrace on the western front of the Capitol were converted into bakeries, where sixteen thousand loaves of bread were baked daily. The chimneys from the ovens pierced the terrace where now the freestone pavement joins the grassy slope, and for months smoke poured out of these in dense black volumes. The greater part of the loaves supplied to the Army of the Potomac up to the summer of 1864 were baked in Washington, Alexandria, and at Fort Monroe, Virginia. The ovens of the latter place had a capacity of thirty thousand loaves a day. But even with all these sources worked to their uttermost, brigade commissaries were obliged to set up ovens near their respective depots, to eke out enough bread to fill orders. These were erected on the sheltered side of a hill or woods, then enclosed in a stockade, and the whole covered with old canvas. . . .

I began my description of the rations with the bread as being the most important one to the soldier. Some old veterans may be disposed to question the judgment which gives it this rank, and claim that *coffee*, of which I shall speak next, should take first place in importance. . . .

It would have interested a civilian to observe the manner in which this ration was served out when the army was in active service. It was usually brought to camp in an oat-sack, a regimental quartermaster receiving and apportioning his among the ten companies, and the quartermaster-sergeant of a battery apportioning his to the four or six detachments. Then the orderly-sergeant of a company or the sergeant of a detachment must devote himself to dividing it. One method of accomplishing this purpose was to spread a rubber blanket on the ground—more than one if the company was large,—and upon it were put as many piles of the coffee as there were men to receive rations; and the care taken to make the piles of the same size to the eye, and to keep the men from growling, would remind one of a country physician making his powders, taking a little from one pile and adding to another. The sugar which always accompanied the coffee was spooned out at the same time on another blanket. When both were ready, they were given out, each man taking a pile, or, in some companies, to prevent any charge of unfairness or injustice, the sergeant would turn his back on the rations, and take out his roll of the company. Then, by request, some one else would point to a pile and ask, "Who shall have this?" and the sergeant, without turning, would call a name from his list of the company or detachment, and the person thus called would appropriate the pile specified. This process would be continued until the last pile was disposed of. There were other plans for distributing the rations; but I have described this one because of its being quite common.

The manner in which each man disposed of his coffee and sugar ration after receiving it is worth noting. Every soldier of a month's experience in campaigning was provided with some sort of bag into which he spooned his coffee; but the *kind* of bag he used indicated pretty accurately, in a general way, the length of time he had been in the service. For example, a raw recruit just arrived would take it up in a paper, and stow it away in that well known receptacle for all eatables, the soldier's haversack, only to find it a part of a general mixture of hardtack, salt pork, pepper, salt, knife, fork, spoon, sugar, and coffee by the time the next halt was made. A recruit of longer standing, who had been through this experience and had begun to feel his wisdom-teeth coming, would take his up in a bag made of a scrap of rubber blanket or a *poncho;* but after a few days carrying the rubber would peel off or the paint of the *poncho* would rub off from contact with the greasy pork or boiled meat ration which was its travelling companion, and make a black, dirty mess, besides leaving the coffee-bag unfit for further use. Now and then some young soldier, a little starchier than his fellows, would bring out an oil-skin bag lined with cloth, which his mother had made and sent him; but even oil-silk couldn't stand everything, certainly not the peculiar inside furnishings of the average soldier's haversack, so it too was not long in yielding. But your plain, straightforward old veteran, who had shed all his poetry and romance, if he had ever possessed any, who had roughed it up and down "Old Virginny," man and boy, for many months, and who had tried all plans under all circumstances, took out an oblong plain cloth bag, which looked as immaculate as the every-day shirt of a coal-heaver, and into it scooped without ceremony both his sugar and coffee, and stirred them thoroughly together. . . .

The coffee ration was most heartily appreciated by the soldier. When tired and foot-sore, he would drop out of the marching column, build his little camp-fire, cook his mess of coffee, take a nap behind the nearest shelter, and when he woke, hurry on to overtake his company. Such men were sometimes called stragglers; but it could, obviously, have no offensive meaning when applied to them. Tea was served so rarely that it does not merit any particular description. In the latter part of the war, it was rarely seen outside of hospitals.

One of the most interesting scenes presented in army life took place at night when the army was on the point of bivouacking. As soon as this fact became known along the column, each man would seize a rail from the nearest fence, and with this additional arm on the shoulder would enter the proposed camping-ground. In no more time than it takes to tell the story, the little camp-fires, rapidly increasing to hundreds in number, would shoot up along the hills and plains, and as if by magic acres of territory would be luminous with them. Soon they would be surrounded by the soldiers, who made it an almost invariable rule to cook their coffee first, after which a large number, tired out with the toils of the day, would make their supper of hardtack and coffee, and roll up in their blankets for the night. If a march was ordered at midnight, unless a surprise was intended, it must be preceded by a pot of coffee; if a halt was ordered in mid-forenoon or afternoon, the same dish was inevitable, with hardtack accompaniment usually. It was coffee *at* meals and *between* meals; and men going on guard or coming off guard drank it at all hours of the night, and to-day the old soldiers who can stand it are the hardest coffee-drinkers in the community, through the schooling which they received in the service.

—Billings, *Hardtack and Coffee*

11. "STARVATION, RAGS, DIRT, AND VERMIN"

At school in Pennsylvania when the war broke out, Randolph Shotwell left at once for his native Virginia, determined to join the first Confederate outfit that he found. He served through the whole of the war, until 1864, when he was captured; we shall read later his bitter description of conditions in Federal prisons. After the war he went into journalism in North Carolina, and was active, for a time, in the Ku Klux Klan and in politics. The conditions which he describes so vividly were not characteristic of the whole of the Confederate Army, but were doubtless to be found quite commonly toward the end of the war when the whole economic machinery of the South seemed to be breaking down.

OUR Quarter Master's department . . . really did a great deal more to break down the army than to keep it up. I mean that their shortcomings, their negligence, improvidence, and lack of energy counterbalanced their services. It is a well-known fact, and a most disgraceful one, that when General Lee crossed the Potomac fully *ten thousand* of his men were *barefooted, blanketless,* and *hatless!* The roads were lined with stragglers limping on swollen and blistered feet, shivering all night, (for despite the heat of the day the nights were chilly), for want of blankets; and utterly devoid of underclothes—if indeed they possessed so much as one shirt!

And the lack of proper equipment gradually made itself felt on the *morale* of the men. In the earlier stages of the war when our men were well dressed and cleanly—every company having its wagon for extra baggage—enabling the private soldier to have a change of clothing and necessary toilet articles—the men retained much of their individuality as *citizen*-soldiers, volunteering to undergo for a time, the privations and perils of army life, but never forgetting that they were *citizens* and *gentlemen*, with a good name and reputation for gentlemanliness to maintain. Hence, when in battle array, these gallant fellows, *each had a pride in bearing himself bravely;* and when the hour of conflict arrived they rushed upon the foe with an impetuosity and fearlessness that amazed the old army officers; and caused foreign military men to declare them the best fighters in the world. After a while the spirit of the men became broken. Constant marching and fighting were sufficient of themselves to gradually wear out the army; but it was more undermined by the continual neglect and ill-provision to which the men were subjected.

Months on months they were without a change of underclothing, or a chance to wash that they had worn so long, hence it became actually coated with grease and dust, moistened with daily perspiration under the broiling sun.

Pestiferous vermin swarmed in every camp, and on the march—an indescribable annoyance to every well-raised man yet seemingly uneradicable. Nothing would destroy the little pests but *hours of steady boiling*, and of course, we had neither kettles, nor the time to boil them, if we had been provided with ample means.

As to purchasing clothes, the private soldiers did not have an opportunity of so doing once in six months, as their miserable pittance of $12 per month was generally withheld that length of time, or longer—(I only drew pay *three* times in *four years*, and after the first year, I could not have bought a *couple of shirts* with a *whole month's pay*.) Naturally fastidious in tastes, and habituated to the strictest personal cleanliness and neatness, I chafed from morning till night at the insuperable obstacles to decency by which I was surrounded, and as a consequence there was not one time in the whole four years of the war that I could not have blushed with mortification at meeting with any of my old friends.

It is impossible for such a state of things to continue for years without breaking down one's self-respect, wounding his *amour propre*, stirring his deepest discontent, and very materially impairing his efficiency as a soldier.

Starvation, rags, dirt, and vermin may be borne *for a time* by the neatest of gentlemen; but when he has become habituated to them, he is no longer a gentleman. The personal pride which made many a man act the *hero* during the first year of the war was gradually worn out, and undermined by the open, palpable neglect, stupidity, and indifference of the authorities until during the last year of the war, the hero became a "shirker," and finally a "deserter."

—SHOTWELL, "Three Years in Battle"

12. VOTING IN THE FIELD

The problem of the soldier vote agitated the Civil War as it did World War II. The Republican party was particularly eager to provide opportunity for soldiers to go home to vote or machinery for voting in the field. Both methods were widely used in the state elections of 1863 and the Presidential election of 1864. The Wisconsin soldier vote—which James Leonard describes—was decisive in the election of a chief justice. That the soldier vote was decisive in the 1864 election, too, is generally conceded—and this notwithstanding such support for McClellan as is revealed by George Breck, of Rochester, New York. Thousands of soldiers were furloughed home at voting time. Lincoln wrote to Sherman, for example, that it might be well to

let Indiana's soldiers "or any part of them go home and vote at the state elec-
tions," and so enthusiastically did Sherman act on the suggestion that the 19th
Vermont Volunteers found themselves voting in the Indiana elections—which
the Republicans carried. Some states—New York, for example, and Ohio—
arranged for voting in the field, and the overwhelming majority of these votes
went to Lincoln. The most careful student of the subject concludes that
"without the soldiers' vote in six crucial states, Lincoln would have lost the
election."

A. Electioneering in the Camps

Camp near White Oak Church, May 14, 1863

Let me state a simple instance as regards myself and the late election that
took place in Co. A for Chief Justice of Wisconsin The morning of election
day the Captain and Lieutenants asked me and the Orderly our opinion in
regard to holding an election, The Captain was rather against it, fearing that
very few of the boys would vote as was the case last fall, I almost sided with
him but I and the Orderly both advised to open a poll, and take what votes
could be got, He finally consented to commence on the condition that I
would act as runner and speak to, or rather electioneer the boys in the
company, I declined at first, advising the selection of some one who as I
thought had more influence than myself Finally however I consented just
to satisfy the Captain and Lieutenant but satisfied in my own mind that I
could accomplish but little I went to work and first brought up all those
whom I knew to be sure and then I set at those who were a little wavering
or careless and by some talking got them up, then I went at those who are
true Union men but still cling to party, all that was needed with them, was
to satisfy them that Mr. Cothren was a Copperhead and we had the papers
to do that The result was that 53 votes were polled every man in the company voting who was old enough, save one before the polls were opened I
would not have believed that 30 votes could be obtained unless he set some
one to work who had more influence than me, I wish though that I could
have more influence in the temperance cause here Whiskey rations are occasionally dealt out now and I am the only one in our Co who does not use
his ration, it is rather embarrassing to be thus the odd member of a family
with the rest joking you on the matter, but I have withstood these temptations thus far and I hope by the sustaining grace of God to hold out firm to
the end.

—James A. Leonard, "Letters of a Fifth Wis. Volunteer"

B. President Lincoln Needs the Soldier Vote

To General W. T. Sherman.

Executive Mansion, Washington, September 19, 1864

Major-General Sherman:

The State election of Indiana occurs on the 11th of October, and the loss
of it, to the friends of the Government would go far toward losing the whole
Union cause. The bad effect upon the November election, and especially the

giving the State government to those who will oppose the war in every possible way, are too much to risk if it can be avoided. The draft proceeds, notwithstanding its strong tendency to lose us the State. Indiana is the only important State voting in October whose soldiers cannot vote in the field. Anything you can safely do to let her soldiers, or any part of them, go home and vote at the State election will be greatly in point. They need not remain for the Presidential election, but may return to you at once. This is in no sense an order, but is merely intended to impress you with the importance to the Army itself of your doing all you safely can, yourself being the judge of what you can safely do.

Yours truly,

A. LINCOLN.

—The Complete Works of Abraham Lincoln

C. VOTING FOR MCCLELLAN

"Fort Keen," Va., Oct. 23, 1864

My dear Ellen

It seems a long time since I have written home, and so it is indeed, nearly three weeks, if I mistake not. You have, perhaps, thought I must be sick, but no, I have enjoyed the best of health. I have been very, very busy, however, with company matters, and with politics also. Last week was devoted, or a good share of it, evenings principally, to the polling of votes from the company and from outside commands. Battery L. cast 108 votes, 61 for McClellan and 47 for Lincoln. Quite a strong vote was cast for Lincoln in consequence of a number of new recruits, between thirty and forty, having joined the Battery very recently, one year men, from the strong Republican district of St. Lawrence Co., men who got $1000 to $1300 bounty each. Nearly all the old men voted for McClellan. I shall send my vote home by Lieut. Anderson to give to Father to poll. Quite a form has to be gone through by New York soldiers who vote, giving power of attorney to some legal voter where they reside to cast their votes for them, taking an oath that they are legal voters etc. all of which requires a good deal of writing. The affidavits are administered by some commanding officer, and I being such, I have administered something in the neighborhood of 500 oaths. About that number of votes have been polled by Lieut. Anderson and I for "Little Mac," which would never have been cast, had we not interested ourselves in the matter. Such mean, contemptible favoritism or partisanship as has been and is shown for Lincoln, by many officers in the army, representatives of the Sanitary and Christian Commissions, etc., you little imagine. Hundreds of soldiers have been literally proscribed from voting for McClellan by their officers, and they have been obliged to get McClellan ballots from other sources and to get other officers to administer the necessary oath to them. I think I shall have to write a letter to the *Union* about the matter, which I think would tell for *our* side, and it might tell in such a manner as to eject me from the army. . . .

—"George Breck's Civil War Letters"

13. RED TAPE, NORTH AND SOUTH

It is the complaint of soldiers and civilians alike that every war is cursed by red tape. The Civil War was no exception; indeed, in some respects, it was the worst administered of all American wars.

Samuel Fiske—or Dunn Browne as he was known—was a Massachusetts clergyman who enlisted in the 14th Connecticut Volunteers, became a captain, fought at Chancellorsville and Gettysburg, spent two weeks in Libby prison, was exchanged, and killed in the Wilderness. During the war he contributed a series of letters to the Springfield Republican; *these were published posthumously as* Dunn Browne's Experiences in the Army. *It is interesting to note that Randolph Shotwell's complaints about red-tapism in the Confederacy parallel those of Samuel Fiske.*

A. Dunn Browne Has Trouble with the War Department

JUDGE of this other case I will relate: about a fair specimen of my experience. An errand at the adjutant-general's office. Went up at ten o'clock. Found a fat doorkeeper. Asked him if I could see any of the assistant adjutant-generals or their clerks. No: couldn't see anybody on business till eleven o'clock. Departed. Came back at eleven. Found a long string of people passing in slowly to one of the rooms. Took my turn. Got a word at last with the clerk. Found it wasn't his specialty to answer questions of the sort I asked him. Was referred by him to another clerk who perhaps could. Went to another room. Stopped by a doorkeeper. At last, permitted to enter, after some other people had come out. Stated my case to the clerk at the desk: "Pay of certain officers of my regiment stopped by order from your office near four months since. No reason assigned. No notice given. Come to you for reason."

"Why don't you send up your request through the proper military channels, sir?"

"Request was so sent up eight weeks ago, enclosing a precise copy of the order issued from your own office to the paymaster. Instead of looking in your own office to find the reason of your own order, you sent our request over to the paymaster-general, asking him why the order was issued. He sent it back indorsed with the statement, that no such order of stoppage was recorded in the pay-department. This you sent back to us 'through the regular channel' as eminently satisfactory. So it would be, only the paymaster, having your positive order not to pay us, and no order countermanding it, refuses to come down with the greenbacks. Another paper came up to you from us several weeks ago, and has not been heard from. This is the progress of eight weeks through the regular channel."

"Why don't you ask the paymaster to find out about the matter?"

"We have done so. He says he has been repeatedly to your office, which, of course, is the only place where information can be obtained, and is unable to get any satisfactory reply."

"Why don't you go to the ordnance and quartermasters departments, and see if your accounts are all right there?"

"We have done so, and find it a reasonable certainty that no stoppages against us have been ordered there. Moreover, they would not stop through your department. The order came from you. You had a precise copy of it sent you with our application. Where could we apply for information as to the reason of your acts save to you?"

"Very well: we'll try to look it up."

"But, sir, if you would let a clerk look at your orders of that date, and answer us to-day, we can perhaps get our pay; otherwise we shall not have access to the paymaster again for two or three months."

The clerk, utterly disgusted at such pertinacity, dismisses us with an appointment to call again at two o'clock. He will see what he can do for us. Call again at two o'clock. Doorkeeper refuses to let us in. No person seen on business after two o'clock. Finally work our way through with the plea of the special appointment. Find, of course, that nothing has been done. "What shall be our next course?"

"Oh! send up another paper through the regular channel."

—[Samuel Fiske], *Mr. Dunn Browne's Experiences in the Army*

B. A Confederate Lieutenant Complains That Red-Tapeism Will Lose the War

Red Tapeism at Richmond threatens to work our everlasting ruin! Some of our junior officers say that anyone under the rank of Brigadier-General can rarely gain so much as access to the Departments, and even the Brigadiers got but little attention if they happen to be out of favor with the "parlour Cabinet" at the Executive Mansion. The President now has *six* aides, ranking as colonels, and decked in all the bravery of gold lace, and feathers, to some-one of whom the "commoner," or "common soldier" must make the "*grande salaam*," and have his plea for audience first "*vised*" by the popinjay before he may approach the "magic circle" within which is his Supreme Excellency—"clothed with the divinity which doth hedge" a "*servant of the people.*"

All members of this noble Court are beginning to "feel their dignity" in the same manner. Secretary of the Treasury Memminger, (said to be a born *Hessian*) whose chief duties consist in writing his autograph upon unlimited quantities of half-worthless "bank-notes" "so-called," has adopted a set of rules governing all applicants for permission to interview his Royalty. A favorite clerk named Jacques —— is posted in the ante-chamber to scrutinize all callers, and *vise* the talismanic bit of cardboard which shall be your "Open Sesame," to audience with his secretaryship. *Some* gentlemen are not willing to be catechized by Jacques as to their business, wishes, etc., consequently retire enraged at the Royal customs of our not too firmly established *Republic.*

Oh! that Mr. Davis could see and realize, the fallacy of undermining our cause by wearying the people with red tape regulations, and nice points of etiquette, instead of showing common fraternity and sympathy with one and all, the poorest and most tiresome citizen as well as the epauletted Major General.

General Winder rules Richmond like a military Camp; nay, not like a well-disciplined camp, for his rule gives annoyance merely to honest men and faithful soldiers, while permitting the city to be over-run by rogues, spies, speculators, foreigners, blockade runners, and fellows of that ilk. His police force is mainly composed of ex-"Plugs" and "Roughs" from Baltimore and Washington, who care little for the cause, and less for honesty, so that it is a matter of common notoriety that any one who has a hundred or two hundred in greenbacks, or a less sum in specie, can not only travel over the whole South—spying out the weakness of the land—but pass through the "underground road" to the North whenever so minded.

Whereas veteran soldiers—armed with furlough, or special order from their general—must lose a day or two—at their own expense—kicking their heels at the doors of the Pass Port Bureau, awaiting the convenience of some dandified clerk within. Is it any wonder that the veteran grows *soured*, and in telling his family, or his comrades in camp how he had been treated sows the seeds for discontent, and ultimate desertion?

How sad to see the enthusiasm and energies of a great people gradually relaxing under the ill-shaped, negligent, insensate policy of the appointed agents for the administration of the government!

I verily believe if we shall ultimately fail in our efforts to secure independence (which God forbid!) the causes of such failure will be found in the fact that all our great military and civil leaders have become infatuated with the idea that success is assured, and that they can conduct the war as if we were an old established nation, or as France and England would conduct it. They do not seem at all aware that if once the spirit and faith of *the people* is broken all will be lost.

Instances of mismanagement by the Red Tape-ists are coming to light by every mail. The great "Flour Contract" of Secretary Randolph, giving Crenshaw, Haxall, and Company, an exclusive monopoly of the flour furnishing business is causing much comment. Aside from the reports of undue influences in the execution of the original contract, it is evident that the monopoly thus created is working injury to the people. Flour is now $40, a barrel in Richmond, and cornmeal $3.50 a bushel, and no doubt these prices will be considered *cheap* before spring.

"Crenshaw Mills," by the terms of the contract are allowed the preference in the use of the railways in the shipment of grain, so that while the depots are full of goods and flour only $8.00 per barrel in the upper valley, the people of Richmond must pay four times that amount or starve!

The Government seems to have less discretion and good judgment than would be found in "an old field school" debating society. Thus, for instance, when we lay at Manassas and Centreville last year, and could easily have drawn supplies from the rich regions of Loudon, Farquier, Warren, and from the valley, via the Manassas and Strasburg Railroad—all our rations and stock-provender was hauled all the way from Richmond—to which it must first have been hauled—merely because Red-Tapeism had its "system" and wanted a "regular issue," and to have things done "through proper channels," and as the result the fine resources of the region referred to, were left untouched to be gathered by the marauders of Pope, Fremont, Banks and Sigel, while that portion of Virginia which should have been reserved to feed the besieged city nine months later, was drained of its provisions to ship to an army surrounded by adjacent supplies! . . .

I haven't a doubt of Mr. Davis' patriotism, or his intention to do *right*, but he is dreadfully mistaken in his selection of Cabinet officers, and in his whole civil policy of administration. . . . I am more and more convinced that our chief chance of success lies in a short, sharp, aggressive warfare.

—SHOTWELL, "Three Years in Battle"

14. THE CONFEDERATES GET RELIGION

The generation that fought the war, North and South alike, was a deeply religious one. Chaplains were customarily attached to regiments of both armies, and numerous preachers visited the troops with or without official status. One of the most interesting features of the history of the Confederacy was the series of revivals that swept the armies, both East and West, throughout the war. There were a few revivals in the winter of 1861-62, but the "great revival" came in the Army of Northern Virginia in the winter and spring of 1863 and spread to the armies of the West. The Reverend John W. Jones, whose Christ in the Camp *is perhaps the best history of this great revival, estimates that no less than 150,000 soldiers "got religion" that year. What is equally interesting is that the religious revival affected the leaders of the Confederacy as well as the rank and file. It was at this time that Jefferson Davis, Generals Bragg, Ewell, Hood, Hardee, and Joseph E. Johnston all entered the church. It is entirely possible that General Lee's deep piety played a role here.*

The two brief excerpts given here describe the great revival of 1863 in the Army of Northern Virginia. Benjamin W. Jones was a private in the 3rd Virginia Infantry Regiment; John Dooley a Virginia boy who left Georgetown College in 1862 to enlist in the famous 1st Virginia Infantry—a regiment whose history dated from 1661. We shall meet him again.

A. RELIGION IN THE CONFEDERATE ARMY

Camp Roper, Va., Feby. 20, 1863

My dear Friend:

I hear that a great religious spirit and revival is spreading throughout Lee's army, and some of the other armies of the South, and there are some evidences of it here, and in other camps about Richmond. Old professors that had become lukewarm in their zeal, are arousing to a sense of their duty, and many of the openly sinful are growing more temperate and reverent in their conversation and regard for religious things. There is less of cursing and profligacy, and much less of card playing in our Company now than formerly. The voice of prayer is often heard in camp among the men, and many commands now have regular, or at least, occasional, preaching. Many ministers have gone out as evangelists to the armies, and some have gone into the ranks as private soldiers, or have become regular chaplains in some command. Their example and teaching are exerting a wide-spread and salutary influence. Rev. J. W. Ward, of Isle of Wight, has preached to our Company once recently, and other ministers hold meetings near us occasionally.

Almost nightly now, before the tattoo is sounded, we hear the voice of song in our camp, religious and revival songs and hymns. There are several men here who sing well, and these assemble together and pass an hour or two together at night very pleasantly. Sergeant N. B. Pond's tent is headquarters for these exercises, and doubtless, to some extent, this method of praise and prayer is doing good here and toning down some of the rougher vices of the men. May it lead finally to a great outpouring of the Holy Spirit upon all the armies, and all the people of all the South. A soldier may fight and be a religious and God-fearing man, too.

But let me tell you of a little incident that has really taken place in our camp lately—one of the little comedies, not altogether innocent, but wholly harmless, that are occasionally happening and which serve as safety-valves to let off the superfluous steam engendered by the life of confinement and idleness in camp.

One of the songs that were being sung quite frequently, almost nightly in fact, by our religious choir was that somewhat eccentric refrain:

"Scotland's burning! Scotland's burning!
Cast on water! Cast on water!"

and so some of the prankish set among our boys conceived the idea of turning a little joke on the men in Sergeant Pond's tent. As a few of the tents had been fixed up with rude dirt chimneys for fireplaces, and Sergeant Pond's was one of these, it gave the boys a fine chance to play their game. And so, one night, one of the smallest among the men, with a bucket of water in hand, was lifted up by a big, strong fellow to the top of the little stick chimney. And just as the choir rang out the alarm,

"Scotland's burning!
Cast on water!"

the little fellow on the chimney cast his bucket of water down upon the fire inside, which deluged the whole fireplace, put out the fire, and scattered the embers in every direction.

Of course, too, it put a sudden stop to the song, and sent the men quickly out of the tent after the offenders. But not in time to discover who they were. Before they were fairly out of the tent, the boys had gained their own bunks, and were enjoying the fun at a distance.

The choir soon saw the joke, and, as they could do no more, submitted quietly. But it is presumed that nothing more will be heard of "Scotland's burning" for some time.

With a prayer for your continued safety and welfare at home, I remain,

Your friend, B.

—Jones, *Under the Stars and Bars*

B. John Dooley Describes Prayer Meetings

Perhaps this is the night for prayer meeting, for the parsons, taking advantage of this period of calm, are indefatigable in their efforts to draw the soldiers together to sing psalms and assist at prayer. Hundreds and thousands respond to their call and the woods resound for miles around with the unscientific but earnest music of the rough veterans of Lee's army. In doleful contrast to the more enlivening notes of the initiated, the chorus of the 'Mourners' may often be recognized; for conversions among the non-religious members of the army of Lee are of daily occurrence, and when they establish themselves upon the 'Mourners'' Bench, it is evident to all how deep and loud is their repentance. There is something very solemn in these immense choruses of earnest voices, and there are, I am sure, hundreds of these honest soldiers truly sincere in believing that they are offering their most acceptable service to God.

Some of the parsons or chaplains are very zealous and persevering in assembling the soldiers to prayer; especially the chaplain of the eleventh Va. and the seventh. The latter is held in high esteem by all, whether members of religion or not; for, they say, in times of action, he is as bold as the bravest and is to be seen in the first and fiercest battles, consoling and assisting the wounded. 'Florence McCarthy' of Richmond, chaplain of the 7th inf., is also distinguished for his preaching and zeal among the soldiers. They say he told his congregation the other day that when they heard the doors and windows of the church slamming while the minister of God was preaching, they might be sure that the devil was at work trying to hinder the faithful from listening to the divine word. Some might very naturally presume from this that his Satanic Majesty was most at large during the blustering month of March than at any other time in the year.

—Durkin, ed., *John Dooley, Confederate Soldier*

Incidents of Army Life: Eastern Front

THE *war was not all fighting, and the fighting was not all in the pitched battles that have been commemorated in history. Judge Oliver Wendell Holmes liked to say that war was an organized bore, but it was Holmes, too, who observed that "accidents may call up the events of the war. You see a battery of guns go by at a trot and for a moment you are back at the White Oak Swamps, or Antietam, or on the Jerusalem Road. You hear a few shots fired in the distance, and for an instant your heart stops as you say to yourself, The Skirmishers are at it, and listen for the long roll of fire from the main line." For most of the soldiers, boys from farms and villages who had lived quietly and simply, the war was exciting enough, and most of the veterans came to look back on the war with pride and nostalgia—witness the enthusiastic reunions of the GAR and the Confederate Veterans. It was filled with minor adventures—scouting, foraging, the picket line, the forced march; it was memorable for good fellowship and lasting friendship; it had humor as well as pathos and tragedy; it was a microcosm of life.*

What we have here is a series of incidents, episodes and experiences that illustrate the vicissitudes of fighting. Some of the circumstances here set forth were peculiar, but that, too, was typical: it was not only (as Winston Churchill said of World War I) a "very dangerous war," it was, in many respects, a very odd war—a war where enemies fraternized between battles, where newspapers kept correspondents in enemy capitals, where the line between regulars and guerillas was tenuous; where foreigners with strange names were always turning up as observers, or sometimes in uniform; where soldiers were expected to take care of themselves and to exercise their ingenuity; where there was opportunity for play and high jinks as well as for fighting.

No collection of excerpts can describe the whole of these varied experiences; all we can hope to do is to submit some that are illustrative and that suggest the dangers and adventures and vicissitudes of the war. There is little continuity in this series of incidents, and we shall content ourselves with notes on the authors and on those episodes which may have some more general significance.

1. HOW IT FEELS TO BE UNDER FIRE

It must not be forgotten that both Federal and Confederate armies were made up largely of volunteers who had never before had experience in battle, and that only a small proportion even of the Regular Army had ever been under fire. Frank Holsinger, who here recalls what it was like to be under fire, was a captain of the 19th U. S. Colored Infantry who was given brevet rank of major at the end of his service, and settled later in Kansas.

THE influence of a courageous man is most helpful in battle. Thus at Antietam, when surprised by the Sixth Georgia Regiment, lying immediately behind the fence at the celebrated cornfield, allowing our regiment to approach within thirty feet, and then pouring in a volley that decimated our ranks fully one-half; the regiment was demoralized. I was worse—I was stampeded. I did not expect to stop this side of the Pennsylvania line. I met a tall, thin young soldier, very boyish in manner, but cool as a cucumber, his hat off, which he was lustily swinging, who yelled: "Rally, boys, rally! Die like men; don't run like dogs!" Instantly all fear vanished. "Why can I not stand and take what this boy can?" I commenced loading and firing, and from this on I was as comfortable as I had been in more pleasant places.

How natural it is for a man to suppose that if a gun is discharged, he or some one is sure to be hit. He soon finds, however, that the only damage done, in ninety-nine cases out of a hundred, the only thing killed is the powder! It is not infrequently that a whole line of battle (this among raw troops) will fire upon an advancing line, and no perceptible damage ensue. They wonder how men can stand such treatment, when really they have done no damage save the terrific noise incident to the discharge. To undertake to say how many discharges are necessary to the death of a soldier in battle would be presumptuous, but I have frequently heard the remark that it took a man's weight in lead to kill him.

In presentiments of death I have no confidence. While I have seen men go into battle predicting truthfully their own death, yet I believe it is the belief of nine out of ten who go into battle that that is their last. I have never gone into battle that I did not expect to be killed. I have seen those who had no thought of death coming to them killed outright. Thus Corporal George Horton, wounded at South Mountain, wrapped his handkerchief around his wounded arm and carried the colors of our regiment to Antietam. Being asked why he did not make the best of it and go to the hospital, that he was liable to be killed, he answered, "The bullet has not been moulded to kill me." Alas! he was killed the next day.

My sensations at Antietam were a contradiction. When we were in line "closed *en masse*," passing to the front through the wood at "half distance," the boom of cannon and the hurtling shell as it crashed through the trees or exploding found its lodgment in human flesh; the minies sizzing and savagely spotting the trees; the deathlike silence save the "steady men" of our officers. The shock to the nerves were indefinable—one stands, as it were, on the brink of eternity as he goes into action. One man alone steps from the ranks and cowers behind a large tree, his nerves gone; he could go no farther. General Meade sees him, and, calling a sergeant, says, "Get that man in ranks." The sergeant responds, the man refuses; General Meads rushes up with, "I'll move him!" Whipping out his saber, he deals the man a blow, he falls—who he was, I do not know. The general has no time to tarry or make inquiries. A lesson to those witnessing the scene. The whole transaction was like that of a panorama. I felt at the time the action was cruel and needless on the part of the general. I changed my mind when I became an officer, when with sword and pistol drawn to enforce discipline by keeping my men in place when going into the conflict.

When the nerves are thus unstrung, I have known relief by a silly remark. Thus at Antietam, when in line of battle in front of the wood and exposed to a galling fire from the cornfield, standing waiting expectant with "What next?" the minies zipping by occasionally, one making the awful *thud* as it struck some unfortunate. As we thus stood listlessly, breathing a silent prayer, our hearts having ceased to pulsate or our minds on home and loved ones, expecting soon to be mangled or perhaps killed, some one makes an idiotic remark; thus at this time it is Mangle, in a high nasal twang, with "D——d sharp skirmishing in front." There is a laugh, it is infectious, and we are once more called back to life.

The battle when it goes your way is a different proposition. Thus having reached the east wood, each man sought a tree from behind which he not only sought protection, but dealt death to our antagonists. They halt, also seeking protection behind trees. They soon begin to retire, falling back into the corn-field. We now rush forward. We cheer; we are in ecstasies. While shells and canister are still resonant and minies sizzing spitefully, yet I think this one of the supreme moments of my existence. . . .

The worst condition to endure is when you fall wounded upon the field. Now you are helpless. No longer are you filled with the enthusiasm of battle. You are helpless—the bullets still fly over and about you—you no longer are able to shift your position or seek shelter. Every bullet as it strikes near you is a new terror. Perchance you are enabled to take out your handkerchief, which you raise in supplication to the enemy to not fire in your direction and to your friends of your helplessness. This is a trying moment. How slowly times flies! Oh, the agony to the poor wounded man, who alone can ever know its horrors! Thus at Bermuda Hundreds, November 28th, being in charge of the picket-line, we were attacked, which we repulsed and were rejoiced, yet the firing is maintained. I am struck in the left forearm, though not disabled; soon I am struck in the right shoulder by an explosive bullet, which is imbedded in my shoulder-strap. We still maintain a spiteful fire. About 12 M. I am struck again in my right forearm, which is broken and the main artery cut; soon we improvise a tourniquet by using a canteen-strap, and with a bayonet the same is twisted until blood ceases to flow. To retire is impossible, and for nine weary hours, or until late in the night, I remain on the line. I am alone with my thoughts; I think of home, of the seriousness of my condition; I see myself a cripple for life—perchance I may not recover; and all the time shells are shrieking and minie bullets whistling over and about me. The tongue becomes parched, there is no water to quench it; you cry, "Water! water!" and pray for night, that you can be carried off the field and

to the hospital, and there the surgeons' care—maimed, crippled for life, perchance die. These are your reflections. Who can portray the horrors coming to the wounded?

The experiences of a man under fire differ materially between his first and
subsequent engagements. Why? Because of discipline. "Familiarity with
death begets contempt" is an old and true saying. With the new troops, they
have not been called on to train or restrain their nerves. They are not only
nervous, but they blanch at the thought of danger. They want education.
What to them, on joining the service, was a terrible mental strain, is soon
transformed into indifference. It is brought about by discipline.

—HOLSINGER, "How Does One Feel Under Fire?"

2. THE THIRD OHIO IS FLOODED OUT IN WEST VIRGINIA

*At the beginning of the war the Federals planned to attack the Confeder-
acy across the Ohio in western Virginia—a mountainous region which had
already seceded from Virginia and set up as the independent state of West
Virginia. Here both McClellan and Lee saw their first Civil War fighting;
though that fighting was inconclusive McClellan emerged with reputation
enhanced, Lee—from whom so much had been expected—with reputation
somewhat clouded.*

*Colonel John Beatty, who here recalls some of the hardships of campaign-
ing in this difficult country, was an Ohio banker and politician who had been
appointed lieutenant colonel of the 3rd Ohio Volunteer Infantry on its
organization in April 1861. He fought through most of the war in the West,
was promoted to a brigadier generalship, and later served in Congress. We
shall meet him again.*

August 20 [1861]. These mountain streams are unreliable. We had come
to regard the one on which we had encamped as a quiet, orderly little river
that would be good enough to notify us when it proposed to swell out and
overflow the adjacent country. In fact we had bragged about it, made all
sorts of complimentary mention of it, put our tents on its margin, and allowed it to encircle our sick and wounded; but we have now lost all confidence in it. Yesterday, about noon, it began to rise. It had been raining, and
we thought it natural that the waters should increase a little. At four o'clock
it had swelled very considerably, but still kept within its bed of rock and
gravel, and we admired it all the more for the energy displayed in hurrying
along branches, logs, and sometimes whole trees. At six o'clock we found it
was rising at the rate of one foot per hour and that the water had now crept
to within a few feet of the hospital tent, in which lay two wounded and a
dozen or more of sick. Dr. McMeens became alarmed and called for help.
Thirty or more boys stripped, swam to the island, and removed the hospital
to higher ground—to the highest ground, in fact, that the island afforded.
The boys returned, and we felt safe.

At seven o'clock, however, we found the river still rising rapidly. It covered nearly the whole island. Logs, brush, green trees, and all manner of drift went sweeping by at a tremendous speed, and the water rushed over land that had been dry half an hour before, with apparently as strong a current as that in the channel. We knew then that the sick and wounded were in danger. How to rescue them was now the question. A raft was suggested; but a raft could not be controlled in such a current, and if it went to pieces or was hurried away, the wounded must drown. Fortunately a better way was suggested; getting into a wagon, I ordered the driver to go above some distance, so that we could move with the current, and then ford the stream. After many difficulties, occasioned mainly by floating logs and driftwood, and swimming the horses part of the way, we succeeded in getting over.

I saw it was impossible to carry the sick back and that there was but one way to render them secure. I had the horses unhitched and told the driver to swim them back and bring over two or three more wagons. Two more finally reached me, and one team, in attempting to cross, was carried downstream and drowned. I had the three wagons placed on the highest point I could find, then chained together and staked securely to the ground. Over the boxes of two of these we rolled the hospital tent, and on this placed the sick and wounded, just as the water was creeping upon us. On the third wagon we put the hospital stores. It was now quite dark. Not more than four feet square of dry land remained of all our beautiful island; and the river was still rising. We watched the water with much anxiety. At ten o'clock it reached the wagon hubs and covered every foot of the ground; but soon after we were pleased to see that it had gone down a little. Those of us who could not get into the wagons climbed the trees. At one o'clock it commenced to rain again, when we managed to hoist a tent over the sick. At two o'clock the long roll, the signal for battle, was beaten in camp and we could just hear, above the roar of the water, the noise made by the men as they hurriedly turned out and fell into line.

It will not do, however, to conclude that this was altogether a night of terrors. It was, in fact, not so very disagreeable after all. There was a byplay going on much of the time, which served to illuminate the thick darkness and divert our minds from the gloomier aspects of the scene. Smith, the teamster who brought me across, had returned to the mainland with the horses, and then swam back to the island. By midnight he had become very drunk. One of the hospital attendants was very far gone in his cups also. These two gentlemen did not seem to get along amicably; in fact they kept up a fusillade of words all night, and so kept us awake. The teamster insisted that the hospital attendant should address him as Mr. Smith. The Smith family, he argued, was of the highest respectability, and being an honored member of that family, he would permit no man under the rank of a major-general to call him Jake. George McClellan sometimes addressed him by his Christian name; but then George and he were Cincinnatians, old neighbors and intimate personal friends and, of course, took liberties with each other. This could not justify one who carried out pukes and slop buckets from a field hospital in calling him Jake, or even Jacob.

Mr. Smith's allusions to the hospital attendant were not received by that gentleman in the most amiable spirit. He grew profane and insisted he was not only as good a man as Smith but a much better one, and he dared the bloviating mule scrubber to get down off his perch and stand up before him like a man. But Jake's temper remained unruffled, and along toward morning, in a voice more remarkable for strength than melody, he favored us with a song:

> Ho! gif ghlass uf goodt lauger du me;
> > Du mine fadter, mine modter, mine vife;
> Der day's vork vas done, undt we'll see
> > Vot bleasures der vos un dis life.
>
> Undt ve sit us aroundt mit der table
> > Undt ve speak of der oldt, oldt time,
> Ven ve lif un dot house mit der gable,
> > Un der vine-cladt banks uf der Rhine;
>
> . . . . . .
>
> So libft up your ghlass, mine modter,
> > Und libft up yours, Gretchen, my dear,
> Undt lift up your lauger, mine fadter,
> > Und drink du long life and good cheer.

—Beatty, *The Citizen-Soldier*

3. FITZ JOHN PORTER VIEWS THE CONFEDERATES FROM A BALLOON

The use of balloons for observation dates back to the 1790s, but the Civil War was the first war in which they were generally used for military purposes. At the outbreak of the war Thaddeus Lowe was authorized to create an aeronautic service; he built five balloons which were used during the Peninsular and later campaigns. Lowe was the first person in America to take photographs from a balloon. Fitz John Porter, whose ascent is here described, is the general whose career was ruined by charges of disobedience at Second Bull Run; his long struggle to win vindication ended favorably in 1886.

ON the 11th of April [1862] at five o'clock, an event at once amusing and thrilling occurred at our quarters. The commander-in-chief had appointed his personal and confidential friend, General Fitz John Porter, to conduct the siege of Yorktown. Porter was a polite, soldierly gentleman, and a native of New Hampshire, who had been in the regular army since early manhood. He fought gallantly in the Mexican war, being thrice promoted and once seriously wounded, and he was now forty years of age,—handsome, enthusiastic, ambitious, and popular. He made frequent ascensions with Lowe, and learned to go aloft alone. One day he ascended thrice, and finally seemed as cosily at home in the firmament as upon the solid earth. It is needless to say that he grew careless, and on this particular morning leaped into the car and demanded the cables to be let out with all speed. I saw with some surprise that the flurried assistants were sending up the great straining canvas with a single rope attached. The enormous bag was only partially inflated, and the loose folds opened and shut with a crack like that of a musket. Noisily, fitfully, the yellow mass rose into the sky, the basket rocking like a feather in the zephyr; and just as I turned aside to speak to a comrade, a sound came from overhead, like the explosion of a shell, and something striking me across the face laid me flat upon the ground.

Half blind and stunned, I staggered to my feet, but the air seemed full of cries and curses. Opening my eyes ruefully, I saw all faces turned upwards, and when I looked above,—the balloon was adrift.

The treacherous cable, rotted with vitriol, had snapped in twain; one fragment had been the cause of my downfall, and the other trailed, like a great entrail, from the receding car, where Fitz John Porter was bounding upward upon a Pegasus that he could neither check nor direct.

The whole army was agitated by the unwonted occurrence. From battery No. 1, on the brink of the York, to the mouth of Warwick river, every soldier and officer was absorbed. Far within the Confederate lines the confusion extended. We heard the enemy's alarm-guns, and directly the signal flags were waving up and down our front.

The General appeared directly over the edge of the car. He was tossing his hands frightenedly, and shouting something that we could not comprehend.

"O—pen—the—valve!" called Lowe, in his shrill tones; "climb—to—the—netting—and—reach—the—valve—rope."

"The valve!—the valve!" repeated a multitude of tongues, and all gazed with thrilling interest at the retreating hulk that still kept straight upward, swerving neither to the east nor the west.

It was a weird spectacle,—that frail, fading oval, gliding against the sky, floating in the serene azure, the little vessel swinging silently beneath, and a hundred thousand martial men watching the loss of their brother in arms, but powerless to relieve or recover him. Had Fitz John Porter been drifting down the rapids of Niagara, he could not have been so far from human assistance. But we saw him directly, no bigger than a child's toy, clambering up the netting and reaching for the cord.

"He can't do it," muttered a man beside me; "the wind blows the valve-rope to and fro, and only a spry, cool-headed fellow can catch it."

We saw the General descend, and appearing again over the edge of the basket, he seemed to be motioning to the breathless hordes below, the story of his failure. Then he dropped out of sight, and when we next saw him, he was reconnoitring the Confederate works through a long black spy-glass. A great laugh went up and down the lines as this cool procedure was observed, and then a cheer of applause ran from group to group. For a moment it was doubtful that the balloon would float in either direction; it seemed to falter, like an irresolute being, and moved reluctantly southeastward, towards Fortress Monroe. A huzza, half uttered, quivered on every lip. All eyes glistened, and some were dim with tears of joy. But the wayward canvas now turned due westward, and was blown rapidly toward the Confederate works. Its course was fitfully direct, and the wind seemed to veer often, as if contrary currents, conscious of the opportunity, were struggling for the possession of the daring navigator. The south wind held mastery for awhile, and the balloon passed the Federal front amid a howl of despair from the soldiery. It kept right on, over sharpshooters, rifle-pits, and outworks, and finally passed, as if to deliver up its freight, directly over the heights of Yorktown.

The cool courage, either of heroism or despair, had seized upon Fitz John Porter. He turned his black glass upon the ramparts and masked cannon below, upon the remote camps, upon the beleaguered town, upon the guns of Gloucester Point, and upon distant Norfolk. Had he been reconnoitring from a secure perch at the tip of the moon, he could not have been more vigilant, and the Confederates probably thought this some Yankee device to peer into their sanctuary in despite of ball or shell. None of their great guns could be brought to bear upon the balloon; but there were some discharges of musketry that appeared to have no effect, and finally even these demonstrations ceased. Both armies in solemn silence were gazing aloft, while the imperturbable mariner continued to spy out the land.

The sun was now rising behind us, and roseate rays struggled up to the zenith, like the arcs made by showery bombs. They threw a hazy atmosphere upon the balloon, and the light shone through the network like the sun through the ribs of the skeleton ship in the *Ancient Mariner*. Then, as all looked agape, the air-craft "plunged, and tacked, and veered," and drifted rapidly toward the Federal lines again.

The allelujah that now went up shook the spheres, and when he had regained our camp limits, the General was seen clambering up again to clutch the valve-rope. This time he was successful, and the balloon fell like a stone, so that all hearts once more leaped up, and the cheers were hushed. Cavalry rode pell-mell from several directions, to reach the place of descent, and the General's personal staff galloped past me like the wind, to be the first at his debarkation. I followed the throng of soldiery with due haste, and came up to the horsemen in a few minutes. The balloon had struck a canvas tent with great violence, felling it as by a bolt, and the General, unharmed, had disentangled himself from innumerable folds of oiled canvas, and was now the cynosure of an immense group of people. While the officers shook his hands, the rabble bawled their satisfaction in hurrahs, and a band of music marching up directly, the throng on foot and horse gave him a vociferous escort to his quarters.

—TOWNSEND, *Campaigns of a Non-Combatant*

4. STUART'S BALL IS INTERRUPTED BY THE YANKEES

We have met both Von Borcke and Stuart before and know that they are good company. Von Borcke's Memoirs first appeared in Blackwood's Maga-*zine and did much to popularize the Southern cause and leaders in Britain.*

The Memoirs *give us, with* John Esten Cooke's Wearing of the Gray, *the best of all pictures of "Beauty" Stuart.*

WE were indulging in the dreamy sentiment natural to the hour, when the gay voice of Stuart broke in—"Major, what a capital place for us to give a ball in honour of our arrival in Maryland! don't you think we could manage it?" To this there was a unanimous response in the affirmative, which was especially hearty on the part of the ladies. It was at once agreed that the ball should be given. I undertook to make all necessary arrangements for the illumination and decoration of the hall, the issuing of the cards of invitation, &c., leaving to Stuart the matter of the music, which he gladly consented to provide.

A soldier's life is so uncertain, and his time is so little at his own disposal, that in affairs of this sort delays are always to be avoided; and so we determined on our way home, to the great joy of our fair companions, that the ball should come off on the following evening.

There was great stir of preparation at headquarters on the morning of the 8th. Invitations to the ball were sent out to all the families in Urbana and its neighbourhood, and to the officers of Hampton's brigade. The large halls of the Academy were aired and swept and festooned with roses, and decorated with battle flags borrowed from the different regiments. At seven in the evening all was complete, and already the broad avenue was filled with our fair guests, proceeding to the scene of festivity according to their social rank and fortune—some on foot, others in simple light "rockaways," others again in stately family coaches, driven by fat Negro coachmen who sat upon the box with great dignity. Very soon the sound of distant bugles announced the coming of the band of the 18th Mississippi Infantry, the Colonel and Staff of the regiment, who had been invited as an act of courtesy, leading the way, and the band playing in excellent style, the well-known air of Dixie. Amid the loud applause of the numerous invited and uninvited guests, we now made our grand *entrée* into the large hall, which was brilliantly lighted with tallow candles.

As master of the ceremonies, it was my office to arrange the order of the different dances, and I had decided upon a polka as the best for an animated beginning. I had selected the New York Rebel as the queen of the festival, and had expected to open the ball with her as my partner, and my surprise was great indeed when my fair friend gracefully eluded my extended arms, and with some confusion explained that she did not join in round dances, thus making me uncomfortably acquainted for the first time with the fact that in America, and especially in the South, young ladies rarely waltz except with brothers or first cousins, and indulge only in reels and contre-dances with strangers.

Not to be baffled, however, I at once ordered the time of the music to be changed, and had soon forgotten my disappointment as to the polka in a very lively quadrille. Louder and louder sounded the instruments, quicker and quicker moved the dancers, and the whole crowded room, with its many exceedingly pretty women and its martial figures of officers in their best uniforms, presented a most striking spectacle of gaiety and enjoyment.

Suddenly enters an orderly covered with dust, and reports in a loud voice to General Stuart that the enemy have surprised and driven in our pickets and are attacking our camp in force, while at the same moment the sound of shots in rapid succession is distinctly borne to us on the midnight air.

The excitement which followed this announcement I cannot undertake to describe. The music crashed into a *concordia discors*. The officers rushed to their weapons and called for their horses, panic-stricken fathers and mothers endeavoured in a frantic way to collect around them their bewildered children, while the young ladies ran to and fro in most admired despair. General Stuart maintained his accustomed coolness and composure. Our horses were immediately saddled, and in less than five minutes we were in rapid gallop to the front. Upon arriving there we found, as is usually the case in such sudden alarms, that things were by no means so desperate as they had been represented.

Colonel Baker, with the splendid 1st North Carolina regiment, had arrested the bold forward movement of the Yankees. Pelham, with his guns in favourable position, was soon pouring a rapid fire upon their columns. The other regiments of the command were speedily in the saddle. The line of battle having been formed, Stuart gave the order for a general attack, and with great rage and fury we precipitated ourselves upon the foe, who paid, with the loss of many killed and wounded, and a considerable number of prisoners for their unmannerly interruption of our social amusement. They were pursued in their headlong flight for several miles by the 1st North Carolina, until, a little past midnight, they got quite out of reach, and all was quiet again.

It was about one o'clock in the morning when we got back to the Academy, where we found a great many of our fair guests still assembled, awaiting with breathless anxiety the result of the conflict. As the musicians had never dispersed, General Stuart ordered them again to strike up; many of our pretty fugitives were brought back by young officers who eagerly volunteered for that commendable purpose; and as everybody was determined that the Yankees should not boast of having completely broken up our party, the dancing was resumed in less than half an hour, and kept up till the first glimmer of dawn. At this time the ambulances laden with the wounded of last night's engagement were slowly approaching the Academy, as the only building at Urbana that was at all suited to the purposes of an hospital. Of course the music was immediately stopped and the dancing ceased, and our lovely partners in the quadrille at once became "ministering angels" to the sufferers.

—Von Borcke, *Memoirs of the Confederate War for Independence*

5. MAJOR R—— WHIPS THE YANKEES SINGLEHANDED

John Esten Cooke, whom we have met before, was another of Stuart's happy band, and his Major R—— might be Von Borcke himself. Member of a distinguished Virginia family, Cooke early turned from the law, to which he was trained, to literature, and even before the outbreak of the war had become the Virginia Cooper or Sims. An ardent secessionist he fought all through the war; after Appomattox he retired to the Valley and devoted himself to celebrating the heroes of the great conflict and to historical novels. He had already written a biography of Stonewall Jackson; after the war came a biography of Lee, a volume of military essays, Hammer and Rapier, *and the delightful and authentic* Wearing of the Gray *from which this rollicking excerpt is taken.*

A WORD first of the doughty sabreur who figured as hero on the occasion, my friend, Major R——, of the C. S. A.

The Major is stout, rosy, of a portly figure, and from his appearance you would not take him for a very active or dangerous personage. But he is both. No man delights more in movement, adventure, and combat. No man sits a horse with more of the true cavalry ease. You may see from the manner in which he handles his sabre that he is master of that weapon; and in the charge he is a perfect thunderbolt. He fingers his pistol and makes the barrels revolve with admirable grace; his salute with the sabre is simply perfection; his air, as he listens to an order from his superior officer, says plainly, "All I wish is to know what you want me to do, General—if it can be done it will be done." This air does not deceive. It is well known to the Major's friends that his motto is, "Neck or nothing." At Mine Run, when General Meade confronted the Southern lines, the worthy said to me, "A soldier's duty is to obey his orders; and if General Stuart told me to charge the Yankee army by myself, I would do it. *He* would be responsible."

It will be seen from the above sketch of the gallant Major, that he is a thorough soldier. In fact he loves his profession, and is not satisfied with performing routine duty. He is fond of volunteering on forlorn hopes, and in desperate emergencies—when he cannot get at the blue-coats for any length of time—he pines.

This mood came to him in the fall of 1862. Quiet had reigned along the lines so long, that he grew melancholy. His appetite did not fail, as far as his friends could perceive, but something obviously rested on his mind. He was rusting, and was conscious of the process. "Why don't they come out and fight?" the Major seemed to ask with his calm, sad eyes. They were in Virginia for the purpose of "crushing the rebellion,"—why didn't they set about the work?

These questions meeting with no satisfactory response, Major R—— determined himself to take the initiative, and see if he could not bring on a little fight, all on his private account. He would thus relieve his bosom of the perilous stuff which preyed upon his heart. It had, indeed, become absolutely necessary to his peace of mind to come into collision with his friends across the way, and he set about devising the best plan for arriving at his object.

The Southern cavalry to which the Major was attached, at that time occupied the county of Culpepper, and picketed along the Rappahannock.

So did the enemy's horsemen, and the Federal pickets were stationed on the southern bank at every ford. This was the case at Warrenton Springs, where a bridge, afterwards destroyed, spanned the Rappahannock; and at this point Major R—— determined to bring on the little affair which had become so necessary to his happiness. He intended to combine pleasure with business by visiting some young ladies at a hospitable mansion not far from the bridge; and having thus laid out his programme he proceeded to execute it, and "all alone by himself" attack the picket guard of some twenty of the enemy.

Behold the Major now in warlike panoply—that is to say, in fine gray dress coat with burnished buttons (for the eyes of Venus after the conflict with Mars); pistol carefully loaded, in holster on his right side; and sabre in excellent order, jingling against his top boots. It was a saying of the worthy, that he "generally kept his arms in good order," and on this occasion nothing was left to be desired. His pistol revolved at the touch, with a clear ringing click; and you could see your face in his sabre blade. Thus accoutred, and mounted on a good, active horse, he set off from Hazel river, and making a detour around Jeffersonton, came to an elevation in rear of Mr. ——'s house, where he stopped to reconnoitre.

The Federal picket—of nineteen men, as he afterwards discovered—was at the bridge; and in the yard of the mansion were two videttes, with their horses tied to the trees under which they were lying. Whether he could succeed in "driving in" the whole picket was problematical, but the videttes were pretty sure game. He would either run them off or capture them.

With the Major execution followed conception rapidly. Pushing boldly over the crest from behind which he had made his reconnoissance, he charged across the field at a thundering gallop, whirling his burnished sabre around his head, yelling in a manner that was truly awful; and shouting as he rode to a suppositious squadron:

"Charge! charge! cut down every man!"

So portentous was the reverberating shout of onset from the lips of the Major, that the videttes started to their feet, and clutched the bridles of their horses instantly. As the warlike figure, surrounded by the brilliant lightning of the flashing sabre, swept on, the videttes probably saw at least a squadron of "Rebel cavalry" in the dust which rose behind; and hastily mounting, darted away, pursued by the triumphant Major, whose yells were now more tremendous than ever.

Across the broad field, past the house, on toward the bridge, galloped the furious assailant, bent on striking terror to the enemy's hearts, and successfully completing his adventure. Before him fled the frightened videttes—their movements accelerated by several balls, which issued from the Major's pistol, and whistled by their ears. On toward the bridge, and into the midst of the picket fled the videttes; and as the Major's shouts, and vociferous orders to his cavalry to charge, and let no one escape, resounded nearer, the pickets, too, mounted in hot haste, and clattered across the bridge, pursued by the Major's pistol shots.

In vain did the officer in charge of the picket-post shout to his men:
"Halt! halt! Shoot down the rascal! Shoot him down, I say! There's only one of them!"

His voice was unheard or his order unheeded. The picket was composed of stuff less soldierly than their officer, and would not obey him. Before their vivid imaginations rose at least a squadron of Confederate cavalry, sweeping on to ride over them, sword in hand.

The result was that Major R—— in ten minutes had possession of the bridge, and sat his horse defiantly in the middle of it. He then amused himself by sending a few parting shots after the demoralized picket, and having performed this agreeable duty rode back to the house of Mr. ——, laughing low in his peculiar way; his breast completely lightened of the oppressive weight which had so long weighed upon it.

At Mr. ——'s he met with a triumphant reception; was greeted with a perfect ovation. The young ladies of the mansion were crazy almost with delight at the manner in which they had been delivered from the presence of their enemies; and when the hero of the occasion made his appearance they met him as women only can meet their deliverers—with smiles such as shine rarely for the poor "civilian." After all it is something to be a soldier. The trade is hard, but the feminine eye has a peculiar brightness when it rests on the sons of Mars!—of Mars, proverbially the favourite of Venus!

The Major was an old soldier, and in no hurry to depart. He counted on the extent of the "scare" he had given the enemy, and quietly enjoyed himself in the charming society of his hostesses. He had once more become "excellent company." The smile had returned to his lips, the light to his eyes. That melancholy which had made his friends uneasy had quite disappeared, and the Major was "himself again"—that is to say, the gayest and most delightful of companions.

When, rising slowly and carelessly, he bade his friendly entertainers good-bye, he was again happy. He came back to camp, smiling, amiable, the soul of sweetness and cheerfulness. I saw him. He was absolutely radiant. His eloquent eye beamed brightly; his countenance was charming; his movements energetic and elastic; the fullest satisfaction was apparent in every lineament of his face. His gay and friendly smile seemed to say, "I went at nineteen of them; ran them off; held the bridge against them; had an excellent supper, a delightful talk—I am happy!"

—Cooke, *Wearing of the Gray*

6. FOREIGNERS FIGHT IN THE NORTHERN ARMY

The Civil War, like the Revolution, attracted soldiers of fortune and ardent partisans from abroad. Literally dozens of more or less distinguished foreigners served in the Confederate ranks; somewhat fewer were attracted to the Union cause. Most of the visiting warriors preferred to stay in the East, in the armies of Northern Virginia or of the Potomac. Many foreign visitors—the Comte de Paris, Fremantle, Wolseley, Estvan, Trobiand, and others—wrote up their wartime experiences, and we have drawn on these from time to time. This account is taken from McClellan's Own Story.

THE most entertaining of my duties were those which sometimes led me to Blenker's camp, whither Franklin was always glad to accompany me to see the "circus," or "opera," as he usually called the performance. As soon as we were sighted, Blenker would have the "officer's call" blown to assemble his polyglot collection, with their uniform as varied and brilliant as the colors of the rainbow. Wrapped in his scarlet-lined cloak, his group of officers ranged around him, he would receive us with the most formal and polished courtesy. Being a very handsome and soldierly-looking man himself, and there being many equally so among his surroundings, the tableau was always very effective, and presented a striking contrast to the matter-of-fact way in which things were managed in the other divisions.

In a few minutes he would shout, *"Ordinanz numero eins!"* whereupon champagne would be brought in great profusion, the bands would play, sometimes songs be sung. It was said, I know not how truly, that Blenker had been a non-commissioned officer in the German contingent serving under King Otho of Greece.

His division was very peculiar. So far as "the pride, pomp, and circumstance of glorious war" were concerned, it certainly outshone all the others. Their drill and bearing were also excellent; for all the officers, and probably all the men, had served in Europe. I have always regretted that the division was finally taken from me and sent to Fremont. The officers and men were all strongly attached to me; I could control them as no one else could, and they would have done good service had they remained in Sumner's corps. The regiments were all foreign and mostly of Germans; but the most remarkable of all was the Garibaldi regiment. Its colonel, D'Utassy, was a Hungarian, and was said to have been a rider in Franconi's Circus, and terminated his public American career in the Albany Penitentiary. His men were from all known and unknown lands, from all possible and impossible armies: Zouaves from Algiers, men of the "Foreign Legion," Zephyrs, Cossacks, Garibaldians of the deepest dye, English deserters, Sepoys, Turcos, Croats, Swiss, beer-drinkers from Bavaria, stout men from North Germany, and no doubt Chinese, Esquimaux, and detachments from the army of the Grand Duchess of Gerolstein.

Such a mixture was probably never before seen under any flag, unless, perhaps, in such bands as Holk's Jägers of the Thirty Years' War, or the free lances of the middle ages.

I well remember that in returning one night from beyond the picket-lines I encountered an outpost of the Garibaldians. In reply to their challenge I tried English, French, Spanish, Italian, German, Indian, a little Russian and Turkish; all in vain, for nothing at my disposal made the slightest impression upon them, and I inferred that they were perhaps gypsies or Esquimaux or Chinese.

Mr. Seward's policy of making ours "a people's war," as he expressed it, by drumming up officers from all parts of the world, sometimes produced strange results and brought us rare specimens of the class vulgarly known as "hard cases." Most of the officers thus obtained had left their own armies for the armies' good, although there were admirable and honorable exceptions, such as Stahl, Willich, Rosencranz, Cesnola, and some others. Few were of the slightest use to us, and I think the reason why the German regiments so seldom turned out well was that their officers were so often men without character.

Soon after General Scott retired I received a letter from the Hungarian Klapka informing me that he had been approached by some of Mr. Seward's agents to get him into our army, and saying that he thought it best to come to a direct understanding with myself as to terms, etc. He said that he would require a bonus of $100,000 in cash and a salary of $25,000 per annum; that on his first arrival he would consent to serve as my chief of staff for a short time until he acquired the language, and that he would then take my place of general commanding-in-chief. He failed to state what provision he would make for me, that probably to depend upon the impression I made upon him.

I immediately took the letter to Mr. Lincoln, who was made very angry by it, and, taking possession of the letter, said that he would see that I should not be troubled in that way again.

Cluseret—afterwards Minister of War under the Commune—brought me a letter of introduction from Garibaldi, recommending him in the highest terms as a soldier, man of honor, etc. I did not like his appearance and declined his services; but without my knowledge or consent Stanton appointed him a colonel on my staff. I still declined to have anything to do with him, and he was sent to the Mountain Department, as chief of staff, I think. . . .

Of a different order were the French princes who formed part of my military family from September 20, 1861, to the close of the Seven Days. They served as captains, declining any higher rank, though they had fully earned promotion before the close of their connection with the army. They served precisely as the other aides, taking their full share of all duty, whether agreeable or disagreeable, dangerous or the reverse. They were fine young fellows and good soldiers, and deserved high credit in every way.

Their uncle, the Prince de Joinville, who accompanied them as a mentor, held no official position, but our relations were always confidential and most agreeable. The Duc de Chartres had received a military education at the military school at Turin; the Comte de Paris had only received instruction in military matters from his tutors. They had their separate establishment, being accompanied by a physician and a captain of *chasseurs-à-pied*. The latter was an immense man, who could never, under any circumstances, be persuaded to mount a horse: he always made the march on foot.

Their little establishment was usually the jolliest in camp, and it was often a great relief to me, when burdened with care, to listen to the laughter and gayety that resounded from their tents. They managed their affairs so well that they were respected and liked by all with whom they came in contact. The Prince de Joinville sketched admirably and possessed a most keen sense of the ridiculous, so that his sketch-book was an inexhaustible source of amusement, because everything ludicrous that struck his fancy on the march was sure to find a place there. He was a man of far more than ordinary ability and of excellent judgment. His deafness was, of course, a disadvantage to him, but his admirable qualities were so marked that I became warmly attached to him, as, in fact, I did to all the three, and I have good reason to know that the feeling was mutual.

Whatever may have been the peculiarities of Louis Philippe during his later life, it is very certain that in his youth, as the Duc de Chartres, he was a brave, dashing, and excellent soldier. His sons, especially the Ducs d'Orléans, d'Aumale, Montpensier, and the Prince de Joinville, showed the same characteristics in Algiers and elsewhere; and I may be permitted to say that my personal experience with the three members of the family who served with me was such that there could be no doubt as to their courage, energy, and military spirit. The course pursued by the Prince de Joinville and the Duc de Chartres during the fatal invasion of France by the Germans was in perfect harmony with this. Both sought service, under assumed names, in the darkest and most dangerous hours of their country's trial. The duc served for some months as Capt. Robert le Fort, and under that name, his identity being known to few if any beyond his closest personal friends, gained promotion and distinction by his gallantry and intelligence.

—McClellan's Own Story

7. THE MUD CAMPAIGN

After the stunning defeat at Fredericksburg, on December 13, 1862, Burnside withdrew his forces across the Rappahannock and marked time while he planned another assault. None of his division commanders, however, supported this plan. For over a month the two armies watched each other across the swollen Rappahannock. Then on the nineteenth of January Burnside prepared to move northward along the river, possibly with a view to crossing at Banks' Ford. The next day a violent storm came up, turning the Virginia roads to mud; horses and artillery bogged down, pontoons could not be moved; the grand movement of the army became, instead, a "mud march," and on the twenty-fifth Burnside was relieved from command.

The querulous Dunn Browne we have met before.

Jan. 23, 1863

The army has tried to move, and been prevented by reasons over which man has no control. The order came to advance again across the Rappahannock, and meet the enemy. Tuesday morning, camps were broken up, tents struck, knapsacks packed; and soon long lines of troops were in motion over hill and dale all around us. The roads for miles were choked with supply-wagons, ammunition-trains and rumbling batteries. All was noise, confusion, and utmost activity. Trumpets sounded, drums beat, whips cracked, mules squealed, and teamsters cursed. In short, all things showed that a vast army was on the move. Excitement took the place of the quiet that had reigned in our midst for a month. Hearts beat high with hope and patriotic ardor, and spirits sank in dismay at the thought of approaching danger, wounds, and death. Some left couches of sickness, roused to new strength at the call to arms. Some, who had been perfectly well, paled into sudden sickness at the same prospect, and came sneaking round the surgeons' tents, and crawling into hospitals.

For ourselves, under orders to be ready for instant march, our regiment waited through the livelong day, with three days' cooked rations in their haversacks, and sixty rounds of ball-cartridge disposed about their persons; blankets, shelter-tents, &c., rolled up, and guns at hand to march in a moment; all constituting a fair mule's load, and what is, in military phrase, facetiously termed "light marching order,"—waited all day, watching the troops, that rolled like a river unceasingly by us, and wondering when we should be emptied into the stream; but waited, most fortunately for us, in vain. For the clouds gathered all day thicker and darker, and night ushered in a storm of wind and pouring rain, harder for that moving army to encounter than a hundred thousand enemies; a driving rain that drenched and chilled the poor shelterless men and horses, and that poached the ground into mud deeper than the New-England mind can conceive of, and stickier than—well, I am at a loss for a similitude. Pitch, for cohesive attraction, is but as sand compared with it.

So the artillery and the wagons stuck fast on Wednesday; the pontoons couldn't go on wheels; and, though the rain continued in floods, there wasn't quite enough to carry them by water: and so the river rose, and couldn't be crossed; and so every thing got mixed up, and all our fine arrangements spoiled; and we experienced the uncertainty that attends human events, and especially a winter campaign in Virginia. And so our noble Burnside goes up to report his disappointment at Washington; and the army comes dragging back, in the deep mud and drizzling rain, to its old quarters. All yesterday and today, the bedraggled and tired regiments are passing us; and all the roads and streams are full of dead horses and mules (I presume fifty are in sight from the top of the hill back of my tent), and pieces of wagons, and the way obstructed with caissons, and pieces of artillery, and pontoons, and all sorts of vehicles, fast in the mud.

We must wait till the earth is dried up a little from the effects of this storm, and then try it again, running the same risks. And I suppose poor Burnside must take all the blame of failures now; whereas I am disposed to look back to the man who kept us two months in inactivity, after the battle of Antietam, in the most beautiful and precious time of the whole year, to find the shoulders on which to lay the blame. However, finding fault now isn't going to help the past. Something must be done even now, as you and the whole North tell us. Only you must consider what a winter's campaign in these regions really means, when you make up your judgment of us and our doings. It means to the soldiers wet feet every day of the march, the cold ground to lie upon, and insufficient food for them to eat. It means coughs, colds, consumptions, rheumatism, and fevers; a row of unmarked graves all along the track of the army, and desolation and mourning to thousands of pleasant homes. It means the pain of seeing in every company brave fellows sinking right down to death before your eyes, with no possibility of helping them, or even doing much to soothe their last hours.

It means, if battle comes, the wounded left to freeze in the severity of the nights, or to mingle their blood with the deep mud on which they lie. It means every possible form of human suffering, privation, and hardship. Make all allowances for us, then, and pray for our strength, endurance, and success; and drop a tear over the brave fellows who are sacrificed, not merely to the demon of battle, but to the more dreaded severities of the winter season.
—[SAMUEL FISKE], *Mr. Dunn Browne's Experiences in the Army*

8. WITH "EXTRA BILLY" SMITH AT YORK

After Chancellorsville Lee planned once again to move into Pennsylvania, in part to bring the war home to the North, in part to find food for his soldiers and forage for his horses. Early in June the Army of Northern Virginia was on the move, Ewell's corps swinging through the Valley and crossing the upper Potomac near Sharpsburg. Ewell had been authorized by Lee, not only to find flour and horses but, if possible, to capture Harrisburg. On June 27 he reached Carlisle; the same day Early moved out from Gettysburg to York, levying a $28,000 contribution on that town.

It was here that Stiles—whose Four Years *is a minor classic—heard "Extra Billy" Smith haranguing the natives. This "Extra Billy" was one of the fabulous characters of the Confederacy. He had received this curious name a generation earlier when, as local postmaster, he collected so much "extra" money for deliveries. Later he was elected Governor of Virginia; went out to California where he took a prominent part in Democratic politics; returned to Virginia and served as Congressman for the decade before the war; and at the age of sixty-five offered his services to the Confederacy. Appointed brigadier general, he refused that rank and took, instead, the colonelcy of the 49th Virginia Infantry. Serving with distinction, and with reckless daring, he was promoted to major general but resigned in 1864 to accept once again the Governorship of his state.*

Robert Stiles was a major of the famous Richmond Howitzers.

THINGS were not likely to be dull when our old friend "Extra Billy" was about; . . . in fact there was apt to be "music in the air" whenever he was in charge. On the occasion below described, the old Governor seemed to be rather specially concerned about the musical part of the performance.

We were about entering the beautiful Pennsylvania town of York, General Smith's brigade in the lead. Under these conditions, feeling sure there was likely to be a breeze stirring about the head of the column, I rode forward so as to be near the General and not miss the fun. As we approached, the population seemed to be very generally in the streets, and I saw at a glance that the old Governor had blood in his eye. Turning to Fred, his aide,—who was also his son, and about the strongest marked case of second edition I ever saw,—he told him to "go back and look up those tooting fellows," as he called the brigade band, "and tell them first to be sure their drums and horns are all right, and then to come up here to the front and march into town tooting 'Yankee Doodle' in their very best style."

Fred was off in a jiffy, and soon here came the band, their instruments looking bright and smart and glistening in the June sunlight—playing, however, not "Yankee Doodle," but "*Dixie*," the musicians appearing to think it important to be entirely impartial in rendering these national airs, and therefore giving us "Dixie" by way of prelude to "Yankee Doodle."

When they got to the head of the column and struck up "Yankee Doodle," and the Governor, riding alone and bareheaded in front of his staff, began bowing and saluting first one side and then the other, especially every pretty girl he saw, with that manly, hearty smile which no man or woman ever doubted or resisted—the Yorkers seemed at first astounded, then pleased. Finally, by the time we reached the public square they had reached the point of ebullition, and broke into enthusiastic cheers as they crowded about the head of the column actually embarrassing its progress, till the old Governor,— the "Governor-General," we might call him,—nothing loth, acceded to the half suggestion and called a halt, his brigade stacking arms and constituting, if not formally organizing, themselves and the people of York into a political meeting.

It was a rare scene—the vanguard of an invading army and the invaded and hostile population hobnobbing on the public green in an enthusiastic public gathering. The General did not dismount, but from the saddle he made a rattling, humorous speech which both the Pennsylvanians and his own brigade applauded to the echo. He said substantially:

"My friends, how do you like this way of coming back into the Union? I hope you like it; I have been in favor of it for a good while. But don't misunderstand us. We are not here with any hostile intent—unless the conduct of your side shall render hostilities unavoidable. You can see for yourselves we are not conducting ourselves like enemies today. We are not burning your houses or butchering your children. On the contrary, we are behaving ourselves like Christian gentlemen, as we are.

"You see, it was getting a little warm down our way. We needed a summer outing and thought we would take it at the North, instead of patronizing the Virginia springs, as we generally do. We are sorry, and apologize that we are not in better guise for a visit of courtesy, but we regret to say our trunks haven't gotten up yet; we were in such a hurry to see you that we could not wait for them. You must really excuse us.

"What we all need, on both sides, is to mingle more with each other, so that we shall learn to know and appreciate each other. Now here's my brigade—I wish you knew them as I do. They are such a hospitable, wholehearted, fascinating lot of gentlemen! Why, just think of it—of course this part of Pennsylvania is ours to-day; we've got it, we hold it, we can destroy it, or do what we please with it. Yet we sincerely and heartily invite you to stay. You are quite welcome to remain here and to make yourselves entirely at home—so long as you behave yourselves pleasantly and agreeably as you are doing now. Are we not a fine set of fellows? You must admit that we are."

At this point my attention was called to a volley of very heated profanity poured forth in a piping, querulous treble, coming up from the rear, and being mounted and located where I commanded a view of the road I saw that the second brigade in column, which had been some distance in the rear, had caught up and was now held up by our public meeting, which filled and obstructed the entire street. Old Jube (Early), who had ridden forward to ascertain the cause of the deadlock, was fairly blistering the air about him and making furious but for the time futile efforts to get at Extra Billy, who in plain sight and not far off, yet blissfully unconscious of the presence of the major-general and of his agreeable observations and comments, was still holding forth with great fluency and acceptability.

The jam was solid and impervious. As D. H. Hill's report phrased it, "Not a dog, no, not even a sneaking exempt, could have made his way through," and at first and for some time Old Jube couldn't do it, and no one would help him. But at last officers and men were compelled to recognize the division commander, and he made his way so far that, by leaning forward, a long stretch, and a frantic grab, he managed to catch General Smith by the back of his coat collar. Even Jube did not dare curse the old General in an offensive way, but he did jerk him back and around pretty vigorously and half screamed:

"General Smith, what the devil are you about! stopping the head of this column in the cursed town?"

With unruffled composure the old fellow replied:

"Having a little fun, General, which is good for all of us, and at the same time teaching these people something that will be good for them and won't do us any harm."

Suffice it to say the matter was amicably arranged and the brigade and its unique commander moved on, leaving the honest burghers of York wondering what manner of men we were. I should add that General Early had the greatest regard and admiration for General Smith, which indeed he could not well avoid, in view of his intense patriotic devotion and his other sterling and heroic qualities. I have seldom heard him speak of any other officer or soldier in the service, save of course Lee and Jackson, in such exalted terms as of the old "Governor-General."

—STILES, *Four Years Under Marse Robert*

9. BLUE AND GRAY FRATERNIZE ON THE PICKET LINE

The bitterness which characterizes any civil war was ameliorated by friendliness among the soldiers on opposite sides. This friendliness was found among the officers, many of whom belonged to the West Point fraternity or had fought together in Mexican and Indian wars; it was found, no less pervasively, among the rank and file, who, for the most part, respected each other and fought without animosity. Civil War narratives are filled with examples of fraternization across picket lines, the exchange of tobacco and food, acts of courtesy and friendliness.

Alexander Hunter, whose Johnny Reb and Billy Yank *is one of the liveliest of descriptions of life in the ranks, was a college boy who joined the 17th Virginia Regiment at the outbreak of the war.*

IT was the latter part of August [1863]; orders were given to be prepared to go on picket early in the morning; and until a late hour the men were busy cooking rations and cleaning equipments.

Before the mists had been chased by the rising sun, the company in close column of fours marched down the road. Men and animals were in perfect condition, brimful of mettle and in buoyant spirits.

The route lay along the banks of the river, upon the winding course of which, after several hours' riding, the regiment reached its destination and relieved the various pickets. A sergeant and squad of men were left at each post, the company being spread out several miles on the river banks to act as videttes, whose duty it was to watch the enemy on the other side of the Rappahannock.

The next day our squad, Sergeant Joe Reid in command, sauntered down the bank, but seeing no one we lay at length under the spreading trees, smoking as solemnly and meditatively as the redoubtable Wilhelmus Kraft and all the Dutch Council, over the affairs of state.

The Rappahannock, which was at this place about two hundred yards wide, flowing slowly oceanward, its bosom reflecting the roseate-hued morn, was as lovely a body of water as the sun ever shone upon. The sound of the gentle ripple of its waves upon the sand was broken by a faint "halloo" which came from the other side.

"Johnny Reb; I say, J-o-h-n-n-y R-e-b, don't shoot!"

Joe Reid shouted back, "All right!"

"What command are you?"

The spoken words floated clear and distinct across the water, "The Black Horse Cavalry. Who are you?"

"The Second Michigan Cavalry."

"Come out on the bank," said our spokesman, "and show yourselves; we won't fire."

"On your honor, Johnny Reb?"

"On our honor, Billy Yank."

In a second a large squad of blue-coats across the way advanced to the water's brink. The Southerners did the same; then the former put the query.

"Have you any tobacco?"

"Plenty of it," went out our reply.

"Any sugar and coffee?" they questioned.

"Not a taste nor a smell."

"Let's trade," was shouted with eagerness.

"Very well," was the reply. "We have not much with us, but we will send to Fredericksburg for more, so meet us here this evening."

"All right," they answered; then added, "Say, Johnny, want some newspapers?"

"Y-e-s!"

"Then look out, we are going to send you some."

"How are you going to do it?"

"Wait and see."

The Rebs watched the group upon the other side curiously, wondering how even Yankee ingenuity could devise a way for sending a batch of papers across the river two hundred yards wide, and in the meantime each man had his own opinion.

"They will shoot arrows over," said Martin.

"Arrows, the devil!" replied the sergeant; "there never was a bow bent which could cast an arrow across this river."

"Maybe they will wrap them around a cannon ball and shoot them across; we'd better get away from here," hastily answered a tall, slim six-footer, who was rather afraid of big shots.

A roar of laughter followed this suggestion, but the originator was too intent on his own awakened fears to let the slightest movement of the enemy pass unscanned. Eagerly he watched while the others were having all the fun at his expense. Presently he shouted:

"Here they come!" and then in a tone of intense admiration, "I'll be dog-goned if these Yanks are not the smartest people in the world."

On the other side were several miniature boats and ships—such as school-boys delight in—with sails set; the gentle breeze impelled the little crafts across the river, each freighted with a couple of newspapers. Slowly, but surely, they headed for the opposite bank as if some spirit Oberon or Puck sat at the tiller; and in a few minutes had accomplished their voyage and were drawn up to await a favorable wind to waft them back.

Drawing lots, Joe Boteler, who found luck against him, started to town, with a muttered curse, to buy tobacco, leaving his comrades to seek some shady spot, and with pipes in our mouths sink deep in the latest war news from the enemy's standpoint, always interesting reading.

It was a cloudless day,—a day to dream,—and with a lazy *sans souci* manner and half-shut eyes, enjoy to the soul the deep loveliness of the scene which lay around us like some fair creation of the fancy, listening the while to the trills of the blue-bird which sat on the top of a lofty tree industriously practicing his notes like a prima donna getting a new opera by heart.

Joe returned in the evening with a box of plug tobacco about a foot square; but how to get it across was the question. The miniature boats could not carry it, and we shouted over to the Yanks that we had about twenty pounds of cut plug, and asked them what we must do? They hallooed back to let one of us swim across, and declared that it was perfectly safe. We held a council of war, and it was found that none of the Black Horse could swim beyond a few rods. Then I volunteered. Having lived on the banks of the Potomac most of my life, I was necessarily a swimmer.

Sergeant Reid went to a house not far off and borrowed a bread trough, and placing it on a plank, the box of tobacco was shipped, and disrobing I started, pushing my queer craft in front of me. As I approached the shore the news of my coming had reached camp, and nearly all the Second Michigan were lined up along the bank.

I felt a little queer, but I had perfect faith in their promise and kept on without missing a stroke until my miniature scow grounded on the beach. The blue-coats crowded around me and gave me a hearty welcome, and relieving the trough of its load, heaped the craft with offerings of sugar, coffee, lemons, and even candy, till I cried out that they would sink my transport. I am sure they would have filled a rowboat to the gunwhale had I brought one.

There was no chaffing or banter, only roistering welcomes.

Bidding my friends the enemy good-by, I swam back with the precious cargo, and we had a feast that night.

—HUNTER, *Johnny Reb and Billy Yank*

10. LIFE WITH THE MOSBY GUERRILLAS

There is a Robin Hood quality about the Mosby Guerrillas. Mosby himself had served as cavalryman under Stuart in the Peninsular campaign, at Manassas and Antietam, but in January 1863 he set up on his own with a band of some three hundred free spirits, harrying the Federals north of the Rappahannock and, later, in the Valley. While the Federals regarded Mosby's men as outlaws, they operated under a Confederate "partisan ranger" law which made them subject to the same regulations as other soldiers, but permitted them almost complete freedom of action. When, on one occasion, Sheridan executed some of his men, Mosby hung seven prisoners in reprisal. At the close of the war the Mosby Guerrillas consisted of eight companies, well mounted and equipped; Mosby himself had been promoted to a colonelcy.

John Munson, from whose recollections this excerpt has been taken, was himself one of the Mosby Guerrillas.

THE life led by Mosby's men was entirely different from that of any other body of soldiers during the war. His men had no camps nor fixed quarters, and never slept in tents. They did not even know anything about pitching a tent. The idea of making coffee, frying bacon, or soaking hardtack was never entertained. When we wanted to eat we stopped at a friendly farm house, or went into some little town and bought what we wanted. Every man in the Command had some special farm he could call his home.

The people in that part of the state which was designated "Mosby's Confederacy," embracing in a general way the counties of Fauquier and Loudoun, were loyal to the South, though frequently outside the lines of the Southern army, and they were glad to have Mosby's men among them, not only to show their sympathy with the South, but also to have the protection which the presence of the Partisans afforded them.

During the war all local government in that country was suspended. There were no courts nor court officers. The people looked to Mosby to make the necessary laws and to enforce them, and no country before, during or since the war was ever better governed. Mosby would not permit any man to commit a crime, or even a misdemeanor, in his domain. One of our men, in a spirit of deviltry, once turned over an old Quaker farmer's milk cans, and when Mosby heard of it he ordered me to take the man over to the army, which was then near Winchester, and turn him over to General Early, with the message that such a man was not fitted to be a Guerrilla.

As a Command we had no knowledge of the first principles of cavalry drill, and could not have formed in a straight line had there ever been any need for our doing so. We did not know the bugle-calls, and very rarely had roll-call. Our dress was not uniform in make or color; we did not address our officers, except Mosby, by their titles; in fact, we did not practice anything usually required of a soldier; and yet withal there was not another body of men in the army under better or more willing control of their leader. Two things were impressed upon us well, however; to obey orders, and to fight. . . .

Each of Mosby's men was armed with two muzzle-loading Colt's army revolvers of forty-four caliber. They were worn in belt holsters. Some few who could afford it, or who had succeeded in capturing extra pistols or who wanted to gratify a sort of vanity, wore an extra pair in their saddle-holsters or stuck into their boot legs. These weapons were extremely deadly and effective in the hand-to-hand engagements in which our men indulged. Long and frequent practice had made every man in the Command a good shot, and each was as sure with his revolver as every cow-boy is with his six-shooter. As a general thing our real fights were fast and furious and quickly over, one or the other side withdrawing at a dead run when the pistols were empty. . . .

"Something gray" was the one requisite of our dress and the cost of it mattered little. Much of it was paid for by Uncle Sam out of the money we got from him directly and indirectly. Like gamblers we took chances with fate. We had ups and downs; but after our successful raids we were the best dressed, best equipped, and best mounted Command in the Confederate army. There were meek and lowly privates among us, of whom it might truly be said that Solomon in all his glory was not arrayed as one of these. Union army sutlers supplied us with a varied assortment of luxuries, and I cannot recall an instance when we rejected what they had on hand on over-hauling their stock, or when we threatened to take our trade to some competitor. . . .

Some of the Command were extremely fastidious in the matter of dress and affected gold braid, buff trimmings, and ostrich plumes in their hats. After the "greenback raid" when we captured General Sheridan's paymasters with a hundred and seventy thousand dollars in crisp new Government notes, each man received as his share more than twenty-one hundred dollars. The result was that all had clothes and accoutrements such as had never gladdened their hearts before. At all times, whether things went well or ill, the Guerrillas were as vain a lot of dandies as one would wish to see; blithe in the face of danger, full of song and story, indifferent to the events of tomorrow, and keyed up to a high pitch of anticipation; mingled with this was the pride that goes hand in hand with repeated victories and the possession of spoils. . . .

Whenever we made a successful raid, we made it a point to repay the farmers and country people whose bounty we enjoyed, in live stock and supplies. The return from a sutler's raid was a holiday occasion, for everybody got something. On one occasion we captured about two hundred and fifty fat cattle from General Sheridan's supply train, and we gave our country friends half of them, dividing them among all the people living within range.

On one occasion, we got into some sutler's stores at Duffield depot on the Baltimore & Ohio Railroad and the goods were so tempting that I concluded to carry an assortment back to our lady hostess and her household. I loaded up a sack with all sorts of useful and ornamental goods, and fastened it to my saddle securely. Then, going back into the store and looking around, I spied some hoop-skirts which the sutler had no doubt bought for some special order from an army officer's wife. I took these and strapped them to my saddle. Then I made another and final round of the store, and began stuffing my many pockets with notions, such as buttons, hair pins, thread, hooks and eyes, and the like; finally I found a lot of papers of needles, and I thrust a handful of these into my trousers' pocket.

Just then some one poked his head into the door and cried:

"The Yankees are coming."

We made a break for our horses and galloped away with our plunder, and our prisoners; keeping up a pretty fast gait for some miles for fear our burdens would slacken the usual speed we practiced when we were retreating. I had not gone a mile before my papers of needles began to come undone in my pocket, and at every jump of my horse a newly released needle would remind me that I had captured it, until at the end of our run I had dozens of needle marks on my anatomy, and two or three points were left inside, to work upward or downward, or out, as they severally saw fit.

I recollect that I delivered all my presents safely to my kind friends, except needles, and I made no reference to these in my account of the raid. In all my later raids on sutler's stores I contented myself with things that were not likely to prove troublesome, or stick into me, such as boots, and gloves, and furnishing goods; but I ignored needles.

—MUNSON, *Reminiscences of a Mosby Guerrilla*

11. THOMAS WENTWORTH HIGGINSON CELEBRATES LIFE IN A BLACK REGIMENT

Colonel Higginson is one of the romantic figures of the war. A Massachusetts aristocrat, he had early thrown in his lot with the poor and the op-

*pressed, had championed such causes as abolition and woman's rights, taken
part in the attempted rescue of Anthony Burns, and gone to Kansas for the
Emigrant Aid Society. A Unitarian clergyman in Worcester at the outbreak
of the war, he had raised and drilled a company when he was offered the
colonelcy of the first colored regiment—the famous 1st South Carolina. He
joined his regiment at Beaufort, sailed with it to Florida, where he raided
up the St. John's River and temporarily occupied Jacksonville. Bad health
and a wound forced Higginson to resign his commission in '64 and return
to the North.*

*After the war he had a long and distinguished career in literature, writing
novels, short stories, critical essays, biographies of notable literary figures, and
some charming reminiscences,* Cheerful Yesterdays. *It is no exaggeration to
say that the best of all his many literary productions is this classic* Army Life
in a Black Regiment.

Camp Saxton, near Beaufort, S. C., November 27, 1862

Thanksgiving-Day; it is the first moment I have had for writing during
these three days, which have installed me into a new mode of life so
thoroughly that they seem three years. Scarcely pausing in New York or in
Beaufort, there seems to have been for me but one step from the camp of a
Massachusetts regiment to this, and that step over leagues of waves.

It is a holiday wherever General Saxton's proclamation reaches. The
chilly sunshine and the pale blue river seem like New England, but those
alone. The air is full of noisy drumming, and of gunshots; for the prize-
shooting is our great celebration of the day, and the drumming is chronic.
My young barbarians are all at play. I look out from the broken windows
of this forlorn plantation house, through avenues of great live-oaks, with
their hard, shining leaves, and their branches hung with a universal drapery
of soft, long moss, like fringe-trees struck with grayness. Below, the sandy
soil, scantly covered with coarse grass, bristles with sharp palmettos and
aloes; all the vegetation is stiff, shining, semi-tropical, with nothing soft or
delicate in its texture. Numerous plantation-buildings totter around, all
slovenly and unattractive, while the interspaces are filled with all manner of
wreck and refuse, pigs, fowls, dogs, and omnipresent Ethiopian infancy. All
this is the universal Southern panorama; but five minutes' walk beyond the
hovels and the live-oaks will bring one to something so un-Southern that the
whole Southern coast at this moment trembles at the suggestion of such a
thing,—the camp of a regiment of freed slaves.

One adapts one's self so readily to new surroundings that already the full
zest of the novelty seems passing away from my perceptions, and I write
these lines in an eager effort to retain all I can. Already I am growing used
to the experience, at first so novel, of living among five hundred men, and
scarce a white face to be seen,—of seeing them go through all their daily
processes, eating, frolicking, talking, just as if they were white. Each day at
dress-parade I stand with the customary folding of the arms before a regi-

mental line of countenances so black that I can hardly tell whether the men stand steadily or not; black is every hand which moves in ready cadences as I vociferate, "Battalion! Shoulder arms!" nor is it till the line of white officers moves forward, as parade is dismissed, that I am reminded that my own face is not the color of coal. . . .

It needs but a few days to show the absurdity of distrusting the military availability of these people. They have quite as much average comprehension as whites of the need of the thing, as much courage (I doubt not), as much previous knowledge of the gun, and, above all, a readiness of ear and of imitation, which, for purposes of drill, counterbalances any defect of mental training. To learn the drill, one does not want a set of college professors; one wants a squad of eager, active, pliant school-boys; and the more childlike these pupils are the better. There is no trouble about the drill; they will surpass whites in that. As to camp-life, they have little to sacrifice; they are better fed, housed, and clothed than ever in their lives before, and they appear to have few inconvenient vices. They are simple, docile, and affectionate almost to the point of absurdity. The same men who stood fire in open field with perfect coolness, on the late expedition, have come to me blubbering in the most irresistibly ludicrous manner on being transferred from one company in the regiment to another.

In noticing the squad-drills I perceive that the men learn less laboriously than whites that "double, double, toil and trouble," which is the elementary vexation of the drill-master,—that they more rarely mistake their left for their right,—and are more grave and sedate while under instruction. The extremes of jollity and sobriety, being greater with them, are less liable to be intermingled; these companies can be driven with a looser rein than my former one, for they restrain themselves; but the moment they are dismissed from drill every tongue is relaxed and every ivory tooth visible. This morning I wandered about where the different companies were target-shooting, and their glee was contagious. Such exulting shouts of "Ki! ole man," when some steady old turkey-shooter brought his gun down for an instant's aim, and then unerringly hit the mark; and then, when some unwary youth fired his piece into the ground at half-cock, such infinite guffawing and delight, such rolling over and over on the grass, such dances of ecstasy, as made the "Ethiopian minstrelsy" of the stage appear a feeble imitation.

December 3, 1862—7 P.M.

What a life is this I lead! It is a dark, mild, drizzling evening, and as the foggy air breeds sand-flies, so it calls out melodies and strange antics from this mysterious race of grown-up children with whom my lot is cast. All over the camp the lights glimmer in the tents, and as I sit at my desk in the open doorway, there come mingled sounds of stir and glee. Boys laugh and shout,—a feeble flute stirs somewhere in some tent, not an officer's—a drum throbs far away in another,—wild kildeer-plover flit and wail above us, like the haunting souls of dead slave-masters,—and from a neighboring cook-fire comes the monotonous sound of that strange festival, half pow-wow, half prayer-meeting, which they know only as a "shout." These fires are usually enclosed in a little booth, made neatly of palm-leaves and covered in at top, a regular native African hut, in short, such as is pictured in books, and such as I once got up from dried palm-leaves for a fair at home.

This hut is now crammed with men, singing at the top of their voices, in one of their quaint, monotonous, endless, Negro-Methodist chants, with obscure syllables recurring constantly, and slight variations interwoven, all accompanied with a regular drumming of the feet and clapping of the hands, like castanets. Then the excitement spreads: inside and outside the enclosure men begin to quiver and dance, others join, a circle forms; some "heel and toe" tumultuously, others merely tremble and stagger on, others stoop and rise, others whirl, others caper sideways, all keep steadily circling like dervishes; spectators applaud special strokes of skill; my approach only enlivens the scene; the circle enlarges, louder grows the singing, rousing shouts of encouragement come in, half bacchanalian, half devout, "Wake 'em, brudder!" "Stan' up to 'em, brudder!"—and still the ceaseless drumming and clapping, in perfect cadence, goes steadily on. Suddenly there comes a sort of *snap*, and the spell breaks, amid general singing and laughter. And this not rarely and occasionally, but night after night, while in other parts of the camp the soberest prayers and exhortations are proceeding sedately.

A simple and lovable people, whose graces seem to come by nature, and whose vices by training. Some of the best superintendents confirm the first tales of innocence, and Dr. Zachos told me last night that on his plantation, a sequestered one, "they had absolutely no vices." Nor have these men of mine yet shown any worth mentioning; since I took command I have heard of no man intoxicated, and there has been but one small quarrel. I suppose that scarcely a white regiment in the army shows so little swearing. . . . If camp regulations are violated, it seems to be usually through heedlessness. They love passionately three things besides their spiritual incantations; namely, sugar, home, and tobacco. This last affection brings tears to their eyes, almost, when they speak of their urgent need of pay; they speak of their last-remembered quid as if it were some deceased relative, too early lost, and to be mourned forever. As for sugar, no white man can drink coffee after they have sweetened it to their liking.

I see that the pride which military life creates may cause the plantation trickeries to diminish. For instance, these men make the most admirable sentinels. It is far harder to pass the camp lines at night than in the camp from which I came; and I have seen none of that disposition to connive at the offences of members of one's own company which is so troublesome among white soldiers. Nor are they lazy, either about work or drill; in all respects they seem better material for soldiers than I had dared to hope.

December 5, 1862

This evening, after working themselves up to the highest pitch, a party suddenly rushed off, got a barrel, and mounted some man upon it, who said, "Gib anoder song, boys, and I'se gib you a speech." After some hesitation and sundry shouts of "Rise de sing, somebody," and "Stan' up for Jesus, brudder," irreverently put in by the juveniles, they got upon the John Brown song, always a favorite, adding a jubilant verse which I had never before heard,—"We'll beat Beauregard on de clare battle-field." Then came the promised speech, and then no less than seven other speeches by as many men, on a variety of barrels, each orator being affectionately tugged to the pedestal and set on end by his special constituency. Every speech was good, without exception; with the queerest oddities of phrase and pronunciation, there was an invariable enthusiasm, a pungency of statement, and an understanding of the points at issue, which made them all rather thrilling. . . .

The most eloquent, perhaps, was Corporal Prince Lambkin, just arrived from Fernandina, who evidently had a previous reputation among them. His historical references were very interesting. He reminded them that he had predicted this war ever since Fremont's time, to which some of the crowd assented; he gave a very intelligent account of that Presidential campaign, and then described most impressively the secret anxiety of the slaves in Florida to know all about President Lincoln's election, and told how they all refused to work on the fourth of March, expecting their freedom to date from that day. He finally brought out one of the few really impressive appeals for the American flag that I have ever heard.

January 1, 1863 (evening)

A happy New Year to civilized people,—mere white folks. Our festival has come and gone, with perfect success, and our good General has been altogether satisfied. Last night the great fires were kept smouldering in the pit, and the beeves were cooked more or less, chiefly more,—during which time they had to be carefully watched, and the great spits turned by main force. Happy were the merry fellows who were permitted to sit up all night, and watch the glimmering flames that threw a thousand fantastic shadows among the great gnarled oaks. And such a chattering as I was sure to hear whenever I awoke that night!

My first greeting to-day was from one of the most stylish sergeants, who approached me with the following little speech, evidently the result of some elaboration:—

"I tink myself happy, dis New Year's Day, for salute my own Cunnel. Dis day las' year I was servant to a Cunnel ob Secesh; but now I hab de privilege for salute my own Cunnel."

That officer, with the utmost sincerity, reciprocated the sentiment.

About ten o'clock the people began to collect by land, and also by water,—in steamers sent by General Saxton for the purpose; and from that time all the avenues of approach were thronged. The multitude were chiefly colored women, with gay handkerchiefs on their heads, and a sprinkling of men, with that peculiarly respectable look which these people always have on Sundays and holidays. There were many white visitors also,—ladies on horseback, and in carriages, superintendents and teachers, officers, and cavalry-men. Our companies were marched to the neighborhood of the platform, and allowed to sit or stand, as at the Sunday services; the platform was occupied by ladies and dignitaries, and by the band of the Eighth Maine, which kindly volunteered for the occasion; the colored people filled up all the vacant openings in the beautiful grove around, and there was a cordon of mounted visitors beyond. Above, the great live-oak branches and their trailing moss; beyond the people, a glimpse of the blue river.

The services began at halfpast eleven o'clock, with prayer by our chaplain, Mr. Fowler, who is always, on such occasions, simple, reverential, and impressive. Then the President's Proclamation was read by Dr. W. H. Brisbane, a thing infinitely appropriate; a South Carolinian addressing South Carolinians; for he was reared among these very islands, and here long since emancipated his own slaves. Then the colors were presented to us by the Rev. Mr. French, a chaplain who brought them from the donors in New York. All this was according to the programme. Then followed an incident so simple, so touching, so utterly unexpected and startling, that I can scarcely believe it on recalling, though it gave the key-note to the whole day. The very moment the speaker had ceased, and just as I took and waved the flag, which now for the first time meant anything to these poor people, there suddenly arose, close beside the platform, a strong male voice (but rather cracked and elderly), into which two women's voices instantly blended, singing, as if by an impulse that could no more be repressed than the morning note of the song-sparrow.—

> "My Country, 't is of thee,
> Sweet land of liberty,
> Of thee I sing!"

People looked at each other, and then at us on the platform, to see whence came this interruption, not set down in the bills. Firmly and irrepressibly the quavering voices sang on, verse after verse; others of the colored people joined in; some whites on the platform began, but I motioned them to silence. I never saw anything so electric; it made all other words cheap; it seemed the choked voice of a race at last unloosed. Nothing could be more wonderfully unconscious; art could not have dreamed of a tribute to the day of jubilee that should be so affecting; history will not believe it; and when I came to speak of it, after it was ended, tears were everywhere. If you could have heard how quaint and innocent it was! Old Tiff and his children might have sung it; and close before me was a little slave-boy, almost white, who seemed to belong to the party, and even he must join in. Just think of it!—the first day they had ever had a country, the first flag they had ever seen which promised anything to their people, and here, while mere spectators stood in silence, waiting for my stupid words, these simple souls burst out in their lay, as if they were by their own hearths at home! When they stopped, there was nothing to do for it but to speak, and I went on; but the life of the whole day was in those unknown people's song.

—Higginson, *Army Life in a Black Regiment*

12. REBEL AND YANKEE YELLS

We hear a great deal about the Rebel Yell, though no two people seem agreed on just what it was, or even on its origin. It has been variously described as "more overpowering than the cannon's roar" and "a mingling of Indian whoop and wolf-howl"; it was probably born of the hunting field. There is far less information on the Yankee Yell; this was undoubtedly something that varied greatly from army to army.

Harvie Dew was a member of the 9th Virginia Cavalry, attached to Stuart.

THAT there existed a marked difference between the yells of the opposing armies during our late war was a recognized fact, and a frequent source of comment. The notes and tones peculiar to each of them were well defined, and led to their designation as the "Yankee" and the "Rebel" yells. . . .

The Federal, or "Yankee," yell, compared with that of the Confederate, lacked in vocal breadth, pitch, and resonance. This was unquestionably attributable to the fact that the soldiery of the North was drawn and recruited chiefly from large cities and towns, from factory districts, and from the more densely settled portions of the country.

Their surroundings, their circumstances of life and employment, had the effect of molding the character and temperament of the people, and at the same time of restraining their vocal development. People living and working in close proximity to one another have no absolute need for loud or strained vocal efforts, and any screaming or prolonged calling becomes seriously annoying to neighbors. Consequently, all such liberties or inconsiderate indulgences in cities, towns, etc., have long ago been discouraged by common consent. . . .

To afford some idea of the difference between these "yells," I will relate an incident which occurred in battle on the plains at Brandy Station, Virginia, in the fall of 1863. Our command was in full pursuit of a portion of Kilpatrick's cavalry. We soon approached their reserves (ours some distance behind), and found ourselves facing a battery of artillery with a regiment of cavalry drawn up on each side. A point of woods projected to the left of their position. We were ordered to move by the right flank till the woods protected us from the battery, and then, in open field, within a few hundred yards of the enemy, we were ordered to halt and right dress.

In a moment more one of the Federal regiments was ordered to charge, and down they came upon us in a body two or three times outnumbering ours. Then was heard their peculiar characteristic yell—"Hoo-ray! Hoo-ray! Hoo-ray!" etc. (This yell was called by the Federals a "cheer," and was intended for the word "hurrah," but that pronunciation I never heard in a charge. The sound was as though the first syllable, if heard at all, was "hoo," uttered with an exceedingly short, low, and indistinct tone, and the second was "ray," yelled with a long and high tone slightly deflecting at its termination. In many instances the yell seemed to be the simple interjection "heigh," rendered with the same tone which was given to "ray.")

Our command was alone in the field, and it seemed impossible for us to withstand the coming shock; but our commander, as brave an officer as ever drew a saber, frequently repeated, as the charging column approached us, his precautionary orders, to "Keep steady, boys! Keep steady!" and so we remained till the Federals were within a hundred yards of us. Then, waving his sword in air, he gave the final order, loud enough to be heard the field over: "Now is your time, boys! Give them the saber! Charge them, men! Charge!"

In an instant every voice with one accord vigorously shouted that "Rebel yell," which was so often heard on the field of battle. "Woh-who-ey! who-ey! who-ey! Woh-who-ey! who-ey!" etc. (The best illustration of this "true yell" which can be given the reader is by spelling it as above, with directions to sound the first syllable "woh" short and low, and the second "who" with a very high and prolonged note deflecting upon the third syllable "ey.")

A moment or two later the Federal column wavered and broke. In pursuit we chased them to within twenty feet of their battery, which had already begun to retreat. The second regiment to the right and rear of the battery then charged upon us, and for a moment we were forced back; but by that time our reserves were up, and we swept the field.

—Dew, "The Yankee and Rebel Yells"

13. DEATH ON THE BATTLEFIELD

There are many descriptions of death in battle, but few more graphic than this from the pen of Henry Blake describing the aftermath of the minor Battle of Williamsburg, on the Peninsula. Blake was a captain in the 11th Massachusetts Volunteers who served all through the war from First Bull Run to the Wilderness.

THE storm continued after the deadly struggle was ended; but it was not heeded by those who had battled from morning till night. In these hours of rest for the wearied, the non-combatants of the army, the members of the supply departments and ambulance corps, clerks, teamsters, musicians, and stragglers, who remain in the rear in time of action, visited the field, plundered the dead of both armies, and rifled the knapsacks of those who had fought while they were asleep. The sun rose in a cloudless sky upon the 6th [May]; but the enemy, having saved their trains had fled; and Williamsburg was occupied without opposition. Seven cannon had been abandoned, because the horses could not extricate them from the mud; and shot and shell were scattered in the road. The guns had been spiked; dishes, pans, kettles, and Dutch ovens, were demolished in the camps and redoubts; and packs of playing cards had been thrown into the streets of the town.

The soldiers visited every portion of the field to search for wounded or dead comrades, and witnessed without emotion scenes which lost their horror on account of their frequency; and, in many cases in which the death had been instantaneous, the attitude of the slain indicated the last act of their lives. The adjutant of a New-Jersey regiment was shot while he was resting upon one knee, and glancing towards the advancing line of the enemy through a field glass; but his limbs had not relaxed. Many hands, in every motion of loading and firing, clutched with the firm hand of death the rammer, gun, or cartridge. I noticed that a number of the dead of the Union army had been mutilated by bowie-knives, made of large, coarse files which the rebels carried in their sheaths; and gashes disfigured the heads and faces. The brief experience of a single engagement satisfied men of the uselessness of revolvers or dirks for the purposes of war, and they disappeared from both armies. Nearly one hundred of the enemy, in one part of the woods, had been killed while they were lying upon the ground; and the bullets had penetrated their foreheads. Some, who had lived a few hours after they were wounded, grasped photographs or letters, upon which their dying eyes rested when the thoughts of cherished and happy homes banished suffering.

Some of the cartridges used by the foe contained no bullet, but consisted of twelve buckshot. The pockets of friend and enemy had been turned inside out by the army thieves . . . and the buttons of the uniforms of every traitor had been removed. "I wish there was a battle every week," one of those miscreants remarked, in speaking of the amount he had stolen.

In wandering over the field, a corporal found in the pocket of a rebel a piece of tobacco upon which the blood had been coagulated, and the professional army thief had not touched it; but he washed the article, took a "chaw," and reserved the rest for future consumption. Head-boards were erected over the graves of the Union soldiers by their comrades, and the corpses of the enemy were buried by fatigue-parties; and the spot upon which they died was their last resting-place upon the earth. Details interred the horses, large numbers of which had been killed. The woods and abattis upon the battle-field were burned for sanitary reasons; and the unexploded shells which had been thrown during the conflict were continually bursting in the flames. A surgeon ordered the pioneers to dig the grave for an unconscious and wounded rebel, who was supposed to be dying; but the general sent him to the hospital, and he lived.

—BLAKE, *Three Years in the Army of the Potomac*

X

From Fort Donelson to Stones River

WHILE *the war in the East surged back and forth between Washington and Richmond, the Chesapeake Bay and the Valley, the war in the West raged and burned over an enormous territory, from Missouri to the Gulf, from the Alleghenies to the Mississippi, with great outcroppings in Missouri, Arkansas, Louisiana, and even in Texas and New Mexico. Nor is it to be forgotten that the heaviest blows of the war in the East were directed, in the end, from the Western theater, Sherman carrying the war to Georgia and the Carolinas.*

Not only were the geographical circumstances of the war in the West profoundly different from those in the East, the strategic objectives, too, were different. The objectives of fighting in Virginia and Maryland were the capture of the rival capitals and the destruction of the rival armies. The war in the West was of necessity directed to different ends. There was, first, the control of the belt of border states—Kentucky and Missouri—and of eastern Tennessee, heavily Unionist in sentiment and commanding the approaches to the East and the South. There was, second, control of the great arteries of commerce: the Mississippi, the Cumberland, Tennessee, and Red rivers, and the railroads which connected the deep South with the Atlantic coast, the border states with the Gulf. The greatest strategical objective was, of course, control of the Mississippi River, and the separation of the Trans-Mississippi West from the rest of the Confederacy. Almost all the major battles of the Western theater involved some strategic point on some river or railroad: Fort Donelson, Island No. 10, Shiloh, Murfreesboro, Vicksburg, Port Hudson, Chattanooga, and others. The otherwise confusing cavalry raids, too, fall into a logical pattern when we see them against the background of lines of communication; and the cavalry leaders of the Western armies—men like Forrest and Morgan and Grierson—played a very different role from Eastern cavalry leaders like Stuart and Buford.

Most of the campaigns of the West involved control of rivers or railroads. There was one prolonged campaign for the control of the Mississippi—a campaign that began with the minor Battle of Belmont and was concluded with the fall of Port Hudson. A second was directed to the first Confederate line of defense—the line stretching from Columbus to Forts Henry and Donelson and to Bowling Green. A third was directed to the second Confederate line of defense—Memphis to Corinth to Chattanooga. The fourth major campaign—that of Chickamauga and Chattanooga—was for the gateway to Georgia, and was followed by the fifth—the campaign for Atlanta and the march from Atlanta to the sea. There were, to be sure, other campaigns, for different objectives. The confused series of campaigns for Kentucky and eastern Tennessee were directed as much to political as to military or economic ends; the fighting in the Trans-Mississippi area, too, was for the allegiance of that area.

The struggle in the West began at St. Louis and the region to the south. If the Confederates could win Missouri, and above all St. Louis, they could strike into the very heart of the Union—through Illinois and Indiana. As early as July 1861 General Hardee ordered Pillow to reinforce New Madrid on the Missouri side of the Mississippi and Columbus on the Kentucky side; if these could be held it would be easy to mount an offensive toward Cairo at the southern tip of Illinois. Frémont, then in command in Missouri, promptly ordered Brigadier General Grant to go to Cape Girardeau, take command of all the troops in the vicinity of the mouth of the Ohio, strengthen Cairo, and drive the Confederates away from the river. It was a big order. For meantime Pillow had built up a force of almost 15,000 men at Columbus, and was preparing to move either across the river into Missouri or up the river toward Illinois. And meantime, too, the Confederates had built up their defenses at Forts Henry and Donelson on the Tennessee and Cumberland rivers, and General Albert Sidney Johnston had sent Buckner to Bowling Green, threatening Louisville. The Confederates had established their first line of defense; could the Federals break it?

1. U. S. GRANT APPLIES FOR A JOB

Grant was working in his father's store in Galena, Illinois, when the war broke out. A West Pointer, he had made a good record in the Mexican War, and then seen service on distant frontier posts until, in 1854, he had resigned from the army, probably under pressure. With the outbreak of the war he applied for appointments from the Governor of Illinois and probably from the Governor of Ohio, tried to get an appointment under McClellan, who ignored him, and worked in the state adjutant general's office. His application to the adjutant general at Washington was ignored. Finally, in June, Governor Yates appointed him colonel of an unruly regiment, the 21st Illinois. Two months later, somewhat to his surprise, he was made brigadier general.

Galena, Illinois, May 24, 1861

Col. L. Thomas
Adjt. Gen. U. S. A.

Sir:—Having served for fifteen years in the regular army, including four years at West Point, and feeling it the duty of every one who has been educated at the Government expense to offer their services for the support of that Government, I have the honor, very respectfully, to tender my services, until the close of the war, in such capacity as may be offered. I would say, in view of my present age and length of service, I feel myself competent to command a regiment, if the President, in his judgment, should see fit to intrust one to me.

Since the first call of the President I have been serving on the staff of the Governor of this State, rendering such aid as I could in the organization of our State militia, and am still engaged in that capacity. A letter addressed to me at Springfield, Illinois, will reach me.

I am very respectfully,

Your obt. svt.,

U. S. GRANT.

—*Personal Memoirs of U. S. Grant*

2. GRANT WINS HIS SPURS AT BELMONT

After whipping his regiment into shape Grant took it to Missouri, then under the command of John C. Frémont, whose only claim to military ability was his record as an explorer. Frémont was trying, with no great success, to hold Missouri for the Union. Meantime Pillow had built up a strong force at Columbus, just south of Cairo; from Columbus he could not only block the Mississippi but threaten Paducah at the mouth of the Tennessee, Cairo at the junction of the Ohio and the Mississippi, or advance into Missouri to support the Confederates there. To forestall these moves Grant fortified Cairo, then pounced on Paducah; then he asked and obtained permission to make a demonstration against Columbus. Lacking strength for a direct attack he selected instead the little village of Belmont, opposite the great fort, where Pillow had a force of some 2,500 men. Belmont was a minor affair, and it was not very clearly a victory, but it brought Grant recognition.

AUTUMN glided away; the leaves were dropping along the banks of the Potomac and the Ohio; the fairest season of the year would soon be gone. It was a period of disaster and inaction. . . . Grant meantime was busily employed in drilling new troops at Cairo, and probably in wondering why they were not made use of. He always believed that where both sides are equally undisciplined the most active would be the most successful. He saw Columbus grow into an impregnable fortress under the care of Pillow and Polk; he heard that the Tennessee and the Cumberland were to be closed by new fortifications; and he asked his superior officer at St. Louis, Fremont, to be allowed to take Columbus (September 10) while it was yet assailable. At length (November 1, 1861) he received orders to make a demonstration against the fortress, to prevent the enemy from sending reinforcements to their general, Price, in Missouri. Grant resolved finally to turn the movement into an actual attack on Belmont.

Columbus rises on a high bluff above the Mississippi on the Kentucky shore. It was now so strongly fortified as to be quite impregnable; armies might have wasted their strength against its lofty bluff for months without result; its long range of heavy cannon closed up the navigation of the river; and a large force of the enemy filled its walls. But it was Belmont, a post on

The Campaigns in Tennessee and Kentucky

341

the opposite side of the Mississippi, under the guns of Columbus, that Grant meant to threaten or assail. Here a considerable force of rebels had formed their camp, defended by rough lines of felled trees and the fire of Columbus; and it was here that the reinforcements were chiefly ferried over the river to aid Price in Missouri. Grant's aim was to destroy their camp, disperse their troops, and then return to Cairo. He would thus practice his new levies, and at the same time alarm the enemy.

No sooner did the brave Western soldiers at Cairo learn that a real attack was to be made than all was exultation and excitement. They rejoiced to be relieved from the dull monotony of camp-life, and to test their courage in the fierce trial of actual combat. Grant ordered General Smith from Paducah to make a demonstration against Columbus, to employ the enemy's attention on that side of the river, while he himself set out for Missouri. His troops, it should be remembered, were all untried men. His two chief commanders, Logan and M'Clernand, had never heard a shot fired in actual battle, and Grant stood alone in the midst of a brave but inexperienced army. His force numbered about thirty-one hundred men.

After several feints he landed his troops from transports at Hunter's Point, in Missouri, and marched at once against Belmont, about three miles below. The enemy were soon found, and the brave troops, advancing as skirmishers, threw themselves against the rude defenses; the officers behaved like veterans, always in the front of the battle; the soldiers climbed, crept, or sprang over the strong abatis; the enemy were slowly driven back to the shore. Pillow, who had crossed over with reinforcements from Columbus, was forced to give way, and the disordered and broken force, larger in numbers than the assailants, took refuge under the river bank and the fire of Columbus.

A strange scene followed. Grant's troops, carried away by the joy of the moment, having taken several hundred prisoners and the enemy's camp, broke into disorder. Speeches were delivered by excited orators; the captured camp was plundered; in the midst of their enemies the inexperienced soldiers believed themselves secure. Grant ordered the camp to be set on fire to drive the troops to their ranks, and suddenly the heavy guns of Columbus opened upon the Union army. Meanwhile large bodies of rebels had crossed the river, and with the aid of Pillow's men had surrounded their late victors.

A startled aid-de-camp, riding up to Grant, exclaimed in alarm, "General, we are surrounded!"

"Well," said he, "we must cut our way out as we cut our way in."

His calmness reassured his little army, and with Grant, M'Clernand, and Logan at their head, they broke through the enemy's line and passed in good order to the landing. Here the whole force was safely embarked, with but slight loss. Grant acted as his own rear-guard, was the last man on the shore, and at one time found himself not more than one hundred and fifty feet from a line of the enemy. He paused a moment to survey them, then turned his horse's head, rode slowly away, and finally broke into a gallop as he approached the river. He made his way with difficulty upon one of the transports, and then the little flotilla moved on under a heavy fire of musketry from the shore. By five o'clock the last vessel was beyond reach of the enemy, and the successful expedition arrived safely at Cairo.

—EUGENE LAWRENCE, "Grant on the Battle-Field"

3. U. S. GRANT BECOMES UNCONDITIONAL SURRENDER GRANT

Grant had already forestalled a Confederate advance down the Tennessee to the Ohio by seizing Paducah. Now he proposed to General Halleck, who had succeeded the incompetent Frémont, an attack on the bastions of Forts Henry and Donelson. The reduction of these forts would not only clear two great rivers, the Tennessee and the Cumberland, but cut the Confederate line of defense from Columbus to Bowling Green, Kentucky, and force the Confederates to retire from Kentucky to Tennessee. After a good deal of prodding Halleck authorized a joint attack on the forts by Grant and Commodore Foote, the latter to blast the forts from his gunboats. Early in February 1862 Grant's army of 17,000 men advanced on Fort Henry. Meantime the gunboats had already reached the fort, which was promptly abandoned, its small defending force marching overland to the much larger and stronger Fort Donelson.

Here is Grant's own story of how he forced the surrender of this fort. As he makes clear, the surrender was quite unnecessary; the Confederates could have withstood a long siege, or they could have fought their way out—as Forrest did. The capture of these two forts, coming on the heels of the Belmont affair, gave Grant a national reputation and brought him a major generalship.

I WAS very impatient to get to Fort Donelson because I knew the importance of the place to the enemy and supposed he would reinforce it rapidly. I felt that 15,000 men on the 8th would be more effective than 50,000 a month later. I asked Flag-officer Foote, therefore, to order his gunboats still about Cairo to proceed up the Cumberland River and not to wait for those gone to Eastport and Florence; but the others got back in time and we started on the 12th [February 1862]. I had moved McClernand out a few miles the night before so as to leave the road as free as possible. . . .

I started from Fort Henry with 15,000 men, including eight batteries and part of a regiment of cavalry, and, meeting with no obstruction to detain us, the advance arrived in front of the enemy by noon. That afternoon and the next day were spent in taking up ground to make the investment as complete as possible. General Smith had been directed to leave a portion of his division behind to guard forts Henry and Heiman. He left General Lew. Wallace with 2,500 men. With the remainder of his division he occupied our left, extending to Hickman creek. McClernand was on the right and covered the roads running south and south-west from Dover. His right extended to the backwater up the ravine opening into the [Cumberland] south of the village. The troops were not intrenched, but the nature of the ground was such that they were just as well protected from the fire of the enemy as if rifle-pits had been thrown up. Our line was generally along the crest of ridges. The artillery was protected by being sunk in the ground. The men who were not serving the guns were perfectly covered from fire on taking position a little back from the crest. The greatest suffering was from want of shelter. It was midwinter and during the siege we had rain and snow, thawing and freezing alternately. It would not do to allow camp-fires except far down the hill out of sight of the enemy, and it would not do to allow many of the troops to remain there at the same time. In the march over from Fort Henry numbers of the men had thrown away their blankets and overcoats. There was therefore much discomfort and absolute suffering.

During the 12th and 13th, and until the arrival of Wallace and Thayer on the 14th, the National forces, composed of but 15,000 men, without intrenchments, confronted an intrenched army of 21,000 without conflict further than what was brought on by ourselves. Only one gunboat had arrived. There was a little skirmishing each day, brought on by the movement of our troops in securing commanding positions; but there was no actual fighting during this time except once, on the 13th, in front of McClernand's command. That general had undertaken to capture a battery of the enemy which was annoying his men. Without orders or authority he sent three regiments to make the assault. The battery was in the main line of the enemy, which was defended by his whole army present. Of course the assault was a failure, and of course the loss on our side was great for the number of men engaged. In this assault Colonel William Morrison fell badly wounded. Up to this time the surgeons with the army had no difficulty in finding room in the houses near our line for all the sick and wounded; but now hospitals were overcrowded. Owing, however, to the energy and skill of the surgeons the suffering was not so great as it might have been. The hospital arrangements at Fort Donelson were as complete as it was possible to make them, considering the inclemency of the weather and the lack of tents, in a sparsely settled country where the houses were generally of but one or two rooms.

On the return of Captain Walke to Fort Henry on the 10th, I had requested him to take the vessels that had accompanied him on his expedition up the Tennessee, and get possession of the Cumberland as far up towards Donelson as possible. He started without delay, taking, however, only his own gunboat, the *Carondelet*, towed by the steamer *Alps*. Captain Walke arrived a few miles below Donelson on the 12th, a little after noon. About the time the advance of troops reached a point within gunshot of the fort on the land side, he engaged the water batteries at long range. On the 13th I informed him of my arrival the day before and of the establishment of most of our batteries, requesting him at the same time to attack that day so that I might take advantage of any diversion. The attack was made and many shots fell within the fort, creating some consternation, as we now know. The investment on the land side was made as complete as the number of troops engaged would admit of. . . .

Confederate Camp in Virginia

Edwin Forbes

Pulling Artillery into Position, Army of the Potomac

The plan was for the troops to hold the enemy within his lines, while the gunboats should attack the water-batteries at close quarters and silence his guns if possible. Some of the gunboats were to run the batteries, get above the fort and above the village of Dover. I had ordered a reconnaissance made with the view of getting troops to the river above Dover in case they should be needed there. That position attained by the gunboats it would have been but a question of time—and a very short time, too—when the garrison would have been compelled to surrender.

By three in the afternoon of the 14th Flag-officer Foote was ready, and advanced upon the water batteries with his entire fleet. After coming in range of the batteries of the enemy the advance was slow, but a constant fire was delivered from every gun that could be brought to bear upon the fort. I occupied a position on shore from which I could see the advancing navy. The leading boat got within a very short distance of the water battery, not further off I think than two hundred yards, and I soon saw one and then another of them dropping down the river, visibly disabled. Then the whole fleet followed and the engagement was closed for the day. The gunboat which Flag-officer Foote was on, besides having been hit about sixty times, several of the shots passing through near the water-line, had a shot enter the pilot-house which killed the pilot, carried away the wheel, and wounded the flag-officer himself. The tiller-ropes of another vessel were carried away, and she, too, dropped helplessly back. Two others had their pilot-houses so injured that they scarcely formed a protection to the men at the wheel.

The enemy had evidently been much demoralized by the assault, but they were jubilant when they saw the disabled vessels dropping down the river entirely out of the control of the men on board. Of course I only witnessed the falling back of our gunboats and felt sad enough at the time over the repulse. Subsequent reports, now published, show that the enemy telegraphed a great victory to Richmond. The sun went down on the night of the 14th of February, 1862, leaving the army confronting Fort Donelson anything but comforted over the prospects. The weather had turned intensely cold; the men were without tents and could not keep up fires where most of them had to stay; and, as previously stated, many had thrown away their overcoats and blankets. Two of the strongest of our gunboats had been disabled, presumably beyond the possibility of rendering any present assistance. I retired this night not knowing but that I would have to intrench my position, and bring up tents for the men or build huts under the cover of the hills.

On the morning of the 15th, before it was yet broad day, a messenger from Flag-officer Foote handed me a note, expressing a desire to see me on the flag-ship and saying that he had been injured the day before so much that he could not come himself to me. I at once made my preparations for starting. . . .

When I reached the fleet I found the flag-ship was anchored out in the stream. A small boat, however, awaited my arrival and I was soon on board with the flag-officer. He explained to me in short the condition in which he was left by the engagement of the evening before, and suggested that I should intrench while he returned to Mound City with his disabled boats, expressing at the time the belief that he could have the necessary repairs made and be back in ten days. I saw the absolute necessity of his gunboats going into hospital, and did not know but I should be forced to the alternative of going through a siege. But the enemy relieved me from this necessity.

When I left the National line to visit Flag-officer Foote I had no idea that there would be any engagement on land unless I brought it on myself. The conditions for battle were much more favorable to us than they had been for the first two days of the investment. From the 12th to the 14th we had but 15,000 men of all arms and no gunboats. Now we had been reinforced by a fleet of six naval vessels, a large division of troops under General L. Wallace and 2,500 men brought over from Fort Henry belonging to the division of C. F. Smith. The enemy, however, had taken the initiative. Just as I landed I met Captain Hillyer of my staff, white with fear, not for his personal safety, but for the safety of the National troops. He said the enemy had come out of his lines in full force and attacked and scattered Mc-Clernand's division, which was in full retreat. The roads, as I have said, were unfit for making fast time, but I got to my command as soon as possible. The attack had been made on the National right. I was some four or five miles north of our left. The line was about three miles long. In reaching the point where the disaster had occurred I had to pass the divisions of Smith and Wallace. I saw no sign of excitement on the portion of the line held by Smith; Wallace was nearer the scene of conflict and had taken part in it. He had, at an opportune time, sent Thayer's brigade to the support of Mc-Clernand and thereby contributed to hold the enemy within his lines.

I saw everything favorable for us along the line of our left and center. When I came to the right appearances were different. The enemy had come out in full force to cut his way out and make his escape. McClernand's division had to bear the brunt of the attack from this combined force. His men had stood up gallantly until the ammunition in their cartridge-boxes gave out. There was abundance of ammunition near by lying on the ground in boxes, but at that stage of the war it was not all of our commanders of regiments, brigades, or even divisions, who had been educated up to the point of seeing that their men were constantly supplied with ammunition during an engagement. When the men found themselves without ammunition they could not stand up against troops who seemed to have plenty of it. The division broke and a portion fled, but most of the men, as they were not pursued, only fell back out of range of the fire of the enemy. It must have been about this time that Thayer pushed his brigade in between the enemy and those of our troops that were without ammunition. At all events, the enemy fell back within his intrenchments and was there when I got on the field.

I saw the men standing in knots talking in the most excited manner. No officer seemed to be giving any directions. The soldiers had their muskets, but no ammunition, while there were tons of it close at hand. I heard some of the men say that the enemy had come out with knapsacks, and haversacks filled with rations. They seemed to think this indicated a determination on his part to stay out and fight just as long as the provisions held out. I turned to Colonel J. D. Webster, of my staff, who was with me, and said: "Some of our men are pretty badly demoralized, but the enemy must be more so, for he has attempted to force his way out, but has fallen back: the one who attacks first now will be victorious and the enemy will have to be in a hurry if he gets ahead of me." I determined to make the assault at once on our left. It was clear to my mind that the enemy had started to march out with his entire force, except a few pickets, and if our attack could be made on the left before the enemy could redistribute his forces along the line, we would find little opposition except from the intervening abatis. I directed Colonel Webster to ride with me and call out to the men as we passed: "Fill your cartridge-boxes, quick, and get into line; the enemy is trying to escape, and he must not be permitted to do so." This acted like a charm. The men only wanted someone to give them a command. We rode rapidly to Smith's quarters, when I explained the situation to him and directed him to charge the enemy's works in his front with his whole division, saying at the same time that he would find nothing but a very thin line to contend with. The general was off in an incredibly short time, going in advance himself to keep his men from firing while they were working their way through the abatis intervening between them and the enemy. The outer line of rifle-pits was passed, and the night of the 15th General Smith, with much of his division, bivouacked within the lines of the enemy. There was now no doubt but that the Confederates must surrender or be captured the next day. . . .

A council of war was held by the enemy at which all agreed that it would be impossible to hold out longer. General Buckner, who was third in rank in the garrison but much the most capable soldier, seems to have regarded it a duty to hold the fort until the general commanding the department, A. S. Johnston, should get back to his headquarters at Nashville. Buckner's report shows, however, that he considered Donelson lost and that any attempt to hold the place longer would be at the sacrifice of the command. Being assured that Johnston was already in Nashville, Buckner too agreed that surrender was the proper thing. Floyd turned over the command to Pillow, who declined it. It then devolved upon Buckner, who accepted the responsibility of the position. Floyd and Pillow took possession of all the river transports at Dover and before morning both were on their way to Nashville, with the brigade formerly commanded by Floyd and some other troops, in all about 3,000. Some marched up the east bank of the Cumberland; others went on the steamers. During the night Forrest also, with his cavalry and some other troops, about a thousand in all, made their way out, passing between our right and the river. They had to ford or swim over the back-water in the little creek just south of Dover.

Before daylight General Smith brought to me the following letter from General Buckner:

Headquarters, Fort Donelson,
February 16, 1862.

Sir:—In consideration of all the circumstances governing the present situation of affairs at this station, I propose to the Commanding Officer of the Federal forces the appointment of Commissioners to agree upon terms of capitulation of the forces and fort under my command, and in that view suggest an armistice until 12 o'clock to-day.

I am, sir, very respectfully,

Your ob't se'v't,
S. B. BUCKNER
Brig. Gen. C. S. A.

To this I responded as follows:

Headquarters Army in the Field,
Camp near Donelson,
February 16, 1862.

General S. B. Buckner,
Confederate Army.

Sir:—Yours of this date, proposing armistice and appointment of Commissioners to settle terms of capitulation, is just received. No terms except an unconditional and immediate surrender can be accepted. I propose to move immediately upon your works.

I am, sir, very respectfully,

Your ob't se'v't,
U. S. GRANT
Brig. Gen.

To this I received the following reply:

Headquarters, Dover, Tennessee,
February 16, 1862.

To Brig. Gen'l U. S. Grant,
U. S. Army.

Sir:—The distribution of the forces under my command, incident to an unexpected change of commanders, and the overwhelming force under your command, compel me, notwithstanding the brilliant success of the Confederate arms yesterday, to accept the ungenerous and unchivalrous terms which you propose.

I am, sir,

Your very ob't se'v't,
S. B. BUCKNER
Brig. Gen. C. S. A.

. . . I had been at West Point three years with Buckner and afterwards served with him in the army, so that we were quite well acquainted. In the course of our conversation, which was very friendly, he said to me that if he had been in command I would not have got up to Donelson as easily as I did. I told him that if he had been in command I should not have tried in the way I did: I had invested their lines with a smaller force than they had to defend them, and at the same time had sent a brigade full 5,000 strong, around by water; I had relied very much upon their commander to allow me to come safely up to the outside of their works.

—*Personal Memoirs of U. S. Grant*

4. GENERAL POPE CAPTURES NEW MADRID

The fall of Forts Henry and Donelson forced the Confederates back on their second line of defense. Johnston withdrew to Murfreesboro, in Tennessee, and prepared to fall back to Corinth. Polk gave up Columbus but was ordered to hold on to New Madrid and Island No. 10 in the great bend of the Mississippi at the juncture of Missouri, Arkansas, Kentucky and Tennessee. New Madrid was vulnerable from land, but Island No. 10 was almost impregnable.

On March 3 General Pope advanced on New Madrid with 20,000 men; by cutting off access to it he succeeded in starving it into submission in ten days. There was some sharp fighting in the final assault, but the battle was a minor affair.

Far more spectacular was the reduction of Island No. 10. As there was no direct approach to the island by land, Pope cut a channel through the great bend north of the island and ferried his army to Point Pleasant below Island No. 10. Meantime Commodore Foote's gunboats, Commander Walke's Carondelet *in the lead, ran the batteries of the island. Isolated, the Confederates tried to evacuate their forts, but were cut off and forced to surrender 7,000 men and 123 heavy guns on April 7. These two victories gave Pope a reputation which he shortly lost in the East.*

Colonel Gilbert, who here describes the Battle of New Madrid, was a Cincinnati engineeer who helped organize the 39th Ohio Volunteers.

In Camp New Madrid (Mo.)
March 14 1862

My dear Wife

"Glory to God in the highest & on earth peace & good will to men—glory to God for the signal & complete victory that has crowned our arms in the recent conflict with rebellious villains at New Madrid & peace & good will to men which I do hope is soon to follow such successes all over our country. On yesterday morning we arose at 2 oclk & prepared breakfast & at 4 oclk we passed from our Camp into the outer darkness on our way to the battle ground. This time I *knew* we were going into the fight & certainly felt as if it were possible that I might never get back alive. On this occasion I had to part from our good Dr Nixon; I had always had him with me before on all occasions & now he would no more be by my side.

Before daylight we arrived on the ground selected for the battle & in the grey morning took silently our respective positions in order of battle.

The night previous the sappers & miners were engaged all night in placing the heavy guns intended to silence the Gunboats as well as the guns of the Fort. The battery was placed so quietly by our men that the pickets of the enemy stationed within less than three hundred yards were not aware of its being done & when our regiments came up to their positions to support the battery we were fired upon & it was then the grey of the morning & the guns of our battery replied much doubtless to the consternation of said pickets. We took them completely by surprize, the gun boats had no steam up & it was some time before they got into position.

The 39th was given the position of honor & of greatest danger being on the extreme right, that is in the advance of all & our boys behaved splendidly. Gen Pope & all the generals under him paid us the highest compliments. We were under fire of shot & shell for twelve mortal hours & wonderful to say only one man in our whole regiment was wounded & he only a slight round shot. I suppose 300 or 400 shot & large shells passed within thirty to forty feet of our men during the day. The cannonading & bursting of bombs was like continuous peals of thunder. The whizzing of the balls & shell was very peculiar & caused involuntary dodging all around &, notwithstanding the real danger we were constantly in, it was a constant source of amusement & merriment amongst the men. . . . Our business was to lay perfectly still in the position in which we were placed & be ready at any time to repel an attack upon the battery & in consequence our men *lay* on the ground the whole day, none being allowed to rise except for reasonable purposes.

The hair breadth escapes were very numerous. I can only say that a large round shell took off a mans haversack & bent his bayonet hanging by his side without touching the man; another man laying on the ground with his knapsack strapped to his back had a 32 lb shot pop right on his back & bounce off without doing more than knock his breath out of his body *for a time*—the ball of course was nearly spent. A 24 lb shot passed within 18 inches of my head & ploughed into the ground 20 ft beyond me. I was sitting down at the time. The large & small balls bounced about just as if some of the great powers were playing a game of foot ball & the bombs burst over & around us until we really got to regard them more as if it was a pyrotechnic display, than if they were instruments of death, sent from a malignant & treacherous enemy. The enemy got our range very correctly & fired all day right to our position, but we were wonderfully preserved.

I got at one time upon a high stump & with my glass commenced looking all along the levee some 1200 yards off for the position of the gun boats & had not more than got down on the ground than bang bang went the heavy guns from one of the gun boats & the shot & shell came whirling right over head & some 20 shots were fired right in our direction showing that I had been seen by the enemy with their glasses.

A large shot came bounding along the ground in the early part of the day & passing us went right in to the ranks of the 27 Ohio who were on our left & took off the legs of three men & stopped right there as if tired. Another large 32 lb shot struck a large log behind which an officer had just dodged &

bounced up in the air about fifty feet looking like a great foot ball. At times the shot could be distinctly seen as they came along and easily dodged.

When night came on we were ordered to remain on the field in just the same position with the strictest injunctions against either sleeping or allowing a single man to sleep & we prepared to pass the night as best we could. I sent my man to camp for my rubber blanket & buffalo & stood up against a tree most of the night. At about 12 oclk a most terrific rain & thunder storm came on & Heavens artillery outdid in noise that of the day. It was a singular sight to see by the glare of the lightning which was very bright to see two thousand men standing up with their blankets on being thoroughly drenchd in the rain.

At daylight we were relieved & marchd back to camp where we had hardly arrived when we heard loud & continuous cheering in the direction of the Fort & after a while we learned that the enemy had evacuated the place leaving a large amt of stores, tents, 500 head of horses & mules, some 20 or 30 large guns besides many stores in the levee & ample supplies of ammunition—everything in fact was abandoned last night in the greatest confusion & we found we had done them terrible damage yesterday. One or two gun boats very much disabled, guns in the fort badly knocked about & there is no doubt they were terribly frightened at seeing us remain on the field of battle all night lest we should storm their works. They must have had 11000 men. . . . They left tents sufficient for 10,000 men & everything else in proportion.

It is one of the most thorough & complete victories we have had & with very little loss of life. The generalship displayed by Genʲ Pope is entitled to all praise. I am very tired. Good night

ALFRED

—COLONEL A. W. GILBERT, Letter to His Wife

5. HENRY STANLEY FIGHTS WITH THE DIXIE GRAYS AT SHILOH

After the debacle in Kentucky, the Confederates formed a line of defense stretching from Memphis through Corinth to Chattanooga. Johnston collected some 40,000 troops here, and awaited the arrival of Van Dorn with another 20,000 from the west. Halleck, now in command of the entire Western theater, directed Grant and Buell to advance to Savannah on the Tennessee River about 30 miles northeast of Corinth. Grant's army began to arrive at Savannah on March 11, and within a week he had some 35,000 men at and around Savannah and Pittsburg Landing, a few miles below on the western side of the river. Buell, however, made a leisurely advance from Nashville, taking 22 days to cover 135 miles.

All unsuspecting of danger, Grant's army was scattered over a large irregular quadrangle bounded on the east by the Tennessee, on the north by Owl Creek and on the south by Lick Creek; the land was mostly wooded and cut by many gullies and ravines. Early on the morning of April 6

Johnston struck the Federal outposts, drove them in, and pushed on to the main attack. Although taken by surprise the Federals rallied and fought back with great courage and pertinacity. The fighting raged for over 12 hours, the Confederates steadily pushing back the Union right flank and driving toward Pittsburg Landing on the left flank.

During the afternoon, when the situation looked desperate for the Federals, advance detachments of Lew Wallace's division and of Buell's reached the field of battle, and the gunboats joined in the fray. By nightfall victory rested with the Confederates, but they had succeeded neither in destroying Grant's army nor in capturing Pittsburg Landing, and they had lost their leader, the brilliant and beloved Albert Sidney Johnston. By the next day the whole situation was reversed. Grant had 25,000 fresh men to throw into the battle; the Confederates were exhausted, and on the defensive. There was some sharp fighting on the seventh, but the Confederates withdrew and Grant failed to pursue. By the time he did get ready to pursue, the Confederate army had retired to Corinth. Shiloh was, with Antietam, the bloodiest day of the war, and the hardest fought. Union losses were over 13,000—of whom some 2,500 were prisoners; Confederate losses over 10,500.

Our first account of Shiloh is by young Henry M. Stanley, later the world-famous Sir Henry Stanley. Born in Wales as John Rowlands 19 years earlier, he had shipped as a cabin boy to Louisiana, where he was adopted by a New Orleans merchant, Henry Morton Stanley, whose name he took. In 1861 he enlisted in the Dixie Grays. Captured at Shiloh he endured the discomforts of Camp Douglas prison, enlisted briefly in the Federal artillery, was discharged, and returned to England, only to come back to the United States and enlist in the Union Navy. Later he returned to England and to an illustrious career in journalism and exploration. The Autobiography, *from which this account of Shiloh is taken, was written many years after the war; though authentic enough in general, the circumstantial details must be put down to skillful journalism.*

O N April 2, 1862, we received orders to prepare three days' cooked rations. Through some misunderstanding, we did not set out until the 4th; and, on the morning of that day, the 6th Arkansas Regiment of Hindman's brigade, Hardee's corps, marched from Corinth to take part in one of the bloodiest battles of the West. We left our knapsacks and tents behind us. After two days of marching, and two nights of bivouacking and living on cold rations, our spirits were not buoyant at dawn of Sunday, the 6th April, as they ought to have been for the serious task before us. . . .

At four o'clock in the morning, we rose from our damp bivouac, and, after a hasty refreshment, were formed into line. We stood in rank for half an hour or so, while the military dispositions were being completed along the three-mile front. Our brigade formed the centre; Cleburne's and Gladden's brigades were on our respective flanks.

Day broke with every promise of a fine day. Next to me, on my right, was a boy of seventeen, Henry Parker. I remember it because, while we stood-at-ease, he drew my attention to some violets at his feet, and said, "It would be a good idea to put a few into my cap. Perhaps the Yanks won't shoot me if they see me wearing such flowers, for they are a sign of peace."

"Capital," said I, "I will do the same."

We plucked a bunch, and arranged the violets in our caps. The men in the ranks laughed at our proceedings, and had not the enemy been so near, their merry mood might have been communicated to the army.

We loaded our muskets, and arranged our cartridge-pouches ready for use. Our weapons were the obsolete flint-locks, and the ammunition was rolled in cartridge-paper, which contained powder, a round ball, and three buckshot. When we loaded we had to tear the paper with our teeth, empty a little powder into the pan, lock it, empty the rest of the powder into the barrel, press paper and ball into the muzzle, and ram home. Then the Orderly-sergeant called the roll, and we knew that the Dixie Greys were present to a man. . . .

Before we had gone five hundred paces, our serenity was disturbed by some desultory firing in front. It was then a quarter-past five. "They are at it already," we whispered to each other. "Stand by, gentlemen,"—for we were all gentlemen volunteers at this time,—said our Captain L. G. Smith. Our steps became unconsciously brisker, and alertness was noticeable in everybody. The firing continued at intervals, deliberate and scattered, as at target practice. We drew nearer to the firing, and soon a sharper rattling of musketry was heard. "That is the enemy waking up," we said. Within a few minutes, there was another explosive burst of musketry, the air was pierced by many missiles, which hummed and pinged sharply by our ears, pattered through the treetops, and brought twigs and leaves down on us. "Those are bullets," Henry whispered with awe.

At two hundred yards further, a dreadful roar of musketry broke out from a regiment adjoining ours. It was followed by another further off, and the sound had scarcely died away when regiment after regiment blazed away and made a continuous roll of sound. "We are in for it now," said Henry. . . .

"Forward, gentlemen, make ready!" urged Captain Smith. In response, we surged forward, for the first time marring the alignment. We trampled recklessly over the grass and young sprouts. Beams of sunlight stole athwart our course. . . . Nothing now stood between us and the enemy.

"There they are!" was no sooner uttered, than we cracked into them with levelled muskets. "Aim low, men!" commanded Captain Smith. I tried hard to see some living thing to shoot at, for it appeared absurd to be blazing away at shadows. But, still advancing, firing as we moved, I, at last, saw a row of little globes of pearly smoke streaked with crimson, breaking-out with spurtive quickness, from a long line of blue figures in front; and simultaneously, there broke upon our ears an appalling crash of sound, the series of fusillades following one another with startling suddenness, which suggested to my somewhat moidered sense a mountain upheaved, with huge rocks tumbling and thundering down a slope, and the echoes rumbling and receding through space. Again and again, these loud and quick explosions were repeated, seemingly with increased violence, until they rose to the highest pitch of fury, and in unbroken continuity. All the world seemed involved in one tremendous ruin! . . .

Though one's senses were preternaturally acute, and engaged with their impressions, we plied our arms, loaded, and fired, with such nervous haste as though it depended on each of us how soon this fiendish uproar would be hushed. My nerves tingled, my pulses beat double-quick, my heart throbbed loudly, and almost painfully; but, amid all the excitement, my thoughts, swift as the flash of lightning, took all sound, and sight, and self, into their purview. I listened to the battle raging far away on the flanks, to the thunder in front, to the various sounds made by the leaden storm. I was angry with my rear rank, because he made my eyes smart with the powder of his musket; and I felt like cuffing him for deafening my ears! I knew how Captain Smith and Lieutenant Mason looked, how bravely the Dixie Greys' banner ruffled over Newton Story's head, and that all hands were behaving as though they knew how long all this would last. Back to myself my thoughts came, and, with the whirring bullet, they fled to the blue-bloused ranks afront. They dwelt on their movements, and read their temper, as I should read time by a clock. Through the lurid haze the contours of their pink faces could not been seen, but their gappy, hesitating, incoherent, and sensitive line revealed their mood clearly.

We continued advancing, step by step, loading and firing as we went. To every forward step, they took a backward move, loading and firing, as they slowly withdrew. Twenty thousand muskets were being fired at this stage, but, though accuracy of aim was impossible, owing to our labouring hearts, and the jarring and excitement, many bullets found their destined billets on both sides.

After a steady exchange of musketry, which lasted some time, we heard the order: "Fix Bayonets! On the double-quick!" in tones that thrilled us. There was a simultaneous bound forward, each soul doing his best for the emergency. The Federals appeared inclined to await us; but, at this juncture, our men raised a yell, thousands responded to it, and burst out into the wildest yelling it has ever been my lot to hear. It drove all sanity and order from among us. It served the double purpose of relieving pent-up feelings, and transmitting encouragement along the attacking line. I rejoiced in the shouting like the rest. It reminded me that there were about four hundred companies like the Dixie Greys, who shared our feelings. Most of us, engrossed with the musket-work, had forgotten the fact; but the wave after wave of human voices, louder than all other battle-sounds together, penetrated to every sense, and stimulated our energies to the utmost.

"They fly!" was echoed from lip to lip. It accelerated our pace, and filled us with a noble rage. Then I knew what the Berserker passion was! It deluged us with rapture, and transfigured each Southerner into an exulting victor. At such a moment, nothing could have halted us.

Those savage yells, and the sight of thousands of racing figures coming towards them, discomfited the blue-coats; and when we arrived upon the place where they had stood, they had vanished. Then we caught sight of their beautiful array of tents, before which they had made their stand, after being roused from their Sunday-morning sleep, and huddled into line, at hearing their pickets challenge our skirmishers. The half-dressed dead and wounded showed what a surprise our attack had been. We drew up in the enemy's camp, panting and breathing hard. Some precious minutes were thus lost in recovering our breaths, indulging our curiosity, and reforming our line. Signs of a hasty rouse to the battle were abundant. Military equipments, uniform-coats, half-packed knapsacks, bedding, of a new and superior quality, littered the company streets.

Meantime, a series of other camps lay behind the first array of tents. The resistance we had met, though comparatively brief, enabled the brigades in rear of the advance camp to recover from the shock of the surprise; but our delay had not been long enough to give them time to form in proper order of battle. There were wide gaps between their divisions, into which the quick-flowing tide of elated Southerners entered, and compelled them to fall back lest they should be surrounded. Prentiss's brigade, despite their most desperate efforts, were thus hemmed in on all sides, and were made prisoners.

I had a momentary impression that, with the capture of the first camp, the battle was well-nigh over; but, in fact, it was only a brief prologue of the long and exhaustive series of struggles which took place that day.

Continuing our advance, we came in view of the tops of another mass of white tents, and almost at the same time, were met by a furious storm of bullets, poured on us from a long line of blue-coats, whose attitude of assurance proved to us that we should have tough work here. But we were so much heartened by our first success that it would have required a good deal to have halted our advance for long. Their opportunity for making a full impression on us came with terrific suddenness. The world seemed bursting into fragments. Cannon and musket, shell and bullet, lent their several intensities to the distracting uproar. If I had not a fraction of an ear, and an eye inclined towards my Captain and Company, I had been spell-bound by the energies now opposed to us. I likened the cannon, with their deep bass, to the roaring of a great herd of lions; the ripping, cracking musketry, to the incessant yapping of terriers; the windy whisk of shells, and zipping of minie bullets, to the swoop of eagles, and the buzz of angry wasps. All the opposing armies of Grey and Blue fiercely blazed at each other.

After being exposed for a few seconds to this fearful downpour, we heard the order to "Lie down, men, and continue your firing!" Before me was a prostrate tree, about fifteen inches in diameter, with a narrow strip of light between it and the ground. Behind this shelter a dozen of us flung ourselves. The security it appeared to offer restored me to my individuality. We could fight, and think, and observe, better than out in the open. But it was a terrible period! How the cannon bellowed, and their shells plunged and bounded, and flew with screeching hisses over us! Their sharp rending explosions and hurtling fragments made us shrink and cower, despite our utmost efforts to be cool and collected. I marvelled, as I heard the unintermitting patter, snip, thud, and hum of the bullets, how anyone could live under this raining death. I could hear the balls beating a merciless tattoo on the outer surface of the log, pinging it vivaciously as they flew off at a tangent from it, and thudding into something or other, at the rate of a hundred a second. One, here and there, found its way under the log, and buried itself in a comrade's body. One man raised his chest, as if to yawn, and jostled me. I turned to him, and saw that a bullet had gored his whole face, and penetrated into his chest. Another ball struck a man a deadly rap on the head, and he turned on his back and showed his ghastly white face to the sky.

"It is getting too warm, boys!" cried a soldier, and he uttered a vehement curse upon keeping soldiers hugging the ground until every ounce of courage was chilled. He lifted his head a little too high, and a bullet skimmed over the top of the log and hit him fairly in the centre of his forehead, and he fell heavily on his face. But his thought had been instantaneously general; and the officers, with one voice, ordered the charge; and cries of "Forward, forward!" raised us, as with a spring, to our feet, and changed the complexion of our feelings. The pulse of action beat feverishly once more; and, though overhead was crowded with peril, we were unable to give it so much attention as when we lay stretched on the ground. . . .

Our progress was not so continuously rapid as we desired, for the blues were obdurate; but at this moment we were gladdened at the sight of a battery galloping to our assistance. It was time for the nerve-shaking cannon to speak. After two rounds of shell and canister, we felt the pressure on us slightly relaxed; but we were still somewhat sluggish in disposition, though the officers' voices rang out imperiously. Newton Story at this juncture strode forward rapidly with the Dixies' banner, until he was quite sixty yards ahead of the foremost. Finding himself alone, he halted; and turning to us smilingly said, "Why don't you come on, boys? You see there is no danger!" His smile and words acted on us like magic. We raised the yell, and sprang lightly and hopefully towards him. "Let's give them hell, boys!" said one. "Plug them plum-centre, every time!"

It was all very encouraging, for the yelling and shouting were taken up by thousands. "Forward, forward; don't give them breathing time!" was cried. We instinctively obeyed, and soon came in clear view of the blue-coats, who were scornfully unconcerned at first; but, seeing the leaping tide of men coming on at a tremendous pace, their front dissolved, and they fled in double-quick retreat. Again we felt the "glorious joy of heroes." It carried us on exultantly, rejoicing in the spirit which recognises nothing but the prey. We were no longer an army of soldiers, but so many school-boys racing, in which length of legs, wind, and condition tell.

We gained the second line of camps, continued the rush through them, and clean beyond. It was now about ten o'clock. My physical powers were quite exhausted, and, to add to my discomfiture, something struck me on my belt-clasp, and tumbled me headlong to the ground. I could not have been many minutes prostrated before I recovered from the shock of the blow and fall, to find my clasp deeply dented and cracked. My company was not in sight. I was grateful for the rest, and crawled feebly to a tree, and plunging my hand into my haversack, ate ravenously. Within half an hour, feeling renovated, I struck north in the direction which my regiment had taken, over a ground strewn with bodies and the débris of war.

The desperate character of this day's battle was now brought home to my mind in all its awful reality. While in the tumultuous advance, and occupied with a myriad of exciting incidents, it was only at brief intervals that I was conscious of wounds being given and received; but now, in the trail of pursuers and pursued, the ghastly relics appalled every sense. I felt curious as to who the fallen Greys were, and moved to one stretched straight out. It was the body of a stout English Sergeant of a neighbouring company, the members of which hailed principally from the Washita Valley. . . .

Close by him was a young Lieutenant, who, judging by the new gloss on his uniform, must have been some father's darling. A clean bullet-hole through the centre of his forehead had instantly ended his career. A little further were some twenty bodies, lying in various postures, each by its own pool of viscous blood, which emitted a peculiar scent, which was new to me, but which I have since learned is inseparable from a battle-field. Beyond these, a still larger group lay, body overlying body, knees crooked, arms erect, or wide-stretched and rigid according as the last spasm overtook them. The company opposed to them must have shot straight. . . .

It was the first Field of Glory I had seen in my May of life, and the first time that Glory sickened me with its repulsive aspect, and made me suspect it was all a glittering lie. . . . Under a flag of truce, I saw the bearers pick up the dead from the field, and lay them in long rows beside a wide trench; I saw them laid, one by one, close together at the bottom. . . .

I overtook my regiment about one o'clock. . . . The enemy resolutely maintained their ground, and our side was preparing for another assault. The firing was alternately brisk and slack. We lay down, and availed ourselves of trees, logs, and hollows, and annoyed their upstanding ranks; battery pounded battery, and meanwhile we hugged our resting-places closely. Of a sudden, we rose and raced towards the position, and took it by sheer weight and impetuosity. About three o'clock, the battle grew very hot. The enemy appeared to be more concentrated, and immovably sullen. Both sides fired better as they grew more accustomed to the din; but, with assistance from the reserves, we were continually pressing them towards the river Tennessee, without ever retreating an inch.

About this time, the enemy were assisted by the gun-boats, which hurled their enormous projectiles far beyond us; but, though they made great havoc among the trees, and created terror, they did comparatively little damage to those in close touch with the enemy.

The screaming of the big shells, when they first began to sail over our heads, had the effect of reducing our fire; for they were as fascinating as they were distracting. But we became used to them. . . .

As it drew near four o'clock . . . several of our company lagged wearily behind, and the remainder showed, by their drawn faces, the effects of their efforts. Yet, after a short rest, they were able to make splendid spurts. As for myself, I had only one wish, and that was for repose. The long-continued excitement, the successive tautening and relaxing of the nerves, the quenchless thirst, made more intense by the fumes of sulphurous powder, and the caking grime on the lips caused by tearing the paper cartridges, and a ravening hunger, all combined, had reduced me to a walking automaton, and I earnestly wished that night would come. . . .

Finally, about five o'clock, we assaulted and captured a large camp; after driving the enemy well away from it; the front line was as thin as that of a skirmishing body, and we were ordered to retire to the tents. . . .

An hour before dawn, I awoke and, after a hearty replenishment of my vitals with biscuit and molasses, I conceived myself to be fresher than on Sunday morning. While awaiting day-break, I gathered from other early risers their ideas in regard to the events of yesterday. They were under the impression that we had gained a great victory, though we had not, as we had anticipated, reached the Tennessee River. Van Dorn, with his expected reinforcements for us, was not likely to make his appearance for many days yet; and, if General Buell, with his 20,000 troops, had joined the enemy during the night, we had a bad day's work before us. We were short of provisions and ammunition, General Sidney Johnston, our chief Commander, had been killed; but Beauregard was safe and unhurt, and, if Buell was absent, we would win the day.

At daylight I fell in with my Company, but there were only about fifty of the Dixies present. . . . Regiments were hurried into line, but, even to my inexperienced eyes, the troops were in ill-condition for repeating the efforts of Sunday. . . . In consequence of our pickets being driven in on us, we were moved forward in skirmishing order. With my musket on the trail I found myself in active motion, more active than otherwise I would have been, perhaps, because Captain Smith had said, "Now, Mr. Stanley, if you please, step briskly forward!" This singling-out of me wounded my *amour-propre*, and sent me forward like a rocket. In a short time, we met our opponents in the same formation as ourselves, and advancing most resolutely. We threw ourselves behind such trees as were near us, fired, loaded, and darted forward to another shelter. Presently, I found myself in an open grassy space, with no convenient tree or stump near; but, seeing a shallow hollow some twenty paces ahead, I made a dash for it, and plied my musket with haste.

I became so absorbed with some blue figures in front of me, that I did not pay sufficient heed to my companion greys. . . . Seeing my blues in about the same proportion, I assumed that the greys were keeping their position, and never once thought of retreat. However, as, despite our firing, the blues were coming uncomfortably near, I rose from my hollow; but, to my speechless amazement, I found myself a solitary grey, in a line of blue skirmishers! My companions had retreated! The next I heard was, "Down with that gun, Secesh, or I'll drill a hole through you! Drop it, quick!"

Half a dozen of the enemy were covering me at the same instant, and I dropped my weapon, incontinently. Two men sprang at my collar, and marched me, unresisting, into the ranks of the terrible Yankees. *I was a prisoner!*

—*The Autobiography of Sir Henry Morton Stanley*

6. AN ILLINOIS PRIVATE FIGHTS AT THE HORNET'S NEST

The hottest fighting in the Battle of Shiloh—and some of the hottest of the whole war—was at the so-called Hornet's Nest, at the center of the Union line. Here Hulbert, W. H. L. Wallace, and Prentiss held out for hours against a series of savage attacks. In the end Wallace was killed, and only a fragment of his regiments succeeded in fighting their way out.

Leander Stillwell, who here tells us how thrilling it was to see the battle flags of the 36th Indiana come on the field, was an Illinois boy who enlisted at St. Louis in 1862, fought at Shiloh, Corinth, and Vicksburg, and later in Arkansas and Tennessee. His recollections, though written years after the war, are based on letters and diaries.

[April 6, 1862]

We had "turned out" about sunup, answered to roll-call, and had cooked and eaten our breakfast. We had then gone to work, preparing for the regular Sunday morning inspection, which would take place at nine o'clock. The boys were scattered around the company streets and in front of the company parade grounds, engaged in polishing and brightening their muskets, and brushing up and cleaning their shoes, jackets, trousers, and clothing generally.

It was a most beautiful morning. The sun was shining brightly through the trees, and there was not a cloud in the sky. It really seemed like Sunday in the country at home. During week days there was a continual stream of army wagons going to and from the landing, and the clucking of their wheels, the yells and oaths of the drivers, the cracking of whips, mingled with the braying of mules, the neighing of the horses, the commands of the officers engaged in drilling the men, the incessant hum and buzz of the camps, the blare of bugles, and the roll of drums,—all these made up a prodigious volume of sound that lasted from the coming-up to the going-down of the sun. But this morning was strangely still. The wagons were silent, the mules were peacefully munching their hay, and the army teamsters were giving us a rest. I listened with delight to the plaintive, mournful tones of a turtle-dove in the woods close by, while on a dead limb of a tall tree right in the camp a wood-pecker was sounding his "long roll" just as I had heard it beaten by his Northern brothers a thousand times on the trees in the Otter Creek bottom at home.

Suddenly, away off on the right, in the direction of Shiloh church, came a dull, heavy "Pum!" then another, and still another. Every man sprung to his feet as if struck by an electric shock, and we looked inquiringly into one another's faces. "What is that?" asked every one but no one answered.

PLAN OF THE
BATTLE OF SHILOH
April 6th & 7th 1862

Union lines April 6th. morning
Confed.
" " evening
Union " 7th. morning

Those heavy booms then came thicker and faster, and just a few seconds after we heard that first dull, ominous growl off to the southwest, came a low, sullen, continuous roar. There was no mistaking that sound. That was not a squad of pickets emptying their guns on being relieved from duty; it was the continuous roll of thousands of muskets, and told us that a battle was on.

What I have been describing just now occurred during a few seconds only, and with the roar of musketry the long roll began to beat in our camp. Then ensued a scene of desperate haste, the like of which I certainly had never seen before, nor ever saw again. I remember that in the midst of this terrible uproar and confusion, while the boys were buckling on their cartridge boxes, and before even the companies had been formed, a mounted staff officer came galloping wildly down the line from the right. He checked and whirled his horse sharply around right in our company street, the iron-bound hoofs of his steed crashing among the tin plates lying in a little pile where my mess had eaten its breakfast that morning. The horse was flecked with foam and its eyes and nostrils were red as blood. The officer cast one hurried glance around him, and exclaimed: "My God! this regiment not in line yet! They have been fighting on the right over an hour!" And wheeling his horse, he disappeared in the direction of the colonel's tent. . . .

Well, the companies were formed, we marched out on the regimental parade ground, and the regiment was formed in line. The command was given: "Load at will; load!" We had anticipated this, however, as the most of us had instinctively loaded our guns before we had formed company. All this time the roar on the right was getting nearer and louder. Our old colonel rode up close to us, opposite the center of the regimental line, and called out, "Attention, battalion!" We fixed our eyes on him to hear what was coming. It turned out to be the old man's battle harangue.

"Gentlemen," said he, in a voice that every man in the regiment heard, "remember your State, and do your duty today like brave men."

That was all. . . . Immediately after the colonel had given us his brief exhortation, the regiment was marched across the little field I have before mentioned, and we took our place in line of battle, the woods in front of us, and the open field in our rear. We "dressed on" the colors, ordered arms, and stood awaiting the attack. By this time the roar on the right had become terrific. The Rebel army was unfolding its front, and the battle was steadily advancing in our direction. We could begin to see the blue rings of smoke curling upward among the trees off to the right, and the pungent smell of burning gun-powder filled the air. As the roar came travelling down the line from the right it reminded me (only it was a million times louder) of the sweep of a thunder-shower in summer-time over the hard ground of a stubble-field.

And there we stood, in the edge of the woods, so still, waiting for the storm to break on us. . . .

The time we thus stood, waiting the attack, could not have exceeded five minutes. Suddenly, obliquely to our right, there was a long, wavy flash of bright light, then another, and another! It was the sunlight shining on gun barrels and bayonets—and—there they were at last! A long brown line, with muskets at a right shoulder shift, in excellent order, right through the woods they came.

We began firing at once. From one end of the regiment to the other leaped a sheet of red flame, and the roar that went up from the edge of that old field doubtless advised General Prentiss of the fact that the Rebels had at last struck the extreme left of his line. We had fired but two or three rounds when, for some reason,—I never knew what,—we were ordered to fall back across the field, and did so. The whole line, so far as I could see to the right, went back. We halted on the other side of the field, in the edge of the woods, in front of our tents, and again began firing. The Rebels, of course, had moved up and occupied the line we had just abandoned. And here we did our first hard fighting during the day. Our officers said, after the battle was over, that we held this line an hour and ten minutes. How long it was I do not know. I "took no note of time."

We retreated from this position as our officers afterward said, because the troops on our right had given way, and we were flanked. Possibly those boys on our right would give the same excuse for their leaving, and probably truly, too. Still, I think we did not fall back a minute too soon. As I rose from the comfortable log from behind which a bunch of us had been firing, I saw men in gray and brown clothes, with trailed muskets, running through the camp on our right, and I saw something else, too, that sent a chill all through me. It was a kind of flag I had never seen before. It was a gaudy sort of thing, with red bars. It flashed over me in a second that that thing was a Rebel flag. It was not more than sixty yards to the right. The smoke around it was low and dense and kept me from seeing the man who was carrying it, but I plainly saw the banner. It was going fast, with a jerky motion, which told me that the bearer was on a double-quick. About that time we left. We observed no kind of order in leaving; the main thing was to get out of there as quick as we could. I ran down our company street, and in passing the big Sibley tent of our mess I thought of my knapsack with all my traps and belongings, including that precious little packet of letters from home. I said to myself, "I will save my knapsack, anyhow;" but one quick backward glance over my left shoulder made me change my mind, and I went on. I never saw my knapsack or any of its contents afterwards.

Our broken forces halted and re-formed about half a mile to the rear of our camp on the summit of a gentle ridge, covered with thick brush. I recognized our regiment by the little gray pony the old colonel rode, and hurried to my place in the ranks. Standing there with our faces once more to the front, I saw a seemingly endless column of men in blue, marching by the flank, who were filing off to the right through the woods, and I heard our old German adjutant, Cramer, say to the colonel, "Dose are de troops of Sheneral Hurlbut. He is forming a new line dere in de bush." I exclaimed to myself from the bottom of my heart, "Bully for General Hurlbut and the new line in the bush! Maybe we'll whip 'em yet." I shall never forget my feelings about this time. I was astonished at our first retreat in the morning across the field back to our camp, but it occurred to me that maybe that was only "strategy" and all done on purpose; but when we had to give up our camp, and actually turn our backs and run half a mile, it seemed to me that we were forever disgraced, and I kept thinking to myself: "What will they say about this at home?"

I was very dry for a drink, and as we were doing nothing, just then, I slipped out of ranks and ran down to the little hollow in our rear, in search of water. Finding a little pool, I threw myself on the ground and took a copious draught. As I rose to my feet, I observed an officer about a rod above me also quenching his thirst, holding his horse meanwhile by the bridle. As he rose I saw it was our old adjutant. At no other time would I have dared accost him unless in the line of duty, but the situation made me bold.

"Adjutant," I said, "What does this mean—our having to run this way? Ain't we whipped?"

He blew the water from his mustache, and quickly answered in a careless way: "Oh, no; dat is all ride. We yoost fall back to form on the reserve. Sheneral Buell vas now crossing der river mit 50,000 men, and vill be here pooty quick; and Sheneral Lew Vallace is coming up from Crump's Landing mit 15,000 more. Ve vips 'em; ve vips 'em. Go to your gompany." . . . But as the long hours wore on that day, and still Buell and Wallace did not come, my faith in the adjutant's veracity became considerably shaken.

It was at this point that my regiment was detached from Prentiss' division and served with it no more that day. We were sent some distance to the right to support a battery, the name of which I never learned. It was occupying the summit of a slope, and was actively engaged when we reached it. We were put in position of about twenty rods in the rear of the battery, and ordered to lie flat on the ground. The ground sloped gently down in our direction, so that by hugging it close, the rebel shot and shell went over us.

It was here, at about ten o'clock in the morning, that I first saw Grant that day. He was on horseback, of course, accompanied by his staff, and was evidently making a personal examination of his lines. He went by us in a gallop, riding between us and the battery, at the head of his staff. The battery was then hotly engaged; shot and shell were whizzing overhead, and cutting off the limbs of trees, but Grant rode through the storm with perfect indifference, seemingly paying no more attention to the missiles than if they had been paper wads.

We remained in support of this battery until about 2 o'clock in the afternoon. We were then put in motion by the right flank, filed to the left, crossed the left-hand Corinth road; then we were thrown into the line by the command: "By the left flank, march." We crossed a little ravine and up a slope, and relieved a regiment on the left of Hurlbut's line. This line was desperately engaged, and had been at this point, as we afterwards learned, for fully four hours. I remember as we went up the slope and began firing, about the first thing that met my gaze was what out West we would call a "windrow" of dead men in blue; some doubled up face downward, others with their white faces upturned to the sky, brave boys who had been shot to death in "holding the line." Here we stayed until our last cartridge was shot away. We were then relieved by another regiment. We filled our cartridge boxes again and went back to the support of our battery. The boys laid down and talked in low tones. Many of our comrades alive and well an hour ago, we had left dead on that bloody ridge. And still the battle raged. From right to left, everywhere, it was one never-ending, terrible roar, with no prospect of stopping.

Somewhere between 4 and 5 o'clock, as near as I can tell, everything became ominously quiet. Our battery ceased firing; the gunners leaned against the pieces and talked and laughed. Suddenly a staff officer rode up and said something in a low tone to the commander of the battery, then rode to our colonel and said something to him. The battery horses were at once brought up from a ravine in the rear, and the battery limbered up and moved off through the woods diagonally to the left and rear. We were put in motion by the flank and followed it. Everything kept so still, the loudest noise I heard was the clucking of the wheels of the gun-carriages and caissons as they wound through the woods. We emerged from the woods and entered a little old field. I then saw at our right and front lines of men in blue moving in the same direction we were, and it was evident that we were falling back.

All at once, on the right, the left, and from our recent front, came one tremendous roar, and the bullets fell like hail. The lines took the double-quick towards the rear. For awhile the attempt was made to fall back in order, and then everything went to pieces. My heart failed me utterly. I thought the day was lost. A confused mass of men and guns, caissons, army wagons, ambulances, and all the debris of a beaten army surged and crowded along the narrow dirt road to the landing, while that pitiless storm of leaden hail came crashing on us from the rear. It was undoubtedly at this crisis in our affairs that the division of General Prentiss was captured. . . .

It must have been when we were less than half a mile from the landing on our disorderly retreat before mentioned, that we saw standing in line of battle, at ordered arms, extending from both sides of the road until lost to sight in the woods, a long well-ordered line of men in blue. What did that mean? and where had they come from? I was walking by the side of Enoch Wallace, the orderly sergeant of my company. . . . Even he, in the face of this seemingly appalling state of things, had evidently lost heart.

I said to him: "Enoch, what are those men there for?"

He answered in a low tone: "I guess they are put there to hold the Rebels in check till the army can get across the river."

And doubtless that was the thought of every intelligent soldier in our beaten column. And yet it goes to show how little the common soldier knew of the actual situation. We did not know then that this line was the last line of battle of the "Fighting Fourth Division" under General Hurlbut; that on its right was the division of McClernand, the Fort Donelson boys; that on its right, at right angles to it, and, as it were, the refused wing of the army, was glorious old Sherman, hanging on with a bulldog grip to the road across Snake Creek from Crump's Landing by which Lew Wallace was coming with 5,000 men. In other words, we still had an unbroken line confronting the enemy, made up of men who were not yet ready, by any manner of means, to give up that they were whipped. . . .

Well, we filed through Hurlbut's line, halted, re-formed, and faced to the front once more. We were put in place a short distance in the rear of Hurlbut, as a support to some heavy guns. It must have been about five o'clock now. Suddenly, on the extreme left, and just a little above the landing, came a deafening explosion that fairly shook the ground beneath our feet, followed by others in quick and regular succession. The look of wonder and inquiry that the soldiers' faces wore for a moment disappeared for one of joy and exultation as it flashed across our minds that the gunboats had at last joined hands in the dance, and were pitching big twenty-pound Parrott shells up the ravine in front of Hurlbut, to the terror and discomfiture of our adversaries.

The last place my regiment assumed was close to the road coming up from the landing. As we were lying there I heard the strains of martial music and saw a body of men marching by the flank up the road. I slipped out of ranks and walked out to the side of the road to see what troops they were. Their band was playing "Dixie's Land," and playing it well. The men were marching at a quick step, carrying their guns, cartridge-boxes, haversacks, canteens, and blanket-rolls. I saw that they had not been in the fight, for there was no powder-smoke on their faces. "What regiment is this?" I asked of a young sergeant marching on the flank. Back came the answer in a quick, cheery tone. "The 36th Indiana, the advance guard of Buell's army."

I did not, on hearing this, throw my cap into the air and yell. That would have given those Indiana fellows a chance to chaff and guy me, and possibly make sarcastic remarks, which I did not care to provoke. I gave one big, gasping swallow and stood still, but the blood thumped in the veins of my throat and my heart fairly pounded against my little infantry jacket in the joyous rapture of this glorious intelligence. Soldiers need not be told of the thrill of unspeakable exultation they have all felt at the sight of armed friends in danger's darkest hour. Speaking for myself alone, I can only say, in the most heart-felt sincerity, that in all my obscure military career, never to me was the sight of reinforcing legions so precious and so welcome as on that Sunday evening when the rays of the descending sun were flashed back from the bayonets of Buell's advance column as it deployed on the bluffs of Pittsburg Landing.

—STILLWELL, *The Story of a Common Soldier of Army Life in the Civil War*

7. ROSECRANS WHIPS VAN DORN AT CORINTH

After Shiloh Halleck took personal command of the vast Federal army of over 100,000 men. Instead of advancing boldly on the exhausted army of Beauregard—who had temporarily succeeded Johnston—he inched forward in a series of "siege" operations, reaching Corinth on May 30. Then he proceeded to break up his own army, sending Buell off toward Chattanooga—

which he did not reach—and detaching another 20,000 men to guard railroad communications. By this imbecility he reduced his grand army to less than 40,000, and the initiative passed to Bragg, who had superseded Beauregard. Bragg hurried off to Chattanooga, leaving Van Dorn and Price with about 40,000 men to oppose Grant, who commanded an equal number. Grant, however, was expected to protect the whole of western Tennessee: he had 7,000 men at Memphis, 12,000 at Bolivar, 6,000 at Jackson, and 23,000 at Corinth, under Rosecrans. It was this latter force that Van Dorn planned to attack; his hope was to turn the whole Union flank all the way up to Fort Donelson.

The battle was joined on October 3; by sunset the Confederates had driven the Federals into the town of Corinth; the next morning, however, the Federals counterattacked and threw Van Dorn back in confusion. This minor battle had some important consequences. It saved the Federal line from Memphis to Corinth; it made Rosecrans' reputation; and it persuaded President Davis to supplant Van Dorn by General Pemberton, who later lost Vicksburg.

Oscar Jackson, who here tells the story, was a twenty-two-year-old captain of the 63rd Ohio Volunteers who later marched to the sea with Sherman; after the war he had a minor political career in Pennsylvania.

O N the first appearance of dawn, the rebels threw out a cloud of skirmishers that annoyed us seriously, as every few minutes someone was hit and this was annoying. Details were made from the line to go out and drive them off. Five were called for from my company. I asked for volunteers and the whole company offered to go on this specially dangerous detail. I took the five I thought had spoken first. They started out and had a regular Indian fight, giving the enemy their fill of bushwhacking, and driving them back to their main force. I was out to see them and shot a time or two, or more, at a "butternut" who returned the fire, the balls going "zip" quite close to my ear. . . .

About ten o'clock the rebels began pouring out of the timber and forming storming columns. All the firing ceased and everything was silent as the grave. They formed one column of perhaps two thousand men in plain view, then another, and crowding out of the woods another, and so on. I thought they would never stop coming out of the timber. While they were forming, the men were considerable distance from us but in plain sight and as soon as they were ready they started at us with a firm, slow, steady step.

> "Firm paced and slow a fearful front they form,
>   Still as the breeze but dreadful as the storm."

So it seemed to us. In my campaigning I had never seen anything so hard to stand as that slow, steady tramp. Not a sound was heard but they looked as if they intended to walk over us. I afterwards stood a bayonet charge when the enemy came at us on the double-quick with a yell and it was not so trying on the nerves as that steady, solemn advance.

I could see that my men were affected by it. They were in line and I knew that they would stand fire but this was a strong test. I noticed one man examining his gun to see if it was clean, another to see if his was primed right; a third would stand a while on one foot then on the other; whilst others were pulling at their blouses, feeling if their cartridge boxes or cap-pouches were all right, and so on, but all the time steadily watching the advancing foe. It is customary in engagements to have some motto or battle cry given by some commander, such as "Fire low," "Stick to your company," "Remember some battle," (naming it). To draw the attention of my company while the charge was advancing I said: "Boys, I guess we are going to have a fight." This is always a doubtful question to an old soldier until he sees it, but they all believed it this time. "I have two things I want you to remember today. One is, we own all the ground behind us. The enemy may go over us but all the rebels yonder can't drive Company H back. The other is, if the butternuts come close enough, remember you have good bayonets on your rifles and use them." And well did they remember what I said.

When the enemy had advanced about one-third of the distance toward us, we got orders to lie down, and then, when the enemy got close enough, we were to fire by companies. The unevenness of the ground now screened us from their view and the second line of infantry, some distance to the rear, appeared to the rebels to be the first they would have to fight, and when they came upon us it was a surprise to them. My company being on the left of the regiment, and our regiment on the left of the brigade, I was among the nearest to the enemy.

The enemy had to come over a bluffish bank a few yards in front of me and as soon as I saw their heads, still coming slowly, I jumped up and said: "Company H, get up." The column was then in full view and only about thirty yards distant. Captain Smith of our regiment thought only about twenty-five yards. Just in front of me was a bush three or four feet high with sear leaves on it. Hitting this with my sword, I said: "Boys, give them a volley just over this. Ready! aim! (and jumping around my company to get from in front of their guns) fire!" In a few seconds the fire was continued along the whole line.

It seems to me that the fire of my company had cut down the head of the column that struck us as deep back as my company was long. As the smoke cleared away, there was apparently ten yards square of a mass of struggling bodies and butternut clothes. Their column appeared to reel like a rope shaken at the end. I had heard this idea advanced and here I saw it plainly. The enemy were stopped, but deploying their column, returned the fire, and, a fine thing for us, fired too low, striking the ground, knocking the dirt and chips all over us, wounding a very few, not one in my company. We got ahead of them with the next volley which we delivered right in their faces. (The guns were all muzzle-loading). At this close distance we fought for perhaps five minutes, when the enemy gave back in confusion. The leafy bush I struck with my sword, on giving the first command to fire, was stripped almost clean. The boys made a fine volley. The enemy came at us in fine order, moving handsomely, but in retreating, every fellow went as suited him, and it appeared to suit all to go fast.

The column that fought us was led by General Rodgers of Texas who fell dead but a few feet from me. When I saw the enemy retreating in such confusion, I remarked to a comrade that we would not have to fight those men any more today, as I thought it would be impossible to rally them again, but strange to say, in some forty minutes I saw them reformed and coming at us again with that slow, steady step, but they made a change in their tactics, for as they came over the bank, or rather out of ravine in front of us, they came at us with a yell on the double-quick. Our men stood firm with loaded guns and fixed bayonets and gave them a volley that threw them somewhat into confusion, slaughtering them fearfully, but pressing on, and firing at us rapidly, they dashed themselves against us like water against a rock and were a second time repulsed and gave back.

Colonel Sprague had all the while been in the thickest of the fight. I think I see him now rush to where the line wavered and with sabre sweeping the air, exclaim, "What does this mean, men? Company ——, close up!" He then spoke and said, "Men, it is your time to cheer now," and with a hearty good will did they respond.

Some distance to the left and front of me were a pair of parrot guns, that we called Battery Robinett in distinction from the small fort of the same name a short distance in the rear of them. Captain Brown and his Company A supported these guns immediately, that is, were between me and them. He was almost annihilated by the first two charges and between me and the guns was clear ground.

Colonel Sprague gave me this order: "Captain Jackson, move your company up to those guns and hold them."

Saluting, I replied, "I will do it," and turning to my command I added, "Left face, forward march." It was like moving into dead men's shoes, for I had seen one company carried away from there on litters, but without a moment's hesitation we moved up.

I had scarce posted my men in rear of the guns when I saw that the enemy were again coming at us, and that a detachment was moving from the main column toward my guns. I knew what they wanted and, as the guns were not for close action, I moved my men in front of them and waited their approach. On they came, formed in their favorite manner, namely, in a solid square or column. I now had but twenty-four men in line formed in two ranks, but even the detachment of the enemy which veered off towards me were formed in a square. As I afterwards learned, they were dismounted Texan rangers and very few of their guns had bayonets. I am told Colonel Sprague asked permission to move the regiment up to my support, but permission was denied.

The rebel officer in command of the Texans was marching at the left of his men and when he came nigh us he turned and walked backwards and said to his men, "Boys, when you charge, give a good yell." I heard his command distinctly and it almost made the hair stand up on my head. The next instant the Texans began yelling like savages and rushed at us without firing. The ground in front of us was about like that where we stood previously and at the proper moment I gave them a volley that halted them, cutting down their entire front. I saw they meant to overwhelm us and drive us from the guns, as they out-numbered us. I estimated their force at one hundred men. My men began loading at will and the Texan, by a dexterous movement, was putting his bayonets to the front, doing the thing among and literally over his dead and wounded comrades. I saw that he would strike us before we could get another volley at them and I gave the command, "Don't load, boys; they are too close on you; let them have the bayonet." In a second every bayonet was brought down to a charge. I have never lived through moments of such intense excitement. Events happened quicker than I can record them. The rebels rushed toward us and just before they struck us, I yelled, "Charge!" in order to give my men momentum to meet the shock. My men sprang at the enemy as one man. It reminded me of a man cutting heavy grain, striking at a thick place. The hostile guns clashed. For an instant we parried like boxers, when the enemy gave back, firing at us now for the first [time] as they retired.

Never have I felt so proud of anything as I was of my men. I thought that no such company was in that army. Hand to hand we fought them. A few of the enemy rushed around my left to my rear to get at the guns and two rebels were killed in rear of my line in single-handed combat. Corporal Selby, then a private, killed a rebel with his bayonet there, which is a remarkable thing in a battle and was spoken of in the official report. Selby called on the Texan to surrender, but he replied, "We'll see who surrenders," and made a lunge at Selby with his bayonet. Selby's skill in the bayonet exercise, in which they had been well drilled, gave him the advantage and he parried the stroke and plunged his own bayonet through the body of the Texan, who fell dead with Selby's bayonet sticking in his body. Thomas Lady also killed a man with his bayonet. Lady was mortally wounded. During this time, terrible fighting was being done along the whole line.

My company was fearfully cut up in this last charge. I had but eleven men standing when I thought the enemy was repulsed, but just as they went into the ravine, one of the rebels turned toward us and fired. I was at the head of my command and a little in front. I saw the fire was aimed at me and tried to avoid it but fate willed otherwise and I fell right backwards, indeed "with my back to the field and my feet to the foe." I was struck in the face. I felt as if I had been hit with a piece of timber, so terrible was the concussion and a stunning pain went through my head. I thought I was killed. It was my impression that I would never rise, but I was not alarmed or distressd by the thought that I was dying; it seemed a matter of indifference to me. In a little while I tried to rise and found I could do so. I got up and tried to walk to the rear. There was no one wounded in my company after I fell. Just at that time our supports charged and pursued the retreating foe, and the battle closed. The victory was ours.

When I got on my feet I walked to the rear a few yards till I came to the trunk of a fallen tree. I was too weak to cross it, but I observed Private Frank Ingmire standing on the tree trunk and I said "Ingmire, help me over."

"Yes," he replied, "let me help you across," and gave me his left hand.

I then noticed that his right arm was dangling at his side, his hand dripping blood. His wrist had been shattered by a ball. He helped me over the log and I took hold of his left arm with both my hands to support myself, saying, "Ingmire, don't leave me," but I only walked a short distance till I felt my hands slipping off his arm, my knees doubling under me, and I sank to the ground unconscious, and knew nothing more until I came to, in the field hospital two days later.

—JACKSON, *The Colonel's Diary*

8. THE ORPHAN BRIGADE IS SHATTERED
AT STONES RIVER

After Shiloh Braxton Bragg was appointed to command the Army of Tennessee. When Halleck detached Buell for an advance on Chattanooga, Bragg took some 40,000 men and got there before him. From September through December 1862 there was confused marching and countermarching through central Kentucky and Tennessee. One detachment of Bragg's army, under Kirby Smith, reached Frankfort, Kentucky, and inaugurated a secession government in that state. Buell advanced on the Confederates there, and on October 8 struck them at Perryville; the battle was a draw but the Confederates retired into East Tennessee and then to Murfreesboro, on the Stones River, not far from Nashville. Meantime Rosecrans had supplanted Buell in command of the newly organized Army of the Cumberland. He built up supplies at Nashville and, when he was ready, moved out to fight Bragg.

The two armies met December 31, outside Murfreesboro, and one of the most bitterly contested battles of the war ensued. It was, in a sense, another Shiloh. Bragg got the jump on Rosecrans, smashed his right flank, and rolled him up against Stones River. Just as disaster threatened the whole Federal army Thomas turned his artillery on the enemy and held him in check. The next day the Confederates renewed the battle, but the most desperate effort came on the third day, January 2, when the misguided Bragg ordered Breckinridge to attack the Union left.

Lieutenant L. D. Young of the 4th Kentucky "Orphan Brigade" tells the story of the futile attack.

CAPTAIN Bramblett with two of his lieutenants, myself one of them, crawled through the weeds a distance of several hundred yards to a prominent point of observation from which through his field glass and even the naked eye we could see the enemy's concentrated forces near and above the lower ford on the opposite side of the river, his artillery being thrown forward and nearest to the river. His artillery appeared to be close together and covering quite a space of ground; we could not tell how many guns, but there was quite a number. The infantry was seemingly in large force and extended farther down toward the ford.

Captain Bramblett was a man of no mean order of military genius and information, and after looking at, and studying the situation in silence for some minutes, he said to us boys, "that he believed Rosecrans was setting a trap for Bragg." Continuing, he said, "If he means to attack us on this side, why does he not reinforce on this side? Why concentrate so much artillery on the bluff yonder? He must be expecting us to attack that force yonder, pointing to Beatty's position on the hill North of us, and if we do, he will use that artillery on us as we move to the attack." At another time during the afternoon I heard him while discussing the situation with other officers of the regiment use substantially the same argument. I accompanied Captain Bramblett to General Breckinridge's headquarters and heard him make substantially in detail a report containing the facts above recited. . . .

General Breckinridge, to thoroughly and unmistakably understand the situation and satisfy himself, in company with one or two of his staff examined the situation as best he could and I presume reached the same conclusion, and when he (Breckinridge) repaired to Bragg's headquarters and vouchsafed this information and suggested the presumptive plan of the enemy, Bragg said: "Sir, my information is different. I have given the order to attack the enemy in your front and expect it to be obeyed."

What was General Breckinridge to do but attempt to carry out his orders, though in carrying out this unwise and ill-conceived order it should cost in one hour and ten minutes 1,700 of as brave and chivalrous soldiers as the world ever saw. What a terrible blunder, what a bloody and useless sacrifice! . . .

How was this wicked and useless sacrifice brought about? "That subordinate must always obey his superior"—is the military law. In furtherance of Bragg's order we were assembled about three o'clock on the afternoon of January 2, 1863 (Friday, a day of ill luck) in a line North of and to the right of Swain's hill, confronting Beatty's and Growes' brigades, with a battery or two of artillery as support. They being intended for the bait that had been thrown across the river at the lower ford, and now occupied an eminence some three-quarters of a mile to the right-front of the Orphan's position on Swain's hill.

This was the force, small as it was that Bragg was so anxious to dislodge. Between the attacking line and federal position was a considerable scope of open ground, fields and pastures, with here and there a clump of bushes or briars, but the entire space was in full view of and covered by the enemy's batteries to the left of the line on the opposite side of the river previously referred to. If the reader will only carry these positions in his eye, he can readily discover the jaws of the trap in this murderous scheme.

A more imposing and thoroughly disciplined line of soldiers never moved to the attack of an enemy than responded to the signal gun stationed immediately in our rear, which was fired exactly at four o'clock. Every man vieing with his fellowman, in steadiness of step and correct alignment, with the officers giving low and cautionary commands, many knowing that it was their last hour on earth, but without hesitating moved forward to their inevitable doom and defeat. We had gotten only fairly started, when the great jaws of the trap on the bluff from the opposite side of the river were sprung, and bursting shells that completely drowned the voice of man were plunging and tearing through our columns, ploughing up the earth at our feet in front and behind, everywhere. But with steadiness of step we moved on. Two companies of the Fourth regiment, my own and adjoining company, encountered a pond, and with a dexterous movement known to the skilled officer and soldier was cleared in a manner that was perfectly charming, obliquing to the right and left into line as soon as passed.

By reason of the shorter line held by the enemy, our line, which was much longer and the colors of each of our battalions being directed against this shorter line, caused our lines to interlap, making it necessary, in order to prevent confusion and crowding, that some of the regiments halt, until the others had passed forward out of the way. When thus halted they would lie down in order to shield themselves from the enemy infantry fire in front, who had by this time opened a lively fusillade from behind their temporary works.

While lying on the ground momentarily . . . a shell exploded right in the middle of the company, almost literally tearing it to pieces. When I recovered from the shock the sight I witnessed was appalling. Some eighteen or twenty men hurled in every direction, including my dear friend, Lieut. George Burnley of Frankfort. But these circumstances were occurring every minute now while the battle was raging all around and about us. Men moved intuitively—the voice being silenced by the whizzing and bursting shells. On we moved, Beatty's and Growes' lines giving way seemingly to allow the jaws of the trap to press with more and ever increasing vigor upon its unfortunate and discomfited victims. But, on we moved, until the survivors of the decoy had passed the river and over the lines stationed on the other side of the river, when their new line of infantry opened on our confused and disordered columns another destructive and ruinous fire.

Coupled with this condition and correlative to it, a battery of Growes and a part of their infantry had been cut off from the ford and seeing our confused condition, rallied, reformed and opened fire on our advanced right now along the river bank. Confronted in front by their infantry, with the river intervening; swept by their artillery from the left and now attacked by both infantry and artillery by an oblique fire from the right, we found ourselves in a helpless condition, from which it looked like an impossibility to escape; and but for the fact that two or three batteries had been ordered into position to check the threatened advance of the enemy and thereby distract their attention, we doubtless would have fared still worse.

We rallied some distance to the right of where we started and found that many, very many, of our noblest, truest and best had fallen. Some of them were left on the field, among whom was my military preceptor, advisor and dear friend, Captain Bramblett, who fell into the hands of the enemy and who died a few days after in Nashville. I shall never forget our parting, a moment or two before he received his wound—never forget the last quick glance and the circumstances that called it forth. He was a splendid soldier and his loss grieved me very much. Many another gallant Kentuckian, some of our finest line and field officers, were left on the field, a sacrifice to stupidity and revenge. Thirty-seven per cent in one hour and ten minutes—some say one hour—was the frightful summary. Among the first of these was the gallant and illustrious Hanson, whose coolness and bearing was unsurpassed and whose loss was irreparable. He with Breckinridge, understood and was fully sensible of—as indicated by the very seriousness of his countenance—the unwisdom of this move and as shown in their protest to Bragg. What a pity that a strict observance of military rule compelled it to be obeyed against his mature military mind and judgment, causing the loss of such a magnificent soldier and gentleman—uselessly and foolishly.

Comtemplating this awful sacrifice, as he rode by the dead and dying in the rear of our lines, General Breckinridge, with tears falling from his eyes, was heard to say in tones of anguish, "My poor Orphans! My poor Orphans!" little thinking that he was dedicating to them a name that will live throughout the annals of time and crown the history of that dear little band with everlasting immortality.

—YOUNG, *Reminiscences of a Soldier in the Orphan Brigade*

XI

The Struggle for Missouri and the West

THE *war in the Trans-Mississippi West has been unjustly neglected by historians. The outcome of the war was decided, to be sure, in the East—at Gettysburg and Vicksburg, at Chattanooga and Atlanta and the Wilderness—yet the fighting in the West profoundly influenced the course of these Eastern campaigns, and some of these campaigns, in turn, were directed to the severance of the Confederacy along the Mississippi River.*

It was Missouri that was crucial. Had that state gone with the Confederacy the consequences would have been grave and might have been decisive. It outflanked Illinois and the Northwest; controlled the Mississippi; conditioned the fighting in Kentucky and Tennessee. And there was, from the beginning, a likely chance that Missouri would throw in its lot with the Confederacy, or yield to Confederate invasion. It was a slave state; a substantial part of its population was of Southern origin; its government was in the hands of Confederate sympathizers. Fortunately northern Missouri and the large German population were pro-Union; fortunately, too, the powerful Blair family was unalterably opposed to secession.

But at the beginning it was touch and go, and indeed it remained that until the war was well under way. Prompt action saved the St. Louis arsenal for the Union; prompt action, too, prevented Governor Jackson from using Camp Jackson as a rallying center for a secession movement. Meantime the Confederate forces grew apace, and in the fighting of the first year the Confederates had the best of it. Not until the Battle of Pea Ridge, in Arkansas, was Missouri safe for the Union, and even after that Sterling Price and Ben McCulloch, the bold Confederate leaders, tried one invasion after another. Even as late as summer of 1864 there was a major battle along the Missouri-Kansas boundary line at Westport, the "Gettysburg of the West." Meantime Missouri was the scene of the most desperate guerrilla and partisan fighting of the war: no other theater of the war could confess anything like the Lawrence and Baxter Springs massacres.

Much of the fighting in Arkansas was part of the Missouri campaign, and Arkansas, too, saw bitter guerrilla warfare. The campaigns along the Red River were part of the larger campaign for the control of the Mississippi. As the Federals closed both the lower and the upper portions of the Mississippi, the only major route from the West to the eastern Confederacy was the Red River, and the Confederate forces in Louisiana threatened New Orleans,

Baton Rouge, and even the Vicksburg expedition, from the Red River valley. There was, as we shall see, a good deal of marching and some fighting in the Bayou Teche country west of New Orleans.

Even the Far West boasted its campaigns. The Confederacy obtained substantial supplies through Mexico, and in the fall and winter of 1863 Banks had occupied Brownsville at the mouth of the Rio Grande and a number of harbors along the coast to Corpus Christi. In distant New Mexico, too, there was a campaign which ended disastrously for Confederate arms.

In a sense all the miscellaneous fighting over this vast area constitutes one great campaign for the control of the West and of the supplies and men that might come from the West to the East. At the risk therefore of cutting across or violating chronology, we present the various segments of the Trans-Mississippi fighting geographically rather than chronologically.

1. HOW THE ARMS WERE TAKEN FROM THE ST. LOUIS ARSENAL

Nowhere was opinion more sharply—or evenly—divided than in Missouri; Governor Jackson went so far as to characterize Lincoln's call for troops as "illegal, unconstitutional, revolutionary, inhuman and diabolical." Although a state convention had voted against secession, Southern sympathizers planned to swing the state into the Confederacy. The first step in this plan was to seize the Federal arsenal at St. Louis, with 60,000 stand of arms. To forestall this plan Governor Yates of Illinois and Nathaniel Lyon, hero of the Union cause in Missouri, removed the arms to Illinois.

Here is the story of that early and decisive gambit in the chess game of Missouri politics and war.

CAPTAIN James H. Stokes, of Chicago, late of the regular army, volunteered to undertake the perilous mission, and Governor Yates placed in his hands the requisition of the Secretary of War for 10,000 muskets. Captain Stokes went to St. Louis, and made his way as rapidly as possible to the arsenal. He found it surrounded by an immense mob, and the postern gates all closed. His utmost efforts to penetrate the crowd were for a long time unavailing. The requisition was shown. Captain Lyon doubted the possibility of executing it. He said the arsenal was surrounded by a thousand spies, and every movement was watched and reported to the headquarters of the Secessionists, who could throw an overpowering force upon them at any moment. Captain Stokes represented that every hour's delay was rendering the capture of the arsenal more certain, and the arms must be moved to Illinois now or never. Major Callender agreed with him, and told him to take them at his own time and in his own way. This was Wednesday night, 24th April (1861).

Captain Stokes had a spy in the camp, whom he met at intervals in a certain place in the city. On Thursday, he received information that Gov. Jackson had ordered two thousand armed men from Jefferson city, whose movements could only contemplate a seizure of the arsenal, by occupying the heights around it, and planting batteries thereon. The job would have been an easy one. They had already planted one battery on the St. Louis levee, and another at Powder Point, a short distance below the arsenal. Capt. Stokes immediately telegraphed to Alton to have the steamer *City of Alton* drop down to the arsenal landing about midnight. He then returned to the arsenal, and commenced moving the boxes of guns, weighing some three hundred pounds each, down to the lower floor.

About 700 men were employed in the work. He then took 500 Kentucky flint-lock muskets, which had been sent there to be altered, and sent them to be placed on a steamer as a blind to cover his real movements. The Secessionists nabbed them at once, and raised a perfect Bedlam over the capture. A large portion of the outside crowd left the arsenal when this movement was executed; and Capt. Lyon took the remainder, who were lying around as spies, and locked them up in the guard-house. About 11 o'clock the steamer *City of Alton* came alongside, planks were shoved out from the windows to the main deck, and the boxes slid down. When the 10,000 were safely on board, Capt. Stokes went to Capt. Lyon and Major Callender, and urged them, by the most pressing appeals, to let him empty the arsenal. They told him to go ahead and take whatever he wanted. Accordingly, he took 10,000 more muskets, 500 new rifle carbines, 500 revolvers, 110,000 musket cartridges, to say nothing of the cannon and a large quantity of miscellaneous accoutrements, leaving only 7,000 muskets in the arsenal to arm the St. Louis volunteers.

When the whole were on board, about 2 o'clock on Friday morning the order was given by the captain of the steamer to cast off. Judge of the consternation of all hands when it was found that she would not move. The arms had been piled in great quantities around the engines to protect them against the battery on the levee, and the great weight had fastened the bows of the boat firmly on a rock, which was tearing a hole through the bottom at every turn of the wheels. A man of less nerve than Capt. Stokes would have gone crazy on the spot. He called the arsenal men on board, and commenced moving the boxes to the stern.

Fortunately, when about two hundred boxes had been shifted, the boat fell away from the shore, and floated in deep water. "Which way?" said Captain Mitchell, of the steamer. "Straight to Alton, in the regular channel," replied Captain Stokes. "What if we are attacked?" said Captain Mitchell. "Then we will fight," said Captain Stokes. "What if we are overpowered?" said Captain Mitchell. "Run her to the deepest part of the river, and sink her," replied Captain Stokes. "I'll do it," was the heroic answer of Capt. Mitchell; and away they went past the secession battery, past the entire St. Louis levee, and on to Alton, in the regular channel, where they arrived at five o'clock in the morning.

When the boat touched the landing, Capt. Stokes, fearing pursuit by some two or three of the Secession military companies by which the city of St. Louis is disgraced, ran to the market-house and rang the fire-bell. The citi-

Pickets Trading Tobacco and Coffee Across the Rappahannock

J. O. Casler

Edwin Forbes

Checking Confederate Advance at Shiloh

zens came flocking pell-mell to the river, in all sorts of habiliments. Capt. Stokes informed them of the situation of things, and pointed out the freight cars. Instantly, men, women, and children boarded the steamer, seized the freight, and clambered up the levees to the cars. Rich and poor tugged together with might and main for two hours, when the cargo was all deposited in the cars, and the train moved off, amid their enthusiastic cheers, for Springfield.

—*Chicago Tribune*, April 29, 1861

2. COTTON IS KING AT THE BATTLE OF LEXINGTON

On June 12, 1861, Governor Jackson abandoned his pretense of neutrality and declared openly for the Confederacy, calling for 50,000 volunteers to defend the state against the Federal invaders. Not that many were forthcoming, but Sterling Price gathered an army of perhaps 10,000, and was shortly reinforced from Arkansas by Ben McCulloch, a famous Texas Ranger. Nathaniel Lyon moved speedily to get control of the state capital, Jefferson City, then sent General Franz Sigel after Price. The two small armies met at Carthage, on the edge of the Ozarks, and Sigel was roundly beaten. Lyon himself came up to take command, followed the Confederates to Wilson's Creek, and—though outnumbered almost two to one—attacked them, August 10, 1861. The gallant Lyon was killed, and his beaten army fell back on Rolla, which had direct railroad connections with St. Louis. The Confederates marched north to the Missouri, by-passed Jefferson City, and attacked a small force of Federals at Lexington. It was another Confederate victory. After that the incompetent Frémont was removed from command in the West, and the Union organized its strength to drive the Confederates out of Missouri.

This story of the Battle of Lexington is told by an Englishman, Samuel P. Day, correspondent for the London Morning Herald.

THE Union forces, under Colonel Mulligan . . . had for some time previous occupied the town of Lexington, around which they had erected defences. On the night of the 11th September [1861] the attack was initiated by an advance party of Confederate troops, who appeared in front of the Federal entrenchments, when a sharp action took place. Four cannons were planted, so as to command the different points, including the entire semi-circle of the Federal position, and a falling fire was kept up in addition to an incessant discharge of musketry. The Confederates rendered themselves almost invisible, being concealed in the adjacent corn-fields and woods; so the attacked party had no other means of doing execution among them, than by firing in the neighbourhood of the localities designated by the cannon smoke, and now and again taking aim at the sharp-shooters who had ventured out of ambush. . . .

On the morning of Wednesday the 17th, the Confederates, under General Price, opened fire from all their batteries, and kept pouring in a shower of iron hail the entire day upon the enemy's entrenchments; while the practice of the sharp-shooters was excellent, as has been acknowledged by the enemy himself. Some time after the siege had commenced, with a praiseworthy humanity General Price sent a flag of truce to Colonel Mulligan, demanding a surrender, and informing him, that as the force he commanded was so superior as to render it useless for him to contend, he had no desire to fight for the sake of shedding blood. He proposed, moreover, to allow the Federal forces to march out of the town under arms, taking their property and baggage with them. All that General Price required was the position; and, this yielded, General Mulligan was free to go with his command wherever he pleased. Half-way between the lines both Generals met, attended by their respective Staff-officers. General Mulligan was obstinate, and would not accept the liberal proposition made to him. They separated, however, in a seemingly friendly manner, and with mutual expressions of regret that the fortunes of war had made their interest so antagonistic and deadly.

During the afternoon of the 18th a hand-to-hand conflict took place, which was but of short duration, when the Confederate troops attacked and carried a portion of the works. Advancing in a strong and steady line up a slope, after slight opposition they caused the Montgomery Guards to break from their entrenchments and retire in disorder before their approach. A murderous volley was then poured into the dispersed ranks, inflicting the heaviest loss that had been experienced since the opening of the siege. Colonel Mulligan endeavoured to rally his men for a charge, but few of them responded to his call.

Hot shot and shell kept pouring into the town, one ball having fired the College building, in which the Federal provisions had been collected. Nevertheless, the troops succeeded in saving the stores and extinguishing the conflagration. From eight o'clock until midnight was occupied by both belligerents in burying their dead. When the truce had expired, the cannonade opened again with additional vigour on the Confederate side, which the enemy did not reply to until the morning. So soon as daybreak had revealed localities sufficiently to afford correct aim, the cannonading became more furious still. The firing on both sides was continuous and furious, and nothing could be heard save the heavy boom of artillery and the sharp clank of musketry.

The ingenuity of the Southerners was conspicuously manifested by the invention of a moving breast-work of cotton bales, which received the Federal shot harmlessly, and completely protected the troops from injury. The effect created by this novel appliance of warfare may be estimated by the following account furnished by the Correspondent of a Northern journal:—

"At this juncture our men discovered, with no little dismay, an engine of war, which was being brought to bear upon them, threatening the very consequences which they dreaded most—a safe approach for the enemy, and an ultimate charge in force over the entrenchments. The rebels presented a strong breast-work of hemp-bales, which appeared like a moving barrier, impenetrable to bullets or cannon shot, and swarming with men in the rear. It was about twenty rods in length, and the height of two bales of hemp. The bales were placed with the ends facing our fortifications, affording a thickness of about six feet. This immense breast-work commenced moving forward, not by detachments or singly, but in one vast body, unbroken and steady, as though it slid along the ground at its own volition. It advanced steadily over the smooth surface, parting to pass trees, and closing up again, as impenetrable as a rock. Behind it were hundreds of men pushing and urging with levers, while others held the bales steadily to their places, and others still, whose numbers were almost indefinite, firing between the crevices and over the top at our soldiers.

"Our men looked at the moving monster in astonishment. It lay like a large serpent, winding over the hills and hollows, apparently motionless, yet moving broadside on, to envelop and destroy them in its vast folds. In vain the cannon were turned upon it. The heavy bales absorbed the shot harmlessly, or quietly resumed the positions from which they were displaced, seemingly moving without hands, but in reality controlled by strong arms, which were unseen. In vain the musket bullets rained upon it in unremitting showers. The thousands that it concealed were safe from such puny assaults, and slowly gliding along, they waited with eagerness the time when their position should warrant them in bursting through its walls and storming up to the intrenchments. Our brave soldiers could only watch it with keen anxiety, and wait for the fearful result."

After having been desperately attacked upon various sides, and finding it useless to resist, about four o'clock on the afternoon of Wednesday, Major Becker, who commanded the Home Guards, crawled out to an advanced breast-work, and ran up a white flag.

The Home Guards deserted their trenches at the order of Major Becker, and rushed into the inner fortification, where they again raised the white flag, and kept it flying. Immediately upon this the Confederates ceased firing, and the garrison was thrown into the greatest confusion. Word was passed around that a surrender had been made, and the men left their entrenchments in disorder to ascertain the truth. Consternation reigned in all directions—Colonel Mulligan, it is said, being on the opposite side, and nobody present to assume control. Word was sent to him, and he ordered the flag down; but the Captains, who by this time realized their true position, and saw nothing but death or surrender before them, implored him to save the men.

Meanwhile the hemp breast-works had moved up under cover of the general confusion, until they had got within a few yards of the Federal entrenchments. The Confederate forces advanced, and everything indicated that the moment had arrived when the crowning assault was to be attempted. In this emergency Colonel Mulligan ordered his men to lay down their arms, and an officer was dispatched to General Price with a flag of truce.

—DAY, *Down South*

3. GUERRILLA WARFARE IN MISSOURI

This long succession of Confederate victories heartened Southern sympa-
thizers not only in Missouri but in Kansas and Arkansas as well. Guerrilla
bands harried Union sympathizers everywhere, and some of them were not
too careful whom they attacked; from Kansas came the Jay Hawkers—a term
applied indiscriminately to Unionists and Confederates—to join in the civil
war.

We have here two accounts of guerrilla warfare after Wilson's Creek
and Lexington. The first is from the pen of young William Gulick of the
1st Iowa Cavalry, who fought through the campaigns in Missouri and Ar-
kansas until his death, in September 1864; the fighting he describes was in
Bates County, on the border of Kansas. The second comes from Colonel
Monks and describes conditions in Ozark County, on the Arkansas border,
in 1862.

A. "THE CONTEMPTABLE JAY HAWKERS"

Butler, Bates Co. Mo. June 1 [1862]

Dear Sister Cynthia.

The 29th the wind blew hard & the Tents as well as every thing else was
a cloud of dust. Next day I was on Guard, & yesterday I just comencd this
letter when a messenger came from Johnstown with foaming stead stating
that a small party with baggage train from here to Osceola had been attacked
by a larger party of Rebel J[ay] H[awkers]. I volunteered with two other
of our Co. & as many from each of the six Cos here to go to the rescue. In less
than twenty minutes we were on the raod. Our Horses were let out to Fourteen miles an hour all hands expecting for once to have some fighting. But it
turned out as usual we were to late, for about Fifteen minutes after the
engagement commenced a party of Co. L. came up. They were on their way
from Clinton to this place. The rebels took to the brush.

Our boys followed them but the brush is so thick at this season of the year
that they all escaped. One or two of there men were wounded. Our loss
was one horse killed. One man shot in the foot. One through his coat collar,
another through the hat.

The contemptable J. H.s have the advantage of us now & they use it too.
It is folly to even *attempt* to hunt them in the brush. They lay in ambush &
shoot a Soldier where ever they can. Not long since Three of our men
were killed & one severely wounded while out after Forage. The rebels fired
at them while watering at a creek. One escaped to give the alarm. the killed
were bruitaly stabed and heads nearly mashed in the ground also Robed of
every thing they had even boots. The men killed were from Cos C. & D.—
Last week Three men were killed at Osceola in nearly the same manner. . . .
A man was also shot from Co. I. Three or Four days ago near this place. as
yet we have only succeeded in killing one of the miscreants. But now a
special order has been issued to shoot Two of the prisoners we have in our

prison for every soldier that is shot. I think this order will be carried out. We have some hard cases in prison here & about Forty of them too. nearly every night some of our Pickets are fired at, or fire to some one. I am one of the unfortunate ones I can never get a shot or scarcely ever have an occasion to shoot. I go on nearly every scout but cannot shoot a secesh. They say we will not scout much more here. I hope then we will leave this miserable God forsaken country where we will have something to do. I observe those that lay around camp the most are the most sickly. There is a lot in every Co. that is never ready for duty, never go a scouting or scarcely anything else, *except to their rations*, and they are always behind. they think *so much gained*. But they mistake for it is an injury to their health. Our Co. is Generally healthy. as for myself I weigh One hundred Fifty Eight lbs. never better in my life.

Truly Yours

Wm O. Gulick

—Guyer, ed., "Journal and Letters of Corporal William O. Gulick"

B. The Displaced Persons of Southern Missouri

THE rebels being encouraged by the late victory, determined to rid the country of all Union men at once. About that time about 350 men, mostly from Oregon county, commanded by two very prominent men, made a scout into Ozark county, Mo. On reaching the North Fork of White River they went into camp at what was known as Jesse James' mill. The owner, a man of about 55 or 60 years of age, as good a man as resided in Ozark county, was charged with grinding corn for Union men and their families; at the time he and a man by the name of Brown were cutting saw logs about two miles from home in the pinery. They went out and arrested them, arrested an old man by the name of Russell and several others, carried them to a man's house, who was a Union man, and had fled to prevent arrest. They took Brown and James about 300 yards from the house, procured a rope, hunted a long limb of a tree, rolled a big rock up to the tree where the first rope was tied to the limb, placed the noose about James' neck, stood him on the rock, rolled the rock out from under him and left him swinging, rolled the rock to the next rope, stood Brown on it, placed the noose around his neck, rolled the rock out and left Brown swinging in the air, went to the third rope, placed Russell on the rock, and just as they aimed to adjust the noose, word came that the home guards and Federals were right upon them in considerable force. They fled, leaving Russell standing upon the rock and both Brown and James dangling in the air.

Every Union man now having fled in fear of his life, the next day the wives of Brown and James, with the help of a few other women, buried them as best they could. They dug graves underneath the swinging bodies, laid bed clothing in the graves and cut them loose. The bodies fell into the coffinless graves and the earth was replaced. So the author is satisfied that the bones of these men still remain in the lonely earth underneath where they met their untimely death with no charge against them except that they had

THE STRATEGIC POSITION OF MISSOURI

been feeding Union men, with no one to bury them but their wives and a few other women who aided. . . .

A short time after this hanging there was a man by the name of Rhodes, who resided at the head of Bennett's Bayou in Howell County. He was about eighty years of age and had been a soldier under General Jackson. His head was perfectly white and he was very feeble. When he heard of the hanging of Brown and James he said openly that there was no civil war in that, and that the men who did it were guilty of murder.

Some two weeks from the date of the hanging of Brown and James, about twenty-five men, hearing of what he had said, organized themselves and commanded by Dr. Nunly and William Sapp, proceeded to the house of Rhodes, where he and his aged wife resided alone, calling him out and told him they wanted him to go with them. His aged wife came out, and being acquainted with a part of the men, and knowing that they had participated in the hanging and shooting of a number of Union men, talked with them and asked: "You are not going to hurt my old man?" They said: "We just want him to go a piece with us over here." Ordering the old man to come along, they went over to a point about a quarter of a mile from the house and informed him of what he had said. There they shot him, cut his ears off and his heart out. Dr. Nunly remarked that he was going to take the heart home with him, pickle it and keep it so people could see how a black Republican's heart looked.

In the meantime, Rhodes not having returned home, and not a single Union man left in the country that Mrs. Rhodes could get to look after him, and having heard when they reached Joseph Spears' that the old man was not with them, although very feeble, she still continued the search; on the second day, about fifty yards from the road and about a quarter of a mile from home, she heard hogs squealing and grunting as though they were eating something. She proceeded to the place and found the hogs were just about to commence eating the remains of her husband. The Union men having fled, she notified some of the neighbors, and the women came in and helped dress the body and buried him the best they could.

There never was a man arrested by the Confederate authorities, or a single word of condemnation uttered, but as far as could be heard there was general approval. It was said that the means were desperate, but that was the only way to get rid of the men and strike terror to them so they could neither give aid nor countenance to the lop-eared Dutch. . . .

After they had hung, shot, and captured and driven from the country all of the Union men, they called a public meeting for the purpose of taking into consideration what should be done with the families of the Union men, which meeting had a number of preachers in it. After discussing the premises, they arrived at the conclusion that if they let the families of the Union men, who had escaped and gone into the Federal lines, remain, they would return and bring in the lop-eared Dutch. They didn't believe that both parties could ever live together, and as they now had the country completely rid of the Union men, they would force their families to leave. They at once appointed men, among whom were several preachers, to go to each one of the Union families and notify them that they would not be allowed to remain; because if they let them stay, their men would be trying to come back, and they didn't believe both parties could live together. They stated at the same time that they were really sorry for the women and children, but nobody was to blame but their husbands and sons, who had cast their lot with the lop-eared Dutch. Also, as they had taken up arms against the Confederate States, all the property they had, both real and personal, was subject to confiscation and belonged to the Confederate authorities; but they would allow them to take enough of their property to carry them inside of the lines of the lop-eared Dutch, where they supposed their men were and where they could care for them.

They said they might have a reasonable time to make preparations to leave the country, and if they didn't leave, they would be forced to do so, if they had to arrest them and carry them out.

The wildest excitement then prevailed among the women and children. They had no men to transact their business and make preparations to leave. Little had they thought, while they were chasing, arresting, hanging and shooting their men, that they, too, would become victims of the rebel hatred and be forced to leave house and home, not knowing where their men were or whether they were dead or alive. All they knew of their whereabouts was, that those who escaped arrest had left their homes, aiming to reach the nearest Federal lines.

Women were at once dispatched to reach the nearest Federal lines, if possible, and inform them of the Confederate order, and procure help to take them out. Their homes and houses were being continually raided by small bands of Confederates roaming over the country, claiming that they were hunting Union men, taking all classes of property that they might see proper to take, without any restraint whatever.

The suffering that followed the women and children is indescribable. They had to drive their own teams, take care of the little ones, travel through the storms, exposed to it all without a man to help them, nor could they hear a single word of comfort spoken by husband, son or friend. On reaching the Federal lines, all vacant houses and places of shelter were soon filled, and they were known and styled as refugees. Many of them went into soldier huts, where the soldiers had wintered and covered the tops of their huts with earth. They had to leave home with a small amount of rations, and on the road the rebels would stop them and make them divide up the little they had started with, and reaching the Federal lines they would be almost destitute of food and many of them very scantily clothed.

—Monks, "A History of Southern Missouri and Northern Arkansas"

4. THE TIDE TURNS AT PEA RIDGE

Halleck was now in command in the West. In December he sent Pope out with greatly strengthened forces to restore Union control of northern and central Missouri. Price had retreated to Springfield; he now moved south-ward to Arkansas where he was joined by Ben McCulloch with a force that included some 5,000 Indians from the Five Civilized Nations. Their combined force numbered over 20,000, and was under the command of General Van Dorn. After him went General Samuel Curtis. The two armies met at Pea Ridge, Arkansas, at the southernmost tip of the Ozarks. With almost a two-to-one superiority Van Dorn thought it safe to divide his army and try an attack from front and rear. The attempt miscarried. While the Confederate left flank was successful, the right under McCulloch was thrown back with heavy loss. The next day, March 8, 1862, Curtis extended his line around both Confederate flanks, enfiladed the Confederates with artillery fire, and forced them to retreat. It was a decisive victory; thereafter Missouri was safe for the Union.

Curtis was one of the ablest—and most neglected—officers in the Union Army. A graduate of West Point he served as colonel of the 3rd Ohio in the Mexican War, became chief engineer of St. Louis, joined the Republican party and served as Congressman from Iowa from 1858 to 1861. Appointed brigadier general he was sent west and commanded the troops at Pea Ridge; later he was in command at the important Battle of Westport.

General Franz Sigel, who tells this story, was one of the noble band of '48ers who had fought for liberalism in Germany. He fled to Switzerland and later to England, and came to the United States in 1852. The outbreak of the war found him director of public schools of St. Louis; he was appointed general of the 2nd Missouri Brigade, fought at Pea Ridge, and went with Pope to Virginia. After the war Sigel moved to New York City, where he had a long and distinguished career as editor.

IT was a little after 6 o'clock in the morning [March 8] when I sent out Colonel Osterhaus with Captain Asmussen of my staff to reconnoiter the ground on which I intended to deploy, and to find the nearest road leading to it. The 44th Illinois followed the two officers for the purpose of marking the right of the position to be taken, but with orders to keep concealed as much as possible, and not to enter into an engagement unless attacked. Half an hour later, I was standing in front of my tent, ready to mount, and anxiously awaiting the return of the staff-officers, when suddenly a few cannon-shots in our front, from Davidson's Union battery, announced the conflict. At this moment General Curtis, to whom I had sent word during the night where my two divisions were assembling, and that they would be ready for action in the morning, rode toward me from the direction where the firing had begun, and, somewhat excitedly, said: "General, I have opened the battle; it will be a hard fight; Davis is already there. Please bring your troops in line as quickly as possible."

I confess that I did not understand the reason why a cannonade was commenced on our side when we were not ready to meet a counter-attack of the enemy with a good chance of success, the more so, as I had been out in our front before General Curtis met me, and had found that our line was weak, stretched out in an open field, the Telegraph road obstructed by artillery, ammunition-wagons, and other vehicles, and that there was no room to deploy my divisions, except behind the first line and masked by it; nor on the left, unless immediately exposed to and raked by the fire of the enemy, whose batteries were supposed to be posted in the margin of the woods, whence they could reach my troops at point-blank range. I explained this to General Curtis, made him acquainted with the object in view, told him that I expected Colonel Osterhaus and Captain Asmussen back every moment, and finally asked him to give me ten minutes' time to wait for them, when I would move immediately to the position selected and commence the attack. Even if our troops on the right should be compelled to yield, it could only be momentarily, as the enemy would have to direct his whole attention to my attack on his flank and rear. I never felt more relieved than when General Curtis, evidently encouraged by this proposition, said: "Well, General, do what you propose." I must add here that I had not seen General Curtis during the night and before I met him near my tent; he could, therefore, not have been fully aware of what I had experienced in my position away from him on the left, and what my intention was to do in the morning, although I had sent Captain Asmussen to his headquarters to report to him, receiving, however, no orders from him in return. After our conversation, which lasted only a few minutes, the two officers came back in all haste, and reported that they had found an excellent position; that no enemy was in sight, and that Colonel Knobelsdorff, with his regiment, was posted as directed. General Curtis declared himself satisfied and rode off, but scarcely had he left me when the cannonade in front became very brisk, some of the hostile missiles bursting over our heads.

I mounted, told Colonel Osterhaus to take charge of our column and move it to the position to be occupied; then, accompanied by Captain Asmussen, I rode to the front, where Davis's division had formed into line, to see what was going on. I found one of our batteries hotly engaged, but compelled to withdraw, which exposed the infantry on the right to an enfilading fire, and also forced it to change its position. One of the regiments—I think it was the 22d or the 8th Indiana—was thrown into momentary disorder by this surprise, and the men fell back toward an eminence on the right of the road on which I was halting. I assisted their brave commander to rally them, which did not take long, and spoke a few words to them, saying that if the right could hold out for half an hour, assistance would come, and all would be well. Meanwhile another regiment had formed on the left, the battery had taken position again and was supported by four other guns (of White's brigade), farther to the left, diverting the enemy's fire.

The line stood firm, and as no hostile infantry appeared, I took leave of the commander of the "Indiana boys," and hastened to my own troops. I reached the head of the column when it was just debouching from the woods, and the first battery that arrived took position on the left of the 44th Illinois, which was kneeling behind a fence. In about 15 minutes the First Division (Osterhaus's) was formed into line, with the artillery in the intervals between the infantry, the Second Division in reserve, about 250 paces behind our right, with General Asboth at its head, who, in spite of his wound received on the 7th, was again in the saddle. Our position, in full view of the open fields, which sloped gently down toward the long skirt of woods, where the enemy's artillery and infantry were posted, was excellent, and allowed the full development of our forces. The enemy's batteries received us well, but many of their shots were either aimed too high, or struck the ground and were buried a short distance in front of us. When well in action, we advanced slowly from position to position, at the same time contracting our line, the infantry following, rising quickly, and as soon as they had reached a new position lying down again. . . .

It was now a little after 11 o'clock; most of the enemy's batteries (about fifty guns) were silenced one after another, by our concentric fire; his infantry, not venturing out of the woods into the open fields, was now treated with a shower of shell and shrapnel. Opposite our extreme left, however, near Elkhorn Tavern, Van Dorn made a determined effort to hold the high spur of hills, the top of which was crowned and protected by rocks and bowlders. Some of Price's infantry had already taken possession of it, and a battery was being placed in position, when Hoffmann's and Elbert's batteries were ordered to direct their fire against them chiefly with solid shot. Not more than fifteen minutes elapsed before the enemy evacuated this last stronghold, while our infantry on the left—the 36th Illinois, and the 2d, 3d, and 17th Missouri—rushed up the steep hill and forced the remnants of the enemy's troops down into Cross Timber Hollow. Almost simultaneously the 12th Missouri, the 25th and the 44th Illinois advanced in double-quick from the center and right into the woods, engaged the enemy's infantry, drove it back, and one of our regiments (the 12th Missouri) captured the "Dallas Battery." On the extreme right, where General Curtis had directed the movements of the troops, Davis's division and a part of Carr's, assisted by Hayden's and Jones's batteries (the latter commanded by Lieutenant David), pushed forward against the left wing of the enemy and forced it to leave the field. The army of Van Dorn and Price, including about two-thirds of McCulloch's troops under Churchill and Greer, and one-third of Pike's Indian Brigade, all of whom had joined Price during the night, were now in precipitate retreat in all directions, pursued by the First and Second Divisions as far as Keetsville, 9 miles to the north, and by a cavalry force under Colonel Bussey with 2 mountain howitzers to the south-west beyond Bentonville. So ended the battle of Pea Ridge, and our little army, instead of being "beaten and compelled to surrender," had gained a decisive victory.

—SIGEL, "The Pea Ridge Campaign"

5. THE CONFEDERATES SCATTER AFTER PEA RIDGE

Confederate losses at Pea Ridge had been shattering; the losses on the retreat were doubtless as heavy. Alarmed at the situation in western Tennessee and in Mississippi, the Confederate government ordered Van Dorn to

transfer his army to Memphis. This put an effective end to the formal fight-
ing in Arkansas; guerrilla warfare continued.

William Watson, who here tells us something of the retreat and disin-
tegration of Confederate forces after Pea Ridge, was a Scotsman engaged in
business at Baton Rouge. He enlisted in the Confederate Army; fought in
the Missouri and Arkansas campaigns and at Corinth; was mustered out and
re-enlisted; was captured and exchanged. Later he was active in blockade-
running. His Life in the Confederate Army *is one of the liveliest accounts*
of the nonmilitary aspects of the war in the West.

WE had now the march before us, and we must undertake it, without
provisions, without tents or cooking utensils, without blankets or overcoats, and our thin clothing now worn and ragged. I have never seen or read
either in newspaper or history any details of this miniature Moscow retreat.
It was, perhaps, one of those black or blurred pages in history that is un-
readable, and is best to be torn out.

We proceeded to scramble along the best way we could, wading through
creeks and rivers and scrambling over rocks and through brushwood. At
night we kindled large fires and took off our wet clothes, wrung the water
out of them, and dried them the best way we could. Occasionally we passed
a small settlement from which the inhabitants had fled, but everything had
been carried away by Price's army. In the gardens we sometimes found the
remains of some turnips or onions, which were eagerly dug out of the ground
with our sabres and eaten raw. Everything like military order of march was
at an end, but the battalions and companies kept in their places, and discipline was still maintained, although to leave the line in search of something
to eat could no longer be strictly forbidden. Several times it was found that
we had taken the wrong road and had to turn back. Sometimes we passed
through rather better tracts of country which had been settled, but the few
settlers had all fled from their homes and the houses were deserted, and everything in the shape of food had been taken by Price's troops. . . .

About the seventh night we halted on the sloping banks of a creek which
ran at the bottom of a pretty deep valley. On the near side of the creek
there was abundance of dry grass, making a fine place to bivouac; and, what
was better, the weather had suddenly changed, and the afternoon and evening were warm and sultry. We expected to get some sleep to-night if the
pangs of hunger would allow us. How the other companies were faring
we were not sure, but supposed they had just their little chances same as
ourselves.

Notwithstanding the wretchedness of our condition, there was throughout the whole of this trying campaign still kept up a continual animation by
light merry-making. Joking was always the order of the day. The most disagreeable and trying privations were alleviated and smoothed over by turning
them into a cause for laughter. If some became sullen and desponding, there
were always some spirits who could by some comical expressions raise the
merry laugh and incite good humour, and put animation into the men. . . .

When daylight came, and we were about to proceed on our march, we found we were in something of a fix.

Our line of march was across the creek, and we had not followed the rules, which was that a creek should always be crossed and the troops to bivouac on the far side. This rule had been departed from at this time, because on the far side of the creek there was not for some distance any suitable place for bivouacing, besides creeks here were so plentiful, and had to be crossed so often, that if we got on the far side we were not far from the near side of another. However, in this case the meaning or object of the rule was very well demonstrated.

The creek, by the sudden storm, was swollen to a great extent, so that it was impossible to cross, and we could not proceed; and if the enemy had been harassing our rear we would have been in the same position as the Israelites at the Red Sea. What was now to be done? No other route was possible; we were pressed by starvation, and no food was to be obtained in the neighbourhood. It would be at least two days before the creek was passable, and if more rain fell it was quite uncertain when we might get across. There was only the remnant or wreck of the 2nd brigade here, but who was in command of it, or whether it had any commander, we did not know, every regiment seeming to act for itself, and every company to act for itself.

After a consultation among the officers of our regiment, it was agreed that the regiment should separate and each company act for itself, and get along the best way they could to Van Buren, and there join again.

Each company then started to shift for itself as they best could. The novelty of the thing was pleasing, as they were now comparatively free. Our company, amounting in the aggregate to 32, proceeded by itself. We had two axes which we carried along for cutting wood for fires, etc., but that was all the company property we had beyond our arms. We proceeded along the creek to see if there was any possibility of finding a place where we might effect a crossing by felling trees so as to fall across it.

We had some splendid fellows for such an emergency, who could handle the axe as well as the rifle, one of whom we called Canada, as he was a native of that country.

Some gigantic trees grew along the edge of the creek in some places, and soon one of them fell across the stream, but it went whirling away with the roaring torrent as if it had been chips. Another and another was cut, but all were carried away.

At length we came to a place where the creek was narrow and the banks high, but there did not seem to be any tree large enough and sufficiently near the bank to fall across, and at this narrow part all were eagerly looking for a tree that would, if felled, span the creek.

"Here, sergeant! here, sergeant," cried Tim D., in great ecstasy, "here is a fine one."

I hastened to where he was. "Where is it?" said I.

"Over yonder," said he, pointing to a tree on the opposite side of the creek, "if we could only manage to get over to cut it."

"You confounded fool," said I, "if we could only manage to get over to it, it would be of no use to us, because we would not want it."

"What is that?" cried some one.

"Oh, it is one of Tim's bulls," said I. "He proposes that we cross the river first, and then cut a tree on the other side."

"Throw him in the river!" cried two or three of the boys.

"Well, now, that was not what I said at all," cried Tim. "I said, There is a fine tree over there, and if some of yees would go over and cut it, we would all get over; and if you would just come and see the tree, you would say yourself that it was a splendid one."

"Then, go over and cut it;" cried two or three of the boys.

At that time Lieutenant G. and Canada, the axe-man, came up; we looked across at the tree and pondered. "Well, certainly, if any one was on that side to cut that tree it would just fall across and make a splendid bridge. I wonder if there could be no means of getting one man across to cut it."

There was a place a little farther down, where the stream ran through a narrow chasm, where the banks were high on each side, and not quite 30 feet from bank to bank, but there were no trees near the place. It was suggested that we might get one of the tall ash trees, which grew higher up the bank, and carry it down, and raise it on end and let it fall across, and if it did not break it would be strong enough for some active fellow to straddle over upon, and then we could throw him over the axe to cut the tree.

"The very thing!" cried Canada, "and I will volunteer to cross on it." And he was off at once to select a suitable ash tree.

One was soon cut down and trimmed, and all hands carried it to the place, and a hole was dug in the ground with our sabres to put the thick end into, while the men got about it, and with the aid of long forked sticks got it raised to the perpendicular; and it was thrown across, and landed successfully on the other side.

The roaring torrent below looked rather trying to the nerves.

"Here, Tim," cried some of the boys, "go over now and cut the tree."

Tim said he would go, but, as he was no axe-man, he could not cut the tree.

"Then stand aside, you useless bog-trotter."

The end of the tree was firmly bedded, and held tight to keep it from rolling, while Canada straddled across, like Blondin, crossing Niagara Falls on the tight rope. He landed safely on the other side, amidst the cheers of the boys; while another immediately crossed after him, and we threw them over the two axes. Of course, they cried back in a joke, pretending to bid us goodbye, as they were going to proceed on and leave us, but we could not hear them for the roaring of the torrent.

They both set to work with a will and the tree, a very large one, soon fell across the creek, forming an excellent bridge, and in a few minutes all had scrambled over.

We ascended the banks on the opposite side, where we looked back and saw some of the other companies along on the banks, vainly searching for a place to cross. We gave a loud cheer to attract their attention. There was soon a commotion among them, and a cry of—"Hilloa, the rifles are over!"

We pointed in the direction of where we had crossed, that they might see our bridge and make use of it, and we proceeded on our way.

"Now, don't yees see," said Tim D., "that I was right after all; you talk about bulls and bog-trotters, but if it had not been for me you would all have been left behind."

"Why, what did you do?"

"Well, it was my tree that was the right tree, and if it had not been the right tree you might all have been drowned in the river, and then you would have said that I had been right." . . .

We now got on to the regular road, and the track of an army was now only too plainly visible—every house was deserted, and everything in the shape of food or forage was carried away, and a good deal of property seemed to have been wantonly destroyed.

We saw some stragglers on the road before us, and we hastened to overtake them, thinking that they might be a part of our regiment, or perhaps Lieutenant G.'s party. When we overtook them we found them to be mostly of our regiment, but not more than a dozen in all, and among them were two of our company, from Lieutenant G.'s party.

Upon inquiring how it was with the party, and why they were separated from it, they said that Lieutenant G. had heard something about some of the missing from our company, and that our 2nd lieutenant, B., was lying very ill somewhere, and some others were also in distress, and he was going to try to render them assistance; and that he had told these two to go and see if they could meet with our party, and tell us not to wait for them, but to push on to Van Buren.

The effects of an army passing over a country distracted by war were now clearly to be seen. Be that army friend or foe, it passes along like a withering scourge, leaving only ruin and desolation behind.

We found it needless to attempt to procure anything like food on the way, and it was only a loss of time and strength going off the road to look for it. We therefore resolved to push on and reach Van Buren as soon as possible, as the road was now plain before us.

At length we drew near to the place. The poor fellows were brightened up with hope, but they were in a sorry plight. They were actually staggering from want and fatigue. Their shoes were worn off their feet, from passing over rocks and boulders, and through creeks. Their clothes were in rags from scrambling through the woods and briars, and burnt in holes from crouching too close to the camp fires in their broken slumbers. Their eyes were bleared and bloodshot, from want of sleep and the smoke of the wood-fires, and their bodies were emaciated by hunger. But now their difficulties were overcome, and their privations supposed to be at an end for the time at least.

It was about three o'clock in the afternoon when we entered Van Buren.
—Watson, *Life in the Confederate Army*

6. QUANTRILL AND HIS GUERRILLAS SACK LAWRENCE

William C. Quantrill is probably the most unsavory figure of the Civil War. Born in Ohio, he moved to Kansas in 1857, where he lived something of a Jekyll-Hyde life, teaching school as William Quantrill, gambling and steal-ing—and perhaps murdering—as Charley Hart. With the outbreak of the war he raised an irregular band of Confederate sympathizers in the border country of Kansas and Missouri, fought at Lexington, and then embarked upon a career of guerrilla warfare. The Federal government declared him an outlaw, but the Confederates mustered him into service and commissioned him captain. In August 1863 he rode into Lawrence, Kansas, at the head of some 450 men, killed upward of 150 men, women, and children, pillaged the town and left it in ashes. Two months later he repeated this exploit at Baxter Springs, Missouri. All efforts to capture him were vain; in 1865 he appeared in Kentucky, but there he was surprised and fatally wounded.

This story of the infamous Lawrence massacre is by one of the few men who escaped, Gurden Grovenor.

THE raid occurred on the morning of Aug. 21st, 1863. It was a clear, warm, still morning, in the midst of one of the hot, dry, dusty spells of weather common in Kansas in the month of August. The guerrillas reached Lawrence just before sunrise after an all night's ride from the border of Missouri. Myself and family were yet in bed and asleep. They passed directly by our house, and we were awakened by their yelling and shouting.

I thought at first that the noise came from a company of colored recruits who were camped just west of our house; thought that they had got to quarrelling among themselves. I got up and went to the window to see what was the matter, and as I drew aside the curtain the sight that met my eyes was one of terror—one that I never shall forget. The bushwhackers were just passing by my house. There were 350 of them, all mounted and heavily armed; they were grim and dirty from their night's ride over the dusty roads and were a reckless and bloodthirsty set of men. It was a sight we had some-what anticipated, felt that it might come, and one that we had dreaded ever since the commencement of the war. I turned to my wife and said: "The bushwhackers are here."

They first made for the main street, passing up as far as the Eldridge House to see if they were going to meet with any opposition, and when they found none they scattered out all over town, killing, stealing and burning. We hastily dressed ourselves and closed up the house tightly as possible and began to talk over what was best to do. My first thought was to get away to some hiding place, but on looking out there seemed no possibility of that as the enemy were everywhere, and I had a feeling that I ought not to leave my family, a young wife and two children, one a babe of three months old, and so we sat down and awaited developments. We saw men shot down and fires shooting up in all directions.

Just on the north of our house, a half a block away and in full view was a camp of recruits twenty-two in all, not yet mustered into service and un-armed. They were awakened by the noise, got up and started to run but were all shot down but five. I saw this wholesale shooting from my window, and it was a sight to strike terror to a stouter heart than mine. But we had not long to wait before our time came. Three of the guerrillas came to the house, stepped up on the front porch, and with the butt of a musket smashed in one of the front windows; my wife opened the door and let them in. They ransacked the house, talked and swore and threatened a good deal, but offered no violence. They set the house on fire above and below, took such things as they fancied, and left. After they had gone I put the fire out below, but above it had got too strong a hold, and I could not put it out.

Not long after a single man rode up to the front gate; he was a villainous looking fellow, and was doubly villainous from too much whiskey. He saw me standing back in the hall of the house, and with a terrible oath he ordered me to come out. I stepped out on the piazza, and he leveled his pistol at me and said; "Are you union or secesh?"

It was my time of trial; my wife with her little one in her arms, and our little boy clinging to her side, was standing just a little ways from me. My life seemingly hung on my answer, my position may be imagined but it can-not be described. The thought ran through me like an electric shock, that I could not say that I was a secessionist, and deny my loyalty to my country; that I would rather die than to live and face that disgrace; and so I answered that I was a union man. He snapped his pistol but it failed to fire. I stepped back into the house and he rode around to the north door and met me there, and snapped his pistol at me again, and this time it failed. Was there a providence in this?

Just then a party of a half dozen of the raiders came riding towards the house from the north, and seeing my enemy, hallooed to him "Don't shoot that man." They rode up to the gate and told me to come there; I did so and my would be murderer came up to me and placed the muzzle of his revolver in my ear. It was not a pleasant place to be in, but the leader of the new crowd told him not to shoot, but to let me alone until he could inquire about me, so he asked me if I had ever been down in Missouri stealing niggers or horses; I told him "No that I never had been in Missouri, except to cross the state going and coming from the east." This seemed to be satisfactory so he told my old enemy to let me alone and not to kill me. This seemed to make him very angry, and he cursed me terribly, but I ventured to put my hand up and push away his revolver. The leader of the party then told me if I did not expect to get killed, I must get out of sight, that they were all getting drunk, and would kill everybody they saw; I told him that that was what I had wanted to do all the morning, but I could not; "Well," he says, "you must hide or get killed." And they all rode away.

After they had gone I told my wife that I would go into the cellar, and stay until the fire reached me, and if any more of the raiders inquired for me to tell them that I had been taken a prisoner and carried off. Some years ago

I read an article in the Sunday School Times, saying that a lie under any circumstances was a sin. I thought then that I should like to see that writer try my experiences at the time of the raid and see what he would think then; I did not feel my lie a sin then and never have since.

The cellar of my house was under the ell and the fire was in the front and in the upper story. There was an outside bulk-head door, where I knew I could get out after the fire had reached the floor above me. I had not been in the cellar long before my wife came and said they had just killed my neighbor across the street.

Soon after the notorious Bill Anderson, passing by the house, saw my wife standing in the yard, stopped and commenced talking with her; told her how many men he had killed that morning, and inquiring where her husband was; she told him that he had been taken prisoner and carried away—was it my wife's duty to tell him the truth, tell him where I was and let him come and shoot me as he would a dog, which he would have done? Awhile after my wife came and said she thought the raiders had all gone, and so I came out of my prison just as the fire was eating through the floor over my head, thankful that I had passed through that dreadful ordeal and was safe.

Such was my experience during those four or five terrible hours. Our home and its contents was in ashes, but so thankful were we that my life was spared that we thought but little of our pecuniary loss. After the raiders had left and the people could get out on the street, a most desolate and sickening sight met their view. The whole business part of the town, except two stores, was in ashes. The bodies of dead men, some of them partly burned away, were laying in all directions. A large number of dwellings were burned to the ground, and the moaning of the grief stricken people was heard from all sides. Gen. Lane, who was in the city at the time, told me that he had been over the battleground of Gettysburg a few days before, but the sight was not so sickening as the one which the burned and sacked city of Lawrence presented. The exact number killed was never known, but it was about 150, many of them of the best citizens.

—Grovenor in *Quantrill and the Border Wars*

7. COLONEL BAILEY DAMS THE RED RIVER

Early in 1864 General Halleck projected an elaborate plan for crushing remaining Confederate resistance in Arkansas and Louisiana. Banks was ordered to move up the Red River to Alexandria, where we would be joined by General Steele, coming down from Arkansas. Together they were to advance on Shreveport and crush the Confederate forces under Kirby Smith and Taylor. The whole expedition was to be supported by a flotilla of gunboats and transports.

From the beginning things went wrong. Taylor dug in at Mansfield, and repulsed a Federal attack with heavy loss. Taylor in turn advanced, only to be repulsed. But Banks decided to retreat to Alexandria. Meantime however the spring floods had not materialized and the Red River, already low, threatened to fall so low that the fleet would be isolated.

At this juncture Colonel Bailey, chief engineer for the defenses of New Orleans and in the Port Hudson campaign, saved the day by constructing a series of wing dams which got the boats over the falls at Alexandria. For this service Bailey was promoted to a brigadier generalship. After the war he went to Missouri, was elected sheriff of his county, and was murdered by two bushwhackers whom he had arrested.

The story of this exploit is here told by Admiral Porter in a report to Secretary of the Navy Gideon Welles.

MISSISSIPPI SQUADRON, FLAGSHIP BLACK HAWK,
MOUTH RED RIVER, MAY 16TH, 1864.

Sir: I have the honor to inform you that the vessels lately caught by low water above the falls at Alexandria, have been released from their unpleasant position. The water had fallen so low that I had no hope or expectation of getting the vessels out this season, and, as the army had made arrangement to evacuate the country, I saw nothing before me but the destruction of the best part of the Mississippi squadron.

There seems to have been an especial Providence looking out for us in providing a man equal to the emergency. Lieut.-Col. Bailey, Acting Engineer of the 19th Army Corps, proposed a plan of building a series of dams across the rocks at the falls, and raising the water high enough to let the vessels pass over. This proposition looked like madness, and the best engineers ridiculed it; but Col. Bailey was so sanguine of success that I requested to have it done, and he entered heartily into the work. Provisions were short and forage was almost out, and the dam was promised to be finished in ten days or the army would have to leave us. I was doubtful about the time, but I had no doubt about the ultimate success, if time would only permit. Gen. Banks placed at the disposal of Col. Bailey all the forces he required, consisting of some three thousand men and two or three hundred wagons. All the neighboring stream-mills were torn down for material; two or three regiments of Maine men were set to work felling trees, and on the second day after my arrival in Alexandria, from Grand Écore, the work had fairly begun.

Trees were falling with great rapidity, teams were moving in all directions, bringing in brick and stone; quarries were opened; flat-boats were built to bring stone down from above, and every man seemed to be working with a vigor I have seldom seen equalled, while perhaps not one in fifty believed in the undertaking. These falls are about a mile in length, filled with rugged rocks, over which at the present stage of water it seemed to be impossible to make a channel.

The work was commenced by running out from the left bank of the river a tree dam, made of the bodies of very large trees, brush, brick, and stone, cross-tied with heavy timber, and strengthened in every way which ingenuity could devise. This was run out about three hundred feet into the river; four large coal barges were then filled with brick and sunk at the end of it. From the right bank of the river, cribs filled with stone were built out to meet the barges, all of which were successfully accomplished, notwithstanding there was a current running of nine miles an hour, which threatened to sweep every thing before it.

It will take too much time to enter into the details of this truly wonderful work; suffice it to say that the dam had nearly reached completion in eight days' working time, and the water had risen sufficiently on the upper falls to allow the *Fort Hindman, Osage,* and *Neosho,* to get down and be ready to pass the dam. In another day it would have been high enough to enable all the other vessels to pass the upper falls. Unfortunately, on the morning of the 9th inst., the pressure of water became so great that it swept away two of the stone-barges which swung in below the dam on one side. Seeing this unfortunate accident, I jumped on a horse and rode up to where the upper vessels were anchored, and ordered the *Lexington* to pass the upper falls if possible, and immediately attempt to go through the dam. I thought I might be able to save the four vessels below, not knowing whether the persons employed on the work would ever have the heart to renew the enterprise.

The *Lexington* succeeded in getting over the upper falls just in time, the water rapidly falling as she was passing over. She then steered directly for the opening in the dam, through which the water was rushing so furiously that it seemed as if nothing but destruction awaited her. Thousands of beating hearts looked on anxious for the result.

The silence was so great as the *Lexington* approached the dam that a pin might almost have been heard to fall. She entered the gap with a full head of steam on, pitched down the roaring torrent, made two or three spasmodic rolls, hung for a moment on the rocks below, was then swept into deep water by the currents, and rounded to safely into the bank.

Thirty thousand voices rose in one deafening cheer, and universal joy seemed to pervade the face of every man present. The *Neosho* followed next—all her hatches battened down, and every precaution taken against accident. She did not fare as well as the *Lexington,* her pilot having become frightened as he approached the abyss, and stopped her engine when I particularly ordered a full head of steam to be carried. The result was that for a moment her hull disappeared from sight, under the water. Every one thought she was lost. She rose, however, swept along over the rocks with the current, and fortunately escaped with only one hole in her bottom, which was stopped in the course of an hour. The *Hindman* and *Osage* both came through beautifully without touching a thing, and I thought if I was only fortunate enough to get my large vessels as well over the falls my fleet once more would do good service on the Mississippi.

The accident to the dam, instead of disheartening Col. Bailey, only induced him to renew his exertions, after he had seen the success of getting four vessels through. The noble-hearted soldiers, seeing their labor of the last eight days swept away in a moment, cheerfully went to work to repair damages, being confident now that all the gunboats would be finally brought over. The men had been working for eight days and nights, up to their necks in water, in the broiling sun, cutting trees and wheeling bricks, and nothing but good humor prevailed among them. On the whole, it was very fortunate the dam was carried away, as the two barges that were swept away from the centre swung around against some rocks on the left and made a fine cushion for the vessels, and prevented them, as it afterward appeared, from running on certain destruction.

The force of the water and the current being too great to construct a continuous dam of six hundred feet across the river in so short a time, Col. Bailey determined to leave a gap of fifty-five feet in the dam, and build a series of wing dams on the upper falls. This was accomplished in three days' time, and on the 11th instant the *Mound City*, the *Carondelet*, and *Pittsburgh* came over the upper falls, a good deal of labor having been expended in hauling them through, the channel being very crooked, scarcely wide enough for them. Next day the *Ozark, Louisville, Chillicothe,* and two tugs also succeeded in crossing the upper falls.

Immediately afterward the *Mound City, Carondelet,* and *Pittsburgh* started in succession to pass the dam, all their hatches battened down and every precaution taken to prevent accident.

The passage of these vessels was a most beautiful sight, only to be realized when seen. They passed over without an accident except the unshipping of one or two rudders. This was witnessed by all the troops, and the vessels were heartily cheered when they passed over. Next morning at ten o'clock, the *Louisville, Chillicothe, Ozark,* and two tugs passed over without any accident except the loss of a man, who was swept off the deck of one of the tugs. By three o'clock that afternoon, the vessels were all coaled, ammunition replaced, and all steamed down the river with the convoy of transports in company. A good deal of difficulty was anticipated in getting over the bars in lower Red River—depth of water reported only five feet; gunboats were drawing six. Providentially, we had a rise from the back-water of the Mississippi—that river being very high at that time—the back water extending to Alexandria, one hundred and fifty miles distant, enabling it to pass all the bars and obstructions with safety.

Words are inadequate to express the admiration I feel for the ability of Lieut.-Col. Bailey. This is without doubt the best engineering feat ever performed. . . .

I have the honor to be, very respectfully, your obedient servant,

DAVID D. PORTER, Rear-Admiral.

—Letter from David D. Porter to Gideon Welles

8. DEFEAT AND RETREAT ON THE RED RIVER

After Pea Ridge the Confederates were never able to establish a strong force in Arkansas or Missouri; they contented themselves with occasional raids. Curtis had advanced to Batesville; later the forces in northern Arkansas

*were transferred to Union General Frederick Steele, who in August 1863
advanced on Little Rock and captured that capital. The next spring General
Banks was directed to advance up the Red River toward Shreveport, Confederate headquarters for the Southwest. The plan was for Banks to drive up
from the south, Steele to come down from Little Rock, and the two armies
to converge on Kirby Smith and destroy him. Like so many plans in which
Banks was involved, this one miscarried. Banks took Alexandria and moved
north on Shreveport but was stopped by General Taylor at Mansfield. At
the Battle of Sabine Crossing, April 8, 1864, Banks was repulsed, and retreated.
We have seen how he—or Colonel Bailey—got the fleet over the falls of the
Red River. Banks continued his retreat toward the Mississippi, harassed by
Kirby Smith, while Steele fell back on Little Rock.*

Lawrence Van Alstyne here tells the story of Banks's repulse and retreat.

May 18, 1864. *Wednesday.* The rear guard was just coming in sight this
morning when we heard firing at the rear. Soon aides came riding down the
line, halting some and turning others out of the way. They raced across the
bridge and in a little while troops were hurrying back across the bridge from
the front.

It beat all how soon the scene was changed. The firing in the rear kept
increasing and grew plainer to hear. The 90th stood at attention on the bank,
which overlooked the whole plain where the trouble seemed to be centering.
Unless the bridge was attacked we had only to look on, and it was a sight
worth a lifetime to see. The ground, except where worn down by the passing army, was covered with weeds and bushes, which hid the skirmish line
from our view until they rose up and fired almost in each others' faces.
Smoke soon hid the battleground. There was no wind and the smoke rose
up like a cloud instead of spreading. The smoke came nearer and it began
to look as if our turn would soon come, but by and by it stood still and then
began to move back. By noon it was plain to see that the fight was ours, for
the smoke cloud went faster and the firing grew less. By 4 P.M. it was over
and the troops began recrossing toward the front.

The surgeons had their shop under a big tree near the bridge. I heard
one of them say to another that he had never seen so few slight wounds
among so many. Most of those that were hit were either killed outright or
mortally wounded. Only a few legs or arms were cut off. The saddest sight
I saw was the killing of a boy, son of a colonel somebody, whose name or
regiment I could not get. I had often seen the boy while at Alexandria and
wondered why such a child should be in such a place. He rode a handsome
bay pony and wore the infantry uniform, even to a little sword. When the
fight began he was somewhere in the advance, and came riding back at the
head of his regiment by the side of his father. They went into the cloud of
smoke and in a few minutes a man came leading the pony back with the little
fellow stretched across the saddle, his hands and feet hanging down on either
side. He was taken back toward the front and I suppose his body will be
sent home. . . .

May 19, *Tuesday*. Our dead were picked up and brought to the bayou where they were laid in rows on the ground. Those that were identified were buried in separate graves, and the others put crosswise in a wide ditch, with blankets spread under and over them. Our loss was estimated at 500 and that of the Rebs at 800. That must mean killed and wounded, for no such number was buried. The rebel dead were buried in the field, I suppose, for none of them were brought in.

Later. A couple of our men are sick and Dr. Warren called in another doctor to look at them. They called it smallpox, and the men were put in a wagon and carted off right away. When the team came back the driver said they were put in the first house they came to, and a man who has had the disease was left to give them medicine. By night everything but the rear guard was across the bridge, and we had orders to be ready to march. We settled down to get some sleep if we could, but the long roll soon sounded and we sprang to our places. No enemy appearing, we built fires and made coffee, and then sat round nodding our sleepy heads until 4 o'clock in the morning.

May 20, *Friday*. By 4 A.M. the troops were across and the pontoons loaded. We marched at quick time and at 6 o'clock were at Simmsport, where we stopped for breakfast of hard-tack and coffee. While at it a man rode in saying the Rebs were already bridging Yellow Bayou. Simmsport is on the Atchafalaya River, and the same Colonel who planned the dam at Alexandria had built a bridge of boats for us to cross over. Twenty-four steamboats were lashed together side and side, and reached from shore to shore. Across the bows of these the artillery, cavalry and wagons were passing in a continuous stream, and infantry was crossing through and among them as best they could. Other boats were busy ferrying the troops, and such getting across a river I never saw. The *Liberty* took us across and we marched down the opposite side for an hour, and halted for the line to straighten out.

And so the whole day went, first starting and then stopping again, but expecting every minute to set out for good. The time we were waiting, if all put together, would have given us a good rest, and the marching we did would have been good exercise. But as it was, we had a hard day of it. It was pitch dark when we finally started. We came to woods and the darkness could be felt. The train got stalled in the narrow road and then another wait. I was so dead sleepy that twice I fell flat on the ground as I was walking along. The fall woke me up each time and I kept going some way. Men had given out and were sleeping all along beside the road like dead men. Daylight never seemed so long coming. We got through the woods and could see much better. My naps as we walked along, and the falls I had in consequence of them, helped to drive off the dreadful drowsiness and by daylight I was wide awake.

May 21, *Saturday*. When daylight came we were passing the mouth of the Atchafalaya and were again on the banks of the Red River. About sunrise we halted. Lieutenant Moody and I sat down and began to figure up how long we had been awake, when we both tumbled over on the ground and were fast asleep. The next thing I knew Moody was shaking me and asking if I was hurt. His face was bloody and I supposed he had been shot. But we soon found that a horse had run over us, his hoofs striking between our heads and scraping the skin off Moody's forehead as he picked them up.

We soon started again, and at 8 o'clock stopped for breakfast, after which we took a livelier gait than ever. The day was hot. The horses and mules showed the strain as well as the men, and it was impossible to rouse them from the deathlike sleep that had overtaken them. There was nothing to do but pull them out of the road and leave them, for every horse and vehicle was loaded with all it could carry. No stop was made for dinner. On we went, and by 6 o'clock the men were lying all along by the roadsides. Teams gave out and were left panting, their sides showing how cruelly they had been whipped to get the very last effort out of them. My feet were blistered, I knew by the feeling, though I had no time to see or attend to them. The pain each step gave me was, I think, the only thing that kept me awake and going.

About sundown we passed a little village and turned from the road across the country, which was said to be the nearest way to the Mississippi. It was a beautiful country, much like the Teche country, which is sometimes called the "Garden of Louisiana." There were some cattle, and a drove of them was gathered and driven along for our supper. . . .

At 9 P.M. we reached the Mississippi at Morgan's Bend or Morganzia. The cattle had been shot and were lying as they fell. It was everyone for himself. Chunks were cut out and were being eaten before the animal was done kicking. A pack of wolves never acted more ravenous and bloodthirsty. I managed to get my hand between the ribs of one and hold of the liver. I couldn't pull my hand out without straightening the fingers and so got only shreds, but I kept it up until I had taken the edge off my appetite and then lay over on my back and was sound asleep. I suppose a hundred men stepped over me and maybe on me, but nothing disturbed my slumbers. I slept like a dead man.

—Van Alstyne, *Diary of an Enlisted Man*

9. PRICE INVADES THE NORTH AND IS DEFEATED AT WESTPORT

As Banks moved toward the Mississippi, Steele retired on Little Rock. Swollen rivers delayed his retreat, and at the end of April 1864 the forces of Price and Kirby Smith caught up with him at Jenkins's Ferry on the Saline River. The Confederates were repulsed, and Steele made good his retirement. Emboldened by their success, however, the Confederates decided to launch another offensive into Missouri.

Wiley Britton of the 6th Kansas Cavalry—later the historian of the fight-

ing in the Trans-Mississippi area—here tells the story of the confused fighting of the last six months, culminating in the smashing Union victory at Westport.

AFTER the battle of Jenkins's Ferry [April 30, 1864], instead of making preparations to attack the Federal forces at Little Rock and Fort Smith, Price commenced organizing his forces for an expedition into Missouri, to be led by him in person. The Confederate troops under Cooper, Maxey, and Gano, in the Indian Territory and western Arkansas, were to make demonstrations against Fort Smith and Fort Gibson, and the line of communication between those points and Kansas, while another part of the Confederate army was to threaten Little Rock. Price's army for the invasion of Missouri numbered some 15,000 men and 20 pieces of artillery before crossing the Arkansas River, and consisted of three divisions, commanded by Generals Fagan, Marmaduke, and Shelby. These troops were mostly veterans, having been in active service since the first year of the war.

About the 1st of September, while strong demonstrations were being made against Fort Smith and Little Rock, Price, with his army, crossed the Arkansas River about half-way between those points at Dardanelle, and marched to the northern part of the State without opposition, and, in fact, without his movements being definitely known to General Rosecrans, who then commanded the Department of the Missouri at St. Louis. When the Confederate forces entered Missouri they were met by detachments of the State militia, who captured several Confederate prisoners, from whom it was ascertained that the invading force was much larger than had been supposed, and that Price was marching direct for St. Louis. Rosecrans at once commenced collecting his forces to meet and check the enemy. General Thomas Ewing, Jr., was in command of the District of South-east Missouri. Pilot Knob, near Iron Mountain, was a post of importance, with fortifications of considerable strength, and was on Price's direct line of march to St. Louis, which was only eighty-six miles distant.

Finding that General Price was certainly advancing toward St. Louis, Ewing, in order to defend Pilot Knob, drew in the detachments of his command stationed at different points in south-east Missouri. As the Federal forces around and in the vicinity of St. Louis were considered inadequate to defend the city against the reported strength of Price's veteran army, on the request of Rosecrans General A. J. Smith's veteran division of the Army of the Tennessee, 4500 strong, passing up the Mississippi River to join Sherman's army, was detained at Cairo to assist in checking the advance of the Confederate army.

Price arrived before Pilot Knob in the afternoon of September 26th, and skirmished until night with detachments of Federal cavalry, which had been thrown out to meet his advance. Ewing had 1051 men at that post, which were only enough to man the works. Having got his troops and artillery all up, Price opened the attack on the fort at daylight on the 27th, and kept it up all day with great resolution. But Ewing's well-served artillery of eleven pieces and his thousand small-arms repulsed every assault made by the Confederates. When night came, however, Ewing was satisfied that he could not hold out another day against the superior attacking force, and he determined to evacuate the fort. Shortly after midnight his troops marched out, and a few moments later his magazine was blown up, and the ammunition which could not be taken along was destroyed. Ewing then marched with his force and joined the troops engaged in the defense of St. Louis and of Jefferson City. On hearing the explosion of the magazine, Price suspected the retreat of the garrison, and immediately ordered his generals to start in pursuit. Continuing his march north with his army he came up and attacked the defenses of St. Louis some miles south of the city, but was repulsed by General A. J. Smith's veterans and other troops, and then changed his line of march and moved westward toward Jefferson City, the State capital.

While Price's plans were not definitely known, his movements indicated that he would endeavor to take Jefferson City. But Rosecrans determined not to allow the State capital to fall into the hands of the invader, and not only called out the enrolled militia of central Missouri for its defense, but also ordered General John B. Sanborn, commanding the District of Southwest Missouri at Springfield, and General John McNeil, commanding the District of Rolla, to march to its defense with their available forces, with the least possible delay. General E. B. Brown and General Clinton B. Fisk, commanding districts in central and north Missouri, were also directed to bring forward to Jefferson City all the State militia that could be spared from their respective districts. General Price moved forward and attacked the capital, but as he was closely pursued by the Federal forces from St. Louis he was soon driven off, and continued his march westward up the south side of the Missouri River.

His next objects were understood to be the capture of Kansas City, and Fort Leavenworth, Kansas, and more particularly the invasion and desolation of Kansas. He conscripted and pressed into service every man and youth found at home able to bear arms. Major-General S. R. Curtis, commanding the Department of Kansas and the Indian Territory, the moment he was advised of the approaching storm, began collecting all his forces along the eastern border of the State south of Kansas City, and urged Governor Carney, of Kansas, to call out the militia to coöperate with the volunteers in resisting the threatened invasion. In response to the governor's call, twenty-four regiments of militia were hastily organized, and took position along the eastern line of the State. Early in these preparatory operations for the defense of the border, Major-General George Sykes, commanding the District of South Kansas, was, at his own request, relieved, and Major-General James G. Blunt was placed in command. As soon as information was received that Price had been driven from Jefferson City and was moving westward, Curtis and Blunt took the field in person to direct the operations of their forces in defense of the border. Blunt took the available force of the volunteers and several sections of artillery, and moved down to Lexington, some forty miles, to meet and hold the enemy as long as possible, so that Rosecrans's forces in pursuit from St. Louis and Jefferson City, under Generals Alfred Pleasonton and A. J. Smith, could come up and attack Price in the rear.

On the afternoon of October 20th Price's advance under Shelby came within sight of Lexington on the south side of the city. Sharp fighting at once commenced between the opposing forces, and lasted until night, when Blunt, having ascertained the strength of the enemy, fell back to Little Blue River, a few miles east of Independence, to form a new line of battle. As this stream was fordable at different points above and below where the Independence and Lexington road crossed it, Blunt's forces, under Colonel Thomas Moonlight, were obliged, on the 21st, to abandon the position taken up behind it after an engagement with Shelby's division, lasting several hours, and fall back behind the Big Blue River, a few miles west of Independence. Here a new line of battle was formed with all Curtis's available troops, including most of the Kansas State militia, who had consented to cross the State line into Missouri. Curtis and Blunt determined to hold Price's army east of the Big Blue as long as practicable in the hope of receiving assistance from Rosecrans, who, it was thought, was following close upon the rear of the Confederate army.

While Curtis's forces were thus fighting and skirmishing with the enemy over nearly every foot of the ground from Lexington to Big Blue, Pleasonton's provisional cavalry division of Rosecrans's army was marching day and night from Jefferson City to overtake the invading force. On the 22d, just as Curtis's troops were being driven from the line of the Big Blue back upon the State line and Kansas City, Pleasonton's cavalry came up and attacked the rear of Price's army, east of Independence, and routed it and drove it in great disorder through the town. Pleasonton at once sent a messenger to Curtis, announcing his presence upon the field. The night of the 22d Price's army encamped on the west side of the Big Blue, just south of Westport. Pleasonton's cavalry encamped that night around and in the neighborhood of Independence, east of the Big Blue. Curtis's forces were encamped from Kansas City to Westport and along the State line west of Westport.

At daylight on the 23d the columns of Pleasonton began to move west, and those of Curtis to move south, and in a short time afterward they became warmly engaged with the Confederates, who were drawn up in the line of battle two and a half miles south of Westport. The opposing armies fought over an area of five or six square miles, and at some points the fighting was furious. At times there were as many as forty or fifty guns throwing shot and shell and grape and canister. About the middle of the afternoon Price's lines began to give way, and by sundown the entire Confederate army was in full retreat southward along the State line, closely pursued by the victorious Federal forces. . . .

The "Price raid," as it was called in the West, was the last military operation of much consequence that took place in Missouri and Arkansas. It is certain that Price lost more than he gained in war material and that the raid did not tend to strengthen the Confederate cause in the West.

—BRITTON, "Resumé of Military Operations in Arkansas and Missouri"

10. THE CONFEDERATES WIN AN EMPTY VICTORY AT GLORIETTA PASS

Even distant New Mexico saw some fighting. In July 1861 the Confederate government authorized General Sibley to organize a brigade for the conquest of New Mexico, and that November Sibley moved out from San Antonio with a force of almost 3,700. The Union forces were under the command of Colonel Canby, a West Pointer who happened to be stationed at Fort Defiance, New Mexico. In January 1862 Sibley advanced up the Rio Grande to Valverde, Canby moved out to meet him, there was a fierce fight in which the Confederates gained the upper hand, and Canby retired to the defenses of Fort Craig. Sibley advanced on Albuquerque and Santa Fe and captured that capital, its defenders retiring to Fort Union in the north-eastern corner of the territory. Meantime the Federals had been reinforced by Colonel Slough with the 1st Colorado Volunteers.

The opposing forces met in the rugged Apache Cañon, on the Pecos River, and there ensued the Battle of Apache Cañon or Glorietta Pass which is here described by Colonel Scurry, the Confederate commander. Glorietta was technically a Confederate victory, but it was a barren one. As Canby came up to join Slough, the Confederates started their retreat—a harrowing trek through 200 miles of desert country. Sibley had started out with 3,700 men; he returned with less than 2,000.

Although this campaign took place early in 1862 it was an isolated affair and is placed here to avoid interrupting the continuity of the story of the fighting in Missouri and Arkansas.

Santa Fe, New Mexico, March 31, 1862

To Major A. M. Jackson,

   A. A. General, Army New Mexico.

Major: Late on the afternoon of the 26th, while encamped at Galistoe, an express from Major Pyron arrived with the information that the major was engaged in a sharp conflict with a greatly superior force of the enemy, about sixteen miles distant, and urging me to hasten to his relief.

The critical condition of Major Pyron and his gallant comrades was made known to the command, and in ten minutes the column was formed, and the order to march given. Our baggage train was sent forward under a guard of one hundred men, under the command of Lieut. Taylor, of the 7th regiment, to a point some six miles in the rear of Major Pyron's position; the main command marching directly across the mountains to the scene of conflict. It is due to the brave men making this cold night march to state, that where the road over the mountain was too steep for the horses to drag the artillery, they were unharnessed, and the men cheerfully pulled it over the difficulties of the way by hand. About three o'clock in the morning we reached Major Pyron's encampment at Johnson's ranche in *canon* Cito. There had been an agreed cessation of hostilities until eight o'clock the next morning. Too much praise cannot be bestowed upon the courage of the officers and men engaged in the affair of the 26th.

As soon as daylight enabled me, I made a thorough examination of the ground, and so formed the troops as to command every approach to the position we occupied, which was naturally a very strong one. The disposition of the troops was soon completed, and by 8 o'clock were ready to receive the expected attack. In this position we remained until the next morning. The enemy still not making their appearance, I concluded to march forward and attack them. Leaving a small wagon guard, I marched in their direction with portions of nine companies of the 4th regiment. . . . From details and other causes they were reduced, until, all combined, they did not number over six hundred men fit for duty. At about six miles from our camp the advance guard gave notice that the enemy were near, in force. I hastened in front to examine their position, and found they were about one mile west of "Pigeon's Ranche," in *canon Glorietta.*

The mounted men who were marching in front were ordered to retire slowly to the rear, dismount, and come into the action on foot. The artillery was pushed forward to a slight elevation in the *canon,* and immediately to open fire. The infantry were rapidly deployed into line, extending across the *canon* from a fence on our left up into the pine forest on our right.

About the time these dispositions were made, the enemy rapidly advanced in separate columns, both upon our right and left. I dispatched Major Pyron to the right to check them in that direction, and placing the centre in command of Major Ragnet, I hastened with the remainder of the command to the left.

A large body of infantry, availing themselves of a gulch that ran up the centre of an inclosed field to our left, were moving under its cover past our left flank to the rear of our position.

Crossing the fence on foot, we advanced over the clearing some two hundred yards under a heavy fire from the foe, and dashed into the gulch in their midst, pistol and knife in hand. For a few moments a most desperate and deadly hand to hand conflict raged along the gulch, when they broke before the steady courage of our men, and fled in the wildest disorder and confusion. . . .

Sending to the rear to have two of the guns brought back to the field, a pause was made to reunite our forces, which had become somewhat scattered in the last rencontre. When we were ready to advance, the enemy had taken cover, and it was impossible to tell whether their main body was stationed behind a long adobe wall that ran nearly across the *canon,* or had taken position behind a large ledge of rocks in the rear. . . .

I took command of the right and immediately attacked the enemy, who were at the ranche. Majors Ragnet and Pyron opened a galling fire upon their left from the rock on the mountain side, and the centre charging down the road, the foe were driven from the ranche to the ledge of rocks before alluded to, where they made their final and most desperate stand. At this point three batteries of eight guns opened a furious fire of grape, canister, and shell upon our advancing troops.

Our brave soldiers, heedless of the storm, pressed on, determined, if possible, to take their battery. A heavy body of infantry, twice our number, interposed to save their guns. Here the conflict was terrible. Our men and officers, alike inspired with the unalterable determination to overcome every obstacle to the attainment of their object, dashed among them. The right and centre had united on the left. The intrepid Ragnet, and the cool, calm, courageous Pyron, had pushed forward among the rocks, until the muzzle of the opposing forces' guns passed each other. Inch by inch was the ground disputed, until the artillery of the enemy had time to escape with a number of their wagons. The infantry also broke ranks and fled from the field. So precipitate was their flight, that they cut loose their teams and set fire to two of their wagons. The pursuit was kept up until forced to halt from the extreme exhaustion of the men, who had been engaged for six hours in the hardest contested fight it had ever been my lot to witness. The enemy is now known to have numbered fourteen hundred men, Pike's Peak miners and regulars, the flower of the United States army.

During the action, a part of the army succeeded in reaching our rear, surprising the wagon guard, and burning our wagons, taking at the same time some sixteen prisoners. About this time a party of prisoners, whom I had sent to the rear, reached there, and informed them how the fight was going in front, whereupon they beat a hasty retreat, not, however, until the perpetration of two acts which the most barbarous savage of the plains would blush to own. One was the shooting and dangerously wounding the Rev. L. H. Jones, chaplain of the 4th regiment, with a white flag in his hand; the other an order that the prisoners they had taken be shot in case they were attacked on their retreat. These instances go to prove that they have lost all sense of humanity, in the insane hatred they bear to the citizens of the Confederacy, who have the manliness to arm in defence of their country's independence.

W. R. Scurry,
Colonel commanding A. N. M.
—Scurry, "Report of the Battle of Glorietta"

XII

How the Soldiers Lived : Western Front

ON THE *whole Americans were the same, East and West, the Army of Ten-nessee much like the Army of Northern Virginia, the Army of the Cumber-land much like the Army of the Potomac. Not only this but the troops were, in fact, very mixed; Illinois and Minnesota, Texas and Alabama regiments fought in Virginia. But the Western armies were made up, almost wholly, from the region west of the Alleghenies, though this was less true of the Confederate than of the Union armies. There were, however, minor differ-ences.*

There was probably a larger proportion of foreign-born soldiers in the Union armies in the West—Germans and Scandinavians particularly. The war in this theater was somewhat more of a real civil war: in Missouri and Arkansas, in Kentucky and particularly in Tennessee, the division of Union and Confederate sentiment ran right through society. In the East only Mary-land had regiments in both armies; but the Army of the Tennessee (Union) included a "1st Alabama" cavalry brigade, while there were many Kentucky and Missouri regiments in the Confederate ranks.

A third difference was imposed by geography and grand strategy. The Western armies fought over an enormous territory, and it is suggestive that there are half a dozen accounts of the hardships of long marches from the West for every one from the East. Cavalry played, perhaps, a larger role—not the cavalry charge but the long raids and the harassment of lines of com-munication. Climate and geography permitted more winter campaigns. The necessity of co-operating with the navy for control of the Mississippi, the Tennessee and the Cumberland, and the Red rivers made operations more nearly a joint affair, and there are examples even of amphibious operations.

Yet on the whole the excerpts we give here need little elaboration. Life in camp; the forced march; religion and play; relations with civilians; the roles of the commissary and of the sutler—these things were pretty much the same East as West, and North as South. It will be sufficient to introduce some of the chroniclers themselves.

1. JOHN CHIPMAN GRAY VIEWS THE WESTERN SOLDIER

Member of a distinguished Massachusetts family, and graduate of the Harvard Law School, Gray enlisted in the 41st Massachusetts Volunteers in 1862 and fought for a year in the Valley and the Peninsular campaigns. In

1863 he was appointed assistant judge advocate and the following year judge advocate, assigned to the Department of the South. All through the war he corresponded with his law school friend, John Codman Ropes—future historian of the Civil War—and this letter, so Eastern in its point of view, is part of that correspondence.

On Board Steamboat 'Bostona No. 2'
White River, Arkansas, July 24, 1864

My Dear John,—

With regard to the general appearance of the Westerners, it is not so different from our own as I had supposed, but certain it is that discipline is most astonishingly lax. We came up from New Orleans to Memphis with veterans of the 49th Indiana Regiment going home on furlough. They were on terms of great familiarity with their officers, eating, drinking and playing cards with them; yet I must say a finer, cleaner, more orderly and well behaved set of men I never saw; the bar was open all the time and was always filled with men and officers, but I did not see an officer or man drunk and indeed in all my boating on these rivers, I have seen but two men at all affected by liquor, though this may be in some measure due to the exceeding weakness of the tipple concocted at the bar. Other western troops that I have seen have not been so clean and good looking as these Indiana men, but the same lack of discipline exists in all. This is carried to so great an extent that General Gordon, whom you will not suppose to be lax in this respect, says he thinks it very doubtful whether it would be worth while to attempt to impart a severer discipline to troops who have been brought up as these have for more than three years. In Memphis there was a sentry whom I had to pass daily, he was always seated in an arm-chair, his gun rested on the wall near his side, he was often reading, and had another chair by him for the convenience of any friend who might like to stop and chat a while. This is no solitary instance, I might tell you of a dozen things as strange.

Our white troops manage to get along though indifferently, on account of the individual character of the men, but I cannot conceive that the Negro troops commanded by officers taken from the ranks of white regiments, and with men taken from the lowest state of degradation can be anything but a burden to the Government and all the Negro troops I have seen in the West (not many to be sure) have been squalid and miserable in the extreme, very different in look from some of the fine Massachusetts and Maryland Regiments that I have seen in the Department of the South.

The run of officers and citizens that one meets in the towns and on the boats is much less rough than I had anticipated, and I have never seen officials more civil and accommodating than the Captains and Clerks of the river boats. My prejudices against the West have been materially lessened by the experience I have had.

There has been and is undoubtedly an immense deal of contraband cotton dealing and other trading, and almost every commanding officer is accused of having a hand in it. The army accuse the navy and the navy accuse the army. The profligacy too in all the large towns in this region is great. Partly from natural causes and partly from want of the means of life, the prostitution in all this region is astonishing. General Steele at Little Rock lives quite like an Eastern Prince with his harem, wines, dogs, horses, equipages and everything in great style. There is something almost romantic in the existence of all these appliances of luxury and civilization in a little town in the midst of a howling wilderness of bloodthirsty enemies.

—FORD, ed., *War Letters of John Chipman Gray and John Codman Ropes*

2. A WISCONSIN BOY COMPLAINS OF THE HARDSHIPS OF TRAINING

A farm boy from the Wisconsin frontier, Chauncey Cooke was barely sixteen when he went to La Crosse to enlist in the 25th Wisconsin Infantry. He was with Pope in the abortive Sioux campaign of 1862; then in the following year his regiment was sent south, where it fought through the Vicksburg and subsequent campaigns. His letters home have an unpretentious and authentic quality that commends them to the historian of the war. This letter—not the last that we shall read—describes training at a camp outside Madison.

Madison, Wis. Dec. 25th, 1862
Co. G., 25th Regt.

Dear Mother:

You see my paper don't have the regulation picture on it of Soldiers in file or in battle array. I am tired of such flummery. The meaning of the whole thing is to make money for the inventor and not for the soldier. We are told that the life of the Nation is at stake, and every fellow that enlists offers himself as a martyr to save his country. I was thinking these things over last, about 2 P.M. in the morning when I was nearly froze and the relief guard came around and I was off duty to go to my tent and get some sleep. It seems like foolery to the common soldier that for two hours we must stand in a temperature of 30 or 40 degrees when we are a thousand miles from the enemy. I had to walk and walk to keep from freezing. The mercury was down near 40 below zero and the guard house where we sat down between reliefs or lay down was little better than out of doors.

The health of our Regiment is none too good. One man dies on an average every day. As I write this letter the drum is beating. The food we get is to blame for our bad health. The boys threaten a riot every day for the bad beef and spoilt bread issued to us and all this in our home state of Wisconsin.

I went to meeting yesterday both morning and evening. In the morning at the Baptist, in the evening at the Episcopal church. The preacher discussed the state of the Union. I thot he talked a bit like a traitor. He was sorry the states should go to war over the question of slavery. He hoped the Union would be preserved and he thot Uncle Tom's Cabin was much to blame for the war. Capt. Dorwin said the preacher ought to live in South Carolina.

There is talk that we will get pay tomorrow. I have sent a record of our company home. Hope you got it. I shall send you a lot of clothing just before we leave.

From your son,

CHAUNCEY

—COOKE, "Letters of a Badger Boy in Blue"

3. AN OFFICER'S QUARTERS IN CAMP CURTIS

Life in camp could be pleasant enough, especially for an officer. William W. Orme—he was commissioned brigadier general the day this letter was written—was colonel of the 94th Illinois Volunteers. An Illinois lawyer, and a friend of Lincoln's, he had been commissioned at the outbreak of the war, fought in Missouri and Tennessee and at Vicksburg, and was later in command at Camp Douglas.

Camp Curtis—Mo. Nov. 29, 1862

Dearest wife—

It is now half past seven o'clock Saturday night. The band is now playing the regular evening tattoo, and everything has the sound of martial life; but it is nothing unusual.

By the way did you know that in our camp life we move by the music of the band. We rise in the morning by the tune the band plays at Reveille, and we go to bed by the martial music at tattoo and taps.

There are some things delightfully pleasant in camp life, and some things terribly monotonous. . . .

You ask me about myself; well! I'll tell you how I live now. I go to bed when I feel like it; sometimes at 7, sometimes at 9, sometimes later. There being no limit to the hours of an officer. My bed consists of my cot laid on the ground flat for purposes of warmth; it being warmer on the ground than if raised on the legs. I have two blankets and my buffalo robe under me, and three blankets over me. If the night is very cold I throw my overcoat over my feet. I sleep very soundly—I am not troubled with much undressing or dressing as I only take off my coat, vest, and boots. I rise in the morning at various hours from 6 to 8 o'clock. Ike (or Zach, is his proper name—Zachariah Lawson) comes into my tent about daylight and starts a fire in my little camp stove—brings me water to wash in, blacks my boots &c. My camp stove is a little round sheet iron drum, set flat on the ground with a little stove pipe running out of the side of the tent. Ike has spread a piece of bagging by the side of my cot for a carpet. So you see I live in fine style. Breakfast is announced at about 8 o'clock, Dinner about 1, and supper about 6. Sometimes we have plenty to eat and sometimes we dont. Tonight we had mush and milk. The ordinary routine of camp duties, such as business drill &c. occupies the day; & so day after day whiles away—while we wonder each succeeding day when and where we'll march. I take a ride every day; pay my respects to the general, trot around the camp &c. & back to my quarters.

It is now after 8 O'clock. I am getting sleepy. We are all well and hearty. There is nothing new. Kiss the dear ones. Tell me if Willy & Berry read their letters themselves. My love to all at home. And as for yourself you possess me entirely my constant love & thoughts.

As ever devotedly yours,
W<small>M</small>.

—"Civil War Letters of Brigadier General William Ward Orme"

4. RELIGION AND PLAY IN THE ARMY OF THE TENNESSEE

There is nothing dramatic or stirring about this simple chronicle of daily life in camp. Jenkin Jones was another of the many Wisconsin boys who fought in the Army of the Tennessee. Born in Wales he had been brought to this country as a baby; enlisted, at nineteen, in the 6th Wisconsin Battery; fought at Corinth, Vicksburg, Chattanooga, and in Georgia. After the war Jones became a prominent Unitarian preacher and editor. His diary is one of the most revealing about soldier life in the Western theater.

Huntsville [Alabama], Sunday, Jan 17, 1864. A pleasant day. Meeting was announced to be had at 2 P.M. in the Presbyterian Church. Obtained permission and went down, but found none, it being held at 6 P.M. Walked over town. Visited the waterworks of the city, which is the largest of the kind South, with the exception of one at Columbia, S. C. A large stream gushes out of the solid rock under the courthouse, which is dammed about four feet and propels a large water wheel which works a powerful force pump that forces water all over the city, furnishing a hydrant at every corner. Pump is enclosed in a neat stone house. Returned to camp for supper and evening roll-call, then we walked back again. The church was very neat and filled with soldiers, but one woman in the audience. Chaplain of 18th Wisconsin officiated, of the Calvinistic school, and but ill agreed with my views, but it seemed good to be once more listening to an earnest speaker and hear the old-fashioned tunes swell in the bass voices that filled the room. Returned to camp, if not better, a more thoughtful man. It was the second sermon I have listened to since leaving home, and in common with all soldiers, I have acquired a careless and light way of passing time.

Sunday, Feb. 7. Rough night for the guard. Rainy and cold. The countersign "Vicksburg" which gave rise to musings which aided in forgetting time. Relieved at 9 A.M. Attended church in company with Griff, E. W. and D. J. D. Service was held in the Methodist, Presbyterian and Epsicopal churches at the same hour (10 A.M.) Curiosity prompted to attend the latter, an elegant furnished church of unique construction, Gothic style, poorly arranged for sound. The civilians were apparently of the aristocratic class, mostly women, equalling the military in numbers. The white-robed minister was a young intelligent Irishman, I should judge. A good choir with the deep-toned organ opened the service with fitting music, after which prayers were read and ceremonies performed for nearly an hour and a half, which to me was mere mockery of religion, reading their desires to God from an established formula, but careful always to omit the prayer for the President of the U. S. A. It was not worship. Ah no! the heart was cold. It was but Phariseeical affectations. A short sermon on charity was read at the close. Very good, the effect of which was tested by passing the plates which were returned well laden with "soldier greenbacks." The money of that government they will not pray for is very acceptable.

I returned to camp, although not pleased with the exercise, yet I trust, benefited. The solemn notes of the organ had awakened feelings that are too apt to lie dormant in the soldier's breast, those that raise the mind above the din of common life, and look to a future of immortality, purity, which all hope to obtain ere long. "Heaven is my home."

Saturday, Feb. 20. As soon as breakfast was over I hitched a new team and drove out to a confiscated fence, a mile off, for a load of lumber, as the two Hungerfords were desirous of coming in with us, and we must build a larger one [hut]. After we were all loaded, a guard commanded us to unload, but after some talk allowed us to leave in quiet with our lumber. Tore down our "humble cot" and six of us went to work in earnest to erect a more commodious one. Had no tent. Built it entirely of lumber. Had it almost completed by night. Was quite tired, with a settled cold on my lungs, almost sick.

Friday, March 4. Evie Evans and myself went to the city on pass. Visited the Christian Commission rooms. Bought stamps. Also went to the colored school under charge of Chaplain of 17th Colored. Had school-teachers, being volunteers from the ranks, teaching the little wooly-heads their "A. B. C.'s." One class of youngsters was taught by a large Negro. A class of young ladies was reading in the *Second Reader*. All seemed attentive and anxious to receive the instruction but poorly imparted to them. Harnesses were opened and distributed to the platoons. I was given one set. No horses.

Sunday, March 13. A delightful Sabbath morning. T. J. Hungerford very sick, heavy fever and hard breathing. Afraid he is going to have a fever. Bathed him, towels kept around him, and all we can do for him is done gladly. After inspection 8 A.M. attended Sabbath school and meeting at the Methodist Church. . . . The minister preached from the 35th and 36th verses of the fourth chapter of St. John, a discourse filled with hell fire and eternal misery, with but little consolation to the many bereaved mothers and sisters present who had lost their all in the Confederate army. Although enemies, I could but feel for their distressing sobs, that were audible all over the room. In the afternoon the day was so cheering that I could not resist the temptation of another walk to town, where in a crowded house of soldiers and citizens I listened to an excellent practical sermon on the ten virgins, wise and foolish.

Tuesday, March 29. Our camp was visited to-day by Mother Bickerdyke with four mule teams loaded with good things from the North for the soldiers. Left us three barrels of potatoes, turnips, carrots, etc., one barrel of sourkraut with one of dried apples. *Noble woman.* I still remember with gratitude the motherly interest she took in my welfare while lying in the hospital at Corinth. Here again she comes with that which she has gathered by her own labor in the North, not leaving it to be wholly absorbed by surgeons, directors and officers, as is too often the case with sanitary goods. She comes along in a mule wagon and delivers it herself to the "good boys" as she terms us, without seeking the officers. She drew a large crowd around her soon. Her glowing, welcoming face, filled with cordiality, had a magnetic influence upon the hearts of all, such a contrast to the haughty, disdainful looks we are accustomed to receive from women in general. May God bless her noble, self-sacrificing spirit, is the soldier's prayer.

Monday, April 4. A cloudy rainy day. Orders given us at 8 A.M. to put our tents in order preparatory to an inspection by medical director. All filth to be removed. Dirty clothes were washed, etc. In the evening the artillery boys listened to a stirring speech on the parade ground by Rev. Collins, chaplain 57th Illinois, a spicy and able speaker. Kept the crowd laughing much of the time, at the same time encouraging and instructing each one in the duty of the hour, and had a good effect. Sold several tracts.

Monday, April 11. Spent the day in the usual way. Two hours' gun drill in the morning, then game of ball; an hour company drill in the afternoon; a game or two of chess, then parade 4 P.M.; reading, writing, the remainder of the time till retreat at 8 P.M. when I made down my cot. In the quiet of alone I lay down, a few yearning thoughts of home, mother, etc. and all is oblivion till reveille calls me forth from the land of nod. A little after noon we were startled by a terrible explosion near the depot. A caisson of the Illinois Battery had exploded while returning from drill, killing six cannoneers instantly and wounding two. A very sad affair. Bodies torn to shreds.

Sunday, April 17. A beautiful and holy Sabbath morning. Warmed even the coldest heart to softness and filled the thoughtful mind with piety, though to many imperceptibly. Knapsack inspection at 8 A.M. Afterwards D. J. D. Griff and myself attended Sabbath school taught by a chaplain. The presiding elder of the Methodist church was sick, and to my astonishment the Yankee chaplain was invited to preach, which he did very fittingly, delivering an excellent sermon from Romans 8th chapter, XV verse. Went down in the afternoon to witness the baptizing at the Methodist church, but we were too late. Visited the new font that is going up, and caught in heavy rain storm before we got back.

Sunday, April 24. Awoke to hear the rain pattering thick and fast on the pine boards overhead. At first I was dissatisfied with the anticipation of a wet day with mud—very blue, but at the thought of yesterday's dusty ordeal I could but say "blessed be the rain that clears the atmosphere and makes all nature look more pleasing when it ceases." Cleared off into a most delightful day by 9 A.M., and I listened to a thorough scientific sermon from Dr. Ross upon technical points, existence of evil. His arguments were very concise and binding. Although differing in opinion I received many new

ideas. He is one of the leading Southern clergy and formerly a rabid secessionist, and to-day he touched upon the war, but so nicely that it could not
displease any of his audience which was composed of the two extremes, viz:
Yankee soldiers and secesh women. He sat way up, he said, upon his faith in
God, "looking down upon the struggle with as much composure as though
they were but the convulsions of so many pigmies—God would do it right."
Just found it out I suppose.

Monday, May 2. A cold, windy day for this time of the year. At night a
fire was very comfortable. Expect to move camp nearer to town soon so as
to shorten the picket line. The left wing of the 16th Corps under Dodge was
moving in all day. Stood on the roadside most of the afternoon, the first time
we were ever permitted to see a moving column without ourselves forming
a part of it. 26th Wisconsin passed. Many of our boys found acquaintances
and friends. In the same Brigade was a regiment of Yanks all the way from
Jersey, regular blue-blooded Yankees. Made a strange appearance in their
leggins and yellow tassels. Physically made a poor comparison by the side
of our sturdy Western boys.

Tuesday, May 10. . . . All the Negroes in town pressed in and put to work.
Twenty of us detailed with Corporal Ferris to load a train with 3 by 8 stuff
for gun platforms to obtain which we had to tear down an old machine shop.
Returned and unloaded by noon.

All the details marched up in line to McBride's headquarters, where
whiskey rations were freely issued to all that wanted, many of the most
greedy drinking in several different details. After this issue the Captain
mounted a table and read a dispatch from Sherman by telegraph, of glorious
news from Grant. Whips Lee and in full pursuit. Butler in Petersburg within
ten miles of Richmond. The news and whiskey brought forth thundering
acclamations from the soldiers. After stating the importance of the immediate completion of the works, we were dismissed for dinner and started home.
Deplorable sight. The intemperate indulgence by those but little used to the
poison, caused a large portion of them to be beastly drunk, and our march
through town was filled with demoniac yells, tumbling in the mud and mire.
I felt ashamed to be seen in the crowd. Such mistaken kindness tends to
demoralize the army as well as to increase the hatred of our enemy. Many
of the boys had to be carried to their tents, and were unable to return to
the work in the afternoon. Rained heavy all the afternoon. Worked hard.
After night a terrible thunder storm deluged our camp, water standing in
one of the tents eighteen inches deep. Our floor was all afloat, and we had
to climb into our bunks to keep dry. Dry land could not be seen. Much noise
and fun in order to forget the disagreeable in the humorous.

—JONES, *An Artilleryman's Diary*

5. THE GREAT REVIVAL IN THE ARMY OF TENNESSEE

*In 1863 and 1864 the Army of Tennessee, like the Army of Northern
Virginia, was swept by a "great revival." Officers and men alike were bap-*

tized, and piety spread—perhaps with despair. These letters are from the Reverend T. J. Stokes, a member—probably chaplain—of the 10th Texas. Mrs. Gay, who reproduces them in her charming Life in Dixie, *lived in Decatur, Georgia.*

Near Dalton, April 5th, 1864.—We have had for some weeks back very unsettled weather, which has rendered it very disagreeable, though we haven't suffered; we have an old tent which affords a good deal of protection from the weather. It has also interfered some with our meetings, though there is preaching nearly every night that there is not rain. Brother Hughes came up and preached for us last Friday night and seemed to give general satisfaction. He was plain and practical, which is the only kind of preaching that does good in the army. He promised to come back again. I like him very much. Another old brother, named Campbell, whom I heard when I was a boy, preached for us on Sabbath evening. There was much feeling, and at the close of the services he invited mourners to the anxious seat, and I shall never forget that blessed half-hour that followed; from every part of that great congregation they came, many with streaming eyes; and, as they gave that old patriarch their hands, asked that God's people would pray for them. Yes, men who never shrank in battle from any responsibility, came forward weeping. Such is the power of the Gospel of Christ when preached in its purity. Oh, that all ministers of Christ could, or would, realize the great responsibility resting upon them as His ambassadors. . . .

Since my return we have established a prayer-meeting in our company, or, rather, a kind of family service, every night after roll call. There is one other company which has prayer every night. Captain F. is very zealous. There are four in our company who pray in public—one sergeant, a private, Captain F. and myself. We take it time about. We have cleared up a space, fixed a stand and seats, and have a regular preaching place. I have never seen such a spirit as there is now in the army. Religion is the theme. Everywhere, you hear around the camp-fires at night the sweet songs of Zion. This spirit pervades the whole army. God is doing a glorious work, and I believe it is but the beautiful prelude to peace. I feel confident that if the enemy should attempt to advance, that God will fight our battles for us, and the boastful foe be scattered and severely rebuked.

I witnessed a scene the other evening, which did my heart good—the baptism of three men in the creek near the encampment. To see those hardy soldiers taking up their cross and following their Master in His ordinance, being buried with Him in baptism, was indeed a beautiful sight. I really believe, Missouri, that there is more religion now in the army than among the thousands of skulkers, exempts and speculators at home. There are but few now but who will talk freely with you upon the subject of their soul's salvation. What a change, what a change! when one year ago card playing and profane language seemed to be the order of the day. Now, what is the cause of this change? Manifestly the working of God's spirit. He has chastened His people, and this manifestation of His love seems to be an earnest of the good things in store for us in not a far away future. "Whom the Lord loveth He chasteneth, and scourgeth every son whom He receiveth." Let all the people at home now, in unison with the army, humbly bow, acknowledge the afflicting hand of the Almighty, ask Him to remove the curse upon His own terms, and soon we will hear, so far as our Nation is concerned, "Glory to God in the highest, on earth peace, good will toward men!"

Your affectionate brother,

T. J. STOKES.

In Camp, Near Dalton, Ga., April 18, 1864,—

The good work still goes on here. Thirty-one men were baptized at the creek below our brigade yesterday, and I have heard from several other brigades in which the proportion is equally large (though the thirty-one were not all members of this brigade). Taking the proportion in the whole army as heard from (and I have only heard from a part of one corps), there must have been baptized yesterday 150 persons—maybe 200. This revival spirit is not confined to a part only, but pervades the whole army. . . . Brother Hughes was with us the other night, but left again the next morning. The old man seemed to have much more influence in the army than young men. I have preached twice since writing to you, and the Spirit seemed to be with me. . . . Many presented themselves, and I could hear many among them, with sobs and groans, imploring God to have mercy upon them; and I think the Lord did have mercy upon them, for when we opened the door of the church six united with us. Every Sabbath you may see the multitude wending their way to the creek to see the solemn ordinance typical of the death, burial and resurrection of our Savior. . . .

If this state of things should continue for any considerable length of time, we will have in the Army of Tennessee an army of believers. Does the history of the world record anywhere the like? Even Cromwell's time sinks into insignificance. A revival so vast in its proportions, and under all the difficulties attending camp life, the bad weather this spring, and innumerable difficulties, is certainly an earnest of better, brighter times not far in the future.

Near Dalton, May 5th, 1864.

The great revival is going on with widening and deepening interest. Last Sabbath I saw eighty-three immersed at the creek below our brigade. Four were sprinkled at the stand before going down to the creek, and two down there, making an aggregate within this vicinity of eighty-nine, while the same proportion, I suppose, are turning to God in other parts of the army, making the grand aggregate of many hundreds. Yesterday I saw sixty-five more baptized, forty more who were to have been there failing to come because of an order to be ready to move at any moment. They belong to a more distant brigade. . . . If we do not move before Monday, Sabbath will be a day long to be remembered—"the water will," indeed, "be troubled." Should we remain three weeks longer, the glad tidings may go forth that the Army of Tennessee is the army of the Lord. But He knoweth best what is for our good, and if he sees proper can so order His providence as to keep us here. His will be done.

—GAY, *Life in Dixie during the War*

6. FROM REVEILLE TO TAPS

Most of the accounts of marching emphasize its hardships. Here is a simple factual account of how an army on the march spends its day. The auspices were, of course, favorable, for this is Sherman's army marching through Georgia. A young man of twenty-four or five when he joined the army, George Ward Nichols had already lived a busy life. Born in Maine and educated in Boston, he had worked as a journalist, taken part in the struggle for free Kansas, studied art in France, and become art editor on the New York Evening Post. *Shortly after the outbreak of the war he joined Frémont's staff; then went as provost marshal to Wisconsin; and ended up as aide-de-camp to General Sherman. His* Story of the Great March *from which this excerpt is taken was one of the most popular of all postwar books, published in England and translated into many European languages. After the war Nichols had a long and distinguished career promoting art and music in Cincinnati.*

AMONG the most characteristic features of the soldier's life is the important step of breaking camp, which is at once the close of a season of monotonous inactivity and the preliminary stage of a phase of exciting adventure. The same general details are on such occasions observed throughout the entire army, differing slightly in some of the corps, when the division which was in the centre or rear marches first, taking the place of the division which was in advance the day before.

The order of march is issued by the army commanders the preceding night, from them to the corps commanders, and then passed along until every soldier, teamster, and camp-follower knows that an early start is to be made. "The second division will be on the Milledgeville road promptly at five o'clock" reads an order, by way of instance.

At three o'clock the watch-fires are burning dimly, and, but for the occasional neighing of horses, all is so silent that it is difficult to imagine that twenty thousand men are within a radius of a few miles. The ripple of the brook can be distinctly heard as it breaks over the pebbles, or winds petulantly about the gnarled roots. The wind sweeping gently through the tall pines overhead only serves to lull to deeper repose the slumbering soldier, who in his tent is dreaming of his far-off Northern home.

But in an instant all is changed. From some commanding elevation the clear-toned bugle sounds out the *reveillé*, and another and another responds, until the startled echoes double and treble the clarion calls. Intermingled with this comes the beating of drums, often rattling and jarring on unwilling ears. In a few moments the peaceful quiet is replaced by noise and tumult, arising from hill and dale, from field and forest. Camp-fires, hitherto extinct or smouldering in dull gray ashes, awaken to new life and brilliancy, and send forth their sparks high into the morning air. Although no gleam of sunrise blushes in the east, the harmless flames on every side light up the scene, so that there is no disorder or confusion.

The æsthetic aspects of this sudden change do not, however, occupy much of the soldier's time. He is more practically engaged in getting his breakfast ready. The potatoes are frying nicely in the well-larded pan; the chicken is roasting delicately on the red-hot coals, and grateful fumes from steaming coffee-pots delight the nostrils. The animals are not less busy. An ample supply of corn and huge piles of fodder are greedily devoured by these faithful friends of the boys in blue, and any neglect is quickly made known by the pawing of neighing horses and the fearful braying of the mules. Amid all is the busy clatter of tongues and tools—a Babel of sound, forming a contrast to the quiet of the previous hour as marked as that between peace and war.

Then the animals are hitched into the traces, and the droves of cattle relieved from the night's confinement in the corral. Knapsacks are strapped, men seize their trusty weapons, and as again the bugles sound the note of command, the soldiers fall into line and file out upon the road, to make another stage of their journey—it may be to win fresh laurels in another victory, or perhaps to find a rest which shall only be broken by the *reveillé* of the last trump.

A day's march varies according to the country to be traversed or the opposition encountered. If the map indicates a stream crossing the path, probably the strong party of mounted infantry or of cavalry which has been sent forward the day before has found the bridges burned, and then the pontoons are pushed on to the front. If a battle is anticipated, the trains are shifted to the rear of the centre. Under any circumstances, the divisions having the lead move unencumbered by wagons, and in close fighting trim. The ambulances following in the rear of the division are in such close proximity as to be available if needed. In the rear of each regiment follow the pack-mules, laden with every kind of camp baggage, including blankets, pots, pans, kettles, and all the kitchen-ware needed for cooking. Here will be found the led horses, and with them the Negro servants, who form an important feature of the *ménage*.

Having placed the column upon the road, let us now follow that long line of muskets gleaming in the rays of the morning sunlight, and ride, heedless of the crack of the rifles, to the head of the column. The advance are driving a squad of Rebel cavalry before them so fast that the march is not in the least impeded. The flankers spread out, on a line parallel to the leading troops, for several hundred yards, more or less, as the occasion may require. They search through the swamps and forests, ready for any concealed foe, and anxiously looking out for any line of works which may have been thrown up by the enemy to check our progress. Here the General of the division, if a fighting man, is most likely to be found; his experienced eye noting that there is no serious opposition, he orders up a brigade or another regiment, who, in soldier's phraseology, send the Rebel rascals "kiting," and the column moves on. A large plantation appears by the road-side. If the "bummers" have been ahead, the chances are that it has been visited, in which event the interior is apt to show evidences of confusion; but the barns are full of corn and fodder, and parties are at once detailed to secure and convey the prize to the road-side. As the wagons pass along they are not allowed to halt, but the grain or fodder is stuffed into the front and rear of the vehicles as they pass, the unhandy operation affording much amusement to the soldiers, and not unfrequently giving them a poor excuse for swearing as well as laughing.

When the treasure-trove of grain, and poultry, and vegetables has been secured, one man is detailed to guard it until the proper wagon comes along. Numbers of these details will be met, who, with proper authority, have started off early in the morning, and have struck out miles away from the flank of the column. They sit upon some cross-road, surrounded with their spoils—chickens, turkeys, geese, ducks, pigs, hogs, sheep, calves, nicely-dressed hams, buckets full of honey, and pots of fresh white lard. . . .

There is a halt in the column. The officer in charge of the pioneer corps, which follows the advance guard, has discovered an ugly place in the road, which must be "corduroyed" at once, before the wagons can pass. The pioneers quickly tear down the fence near by and bridge over the treacherous place, perhaps at the rate of a quarter of a mile in fifteen minutes. If rails are not near, pine saplings and split logs supply their place. Meanwhile the bugles have sounded, and the column has halted. The soldiers, during the temporary halt, drop out of line on the road-side, lying upon their backs, supported by their still unstrapped knapsacks. If the halt is a long one, the different regiments march by file right, one behind the other, into the fields, stacking their muskets, and taking their rest at ease, released from their knapsack.

These short halts are of great benefit to the soldier. He gains a breathing-spell, has a chance to wipe the perspiration from his brow and the dust out of his eyes, or pulls off his shoes and stockings to cool his swollen, heated feet, though old campaigners do not feel the need of this. He munches his bit of hard bread, or pulls out a book from his pocket, or oftener a pipe, to indulge in that greatest of luxuries to the soldier, a soothing, refreshing smoke. Here may be seen one group at a brook-side, bathing their heads and drinking; and another, crowded round an old song-book, are making very fair music. One venturesome fellow has kindled a fire, and is brewing a cup of coffee. All are happy and jolly; but when the bugle sounds "fall in," "attention," and "forward," in an instant every temporary occupation is dropped, and they are on the road again.

This massing of brigades and wagons during a halt is a proper and most admirable arrangement. It keeps the column well closed up; and if a brigade or division has by some means been delayed, it has the opportunity to overtake the others. The 20th Corps manage this thing to perfection.

A great many of the mounted officers ride through the fields, on either side of the line of march, so as not to interfere with the troops. General Sherman always takes to the fields, dashing through thickets or plunging into the swamps, and, when forced to take the road, never breaks into a regiment or brigade, but waits until it passes, and then falls in. He says that they, and not he, have the right to the road.

Sometimes a little creek crosses the path, and at once a foot-bridge is made upon one side of the way for those who wish to keep dry-shod; many, however, with a shout of derision, will dash through the water at a run, and then they all shout the more when some unsteady comrade misses his footing and tumbles in at full length. The unlucky wight, however, takes the fun at his expense in the best of humor. Indeed, as a general rule, soldiers are good-humored and kind-hearted to the last degree. I have seen a soldier stand at a spring of water for ten minutes, giving thirsty comers cool draughts, although it would delay him so that he would have to run a quarter of a mile or more to overtake his company. The troops, by the way, kept their ranks admirably during this Georgia campaign. Occasionally, however, they would rush for a drink of water, or for a bee-hive which they would despoil of its sweets with a total disregard of the swarm of bees buzzing about their ears, but which, strange to say, rarely stung.

But the sun has long since passed the zenith, the droves of cattle which have been driven through the swamps and fields are lowing and wandering in search of a corral, the soldiers are beginning to lag a little, the teamsters are obliged to apply the whip oftener, ten or fifteen miles have been traversed, and the designated halting-place for the night is near. The column must now be got into camp.

Officers ride on in advance to select the ground for each brigade, giving the preference to slopes in the vicinity of wood and water. Soon the troops file out into the woods and fields, the leading division pitching tents first, those in the rear marching on yet farther, ready to take their turn in the advance the next day.

As soon as the arms are stacked, the boys attack the fences and rail-piles, and with incredible swiftness their little shelter-tents spring up all over the ground. The fires are kindled with equal celerity, and the luxurious repast prepared, while "good digestion waits on appetite, and health on both." After this is heard the music of dancing or singing, the pleasant buzz of conversation, and the measured sound of reading. The wagons are meanwhile parked and the animals fed. If there has been a fight during the day, the incidents of success or failure are recounted; the poor fellow who lies wounded in "the anguish-laden ambulance" is not forgotten, and the brave comrade who fell in the strife is remembered with words of loving praise.

By-and-by the tattoo rings out on the night air. Its familiar sound is understood. "Go to rest, go to rest," it says, as plainly as organs of human speech.

Shortly after follows the peremptory command of "Taps." "Out lights, out lights, out lights!" The soldier gradually disappears from the camp-fire. Rolled snugly in his blanket, the soldier dreams again of home, or revisits in imagination the battle-fields he has trod. The animals, with dull instinct, lie down to rest, and with dim gropings of consciousness ruminate over "fresh fields and pastures new." The fires, neglected by the sleeping men, go out, gradually flickering and smouldering, as if unwilling to die.

All is quiet. The army is asleep. Perhaps there is a brief interruption to the silence as some trooper goes clattering down the road on an errand of speed, or some uneasy sleeper turns over to find an easier position. And around the slumbering host the picket-guards keep quiet watch, while constant, faithful hearts in Northern and Western homes pray that the angels of the Lord may encamp around the sleeping army.

—Nichols, *The Story of the Great March*

7. FORCED MARCHES IN THE TECHE COUNTRY

There was no more difficult marching or fighting country than the Teche country stretching west of New Orleans. An alluvial region filled with lakes and swamps, almost impassable, and cursed by heat and mosquitoes in the summer, it presented very real difficulties to Northern boys.

John De Forest, who here describes the cruel hardships of a forced march through the Teche country in the spring of 1863, was an historian and novelist who returned from Europe, on the outbreak of the war, to recruit a company for the 12th Connecticut Volunteers. He served with Banks in the Southwest and later in the Shenandoah Valley. His essays on the war, contributed to Harper's *and* The Galaxy, *were later collected as* A Volunteer's Adventures; *of his many novels the best known is* Miss Ravenel's Conversion from Secession to Loyalty, *one of the earliest forays into realism.*

SLING blankets and shoulder arms was the order now, and we set off on our long chase to Alexandria [Louisiana]. Mouton had gained five or six hours the start of us, and Texans on horseback can travel faster than Yankees on foot, so that, although we marched furiously that hot day, making twenty-four miles before nightfall, Grover had finished his battle long before we reached him. Unacquainted with the country and ordered to the wrong place, he had gone to the wrong place. He had posted himself on one of two parallel roads, instead of where the two met in one, affording him a chance to fight decisively. The consequence was a sidelong battle, both sides suffering, but the enemy escaping.

Forward at full speed the next day and the day after, scurrying and popping of cavalry in the front, as our van skirmished with their rear. At times a great distant dust, showing how close we were upon the Rebel flight. It is a solemn and menacing phenomenon, the dust of a marching enemy, but more particularly so, of course, when it is advancing upon you. The smoke of burning cotton streaked the day, and the flare of it luridly starred the night; for even in his haste Mouton was determined that no fraction of the financial king should fall to the Yankees. Stragglers in grey and butternut dropped back among us with pacific waving of caps and handkerchiefs; for although we could not catch the Texan horsemen, we were marching the Louisiana infantry to tatters. It seemed like meeting old friends to come across the fellows of the Crescent regiment, whom we had encountered six months before at Labadieville, or Georgia Landing. Shouts of recognition took place, gayer on our side than on theirs. They told us that their officers were driving the men on with drawn sabres, or the whole force would have gone to pieces under the exhaustion of the retreat. Mightily encouraged by these statements, we blistered our soles with renewed energy.

Oh, the horrors of marching on blistered feet! It is an incesant bastinado applied by one's own self, from morning to night. I do not mean a single blister, as big as a pea, but a series of blisters, each as large as a dollar, or, to judge by one's sensations, as large as a cartwheel. I have had them one under the other, on the heel, behind the heel, on the ball of the foot, on every toe, a network, a labyrinth, an archipelago of agony. Heat, hunger, thirst, and fatigue are nothing compared with this torment. When you stand, you seem to be on red-hot iron plates; when you walk, you make grimaces at every step. In the morning the whole regiment starts limping, and by noon the best soldiers become nearly mutinous with suffering. They snarl and swear at each other; they curse the general for ordering such marching; they curse the enemy for running away instead of fighting; they fling themselves down in the dust, refusing to move a step further. Fevered with fatigue and pain, they are actually not themselves. Meantime, the company officers, as sore-footed as anyone, must run about from straggler to straggler, coaxing, arguing, ordering, and, perhaps, using the flat of the sabre. Instead of marching in front of my company, I followed immediately in the rear, so that I could see and at once pounce upon everyone who fell out.

It was curious to note how cheerful everyone became if cannon in front told of the proximity of the enemy. We were ready to fight the bloodiest of combats rather than march a mile further. We filed into line of battle delighted, and then resumed our pursuit heartsick.

It will be asked, perhaps, whether I, an officer and claiming, of course, to to be a patriot, preserved my staunchness under these trials. I must confess, and I do it without great shame, conscious of being no more than human, that in my inmost soul I was as insubordinate as the worst men were in speech and behavior. In my unspeakable heart I groaned and raved. I wished the bridges would break down—I wished the regiment would refuse to take another step—it seemed to me that I should have been silent in the face of mutiny. But nothing of all this passed my lips, and none could suspect it from my actions.

When we bivouacked at night came the severest trial. Our regiment was on the left of the brigade, and as we always slept in line of battle, this threw us half a mile from the bayou, along which we marched, and which was our only source of water. It was necessary to order a squad of the blistered and bloody-footed men to bring water for the company's coffee. The first sergeant takes out his book and reads off the fatigue detail: "Corporal Smith,

Privates Brown, Jones, Robinson, and Brown second, fall in with canteens to get water."

Now ensues a piteous groaning, pleading, and showing of bloody heels or blistered soles, on the part of the most fagged or least manly of the victims of rotation in labor. The first sergeant feels that he has no discretion in the matter, and he knows, moreover, that the other men are fully as incapable of marching as these. He stands firm on his detail, and the opposition grumblingly yields. Slowly and sadly Messrs. Brown, Jones, Robinson, and Brown second take up the canteens of the company, each backing six or eight, and limp away to the river, returning, an hour later, wet, muddy, dragged out, and savage.

Somewhat similar scenes happened on the march. Aides passed down the length of the trailing column with the order, "Water half a mile in front; details will be sent forward with canteens." Under these circumstances, roguish soldiers would sometimes use the chance to forage, falling in an hour later with a load of chickens as well as of fluid.

Having tried various alleviations for the hardships of marching, without much benefit, I conclude that man was not made to foot it at the rate of thirty miles a day. Soaping the inside of the stockings does some good, by diminishing the friction and, as a consequence, the blistering. It is also advisable to wash the feet before starting, always providing you have sufficient time and water. Beware of washing them at night; it cracks the heated skin and increases the misery. Beware, too, of trying to march on the strength of whiskey; you go better for a few minutes, and then you are worse off than ever. Opium is far superior as a temporary tonic, if I may judge by a single day's experience. I started out sick, took four grains of opium, marched better and better every hour, and at the end of twenty-two miles came in as fresh as a lark.

It must be understood by the non-military reader that company officers of infantry are not permitted to mount horses, whether by borrowing or stealing, but must foot it alongside of their men, for the double purpose of keeping them in order and of setting them an example of hardihood. On this march, General Banks impounded, at a certain point on the road, more than a dozen infantry officers who were found astride of animals, causing each to rejoin his command as it passed, placing some under arrest and summarily dismissing one from the service. They looked exceedingly crestfallen as they stood there, cooped up in a barnyard under charge of the provost guard. The passing soldiers grinned at them, hooted a little, and marched on, much cheered by the spectacle.

If it had not been for the counter irritant of blistered feet, we should have heard a mutinous deal of grumbling on account of thirst. A man strapped up as a soldier is, and weighted with forty rounds of ammunition, knapsack, three days' rations, canteen containing three pints, and rifle, perspires profusely. I have seen the sweat standing on the woolly fibres of their flannel sacks like dew. To supply this waste of moisture they pour down the warm water of their canteens, and are soon begging for leave to fall out of the ranks in search of incredibly situated springs and rivulets. It will not do to accede to the request, for if one man goes, all have a right to go, and, moreover, the absence would probably terminate in a course of foraging or pillaging. Mindful of his duty and the orders of his superiors, the captain grimly responds, "Keep your place, sir," and trudges sufferingly on, cursing inwardly the heat, the dust, the pace and, perhaps, the orders. He knows that if his fellows are caught a mile to the rear wringing the necks of chickens, he may be sent after them; and, in view of his blisters and the fifteen miles already marched and the indefinite miles yet to go, he has no fancy for such an expedition. . . .

In describing the miseries of marching, I must not forget the dust. The movement of so many thousands of feet throws up such dense and prodigious clouds that one who has not witnessed the phenomenon will find it difficult to imagine it in all its vastness and nuisance. The officers dodge from side to side of the road to escape the pulverous suffocation; and the men, bound to their fours, choke desperately along in the midst of it. The faces become grimed out of all human semblance; the eyelashes are loaded, the hair discolored, and the uniform turns to the color of the earth. It frequently happens that you cannot see the length of your regiment, and it has occurred to me that I have been unable to see the length of my own company of perhaps twenty files. Of course, this annoyance varies greatly in magnitude, according to the nature of the earth.

Rain is good or bad, according to circumstances. In hot weather it cools the skin, invigorates the muscles, and is a positive comfort, except in so far as it spoils the footing. On the second day of this advance we had a pelting shower, which soaked everybody, including General Banks—which last circumstance was a source of unmixed satisfaction to the soldiers. Enlisted men like to see officers bear their share of the troubles of war; and, moreover, our fellows held the general responsible for the tearing speed at which we were going. But rain, although pleasant to the skin in warm weather, will reach the earth and make puddles; and to infantry in march a puddle in the road is a greater nuisance than people in carriages would imagine. No man, however wet he may be, wants to step into it; he crowds his next comrade, and so gets into a growling bout; or he hangs back, and so checks the succeeding files. A large puddle always produces a tailing-off of the regiment, which must be made up presently by double-quicking, much to the fatigue and wrath of the rearmost. Oh, miserable left of the column! how many times a day it has to run in order to catch up with the right! and how heartily it hates the right in consequence! Put a regiment or a brigade "left in front," and see how it will go. The men who usually march in the rear are now in the lead, and they are sure to give the fellows at the other end of the line a race. This opening out of the column of march is a constant evil, and one which officers soon learn to struggle against with incessant watchfulness. I believe that I used to shout, "Close up, men," at least a hundred times a day, in every conceivable tone of authority, impatience, and entreaty.

But are there no comforts, no pleasures, in forced marching? Just one:

stopping it. Yes, compared with the incessant anguish of going, there was a keen luxury in the act of throwing one's self at full length and remaining motionless. It was a beast's heaven; but it was better than beast's hell—insupportable fatigue and pain. The march done, the fevered feet bare to the evening breeze, the aching limbs outstretched, the head laid on the blanket roll which had been such a burden through the day, the pipe in mouth, nature revived a little and found that life retained some sweetness. Delicious dreams, too—dreams wonderfully distinct and consecutive—made slumber a conscious pleasure. All night I was at home surrounded by loving faces. No visions of war or troubles; no calling up of the sufferings of the day, nor anticipation of those of the morrow; nothing but home, peace, and friends. I do not know why this should be, but I have always found it so when quite worn out with fatigue, and I have heard others say that it was their experience.

I have already said that we were *en bivouac*. Shelter tents were as yet unknown in the Department of the Gulf, and our wall tents, as well as every other article of not absolutely essential baggage, had been left at Brashear City. For cover, our servants made hasty wigwams or lean-tos of rails, over which we threw our rubber blankets to keep out the "heft" of the showers. If it rained we sat up with our overcoats over our heads, or perhaps slept through it without minding. Not until August, more than three months later, did we again enjoy the shelter of a tent; and during that time we had only two brief opportunities for providing ourselves with board shanties. Meantime we became as dirty and ragged as beggars, and eventually as lousy.

For some time I supposed that what I ate was the free gift of the colored population, and rejoiced in the gratitude of the emancipated slaves who shared their food with their deliverers. My man George, a sly and slippery darkey, brought in sheep, chickens and corn-dodgers, saying that they had been given to him. Given they were, but by the providence of war, and not by the willing hands of emancipated men and brethren. George, representative of hungry Mars, entered whatever dwelling came handiest, whether of white or black, and took therefrom whatever was good to eat without offering to pay or consulting the inclination of the proprietor. I soon discovered this, but I had not the stomach to stop it. To march without food was impossible, and to buy without money was equally out of the question.

Let me suggest, in passing, that the irregular payments of the army were a fruitful source of demoralization. The officer cannot draw rations, and if his money is withheld from for six or eight or twelve months, as was frequently the case, he must allow his servant to forage for him, or he must starve. If he forages, the men will follow the example, although not driven by the same necessity, inasmuch as they are provided with food and clothing. The result is widespread straggling and often atrocious plundering. . . .

At Opelousas our pursuit of Mouton ceased for a few days. Even to this moment I am grateful for that halt and smile with pleasure over the recollection of it. Our provisions were out, and we thanked heaven for it, seeing starvation on the morrow to be pleasanter than marching today. So, until the Teche could be cleared of sunken gunboats, and the transports could come up with additional salt beef and hardtack, we rested in the green Opelousas. Oh, rest! oh, sleep! Three days and nights of solid sleep! It was better than kingdoms and the glory thereof. Except when I was on duty, or eating, I did little but lie folded in slumber. The hard ground was miraculously softened, and fitted my weary limbs like down. No one can imagine the luxury of rest to the utterly weary; it is like the first draught of water to one who has pined with thirst; it must be proven to be comprehended.

For one poor fellow of my company there was no repose, even now. Sick at Brashear City, he had voluntarily left hospital for the sake of fighting; had behaved nobly at Camp Beaseland, but failed rapidly under the severities of the pursuit. During this last day he staggered along between men detailed to support him, agonized with fever and half delirious, moaning: "We never rest! Oh, when shall we ever rest?" Now, with no bedding but his blanket, he lay on the ground, quite out of his head and muttering constantly, "Fall in!" as if he were still on the march. Ambulances we had none in the army, but he was sent in a country cart to hospital, and, after a long sickness, recovered.

On the arrival of the regiment it had been placed on picket, two miles north of the town; and when, next day, an order came to relieve it, men and officers begged to be allowed to remain undisturbed. Watching and the chance of fighting were trifles compared with even two miles of marching on those unhealed blisters. The petition was granted, and the Twelfth continued its picket duty, looking contentedly out over the great bare plain which led northward. No one would have wondered at our choice who had seen the plight in which the regiment reached this blessed bivouac. Seventy-five men and officers dragged along with the colors, while four hundred others lay gasping by the roadside for miles rearward, fagged nigh unto death with speed and the scorching rays of the Louisiana sun. In the whole history of the Twelfth, before and after, there never was such another falling out—not even when it was following Early up the Shenandoah, under cavalry Sheridan. The truth is that Banks was the most merciless marcher of men that I ever knew.

Our blisters had scarcely well hardened to callosities when orders reached Weitzel's brigade to break camp, overtake Dwight, who was five miles ahead, and push the enemy as rapidly as possible to Alexandria. I was at this time on a court-martial at Opelousas, and we might, I suspect, have remained on that duty, and so have escaped the three days of misery which followed; but, anticipating a battle, we enthusiastically deemed it our duty to adjourn to the General's headquarters and beg leave to join the column.

Starting at five in the afternoon, we reached a broken bridge about seven, made it passable by dint of several hours of labor, and then pushed on until three in the morning. Next to the stupidity and fruitless worry of night fighting comes the stupidity and fruitless worry of night marching. Except under extraordinary circumstances, the results which it achieves do not half compensate for the mischief which it works on the discipline of an army, and the morale and physique of the individual soldier. The officer cannot see his men, and they straggle in spite of him. There is constant falling, stumbling, and unrewarded waste of strength, accompanied by irritation, quarrelling, and disorderliness. Every molehill seems a mountain; every unusual darkness in the path shows like an abyss; the line is continually opening and must be closed up by laborious double-quicking. The men stagger against each other, and slumber marching. At every halt to rest, some fall asleep and are left behind in the darkness. When we bivouacked at three in the morning, ten hours from our starting point, we had made only sixteen miles, and were as exhausted as if we had gone thirty. My company was immediately sent out on picket, and this duty kept me moving and watching until sunrise. After a breakfast of hardtack and coffee, I dozed a few minutes while the fall-in call was beating, and then set off on a day's march of twenty-seven miles, coming in after nightfall well blistered.

The next day, bivouacked on rolling turf by the side of a lovely stream, we bathed and rested. Before dawn on the third morning, having as yet had less than ten hours' sleep since leaving Opelousas, I commenced the hardest day's work of my life. Starting lame, and improving from hour to hour, like foundered horses, we accomplished twenty-four miles by three in the afternoon. As usual, we had halted ten minutes in every hour, closing up, coming to a front, dressing the line, stacking arms, and dropping down by the side of the road to rest. The men had kept well together; such few as had fallen out had come up during the long pause which took place at three; and we were, so far, proud of our march and rather pleased at having done so much. But this sentiment was based on the expectation that we would presently go into bivouac. When, therefore, General Banks joined the column, and some one heard him say that we must reach Alexandria that night, and the horrible tale passed down along the line of stacks, our hearts were suddenly full of despair and growling.

For the next ten miles it was a fight against nature. Every effort was made to cheer the men onward and beguile them from a sense of their miseries. The staggering drummers were forced to beat the march for the staggering regiments. Some of the field officers dismounted and walked at the head of their commands. At one halt, Lieutenant Colonel Van Petten ran foot races in his big boots with a private, to make the soldiers laugh at the unusual buffoonery. Staff officers rode up and down the line, giving orders to yell and setting the example of uproar. The company officers carried the rifles of tottering men, and hastened from straggler to straggler, cheering, ordering, and threatening, but, I think, never striking; for no one could find it in his heart to maltreat poor fellows who were almost at the last gasp with pain and fatigue. We reeled, crawled, and almost rolled toward Alexandria.

As night fell, the pace increased, and the whooping became continuous, and we seemed like a column of maniacs. But in the last two miles, in the pitchy darkness between eight and nine of the evening, a silence of despair descended upon us, and then the regiments melted like frost in sunshine. I could not see who fell out of my company, and I did not care. My whole official sentiment of honor was concentrated, under the flame of intense physical suffering, into the one little idea of getting myself to Alexandria with the colors, no matter who else dropped by the way. The few men remaining in the organization reeled on speechlessly. If they passed a dying artillery horse, they no longer shouted, with savage defiance, "Fresh horses! bring on your horses!" They had stopped muttering curses against Banks and the Confederates—those two enemies. They were at the point, morally, of unspeakable desperation and, physically, of mere movement in one direction, without a thought or a sentiment beyond what was necessary to put one foot before the other, and to lean toward Alexandria.

If the enemy had been there we could not have fought him nor run away from him. But, fortunately, there was no enemy within twenty miles of us, as there had been none from the hour we started. God alone knows why we marched thus; our commander has probably forgotten. We had nothing more to boast of than that we had accomplished thirty-four miles in one day, and eighty-seven miles in the whole burst of seventy-six hours, to which Company D of the Twelfth Connecticut had added five miles by a nocturnal foraging expedition. About one third of the regiment stacked arms in the little wood where we bivouacked, and nearly all the remainder straggled in before morning. That night I was too tired to eat, and went contentedly to sleep without supper. . . .

Longer and more rapid forced marches than this of ours have been made, but I am glad that I was not called upon to assist at the performance. We should not have suffered so much as we did, had it not been for the heat, which not only wore out our muscular forces, but greatly increased the blistering of our feet.

Perhaps it is worth while to mention that, after two or three days of repose, we were excessively proud of our thirty-four miles in a day, and were ready to march with any other brigade in the army for a wager.

—DE FOREST, "Forced Marches"

8. AN INDIANA BOY REASSURES HIS MOTHER ABOUT MORALS IN THE ARMY

Theodore Upson was barely seventeen when he enlisted in the 100th Regiment of Indiana Volunteers. Brought up in a strict Presbyterian household, he was much concerned to reassure his parents about such matters as drinking, swearing, and gambling. On the whole the morals of both armies were remarkably good. There was comparatively little drunkenness and, by modern standards, little gambling. While there was a great deal of pillaging, especially among the invaders, crimes against persons were rare and sex offenses almost unknown. Young Upson fought at Vicksburg and Chattanooga and was with Sherman in his March to the Sea.

Bellefont, Ala., April 2, 1864

Dear Mother—

I have had several letters from the home people asking me about drinking in the Army, and Father has written me saying he hopes I am not getting to be a d[r]unkard as he hears many of the soldiers are. I think you good people at home must imagine we keep a barell of whisky on tap all of the time. Now for the truth about this and other things that are told about our boys. There is some drinking in the Army, I am sorry to say, but it is the exception rather than the rule. Some of our officers may take a social glass when they get together at times but few if any of them drink to excess, and I think drinking among the officers is less now than ever before. Good officers know that when wine is in, wit is out. They know too that the men distrust and have no confidence in an intemperate officer, in fact will make fun of him. And an officer whose men make fun of him had better resign as some *have done*, for his usefulness is at an end. I know what I am talking about for I have been around Hd Quarters enough to have learned the habits of our Generals. Grant does not drink at all; Sherman but little, if any; I don't think any. Howard never; McPherson, I think, never; Logan is no tippler; and in our Division and Brigade officers all, or nearly all, are total abstainers.

As to the rank and file hardly a man is a drinker. It is not so easy for a soldier to get liquor as most people seem to think. First, he has to have an order from a commissioned officer. Not so easy to get as the officers do not want thier men to drink. Next, it takes money which the men are often without. Another thing, good hard experience has taught them that liquour is no good, that they need clear heads and sound bodies to stand the strain and hardships of Army life. A soldier must be above all temperate in all things.

As to profanity a good many of the boys do use swear words, some liberaly, some not at all. But this is a strenuous life. Men will do here what they would not do at home and I know this. Profanity is not deep nor vicious. Let a Chaplain come along who the men respect and the most of them will be gaurded in thier talk. Why? Because all the time thier better selves are lying dormant and under different conditions would assert themselves. We have a good many men, Uncle Aaron Woflord, for instance, who set a good quiet example which is respected, to say the least, by the roughest.

As to gambling, there is very little of it. The men play cards a good deal, it is true, sometimes for small stakes, but it is for amusement alone. No gambling about it. A real gambler would not be held in any respect by the men.

As to other vices, I think I am safe in saying that you might search the world over and not find as clean a lot of men as comprise the Army today. I do not say it has always been so, but the men who compose the great Army to which I have the honor to belong have passed through the trials and temptations of the soldiers life and now are like gold—cleared of its dross. And when this war is ended and what are left of this Army return to civil life, you will see that they will be accepted as among the best and highest of ideal American citizens. All the roughness will fall away and they will be shining lights in thier chosen walks of life. As for myself, I am too proud to dabble in mud and mire. So do not worry, Father mine, I am not going to the dogs; neither are any of the other boys you know.

I have at one time mentioned our excellent Chaplain, Rev John A Brouse, father of Captain Charles Brouse, who was so teribly wounded at Mission Ridge. Chaplain Brouse is a valient soldier, not only of the Cross, but also of this war. He never seems to think of himself and was right on the firing line helping care for the wounded and saying words of comfort to the dying. A noble man is Chaplain Brouse and the boys love him as a Father. There is also a Chaplain of the 90 Ill, a Catholic Preist, who is greatly loved and respected by all of the men of his and other Regiments. So you see this war is breaking down the barriers between beliefs and creeds as well as doing many other things you may think more or less desirable. And another thing I know you will find it hard to understand, money has but little value with the boys now. They all seem to think the pittance paid them by the Government is an incident of the service, that they are giving this part of thier lives for a principle and do not expect to gain any personal profit from it in any way.

—WINTHER, ed., *Journal of Theodore Upson*

9. AN ILLINOIS PRIVATE COMPLAINS OF BAD COOKING

The food provided for the Union soldiers was adequate quantitatively, but that is about all that can be said for it. The normal ration consisted of a pound of hardtack, or its equivalent, three-quarters pound of bacon or salt pork or a pound of beef, plus coffee, sugar and salt. By modern dietary standards this diet was calculated to break down the strongest constitutions. Not only was it badly planned, and monotonous, but it was generally badly cooked. Cooking was commonly assigned not to trained cooks but to soldiers detailed for brief periods to that unpleasant job. Fortunately many of the soldiers supplemented their regular rations by setting up their own messes, by boxes from home, or—more commonly in the West—by foraging.

We have met Leander Stillwell before, in the midst of battle.

I RETAIN a vivid recollection of the kind of army cooking we had for the first few months in Tennessee. At Camp Carrolton and Benton Barracks we had company cooks who prepared the food for the entire company. They were merely enlisted men, detailed for that purpose, and while their cooking was nothing to brag about, it was vastly superior to what now ensued. We divided up into messes, of four, eight, or twelve men, or thereabouts, to the mess, and generally would take turns in the culinary line. Very few of us knew anything whatever about cooking, and our exploits in that regard would have been comical if the effects had not been so pernicious. Flour was issued to us after our arrival at Pittsburg Landing, but we had no utensils in which we could cook biscuits, or loaves. So we would make a batter out of flour, water, grease, and salt, and cook it in a mess pan, the product being the army "flapjack." It invariably was tough as a mule's ear, about as heavy as lead, and very indigestible. Later we learned to construct ovens of wood, daubed with mud, or of stone, and in them, in the course of time, we acquired the knack of baking good bread. But with us in the west the hardtack was generally our standard bread diet, and nothing could beat it.

And for some time our cooking of "Yankee beans," as we called them, was simply atrocious. As you know, beans should be cooked until they are thoroughly done; otherwise they are decidedly harmful. Well, we would not cook them much more than half enough, the result being a sloppy, slimy mess, its looks alone being well-nigh sufficient to extinguish one's appetite. And as for the rice—the horrible messes we would make of that defy description. I know that one consequence with me was I contracted such an aversion to rice that for many years afterwards, while in civil life, I just couldn't eat it in any form, no matter how temptingly it was prepared.

Owing to improperly cooked food, change of climate and of water, and neglect of proper sanitation measures in the camps, camp diarrhea became epidemic at Pittsburg Landing, especially among the "green" regiments like ours. And for about six weeks everybody suffered, more or less, the difference being only in degree. The fact is, the condition of the troops in that quarter during the prevalence of that disorder was simply so bad and repulsive that any detailed description thereof will be passed over. I never saw the like before, and never have seen it since. I always thought that one thing which aggravated this trouble was the inordinate quantity of sugar some of the men would consume. They would not only use it to excess in their coffee and rice, but would frequently eat it raw, by handfuls.

I happen to think, right now, of an incident that illustrates the unnatural appetite of some of the men for sugar. It occurred in camp one rainy day during the siege of Corinth. Jake Hill, of my company, had covered the top of a big army hardtack with sugar in a cone-like form, piling it on as long as the tack would hold a grain. Then he seated himself on his knapsack and proceeded to gnaw away at his feast, by a system of "regular approaches." He was even then suffering from the epidemic before mentioned, and was so weak he could hardly walk.

Some one said to him, "Jake, that sugar ain't good for you in your condition."

He looked up with an aggrieved air and responded in a tone of cruelly injured innocence, "Haven't I the right to eat my r-a-a-tion?"

Strange to say, Jake got well, and served throughout the war. He was a good soldier, too. . . .

In consequence of the conditions at Pittsburg Landing that have been alluded to, men died by the score like rotten sheep. And a great many more were discharged for disability and thereby were lost to the service. It is true that some of these discharged men, especially the younger ones, subsequently re-enlisted, and made good soldiers. But this loss to the Union armies in Tennessee in the spring of '62 by disease would undoubtedly surpass the casualties of a great battle, but, unlike a battle, there was no resulting compensation whatever.

—STILLWELL, *The Story of a Common Soldier of Army Life in the Civil War*

10. HOW TO MAKE MONEY IN THE ARMY

There were fraud and chicanery in American business a-plenty in the sixties, and inevitably they made their appearance in the armies, North and South. As Federal soldiers had more money to spend—and more things to spend it on—there was more of the sort of thing described here in the North than in the South.

E. W. Locke, who here recalls the various methods of preying on the soldiers, was a professional singer, author of such popular songs as "Down by the Sea" and "I Feel I'm Growing Old, Lizzie," and temperance lecturer who "attached" himself to General Abercrombie's division.

FOR a time, peddling watches in the camps was a great business; they were made almost expressly for the Army, showy, cheap as possible, and if they would only run for a short time, it mattered little whether they would keep time or not. But will the soldier, who in the first year of the war gets but eleven dollars a month, spend twenty dollars for a watch, and especially without knowing whether it is good or worthless? Those only who are ignorant of the tastes of young people will ask this question. Of course he will, unless he thinks he wants something else more. . . .

Watch-peddling was a business in the Army not to be sneered at. One Jew, who has been dodging in and out of the tents of one regiment all day, has sold twenty-seven before sundown, and he will sell many more before tattoo. They are all of one pattern, and very taking to the eye. They may run a month or a year, and they may keep tolerably correct time. But they were made more for sale than service, and they sell. . . .

Among the most useful of the camp-followers were the picture-makers. This business continued in the camp, with short intervals of exclusion, to the end of the war; and the number was small, indeed, who did not send home likenesses. If the friends at home have not seen the boy in soldier-clothes, he is anxious to show them how he looks. If he has been promoted to a Corporal, with two stripes on his arm, or a Sergeant, with three, or an Orderly, with stripes and a square, the picture sent home will tell the story better than a letter. Jealous neighbors cannot gainsay the ambrotype. The Lieutenant, the Captain, the Major, the Colonel, all must go to the artist as soon as they receive the insignia of their promotion. It is not necessary to write that a Lieutenant has become a Captain, those two bars on that shoulder-strap tell the news.

Some of the artists made considerable money, but they earned all they received. It sometimes happened that a shell, or other missile, would come whizzing along, while the operator was adjusting the lenses. Squinting at his man, through the camera, suddenly his apparatus is *non est*.

Often the picture taken in camp is the last and most precious memento the home-circle has of him who sleeps they know not where. These mementos exist in every town and hamlet in our country.

Another most useful class of camp-followers were the soldiers' memorial agents. We see these significant lithographs hanging in many a house. When my eye catches one of them in a stranger's house, I know at once that family had a near friend in the war. There is one name on that paper, perhaps more, very precious to them. . . . The day will come when they will be to many families precious as a coat of arms. A hundred years hence, and they will be shown with pride, and exultant men will say, "That was my grandfather's brother, or that was my great-uncle. He died for the flag."

Every one has seen these memorials; but all do not know how they were prepared. A lithographer executed the design on stone, leaving blank space for printing in the names, company, regiment, and other items of interest, such as time of enlistment, discharge, or death. The lithograph, as it comes from the stone, is as good for one regiment as another. Agents visit the camp, and obtain all the necessary items for printing, take orders, at perhaps a dollar and a half each, return to have the printing done, and, in due time, probably soon after pay-day, reappear in camp to furnish the subscribers with the coveted memorial. If a battle has occurred in the agent's absence, many of his orders are worthless. "Fell in battle." An asterisk at their names directs to these fearful words. At one time this was a largely-paying business.

Taking butter to the Army was, at times, a profitable speculation. If the trader was shrewd, he would time his shipment so that it would reach the camp about pay-day. I do not remember, however, to have met any one who made a fortune in this business.

Many made considerable money in purchasing the hides of the slaughtered cattle. But there were rings in the Army, as there are out; and if you were not in the ring, you could not purchase hides.

An enterprising, but not very shrewd Yankee, visited Chatanooga, in the winter of '64, and seeing the great number of hides that were daily accumulating, endeavored to buy them; but some were ahead of him, or were in the ring, while our Yankee was out. He would then purchase the tallow. "O, yes; he could have the tallow;" for as yet there was no tallow-ring, and speedily there is a large candle-factory in operation, not in Chatanooga, Murfreesboro', or Nashville, but in the brain of the speculator. He has learned the price of candles, and is not long in coming to the conclusion, that with tallow at two, and candles at twelve cents per pound, there is a moderate fortune in the business. Hurrying to Nashville for a quantity of moulds, some large kettles, and one or two experts to assist in the new speculation, he soon has his plans well matured. But it requires time to make the moulds, and before the army candle-factory is completed, the short evenings have come, the Army is ready to move, and the anticipated fortune vanishes.

While the Army lay in winter quarters, it was a good field for theatrical and minstrel troupes. I know one man who made thirty thousand dollars in two seasons, in this line. Just how he did it, I am not able to say; but this I know, he went there with nothing, and came away at the end of the second winter with that amount of money.

Many made a great deal of money by circulating bills of worthless banks.

I met one man who had a thousand dollars in notes of the Bank of Tecumseh, Michigan. They, of course, were worthless at home; but I doubt not they brought him their face in whatever he wished to buy. Notes of broken banks were sent to the Army, and sold to shrewd, unscrupulous men, as counterfeit money is sold, and the dealers made small fortunes. "But how could this be done to any extent?" If one had a nominal thousand dollars in these notes, he could easily sell them at half price, it answering as well as good money to purchase anything the Southern people or Negroes had to sell. For a year after greenbacks were issued, the Southern people preferred notes of State banks, whether good or not, to them. It sometimes happened that our troops would advance on a place, as, for example, Winchester, hold it a short time, retire for a season, and then reoccupy. If they had distributed greenbacks at the first occupation, at the second there was an opportunity to gather them in exchange for State bills. Then was the time for the dealer in notes of broken banks.

The most cruel swindles were perpetrated on the Southern people and Negroes, after the issue of facsimile Confederate notes. These could be bought for a trifle. At times the Negroes made quite a business of washing, baking hoe-cakes, picking cherries, and other fruit, and bringing sweet pota- toes to camp. It was cruel to pretend to pay them for their hard toil in this worthless stuff, yet the quantity thus disposed of no doubt amounted to a million of dollars. . . .

If I knew the mysteries of cotton-buying, I could make this chapter in- tensely interesting. I saw it brought in by ten, twenty and fifty bales, but never a pound sold. Here was a ring that only the favored few could enter. Expeditions failed through the avarice of the leading officers. Men preferred making five hundred thousand dollars to gaining a victory.

I always noticed when cotton was brought in, that some of the officers connected with the Provost-Marshal's Department took special interest in it. I noticed, furthermore, that when a citizen of the North came to the Army with funds, and the hope of buying this article, there was always something in the way. The authorities at Washington were not granting permits, or the Army was to advance shortly, or it would be extremely hazardous to attempt to move it. I was told by one of these citizens that he was informed by one of the officers who stood very near the General commanding, that he could not only obtain a permit to buy cotton, but have the exclusive privilege of the department, by furnishing the requisite capital, taking all risks, and divid- ing the profits. . . .

Many persons made money by smuggling quinine, and other articles which brought a great price. In taking my trunk to the depot at Louisville one morning, I noticed a woman of middle age, dressed in black, standing by her trunk, waiting, as we all were, to have our baggage carefully inspected, before it could be taken aboard the train for Nashville. Inspecting the articles in due order, the officer comes to the lady's trunk, which she has already opened, and proceeds to examine dresses, skirts, and other articles of female apparel, which, having done to his satisfaction, he locks the trunk, and politely hands her the key. Turning it on end to mark it, his suspicions are aroused, and he demands the key again, opening it, running his cane down inside, then measuring to the floor, he sees that the trunk has a false bottom. The articles are removed, the thin board split out with his cane, and there are needles enough to supply a good sized town for a year; neither she nor her trunk went to Nashville on that train. The last I saw of her she was turning a corner with an officer, who was escorting her to the office of the Provost-Marshal. How she expected to get these needles through the lines, and how much profit there would have been on the sales had her enterprise been successful, I know not.

Judging from what I saw of the people where we went, I should think needles were the last things to smuggle. The articles most needed were wheat and soap.

—LOCKE, *Three Years in Camp and Hospital*

11. GRAFT AND CORRUPTION IN THE CONFEDERATE COMMISSARY

Complaints against the commissary were ardent, on both sides. The simple fact was that there was no such organization of the commissary department, during the Civil War, as we are familiar with from the First and Second World Wars. Nor was there any adequate check on the food and drink that went through the commissary, or on the activities of the sutlers.

This picture of graft in the Confederate commissary is doubtless accurate enough for Watson's particular outfit, but it is by no means a faithful picture of conditions generally in the Confederate armies. We have already met the irrepressible Watson on the retreat from Pea Ridge.

THE army was furnished, through the quarter master's department, with quarters, whether houses or tents, camp equipage, arms, ammunition, accoutrements, and clothing, and all means of transport. These the department obtained from contractors, and the shocking quality of the materials furnished showed corruption to a great extent. The soldier, of course, knew nothing about the contracts, and in the South they had always the excuse that good materials were not to be got; but the things which mostly affected the soldier personally were shoes and clothing, and these, to a great extent, they managed to provide for themselves, or they were sent to them by their friends at home.

The system pursued by the commissaries, even making allowance for the difficulties they were subject to, were simply disgraceful. I do not exaggerate when I say that on an average from every requisition of rations said to be issued to the troops, the commissary took off one-third and sold it, putting the proceeds in his pocket. The cause of this peculation lay greatly in the system of management. I might say that the system, as it then existed, was such that even a man of the most sterling integrity, and of honest and upright principles, if appointed commissary of a regiment on active service could hardly, after six months, remain an honest man. If so, he would deserve the greatest credit for it.

The system was this: The commissary received a supply of provisions from the depot. He got with it an invoice detailing quantity and price. From these he issued to the non-commissioned officers and soldiers, on requisitions signed by the orderly-sergeants and captains of companies. He sold for money to all officers and men pertaining to the army. He had to account for the amount of the consignment (losses and casualties excepted) by money and requisitions. The practice was this: An orderly sergeant made out a requisition for his company—say for 100 men for one day—flour, 100 lb.; beef, pork, or bacon, 75 lb.; coffee, seven lb.; sugar, 14 lb.; rice or pease, six lb.; soap, two lb.; salt, pepper, vinegar, etc. This requisition was signed by the captain, and men were detailed to go to the commissary store to draw these rations. The commissary takes the requisition and calls his assistant, and says to the men, "Well, you can get three-quarter ration of flour, half ration of pork, half ration of coffee, and half ration of sugar, and that is all." The men would grumble and say, "We only got half rations yesterday." "Can't help it, I am short of provisions, and there are other companies to serve as well as you, and all must get their share." He then sticks the requisition on the file, and his assistant weighs out the rations. "Will we get the back rations when the supplies come up?" some mischievous young rascal would say as he dodged behind a barrel. The commissary would put his hand on his revolver, but restrain himself, and pretend to take no notice of a thing so absurd, and buries his face in his book, while he credits himself with full rations issued to 100 men as per requisition, while his assistant and the men would laugh at the audacity of the offender, "no back rations" being the commissary's watchword, and, what was more strange, no requisition would be received unless it was made out for the full amount.

Thus the commissary had a voucher for and was credited with supplying a full requisition when he had only supplied a small part of it, and he had the rest to sell for his own benefit. I have frequently known instances of a company, after giving the full requisition and being supplied with half rations on the grounds that provisions were scarce, getting one of the army waggon drivers, and giving him money to go to the commissary store and purchase four or five pounds of coffee, or other necessaries, which had been kept off them, which he would obtain for money without the least trouble, and this system was carried on quite openly. I more than once nearly got into serious difficulty by insisting on marking on the requisition the actual quantity of provisions delivered.

In the post-commissaries and depots there was another system of peculation.

In these depots there were immense stocks of provisions stored for army use. These were periodically inspected by officers, generally of the sinecure kind appointed through favour for such purposes, and there was always a considerable quantity marked "condemned" as being unfit for use. The ceremony of inspecting was generally done in this way: The inspecting officers would come to the depot, where they would be met by the post-commissary, who would receive them in the most friendly manner, and conduct them into the large stores. On each side along the wall would be piled up on the top of each other with their ends exposed, a great many barrels of beef, pork, flour, biscuit, etc.

"These," says the commissary, "are what I have myself picked out as being bad. Those on this side are good, but you can inspect for yourself. Cooper, open one or two of these barrels." The cooper opens a barrel which of course had been already selected. The unsavoury brine spurts out. The officers stand back to save their handsome uniforms. Other barrels are examined of flour, biscuit, etc., similarly selected. Then all on that side, the bulk of which were probably the best provisions, are ordered to be marked condemned. The officers would take a list of the numbers to make their report, and then go and inspect the hospital stores of wines, brandies, etc., of which they would acknowledge they were better judges. A few days' notice would then be given of a sale of "condemned army stores" and they would be auctioned off for a mere trifle. The commissary of course has an agent present who knew what lots to purchase.

Thus it was said large quantities of the very best stores were often marked "Condemned" and sold off at a mere trifle, the commissary having an agent on the ground to buy them in.

—WATSON, *Life in the Confederate Army*

12. THE SOLDIERS GET PAID AND THE SUTLER GETS THE MONEY

By European standards the United States paid its soldiers well; by American standards the pay was shockingly low. At the beginning of the war it was 11 dollars a month for privates, plus a clothing allowance; this was raised to 13 and then to 16 dollars, but the depreciation of money meant that the purchasing value of this pay actually declined during the war. It should be remembered, however, that soldiers' pay was supplemented by Federal and state bounties. The pay of Confederate soldiers was even lower, and the rapid depreciation of Confederate currency meant that most soldiers were fighting without pay.

Not only was Civil War pay low, but soldiers were expected to supply most of the services and comforts that the government furnished in later wars. Thus they had to do their own wash, or find some camp hanger-on to do it; they supplemented their food by private purchases; they even bought their own stoves. Sutlers, who supplied luxuries to the soldiers—tobacco, fruit, cheese, and sometimes liquor—held a semiofficial position. In an effort to regulate them, Congress provided that a board of officers should fix the prices charged, and that no sutler might take a lien on more than one sixth of a soldier's pay in any one month, but these provisions were generally ignored.

AT intervals, various in duration, we were visited by the paymaster, who paid us what was coming from the Government. A paymaster had the rank of Major in the regular army. To us in the field he always came with his "strong box" conveyed in an ambulance, or army wagon, and well guarded by a troop of cavalry with loaded carbines in their hands. Reaching a particular regiment he would go over the amount due each man, as reported by the Adjutant, and, if this was found correct, the specified sum would be put in a pay envelope; then the men would be formed in line, and when the name of a given soldier was called he would step forward and receive his money, which was always in currency or "greenbacks." Even small fractional amounts were paid in paper money, as neither gold, silver, nor even copper was in circulation.

The paymaster always had on a bright, new uniform, his linen was immaculate, and his boots never failed to be glossy black. In all this he presented a striking contrast to the other officers in active service in the field.

The more thrifty among the soldiers sent, by far, the greater part of their pay home. In most instances this was done through express companies which followed us in the field, and were new institutions to practically all of us. The prudent soldier, if so disposed, had opportunity to lay by substantially all his wages, which, in the early part of the war, was for the private soldier $13 per month, but later was advanced to $16. The ration furnished by the Government was ample, and so was the clothing allowed each man. Indeed, some of the more thrifty did not use all that was allowed in this way, and consequently received commutation in the way of small, but by no means, intangible amounts of money.

As said above, a few men sent their pay home to almost the last cent. In contrast to these of the more thrifty there was a pitiful minority who had squandered their last farthing in a few hours after being paid off. How? Some of them in gambling with cards, some of them at dice, and others by indulging in what was called "chuck-a-luck." This last was a game of chance, with the *chances* very greatly against the poor soldier victim on the outside.

Not a few "blew-in" all they had received from the paymaster at the Sutler's tent. The Sutler was the recognized regimental merchant. After securing the consent of the commanding officer the Sutler proceeded to lay in a stock of such things as he thought the men would need in the field, and in amount about what could be loaded in a wagon.

His stock included such articles as tobacco, cigars, lemons, oranges, apples, candy, raisins, soda crackers, cakes, canned fruits of various kinds, loaf sugar, mackerel, salt fish, bacon, ginger ale, "pop" and other "soft" drinks. Nearly all these articles were outside the soldier's rations, and were hence, by him, regarded as luxuries which the more provident refused to buy.

Arrived in camp the Sutler transferred his goods to a strong tent of proper size, which through the day, was open in front and, at which, was a wide transverse board which served the double purpose of counter and showcase. The sides of the tent came well down and were securely fastened. The Sutler always slept in his tent and in the midst of his stock. However, sometimes a thief would take advantage of the darkness to rip a hole in the sides of the tent and make a hasty dash for whatever he might be able to lay his hands on.

That the Sutler's prices were always high, and sometimes even exorbitant, can well be imagined. But to make a good profit he had to mark his goods high, for he necessarily incurred great risk. In the field he was in danger of capture. Then, when the regiment had orders to move on short notice, he had to pack his stock hurriedly and often put it "pell-mell" in a wagon for transfer to the next camping place. Furthermore, unless quickly turned some of his goods would grow stale on his hands. One article of this nature was butter, which not infrequently became so rancid as to be wholly unusable.

As to the Sutler himself, he might be long or short. He might be a blonde or brunette. He might be a native or foreigner. But one thing he was always sure to be, namely, "on the make." At the time the average regiment was organized those who joined it were actuated by motives more or less mixed in character. But with the Sutler it was different, for his sole motive was gain.

An "easy-mark" for the Sutler was the financial "tenderfoot," the "live-to-day-and-starve-to-morrow" man who was in every regiment, in every company, and indeed, in practically every squad. And no sooner had this "come-easy-go-easy" specimen received his pay than he forthwith went to the Sutler's tent and proceeded to get "outside" a good deal that, for the man's good, had far better have been left on the shelves.

But not only would these "easy-goers" get rid of their money, but often-times the stuff they ate would make them sick. Indeed, in every regiment more than one death could primarily be attributed to certain articles in the Sutler's tent.

—CHARLES BENEULYN JOHNSON, *Muskets and Medicine*

13. SONG AND PLAY IN THE ARMY OF TENNESSEE

The period which Bromfield Ridley here describes was toward the end of the war, when things looked blackest for the Confederacy. By that time Johnston's army had been driven out of South Carolina and into North Carolina. In the midst of this scene of disaster Ridley took the opportunity to recall some of the more cheerful aspects of army life. What he recorded is of interest alike to students of social history and of the American language. Ridley was a first lieutenant, attached to the staff of General A. P. Stewart.

ONE night, one of Colonel McLemore's captains formed a line of battle by saying: "Boys, you can't see me, but dress up on my voice." Colonel Anderson would say, "Dress up on my friend Brit." These things got to be by-words in those commands. Instead of "Blow the Bugle," it was "Toot the Dinner Horn." That takes me to some of our greenhorns in the drill. When we first started, a fellow in East Tennessee began drilling his company thus: "Men, tangle in fours! By move forward! Put! Wheel into line! By turn around! Git!" A Middle Tennessee captain, wanting his company to cross a creek on a log, said: "Attention, company! In one rank to walk a log! Walk a log! March!"

It carried you back to old times to hear the guards around a regiment halloo out, "T-w-e-l-v-e o'-c-l-o-c-k and a-l-l-'s well!" The rude and untrained soldier would play on that and say: "T-w-e-l-v-e o'-c-l-o-c-k, and sleepy as h—l!" When a soldier goes out foraging it is called going on a "lark;" when he goes stealing, it is "impressing it into service;" when a Quartermaster wants to shield his rascality, he has a favorite abstract called "L," which is used, and means "Lost in the service;" when a squad runs from the enemy, it is "Skedadling;" the ricochetting of a cannon ball is "Ski-ugling"—words whose origin began with the war. Let a stranger or soldier enter camp and call for a certain company—say, Company F. Some soldier will say, "Here's Company F!" By the time he can get there, another will cry out at the far part of the regiment, "Here's Company F!" Then the whole command will take up the refrain, until the poor fellow in vexation will sulk away. Let an old soldier recognize a passing friend, and say, "How are you Jim?" a marching division will keep it up, with "How are you, Jim?" until the poor fellow swoons.

In the army we have some of the finest mimics in the world. Let one cackle like a hen, and the monotony of camp is broken by the encore of "S-h-o-o!" Then other cacklers take it up, until it sounds like a poultry yard stirred up over a mink or a weasel. Let one bray like an ass, others take it up until the whole regiment will personate the sound, seemingly like a fair ground of asses. As mimics they are perfect; as musicians, also. I met one once who said, "If you will give me a jigger, I'll give you some chin music." He put his hands to his chin, and with his teeth made a sound like rattling bones, keeping time to his pat and song. Some of the finest singers I ever heard were soldiers and some of the best acting I ever saw was done by them. In camp it is so delightful to hear the brass band dispensing music in the sweetest strains. Near Atlanta, a Dutch battery entertained us every fifteen minutes, and whilst we kept our eyes open to the music of the shells from far away would beat upon our ears the music of the enemy's brass bands; our bands would tune up and make us oblivious to the roar of that old battery. I tried once in the progress of the battle to assimilate it to music. The sound of the minnie ball—Zip! Zip!—I dubbed the soprano; the roar of the musketry, the alto; the lingering sound of battle, the tenor; the artillery, the basso. Now, intersperse it with the interlude of an old Rebel yell, and you've got it.

As to wit and sarcasm you hear in camp, I'd defy the world to beat it. Anyone attempting to be consequential, or unnatural, is the character to work on, and the gravest of the Chaplains cannot look upon their ridicule without smiling. A psalm-singing soldier one day gave out a distich for song, to sing to the long meter hymn of St. Thomas. Some blasphemous fellow changed it to

C. Parsons

Gun and Mortar Boats on the Mississippi

A. C. Redwood

Confederate Sharpshooters Attacking Mortar Boats

"The possum am a cunning fowl,
He climbs upon a tree."

The regiment broke out with the chorus.

"Rye-straw! Rye-straw! Rye-straw!"
"And when he wraps his tail 'round a limb,
He turn and looks at me."
"Rye-straw! Rye-straw! Rye-straw! Rye-straw!"

This is shocking to us now, but when you reflect upon the idea that in their daily walk the soldiers had no way of entertainment, it was excusable to find some means of pastime and of keeping cheerful, if sacrilege is pardonable.

Some of the parodies on our Southern songs should be remembered. I copy a verse to the tune of "My Maryland." (If you know the tune, sing it.)

Old Stonewall Jackson's in the field,
Here's your mule, Oh, here's your mule!
And he has the boys that will not yield,
Here's your mule, Oh, here's your mule!
And when you hear the old man pray,
You may be sure that on next day,
The very Devil will be to pay—
Here's your mule, Oh, here's your mule!

And now since my native place is Old Jefferson, Tennessee, within a stone's throw of the battlefield of Murfreesboro (Stone's river), I think of the devastation and desolation created there by war. I will give a verse of my parody that I used to sing, as I rode along in Ward's regiment, Morgan's cavalry.

Also to enjoy it sing it as you read.

The Yankee's heel is on the street,
Jefferson, Old Jefferson!
I hear the tramp of the vandal's feet,
Jefferson, Old Jefferson!
Hark! I hear a rooster squall,
The vandal takes them hen and all,
And makes the men and women bawl,
Jefferson, Old Jefferson!

One more on the Happy Land of Canaan, and I am done. (If you know the tune sing it.)

I will sing you a song, as the ladies pass along,
All about the times we are gaining; aha!
I will sing it in rhymes, and suit it to the times,
And we'll call it the "Happy Land of Canaan."—Chorus.

Oh me! Oh my! The pride of our Southern boys am coming; aha!
So it's never mind the weather, but get over double trouble,
For I'm bound for the Happy Land of Canaan.

In the Harper's Ferry section, there was an insurrection,
Old John Brown thought the niggers would sustain him, aha!
But old Governor Wise put his specks upon his eyes,
And sent him to the Happy Land of Canaan.—CHORUS.

Old John Brown is dead, and the last words he said,
"Don't keep me here a long time remaining;" aha!
So we led him up a slope, and hung him on a rope,
And sent him to the Happy Land of Canaan.—CHORUS.

                    —RIDLEY, *Battles and Sketches of the Army of Tennessee*

XIII

Incidents of Army Life: Western Front

FUNDAMENTALLY, *as we have already observed, the war in the East and in the West was pretty much the same. The same soldiers fought, the same officers commanded; the same weapons and techniques were used. Differences were imposed by considerations of geography rather than by social or psychological considerations. Thus warfare in the West was more mobile, more fluid. Armies fought over vast areas and army corps and divisions were shifted back and forth from Missouri to Mississippi to Tennessee. Occasionally—as with Rosecrans' army at Murfreesboro, between Stones River and the Tullahoma campaigns—the Western armies did stay put for some length of time, but normally they were on the move. The soldiers got a chance to see more varied types of society and economy than in the fighting in Virginia.*

There was another difference—in degree rather than in kind, to be sure. As has been mentioned, the fighting in the West was more nearly a civil war than was the fighting in the East. Family fought against family, brother against brother. The pillaging was about as bad in the East as in the West, but there was nothing in the East so savage as the guerrilla warfare in Missouri, nor was there anything like the bitterness in West Virginia that was found in eastern Tennessee.

Because of these circumstances of geography and history there is, about the fighting in the West, a more personal and perhaps a more casual character than is to be found elsewhere. Thus Mark Twain tells us how uncertain he and his friends were whether they were Confederates or Unionists. Thus there seemed to be—perhaps it is an illusion—a more personal quality about the cavalry fighting; Forrest and Morgan roamed pretty much where they would; Grierson seemed to be on his own; Wilson raised his cavalry his own way.

It is perhaps not too bold a generalization to say that the warfare in Virginia approached more nearly the traditional warfare of the Old World, while the warfare in the West kept a bit more its casual independence and almost its frontier character.

1. MARK TWAIN RECALLS A CAMPAIGN THAT FAILED

As a young man of twenty-two Mark Twain was apprenticed to a river pilot—the most glorious of all professions, he thought—and four years on the river gave him the material for Life on the Mississippi. *The Civil War closed*

the river to ordinary steamboat traffic, and he returned to his boyhood town,
Hannibal, Missouri. There he joined a volunteer company of a dozen or so,
which, according to his own story, was ready to fight on either side. "Out
West," he wrote, "there was a good deal of confusion in men's minds during
the first months of the great trouble. . . . It was hard for us to get our bear-
ings." His campaign came to an inglorious end when he sprained an ankle
falling out of a barn hayloft. One of the "Marion Rangers," Absalom Grimes,
later became a famous Confederate scout. As Mark Twain himself says, this
is not an unfair picture of what went on in the border states during the early
months of the war.

YOU have heard from a great many people who did something in the war;
is it not fair and right that you listen a little moment to one who started
out to do something in it, but didn't? Thousands entered the war, got just a
taste of it, and then stepped out again, permanently. These, by their very
numbers, are respectable, and are therefore entitled to a sort of voice,—not a
loud one, but a modest one; not a boastful one, but an apologetic one. They
ought not to be allowed much space among better people—people who did
something—I grant that; but they ought at least to be allowed to state why
they didn't do anything, and also to explain the process by which they
didn't do anything. Surely this kind of light must have a sort of value.

Out West there was a good deal of confusion in men's minds during the
first months of the great trouble—a good deal of unsettledness, of leaning first
this way, then that, then the other way. It was hard for us to get our bear-
ings. I call to mind an instance of this. I was piloting on the Mississippi when
the news came that South Carolina had gone out of the Union on the 20th
of December, 1860. My pilot-mate was a New Yorker. He was strong for
the Union; so was I. But he would not listen to me with any patience; my
loyalty was smirched, to his eye, because my father had owned slaves. I said,
in palliation of this dark fact, that I had heard my father say, some years
before he died, that slavery was a great wrong, and that he would free the
solitary Negro he then owned if he could think it right to give away the
property of the family when he was so straitened in means. My mate re-
torted that a mere impulse was nothing—anybody could pretend to a good
impulse; and went on decrying my Unionism and libeling my ancestry. A
month later the secession atmosphere had considerably thickened on the
Lower Mississippi, and I became a rebel; so did he. We were together in
New Orleans, the 26th of January, when Louisiana went out of the Union.
He did his full share of the rebel shouting, but was bitterly opposed to
letting me do mine. He said that I came of bad stock—of a father who had
been willing to set slaves free. In the following summer he was piloting a
Federal gun-boat and shouting for the Union again, and I was in the Confederate army. I held his note for some borrowed money. He was one of
the most upright men I ever knew; but he repudiated that note without
hesitation, because I was a rebel, and the son of a man who owned slaves.

In that summer—of 1861—the first wash of the wave of war broke upon the shores of Missouri. Our State was invaded by the Union forces. They took possession of St. Louis, Jefferson Barracks, and some other points. The Governor, Claib Jackson, issued his proclamation calling out fifty thousand militia to repel the invader.

I was visiting in the small town where my boyhood had been spent—Hannibal, Marion County. Several of us got together in a secret place by night and formed ourselves into a military company. One Tom Lyman, a young fellow of a good deal of spirit but of no military experience, was made captain; I was made second lieutenant. We had no first lieutenant; I do not know why; it was long ago. There were fifteen of us. By the advice of an innocent connected with the organization, we called ourselves the Marion Rangers. I do not remember that any one found fault with the name. I did not; I thought it sounded quite well. The young fellow who proposed this title was perhaps a fair sample of the kind of stuff we were made of. He was young, ignorant, good-natured, well-meaning, trivial, full of romance, and given to reading chivalric novels and singing forlorn love-ditties. He had some pathetic little nickel-plated aristocratic instincts, and detested his name, which was Dunlap; detested it, partly because it was nearly as common in that region as Smith, but mainly because it had a plebeian sound to his ear. So he tried to ennoble it by writing it in this way: *d'Unlap.* That contented his eye, but left his ear unsatisfied, for people gave the new name the same old pronunciation—emphasis on the front end of it. He then did the bravest thing that can be imagined,—a thing to make one shiver when one remembers how the world is given to resenting shams and affectations; he began to write his name so: *d'Un Lap.* And he waited patiently through the long storm of mud that was flung at this work of art, and he had his reward at last; for he lived to see that name accepted, and the emphasis put where he wanted it, by people who had known him all his life, and to whom the tribe of Dunlaps had been as familiar as the rain and the sunshine for forty years. . . .

That is one sample of us. Another was Ed Stevens, son of the town jeweler,—trim-built, handsome, graceful, neat as a cat; bright, educated, but given over entirely to fun. There was nothing serious in life to him. As far as he was concerned, this military expedition of ours was simply a holiday. I should say that about half of us looked upon it in the same way; not consciously, perhaps, but unconsciously. We did not think; we were not capable of it. As for myself, I was full of unreasoning joy to be done with turning out of bed at midnight and four in the morning, for a while; grateful to have a change, new scenes, new occupations, a new interest. In my thoughts that was as far as I went; I did not go into the details; as a rule one doesn't at twenty-four. . . .

These samples will answer—and they are quite fair ones. Well, this herd of cattle started for the war. What could you expect of them? They did as well as they knew how, but really what was justly to be expected of them? Nothing, I should say. That is what they did.

We waited for a dark night, for caution and secrecy were necessary; then, toward midnight, we stole in couples and from various directions to the Griffith place, beyond the town; from that point we set out together on foot. Hannibal lies at the extreme south-eastern corner of Marion County, on the Mississippi River; our objective point was the hamlet of New London, ten miles away, in Ralls County.

The first hour was all fun, all idle nonsense and laughter. But that could not be kept up. The steady trudging came to be like work; the play had somehow oozed out of it; the stillness of the woods and the somberness of the night began to throw a depressing influence over the spirits of the boys, and presently the talking died out and each person shut himself up in his own thoughts. During the last half of the second hour nobody said a word.

Now we approached a log farm-house where, according to report, there was a guard of five Union soldiers. Lyman called a halt; and there, in the deep gloom of the overhanging branches, he began to whisper a plan of assault upon that house, which made the gloom more depressing than it was before. It was a crucial moment; we realized, with a cold suddenness, that here was no jest—we were standing face to face with actual war. We were equal to the occasion. In our response there was no hesitation, no indecision: we said that if Lyman wanted to meddle with those soldiers, he could go ahead and do it; but if he waited for us to follow him, he would wait a long time.

Lyman urged, pleaded, tried to shame us, but it had no effect. Our course was plain, our minds were made up: we would flank the farm-house—go out around. And that is what we did.

We struck into the woods and entered upon a rough time, stumbling over roots, getting tangled in vines, and torn by briers. At last we reached an open place in a safe region, and sat down, blown and hot, to cool off and nurse our scratches and bruises. Lyman was annoyed, but the rest of us were cheerful; we had flanked the farm-house, we had made our first military movement, and it was a success; we had nothing to fret about, we were feeling just the other way. Horse-play and laughing began again; the expedition was become a holiday frolic once more.

Then we had two more hours of dull trudging and ultimate silence and depression; then, about dawn, we straggled into New London, soiled, heel-blistered, fagged with our little march, and all of us except Stevens in a sour and raspy humor and privately down on the war. We stacked our shabby old shot-guns in Colonel Ralls's barn, and then went in a body and break-fasted with that veteran of the Mexican war. Afterwards he took us to a distant meadow, and there in the shade of a tree we listened to an old-fashioned speech from him, full of gunpowder and glory, full of that adjective-piling, mixed metaphor, and windy declamation which was regarded as eloquence in that ancient time and that remote region; and then he swore us on the Bible to be faithful to the State of Missouri and drive all invaders from her soil, no matter whence they might come or under what flag they might march. This mixed us considerably, and we could not make out just what service we were embarked in; but Colonel Ralls, the practiced politician and phrase-juggler, was not similarly in doubt; he knew quite clearly that he had invested us in the cause of the Southern Confederacy. He closed the solemnities by belting around me the sword which his neighbor, Colonel Brown, had worn at Buena Vista and Molino del Rey; and he accompanied this act with another impressive blast.

Then we formed in line of battle and marched four miles to a shady and pleasant piece of woods on the border of the far-reaching expanses of a flowery prairie. It was an enchanting region for war—our kind of war.

We pierced the forest about half a mile, and took up a strong position, with some low, rocky, and wooded hills behind us, and a purling, limpid creek in front. Straightway half the command were in swimming, and the other half fishing. The ass with the French name gave this position a romantic title, but it was too long, so the boys shortened and simplified it to Camp Ralls.

We occupied an old maple-sugar camp, whose half-rotted troughs were still propped against the trees. A long corn-crib served for sleeping quarters for the battalion. On our left, half a mile away, was Mason's farm and house; and he was a friend to the cause. Shortly after noon the farmers began to arrive from several directions, with mules and horses for our use, and these they lent us for as long as the war might last, which they judged would be about three months. The animals were of all sizes, all colors, and all breeds. They were mainly young and frisky, and nobody in the command could stay on them long at a time; for we were town boys, and ignorant of horsemanship. The creature that fell to my share was a very small mule, and yet so quick and active that it could throw me without difficulty; and it did this whenever I got on it. Then it would bray—stretching its neck out, laying its ears back, and spreading its jaws till you could see down to its works. It was a disagreeable animal, in every way. If I took it by the bridle and tried to lead it off the grounds, it would sit down and brace back, and no one could budge it. However, I was not entirely destitute of military resources, and I did presently manage to spoil this game; for I had seen many a steamboat aground in my time, and knew a trick or two which even a grounded mule would be obliged to respect. There was a well by the corn-crib; so I substituted thirty fathom of rope for the bridle, and fetched him home with the windlass.

I will anticipate here sufficiently to say that we did learn to ride, after some days' practice, but never well. We could not learn to like our animals; they were not choice ones, and most of them had annoying peculiarities of one kind or another. Stevens's horse would carry him, when he was not noticing, under the huge excrescences which form on the trunks of oak-trees, and wipe him out of the saddle; in this way Stevens got several bad hurts. Sergeant Bowers's horse was very large and tall, with slim, long legs, and looked like a railroad bridge. His size enabled him to reach all about, and as far as he wanted to, with his head; so he was always biting Bowers's legs. On the march, in the sun, Bowers slept a good deal; and as soon as the horse recognized that he was asleep he would reach around and bite him on the leg.

His legs were black and blue with bites. This was the only thing that could ever make him swear, but this always did; whenever the horse bit him he always swore, and of course Stevens, who laughed at everything, laughed at this, and would even get into such convulsions over it as to lose his balance and fall off his horse; and then Bowers, already irritated by the pain of the horse-bite, would resent the laughter with hard language, and there would be a quarrel; so that horse made no end of trouble and bad blood in the command.

However, I will get back to where I was—our first afternoon in the sugar-camp. The sugar-troughs came very handy as horse-troughs, and we had plenty of corn to fill them with. I ordered Sergeant Bowers to feed my mule; but he said that if I reckoned he went to war to be dry-nurse to a mule, it wouldn't take me very long to find out my mistake. I believed that this was insubordination, but I was full of uncertainties about everything military, and so I let the thing pass, and went and ordered Smith, the blacksmith's apprentice, to feed the mule; but he merely gave me a large, cold, sarcastic grin, such as an ostensibly seven-year-old horse gives you when you lift his lip and find he is fourteen, and turned his back on me. I then went to the captain, and asked if it was not right and proper and military for me to have an orderly. He said it was, but as there was only one orderly in the corps, it was but right that he himself should have Bowers on his staff. Bowers said he wouldn't serve on anybody's staff; and if anybody thought he could make him, let him try it. So, of course, the thing had to be dropped; there was no other way.

Next, nobody would cook; it was considered a degradation; so we had no dinner. We lazied the rest of the pleasant afternoon away, some dozing under the trees, some smoking cob-pipes and talking sweethearts and war, some playing games. By late suppertime all hands were famished; and to meet the difficulty all hands turned to, on an equal footing, and gathered wood, built fires, and cooked the meal. Afterward everything was smooth for a while; then trouble broke out between the corporal and the sergeant, each claiming to rank the other. Nobody knew which was the higher office; so Lyman had to settle the matter by making the rank of both officers equal. The commander of an ignorant crew like that has many troubles and vexations which probably do not occur in the regular army at all. However, with the song-singing and yarn-spinning around the camp-fire, everything presently became serene again; and by and by we raked the corn down level in one end of the crib, and all went to bed on it, tying a horse to the door, so that he would neigh if any one tried to get in.

We had some horsemanship drill every forenoon; then, afternoons, we rode off here and there in squads a few miles, and visited the farmers' girls, and had a youthful good time, and got an honest good dinner or supper, and then home again to camp, happy and content.

For a time, life was idly delicious, it was perfect; there was nothing to mar it. Then came some farmers with an alarm one day. They said it was rumored that the enemy were advancing in our direction, from over Hyde's prairie. The result was a sharp stir among us, and general consternation. It was a rude awakening from our pleasant trance. The rumor was but a rumor—nothing definite about it; so, in the confusion, we did not know which way to retreat. Lyman was for not retreating at all, in these uncer= tain circumstances; but he found that if he tried to maintain that attitude he would fare badly, for the command were in no humor to put up with in- subordination. So he yielded the point and called a council of war—to con- sist of himself and the three other officers; but the privates made such a fuss about being left out, that we had to allow them to be present. I mean we had to allow them to remain, for they were already present, and doing the most of the talking too. The question was, which way to retreat; but all were so flurried that nobody seemed to have even a guess to offer. Except Lyman. He explained in a few calm words, that inasmuch as the enemy were ap- proaching from over Hyde's prairie, our course was simple: all we had to do was not to retreat *toward* him; any other direction would answer our needs perfectly. Everybody saw in a moment how true this was, and how wise; so Lyman got a great many compliments. It was now decided that we should fall back on Mason's farm.

It was after dark by this time, and as we could not know how soon the enemy might arrive, it did not seem best to try to take the horses and things with us; so we only took the guns and ammunition, and started at once. The route was very rough and hilly and rocky, and presently the night grew very black and rain began to fall; so we had a troublesome time of it, struggling and stumbling along in the dark; and soon some person slipped and fell, and then the next person behind stumbled over him and fell, and so did the rest, one after the other; and then Bowers came with the keg of powder in his arms, whilst the command were all mixed together, arms and legs, on the muddy slope; and so he fell, of course, with the keg, and this started the whole detachment down the hill in a body, and they landed in the brook at the bottom in a pile, and each that was undermost pulling the hair and scratching and biting those that were on top of him; and those that were being scratched and bitten scratching and biting the rest in their turn, and all saying they would die before they would ever go to war again if they ever got out of this brook this time, and the invader might rot for all they cared, and the country along with him—and all such talk as that, which was dismal to hear and take part in, in such smothered, low voices, and such a grisly dark place and so wet, and the enemy may be coming any moment.

The keg of powder was lost, and the guns too; so the growling and complaining continued straight along whilst the brigade pawed around the pasty hillside and slopped around in the brook hunting for these things; con- sequently we lost considerable time at this; and then we heard a sound, and held our breath and listened, and it seemed to be the enemy coming, though it could have been a cow, for it had a cough like a cow; but we did not wait, but left a couple of guns behind and struck out for Mason's again as briskly as we could scramble along in the dark. But we got lost presently among the rugged little ravines, and wasted a deal of time finding the way again, so it was after nine when we reached Mason's stile at last; and then before we could open our mouths to give the countersign, several dogs came bounding over the fence, with great riot and noise, and each of them took a soldier by the slack of his trousers and began to back away with him. We could not shoot the dogs without endangering the persons they were attached to; so we had to look on, helpless, at what was perhaps the most mortifying spectacle of the civil war. There was light enough, and to spare, for the Masons had now run out on the porch with candles in their hands. The old man and his son came and undid the dogs without difficulty, all but Bowers's; but they couldn't undo his dog, they didn't know his combination; he was of the bull kind, and seemed to be set with a Yale time-lock; but they got him loose at last with some scalding water, of which Bowers got his share and returned thanks. Peterson Dunlap afterwards made up a fine name for this engagement, and also for the night march which preceded it, but both have long ago faded out of my memory.

We now went into the house, and they began to ask us a world of questions, whereby it presently came out that we did not know anything concerning who or what we were running from; so the old gentleman made himself very frank, and said we were a curious breed of soldiers, and guessed we could be depended on to end up the war in time, because no government could stand the expense of the shoe-leather we should cost it trying to follow us around. "Marion *Rangers!* good name, b'gosh!" said he. And wanted to know why we hadn't had a picket-guard at the place where the road entered the prairie, and why we hadn't sent out a scouting party to spy out the enemy and bring us an account of his strength, and so on, before jumping up and stampeding out of a strong position upon a mere vague rumor—and so on and so forth, till he made us all feel shabbier than the dogs had done, not half so enthusiastically welcome. So we went to bed shamed and low-spirited; except Stevens. Soon Stevens began to devise a garment for Bowers which could be made to automatically display his battle-scars to the grateful, or conceal them from the envious, according to his occasions; but Bowers was in no humor for this, so there was a fight, and when it was over Stevens had some battle-scars of hs own to think about.

Then we got a little sleep. But after all we had gone through, our activities were not over for the night; for about two o'clock in the morning we heard a shout of warning from down the lane, accompanied by a chorus from all the dogs, and in a moment everybody was up and flying around to find out what the alarm was about. The alarmist was a horseman who gave notice that a detachment of Union soldiers was on its way from Hannibal with orders to capture and hang any bands like ours which it could find, and said we had no time to lose. Farmer Mason was in a flurry this time, himself. He hurried us out of the house with all haste, and sent one of his Negroes with us to show us where to hide ourselves and our tell-tale guns among the ravines half a mile away. It was raining heavily.

We struck down the lane, then across some rocky pasture-land which offered good advantages for stumbling; consequently we were down in the mud most of the time, and every time a man went down he blackguarded the war, and the people that started it, and everybody connected with it, and gave himself the master dose of all for being so foolish as to go into it. At last we reached the wooded mouth of a ravine, and there we huddled ourselves under the streaming trees, and sent the Negro back home. It was a dismal and heart-breaking time. We were like to be drowned with the rain, deafened with the howling wind and the booming thunder, and blinded by the lightning. It was indeed a wild night. The drenching we were getting was misery enough, but a deeper misery still was the reflection that the halter might end us before we were a day older. A death of this shameful sort had not occurred to us as being among the possibilities of war. It took the romance all out of the campaign, and turned our dreams of glory into a repulsive nightmare. As for doubting that so barbarous an order had been given, not one of us did that.

The long night wore itself out at last, and then the Negro came to us with the news that the alarm had manifestly been a false one, and that breakfast would soon be ready. Straightway we were lighted-hearted again, and the world was bright, and life as full of hope and promise as ever—for we were young then. . . .

The mongrel child of philology named the night's refuge Camp Devastation, and no soul objected. The Masons gave us a Missouri country breakfast, in Missourian abundance, and we needed it: hot biscuits; hot "wheat bread" prettily criss-crossed in a lattice pattern on top; hot corn pone; fried chicken; bacon, coffee, eggs, milk, buttermilk, etc.;—and the world may be confidently challenged to furnish the equal to such a breakfast, as it is cooked in the South.

We staid several days at Mason's. . . . At last it was with something very like joy that we received news that the enemy were on our track again. With a new birth of the old warrior spirit, we sprang to our places in line of battle and fell back on Camp Ralls.

Captain Lyman had taken a hint from Mason's talk, and he now gave orders that our camp should be guarded against surprise by the posting of pickets. I was ordered to place a picket at the forks of the road in Hyde's prairie. Night shut down black and threatening. I told Sergeant Bowers to go out to that place and stay till midnight; and, just as I was expecting, he said he wouldn't do it. I tried to get others to go, but all refused. Some excused themselves on account of the weather; but the rest were frank enough to say they wouldn't go in any kind of weather. This kind of thing sounds odd now, and impossible, but there was no surprise in it at the time. On the contrary, it seemed a perfectly natural thing to do. There were scores of little camps scattered over Missouri where the same thing was happening. These camps were composed of young men who had been born and reared to a sturdy independence, and who did not know what it meant to be ordered around by Tom, Dick, and Harry, whom they had known familiarly all their lives, in the village or on the farm. It is quite within the probabilities that this same thing was happening all over the South. . . .

It was quite the natural thing. One might justly imagine that we were hopeless material for war. And so we seemed, in our ignorant state; but there were those among us who afterward learned the grim trade; learned to obey like machines; became valuable soldiers; fought all through the war, and came out at the end with excellent records. One of the very boys who refused to go out on picket duty that night, and called me an ass for thinking he would expose himself to danger in such a foolhardy way, had become distinguished for intrepidity before he was a year older.

I did secure my picket that night—not by authority, but by diplomacy. I got Bowers to go, by agreeing to exchange ranks with him for the time being, and go along and stand the watch with him as his subordinate. We staid out there a couple of dreary hours in the pitchy darkness and the rain, with nothing to modify the dreariness but Bowers's monotonous growlings at the war and the weather; then we began to nod, and presently found it next to impossible to stay in the saddle; so we gave up the tedious job, and went back to the camp without waiting for the relief guard. We rode into camp without interruption or objection from anybody, and the enemy could have done the same, for there were no sentries. Everybody was asleep; at midnight there was nobody to send out another picket, so none was sent. We never tried to establish a watch at night again, as far as I remember, but we generally kept a picket out in the daytime.

In that camp the whole command slept on the corn in the big corn-crib; and there was usually a general row before morning, for the place was full of rats, and they would scramble over the boys' bodies and faces, annoying and irritating everybody; and now and then they would bite some one's toe, and the person who owned the toe would start up and magnify his English and begin to throw corn in the dark. The ears were half as heavy as bricks, and when they struck they hurt. The persons struck would respond, and inside of five minutes every man would be locked in a death-grip with his neighbor. There was a grievous deal of blood shed in the corn-crib, but this was all that was spilt while I was in the war. . . .

The rest of my war experience was of a piece with what I have already told of it. We kept monotonously falling back upon one camp or another, and eating up the country. I marvel now at the patience of the farmers and their families. They ought to have shot us; on the contrary, they were as hospitably kind and courteous to us as if we had deserved it. In one of these camps we found Ab Grimes, an Upper Mississippi pilot, who afterwards became famous as a dare-devil rebel spy, whose career bristled with desperate adventures. The look and style of his comrades suggested that they had not come into the war to play, and their deeds made good the conjecture later. They were fine horsemen and good revolver-shots; but their favorite arm was the lasso. Each had one at his pommel, and could snatch a man out of the saddle with it every time, on a full gallop, at any reasonable distance.

In another camp the chief was a fierce and profane old blacksmith of sixty, and he had furnished his twenty recruits with gigantic home-made bowie-knives, to be swung with the two hands, like the *machetes* of the Isth-

mus. It was a grisly spectacle to see that earnest band practicing their murderous cuts and slashes under the eye of that remorseless old fanatic.

The last camp which we fell back upon was in a hollow near the village
of Florida, where I was born—in Monroe County. Here we were warned,
one day, that a Union colonel was sweeping down on us with a whole regiment at his heels. This looked decidedly serious. Our boys went apart and
consulted; then we went back and told the other companies present that the
war was a disappointment to us and we were going to disband. They were
getting ready, themselves, to fall back on some place or other, and were only
waiting for General Tom Harris, who was expected to arrive at any moment; so they tried to persuade us to wait a little while, but the majority of us
said no, we were accustomed to falling back, and didn't need any of Tom
Harris's help; we could get along perfectly well without him—and save time
too. So about half of our fifteen, including myself, mounted and left on the
instant; the others yielded to persuasion and staid—staid through the war.

An hour later we met General Harris on the road, with two or three people in his company—his staff, probably, but we could not tell; none of them
were in uniform; uniforms had not come into vogue among us yet. Harris
ordered us back; but we told him there was a Union colonel coming with a
whole regiment in his wake, and it looked as if there was going to be a
disturbance; so we had concluded to go home. He raged a little, but it was
of no use; our minds were made up. We had done our share; had killed one
man, exterminated one army, such as it was; let him go and kill the rest, and
that would end the war. I did not see that brisk young general again until last
year; then he was wearing white hair and whiskers.

In time I came to know that Union colonel whose coming frightened me
out of the war and crippled the Southern cause to that extent—General
Grant. I came within a few hours of seeing him when he was as unknown as
I was myself; at a time when anybody could have said, "Grant?—Ulysses S.
Grant? I do not remember hearing the name before." It seems difficult to
realize that there was once a time when such a remark could be rationally
made; but there *was*, and I was within a few miles of the place and the occasion too, though proceeding in the other direction.

The thoughtful will not throw this war-paper of mine lightly aside as
being valueless. It has this value: it is a not unfair picture of what went on
in many and many a militia camp in the first months of the rebellion, when
the green recruits were without discipline, without the steadying and heart-
ening influence of trained leaders; when all their circumstances were new
and strange, and charged with exaggerated terrors, and before the invaluable
experience of actual collision in the field had turned them from rabbits into
soldiers. If this side of the picture of that early day has not before been put
into history, then history has been to that degree incomplete, for it had and
has its rightful place there. There was more Bull Run material scattered
through the early camps of this country than exhibited itself at Bull Run.
And yet it learned its trade presently, and helped to fight the great battles
later. I could have become a soldier myself, if I had waited. I had got part of

it learned; I knew more about retreating than the man that invented retreating.

    —Mark Twain, "The Private History of a Campaign That Failed"

2. MAJOR CONNOLLY LOSES FAITH IN THE CHIVALRY OF THE SOUTH

One of the best of all Civil War commentators, Major James A. Connolly was an Illinois lawyer who in 1862 raised a company which promptly elected him captain. Later he was made major in the 123rd Illinois Infantry and at the end of the war had been promoted to lieutenant colonel. After Chickamauga he was assigned as division inspector in the XIV Army Corps, and went with Sherman to the sea and beyond. He wrote of his Civil War diary that "like an old army ambrotype it may not be a delight, but it is a true picture just as it was taken in the stirring days." We shall turn to him again for lively pictures of the battlefield. After the war Connolly was U. S. Attorney for the Southern District of Illinois and a member of Congress. He tells us here of a holiday trip from Cairo up the Ohio and the Cumberland to Fort Donelson shortly after its capture.

                                     March 10th, '62

Dear ——:

    The Cumberland was on a regular bender. We passed several small villages, completely inundated; some of the houses floating off and others stationary with nothing but the chimneys visible.

    In the villages built higher up on the bluffs everything appeared like a Sunday; no smoke visible, except from an occasional chimney—no doors open—no signs of life—no citizens except occasionally a solitary butternut as the soldiers called them. Most of the farm houses along the river are built of logs in very primitive style, and nearly every one we saw was surrounded by water, so that their occupants had to go around the premises in rude canoes made of logs. It is probable that I am prejudiced, but I certainly thought I never saw such miserable looking creatures as inhabit the banks of the Cumberland, and their habitations looked more wretched than themselves. We frequently sailed so close to farm houses that we could easily hold conversation with the occupants, and wherever a man appeared the soldiers invariably made him swing his hat, the boys consoling themselves with the idea that the swinging of the hat was an evidence of respect for the Union and for "Yankee" soldiers. One instance I recollect, where we must have sailed through the door yard of a cabin (if cabins have such things in Dixie,) the inmates were assembled on the rude porch, five dirty children, three dirty, tangle haired, parchment faced women, sans crinoline, sans shoes, sans stockings,—half a dozen dogs of low degree, and one middle-aged, lantern jawed, long haired butternut clad concern such as they called a man in Dixie.

    As we neared the cabin the soldier boys called out "swing your hat and hurrah for the Union, old butternut;" no response from butternut who leans lazily against his porch, and throws a sullen, defiant look toward the passing steamer; that don't suit the boys; they never pass a native without making him do some reverence toward the Union, so they hail him again, still he is silent; then the boys clamor to have the boat stopped; they want to "clean him out," "set his cabin adrift," "take him in out of the wet," and all such expressions are heard amongst the soldiers, but one cool fellow picks up his musket as the boat is just opposite the cabin, and pointing it at the butternut, takes aim at him; butternut darts within the cabin door amid the shouts of the soldiers, and the women follow him; in an instant out comes a woman with a dirty white rag which she swings lustily, and after a swing or two of the rag out comes the man again, and swinging his slouch hat vigorously, gives three rousing yells; the boys conclude they have converted him—made a Union man of him, so they gave him three such cheers as a regiment of Western boys can give when they are in good humor, and they sail on satisfied, to produce similar conversions on all refractory butternuts they meet. The last I saw of the cabin, as we turned a bend in the river, the man was swinging his hat and the women white rags at a steamer loaded with soldiers just behind us.

We passed several double log houses that were probably the residences of well to do farmers, judging alone from the number of "niggers" around. In every instance the blacks would manifest the most extravagant delight; jumping up and down, clapping their hands, the little nigs rolling and tumbling on the ground, performing as many antics as so many monkeys. We passed several large iron works surrounded by the little cabins of the operatives, and generally one large fine brick mansion—the residence, probably of the manager. But all was silent—no smoke curling from the chimneys—sounds of machinery hushed—the operatives scattered on battle fields, within prison walls, and in rude graves, the children of these iron villages orphaned and with the taint of treason on their lives—the mothers widowed and the proprietors ruined. The banks of the Cumberland are desolated, not by "Yankee invaders" but by the mad folly of the inhabitants; they had been traitors all the way up the river, and their new born respect for the Union was only begotten by the thunder of Grant's guns at Fort Donelson. My faith in the superior chivalry of the South is gone. It is mere gasconade. They boast of their chivalry and courage, but so did Don Quixote and the renowned Jack Falstaff. Their boasted chivalry will in the end avail no more than the chivalry of Lilliput in the grasp of Gulliver. Many of them no doubt had been Union men at the commencement of the struggle, but the slow progress of the Union army led them to believe rebellion would triumph and so their want of faith in the old Union led them to embrace the rebel cause.

They thought they won the race at "Bull Run," but that proved only to be "false start." We steamed on up the river, the same appearance of desolation on every hand, the same sport with the soldiers and "butternuts" on the banks, the same deserted villages and jubilant darkies, until the word passed around, "Three miles to Fort Donelson." Then came a scene of excitement, all crowding to the bow of the boat, every eye strained to catch the first glimpse of the rebel stronghold. We turn a bend in the river and the fort is in view, the stars and stripes floating over it. A cheer bursts from the soldiers on board, the band strikes up the "Star Spangled Banner" and we sail gaily over the same waters that our gunboats breasted a few days before in a murderous hail of rebel shot and shell. We passed the batteries and went up the river about half a mile to the landing at the village of Dover. I was soon ashore and wandering through the city of tents, in search of my home company. I found it in about an hour, and was soon surrounded by the company answering inquiries about home, the wounded, etc. They had supper before I found them, but a fire was soon lighted, some coffee made, some fat pork fried, and with the ground for my table and seat, a tin pan full of fried pork, a tin cup full of coffee and plenty of "hard tack," I ate a hearty supper. . . .

The battle was fought in dense timber, on very high hills and deep ravines, and nearly the whole of the fighting was done by the enemy outside of their entrenchments. The lines of the battle extended over a space of three or four miles, and the whole distance is thickly strewn with the pits of the dead. . . .

I saw a great many taken up. I saw one pit containing five opened and the dead taken out to be sent home. They lay there side by side, with uniform and cartridge box on, just as they fell, covered over with blankets and the dirt thrown in on them. From the best estimate I could make I should say there were 500 of our men buried on the field and at least an equal number of rebels; and I should think there were 1,500 of our men wounded so as to be obliged to go into hospital, and probably 500 more who were wounded, but not seriously enough to go into hospital. A very small proportion of our wounded, however, will, for most of their wounds are from buckshot and are not very serious. . . . A great many horses were lying on the field, just where they fell, scattered all over the field, singly, by twos, threes and fours. Frozen pools of blood were visible on every hand, and I picked up over twenty hats with bullet holes in them and pieces of skull, hair and blood sticking to them inside.

The ground was strewn with hats, caps, coats, pants, canteens, cartridge boxes, bayonet scabbards, knapsacks, rebel haversacks filled with biscuits of their own making, raw pork, broken guns, broken bayonets, dismounted cannon, pieces of exploded shells, six and twelve-pound balls, and indeed all sorts of things that are found in an army. There was such a profusion of everything that I scarcely could determine what to take as a memento of that terrible field, which is probably the only one I shall ever have a chance to see. You can form no conception of what a battlefield looks like. No pen and ink description can give you anything like a true idea of it. The dead were buried from two to two and a half feet deep; the rebels didn't bury that deep and some had their feet protruding from the graves. . . .

The ignorance of many of the rebels surprised me and I should not have believed it had I not talked with them myself. Some of them told me, and they seemed to be honest in it, that they thought they had been fighting for the Union; others told me they thought our army was coming down there to carry off all the "niggers;" they told me they thought none but abolitionists were in our army, and that they were surprised when they found there were more Democrats than abolitionists in it. An amusing incident occurred at the Fort in a conversation between an Illinoisan and a Mississippi captain. The Mississippian remarked that they could whip the New England Yankees every time, and went on to speak of the New England Yankee as a dried up, bloodless specimen of humanity, without courage or physical power, and without a single idea higher than money. The Illinoisan heard him through and then pointing to a Federal captain standing in sight, about 6 feet 3 in height and weighing at least two hundred pounds, remarked: "There is a New England Yankee, born and raised in the state of Maine, and he was among the first men who climbed over your breastworks and ran over your guns." The Mississippian changed the topic of conversation speedily.

—"Major Connolly's Letters to His Wife"

3. THE GREAT LOCOMOTIVE CHASE IN GEORGIA

General Ormsby McK. Mitchel, who organized this locomotive raid, was one of the most remarkable minor figures of the war. Born in Kentucky and a graduate of West Point, Mitchel was a combination engineer, philosopher, and astronomer—chief engineer for the Little Miami Railroad, professor of philosophy and astronomy at Cincinnati College with the largest telescope on the continent. Appointed brigadier at the outbreak of the war he served in the Department of Ohio and later under Buell in Tennessee and Alabama. Quarreling with Buell he resigned late in 1862 but was transferred, instead, to Hilton Head, South Carolina, where he contracted yellow fever and died.

The locomotive raid was designed to disrupt Confederate communications far behind the lines. William Pittenger of the 2nd Ohio Volunteers was a member of the "Andrews Raiders" who carried out this assignment. Twenty-two of the raiders were captured and of these eight were hanged and eight escaped. Pittenger later became a Methodist minister.

THE railroad raid to Georgia, in the spring of 1862, has always been considered to rank high among the striking and novel incidents of the civil war. At that time General O. M. Mitchel, under whose authority it was organized, commanded Union forces in middle Tennessee, consisting of a division of Buell's army. The Confederates were concentrating at Corinth, Mississippi, and Grant and Buell were advancing by different routes toward that point. Mitchel's orders required him to protect Nashville and the country around, but allowed him great latitude in the disposition of his division, which, with detachments and garrisons, numbered nearly seventeen thousand men. His attention had long been strongly turned toward the liberation of east Tennessee, which he knew that President Lincoln also earnestly desired, and which would, if achieved, strike a most damaging blow at the resources of the rebellion. . . . He determined, therefore, to press into the heart of the enemy's country as far as possible, occupying strategical points before they were adequately defended and assured of speedy and powerful reinforcement. To this end his measures were vigorous and well chosen.

On the 8th of April, 1862, ... he marched swiftly southward from Shelbyville, and seized Huntsville in Alabama on the 11th of April, and then sent a detachment westward over the Memphis and Charleston Railroad to open railway communication with the Union army at Pittsburg Landing. Another detachment, commanded by Mitchel in person, advanced on the same day seventy miles by rail directly into the enemy's territory, arriving unchecked with two thousand men within thirty miles of Chattanooga,—in two hours' time he could now reach that point,—the most important position in the West. Why did he not go on? The story of the railroad raid is the answer. The night before breaking camp at Shelbyville, Mitchel sent an expedition secretly into the heart of Georgia to cut the railroad communications of Chattanooga to the south and east. The fortune of this attempt had a most important bearing upon his movements, and will now be narrated.

In the employ of General Buell was a spy named James J. Andrews, who had rendered valuable services in the first year of the war, and had secured the full confidence of the Union commanders. In March, 1862, Buell had sent him secretly with eight men to burn the bridges west of Chattanooga; but the failure of expected coöperation defeated the plan, and Andrews, after visiting Atlanta, and inspecting the whole of the enemy's lines in that vicinity and northward, had returned, ambitious to make another attempt. His plans for the second raid were submitted to Mitchel, and on the eve of the movement from Shelbyville to Huntsville Mitchel authorized him to take twenty-four men, secretly enter the enemy's territory, and, by means of capturing a train, burn the bridges on the northern part of the Georgia State Railroad, and also one on the East Tennessee Railroad where it approaches the Georgia State line, thus completely isolating Chattanooga, which was virtually ungarrisoned.

The soldiers for this expedition, of whom the writer was one, were selected from the three Ohio regiments belonging to General J. W. Sill's brigade, being simply told that they were wanted for secret and very dangerous service. So far as known, not a man chosen declined the perilous honor. Our uniforms were exchanged for ordinary Southern dress, and all arms except revolvers were left in camp. On the 7th of April, by the roadside about a mile east of Shelbyville, in the late evening twilight, we met our leader. Taking us a little way from the road, he quietly placed before us the outlines of the romantic and adventurous plan, which was: to break into small detachments of three or four, journey eastward into the Cumberland Mountains, then work southward, traveling by rail after we were well within the Confederate lines, and finally, the evening of the third day after the start, meet Andrews at Marietta, Georgia, more than two hundred miles away. When questioned, we were to profess ourselves Kentuckians going to join the Southern army.

On the journey we were a good deal annoyed by the swollen streams and the muddy roads consequent on three days of almost ceaseless rain. Andrews was led to believe that Mitchel's column would be inevitably delayed; and as we were expected to destroy the bridges the very day that Huntsville was entered, he took the responsibility of sending word to our different groups that our attempt would be postponed one day—from Friday to Saturday, April 12. This was a natural but a most lamentable error of judgment.

One of the men detailed was belated, and did not join us at all. Two others were very soon captured by the enemy; and though their true character was not detected, they were forced into the Southern army, and two reached Marietta, but failed to report at the rendezvous. Thus, when we assembled very early in the morning in Andrews's room at the Marietta Hotel for final consultation before the blow was struck we were but twenty, including our leader. All preliminary difficulties had been easily overcome, and we were in good spirits. But some serious obstacles had been revealed on our ride from Chattanooga to Marietta the previous evening. The railroad was found to be crowded with trains, and many soldiers were among the passengers. Then the station—Big Shanty—at which the capture was to be effected had recently been made a Confederate camp.

To succeed in our enterprise it would be necessary first to capture the engine in a guarded camp with soldiers standing around as spectators, and then to run it from one to two hundred miles through the enemy's country, and to deceive or overpower all trains that should be met—a large contract for twenty men. Some of our party thought the chances of success so slight, under existing circumstances, that they urged the abandonment of the whole enterprise. But Andrews declared his purpose to succeed or die, offering to each man, however, the privilege of withdrawing from the attempt—an offer no one was in the least disposed to accept. Final instructions were then given, and we hurried to the ticket-office in time for the northward-bound mail-train, and purchased tickets for different stations along the line in the direction of Chattanooga.

Our ride, as passengers, was but eight miles. We swept swiftly around the base of Kenesaw Mountain, and soon saw the tents of the Confederate forces camped at Big Shanty gleam white in the morning mist. Here we were to stop for breakfast, and attempt the seizure of the train. The morning was raw and gloomy, and a rain, which fell all day, had already begun. It was a painfully thrilling moment. We were but twenty, with an army about us, and a long and difficult road before us, crowded with enemies. In an instant we were to throw off the disguise which had been our only protection, and trust to our leader's genius and our own efforts for safety and success. Fortunately we had no time for giving way to reflections and conjectures which could only unfit us for the stern task ahead.

When we stopped, the conductor, the engineer, and many of the passengers hurried to breakfast, leaving the train unguarded. Now was the moment of action. Ascertaining that there was nothing to prevent a rapid start, Andrews, our two engineers, Brown and Knight, and the firemen hurried forward, uncoupling a section of the train consisting of three empty baggage or box-cars, the locomotive, and the tender. The engineers and the firemen sprang into the cab of the engine, while Andrews, with hand on the rail and foot on the step, waited to see that the remainder of the party had gained entrance into the rear box-car. This seemed difficult and slow, though it really consumed but a few seconds, for the car stood on a considerable bank, and the first who came were pitched in by their comrades, while these in turn dragged in the others, and the door was instantly closed. A sentinel, with musket in hand, stood not a dozen feet from the engine, watching the whole proceeding; but before he or any of the soldiers or guards around could make up their minds to interfere all was done, and Andrews, with a nod to his engineer, stepped on board. The valve was pulled wide open, and for a moment the wheels slipped round in rapid, ineffective revolutions; then, with a bound that jerked the soldiers in the box-car from their feet, the little train darted away, leaving the camp and the station in the wildest uproar and confusion. The first step of the enterprise was triumphantly accomplished.

According to the time-table, of which Andrews had secured a copy, there were two trains to be met. These presented no serious hindrance to our attaining high speed, for we could tell just where to expect them. There was also a local freight not down on the time-table, but which could not be far distant. Any danger of collision with it could be avoided by running according to the schedule of the captured train until it was passed; then at the highest possible speed we could run to the Oostenaula and Chickamauga bridges, lay them in ashes, and pass on through Chattanooga to Mitchel at Huntsville, or wherever eastward of that point he might be found, arriving long before the close of the day. It was a brilliant prospect, and so far as human estimates can determine it would have been realized had the day been Friday instead of Saturday. On Friday every train had been on time, the day dry, and the road in perfect order. Now the road was in disorder, every train far behind time, and two "extras" were approaching us. But of these unfavorable conditions we knew nothing, and pressed confidently forward.

We stopped frequently, and at one point tore up the track, cut telegraph wires, and loaded on cross-ties to be used in bridge-burning. Wood and water were taken without difficulty, Andrews very coolly telling the story to which he adhered throughout the run—namely, that he was one of General Beauregard's officers, running an impressed powder-train through to that commander at Corinth. We had no good instruments for track-raising, as we had intended rather to depend upon fire; but the amount of time spent in taking up a rail was not material at this stage of our journey, as we easily kept on the time of our captured train. There was a wonderful exhilaration in passing swiftly by towns and stations through the heart of an enemy's country in this manner. It possessed just enough of the spice of danger, in this part of the run, to render it thoroughly enjoyable. The slightest accident to our engine, however, or a miscarriage in any part of our program, would have completely changed the conditions.

At Etowah we found the "Yonah," an old locomotive owned by an iron company, standing with steam up; but not wishing to alarm the enemy till the local freight had been safely met, we left it unharmed. Kingston, thirty miles from the starting-point, was safely reached. A train from Rome, Georgia, on a branch road, had just arrived and was waiting for the morning mail—our train. We learned that the local freight would soon come also, and, taking the side-track, waited for it. When it arrived, however, Andrews saw, to his surprise and chagrin, that it bore a red flag, indicating another train not far behind. Stepping over to the conductor, he boldly asked: "What does it mean that the road is blocked in this manner when I have orders to take this powder to Beauregard without a minute's delay?" The answer was interesting, but not reassuring: "Mitchel has captured Huntsville, and is said to be coming to Chattanooga, and we are getting everything out of there." He was asked by Andrews to pull his train a long way down the track out of the way, and promptly obeyed.

It seemed an exceedingly long time before the expected "extra" arrived, and when it did come it bore another red flag. The reason given was that the "local," being too great for one engine, had been made up in two sections, and the second section would doubtless be along in a short time. This was terribly vexatious; yet there seemed nothing to do but to wait. To start out between the sections of an extra train would be to court destruction. There were already three trains around us, and their many passengers and others were all growing very curious about the mysterious train, manned by strangers, which had arrived on the time of the morning mail. For an hour and five minutes from the time of arrival at Kingston we remained in this most critical position. The sixteen of us who were shut up tightly in a box-car,—personating Beauregard's ammunition,—hearing sounds outside, but unable to distinguish words, had perhaps the most trying position. Andrews sent us, by one of the engineers, a cautious warning to be ready to fight in case the uneasiness of the crowd around led them to make any investigation, while he himself kept near the station to prevent the sending off of any alarming telegram. So intolerable was our suspense, that the order for a deadly conflict would have been felt as a relief. But the assurance of Andrews quieted the crowd until the whistle of the expected train from the north was heard; then as it glided up to the depot, past the end of our side-track, we were off without more words.

But unexpected danger had arisen behind us. Out of the panic at Big Shanty two men emerged, determined, if possible, to foil the unknown captors of their train. There was no telegraph station, and no locomotive at hand with which to follow; but the conductor of the train, W. A. Fuller, and Anthony Murphy, foreman of the Atlanta railway machine-shops, who happened to be on board of Fuller's train, started on foot after us as hard as they could run. Finding a hand-car they mounted it and pushed forward till they neared Etowah, where they ran on the break we had made in the road, and were precipitated down the embankment into the ditch. Continuing with more caution, they reached Etowah and found the "Yonah," which was at once pressed into service, loaded with soldiers who were at hand, and hurried with flying wheels toward Kingston. Fuller prepared to fight at that point, for he knew of the tangle of extra trains, and of the lateness of the regular trains, and did not think we should be able to pass.

We had been gone only four minutes when he arrived and found himself stopped by three long, heavy trains of cars, headed in the wrong direction. To move them out of the way so as to pass would cause a delay he was little inclined to afford—would, indeed, have almost certainly given us the victory. So, abandoning his engine, he with Murphy ran across to the Rome train, and, uncoupling the engine and one car, pushed forward with about forty armed men. As the Rome branch connected with the main road above the depot, he encountered no hindrance, and it was now a fair race. We were not many minutes ahead.

Four miles from Kingston we again stopped and cut the telegraph. While trying to take up a rail at this point we were greatly startled. One end of the rail was loosened, and eight of us were pulling at it, when in the distance we distinctly heard the whistle of a pursuing engine. With a frantic effort we broke the rail, and all tumbled over the embankment with the effort. We moved on, and at Adairsville we found a mixed train (freight and passenger) waiting, but there was an express on the road that had not yet arrived. We could afford no more delay, and set out for the next station, Calhoun, at terrible speed, hoping to reach that point before the express, which was behind time, should arrive. The nine miles which we had to travel were left behind in less than the same number of minutes. The express was just pulling out, but, hearing our whistle, backed before us until we were able to take the side-track. It stopped, however, in such a manner as completely to close up the other end of the switch. The two trains, side by side, almost touched each other, and our precipitate arrival caused natural suspicion. Many searching questions were asked, which had to be answered before we could get the opportunity of proceeding. We in the box-car could hear the altercation, and were almost sure that a fight would be necessary before the conductor would consent to "pull up" in order to let us out. Here again our position was most critical, for the pursuers were rapidly approaching.

Fuller and Murphy saw the obstruction of the broken rail in time, by reversing their engine, to prevent wreck, but the hindrance was for the present insuperable. Leaving all their men behind, they started for a second foot-race. Before they had gone far they met the train we had passed at Adairsville, and turned it back after us. At Adairsville they dropped the cars, and with locomotive and tender loaded with armed men, they drove forward at the highest speed possible. They knew that we were not many minutes ahead, and trusted to overhaul us before the express train could be safely passed.

But Andrews had told the powder story again with all his skill, and added a direct request in peremptory form to have the way opened before him, which the Confederate conductor did not see fit to resist; and just before the pursuers arrived at Calhoun we were again under way. Stopping once more to cut wires and tear up the track, we felt a thrill of exhilaration to which we had long been strangers. The track was now clear before us to

Chattanooga; and even west of that city we had good reason to believe that we should find no other train in the way till we had reached Mitchel's lines. If one rail could now be lifted we would be in a few minutes at the Oostenaula bridge; and that burned, the rest of the task would be little more than simple manual labor, with the enemy absolutely powerless. We worked with a will.

But in a moment the tables were turned. Not far behind we heard the scream of a locomotive bearing down upon us at lightning speed. The men on board were in plain sight and well armed. Two minutes—perhaps one— would have removed the rail at which we were toiling; then the game would have been in our own hands, for there was no other locomotive beyond that could be turned back after us. But the most desperate efforts were in vain. The rail was simply bent, and we hurried to our engine and darted away, while remorselessly after us thundered the enemy.

Now the contestants were in clear view, and a race followed unparalleled in the annals of war. Wishing to gain a little time for the burning of the Oostenaula bridge, we dropped one car, and, shortly after, another; but they were "picked up" and pushed ahead to Resaca. We were obliged to run over the high trestles and covered bridge at that point without a pause. This was the first failure in the work assigned us.

The Confederates could not overtake and stop us on the road; but their aim was to keep close behind, so that we might not be able to damage the road or take in wood or water. In the former they succeeded, but not in the latter. Both engines were put at the highest rate of speed. We were obliged to cut the wire after every station passed, in order that an alarm might not be sent ahead; and we constantly strove to throw our pursuers off the track, or to obstruct the road permanently in some way, so that we might be able to burn the Chickamauga bridges, still ahead. The chances seemed good that Fuller and Murphy would be wrecked. We broke out the end of our last box-car and dropped cross-ties on the track as we ran, thus checking their progress and getting far enough ahead to take in wood and water at two separate stations. Several times we almost lifted a rail, but each time the coming of the Confederates within rifle-range compelled us to desist and speed on. Our worst hindrance was the rain. The previous day (Friday) had been clear, with a high wind, and on such a day fire would have been easily and tremendously effective. But to-day a bridge could be burned only with abundance of fuel and careful nursing.

Thus we sped on, mile after mile, in this fearful chase, round curves and past stations in seemingly endless perspective. Whenever we lost sight of the enemy beyond a curve, we hoped that some of our obstructions had been effective in throwing him from the track, and that we should see him no more; but at each long reach backward the smoke was again seen, and the shrill whistle was like the scream of a bird of prey. The time could not have been so very long, for the terrible speed was rapidly devouring the distance; but with our nerves strained to the highest tension each minute seemed an hour. On several occasions the escape of the enemy from wreck was little less than miraculous. At one point a rail was placed across the track on a curve so skilfully that it was not seen till the train ran upon it at full speed. Fuller says that they were terribly jolted, and seemed to bounce altogether from the track, but lighted on the rails in safety. Some of the Confederates wished to leave a train which was driven at such a reckless rate, but their wishes were not gratified.

Before reaching Dalton we urged Andrews to turn and attack the enemy, laying an ambush so as to get into close quarters, that our revolvers might be on equal terms with their guns. I have little doubt that if this had been carried out it would have succeeded. But either because he thought the chance of wrecking or obstructing the enemy still good, or feared that the country ahead had been alarmed by a telegram around the Confederacy by the way of Richmond, Andrews merely gave the plan his sanction without making any attempt to carry it into execution.

Dalton was passed without difficulty, and beyond we stopped again to cut wires and to obstruct the track. It happened that a regiment was encamped not a hundred yards away, but they did not molest us. Fuller had written a despatch to Chattanooga, and dropped a man with orders to have it forwarded instantly, while he pushed on to save the bridges. Part of the message got through and created a wild panic in Chattanooga, although it did not materially influence our fortunes. Our supply of fuel was now very short, and without getting rid of our pursuers long enough to take in more, it was evident that we could not run as far as Chattanooga.

While cutting the wire we made an attempt to get up another rail; but the enemy, as usual, were too quick for us. We had no tool for this purpose except a wedge-pointed iron bar. Two or three bent iron claws for pulling out spikes would have given us such incontestable superiority that, down to almost the last of our run, we should have been able to escape and even to burn all the Chickamauga bridges. But it had not been our intention to rely on this mode of obstruction—an emergency only rendered necessary by our unexpected delay and the pouring rain.

We made no attempt to damage the long tunnel north of Dalton, as our enemies had greatly dreaded. The last hope of the raid was now staked upon an effort of a kind different from any that we had yet made, but which, if successful, would still enable us to destroy the bridges nearest Chattanooga. But, on the other hand, its failure would terminate the chase. Life and success were put upon one throw.

A few more obstructions were dropped on the track, and our own speed increased so that we soon forged a considerable distance ahead. The side and end boards of the last car were torn into shreds, all available fuel was piled upon it, and blazing brands were brought back from the engine. By the time we approached a long, covered bridge a fire in the car was fairly started. We uncoupled it in the middle of the bridge, and with painful suspense waited the issue. Oh for a few minutes till the work of conflagration was fairly begun! There was still steam pressure enough in our boiler to carry us to the next wood-yard, where we could have replenished our fuel by force, if necessary, so as to run as near to Chattanooga as was deemed prudent. We did not know of the telegraph message which the pursuers had sent ahead. But, alas! the minutes were not given. Before the bridge was extensively fired the enemy was upon us, and we moved slowly onward, looking back to see what they would do next. We had not long to conjecture. The Confederates pushed right into the smoke, and drove the burning car before them to the next side-track.

With no car left, and no fuel, the last scrap having been thrown into the engine or upon the burning car, and with no obstruction to drop on the track, our situation was indeed desperate. A few minutes only remained until our steed of iron which had so well served us would be powerless.

But it might still be possible to save ourselves. If we left the train in a body, and, taking a direct course toward the Union lines, hurried over the mountains at right angles with their course, we could not, from the nature of the country, be followed by cavalry, and could easily travel—athletic young men as we were, and fleeing for life—as rapidly as any pursuers. There was no telegraph in the mountainous districts west and northwest of us, and the prospect of reaching the Union lines seemed to me then, and has always since seemed, very fair. Confederate pursuers with whom I have since conversed freely have agreed on two points—that we could have escaped in the manner here pointed out, and that an attack on the pursuing train would likely have been successful. But Andrews thought otherwise, at least in relation to the former plan, and ordered us to jump from the locomotive one by one, and, dispersing in the woods, each endeavor to save himself. Thus ended the Andrews railroad raid.

It is easy now to understand why Mitchel paused thirty miles west of Chattanooga. The Andrews raiders had been forced to stop eighteen miles south of the same town, and no flying train met him with the expected tidings that all railroad communications of Chattanooga were destroyed, and that the town was in a panic and undefended. He dared advance no farther without heavy reinforcements from Pittsburg Landing or the north; and he probably believed to the day of his death, six months later, that the whole Andrews party had perished without accomplishing anything.

A few words will give the sequel to this remarkable enterprise. There was great excitement in Chattanooga and in the whole of the surrounding Confederate territory for scores of miles. The hunt for the fugitive raiders was prompt, energetic, and completely successful. Ignorant of the country, disorganized, and far from the Union lines, they strove in vain to escape. Several were captured the same day on which they left the cars, and all but two within a week. Even these two were overtaken and brought back when they supposed that they were virtually out of danger. Two of those who had failed to be on the train were identified and added to the band of prisoners.

Now follows the saddest part of the story. Being in citizens' dress within an enemy's lines, the whole party were held as spies, and closely and vigorously guarded. A court-martial was convened, and the leader and seven others out of the twenty-two were condemned and executed. The remainder were never brought to trial, probably because of the advance of Union forces, and the consequent confusion into which the affairs of the departments of east Tennessee and Georgia were thrown. Of the remaining fourteen, eight succeeded by a bold effort—attacking their guard in broad daylight—in making their escape from Atlanta, Georgia, and ultimately in reaching the North. The other six who shared in this effort, but were recaptured, remained prisoners until the latter part of March, 1863, when they were exchanged through a special arrangement made with Secretary Stanton. All the survivors of this expedition received medals and promotion. The pursuers also received expressions of gratitude from their fellow-Confederates, notably from the governor and the legislature of Georgia.

—PITTENGER, "The Locomotive Chase in Georgia"

4. CAPTAIN CANFIELD TRIES TO FREE SLAVES

The attitude of the Union government and the Union Army toward slaves was, from the beginning, anomalous. On the one hand the war was actually over slavery, and a large segment of Northern opinion took for granted that it was a war to end slavery. Not only this but in so far as slaves performed essential labor, they contributed to Confederate military strength. On the other hand the official position of Congress and of the President was that the Federal government had no power over slavery in the states, and that the war was one for the restoration of the Union. Very early in the war slaves began pouring into the Union armies, and as these armies advanced into the South the problem of disposing of the Negroes became acute. Generals Frémont and Hunter proclaimed emancipation, on their own, and were repudiated by Lincoln. General Butler tried to solve the problem by declaring slaves "contraband of war" and the term "contrabands" stuck.

Not until July 1862 did Congress try to deal with the problem in a general fashion. An act of that month provided that slaves of persons engaged in or contributing to the rebellion were forfeited, and that all slaves of persons in rebellion were to be free on entering Union lines. What this meant was that claimants of fugitive slaves were required to prove their loyalty. The administration of the act varied greatly from commander to commander. As Captain Canfield's account—written partly in the third person—makes clear, a commanding officer hostile to emancipation—and there were many of these—could in effect nullify the act. Canfield was a captain in the 21st Ohio Volunteers.

WHILE at Athens the black calaboose of the south nearly terminated the usefulness of our regiment. Slaves came to us bringing information of the enemy far south of our lines, and expecting protection and freedom, to be greatly disappointed.

Individual members of the regiment often secreted them or steered them on to the north, but they were usually surrendered to their masters, who came boldly after them.

In one case at least, a slave was not allowed to enter our lines, but was detained at the outpost, and surrendered to his master for ten dollars; and it was a republican who took the money. This was reported at regimental headquarters, but nothing was done about it. Lieutenant Colonel Neibling was a pronounced pro-slavery man, and did not hesitate to voluntarily detain slaves in the county jail until their masters came for them.

Slaves were often surrendered, to be taken south beyond the lines of our army, in violation of orders of the Secretary of War.

The fore part of August, Captain Canfield and Lieutenants Wicker and Patterson, each employed a colored servant. About the middle of the month Lieutenant Colonel Niebling went to Co. K's quarters, and thus ordered Lieutenant Wickers servant: "Van! come out of there and go with your master," whereupon the Lieutenant Colonel and Lieutenant Patterson had some harsh words passed between them.

This, and what was termed rebel influence had now provoked much indignation, and the men of Company K declared if another man came into camp hunting slaves, they would throw him into a slop hole.

On the 23d a planter came near camp, and meeting Captain Canfield, said he heard his servant was in his (Canfield's) camp, and asked the captain if he had any objection to his going to see. "Oh no," said the captain, "not in the least;" but seeing several groups of men casting significant glances toward the stranger, he added, "You will not consider me responsible for anything that happens."

Hearing this the stranger turned back. Shortly after the Lieutenant Colonel's orderly came with an order dated and directed to Captain Canfield, saying:

$\left\{\begin{array}{l}\text{HEADQUARTERS 21ST, O. V. I.}\\ \text{Athens, Ala., Aug. 23d, 1862.}\end{array}\right.$

Negro boy Pat in your company is the property of ——. You will deliver him outside camp lines to his master. Signed,

J. M. NIEBLING.

Lieut. Col. Comdg. Regt.

Captain Canfield wrote in answer, acknowledging the receipt of the order, and added, "I respectfully decline to obey it," signed it officially, as Captain Commanding Company, and kept a copy of the correspondence. Nothing further was said or done about this, however.

Matters were in this condition, when for the first time in two months I was detailed as officer of the day, a duty I should often have performed before. I received my order in the evening, and that night I made up my mind that when I went on duty the next morning, I would break up the slave trade in the regiment for twenty-four hours at least; and my success surprised me. The county jail was full of prisoners, chiefly fugitive slaves, who were not turned over to me, but one of my sentinels was posted there, and I assumed whatever authority I lacked to investigate the reason of their detention. I knew very well there were no charges against the black men. After my guard was fully posted and every duty performed, I took a non-commissioned officer and file of men for escort, and reported to Lieutenant Colonel Niebling for any orders he might be pleased to give me. I found him sitting in the shade of a public house near the depot, surrounded by a number of gentlemen of the town. After informing me that there were no new orders for me, I was turning away to leave him, when he called out to me, "Where are you going with that guard?" to which I answered, "I am going down to release the prisoners in the jail, against whom there are no charges."

He answered, "Sir, I order you not to do it."

I then said with deference of manner, "Colonel, will you be so good as to have charges preferred against them."

He replied in a towering rage, it was none of my damned business, and that I should go to my quarters in arrest. Of course I obeyed the order of arrest, and quite crestfallen, went to my tent, followed by the boisterous laughter and jeers of Colonel Niebling's companions, who were sitting about him and heard all that was said.

I had up to this time been considered a severe disciplinarian, and had incurred the displeasure of many officers and men of the regiment on that account, and their judgment at first was, that I was served just right. But before sundown that day, all the slaves were relieved by Colonel Niebling himself, and the regiment was in rebellion against its commanding officer, and my arrest was made the pretext for the mutiny.

That night a meeting of officers was held in the court house, and an address prepared, wherein they told Colonel Niebling of his sins, which was presented to him next day. A committee of which Captain Silas S. Canfield was chairman, was appointed to prefer charges against him, and eight counts were agreed upon, provided he did not resign his commission at once.

Yet the outcome of it all was, that the slave trade was abolished effectually, and while there was no doubt that grave charges could have been sustained against Colonel Niebling, none were ever preferred. It was understood that General Buell, who commanded the army at that time, approved of his course in surrendering fugitive slaves, and nothing could have saved the officers concerned in that address, but he never referred it. I was released from arrest without any explanation whatever, and returned to the command of my company.

—CANFIELD, *History of the 21st Regiment Ohio Volunteer Infantry*

5. A BADGER BOY MEETS THE ORIGINALS OF *UNCLE TOM'S CABIN*

Here is our old friend Chauncey Cooke again—the Wisconsin boy who enlisted at sixteen, fought the Sioux Indians, and then was sent to Kentucky to take part in the campaign against Bragg. It is not to be supposed that all Union soldiers saw the Negroes through the eyes of Harriet Beecher Stowe;

many of them—like Colonel Niebling—were bitterly hostile to emancipation.

Columbus, Ky., March 5th, 1863
25th Wis. Vol. Infantry

Dear Folks at Home:

I sent you a letter a day or two ago and maybe I will hear from you soon. I hope I shall. I am well and we are hearing and seeing things and the days are not so heavy as at Madison. The weather is fine—most of the time warm and clear.

We drill every day, do police work, cleaning round the camp, and take a stroll now and then back in the country, far as the pickets will let us. We are really in the "Sunny South." The slaves, contrabands, we call them, are flocking into Columbus by the hundred. General Thomas of the regular army is here enlisting them for war. All the old buildings on the edge of the town are more than full. You never meet one but he jerks his hat off and bows and shows the whitest teeth. I never saw a bunch of them together, but I could pick out an Uncle Tom, a Quimbo, a Sambo, a Chloe, an Eliza, or any other character in *Uncle Tom's Cabin.* The women take in a lot of dimes washing for the soldiers, and the men around picking up odd jobs. I like to talk with them. They are funny enough, and the stories they tell of slave life are stories never to be forgotten. Ask any of them how he feels and the answer nearly always will be, "Sah, I feels might good, sah," or "God bress you, massa, I'se so proud I'se a free man." Some are leaving daily on up-river boats for Cairo and up the Ohio River. The Ohio has always been the river Jordan to the slave. It has been the dream of his life even to look upon the Ohio River.

The government transports returning from down river points where they had been with troops or supplies would pick up free men on every landing and deliver them free of charge at places along the Ohio and upper Mississippi points.

The slaves are not all black as we in the North are apt to suppose. Some of them are quite light. Those used as house servants seem to have some education and don't talk so broad. A real pretty yellow girl about 18 was delivering some washing to the boys yesterday. She left her master and mistress in December and came to Columbus. In answer to the questions of the boys she said she left home because her mistress was cross to her and all other servants since Lincoln's emancipation. She said her mother came with her. One of the boys asked her why her father did not come with her. She said, "My father hain't no colored man, he's a white man." When the boys began to laugh she picked up her two-bushel basket of clothes, balanced it on her head, and went her way. That girl must have made fifty stops among the tents leaving her basket of clothes. I wonder if she heard the same dirty talk in each of them. The talk wasn't clean, but some of us who tho't so just let it pass and kept still. . . .

Your son,
CHAUNCEY

Columbus, Ky., March 21st., 1863
25th Wisconsin Vol.

Dear Mother:

After drill went out in the edge of the woods. Its more peaceful and homelike than the racket of the camp. I can see the picket guard beyond me slowly pacing his beat. There is no enemy about but the discipline and regulations are just as rigid as they are in Georgia. No white man can come within the picket line except he has the password. A Negro is allowed to come in. We are afraid that the whites may be spies, we know the blacks are our friends.

The health of the regiment is good save a few cases of bowel trouble. The boys call it the Kentucky quickstep. There is more sickness among the poor lazy blacks. They are filling all the vacant houses and even sleeping under the trees, so anxious are they to get near "de Lincoln soldiers." They live on scraps and whatever they can pick up in camp and they will shine our shoes or do any camp work for an old shirt or cast-off coat. They had a revival meeting at the foot of the bluff last night and such shouting and singing and moaning. It was Massa Lincoln was a savior that came after two hundred years of tribulation in the cotton fields and cane. They had long known that something was going to happen because so many times their massa had visitors and they would tell the servants to stay in their cabins and not come to the "big house" until they were called. Then some of the house servants would creep round under the windows and hear the white folks talking about war and that the slaves were going to be free. And when the one that was sent to listen would come back and tell the others, they would get down on their knees and pray in whispers and give thanks to the Lord. Everything with the darkies is Lord, Lord. Their faith that the Lord will help them has held out more than 200 years.

I sometimes wonder if the Lord is not partial to the white race and rather puts it onto the black race because they are black. We sometimes get terribly confused when we try to think of the law of Providence. This black race for instance, they can't talk ten words about slavery and old Massa and old Missus, but they get in something about "de blessed Lord and de lovely Jesus" and yet in this land of Washington, God has permitted them to be bought and sold like our cattle and our hogs in the stockyards for more than 200 years.

I listened for two hours this morning to the stories of a toothless old slave with one blind eye who had come up the river from near Memphis. He told me a lot of stuff. He said his master sold his wife and children to a cotton planter in Alabama to pay his gambling debts, and when he told his master he couldn't stand it, he was tied to the whipping post stripped and given 40 lashes. The next night he ran to the swamps. The bloodhounds were put on his track and caught him and pulled him down. They bit him in the face and put out his eye and crushed one of his hands so he could not use it. He stripped down his pants and showed me a gash on one of his hips where one of the hounds hung unto him until he nearly bled to death.

This happened in sight of Nashville, the capitol of Tennessee. I told this to some of the boys and they said it was all bosh, that the niggers were lying to me. But this story was just like the ones in Uncle Tom's Cabin, and I believe them. And father knows of things very much like this that are true.

I will write you again soon,

Your son

CHAUNCEY

—COOKE, "Letters of a Badger Boy in Blue"

6. INCIDENTS OF THE PICKET LINE AT CHATTANOOGA

We have met the vivacious Joseph Polley before. His Texas Brigade was sent west with Longstreet to support Bragg at Chickamauga, and it was in that fierce battle that its leader, Hood, lost his leg. After Chickamauga Bragg's forces moved onto the heights above Chattanooga where they hoped to starve Rosecrans out. The incidents which Polley recalls here are from the short period of watchful waiting between the two great battles.

Chattanooga, Tenn. Oct. 1, 1863

I was lucky enough to be on picket duty a few nights ago with my friends Will Burges and John West, of Companies D and E of the Fourth, each of whom is not only a good soldier, but a most entertaining companion. As the night advanced, it became cold enough to make a fire very acceptable, and, appropriating a whole one to ourselves, we had wandered from a discussion of the war and of this particular campaign that was little flattering to General Bragg, into pleasant reminiscences of our homes and loved ones, when someone on horseback said, "Good evening, gentlemen." Looking hastily up, we discovered that the intruder was General Jenkins, alone and unattended by either aide or orderly, and were about to rise and salute in approved military style, when, with a smile plainly perceptible in the bright moonlight, he said, "No, don't trouble yourselves," and, letting the reins drop on his horse's neck, threw one leg around the pommel of his saddle and entered into conversation with us.

Had you been listening for the next half hour or so, Charming Nellie, you would never have been able to guess which of us was the General, for, ignoring his rank as completely as we careless Texans forgot it, he became at once as private a soldier as either of us, and talked and laughed as merrily and unconcernedly as if it were not war times. I offered him the use of my pipe and smoking tobacco, Burges was equally generous with the plug he kept for chewing, and West was even polite enough to regret that the whisky he was in the habit of carrying as a preventive against snake bites was just out; in short, we were beginning to believe General Jenkins of South Carolina the only real general in the Confederate service, when, to our surprise and dismay, he straightened himself up on his saddle, and climbing from "gay to grave, from lively to severe," announced that at midnight the picket line would be expected to advance and drive the Yankees to the other side of the creek.

We might easily have forgiven him for being the bearer of this discomforting intelligence had that been the sum total of his offending; but it was not; he rode away without expressing the least pleasure at having made our acquaintance, or even offering to shake hands with us—the necessary and inevitable consequence of such discourtesy being that he descended at once in our estimation to the level of any other general.

But midnight was too near at hand to waste time in nursing indignation. Instant action was imperative, and resolving ourselves into a council of war with plenary powers, it was unanimously decided by the three privates there assembled that our recent guest was an upstart wholly undeserving of confidence; that the contemplated movement was not only foolish and impracticable, but bound to be dangerous; and that, if a single shot were fired at us by the enemy, we three would just lie down and let General Jenkins of South Carolina do his own advancing and driving. Being veterans, we knew far better than he how easy it was at night for opposing lines to intermingle with each other and men to mistake friends for enemies, and we did not propose to sanction the taking of such chances.

All too soon the dreaded and fateful hour arrived; all too soon the whispered order "Forward" was passed from man to man down the long line, and, like spectral forms in the ghastly moonlight, the Confederate pickets moved slowly out into the open field in their front, every moment expecting to see the flash of a gun and hear or feel its messenger of death, and all awed by the fear the bravest men feel when confronting unknown danger. Not ten minutes before, the shadowy forms of the enemy had been seen by our videttes, and if the line of the creek was worth capturing by us, it surely was worth holding by the Yankees. But all was silent and still; no sight of foe, no tread of stealthy footstep, no sharp click of gunlock—not even the rustling of a leaf or the snap of a twig came out of the darkness to relieve our suspense and quiet the expectant throbbing of our hearts.

Under these circumstances, West, Burges, and your humble servant, like the brave and true men they are, held themselves erect and advanced side by side with their gallant comrades until the terra incognita and impenetrability of the narrow but timbered valley of the stream suggested ambush and the advisability of rifle-pits. Working at these with a will born of emergency, we managed to complete them just as the day dawned, and jumping into them with a sigh of inexpressible relief—our courage rising as the night fled— waited for hostilities to begin. But the Yankees had outwitted us, their withdrawal, by some strange coincidence, having been practically simultaneous with our advance—they taking just enough start, however, to keep well out of our sight and hearing. West remarked next morning, "It's better to be born lucky than rich," but whether he referred to our narrow escape, or to that of the Yankees, he refused to say. . . . Soon afterward a truce along the picket lines in front of the Texans was arranged; that is, there was to be no more shooting at each other's pickets—the little killing and wounding done by

C. F. Johnson

The Hut Picket

C. F. Johnson

In the Hut

"Fall in for Soup"

the practice never compensating for the powder and shot expended, and the discomfort of being always on the alert, night and day.

But the South Carolinians, whose picket line began at our left, their first rifle-pit being within fifty feet of the last one of the First Texas, could make no terms, whatever. The Federals charge them with being the instigators and beginners of the war, and, as I am informed, always exclude them from the benefit of truces between the pickets. It is certainly an odd spectacle to see the Carolinians hiding in their rifle pits and not daring to show their heads, while, not fifty feet away, the Texans sit on the ground playing poker, in plain view and within a hundred yards of the Yankees. Worse than all, the palmetto fellows are not even permitted to visit us in daylight, except in disguise—their new uniforms of gray always betraying them wherever they go. One of them who is not only very fond of, but successful at, the game of poker, concluded the other day to risk being shot for the chance of winning the money of the First Texas, and, divesting himself of his coat, slipped over to the Texas pit an hour before daylight, and by sunrise was giving his whole mind to the noble pastime.

An hour later a keen-sighted Yankee sang out, "Say, you Texas Johnnies! ain't that fellow playing cards, with his back to a sapling, one of them d——d South Carolina secessionists? Seems to me his breeches are newer 'n they ought to be." This direct appeal for information placed the Texans between the horns of a dilemma; hospitality demanded the protection of their guest—prudence, the observance of good faith toward the Yankees. The delay in answering obviated the necessity for it by confirming the inquirer's suspicions, and, exclaiming, "D—n him, I just know it is!" he raised his gun quickly and fired. The South Carolinian was too active, though; at the very first movement of the Yankee, he sprang ten feet and disappeared into a gulch that protected him from further assault. . . .

Jack Smith, of Company D, is sui generis. A brave and gallant soldier he is yet an inveterate straggler, and is therefore, not always on hand when the battle is raging, but at Chickamauga he was, and, singularly enough, counted for two.

Another member of Company D is constitutionally opposed to offering his body for sacrifice on the altar of his country, and, when he cannot get on a detail which will keep him out of danger, is sure to fall alarmingly sick. Jack determined to put a stop to this shirking, so early on the morning of the 19th, he took the fellow under his own protecting and stimulating care, and, attacking him in the most vulnerable point, to the surprise of everybody, carried him into and through the fight of that day.

"Come right along with me, Fred, and don't be scared a particle," Jack was heard to say in his coaxing, mellifluous voice as we began to advance on the enemy, "for I'll shoot the head off the first man who points a gun in front of you, and I'll watch out for your carcass, and after we have whipped the Yanks you an' me'll finish them bitters in my haversack."

"But I don't like bitters," protested Fred in a trembling voice.

"I know that, ole feller, an' I don't generally like 'em myself, but these are

made on the old nigger's plan—the least mite in the world of cherry bark, still
less of dogwood, and then fill up the bottle with whisky."

Needless to say that after the battle was over and Jack had brought his
protege safely through its perils, quite a number of comrades looked long-
ingly at the bottle. In vain, however; Jack was loyal to his promise and he
and Fred were the merriest men in Company D that night.

—POLLEY, *A Soldier's Letters to Charming Nellie*

7. THE CONFEDERATES ESCAPE IN THE TECHE COUNTRY

*Before he could support Grant in the Vicksburg-Port Hudson campaign
General Banks, who had replaced Butler in New Orleans, felt that he had to
dispose of the Confederate forces in the Teche country west of the city, a
country of bayous, lakes, and swamps. In January 1863 Banks organized the
first of his expeditions against General Taylor's miscellaneous forces, but this
petered out. A second advance took place in April and met with some success. It is this advance that is recorded here. Later that summer General
Taylor, whom we have already met in the Valley campaign, and his subordinate Mouton struck back, recovering the whole Teche country up to
the gates of New Orleans. The fall of Port Hudson released large forces for
a counterattack, however, and Taylor retreated to the Red River country.*

It is, once more, the novelist De Forest who tells the story.

THE Teche country was to the war in Louisiana what the Shenandoah
Valley was to the war in Virginia. It was a sort of back alley, parallel
to the main street wherein the heavy fighting must go on; and one side or
the other was always running up or down the Teche with the other side
in full chase after it. There the resemblance ends, for the Teche country is
a long flat, hemmed in by marshes and bayous, which, as everybody but a
blind man can see, is a very different thing from a rolling valley bordered by
mountains. . . .

My first adventure in this region was in January, 1863. Weitzel dashed
up to the confluence of the Teche and Atchafalaya with five or six regiments,
scared Mouton out of his position there, smashed the Confederates' new ironclad gunboat *Cotton*, and returned next morning. Although pestered with
cold and hunger, our march homeward was as hilarious as a bacchanal
procession. It was delightful to have beaten the enemy, and it was delightful
to be on the way back to our comfortable quarters. The expedition was
thus brief because it had fulfilled its object, which was to weaken the Confederate naval power on the Teche, and thus enable Banks to take the back
alley in his proposed advance on Port Hudson.

But why should he go by the back alley of the Teche instead of by the
main street of the Mississippi? Because it was necessary to destroy the army
of Mouton, or, at least, to drive it northward as far as possible, in order to
incapacitate it from attacking New Orleans while we should be engaged with
the fortress of the bluffs. The story ran in our brigade that this sensible plan

originated in the head of our own commandant, Weitzel. I believed it then, and I have learned no better since, although I can affirm nothing. The reader will please to remember that there is a great deal of uncertainty in war, not only before but after.

About the middle of April, 1863, I was once more at the confluence of the Teche and the Atchafalaya. This time Mouton was there in strong force, posted behind entrenchments which seemed to me half a mile in length, with an impassable swamp on his right and armored gunboats on his left. Banks's army was far superior in numbers and, supported as it was by a sufficient fleet of gunboats, could doubtless have carried the position; but the desirable thing to do was of course, not so much to beat Mouton as to bag him, and so finish the war in this part of Louisiana. Accordingly, by mysterious water-ways of which I know nothing, Grover's division was transported to Irish Bend, in Mouton's rear, while Emory's and Weitzel's divisions should amuse him in front.

And here I am tempted . . . to describe this same amusement. The first part of the joke was to push up Weitzel's brigade to draw the enemy's fire. In a single long line, stretching from the wood on the left well toward the river on the right, the brigade advanced directly toward the enemy's works, pros-trating or climbing fences, and struggling amid horrible labyrinths of tangled sugar cane. Rush through a mile of Indian corn, taking the furrows diago-nally, then imagine yourself three times as tired and breathless as you are, and you will form some conception of what it is to move in line through a cane-field. At first you valiantly push aside the tough green obstacles; then you ignominiously dodge under or around them; at last you fall down with your tongue out. The ranks are broken; the regiment tails off into strings, the strongest leading; the ground is strewn with panting soldiers; the organiza-tion disappears.

The cane once passed, stragglers began to come up and find their places; the ranks counted off anew while advancing, and we had once more a regi-ment. Now we obtained a full view of the field of projected amusement. Before us lay a long and comparatively narrow plain, bounded by forests rising out of swamps, and decorated by a long low earthwork, a third of a mile ahead of us, and barely visible to the naked eye. Away to our right were two half-demolished brick sugar-houses, near which there was a scurry-ing of dust to and fro, bespeaking a skirmishing of cavalry. Otherwise the scene was one of perfect quietness and silence and desertion.

Of a sudden *bang, bang, bang,* roared an unseen battery, and *jiz, jiz, jiz,* screeched the shells over our heads. Evidently the enemy was too much amused to keep his mouth shut. Then our own batteries joined in with their *bang, bang, bang, jiz, jiz, jiz,* and for twenty minutes or more it was as dis-gusting as a Fourth of July. The shelling did not hurt us a bit, and con-sequently did not scare us much, for we were already accustomed to this kind of racket, and only took it hard when it was mingled with the cries of the wounded. I never assisted, as the French phrase it, at a noisier or a more harmless bout of cannonading. Not a man in my regiment was injured, although the shells hummed and cracked and fought each other in flights over our heads, dotting the sky with the little globes of smoke which marked their explosions, and sending buzzing fragments in all directions.

Meantime our point was gained; the enemy had defined his position. There was a battery in the swampy wood on his right, which would enfilade an attacking column, while on his left the same business would be performed by his armored gunboats in the Teche. Now came an order to take the brigade to the rear. A greenhorn of an aide, shrieking with excitement, galloped up to our commander and yelled: "Colonel, double-quick your men out of range. Double-quick!"

I remember the wrath with which I heard this order. Run? Be shot if I would run or let a man of my company run. The regiment, hearing the command, had faced about and was going to the rear at a pace which threatened confusion and panic. I rushed through the ranks, drew my sword, ordered, threatened, and brought my own company from a double-quick down to the ordinary marching step. Every other officer, from the colonel downward, instinctively did the same; and the regiment moved off in a style which we considered proper for the Twelfth Connecticut.

That night we bivouacked with mosquitoes, who drew more blood than the cannonade of the afternoon. Next morning the heavy guns of the opposing gunboats opened a game of long bowls, in which the Parrotts of the Twenty-first Indiana took a part, sending loud-whispering shells into the farthest retreats of the enemy. At ten, the whole army, three lines deep and stretching across the river—a fine martial spectacle—advanced slowly through the canefields toward the entrenchments. Marching in my preferred position, in the front rank of my company and next to the regimental colors, I felt myself to be an undesirably conspicuous person, as we came out upon the open ground in view of the enemy, and received the first discharge of their artillery. It is a grand thing to take the lead in battle, but all the same it is uncomfortable. The first cannon shot which I noticed struck the ground sixty or eighty feet in front of our color guard, threw up the ploughed soil in a little cloud, leaped a hundred feet behind the regiment, and went bounding off to the rear.

"That's bad for the fellows behind us," I said to my men, with that smile which a hero puts on when he makes the best he can of battle, meantime wishing himself at home.

The next shot struck within thirty feet of the line, and also went jumping and whistling rearward. They were evidently aiming at the colors, and that was nearly equivalent to aiming at me.

"You'll fetch him next time," I thought, grimly; and so, doubtless, thought hundreds of others, each for himself.

But at this moment one of our own batteries opened with great violence and evidently shook the nerves of the enemy's gunners, for their next shot screeched over the colors and first struck the ground far in rear of the regiment, and thereafter they never recovered their at first dangerously accurate range. Now came an order to the infantry to halt and lie down, and no veteran will need to be told that we obeyed it promptly. I never knew that order to be disregarded on a field of battle, not even by the most inexperienced and insubordinate of troops, unless, indeed, they were already running.

The battle of Camp Beaseland was an artillery duel of fifteen or twenty pieces on a side, lasting hotly from eleven in the morning till six in the evening, with a dash of infantry charging and heavy musketry on either flank, and a dribble of skirmishing along the whole line. Where we were, it was all artillery and skirmishing, noisy and lively enough, but by no means murderous. Bainbridge's regular battery on our right pitched into a Louisiana battery on our left front, and a little beyond it a battery of the Twenty-first Indiana pounded away at the Confederate gunboats and at an advanced earthwork. The loud metallic spang of the brass howitzers, the dull thud of the iron Parrotts, and the shrieking and cracking of the enemy's shells made up a *charivari* long to be remembered.

Meantime, companies moved out here and there from the line of infantry, deployed as skirmishers, advanced to within two or three hundred yards of the breastworks, and opened fire. This drew the Rebel musketry and made things hotter than ever. The order to lie low passed along, and we did the best we could with the cane-hills, wishing that they were bigger. As I lay on my side behind one of these six-inch fortifications, chewing the hardtack which was my only present creature comfort, several balls cut the low weeds which overhung me. Yet, notwithstanding the stunning racket and the quantity of lead and iron flying about, our loss was very small.

Nor could the enemy have suffered more severely, except on our left. There the Seventy-fifth and 114th New York, drawn up in the swampy wood which at that point separated the two armies, repulsed with a close volley of musketry a swarm of Texans who attempted to ford the morass and turn our flank. There, too, the heaviest fire of our batteries was concentrated and made havoc, as I afterward heard, of the enemy's artillery. An officer of one of our skirmishing companies, whose position enabled him to see this part of the enemy's line, assured me, with a jocose exaggeration founded on fact, that "the air was full of horses' tails and bits of harness." But, in a general way, there was very little slaughter for the amount of powder expended. We were not fighting our hardest; we were merely amusing the enemy. The only serious work done was to smash one or two of his gunboats. Meanwhile, it was hoped that Grover was gaining Mouton's rear and so posting himself as to render escape impossible.

An officer, major of a Texas regiment, as I was told by prisoners, attracted the notice of both armies by riding from left to right of the enemy's position in full view of our line. He was behind the entrenchment, it is true, but that was little more than a rifle pit and hardly concealed the legs of his horse. He was undoubtedly a staff officer engaged in carrying orders to the battery in the wood. As he came back on his perilous mission every skirmisher fired at him, and many men in the line of battle added their bullets to the deadly flight which sought his life, while all our brigade watched him with breathless interest. Directly in front of me the horse reared; the rider dismounted and seemed to examine him; then, remounting, cantered a few yards; then leaned backwards and slid to the ground. Away went the horse, wildly, leaving his gallant master dead.

About five o'clock an order arrived to move out of range of fire. The skirmishers came in; the men rose and took their places in line; and we marched slowly back to our position of the morning. During the night we fought mosquitoes, not with the idea of amusing them, but in deadly earnest. During the night, also, the colonel in charge of the pickets, a greenhorn of some nine-months' regiment, distinguished himself by an exhibition of the minimum of native military genius. Early in the morning he reported to Weitzel that the enemy had vacated their position.

"How do you know?" demanded the startled general.

"I heard their artillery going off about two o'clock."

"Good God, sir! why didn't you inform me of it immediately?"

"Why, General, I thought you wanted them to clear out; and I didn't like to disturb you after such a hard day's work."

Thus collapsed the plan by which we were to stick like a burr to the enemy and pitch into his rear whenever he should attempt to force his way through Grover.

—DE FOREST, "Forced Marches"

8. FORREST'S CAVALRYMEN CAPTURE A COLT

The cavalry, Union and Confederate, always needed horses, and in a region like Middle Tennessee, which had been fought over and pillaged over for three years, the need was acute. Here Private John Milton Hubbard of Forrest's cavalry corps—the 7th Tennessee—tells how the brave raiders captured "Sal's colt."

THAT a little fun can be mixed up with the horrors of war was illustrated on this trip somewhere over in the hills of Wayne. James E. Wood's little chestnut sorrel, the horse which had been tendered by his owner to Captain Tate, as related in the account of the fight at Ripley, and from which that gallant officer was shot, struck the frog of one foot against a stone and was rendered unserviceable. Austin Statler and Tom Joyner set about the task of helping their fellow-soldier to a remount. This was difficult to do in a country which had been stripped of all the good stock. The only animal available appeared to be a three-year-old, standing in an enclosure near an humble cottage. Statler, in his blandest manner, explained the situation to the mistress of the cottage, and alluded in earnest words to the fine points of the lame horse, which needed only a few days' rest to restore him to his former condition of usefulness. No, no; the old lady couldn't see it in the light in which it had been so earnestly presented. There were seven stout daughters standing by ready to assist their mother, who averred that the animal was "Sal's colt," and he couldn't have it upon any terms whatever. Statler persisted until high words resulted, and the soldiers advanced towards "Sal's colt." Thoroughly aroused, and reinforced by her mother and sisters,

Sal herself, a buxom lassie, now came to the rescue, cleared the fence at a bound, and sat astride of the bridleless colt.

Victory now seemed to perch upon the banner of the females, but the soldiers, who had no idea of seeing their comrade hotfoot it along the roads of Wayne, moved to the assault, determined to capture the colt, but anxious to inflict no bruises upon their adversaries, who fought like wildcats. The contest was fast and furious, but in a class entirely by itself. There were blood and hair in evidence, but no mortal casualties. There were pinching and twisting, wrenching and wringing, clutching and hugging, yes, hugging, till the female side had mostly lost its wind and Sal, grasping the mane of the colt with the grip of despair, while she planted her heels in its sides, was gently lifted from her position by the gallant trio. "It was all over but the shouting." The bit was forced and the girth was buckled. "Sal's colt" had changed its politics and been mustered into the service of the Confederacy.

The old lady intimated that "men folks" were at hand and ready to avenge all her wrongs. Statler, as a precautionary measure, rode out in the direction indicated by her and saw three armed citizens approaching. With cocked gun and ready pistol he commanded them, with assumed bravado, to lead the way to the cottage, while he assured them that he, too, had "a whole gang in reach." Tableau vivant: An elderly man "breathing out threatening and slaughter" and declaring that he would have satisfaction before the sun went down; two lusty young men with guns and in the poise of interested spectators; six bouncing young girls well distributed in the ensemble and joining in a chorus of abuse; an elderly woman standing in the kitchen door and wiping the sweat from her neck and ears with her checked apron, beaten but not conquered; Sal perched upon the top rail of the front fence in the attitude of a show girl about to dance a horn pipe, and gazing at three vanishing cavaliers just then turning a corner and making time to overtake the command; lastly, the abandoned warhorse, which had heard the guns at Tishomingo, stripped of his trappings and "turned out to grass," was standing meekly by and looking as if he might be thinking he had no friends at all.

—HUBBARD, *Notes of a Private*

9. GENERAL WILSON RAISES HIS CAVALRY THE HARD WAY

This entertaining episode is from the closing chapter of the war in the West. After Sherman launched his March to the Sea he sent General Thomas to Nashville to collect an army that would hold Tennessee against Hood. The troubles General Wilson had getting horses for his cavalry suggest how that army was improvised.

We will meet James Harrison Wilson again and need not pause here for a lengthy introduction. Only twenty-four when the war broke out, he had a meteoric rise, ending the war with the rank of major general. He was, by general agreement, with Sheridan the most brilliant cavalry commander in the Union armies.

WHILE Hood was advancing from the Tennessee and I had nominally six divisions of cavalry, my actual force with the colors in front of Hood did not exceed five thousand fighting men. Until the movement began I remained at Nashville, engaged night and day in perfecting the paper work, in gathering horses, arms, and equipments, and in making ready for the campaign which was soon to burst upon us. Generally, the supply departments responded promptly to my call, but horses, our greatest want, were scarce, and with the higher requirements and closer inspections I had myself prescribed a few months before, and the advance in price which had naturally followed the advance in quality, the western horse contractors found it impossible to supply our demands. The War Department itself seemed to despair, and while Stanton appeared willing to do what he could, he finally lost patience and his good sense besides, and telegraphed Thomas that if he waited for Wilson to remount his cavalry he would wait "till the crack of doom." But as this was after I had asked and he had granted permission to impress horses from the people wherever they could be found south of the Ohio River, his pessimistic assertion was shortly shown to be both unjust and unfounded.

This arbitrary measure was entirely without precedent within our lines, but it was carried ruthlessly into effect while the contending armies were facing each other in front of Nashville. Within seven days after the Secretary's authority came to hand seven thousand horses were obtained in middle and western Kentucky and our mounted force was thereby increased to twelve thousand, nine thousand of which were actually assembled at Edgefield or within supporting distance. The quartermasters to whom this duty was assigned gave vouchers in proper form for every horse taken and it is believed that no permanent loss or injury was inflicted upon the loyal people.

Every horse and mare that could be used was taken. All street-car and livery stable horses, and private carriage- and saddle-horses, were seized. Even Andrew Johnson, the vice-president-elect, was forced to give up his pair. A circus then at Nashville lost everything except its ponies; even the old white trick horse was taken but it is alleged that the young and handsome equestrienne, who claimed him, succeeded in convincing my adjutant general that the horse was unfit for cavalry service. Be this as it may, a clean sweep was made of every animal that could carry a cavalry-man and the result is shown by the fact that although two brigades of three thousand men were sent to Kentucky in pursuit of Lyon's Confederate cavalry, about ten thousand well mounted men crossed the Cumberland on the night of December 12 [1864] and marched out against the enemy on the morning of the 15th, as soon as the thaw made it possible to move at all.

The great victory which resulted from turning the enemy's flank shows how important the measure was in making the cavalry the tremendous factor it became, not only in that battle but in the campaign which wound up the war.

—WILSON, *Under the Old Flag*

XIV

The Problem of Discipline

WHY *should discipline have been a problem in the Civil War? There are a number of reasons for this, and not all of them are discreditable. Americans had never taken kindly to discipline, either in peace or in war. In civil life every man thought himself as good as his neighbor—even if that neighbor happened to be a merchant or a physician, a mayor or a Congressman—and this attitude was carried over into the armies. There was no military tradition in America, and little understanding of the value of rules and of discipline. This was the first major war in which Americans had ever been engaged, and it was the first to levy on the whole population. From 3,500,000 to 4,000,000 men fought, at one time or another, in Union or Confederate armies—an astonishingly high percentage of the total population of 31,000,000—and all but a handful of these were wholly without previous military experience.*

These considerations suggest that the problem of discipline would have been difficult in the best of circumstances; it was aggravated by the policies of Federal and Confederate governments. There was, for example, no trained officer class, and neither government did anything effective either to use such material as was available or to train officers. At the outbreak of the war the Regular Army consisted of 16,367 officers and men; there were, in addition, a number of graduates of West Point or of the Citadel and the Virginia Military Institute who were available. This nucleus of Regular Army and veterans might have been sufficient to provide officers for the volunteers of 1861 and 1862; by the time of the draft the war had produced a crop of competent officers. But the government did not follow the policy of breaking up the Regular Army, nor did the Confederacy use its officer material to best advantage. Most of the field and many of the general officers were appointed by state governors, usually on political grounds; a great many of these, especially in the North, earned their appointments by raising their own regiments or companies. Lower officers were customarily elected by the rank and file. Most of the officers were totally ignorant of the rules of warfare, of military tactics, and of the requirements of discipline. Some learned quickly; others never learned.

One result of this situation was widespread insubordination, downright disobedience, and a staggeringly high rate of desertion. It was not that the typical American was either disorderly or disobedient; it was rather that while willing enough to fight, he saw no reason for observing discipline when there was no fighting at hand. He had little respect for officers, as such, and many

481

of these were not deserving of respect. He was unfamiliar with the require-
ments of camp sanitation; saw no harm in straggling; was inclined to regard
most regulations as something between a joke and a nuisance. Circumstances,
as well as the inevitable opportunities and temptations of war, encouraged him
to foraging and pillaging.

Punishment for insubordination varied greatly from army to army, from
regiment to regiment, and from time to time. Many officers were lax dis-
ciplinarians because they curried favor with their men; in the long run the
men respected more the strict disciplinarians. Military courts—often drum-
head courts—dealt with more serious cases. The penalty for desertion, or for
sleeping on sentry duty, was death, but this extreme penalty was rarely in-
flicted. Statistics for the Confederacy are wholly wanting; those for the Union
are inadequate and misleading. While there are numerous accounts of execu-
tions and numerous accounts, too, of last-minute reprieves, the surgeon gen-
eral's office gives total executions as 121; when we recall that there were well
over 200,000 desertions from the Union Army, and that some 75,000 of these
were arrested during the last two years of the war, we realize how feeble was
the machinery of enforcement and discipline.

The excerpts which follow are designed to show some of the varied
aspects of the problem of discipline: the causes of soldier discontent, the
manifestations of that discontent in insubordination and desertion, the ravages
of pillaging, the methods of punishment, and the impression that the conduct
and misconduct of the Civil War soldiers made on thoughtful observers.

1. THOMAS WENTWORTH HIGGINSON EXPLAINS
THE VALUE OF TRAINED OFFICERS

Higginson himself was an amateur—a Unitarian clergyman who had
helped raise and train a Massachusetts regiment and then found himself
colonel of the 1st South Carolina colored regiment, where his chief problems
were in the realm of training, discipline, sanitation, the commissary, and so
forth. This essay on the problem of command—one of the very best in our
literature—appeared within a few months of Higginson's retirement from the
army.

NOW that three years have abolished many surmises, and turned many
others into established facts, it must be owned that the total value of the
professional training has proved far greater, and that of the general preparation far less, than many intelligent observers predicted. The relation between
officer and soldier is something so different in kind from anything which civil
life has to offer, that it has proved almost impossible to transfer methods or
maxims from the one to the other. If a regiment is merely a caucus, and the
colonel the chairman,—or merely a fire-company, and the colonel the foreman,—or merely a prayer-meeting, and the colonel the moderator,—or merely
a bar-room, and the colonel the landlord,—then the failure of the whole thing
is a foregone conclusion.

War is not the highest of human pursuits, certainly; but an army comes very near to being the completest of human organizations, and he alone succeeds in it who readily accepts its inevitable laws, and applies them. An army is an aristocracy, on a three-years' lease, supposing that the period of enlistment. No mortal skill can make military power effective on democratic principles. A democratic people can perhaps carry on a war longer and better than any other; because no other can so well comprehend the object, raise the means, or bear the sacrifices. But these sacrifices include the surrender, for the time being, of the essential principle of the government. Personal independence in the soldier, like personal liberty in the civilian, must be waived for the preservation of the nation. With shipwreck staring men in the face, the choice lies between despotism and anarchy, trusting to the common sense of those concerned, when the danger is over, to revert to the old safeguards. It is precisely because democracy is an advanced stage in human society, that war, which belongs to a less advanced stage, is peculiarly inconsistent with its habits. Thus the undemocratic character, so often lamented in West Point and Annapolis, is in reality their strong point. Granted that they are no more appropriate to our stage of society than are revolvers and bowie-knives, that is precisely what makes them all serviceable in time of war. War being exceptional, the institutions which train its officers must be exceptional likewise.

The first essential for military authority lies in the power of command,—a power which it is useless to analyze, for it is felt instinctively, and it is seen in its results. It is hardly too much to say, that, in military service, if one has this power, all else becomes secondary; and it is perfectly safe to say that without it all other gifts are useless. Now for the exercise of power there is no preparation like power, and nowhere is this preparation to be found, in this community, except in regular army-training. Nothing but great personal qualities can give a man by nature what is easily acquired by young men of very average ability who are systematically trained to command.

The criticism habitually made upon our army by foreign observers at the beginning of the war continues still to be made, though in a rather less degree,—that the soldiers are relatively superior to the officers, so that the officers lead, perhaps, but do not command them. The reason is plain. Three years are not long enough to overcome the settled habits of twenty years. The weak point of our volunteer service invariably lies here, that the soldier, in nine cases out of ten, utterly detests being commanded, while the officer, in his turn, equally shrinks from commanding. War, to both, is an episode in life, not a profession, and therefore military subordination, which needs for its efficiency to be fixed and absolute, is, by common consent, reduced to a minimum. The white American soldier, being, doubtless, the most intelligent in the world, is more ready than any other to comply with a reasonable order, but he does it because it is reasonable, not because it is an order. With advancing experience his compliance increases, but it is still because he better and better comprehends the reason. Give him an order that looks utterly unreasonable,—and this is sometimes necessary,—or give him one which looks trifling, under which head all sanitary precautions are yet to apt to rank, and you may, perhaps, find that you still have a free and independent citizen to deal with, not a soldier. *Implicit* obedience must be admitted still to be a rare quality in our army; nor can we wonder at it.

In many cases there is really no more difference between officers and men, in education or in breeding, than if the one class were chosen by lot from the other; all are from the same neighborhood, all will return to the same civil pursuits side by side; every officer knows that in a little while each soldier will again become his client or his customer, his constituent or his rival. Shall he risk offending him for life in order to carry out some hobby of stricter discipline? If this difficulty exist in the case of commissioned officers, it is still more the case with the non-commissioned, those essential intermediate links in the chain of authority. Hence the discipline of our soldiers has been generally that of a town-meeting or of an engine-company, rather than that of an army; and it shows the extraordinary quality of the individual men, that so much has been accomplished with such a formidable defect in the organization. Even granting that there has been a great and constant improvement, the evil is still vast enough. And every young man trained at West Point enters the service with at least this advantage, that he has been brought up to command, and has not that task to learn.

He has this further advantage, that he is brought up with some respect for the army-organization as it is, with its existing rules, methods, and proprieties, and is not, like the newly commissioned civilian, desposed in his secret soul to set aside all its proprieties as mere "pipe-clay," its methods as "old-fogyism," and its rules as "red-tape." How many good volunteer officers will admit, if they speak candidly, that on entering the service they half believed the "Army Regulations" to be a mass of old-time rubbish, which they would gladly reëdit, under contract, with immense improvements, in a month or two,—and that they finally left the service with the conviction that the same book was a mine of wisdom, as yet but half explored!

Certainly, when one thinks for what a handful of an army our present military system was devised, and with what an admirable elasticity it has borne this sudden and stupendous expansion, it must be admitted to have most admirably stood the test. Of course, there has been much amendment and alteration needed, nor is the work done yet; but it has mainly touched the details, not the general principles. The system is wonderfully complete for its own ends, and the more one studies it the less one sneers. Many a form which at first seems to the volunteer officer merely cumbrous and trivial he learns to prize at last as almost essential to good discipline; he seldom attempts a short cut without finding it the longest way, and rarely enters on that heroic measure of cutting red-tape without finding at last that he has entangled his own fingers in the process.

More thorough training tells in another way. It is hard to appreciate, without the actual experience, how much of military life is a matter of mere detail. The maiden at home fancies her lover charging at the head of his company, when in reality he is at that precise moment endeavoring to convince his company-cooks that salt-junk needs five hours' boiling, or is anxiously deciding which pair of worn-out trousers shall be ejected from a drummer-boy's knapsack. Courage is, no doubt, a good quality in a soldier, and luckily not often wanting; but, in the long run, courage depends largely on the haversack. Men are naturally brave, and when the crisis comes, almost all men will fight well, if well commanded. As Sir Philip Sidney said, an army of stags led by a lion is more formidable than an army of lions led by a stag. Courage is cheap; the main duty of an officer is to take good care of his men, so that every one of them shall be ready, at a moment's notice, for any reasonable demand.

A soldier's life usually implies weeks and months of waiting, and then one glorious hour; and if the interval of leisure has been wasted, there is nothing but a wasted heroism at the end, and perhaps not even that. The penalty for misused weeks, the reward for laborious months, may be determined within ten minutes.

Without discipline an army is a mob, and the larger the worse; without rations the men are empty uniforms; without ammunition they might as well have no guns; without shoes they might almost as well have no legs. And it is in the practical appreciation of all these matters that the superiority of the regular officer is apt to be shown. . . .

Military glory may depend on a thousand things,—the accident of local position, the jealousy of a rival, the whim of a superior. But the merit of having done one's whole duty to the men whose lives are in one's keeping, and to the nation whose life is staked with theirs,—of having held one's command in such a state, that, if at any given moment it was not performing the most brilliant achievement, it might have been,—this is the substantial triumph which every faithful officer has always within reach.

Now will any one but a newspaper flatterer venture to say that this is the habitual standard in our volunteer service? Take as a test the manner in which official inspections are usually regarded by a regimental commander. These occasions are to him what examinations by the School Committee are to a public-school teacher. He may either deprecate and dodge them, or he may manfully welcome them as the very best means of improvement for all under his care. Which is the more common view? What sight more pitiable than to behold an officer begging off from inspection because he has just come in from picket, or is just going out on picket, or has just removed camp, or was a day too late with his last requisition for cartridges?

No doubt it is a trying ordeal to have some young regular-army lieutenant ride up to your tent at an hour's notice, and leisurely devote a day to probing every weak spot in your command,—to stand by while he smells at every camp-kettle, detects every delinquent gun-sling, ferrets out old shoes from behind the mess-bunks, spies out every tent-pole not labelled with the sergeant's name, asks to see the cash-balance of each company-fund, and perplexes your best captain on forming from two ranks into one by the left flank. Yet it is just such unpleasant processes as these which are the salvation of an army; these petty mortifications are the fulcrum by which you can lift your whole regiment to a first-class rank, if you have only the sense to use them. So long as no inspecting officer needs twice to remind you of the same thing, you have no need to blush. But though you be the bravest of the brave, though you know a thousand things of which he is utterly ignorant, yet so long as he can tell you one thing which you ought to know, he is master of the situation. He may be the most conceited little popinjay who ever strutted in uniform; no matter; it is more for your interest to learn than for his to teach. Let our volunteer officers, as a body, once resolve to act on this principle, and we shall have such an army as the world never saw. But nothing costs the nation a price so fearful, in money or in men, as the false pride which shrinks from these necessary surgical operations, or regards the surgeon as a foe. . . .

In those unfortunate early days, when it seemed to most of our Governors to make little difference whom they commissioned, since all were alike un-tried, and of two evils it was natural to choose that which would produce the more agreeable consequences at the next election-time,—in those days of darkness many very poor officers saw the light. Many of these have since been happily discharged or judiciously shelved. The trouble is, that those who remain are among the senior officers in our volunteer army, in their respective grades. They command posts, brigades, divisions. They preside at court-martials. Beneath the shadow of their notorious incompetency all minor evils may lurk undetected. To crown all, they are, in many cases, sin-cere and well-meaning men, utterly obtuse as to their own deficiencies, and manifesting (to employ a witticism coeval with themselves) all the Christian virtues except that of resignation.

The present writer has beheld the spectacle of an officer of high rank, previously eminent in civil life, who could only vindicate himself before a court-martial from the ruinous charge of false muster by summoning a staff-officer to prove that it was his custom to sign all military papers without looking at them. He has seen a lieutenant tried for neglect of duty in allowing a soldier under his command, at an important picket-post, to be found by the field-officer of the day with two inches of sand in the bottom of his gun,—and pleading, in mitigation of sentence, that it had never been the practice in his regiment to make any inspection of men detailed for such duty. That such instances of negligence should be tolerated for six months in any regi-ment of regulars is a thing almost inconceivable, and yet in these cases the regiments and the officers had been nearly three years in service. . . .

The glaring defect of most of our volunteer regiments, from the begin-ning to this day, has lain in slovenliness and remissness as to every department of military duty, except the actual fighting and dying. When it comes to that ultimate test, our men usually endure it so magnificently that one is tempted to overlook all deficiencies on intermediate points. But they must not be overlooked, because they create a fearful discount on the usefulness of our troops, when tried by the standard of regular armies. I do not now refer to the niceties of dress-parade or the courtesies of salutation: it has long since been tacitly admitted that a white American soldier will not present arms to any number of rows of buttons, if he can by any ingenuity evade it; and to shoulder arms on passing an officer is something to which only Ethiopia or the regular army can attain. Grant, if you please, (though I do not grant,) that these are merely points of foolish punctilio. But there are many things which are more than punctilio, though they may be less than fighting.

The efficiency of a body of troops depends, after all, not so much on its bravery as on the condition of its sick-list. A regiment which does picket-duty faithfully will often avoid the need of duties more terrible. Yet I have ridden by night along a chain of ten sentinels, every one of whom should have taken my life rather than permit me to give the countersign without dismounting, and have been required to dismount by only four, while two did not ask me for the countersign at all, and two others were asleep. I have ridden through a regimental camp whose utterly filthy condition seemed enough to send malaria through a whole military department, and have been asked by the colonel, almost with tears in his eyes, to explain to him why his men were dying at the rate of one a day. The latter was a regiment nearly a year old, and the former one of almost two years' service, and just from the old Army of the Potomac.

The fault was, of course, in the officers. The officer makes the command, as surely as, in educational matters, the teacher makes the school. There is not a regiment in the army so good that it could not be utterly spoiled in three months by a poor commander, nor so poor that it could not be altogether transformed in six by a good one. The difference in material is nothing,— white or black, German or Irish; so potent is military machinery that an officer who knows his business can make good soldiers out of almost anything, give him but a fair chance. The difference between the present Army of the Potomac and any previous one,—the reason why we do not daily hear, as in the early campaigns, of irresistible surprises, overwhelming numbers, and masked batteries,—the reason why the present movements are a tide and not a wave,—is not that the men are veterans, but that the officers are. There is an immense amount of perfectly raw material in General Grant's force, besides the colored regiments, which in that army are all raw, but in which the Copperhead critics have such faith they would gladly select them for dangers fit for Napoleon's Old Guard. But the newest recruit soon grows steady with a steady corporal at his elbow, a well-trained sergeant behind him, and a captain or a colonel whose voice means something to give commands.

—HIGGINSON, "Regular and Volunteer Officers"

2. THE NEW YORK SEVENTY-NINTH MUTINIES

Mutiny was in fact very rare; when it occurred, as it did with the 79th New York and a few other regiments, it attracted a great deal of attention. The trouble here seems to have been twofold: misunderstanding about the term of enlistment, and incompetent officers. There was a good deal of drunkenness in the regiment, and over a hundred desertions. When the regiment was ordered to Virginia it refused to march. Firm action on the part of

Colonel Andrew Porter and General Isaac Stevens restored order, and eventually the regiment earned back its colors and its good name, and at Chantilly, as we have seen, it fought gallantly.

Captain William Lusk, who tells the story, was a Yale graduate who returned from medical studies abroad to enlist in this Highland Regiment, was commended for gallantry in action, and helped put down the draft riots in New York. After the war he became one of the nation's leading obstetricians.

Maryland, Camp Causten, Aug. 17th, 1861

My dear Mother:

This has been a busy and painful week for the officers of the Highland Regiment. You have seen various accounts of our troubles in the papers, but they contain nothing authentic, although perhaps about as much as an outsider can understand. The mutiny of Thursday is only the legacy of a quarrel begun among the officers before the Regiment left for the seat of war. The quarrel ended after the battle of Bull Run, in the resignation of several of the officers whose ambition was disappointed as to governing the affairs of the Regiment. . . . Since the battle, owing to the loss through resignations or deaths, of our Colonel, Major and 9 of the 10 Captains, besides that of many of the Lieutenants, we were left in a condition peculiarly unfavorable to discipline; and this much is to be said that the companies of Captain Ellis (my own) and that of Captain Elliot, which were provided with officers, obeyed their orders, and refused to join the mutineers.

The mutiny commenced in the morning by the men's refusing to strike their tents as commanded. They were to have been struck at 5 A.M. and the Regiment was to move at 6 o'clock. Col. Stevens repeated the orders, but they were still silently and sullenly neglected. He then went among the men and used all his powers of persuasion, but they had been told that they had the law on their side, and if they only persevered, they would be able to return home as a militia regiment. Col. Stevens next sent to each company singly and read the articles of war, appending to them such remarks as would enforce in the men the danger of their course; but by this time, the camp, left without sentry, became exposed to the whiskey dealers who made good use of their opportunities.

Soon a scene of the wildest confusion took place. The soldiers, throwing off all authority, presented the hideous and disgusting spectacle of a debauched and drunken Helotry. It was a time trying to one's nerves—more trying far than the musketry or cannonading of Bull Run. The Colonel ordered the officers to strike the tents themselves. This we did amid the jeers, the taunts, and the insults of an infuriated mob. One man brought me his gun, cocked it, showed me it was capped, and reminded me it was intended for one officer at least to die, should our release be attempted. Still we worked quietly on, obeying our orders. Some of the Lieutenants were allowed to take down the tents undisturbed, but on leaving them a moment, they were again pitched by the men. Everywhere we were threatened, and it became equally necessary to show neither fear of the men, nor, on the other hand, to allow ourselves any act of violence which would precipitate bloodshed.

Luckily for us, when the men were most maddened by drink, an old country quarrel broke out among them, viz:—the feud between the Orangemen and the Ribandmen, which we only know of through English novels, and history. We were not, however, altogether forgotten. Names neither poetical, decent, or complimentary were bestowed upon us.

Finally afternoon advanced, and nothing was gained. The Colonel called on the men for the last time to render obedience. Soberness and reflection had begun their work upon a few. These fell into their places, and were stationed around the Camp as a guard over the others. Still, though thus yielding, their sympathies were either extended to their mutinous comrades, or else they were too fearful to render much assistance. It was necessary for the officers to be everywhere, and I confess I was quite exhausted when a body of cavalry and a line of infantry appeared, coming toward us. This was a great relief. The mutineers, all unconscious, were surrounded, and, when it was too late to resist, obeyed the orders issued, a death penalty being promised to those who wavered. You have seen in the papers the punishment awarded to the Regiment—the taking of our colors and the disgrace from which we are suffering.

Dear Mother, I feel heartsick and much depressed. I begin to repent bitterly of having cast my lot with a foreign Regiment. Our men have not the feelings of Americans, and cannot, when a reverse comes, be inspired to renewed efforts by enthusiasm for the cause. I am eager for another battle in order that we may have an opportunity to regain our colors, yet dread to risk it now that our men are much demoralized. I wish old Connecticut had a place for me.

Goodbye, dear mother.
Love to sisters and all.
Affec'y.,
W. T. Lusk.

—War Letters of William Thompson Lusk

3. "IT DOES NOT SUIT OUR FELLOWS TO BE COMMANDED MUCH"

The major difficulty in discipline was with the officers. Captains and lieutenants were customarily elected by the men; as this letter tells, they could be dismissed by the men, too.

Charles Johnson was a Swedish-born boy who enlisted in the Hawkins Zouaves—a New York regiment—and fought through the Peninsular, the Roanoke, and the Antietam campaigns. This letter was written from Fort Clark, near Hampton, Virginia.

Monday, October 28th [1861]

Our Company seems to be not only unfortunate in the choice of officers, but in the officers chosen for us as well. Captain Coppault, certainly a splendid drillmaster and with every outward appearance of a soldier, turns out a failure in the field, and has resigned. Lieutenant Russell is not much better, and perhaps ought to resign. Flemming is the best of men, but too good a fellow for a disciplinarian, and our First Sergeant is so ridiculously boyish that all his discipline loses its effect. Second Sergeant Peret, the slave of a clique which runs the Company, dares not say his soul is his own, and not an intelligent officer in our tribe, except it be Corporal Davis of the Color Guard, and he, being an artist who cares nothing for this military business except for the subjects it furnishes his pencil, is neither appreciated nor understood. And now we are to have one Barnard for our Captain. This man, for shooting a subordinate in the First New York Volunteers, had to fly for his life, but instead of resigning, he was transferred to this Regiment. Colonel Hawkins refused to recognize him, however, and he is, in consequence thereof, under arrest. Lieutenant-Colonel Betts has assigned Barnard to our Company to fill the vacancy caused by the resignation of Captain Coppault.

It does not suit the temper of our fellows to be commanded much, anyway; and for one of our own Regiment even, unless he carried a pretty strong hand, it might be an unpleasant task to take hold of Company I, and that being the case, the feeling of the Company as a whole can easily be imagined. The idea of being controlled by a man for whom most of us felt an abhorrence, seemed entirely intolerable. This feeling, sharpened by the notion that we would be submitting to another indignity put upon us, assisted by the contemptuous opinion we held of Barnard as to his bravery, combined to give the Captain a reception such as perhaps no other officer had ever before had from his subordinates. A variety of insults were heaped upon him openly, the moment he entered our quarters, and last Thursday, when he came out to take command, the Company refused to a man to obey his orders. And this, too, after he had made a speech to the effect that the insulting remarks he had heard must be stopped, and that he would shoot another man under the same circumstances, etc.; but all in vain—our boys insisted that they did not know him and would not obey, and he was obliged to retire, leaving the command to Lieutenant Russell.

During that day he was burned in effigy, a caricature was made on his tent, and a variety of greater indignities suggested, should he ever attempt to take command. On Dress Parade, a general order was read assigning him to our Company with every circumstance of name and rank, which only served to exasperate our men the more. Russell did all he could in a few remarks, laying down the law, but his little speech was instantly followed by three cheers for Russell and three groans for Barnard, and that night the Company's quarters seemed a perfect bedlam, so that the poor man dared not step out of his tent. This was the last of Captain Barnard. In the morning, the Major sent in a request that the Company cease their demonstrations, as Captain Barnard had already sent in his resignation.

—JOHNSON, *The Long Roll*

4. GRIPING IN THE UNION ARMY

Griping is a prerogative of all soldiers; it was probably indulged in more wholeheartedly during the Civil War than in any other American war, and with more justification. What we have constantly to keep in mind is that the nation was wholly unprepared for war, approached it with reluctance and timidity, and looked to its early conclusion.

Nothing is more revealing of this situation than the reluctance with which Lincoln prepared to create an army. With a Regular Army of less than 16,000—many officers and soldiers had gone over to the Confederacy—Lincoln relied on the states to furnish such troops as might be necessary to put down the rebellion. Not until mid-April 1861 did Lincoln call for 75,000 militia—to serve for three months! This, to be sure, was in accordance with the Acts of 1795 and 1803, and as Congress was not in session there appeared to be no authority for raising a volunteer army. There was a rush to the colors—that is to state regiments. Most of those who enlisted expected that they would be permitted to return in three months. After Bull Run it became clear that the war would be a long one, and the Secretary of War called on the state governors to extend the three-months service to three years or the duration of the war. For the most part the volunteers fell in with this arrangement, but in many regiments there was sharp discontent—discontent aggravated by the breakdown of supplies, incompetent officers, delays in pay, and other untoward considerations.

Samuel Partridge here describes some of the causes for discontent in the 13th New York Volunteers, a regiment recruited from around Elmira, New York.

Fort Bennet Virginia, Tuesday Aug. 14, 1861

My dear Mac,

A tent with a wet bottom—and one which sways from side to side and whose skirts flap like sails taken aback with every gust is by no means the most comfortable apartment in which to write. A wet backside and a candle flickering with every gust which soughs through my princely abode are no very great aids. A heavy overcoat does not assist materially in chirographic movements—and two or three hundred bitterly disappointed men—by a continual volley of double distilled profanity which completely silences the storm, and fairly dissipates the heavy fog do not assist to any great degree one's facility of composition or clearness of expression or the beauty of one's style. Amid all these drawbacks I am about to give you a statement of the present condition of the regiment—and to set at rest the conflicting rumors and newspaper reports which I know have reached you ere this does.

What I now write will be but introductory to and explanatory of what I shall probably write tomorrow. Tomorrow, the 14th, completes the three months for which the 13th Regiment of New York Volunteers were sworn into the United States service, and the time at which they fully expected to be mustered out.

First—concerning the promises made them. The mustering officer at Elmira told many of them that they would not be held beyond the time, but would have an opportunity to re-enlist if they chose. Rifles were promised them by the state; the state tried hard to break its word, but by the herculean efforts of our Noble Colonel—the arms were furnished us on the eve of an action.

The state promised us camp and garrison equipage—medical stores and uniforms. The former are now and ever have been very incomplete and uncomfortable. The medical and commissary departments have been with difficulty kept supplied—though much honor is due to the Regimental officers in charge of those departments. Our uniforms were of shoddy—of different shades and of Anakite size—and are now so completely worn out that no two men are dressed alike—and when the Regiment is in line it looks like un-uniformed militia on training day, or rather like a mob or rabble—dozens of men appear in shirts and drawers, many have no shoes or stockings, the pants of those so fortunate as to have any are worn to tatters so as to excuse their nakedness—and some, the seats of whose baggy breeches are gone, have gathered the tattered edges together and bound them with a few straws into a rope as you would fasten the mouth of a bag.

Many of us are gentlemen and this style of dress goes hard with them—but having only been paid as yet to the First of June they have not the means to clothe themselves.

After the dreadful affair of July 21—came a severe rain in which most of the men were obliged to sleep uncovered by the roadside, numbers thereby incurring incurable diseases—many became ruptured on the battle field where the hardest work was entrusted to the 13th Volunteers—Gentleman soldiers instead of the rough regulars.

We were promised a discharge—Gen. Sherman refused to grant applications for furloughs or leaves of absence, saying "You will all *probably* go home in a few days." or—"I am *almost positive though not quite certain* that your regiment will be discharged"—his "uncertainty" leaving him a hole to creep out of.

General McClellan told us verbally—"You shall go home in a few days." These things raised the expectations of the men to the highest pitch—but Secretary Seward dashed the cup of joy from our lips on Sunday afternoon by telling us that we *must* remain two years in accordance with a requisition on Gov. Morgan and a subsequent turning over.

Lieut. Col. [Carl] Stephan and Major [Oliver L.] Terry yesterday called on the Secretary of War—to ascertain the facts. We are to be held because other regiments in the same circumstances would press their own claims based on ours as a precedent, if we were permitted to leave. They make us fair promises—they will arm and equip us as well as any regiment in the service—will allow us to remove to a more salubrious climate. We can choose our own place—

The 13th have been victimized for three months by fair promises—and can not and will not put any more faith in them—nor can I blame them for feeling doubts.

Again I cannot blame them for wishing a discharge—cut up in battle—broken up in health and greatly reduced in numbers—a small regiment at first too—and a valiant one under the deadly fire of the enemy—and not now worth one single dime. You have heard greatly exaggerated reports of their condition heretofore—but now no report can be too bad to be true. We have no discipline whatever. Though the oldest volunteer regiment now in Virginia we are the most demoralized most deplorably so—and if thus impressed into service never will be of any use whatever. I am not writing this in a spirit of discontent. I am satisfied and happy to remain and shall be so if discipline can be maintained. Otherwise you can imagine that I shall [be] somewhat unhappily situated in a body of dissatisfied discontented and mutinous men.

—McKelvey, ed., "Civil War Letters of Samuel S. Partridge"

5. A CAMP OF SKULKERS AT CEDAR MOUNTAIN

There were various kinds and degrees of desertion: failure to report for the draft, bounty jumping, outright desertion, and skulking and straggling to avoid battle.

George Alfred Townsend, whom we have met once before, here describes a camp of skulkers hiding in the woods during the Battle of Cedar Mountain—or, as it is sometimes called, Slaughter Mountain—of August 9, 1862. This was one of the minor engagements preceding the Second Manassas campaign; partly because Banks and McDowell were unable to bring up their full forces, it was a victory for Jackson.

BEYOND this the way was comparatively clear; but as I knew that other guards held the road further on, I passed to the right, and with the hope of finding a rill of water, went across some grass fields, keeping toward the low places. The fields were very still, and I heard only the subdued noises wafted from the road; but suddenly I found myself surrounded by men. They were lying in groups in the tall grass, and started up suddenly, like the clansmen of Roderick Dhu. At first I thought myself a prisoner, and these some cunning Confederates, who had lain in wait. But, to my surprise, they were Federal uniforms, and were simply skulkers from various regiments, who had been hiding here during the hours of battle. Some of these miserable wretches asked me the particulars of the fight, and when told of the defeat, muttered that they were not to be hood-winked and slaughtered.

"I was sick, anyway," said one fellow, "and felt like droppin' on the road."

"I didn't trust my colonel," said another; "he ain't no soldier."

"I'm tired of the war, anyhow," said a third, "and my time's up soon; so I shan't have my head blown off."

As I progressed, dozens of these men appeared; the fields were strewn with them; a true man would rather have been lying with the dead on the field of carnage, than here, among the craven and base. I came to a spring at last, and the stragglers surrounded it in levies. One of them gave me a cup to dip some of the crystal, and a prayerful feeling came over me as the cooling draught fell over my dry palate and parched throat. Regaining the road, I encountered reinforcements coming rapidly out of Culpepper, and among them was the 9th New York. My friend, Lieutenant Draper, recognized me, and called out that he should see me on the morrow, if he was not killed meantime. Culpepper was filling with fugitives when I passed up the main street, and they were sprinkled along the sidewalks, gossiping with each other. The wounded were being carried into some of the dwellings, and when I reached the Virginia Hotel, many of them lay upon the porch. I placed my blanket on a clean place, threw myself down exhaustedly, and dropped to sleep directly.

—Townsend, *Campaigns of a Non-Combatant*

6. "THE ARMY IS BECOMING AWFULLY DEPRAVED"

Away from home, in the enemy's country, and without any inbred sense of discipline or firm officers, many of the soldiers were, indeed, "awfully depraved." Depravity ran the gamut from drunkenness and profanity to theft, pillaging, and murder.

Charles Wills, whose moral sense was deeply affronted by what he saw, was an Illinois boy of twenty-one when he enlisted as a private in the 8th Illinois Infantry. Before the end of the war he had been promoted to lieutenant colonel. He fought in Missouri, Tennessee, and Alabama, and was with Sherman in the March to the Sea. His letters are filled with accounts of immorality and pillaging in the army.

Provost Marshal's Office, Waterford, Miss., December 12, '62

From captain of the provost guard I have been changed to provost marshal. I had charge of two companies, doing the guard duty for the provost of our division until yesterday; the division was ordered forward to Oxford, except our regiment, which was left to guard the railroad between this point and the Tallahatchie river. Headquarters being here, Colonel Dickerman appointed me provost and sent my company to guard a bridge one and one-half miles south of this place. My business is to attend to all prisoners, deal with citizens (administer oaths, take paroles, etc.), give all passes for citizens and soldiers leaving, have charge of all soldiers straggling from their regiments, issue permits to sutlers, etc., and overlook the cotton trade. Altogether, quite enough for any one man to attend to.

The little advantage of having a comfortable house to live in, etc., is worth something; but I kind o' feel as if I would rather be with my company. Another regiment came in to-night, 12th Indiana, and we may possibly be relieved to-morrow. Shall be glad if we can only get with our division again. General Lanman has again taken command of our division, and although we know nothing against McKean, yet we know so much good of Lanman, that we're much pleased. Eight of our companies are guarding bridges, so we only have two here. Confound this railroad guarding; I'm down on it. 'Tis more dangerous than regular soldiering, harder work, and no shadow of a chance for glory. There's a smart chance of fun in my present business, particularly in the citizens branch thereof.

It would have furnished you with amusement enough for a month, could you have heard an old lady talk who visited me to-day. She was a F. F. and blooded, O Lord! We let all come within the lines; but before they can pass out, an oath or parole is required of them. How they squirm! Rebels, though they are, 'tis shocking and enough to make one's blood boil to see the manner in which some of our folks have treated them. Trunks have been knocked to pieces with muskets when the women stood by, offering the keys, bureau drawers drawn out, the contents turned on the floor, and the drawer thrown through the window, bed clothing and ladies' clothing carried off and all manner of deviltry imaginable perpetrated. Of course the scoundrels who do this kind of work would be severely punished if caught, but the latter is almost impossible. Most of the mischief is done by the advance of the army, though, God knows, the infantry is bad enough. The d—d thieves even steal from the Negroes (which is lower business than I ever thought it possible for a white man to be guilty of) and many of them are learning to hate the Yankees as much as our "Southern Brethern" do.

The army is becoming awfully depraved. How the civilized home folks will ever be able to live with them after the war, is, I think, something of a question. If we don't degenerate into a nation of thieves, 'twill not be for lack of the example set by a fair sized portion of our army. Do you remember that I used to write that a man would no sooner lose his morality in the army than at home? I now respectfully beg to recall the remark.

Scottsboro, Ala., January 5, 1864

It's all over now, the mounting part has "played" and that string will not probably be harped on again for this brigade to dance to. I think that today, Sherman, Logan or Ewing would not trust a detachment of this brigade on sorebacked mules if they had only three legs. This little squad of 500 men in the two months they have been mounted have committed more devilment than two divisions of regular cavalry could in five years. Everything you can think of, from shooting Negroes, or marrying these simple country women, down to stealing babies' diapers. From taking $2,700.00 in gold, to snatching a brass ring off the finger of the woman who handed a drink of water. From taking the last "old mar' " the widow had to carry her grist to mill, to robbing the bed of its cord, for halters, and taking the clothes line and bed-clothing "to boot." I'll venture that before we were dismounted, not a well-rope, tracechain, or piece of cord of any kind strong enough to hold a horse could be found in the districts through which we have foraged.

I want you to understand that my command is not responsible for the heavy devilment. I have steadily discountenanced it, and watched my men carefully. I am willing to be responsible for all they did, and will probably have a chance, as I understand a board of inquiry sits on the subject shortly. Some of the officers will, I think, have cause to wish they were never

mounted; and to think that "Mission Ridge" would have been preferable to
the duty they have been on.   —WILLS, *Army Life of an Illinois Soldier*

7. ROBERT GOULD SHAW COMPLAINS THAT WAR IS A DIRTY BUSINESS

*Robert Gould Shaw, member of a prominent Massachusetts merchant
family, was a lieutenant in the 2nd Massachusetts Volunteers when the famous
54th Massachusetts colored regiment was formed; he volunteered for service
and was appointed colonel. His regiment saw duty off the coast of Florida
and Georgia and then in the heroic attack on Battery Wagner, where Shaw
lost his life. Although only a minor figure in the war he has had raised to him
two noble memorials—St. Gaudens' great Shaw Memorial overlooking Boston
Common, and William Vaughn Moody's "Ode in Time of Hesitation."*

St. Simon's Island [Georgia], June 9th, 1863

We arrived at the southern point of this island at six this morning. I went
ashore to report to Colonel Montgomery, and was ordered to proceed with
my regiment to a place called Pike's Bluff, on the inner coast of the island,
and encamp. We came up here in another steamer, the *Sentinel,* as the *De
Molay* is too large for the inner waters, and took possession of a plantation
formerly owned by Mr. Gould. . . .

On Wednesday, a steamboat appeared off our wharf, and Colonel Montgomery hailed me from the deck with, "How soon can you get ready to start
on an expedition?"

I said, "In a half an hour," and it was not long before we were on board,
with eight companies, leaving two for camp-guard.

We steamed down by his camp, where two other steamers, with five
companies from his regiment, with two sections of Rhode Island artillery,
joined us. A little below there we ran aground and had to wait until midnight
for flood-tide, when we got away once more.

At 8 A.M. we were at the mouth of the Altamaha river, and immediately
made for Darien. We wound in and out through the creeks, twisting and
turning continually, often heading in directly the opposite direction from
that which we intended to, and often running aground, thereby losing much
time. Besides our three vessels, we were followed by the gunboat *Paul Jones.*

On the way up, [Colonel] Montgomery threw several shells among the
plantations, in what seemed to me a very brutal way, for he didn't know how
many women and children there might be.

About noon, we came in sight of Darien, a beautiful little town. Our
artillery peppered it a little, as we came up, and then our three boats made
fast to the wharves, and we landed the troops. The town was deserted, with
exception of two white women and two Negroes.

Montgomery ordered all the furniture and movable property to be taken
on board the boats. This occupied some time; and, after the town was pretty
thoroughly disembowelled, he said to me, "I shall burn this town." He

speaks always in a very low tone, and has quite a sweet smile when addressing you. I told him "I did not want the responsibility of it;" and he was only too happy to take it all on his shoulders. So the pretty little place was burnt to the ground, and not a shed remained standing—Montgomery firing the last buildings with his own hand. One of my companions assisted in it, because he ordered them out, and I had to obey. You must bear in mind, that not a shot had been fired at us from this place, and that there were evidently very few men left in it. All the inhabitants (principally women and children) had fled on our approach, and were, no doubt, watching the scene from a distance. Some of our grapeshot tore the skirt of one of the women whom I saw. Montgomery told her that her house and property should be spared; but it went down with the rest.

The reasons he gave me for destroying Darien were, that the Southerners must be made to feel that this was a real war, and that they were to be swept away by the hand of God, like the Jews of old. In theory, it may seem all right to some, but when it comes to being made the instrument of the Lord's vengeance, I myself don't like it. Then he says "We are outlawed, and, therefore, not bound by the rules of regular warfare." But that makes it none the less revolting to wreak our vengeance on the innocent and defenceless.

By the time we had finished this dirty piece of business, it was too dark to go far down the narrow river, where our boat sometimes touched both sides at once: so we lay at anchor until daylight, occasionally dropping a shell at a stray house. The *Paul Jones* fired a few guns as well as we.

I reached camp at about 2 P.M., to-day, after as abominable a job as I ever had a share in.

Remember not to breathe a word of what I have written about this raid, for I have not yet made up my mind what I ought to do. Besides my own distaste for this barbarous sort of warfare, I am not sure that it will not harm very much the reputation of black troops and of those connected with them. For myself, I have gone through the war so far without dishonor, and I do not like to degenerate into a plunderer and robber—and the same applies to every officer in my regiment. . . .

All I complain of is wanton destruction. After going through the hard campaigning and hard fighting in Virginia, this makes me very much ashamed of myself, Montgomery, from what I have seen of him, is a conscientious man, and really believes what he says, "that he is doing his duty to the best of his knowledge and ability." There are two courses only for me to pursue: to obey orders and say nothing, or to refuse to go on any more such expeditions, and be put under arrest, probably court-martialed, which is a serious thing.

—Post, ed., *Soldiers' Letters from Camp, Battle-Field and Prison*

8. THE YANKEE INVADERS PILLAGE AND BURN

With the exception of Lee's two invasions north of the Potomac, Morgan's abortive raid into Indiana, Early's thrust toward Washington, and the fight-

ing in Missouri, the war was fought entirely in the South. This meant not only the devastation and ruin that inevitably accompany the bombardment of cities, pitched battles, the encampment and marching of hostile armies, but destruction and pillaging. Pillaging is to be distinguished from organized and systematic destruction such as that carried out by Sheridan and Hunter in the Valley of Virginia and by Sherman in his March to the Sea; the first was an expression of individual lawlessness, the second systematic and authorized. From the point of view of the victims, to be sure, it made little difference whether their houses were sacked out of motives of high strategy or of wantonness: the result was the same. Pillaging was sometimes inspired by greed, sometimes by the kind of brutal destructiveness familiar to us from the Second World War, sometimes by bitterness and hatred. Some officers made sincere efforts to prevent or at least to control pillaging; others appear to have connived at it. That it was a violation of the rules of war and destructive of discipline is too obvious for emphasis.

The four excerpts which follow speak for themselves, and it will be sufficient to say a word about the circumstances and the authors.

David Cronin—who called himself "Major Eyland"—was a New York artist who returned from studies abroad to join the Union army in April 1861; he fought at Harpers Ferry, in southeastern Virginia, and in the Peninsular campaign, where he was an artist for Harper's Weekly. *It is from his account of that campaign that we have taken this appalling picture of the wanton sacking of the Governor John Page mansion and the destruction of one of the most valuable libraries in the South.*

Francis Pierce, who describes the looting of Fredericksburg—already battered by artillery—was a member of the 108th New York Volunteers.

Sarah Morgan we shall meet again; her lively description of the sacking of the Judge Thomas Gibbes Morgan house in Baton Rouge, Louisiana, is something of a classic.

General Grierson's great raid of 1863, commemorated elsewhere, was merely one of a series by that dashing cavalry officer; the intrepid Elizabeth Beach gives us an incident from one of his raids of the following year.

A. THE YANKEES SACK THE PAGE HOUSE IN WILLIAMSBURG

NEARLY all the residences in town, that had not been entirely deserted by their inhabitants after the battle of Williamsburg, were unmolested by our troops. The presence of even one servant would almost certainly save a dwelling from hostile visitation, and we all know how strict McClellan was in protecting private property; but those that were entirely abandoned had been more or less despoiled. This was notably the case with the ancient mansion of Governor John Page, situated on the Bowling Green, near the remains of the colonial palace of Lord Dunmore. It had been a stately, handsomely furnished relic of the pre-Revolutionary period and in its parlors Washington had executed a minuet and La Fayette had saluted a partner in the dance. It had contained a library scarcely surpassed in value by any other private library then in the United States. Page, who belonged to the Revolutionary epoch, was at one time Governor of Virginia; a personal friend of Washington; a school-mate and intimate associate of Jefferson; a true patriot and one of the ruling political spirits of his age and country. He seems to have been the confidential friend and adviser of many of the more active progenitors of the Revolution.

I was told that the occupants of the Page mansion were at dinner when the battle of Williamsburg began, and that in their haste to get away, they left the house without even a servant to take charge of the premises, and a portion of costly dining-plate remained upon the table. The invaders ransacked the house from cellar to roof; there was no one to ask McClellan to protect it. I have never looked upon a more deplorable picture of the ravages of war than when standing amid the litter of half-destroyed books, papers and documents on the floor of the Governor's library. Shattered marble busts and statuary, fragments of ornamented book-cases, heaps of old engravings, loose manuscripts, vellum bound volumes, torn files of precious colonial newspapers, bills of lading and commercial correspondence, pieces of window glass and crushed stucco, mixed with straw and mud, on every side. Hundreds of heavy-booted and spurred cavalrymen had played football with everything of value in the house.

When I took command, I placed a guard in front of the house and forbade all intrusion. Upon my first visit I picked up a bound volume of the *Virginia Gazette*, the first Virginia newspaper, containing files of 1776 and 1777; a rare old folio edition of Shakespeare's plays, and a copy of the book written by Captain John Smith, giving a general history of his explorations in Virginia, with a queer map of the territory and water ways, drawn by himself, and published in London in 1624. These relics I carried to head-quarters where they attracted the attention of my numerous visitors—principally officers from the command stationed at Fort Magruder. The files of the *Virginia Gazette* were of great interest and value. I recall a letter they contained from Boston, describing an incident at a theatre during the investment of that place. Some one entered the theatre during a performance and shouted "The Red-coats are coming" and immediately the audience arose in great consternation and left the house without ceremony. These files disappeared from my quarters and a long and close search to discover who had taken them was fruitless. The Shakespeare was given to some officer who fancied it. So was Captain Smith's very rare work. The same copy, or another of the same edition, recently sold in New York for a sum a little above a thousand dollars. I regarded these relics with less value at that time because they could not be carried about, and a soldier must be prepared to move at any moment. Indeed, they could possess but a momentary interest to those who were almost constantly in the saddle and facing death every day. Few of my visitors appreciated their true value.

—[David Edward Cronin], *The Evolution of a Life*

B. "The Soldiers Delight in Destroying Everything"

Fredericsburgh [was] given up to pillage and destruction. Boys came into our place *loaded* with *silver* pitchers, *silver* spoons, silver lamps and castors etc. Great 3 story brick houses furnished magnificently were broken into and their contents scattered over the floors and trampled on by the muddy feet of the soldiers. Splended alabaster vases and pieces of statuary were thrown at 6 and 700 dollar mirrors. Closets of the very finest china ware were broken into and their contents smashed onto the floor and stamped to pieces. Finest cut glass ware goblets were hurled at nice plate glass windows, beautifully embroidered window curtains torn down, rosewood pianoes piled in the street and burned or soldiers would get on top of them and dance and kick the keyboard and internal machinery all to pieces—little table ornaments kicking in every direction—wine cellars broken into and the soldiers drinking all they could and then opening the faucets and let the rest run out—boys go to a barrel of flour and take a pailful and use enough to make one batch of pancakes and then pour the rest in the street—everything turned up side down. The soldiers seemed to delight in destroying everything. Libraries worth thousands of dollars were overhauled and thrown on the floor and in the streets—Ed I can't begin to *describe* the scenes of destruction. It was so throughout the whole city and from its appearance very many wealthy families must have inhabited it.

—McKelvey, ed., "Civil War Letters of Francis Edwin Pierce"

C. The Yankees Sack Sarah Morgan's Home

August 13th, 1862.—I am in despair. Miss Jones, who has just made her escape from town, brings a most dreadful account. She, with seventy-five others, took refuge at Doctor Enders', more than a mile and a half below town, at Hall's. It was there we sent the two trunks containing Father's papers and our clothing and silver. Hearing that guerrillas had been there, the Yankees went down, shelled the house in the night, turning all those women and children out, who barely escaped with their clothing, and let the soldiers loose on it. They destroyed everything they could lay their hands on, if it could not be carried off; broke open armoires, trunks, sacked the house, and left it one scene of devastation and ruin. They even stole Miss Jones's braid! She got here with nothing but the clothes she wore.

This is a dreadful blow to me. Yesterday I thought myself beggared when I heard that our house was probably burnt, remembering all the clothing, books, furniture, etc., that it contained; but I consoled myself with the recollection of a large trunk packed in the most scientific style, containing quantities of nightgowns, skirts, chemises, dresses, cloaks—in short, our very best—which was in safety. Winter had no terrors when I thought of the nice warm clothes; I only wished I had a few of the organdy dresses I had packed up before wearing. And now? It is all gone, silver, Father's law papers, without which we are beggars, and clothing! Nothing left!

August 25th.—About twelve at night.—Sleep is impossible after all that I have heard; so, after vainly endeavoring to follow the example of the rest and sleep like a stoic, I have lighted my candle and take to this to induce drowsiness.

Just after supper, when Anna and I were sitting with Mrs. Carter in her room, I talking as usual of home and saying I would be perfectly happy if Mother would decide to remain in Baton Rouge and brave the occasional shellings, I heard a well-known voice take up some sentence of mine from a dark part of the room; and with a cry of surprise, I was hugging Miriam until she was breathless. Such a forlorn creature!—so dirty, tired, and fatigued as to be hardly recognizable. We thrust her into a chair and made her speak. She had just come with Charlie, who went after them yesterday, and had left Mother and the servants at a kind friend's on the road. I never heard such a story as she told. I was heartsick, but I laughed until Mrs. Badger grew furious with me and the Yankees and abused me for not abusing them.

She says when she entered the house she burst into tears at the desolation. It was one scene of ruin. Libraries emptied, china smashed, sideboards split open with axes, three cedar chests cut open, plundered, and set up on end; all parlor ornaments carried off; her desk lay open with all letters and notes well thumbed and scattered around, while Will's last letter to her was open on the floor, with the Yankee stamp of dirty fingers. Mother's portrait, half cut from its frame, stood on the floor. Margaret, who was present at the sacking, told how she had saved Father's. It seems that those who wrought destruction in our house were all officers. One jumped on the sofa to cut the picture down (Miriam saw the prints of his muddy feet) when Margaret cried: "For God's sake, gentlemen, let it be! I'll help you to anything here. He's dead, and the young ladies would rather see the house burn than lose it!"

"I'll blow your damned brains out," was the "gentleman's" answer as he put a pistol to her head, which a brother officer dashed away, and the picture was abandoned for finer sport. All the others were cut up in shreds.

Upstairs was the finest fun. Mother's beautiful mahogany armoire, whose single door was an extremely fine mirror, was entered by crashing through the glass, when it was emptied of every article and the shelves half split and half thrust back crooked. Letters, labeled by the boys private, were strewn over the floor; they opened every armoire and drawer, collected every rag to be found, and littered the whole house with them, until the wonder was where so many rags had been found. Father's armoire was relieved of everything, Gibbes's handsome Damascus sword with the silver scabbard included. All his clothes, George's, Hal's, Jimmy's, were appropriated. They entered my room, broke that fine mirror for sport, pulled down the rods from the bed, and with them pulverized my toilet set, taking also all Lydia's china ornaments I had packed in the washstand. The debris filled my basin and ornamented my bed. My desk was broken open. Over it were spread all my letters and private papers, a diary I kept when twelve years old, and sundry tokens of dried roses, etc., which must have been very funny, they all being labeled with the donor's name and the occasion. Fool! how I writhe when I think of all they saw; the invitations to buggy rides, concerts, "compliments of," etc.! Lilly's sewing machine had disappeared, but as Mother's was too heavy to move, they merely smashed the needles.

In the pillaging of the armoires they seized a pink flounced muslin of Miriam's, which one officer placed on the end of a bayonet and paraded round with, followed by the others who slashed it with their swords, crying: "I have stuck the damned Secesh! That's the time I cut her!" and continued their sport until the rags could no longer be pierced. One seized my bonnet, with which he decked himself, and ran in the streets. Indeed, all who found such rushed frantically around town, by way of frolicking, with the things on their heads. They say no frenzy could surpass it. Another snatched one of my calico dresses and a pair of vases that Mother had when she was married, and was about to decamp when a Mrs. Jones jerked them away and carried them to her boardinghouse, and returned them to Mother the other day. Blessed be Heaven! I have a calico dress! Our clothes were used for the vilest purposes and spread in every corner, at least those few that were not stolen.

Aunt Barker's Charles tried his best to defend the property. "Ain't you 'shamed to destroy all dis here that belongs to a poor widow lady who's got two daughters to support?" he asked of an officer who was foremost in the destruction.

"Poor? Damn them! I don't know when I have seen a house furnished like this! Look at that furniture! They poor!" was the retort, and thereupon the work went bravely on of making us poor indeed.

It would have fared badly with us had we been there. The servants say they broke into the house, crying: "Where are those damned Secesh women? We know they are hid in here, and we'll make them dance for hiding from federal officers!" And they could not be convinced that we were not there until they had searched the very garret. Wonder what they would have done? Charles caught a Captain Clark in the streets, when the work was almost over, and begged him to put an end to it. The gentleman went readily, but though the devastation was quite evident, no one was to be seen, and he was about to leave when, insisting that there was some one there, Charles drew him into my room, dived under the bed, and drew from thence a Yankee captain by one leg, followed by a lieutenant, each with a bundle of the boys' clothes which they instantly dropped, protesting they were only looking around the house. The gentleman captain carried them off to their superior.

Ours was the most shockingly-treated house in the whole town. We have the misfortune to be equally feared by both sides, because we will blackguard neither. So the Yankees selected the only house in town that sheltered three forlorn women, to wreak their vengeance on. From far and near, strangers and friends flocked in to see the ravages committed. Crowds rushed in before, crowds came in after, Miriam and Mother arrived, all apologizing for the intrusion, but saying they had heard it was a sight never before seen. So they let them examine to their hearts' content, and Miriam says the sympathy of all was extraordinary. A strange gentleman picked up a piece of Mother's mirror, which was as thick as his finger, saying: "Madame, I should like to keep this as a memento. I am about to travel through Mississippi and, having seen what a splendid piece of furniture this was and the state your house is left in, should like to show this as a specimen of Yankee vandalism." . . .

Thursday, August 28th—I am satisfied. I have seen my home again. Tuesday I was up at sunrise, and my few preparations were soon completed, and before any one was awake I walked over to Mr. Elder's, through mud and dew, to meet Charlie. Fortunate was it for me that I started so early, for I found him hastily eating his breakfast and ready to leave. He was very much opposed to my going, and for some time I was afraid he would force me to remain, but at last he consented, perhaps because I did not insist; and with wet feet and without a particle of breakfast, I at length found myself in the buggy on the road home.

Our house could not be reached by the front; so we left the buggy in the back yard, and running through the lot without stopping to examine the storeroom and servants' rooms that opened wide, I went through the alley and entered by the front door.

Fortunate was it for this record that I undertook to describe the sacking only from Miriam's account. If I had waited until now, it would never have been mentioned; for as I looked around, to attempt such a thing seemed absurd. I stood in the parlor in silent amazement, and in answer to Charlie's "Well?" I could only laugh. It was so hard to realize. As I looked for each well-known article, I could hardly believe that Abraham Lincoln's officers had really come so low down as to steal in such a wholesale manner. . . .

Bah! What is the use of describing such a scene? Many suffered along with us, though none so severely. Indeed, the Yankees cursed loudly at those who did not leave anything worth stealing. They cannot complain of us on that score. All our handsome Brussels carpets, together with Lydia's fur, were taken, too. What did they not take? In the garret, in its darkest corner, a whole gilt-edged china set of Lydia's had been overlooked; so I set to work and packed it up, while Charlie packed her furniture in a wagon to send to her father.

—SARAH DAWSON, A Confederate Girl's Diary

D. GRIERSON'S RAIDERS ON A RAMPAGE

New Albany Miss. July 29th 1864

Dear Father & Mother

I am seated once more to write to you all. . . . I went up to Mr. Hills in the evening to see Gen Grearson, and asked him to place a guard at my house, told him that his men were searching all over my house and tearing up every thing. Told him that they had already got all I had to eat, that I only asked protection that night, for myself and children. he said certainly he would send me a guard, and if I would treat him right he would protect me untill they left. So he sent one of his body guard, and we rested quietly that night. I treated him very kindly, made him a good pallet in the passage and we were not bothered with any other Yankees that night. They all left next morning, so I thought I had got off tolerably well.

I talked with Greaerson about half an hour. he treated me very politely, but I dont think he has much feeling. You ought to have seen how grand him and his staff looked. There were five of them, him and his adjutant sergeon and two others. They were sitting in Mrs Hills passage *dressed into fits*, with three or four bottles of champaign, and boxes of segars setting around them. They asked me a great many questions about my husband. I told them the truth, told them he had gone off to save his horse, that he had lost four horses by them. he says has he a fine horse now. I told him yes that he could not practice medicine on a sorry one, that good horses were scarce in this country now, and he had got him a good one, and went off to keep them from getting him. Oh! he says he had as well stay at home, we would not bother him nor his horse either. I told him that I knew better than that, that he had been taken once, and his horse every time. . . .

Well next morning Mr Hill got on his horse, came down here and asked Asa to go up and see Luly. They concluded they would then ride up towards Ellistown, and see what the Yankees done up there the night before. They rode up to Mr Hills hitched their horses at the gate, and went in to see the child. Asa put medicine in his pocket for her, and left his saddle bags on his horse, something he very seldom ever does. They had not been in there more than five minutes, before the Yankees came *tearing* down the lane from Langstons right up to Hills house. Mr Hill and Asa broke to run as hard as they could. Mrs. Hill screamed at them to stop they would shoot them. Mr. Hills stopped. They were so close by, but Asa put out and never looked back, untill he was out of hearing. Says he forgot he ever had the rheumatism, he went through the back yard, and horse lot. The Yankees never saw him at all. he did not pretend to go towards his horse. That would have been going right into the Yankees. They were riding round the corner before they knew they wer[e] in ten miles of them. They rode up and took the horses first thing. The one that got Asa's horse says, well I have got a fine horse, rode off saddle-bags, and all. Asa says he would not mind loosing the saddle-bags much, if they had not have had his surgical instruments in them. They cant be replaced. Mr Hill went back in the house and staid untill they left. That was not till next day. They did not bother him.

They staid here all that day, camped in the same place that night, and left next day, but they ruined us all before they left. I cant begin to tell you what they done to other people, it would take so long but will *try* and tell you how they treated us, they came here thicker than they did before if possible. *All day* working like ants, all over the house up stairs and down, in every hole and corner, searching & peeping every where, carried off every irish potatoe beet onion beans, even took time to pick pans of beans took my pillow cases to put them in took towels one new table cloth all my knives but 3 some of my dishes and every pan they could find. Took my shears Asas hatchet. Tore my house all to pieces, it would take me a week to mess it up like they did, pulled all our dirty clothes out of the closets, and examined

R. F. Zogbaum

Questioning a Prisoner

Illustrated London News

Confederate Deserter Coming into Union Lines

Illustrated London News

Punishments in the Federal Camp

them. Took all Asa's clothes they could find. Worked here all day I reckon two hundred had been up stairs looked around and came down I followed after them, untill I was nearly broke down, *scared* nearly to death for fear they would find my things that were hid for I knew that was *my all*, provision clothes bed-clothes blankets and every thing was in there, after awhile about a dozen of the infantry came in, and up stairs they went to searching all about, commenced looking under the floor I had a few things hid under their, they commenced pulling them out, pulled out medicine tobacco cards and other little things, but did not seem to want any thing but the tobacco.

After awhile one *rascal* went up in the corner and in stooping to put his hand under the floor, put it against the planks, and they slipped a little. he pulled them off, and says, by george, boys here is the place, they just ripped the planks off and in they went. One says run down and guard the door, dont let another fellow come up, we'll divide the things amongst us. I had in there, meat, flour sugar, coffee, molasses, lard & salt. All of Asas good clothes, Sarahs mine and the childrens. We all had new shoes in there that we had not worn, in a pillow case. They pulled them all out and looked at them. I stood over them and as they would pull out the shoes & clothes, I would grab them and tell them that they could not have them, but every time they came to anything of Asa's they *would* take it. Took his over coat, a pair of new blue jeans pants, three pair of summer pants all his drawers except the ones he had on, one shirt, a new silk handkerchief. So you know he is very near without clothes. They did not take any of my clothes, except pocket handkerchiefs. Sarah & me both had some new handkerchiefs, they got them all, and would have taken our dresses, if we had not fought over them so, as they pulled them out, I would take them from them, and throw them to Sarah, she would sit down on them, untill she had a large pile under her, she said she would fight over them a long time before they got them. They took two of her dresses, that were left hanging in her room, and Melia's white embroidered dress it was hanging in one of Sarahs. They were taken while we were up stairs *fighting* over the others. We dont know who took them, every room was full at once, we could not watch them all. They were old dresses of Sarahs she hid all her best onces, her pink flounce and dark striped skirt. I hate their taking Melia's, very much, because it came from where it did. I gave Sarah my purple flounce muslin in the place of the one she lost. I have not had it on in three summers. They took one of my best quilts, and three nice blankets but I stole one of them from him after he had got it. he laid it down by him to divide the provision. I slipped up behind him and got it, there was such confusion amongst them he never discovered it.

They left me nothing to eat at all. Took *every solitary* thing I had, except one jar of lard and my salt. There was not even a grain of corn on the place to make hominy after they were gone, and we had enough of every thing to last us till christmas. I hated their taking my chickens and groceries worse than any thing else. I knew we could get meat and bread as soon as they left, but the other things cannot be replaced without sending to Memphis, and we have no cotton. We were living well, but will have to live on meat &

bread after this, and we may not be able to get that all the time. They killed all of Asa's hogs for next years meat, but we happened to save our cows. They killed nearly every bodys cows & calves around here but ours. We have two good cows with young calves. They happened not to come up untill very late. We turned them in the yard and kept them there. My calves were in the orchard. They started to shoot them several times, but I ran after them and begged them not to kill them. Told them they had taken every thing I had to eat, but if they would leave the calves that we could live on milk & bread.

Mr Bond milked fifteen cows. They killed every cow and calf he had he now has no cow at all. They nearly ruined him, burned 40 bags of cotton, and killed all his stock took every thing he had in the house to eat, and *every* Negro he had, went with them. Mrs Bond has all her work to do.

They treated Mr Hill in the same manner took & killed nearly every thing he had. They had a little provision hid that they did not find. Every one of his Negroes went with them there is not a Negro on his place large nor small. Mrs Hill has all her work to do. . . .

Well I will quit writing about the Yankees. I know you are all tired of it. I have not told you half that I could tell you. I must tell you though about their finding Mr Bells money. Mrs Bell heard they were coming, and went and buried the money in the corner of a fence. Not a living soul knew where she put it, they went there and dug it up. They had 25 dollars in gold, 15 in greenback, and 100 Confederate.

I must tell you of another thing too, how bad we were scared, after the Yankees had been gone about five days, the news came here, that they had sent all the Negroes & waggons on to Memphis, and they were coming back burning every house they passed, turning the people out of doors. We heard one evening that they would be here next morning, and burn us out, heard it from several different sources. Every body went to work, bundling up their clothes, to try & save some. We tied up a bundle apiece, to carry of[f] when they set the house on fire, Asa put on his best clothes that were left, took his account books, and left. You would have laughed to seen us next morning. Sarah May Jones me and Kitsy, all had a string of clothes tied under our hoops. Mr Flournoy worked all night carrying things of[f] in the woods, they did not come back though we soon heard it was all false. . . .

You must all write to me as soon as you get this. I would have written sooner, but have not had energy enough to write a letter since the Yankees left untill now. They turned over my molasses, up stairs, spilt all over the house up stairs & down, and I did not have it scoured up in a week, so you see I did not care much for anything. I have got over that now, we are all in good spirits again. . . .

This leaves us all well, children are getting along well and growing fast. Clara's school is broken up, the teacher cant get board. All send love to you

Your affectionate daughter

E. J. BEACH

—SMITH, ed., "The Yankees in New Albany"

9. PUNISHMENTS IN THE UNION AND CONFEDERATE ARMIES

Punishments varied greatly from regiment to regiment and from army to army. Much depended on the character of the commanding officers; much, too, on the circumstances in which the offenses were committed. As might be expected, too, the attitude of the soldiers toward the punishment of their comrades varied considerably. Companies that were badly officered, or that had suffered from a poorly managed commissary, or from other forms of mistreatment and neglect, generally sympathized with the culprits. Sometimes the punishments were brutal; generally they were merely humiliating. Although flogging had been forbidden by law before the Civil War, it is evident that the practice continued in both armies.

We have already met all three of our reporters: Wilder Dwight of the 2nd Massachusetts, who was killed at Antietam; Frank Wilkeson, who went south with bounty jumpers; and the effervescent John Dooley of the 1st Virginia Infantry.

A. Maintaining Discipline in the Army of the Potomac

Pleasant Hill, Camp near Darnestown, September 4, 1861

It is afternoon. You have come to visit the camp of the Massachusetts Second. The General had at once pointed it out last evening. You then admired the regularity of its form. You now admire the neatness and order that you find within.

You go out in front and look over at the opposite hill, where the —— Regiment is in camp. The officer of the day in our camp is administering a punishment. The court-martial had sentenced a drunken and insubordinate fellow to be tied to a tree for one hour three successive days. There he *is tied*. The —— Regiment catch sight of him. At once, in a disorderly mob, they rush to the edge of their hill. They cry out 'Cut him down,' they groan and yell against us. Our guard is called out. Their officers cannot restore order, though they succeed in keeping their men within their lines. The punishment is concluded. Not a man in our lines stirs or speaks. You have contrasted the discipline of the two regiments. You have seen pictures enough, because you want to hear more of this one. Colonel Gordon, as Acting Brigadier, directs the arrest of the ringleaders of the —— Regiment, and their officer of the day. The next morning . . . Colonel —— comes to ask that the man may be tied somewhere where the regiment which he is *commanded by* cannot see him. Colonel Gordon says, No. General Banks, on being consulted by Colonel Gordon, directs him to go on. 'Discipline must be maintained,' says the General. Colonel —— then goes to General Banks, and, by what persuasion we know not, wheedles out of him a recommendation to Colonel Gordon that the punishment be inflicted with less 'publicity.' This recommendation comes just before the time for punishment. General

Banks cannot be found in season to give any explanation of his written recommendation. Colonel Gordon makes up his mind to tie the man in the same place, and in the same way, come what may. It is done without trouble. But the recommendation from headquarters has shaken our confidence.

This illustrates the difficulties under which discipline is maintained. We are the only regiment that attempts it, and even the officers among our neighbors discountenance the severity which alone insures our discipline. But *our men* are getting, every day, a better tone. They pride themselves on the obvious contrast between their regiment and the others. They submit to the rules out of which this contrast comes. But the fact that the other regiments do as they please aggravates our difficulties and endangers our success. We are beginning to long for the direct command of McClellan, who would sustain our system without fear, favor, or affection. A political education does not favor the direct disregard of consequences which belongs to military command. Yet I do not wish to complain of General Banks. I think he means well, but I fear that he lacks a little either of education or confidence to push things through.

I have been working away at the deficiencies of our commissariat. I do not hesitate to say that its condition is disgraceful. No organization, and not even accidental and disproportioned abundance, in any direction. A general short commons. This we hope to remedy. But I do not make much progress. In fact, General Banks's division is not officered in the Quartermaster and Subsistence Departments as it should be.

But enough of this. We are getting on well, and I only grumble because we might do so much better. To-day, again, the man *shall* be tied to the tree.
                              —DWIGHT, *Life and Letters of Wilder Dwight*

B. PUNISHMENTS IN THE ARMY OF THE POTOMAC

The discipline throughout the Army of the Potomac during the winter of 1863-64 was necessarily severe. The ranks of the original volunteers, the men who sprang to arms at the tap of the northern war-drum had been shot to pieces. Entire platoons had disappeared. Regiments that had entered the great camps of instruction formed around Washington in 1861-62 a thousand men strong, had melted before the heat of Confederate battle-fire till they numbered three hundred, two hundred, and as low as one hundred and fifty men. During the winter of 1863-64 these regiments were being filled with bounty-jumpers, and these men had to be severely disciplined, and that entailed punishment. There was no longer the friendly feeling of cordial comradeship between the enlisted men and their officers, which was one of the distinguishing characteristics of the volunteer troops. The whole army was rapidly assuming the character and bearing of regular troops, and that means mercenaries. The lines drawn between the recruits of 1863-64 and their officers were well marked and they were rigid. The officers were resolute in their intention to make the recruits feel the difference in their rank. Breaches of army discipline were promptly and severely punished. . . .

The punishments inflicted on the enlisted men were various, and some of them were horribly brutal and needlessly severe; but they apparently served their purpose, and the times were cruel, and men had been hardened to bear the suffering of other men without wincing. One punishment much affected in the light artillery was called "tying on the spare wheel." Springing upward and rearward from the centre rail of every caisson was a fifth axle, and on it was a spare wheel. A soldier who had been insubordinate was taken to the spare wheel and forced to step upon it. His legs were drawn apart until they spanned three spokes. His arms were stretched until there were three or four spokes between his hands. Then feet and hands were firmly bound to the felloes of the wheel. If the soldier was to be punished moderately he was left, bound in an upright position on the wheel for five or six hours. If the punishment was to be severe, the ponderous wheel was given a quarter turn after the soldier had been lashed to it, which changed the position of the man being punished from an upright to a horizontal one. Then the prisoner had to exert all his strength to keep his weight from pulling heavily and cuttingly on the cords that bound his upper arm and leg to the wheel. I have frequently seen men faint while undergoing this punishment, and I have known men to endure it for hours without a murmur, but with white faces, and set jaws and blazing eyes. To cry out, to beg for mercy, to protest, ensured additional discomfort in the shape of a gag, a rough stick, being tied into the suffering man's mouth. Tying on the spare wheel was the usual punishment in the artillery service for rather serious offences; and no man wanted to be tied up but once. . . .

To be bucked and gagged? Yes, that was severe, but not dangerous. It was highly disagreeable and painful, too, if prolonged, and at all times calculated to make a man's eyes stick out of his head as lobster's eyes do. And then the appearance of a man while undergoing the punishment was highly discreditable. The soldier about to be bucked and gagged, generally a drunken or noisy soldier, was forced to sit on the ground; his knees were drawn up to his chin, then his hands were drawn forward to his shins, and there they were securely bound together. A long stick was then thrust under his knees and over his arms. A gag was then securely bound in his mouth. The soldier who was bucked and gagged could not hurt himself or any one else. He could not speak, but he could make inarticulate sounds indicative of his suffering, and he invariably made them before he was released.

Daily many men were tied up by the thumbs, and that was far from pleasant. The impudent bounty-jumper who had stood on his toes under a tree for a couple of hours to keep his weight off of his thumbs, which were tied to a limb over his head, was exceedingly apt to heed the words of his officers when next they spoke to him. The bounty-jumper lacked the moral qualities which could be appealed to in an honest endeavor to create a soldier out of a ruffian; but his capacity to suffer physically was unimpaired, and that had to be played upon.

Then there was the utterly useless and shoulder-chafing punishment of carrying a stick of cord-wood. The stick that one picked up so cheerfully, and stepped off with so briskly, and walked up and down before a sentinel with so gayly in the early morning, had an unaccountable property of growing heavier and heavier as the sun rose higher and higher. One morning at ten o'clock I dropped a stick that did not weigh more than twelve pounds at sunrise. I sat down by it and turned it over and over. It had not grown, but I was then willing to swear that it had gained one hundred and eighty pounds in weight during the time I had carried it.

—WILKESON, *Recollections of a Private Soldier*

C. Punishments in the Army of Northern Virginia

I would like to tell you how breakers of discipline are treated. All prisoners of the Regt. are consigned to the guard house and if they prove refractory are liable to be *bucked* or gagged. Some times refractory members of companies are sent to the guard house under condemnation either to be bucked or gagged or perhaps to wear a barrel-shirt.

'Bucking' is making the culprit sit in a doubled up posture, clasping his knees with his hands, and whilst his knees almost touch his chin a long stick is inserted between his arms and underneath his knee joints. 'Gagging' is more severe, and is performed by placing a bayonet in the culprit's mouth and fixing it there by tying behind the head strings or cord attached to either end of the implement of torture. Frequently however a stick is used in place of the bayonet on account of the severity of the former instrument. Should the condemned resist or become very insolent, he is shown no mercy until he evinces some marks of repentance and future subordination. Usually neither of these two punishments lasts more than from an hour to two hours.

The barrel shirt punishment is generally inflicted upon such as have been guilty of some petty or shameful misdemeanors and have been sentenced by a court martial to this ignominious and ludicrous mode of expiation. The barrel shirt is simply a flour barrel minus both head and bottom, with two holes made in the staves. The culprit is clothed with this staving garment, thrusts his arms through the holes, gets his chin over the rim, and has to walk up and down a given space under guard for as many hours during the day as are appointed by his sentence. He finds it quite embarrassing and his legs are at a loss how to proceed. I have never seen any one hung up by the thumbs, which punishment, they say, is very frequent in the Yankee army. I have seen however what may be thought a novel punishment for an offense by no means unusual. Some of the men being caught in the act of straggling from their regiments were brought back and made to march in a circle, like horses working a threshing machine, at the same time having billets of wood tied to their ankles in order to impede their progress. But this novelty I have seen but once. . . .

This evening (March 9, 1863) our Brigade is ordered out to witness a horrible sight. One of the 24th Va. Infantry being tried by court martial for cowardice at the battle of Sharpsburg is condemned to be whipped publicly and then dishonorably dismissed from the service. The brigade is to be present at this degrading punishment.

We are all drawn up in line and the poor man is tied to a pole about fifty yards in front of us. His hands are stretched above his head and his shirt stripped to the waist. The executioner then steps forward and with several heavy switches, the executioner being likewise a criminal who is to earn his release from punishment by inflicting this disgrace on his fellow man.

The word being given, the executioner began his disgusting work, the wretched man wincing and his flesh shrinking neath every blow which one after another were delivered in quick succession until 39 were rec'd. by the culprit. In truth it is a horrid sight, and the executioner was so overcome by his feelings that as soon as his work was done his eyes filled with tears and he wept—he wept! This horrible event transpired without the loss of blood to any one, and the wretched creature (or happy individual, had he truly a craven heart) pockets his dishonorable discharge and leaves for parts unknown.

—DURKIN, ed., *John Dooley, Confederate Soldier*

10. EXECUTING DESERTERS

Desertion was the bane of both Union and Confederate armies. The total number of desertions assumed almost astronomical proportions. There was a total of some 260,000 desertions from the ranks in the Union armies, of whom possibly 60,000 returned to service; in addition there were 160,000 who failed to appear when drafted and qualified technically as deserters. The figures for the Confederate Army are unsatisfactory, but desertion here probably ran to about 10 per cent.

The pattern of desertion varied North and South. A large proportion of Confederate desertions was probably absence without leave—soldiers going home to help get in the crops, or to visit their families. While there was widespread evasion of the draft, in the South, much of this was under the masquerade of legality and was connived at by state authorities. Many Confederate deserters, too, were Union sympathizers who had been pressed into Confederate service: this was particularly true in the border states. There are comparatively few examples of Union soldiers deserting to the enemy; toward the end of the war many Confederates went over to the other side. Yet notwithstanding all the temptations and opportunities to desert, Confederate desertions were proportionately slightly lower than Federal.

The penalty for desertion was death, but this penalty was rarely imposed. Statistics here, too, are unreliable, but it is probable that not one deserter in 500 paid the extreme penalty. Clearly both armies would have been better for more effective punishments here. As executions were in fact rare it is sufficient to confine ourselves to a single witness from each army describing these tragic incidents of war.

A. General Sheridan Executes Two Deserters at Chattanooga

Chattanooga, Tennessee, November 14, 1863

My dear Friend—

This town is suffering severely on account of its rebellious sentiments. Since our army came back from the Chickamauga field the town has been pretty roughly handled by the 'merciless Yankees.' Many of the finest residences, particularly those on the more commanding points have been torn down and 'Yankee forts' erected in their stead. Generally where the buildings have been torn down the owners had gone south among their friends. I think they will be somewhat disappointed when they return and find their beautiful homes among the things that were. But 'the way of the transgressor is hard,' at least it seems so in this case.

I witnessed a painful sight this afternoon—the shooting of two federal soldiers. As it may be of interest I will give you a description of it. The two men belonged to Illinois regiments: one to the 44th and the other to the 88th, both of our division, which as you know is commanded by General Sheridan. The men had been tried for desertion, found guilty and sentenced to be shot. One brigade of the division under arms, with colors flying and band playing formed about noon in nearly a hollow square with one side entirely open. Thousands of soldier spectators gathered about those who stood under arms. About one P.M. a solemn procession composed of two details of infantry, one in front of the prisoners and one in the rear, marched into the inclosure. Behind the first company and immediately in front of the prisoners their coffins were borne each upon the shoulders of four men. In the rear of the doomed men marched the second company with their rifles at the right shoulder shift and bayonets fixed. A band playing a solemn tune marched with slow and measured step in front of the little procession. General Sheridan and staff were present. All were mounted and all in full uniform. The General had a broad yellow sash over his shoulder drawn across his breast and down under his sword belt. He sat motionless upon his big black horse which stood just a little in front of the other horsemen. When the procession arrived at the open side of the square it was halted, the coffins were placed upon the ground, when the prisoners knelt and the chaplain prayed. They then arose, apparently very calm, and sat erect each upon his coffin. A bandage was then bound over the eyes of each. A platoon of soldiers with loaded rifles stood a few paces in front. There was a strange silence for a moment and then the voice of command rang out. "Ready!" "Aim!" "Fire!" And each of the prisoners fell back over his coffin, dead.

It was hard to see men thus killed by their own comrades but you have no idea how many have deserted, encouraged by friends at home to do the disgraceful act. Sad as the scene this afternoon was, it will have a wholesome effect upon the whole division.

Truly yours, W. G.
—"Civil War Letters of Washington Gardner"

B. Executing Deserters from the Confederate Army

Camp near Rappahannock River, Va., March 5, 1863

A man was shot near our regiment last Sunday for desertion. It was a very solemn scene. The condemned man was seated on his coffin with his hands tied across his breast. A file of twelve soldiers was brought up to within six feet of him, and at the command a volley was fired right into his breast. He was hit by but one ball, because eleven of the guns were loaded with powder only. This was done so that no man can be certain that he killed him. If he was, the thought of it might always be painful to him. I have seen men marched through the camps under guard with boards on their backs which were labeled, "I am a coward," or "I am a thief," or "I am a shirker from battle," and I saw one man tied hand and foot astride the neck of a cannon and exposed to view for sixteen hours. These severe punishments seem necessary to preserve discipline.

Camp near Orange Court House, Va., September 27, 1863

We had nine more military executions in our division yesterday—one man from Thomas' Brigade, one from Scales' and seven from Lane's. Colonel Hunt was a member of the court-martial which sentenced them, and he tells me that one of the men from Lane's Brigade was a brother of your preacher, and that the two looked very much alike. He said he was a very intelligent man, and gave as his reason for deserting that the editorials in the Raleigh "Standard" had convinced him that Jeff Davis was a tyrant and that the Confederate cause was wrong. I am surprised that the editor of that miserable little journal is allowed to go at large. It is most unfortunate that this thing of shooting men for desertion was not begun sooner. Many lives would have been saved by it, because a great many men will now have to be shot before the trouble can be stopped. . . .

I must close, as a doctor has just come for me to go with him to assist in dissecting two of the men who were shot yesterday.

—WELCH, A Confederate Surgeon's Letters to his Wife

11. GENERAL LEE DISCUSSES THE PROBLEM OF DISCIPLINE

Lee was as gentle as any warrior in history, but he was a professional soldier and a firm disciplinarian. From long experience in the Mexican War, on the border, and as Superintendent of the United States Military Academy, he knew that failure to enforce rules or to maintain discipline leads to demoralization and penalizes the innocent instead of the guilty.

In this letter to President Davis Lee discusses the question of amnesty for deserters and touches on one of the problems which most harassed him. It is worth remembering that when he wrote it the Army of Northern Virginia had been reduced to some 70,000 men and was facing Grant's army of almost twice that size; had the Confederate government been able to round up de-

serters—*many of them hiding behind state exemptions and writs of habeas corpus—he might have brought his army up to a strength sufficient to defeat Grant.*

HD QRS ARMY N. VA.
13th April 1864

His Excy JEFFERSON DAVIS,
Presdt. Confed. States,
Richmond,
MR. PRESIDENT,

. . . I am satisfied that it would be impolitic and unjust to the rest of the army to allow previous good conduct alone to atone for an offence most pernicious to the service, and most dangerous as an example. In this connection, I will lay before your Excellency some facts that will assist you in forming your judgment, and at the same time, present the opinions I have formed on the subject of punishment in the army. In reviewing Court Martial cases, it has been my habit to give the accused the benefit of all extenuating circumstances that could be allowed to operate in their favor without injury to the service. In addition to those parties whose sentences I have remitted altogether or in part, or whom, when capitally convicted, I have recommended to pardon or commutation of punishment, I have kept a list during the past winter of certain offenders, whose cases while they could not be allowed to go unpunished altogether, without injury to the service, had some extenuating features connected with them. I confirmed the sentences, and all of them have undergone a part of their punishment, but recently I remitted the remainder in the order of which I enclose a copy.

Beyond this, I do not think it prudent to go, unless some reason be presented which will enable me to be lenient without creating a bad precedent, and encouraging others to become offenders. I have arrived at this conclusion from experience. It is certain that a relaxation of the sternness of discipline as a mere act of indulgence, unsupported by good reasons, is followed by an increase in the number of offenders. The escape of one criminal encourages others to hope for like impunity, and that encouragement can be given as well by a repetition of a general act of amnesty or pardon, as by frequent exercise of clemency towards individuals. If the convicted offenders alone were concerned, there would be no objection to giving them another trial, as we should be no worse off if they again deserted than before. But the effect of the example is the chief thing to be considered, and that it is injurious, I have no doubt. Many more men would be lost to the service if a pardon be extended in a large number of cases than would be restored to it by the immediate effects of that action.

The military executions that took place to such an extent last autumn, had a very beneficial influence, but in my judgment, many of them would have been avoided had the infliction of punishment in such cases uniformly followed the commission of the offence. But the failure of courts to convict or sentence to death, the cases in which pardon or commutation of punishment had been granted upon my recommendation, and the instances in which the same indulgence was extended by your Excellency upon grounds made known to you by others, had somewhat relaxed discipline in this respect, and the consequences became immediately apparent in the increased number of desertions. I think that a return to the current policy would inevitably be attended with like results. Desertion and absence without leave are nearly the only offences ever tried by our Courts. They appear to be almost the only vices in the army. Notwithstanding the executions that have recently taken place, I fear that the number of those who have escaped punishment in some one of the ways above mentioned has had a bad effect already. The returns for the month of March show 5474 men absent without leave, and 322 desertions during the month. There have been 62 desertions within the present month specially reported, but the whole number I fear considerably exceeds that some of the large number absent without leave, are probably sick men who have failed to report, and some of the deserters are probably absent without leave, but the number is sufficiently great to show the necessity of adhering to the only policy that will restrain the evil, and which I am sure will be found truly merciful in the end. Desertions and absence without leave not only weaken the army by the number of offenders not reclaimed, but by the guards that must be kept over those who are arrested. I think therefore that it would not be expedient to pardon & return to duty any of those now under sentence, or release those under charges, except for good cause shown.

> I have the honour to be
> With great respect
> Your obt. servt.
> R. E. LEE
> *Genl.*

—FREEMAN, ed., *Lee's Confidential Dispatches*

12. AN ENGLISHMAN PRAISES THE GOOD CONDUCT OF AMERICAN SOLDIERS

After hearing so much about misconduct, it is reassuring to read the testimony of that shrewd observer, Edward Dicey, to the effect that the American soldier was better behaved than the European, as indeed he was. Dicey, whom we have met before, was a distinguished journalist and author whose Six Months in the Federal States, *a report on a visit to America in 1862, is one of the most judicious of foreign views of wartime America.*

THE least creditable incident of the war to the Federal cause was the proclamation of General Butler about the women of New Orleans, which appeared at this period. . . . There was, I admit, much force in the explanation which my Northern friends sought to give of it. It is possible, and I believe true, that General Butler *may* have only meant that the women of New Orleans, who insulted the Federal soldiers, should be imprisoned for the night in the lock-up house allotted to the disorderly women of the town. Whatever the intention may have been, there is no question that the strictest care was taken lest the order should be abused; and it is certain that the Southern ladies were grossly insulting in their behaviour to the Union soldiers, using as they did language and gestures which, in a city occupied by troops of any other nation, would have subjected them, without orders, to the coarsest retaliation.

What is more to the point also—as I can state from my own observation—the rank and file of the American army is the most orderly I have ever seen, a circumstance which is due, probably, to the fact of the privates being mostly married, and all men of some kind of education. There is less brutality about the Federal troops, and more respect for women, than amongst any soldiery we are acquainted with in the Old World.

It once happened to me, I may mention here, to have to escort a party of ladies, after dark, across the long chain-bridge of Washington. For about two-thirds of that weary mile's walk, the whole bridge was crowded with a confused mass of Federal soldiers, who were halting there on their march southwards. The men were excited at the prospect of the approaching campaign, and it was obvious many of them had drunk freely on breaking up their camp at Washington. It was so dark, that no discipline could be maintained, and the men were sitting, sleeping, or singing, as they liked best. We had almost to grope our way through the groups of soldiers scattered along the bridge. The number of gentlemen in our party was so small, we could have afforded but little protection to the ladies under our charge, in case any insult had been offered to them. Having some knowledge of what common soldiers are in other countries under similar circumstances, I own that I felt considerable trepidation as to how far we should be able to extricate ourselves from the melee without annoyance. I can only say that, during the whole of that long passage, no remark whatever was addressed to us. The moment it was seen that there were ladies in our party, the soldiers got up from the planks, on which they were lying, to make way for us; and the songs (many of them loose enough), which the men were singing, were hushed immediately at our approach.

Whether a like journey could have been performed through an European army with like results I leave it to any one acquainted with the subject to say. In truth, the almost morbid sentiment of Americans with regard to women, while it renders them ridiculously susceptible to female influence, protects women in that country from the natural consequences of their own misconduct.

—DICEY, *Six Months in the Federal States*

XV

Great Britain and the American Civil War

THE *Civil War was not fought in isolation; the greatest civil war that the Western world had known could not be a purely domestic affair. The issues that were involved, or that seemed to be involved, deeply affected European peoples and nations, and America, in turn, was affected by European attitudes and policies. Yet Britain and Europe were from the first confused about the Civil War. Was the South fighting for self-determination—or for slavery? Was the North fighting for empire—or for freedom? Official declarations of policy, North and South, did little to clarify the situation. Confusion extended even to the legal realm. Was the war in fact a war, in the legal sense? If so it was entirely proper to recognize the belligerency of the Confederacy. The official Northern position was that the struggle was not a war at all, but a domestic insurrection; yet Lincoln proclaimed a blockade, which is an instrument of war, and recognized in fact, if not in law, the belligerency of the South.*

Just as in the American Revolution the role of France was of crucial importance to those fighting for independence, so in the Civil War the role of Britain was crucial. Southerners were ever conscious of that earlier chapter in American history, and the hopes of the South were fixed, from the beginning, on Britain and on France—which would presumably follow the British lead. It was not merely that Southerners thought that they had a good cause and one that would inevitably appeal to the British who, in the words of Henry Adams, "took naturally to rebellion—when foreign." Nor was it merely that they could count on the sympathy of the British upper classes, whose general social system was far closer to that of the South than to that of the more equalitarian North. There were practical considerations as well. Politically—so it was assumed by Southerners—Britain would prefer to see the United States split into two nations, for the United States was a potential rival, and American democracy a potential threat to the British social and economic system. Economically—again so it was assumed—the British would inevitably favor the creation in America of a nation dedicated to free trade. Finally—and this was the trump card—Cotton was King. English spindles depended on Southern cotton; without it the textile mills would shut down, England would lose her markets, unemployment and political disorder would spread. In sheer self-defense Britain would have to recognize the South and break the blockade.

Breaking the blockade would, almost inevitably, mean war. With Eng-land, and doubtless France, as allies how could the Confederacy fail to win!

Thus the stakes were high. But Britain, too, knew that the stakes were high. Would she allow the sympathies of her upper classes to dictate her policy? Would she be so affected by the blockade as to intervene in self-defense? Would she risk war with her American cousins—war which would ally her, willy-nilly, with a slave power?

In Britain itself the Civil War divided classes as had no other foreign con-flict in her history—not even the French Revolution. On the whole, and with important exceptions, the upper classes were pro-Southern, the middle and working classes pro-Northern. The English aristocracy saw in the American conflict a chance to humiliate an upstart nation whose democratic and equalitarian practices they detested; the middle and working classes saw the struggle as one for the vindication of democracy and—after the Emancipa-tion Proclamation—of freedom. The intellectuals were sharply divided. Some, like Acton, for example, saw the American war as a chapter in the great history of freedom, and supported the South as the champion of self-determination. Others, like Leslie Stephen and John Stuart Mill, saw it, too, as a struggle for freedom, but thought of freedom for the Negro. The most influential spokesmen for the North were, however, liberal statesmen and publicists like Cobden, Bright, and Forster, men who were convinced that the progress of democracy in Britain was intimately bound up with the triumph of the Union.

Both the Union and the Confederate governments made strenuous efforts to win English support: propaganda techniques were as skillfully developed during the Civil War as during the World Wars. Lincoln sent over such spokesmen—and spokeswomen—as Henry Ward Beecher and Harriet Beecher Stowe and the egregious Robert Walker; the Confederacy sent over a num-ber of accredited agents, like James Mason and Pierre Rost and John Peyton, or Captain Bullock, who was to arrange for building ships, or Henry Hotze, who established and edited the Index, *a newspaper devoted to presenting the Southern cause.*

On the whole the official English policy was correct, but the expression of that policy was often discourteous. Thus, though the British position in the Trent *affair was technically correct, the manner of stating that position was arrogant, and the widespread demand for war over what was at worst a minor mistake was unpardonable. Nor were the British themselves guiltless of infractions of international law—witness the subsequent* Alabama *award. Even more deplorable, from the point of view of the future relations of the two great English-speaking peoples, was the persistent expression of sym-pathy for the South and hostility to the North in such great papers as the* Times *and the* Standard, *and the almost scurrilous attacks on the North in such magazines as the* Edinburgh, Blackwood's, *the* Quarterly, Punch *and the* Saturday Review. *In short the English aristocracy, the press, the Established Church, and even the universities appeared to be pro-Southern. It took a long time for Americans to forget this.*

1. HENRY RAVENEL EXPECTS FOREIGN INTERVENTION

Here is the way the recognition situation looked to a thoughtful Southern observer, and the way it looked to most Southerners.

Ravenel, the reader will recall, was a South Carolina planter who had won distinction as one of the leading American botanists.

M[onday] 8. [April 1861]—The great European powers, as far as we may judge from their leading papers, seem inclined to favour the new Confederacy.

Old prejudices against our misunderstood domestic institution of African servitude (it is the *word* "slavery" that has blinded their eyes) are giving way before the urgent calls of *Self Interest*, & we only need that they should become more intimately acquainted with it, to dissipate their mistaken notions. In addition to their requiring the produce of the Cotton States to keep their manufacturers in motion, & furnish food & employment to their operatives, new complications have arisen which are favourable to their friendly recognition of our independence. The United States have lately increased their Tariff so high on many articles of European manufacture, as to amount almost to prohibition; whilst the Confederate States have lessened theirs from the old standard, & have it in contemplation to reduce still more. The case then stands thus: We furnish what is absolutely essential to their commercial & manufacturing prosperity, & we alone—We offer them a market for their goods on better terms than heretofore. We invite their vessels to do our carrying trade, or at any rate throw open the door of competition to them, which has been hitherto open only to U. S. vessels. On the other hand the United States, now that the Cotton States have seceded, can furnish but little toward supplying their wants with cotton—They have in addition imposed such a tariff, as to cut off trade in a great measure. The U. S. are mainly a manufacturing & commercial nation, & must necessarily come into competition with them. In a word, what the U. S. have lost by our withdrawal from the Union, they have gained. They know too that we are an agricultural people, & will never compete with them in manufactures & commerce, but will always be their best customers.

These various reasons which lie on the surface, & which they already understand, must have their effect. Self Interest is the ruling power among nations, no less than among individuals.

—CHILDS, ed., *The Private Journal of Henry William Ravenel*

2. *BLACKWOOD'S EDINBURGH MAGAZINE* REJOICES IN THE BREAK-UP OF THE UNION

Most of the English press was implacably hostile to the North. This hostility did not always carry with it friendship to the South. Sometimes it was merely a general hostility to everything American—American republi-

canism, democracy, business, manners, and leaders. Blackwood's Edinburgh
Magazine, *which contained some of the best reporting on the war, was from
the beginning critical of the Federal government. As was the English practice at the time, the articles are unsigned; this one appeared in October 1861.*

OUR constitution has fulfilled its most important and most delicate office—
that of bringing the best of the spirit and intellect of the nation to the
service of the state. . . .

It is notorious that this end has not been fulfilled by the American constitution. Nor was it rational to expect that it should be. Statesmanship is
born of the collision of great principles or of important interests. No such
result can be produced where power is all on one side. When the people have
everything, they need no champions. Therefore, in America, patriotism
means flattery of the people; party spirit is the spirit of rapine; and debates,
instead of eliciting wisdom and truth, are the ignoble squabbles of mediocri-
ties. Where, in American history for the last forty years—that is to say, ever
since the impulse of the Revolution died out—are we to look for her great
statesmen? Yet in that period there is no great nation in Europe that has not
produced men who have secured an enduring fame by their assertion of great
principles, or by the influence they have exerted on the destinies of nations.
And it is not true, as has been said, and quoted with applause, that the nation
is happiest which has no history, for such happiness is stagnation or worse.
The spirit that presides over the public life of America has made itself felt
over the whole nation. The higher minds stand aloof from politics, as Bayard
would turn from a modern prize-ring. The meed for which he had been used
to contend with noble knights—the smiles of ladies, the favour of anointed
kings, and immortal honour—is now a bag of coin handed to the victor in a
pot-house. So the best Americans either betake themselves to other pursuits,
or roam disconsolately over the world, where they see their equals winning
honour in the field from which they are for ever excluded.

That men of this class should countenance the violent measures of the
North is at first sight unaccountable. It is difficult to imagine that intellectual
men should either be friendly to a system which extends its theory of equality
to intellect, and thus neutralises their natural superiority; or should wish
to establish, in its grossest form, the supremacy of a numerical majority, by
the forcible subjugation of the great minority which constitutes the South.
It is quite possible, however, that, while giving their voice to the North, they
may neither be friendly to the Union, nor desirous of seeing the South subjugated. They may wish to see the natural aristocracy to which they belong
raised to its proper position in the state. They may consider that, by quiet
separation, the Union might, with increased compactness and unanimity, re-
recover much of its vitality, and that the system they suffer under might be
indefinitely prolonged. And they may view the present convulsion of that
system as the necessary preliminary of those political changes which, it is
natural to suppose, they must ardently desire. To suppose this is not to im-
pugn their patriotism; for if we have made our views clear in this paper, it is

evident that they may look on such a crisis as now exists as necessary for the regeneration of their most important institutions. They may therefore accompany the movement with the expectation of finding an opportunity to control it.

But we do not suppose that any men possessing the powers requisite for statesmanship can really believe that, if by force of arms the reluctant South should be dragged back to the Union, the Union will be thereby restored on its original basis. Successful coercion would be a greater revolution than the acknowledgment of secession—this only lops the branches, while that strikes at the root. Nor do we imagine that any such men as these are to be found in the ranks of the Abolition party. Clever people may belong to that party. Mrs Beecher Stowe is a very clever woman, and has written a very clever novel; but she is, by the success of that novel, committed to sentiments more adapted to fiction than to politics. She evidently looks on the South as a vast confederation of Legrees, keeping millions of virtuous Uncle Toms in horrible subjection; and quotes Mr Wendell Phillipps as if she believed that mischievous monomaniac to be an inspired apostle. But statesmen must ask themselves how the difficulty presented by the condition of the African race would be solved by setting them free. What is to become of the liberated slaves? and how is their labour to be replaced? are questions the very first to be asked, but which we must not expect a crazy Abolitionist to answer. But such considerations do not occur to those enthusiastic philanthropists who testify to their love of the Negro by their hatred of the planter. The destruction of armies, the ravage and ruin of territory, are as nothing, in their heated fancy, compared with the success of their plan. And if secession were accomplished their plan would be at an end, for they would then have no more concern in the liberation of the slaves of the South than in a crusade to set the Georgian and Circassian ladies free from the harems of the Bosphorus. Thus, under present circumstances, their fanaticism has become sanguinary; they are pledged to their course, and will follow it with all the desperate recklessness and tenacity with which weak minds will cling to their only chance of notoriety.

—Anonymous, "Democracy Teaching by Example"

3. YANCEY AND MANN PLEAD THE CONFEDERATE CAUSE

Even before the outbreak of hostilities the Confederate government had sent commissioners to Britain and France. Their primary task was, of course, to represent the government in the somewhat unlikely event of recognition. Failing this they were to drum up support for the Confederacy, win friends and influence people, spread propaganda, try to get supplies through the blockade, and so forth.

John Peyton, whose description of Yancey and Mann is here reproduced, was himself an agent for the state of North Carolina. Born at Montgomery Hall in Virginia, he studied law at the state university, went to France and Austria for the Fillmore administration, moved to Illinois, and then returned to Virginia. Though opposed to secession Peyton went with his state. He sailed from Charleston in October 1861, did what he could for the Confederate cause abroad, and then settled down, after the war, on the Isle of Guernsey.

Yancey was one of the foremost "hotheads" of the South. He had hoped for high office in the Confederacy—perhaps for the Presidency itself; when not even a Cabinet appointment was forthcoming he accepted a foreign mission, but gave up in 1862 and served briefly in the Confederate Congress until his death the following year.

Ambrose Mann was a seasoned diplomat who had served as special commissioner to various German states, to Kossuth's Hungary, and to Switzerland. He spent one year in England; then went to Belgium, where he somewhat pointlessly cultivated the good will of King Leopold under the illusion that that King could influence Queen Victoria and Napoleon III. In 1863-64 he was commissioner to the Vatican. Like Peyton, Mann remained abroad after the war. He died in Paris in 1889.

THE duties of my mission required me to call upon the Confederate Commissioners immediately upon my arrival in London. Two of them only were in town, Mr. Yancey and Colonel Mann. Judge Rost, the third member, was absent in Paris. They were both sanguine of the immediate recognition of the Confederate States; said it might occur at any moment. I saw at once the source of the great confidence manifested in Richmond. These gentlemen were laboriously occupied, as they had been since their arrival, six months before, in the discharge of their official duties, and believed they were now about to have their labours crowned with success. Mr. Yancey had just attended a dinner at the Fishmonger's Hall, to which he had been specially invited, through the instrumentality of Mr. Samuel Isaacs, surviving partner of the firm of S. Isaacs, Campbell, and Co., who was successfully engaged in blockade-running, and in many ways showing his sympathy with the Confederate cause.

Mr. Yancey occupied the seat of honour to the right of the Prime Warden, by whom he was requested to address the meeting, in response to the sixth regular toast. . . .

In answer to the sixth toast, which had reference to the Civil War in America, Mr. Yancey delivered a brief address, which was most favourably received by the Company and the public. . . .

Mr. Yancey availed himself of the first opportunity after my arrival, when I had but imperfectly recovered from the fatigues of the journey, to hold with me a lengthy and earnest conversation upon the line of private conversation and policy which ought to be adopted by all Confederates in Europe, public and private, official and unofficial. He said that he had discovered since arriving in England, that the real cause of a want of sympathy for the South in the beginning, was the existence among us of slavery, and that we ought to feel it our duty to make Europeans understand that the North was not fighting against slavery, but was willing to guarantee it to the South, provided the Confederate people would lay down their arms and re-enter the Union. . . .

As an orator and statesman, Mr. Yancey enjoyed an extended reputation in America, with which I was familiar, as also with the solid foundations upon which it rested, having read many, if not all of his speeches, while he was a representative in Congress from the State of Alabama, and had heard, probably, the ablest of the popular addresses he delivered during the exciting contest which resulted in the election of Lincoln to the Presidency. During the few months we passed in London, in close and intimate friendship, I conceived even a higher opinion than I had previously entertained of his great abilities. Whatever he said bore the genuine marks of creative intellect, and he argued a point with astonishing fertility of genius. He had never indulged in indolent epicureanism, but his life had been one of labour, chiefly devoted to the study and practice of the law. His mind had not, however, been narrowed by the technicalities of the profession; these studies and pursuits had only given a logical precision to his views. He possessed an extended acquaintance with business affairs, financial and commercial. He was methodical and administrative, deducing order from confusion; he used the subtle weapons of casuistry with consummate skill, and always took a comprehensive view of the whole region of political science. To his rare powers he united an umblemished integrity of character, a fervid patriotism, and a benevolence and purity of private life, which enhanced his influence, and made him a delightful companion and friend.

Though he was not admitted to official circles—these were of course reserved for the ministers of actually recognized governments—he had a considerable acquaintance among the chief personages in London society, mainly through the instrumentality of his co-commissioner Colonel Mann, and was never in any company without making a favourable impression, though his manners were plain, and his style of conversation far from the highest. It was only when he had the whole field to himself, and indulged in what might be termed a discourse, that he at all left the conviction that he was a man of ability and power. . . .

Colonel Mann was in many respects the opposite of Mr. Yancey. His early youth had not been given to laborious preparation for a profession, and his after life had not been spent in the confinement of an attorney's office. He had no professional, but a great deal of general knowledge. Bred upon a Virginian plantation, he had early acquired the fine social habits of the hospitable, but often indolent and luxurious planters. His manners and address were frank and easy. The solid parts of an education which he had obtained in his Virginian home, and among those high-bred planters, had gained a European polish. . . .

With excellent tact and knowledge, Colonel Mann had taken his apartments in the desirable quarter of Albemarle Street, within a stone's throw of Cambridge House, the town residence of Lord Palmerston, while Mr. Yancey was lodged further off, in Bury Street. In this central situation, near the Prime Minister (and on the best of terms with his private secretary, the

Hon. Mr. Evelyn), deferred to by his official associates, consulted by all Confederate agents, Colonel Mann was in a position to know everything of moment transpiring at the chief sources of British power, to labour efficiently for his cause, as also to keep the Government on the banks of the James duly informed as to their progress in reaching that desired goal, recognition, always in view, ever near at hand and never reached!

                                        —PEYTON, *The American Crisis*

4. NORTHERNERS INVOKE ENGLISH UNDERSTANDING

The campaign for foreign understanding and sympathy was carried on by private individuals as well as by governments. Here the North doubtless had the best of it, for the intellectual and financial ties between the North and Britain were intimate.

We give here two typical letters; these might be multiplied a hundredfold. The first is from August Belmont of New York, the second from George Ticknor of Boston. Born in Germany, Belmont had early entered the banking house of Rothschild; in his early twenties he had come to New York and, as agent for the Rothschilds, established what was to be one of the great banking houses of the country. He had served as Minister to the Netherlands and made frequent trips abroad to add to his large art collection. A Democrat, Belmont was an ardent Unionist, and in 1861 helped raise and equip the first German regiment from New York City. Throughout the war he pleaded the Union cause in Britain and on the continent, by letter and in person.

Ticknor is so well known that he needs little introduction. He had long been a major figure in the intellectual life of New England and, as author of the notable History of Spanish Literature, *was known everywhere abroad. Like Belmont, and like his friend Charles Sumner, he was indefatigable in presenting the Union cause to his English and European friends.*

A. AUGUST BELMONT WARNS OF BITTER FEELING BETWEEN AMERICA AND ENGLAND

To Baron Lionel de Rothschild, M. P.

                                        New-York, May 21, 1861

Dear Baron: The telegraphic report of Lord John Russell's declaration in Parliament, on the 6th inst., concerning Southern privateers, has created a painful surprise and disappointment throughout the whole North.

In placing them upon the footing of *belligerents,* the English Government takes an initiative step toward recognizing the Southern Confederacy, because the letters of marque of an unauthorized and unrecognized government in rebellion against the constituted authorities can, under the law of nations, only be regarded by every maritime power as pirates, and treated accordingly.

If Ireland or Scotland should revolt against the British crown, or Canada attempt to dissolve her allegiance to the mother country, would the United

States be justified in recognizing the privateers fitted out by the rebels as belligerents? I am sure that our Government would not assume such an unfriendly position, and give so material a support to a rebellious province in endangering the trade of its allies and of the world at large.

With the blockade of the Southern ports, which, before a fortnight can have elapsed, will be an effective one from the Chesapeake to the Rio Grande, the privateers of Jeff. Davis would have soon disappeared from the ocean, even if they ever made their appearance, had the declaration of Lord John not opened to them the British ports in the West Indies, Canada, and Great Britain.

It may be that the British Government will not condemn any prizes brought by the privateers into its ports, but the fact of their being allowed to run in for supplies and coal, and to escape into the many ports and inlets of the West Indies where our ships-of-war cannot follow them, will attract numerous lawless adventurers under the piratical flag of the Southern rebels.

The position which your Government seems inclined to take in the contest is, in my opinion, a very unfortunate one. It will complicate matters, must prolong the struggle, and result in a very bitter feeling between this country and England.

The whole North, without distinction of party, is determined not to allow our Government and our Union to be destroyed, and I am sure the sword will never be laid down until the American flag floats again from Maine to the Mississippi. The people feel that they are fighting for their national existence, and that no sacrifice can be too great in order to maintain and preserve that boon.

What the South claims now is for us to give up every port, from the Chesapeake to the Mississippi, to a foreign power, which has shown sufficiently within the last few months how far public and private property and obligations are to be respected by it.

In the struggle which is before us we had hoped for the sympathy of Europe, and particularly of England. Your statesmen and your press have at all times taken the most violent and uncompromising stand against slavery, and it is more than strange to see the British Government now give its moral countenance to a power which, under the declaration of its Vice-President (Alex. Stephens), is based upon *slavery* as its principal fundamental strength. That basis will most probably require the re-opening of the slave-trade, as soon as England shall have recognized the Confederacy, and should, in that event, the sympathy of the British Cabinet stop short, and not allow the *cotton-growers* to strengthen the foundations of their Government, then Mr. Jeff. Davis will, of course, put an embargo upon the export of cotton, in order to compel England to consent to the nefarious traffic in human flesh. He could certainly not be charged with a want of logic, by reasoning that the same power which induced England to throw her weight into the scale of a rebellious slave power, trying to overthrow our free institutions, would also be sufficiently potent to compel her to consent to the Confederacy drawing its supplies from Africa, of an element which the founders of that Confederacy had openly declared to the civilized world to be the basis of this young creation, claiming rank among the civilized nations of the world. . . .

Lord John Russell draws an analogy of the Southern rebellion to the struggle for independence by Greece, and asserts that, because England recognized Greece then as a belligerent, the South has to be recognized now by her in the same character. Greece was a conquered and enslaved *province* of a semi-barbarous despotism and had never been completely subjugated. It was a Christian people, tyrannized by fanatical Moslemism, and had the warm and active sympathy of the whole civilized world on its side.

The Southern States, who are now in a state of rebellion against the Federal Government, were free and voluntary parties to a compact of union, which was declared to be perpetual. They cannot point to a single right guaranteed to them by the Constitution which has been violated, and the only ground upon which they justify their rebellion is the *fear* that their peculiar institution of slavery may hereafter be interfered with by the party which put Mr. Lincoln into power.

I am free to say that the simile of Lord John is as unfortunate as the position which he has initiated for his Government in this crisis. The British Cabinet will, if this course should be persisted in, commit the fatal error of losing the good will of the party *which in the end must be successful*, in order to gain the friendship of those whose defeat can only be a question of time. We have three times as large a population, as united and brave as theirs; we have a navy, we have money and credit, in which latter they are most sadly and justly deficient.

Already Davis is again in the market with a loan of fifty millions of dollars. Who will loan a dollar to a confederacy of States, of which four have already repudiated their debts, while the remaining five will in less than three months be in default of their semi-annual dividends, unless it be that the name of Jeff. Davis, notwithstanding his advocacy of repudiation in his own State, Mississippi, should have a sweeter sound to European capitalists than I think he will ever acquire? In less than a year the Confederate States will pay their obligations in treasury warrants, which will have the same ultimate value as the French "assignats."

You know that I have never been in favor of the party which is now at the head of our Government, and my convictions on this point have in no way been changed. I am, however, convinced that the whole North to a man will stand by the Administration in the present struggle, and that, *come what may*, the integrity of the Union and the inviolability of our territory will be maintained to the bitter end.

Civil war is now upon us; no human power can prevent it. A vigorous and gigantic effort, on the part of the North, may, and I am confident will, shorten its horrors and disastrous results. An interference or one-sided neutrality, such as is foreshadowed by Lord John Russell's speech, can only prolong the fratricidal war, and entail ruin, not only upon both sections of our country, but upon the material interests and commerce of the world.

—Belmont, *Letters, Speeches, and Addresses*

B. GEORGE TICKNOR EXPLAINS THE WAR TO HIS ENGLISH FRIENDS

To Sir Charles Lyell.

Boston, February 11, 1862

MY DEAR LYELL,—No doubt, I ought to have written to you before. But I have had no heart to write to my friends in Europe, since our troubles took their present form and proportions. . . .

You know how I have always thought and felt about the slavery question. I was never an Abolitionist, in the American sense of the word, because I never have believed that any form of emancipation that has been proposed could reach the enormous difficulties of the case, and I am of the same mind now. Slavery is too monstrous an evil, as it exists in the United States, to be reached by the resources of legislation. . . . I have, therefore, always desired to treat the South with the greatest forbearance, not only because the present generation is not responsible for the curse that is laid upon it, but because I have felt that the longer the contest could be postponed, the better for us. I have hoped, too, that in the inevitable conflict with free labor, slavery would go to the wall. I remember writing to you in this sense, more than twenty years ago, and the results thus far have confirmed the hopes I then entertained. The slavery of the South has made the South poor. The free labor of the North has made us rich and strong.

But all such hopes and thoughts were changed by the violent and unjustifiable secession, a year ago; and, since the firing of the first gun on Fort Sumter, we have had, in fact, no choice. We must fight it out. Of the results I have never doubted. We shall beat the South. But what after that? I do not see. It has pleased God that, whether we are to be two nations or one, we should live on the same continent side by side, with no strong natural barrier to keep us asunder; but now separated by hatreds which grow more insane and intense every month, and which generations will hardly extinguish. . . .

Our prosperity has entered largely into the prosperity of the world, and especially into that of England and France. You feel it to have been so. And some persons have been unwise enough to think that your interference in our domestic quarrel can do good to yourselves, and perhaps to us, by attempting to stop this cruel and wicked war. It is, I conceive, a great mistake. I have believed, since last August, that France was urging your government to some sort of intervention,—to break the blockade or to enforce a peace,—but the general opinion here has been that England has been the real mover in the matter, thus engendering a bitter hatred of your people, which the unjustifiable tone of your papers and ours increases and exasperates. All this is wrong, and so far as you are excited by it to intervention, it is most unhappy and portentous. The temptation, no doubt, is strong. It almost always is in the case of civil wars, which, from their very nature, invite interested and neighboring nations to interfere. But how rarely has good come to anybody from such interference. In the present instance I am satisfied that it would only exasperate us, and lead to desperate measures. . . .

As to the present comparative condition of North and South, there can be no question. At Richmond, and elsewhere beyond the Potomac, gold is at forty per cent premium, coffee and tea at four or five prices, salt as dear. . . . Beef and bread they have in abundance, and so resolute and embittered are they, that they seem content with this. But it cannot be. The women, I hear, in a large part of the South, will not speak to men who stay at home from the army without obvious and sufficient cause. But the suffering is great, however the proud spirit may bear up against it, and they must yield, unless, what is all but incredible, they should speedily gain great military success. . . .

At the North the state of things is very different. There is no perceptible increase of poverty. . . . Nor is anybody disheartened. If you were here you would see little change in our modes of life, except that we are all busy and in earnest about the war. . . . This, however, is not to last. The government must either impose taxes heavy enough to sustain its credit, as it ought to have done long ago, and then our incomes will all feel it, or it must rush into a paper currency, and then, of course, prices must rise in proportion, and the whole end in disaster. . . .

A country that has shown the resources and spirit of the North—however they may have been misused, and may continue to be—cannot be ruined by a year or two of adverse fortune, or even more. Changed it will be, how, or how much, I cannot guess, nor do I find anybody worth listening to that can tell me. But we are young and full of life. Diseases that destroy the old are cast off by the vigor of youth; and, though I may not live to see it, we shall again be strong and have an honored place among the nations. For the South I have no vaticinations. The blackness of thick darkness rests upon them, and they deserve all they will suffer. I admit that a portion of the North, and sometimes the whole North, has been very unjust to them. . . . But it is all no justification of civil war. . . . It is the unpardonable sin in a really free State.

You will, perhaps, think me shabby if I stop without saying anything about the Trent affair, and so I may as well make a clean breast of it. Except Everett, all the persons hereabout in whose judgment I place confidence believed from the first that we had no case. I was fully of that mind. . . .

As to the complaint about our closing up harbors, we are not very anxious. It is a harsh measure, but there are precedents enough for it,—more than there ought to be. But two will fully sustain the mere right. By the treaty of Utrecht you stipulated not only for the destruction of the fortifications of Dunkirk, but for filling up the port; and in 1777 (I think it was that year) you destroyed the entrance to Savannah, so that appropriations were made, not many years ago, by our Congress, to remove the obstructions, although the river, there, has cut out itself a new channel. I do not think that we have closed any but the minor and more shallow channels by the blockade. . . . However, if England and France want a pretext for interfering with us, perhaps this will do as well as any other. No doubt the "Times" at least, will be satisfied with it.

—*Life, Letters and Journals of George Ticknor*

5. CAPTAIN WILKES SEIZES MASON AND SLIDELL

It was the Trent *affair that brought the first, and perhaps the major, crisis in Anglo-American affairs during the war. The story itself is fully told in Lieutenant Fairfax's narrative. What Fairfax does not tell is the story of the impact of the* Trent *affair on England, and of the subsequent diplomatic controversy.*

James Mason and John Slidell were, respectively, Confederate commissioners to Britain and France. Learning that they had left Havana for England, Captain Wilkes stopped the Trent *and removed them, without specific instructions from his own government. His act was technically a violation of international law; he should have brought the* Trent *to an American port where a prize court would have adjudicated the whole case. What he did, however, was what the British themselves had done scores of times in the early years of the century. Nor did the British government at first hold Wilkes's act contrary to international law. As early as November 11, 1861, Palmerston had written the editor of the* Times *that "this American cruiser might, by our own principles of International Law, stop the West India packet, search her, and if the Southern men and their despatches and credentials were found on board, either take them out or seize the packet and carry her back to New York for trial." Yet when Wilkes did just this a wave of anger swept over England, and the government itself was moved to threats. The British government demanded that the United States release the prisoners and apologize for Wilkes's action, and insisted on an immediate answer. Fortunately the Prince Consort toned down Lord Russell's first letter, but even after toning down it bore the appearance of an ultimatum. Meantime orders were issued to hold the fleet in readiness for action, and thousands of soldiers were shipped over to Canada, while the export of war munitions to America was for a time stopped.*

Lincoln and Seward were in a dilemma. If they did not satisfy Britain they might find themselves with another war on their hands. If they did public opinion—which had made a hero of Wilkes—would be outraged. With his customary skill Seward found a solution. He did not apologize, but congratulated England on at last adopting the principles of international law for which the United States had long contended; then he had Mason and Slidell shipped off to England. American public opinion was on the whole pleased; the English were satisfied. In the long run the Trent *affair cleared the air; like the Venezuela crisis of Cleveland's administration it led both countries to contemplate war and revealed to both that they did not like the prospect. Yet in the lasting sense of resentment which was planted in America, Britain paid a high price for her insistence on a fine point of law.*

Donald Macneill Fairfax, who here tells the story of the removal of Mason and Slidell, was executive officer of the San Jacinto; *he later fought with Farragut at New Orleans, and off Charleston. In 1880 he was named rear admiral.*

IN October, 1861, the United States screw-sloop *San Jacinto*, of which Captain Charles Wilkes was commander and the writer was executive officer, on her return from the west coast of Africa, touched at the island of St. Thomas to coal ship. Here for the first time we learned of the presence in those waters of the Confederate cruiser *Sumter* (Captain Raphael Semmes). Captain Wilkes immediately determined to search for the enemy. At Cienfuegos, on the south coast of Cuba, he learned from the United States consul-general at Havana that Messrs. Mason and Slidell, Confederate commissioners to Europe, and their secretaries and families had recently reached that port from Charleston en route to England. He immediately put to sea, October 26th, with the purpose of intercepting the blockade runner which had brought them out. The commissioners . . . had run the Union blockade successfully . . . and had arrived . . . at Havana on the 17th. There we ascertained that their plan was to leave on the 7th of November in the English steamer *Trent* for St. Thomas on their way to England, and readily calculated when and where in the Bahama Channel we might intercept them. Meanwhile . . . Captain Wilkes continued his cruise after the *Sumter* along the north coast of Cuba, also running over to Key West in the hope of finding the *Powhatan* or some other steamer to accompany him to the Bahama Channel. . . . Here, 240 miles from Havana, and 90 miles from Sagua la Grande, where the channel contracts to the width of 15 miles, at noon on the 8th of November the *Trent* was sighted. . . .

It was evident, even at that early day, that the South had the sympathy of nearly all Europe—particularly of England and France. When Captain Wilkes first took me into his confidence, and told me what he purposed to do, I earnestly reminded him of the great risk of a war with these two Governments, supported as they were by powerful navies; and when we reached Key West I suggested that he consult with Judge Marvin, one of the ablest maritime lawyers. I soon saw, however, that he had made up his mind to intercept and capture the *Trent* as well as to take possession of the commissioners, and I therefore ceased to discuss the affair. As the next in rank to Captain Wilkes, I claimed the right to board the mail-packet. Captain Wilkes fully expected that I would tender my services for this "delicate duty," and rather left to me the plan of carrying out his instructions. I was impressed with the gravity of my position, and I made up my mind not to do anything unnecessary in the arrest of these gentlemen, or anything that would irritate the captain of the *Trent*, or any of his passengers, particularly the commissioners—lest it might occur to them to throw the steamer on my hands, which would necessitate my taking her as a prize.

As the *Trent* approached she hoisted English colors; whereupon our ensign was hoisted and a shot was fired across her bow. As she maintained her speed and showed no disposition to heave to, a shell was fired across her bow which brought her to. Captain Wilkes hailed that he intended to send a boat on board, and I then left with the second cutter.

The manner of heaving the *Trent* to evidently was galling to Captain Moir. When he did stop his steamer, he showed how provoked he was by impatiently singing out through his trumpet, "What do you mean by heaving my vessel to in this manner?" I felt that I must in every way conciliate him when I should get on board. Two boats had been equipped ready to lower and the officers and crews detailed to jump into them. These were not employed until later. The boat I took was a third one, and as the sea was smooth, but a few minutes elapsed before we reached the *Trent*. I instructed the boat's crew to remain alongside for orders, and, boarding the vessel, I was escorted by one of her officers to the upper or promenade deck and was introduced to Captain Moir. . . . I immediately asked if I might see his passenger-list, saying that I had information that Messrs. Mason and Slidell were on board. The mention of Mr. Slidell's name caused that gentleman to come up and say, "I am Mr. Slidell; do you want to see me?" Mr. Mason, whom I knew very well, also came up at the same time, thus relieving me from Captain Moir's refusal, which was very polite but very positive, that I could not under such circumstances be shown any list of passengers. . . . In the briefest time . . . I informed Captain Moir that I had been sent by my commander to arrest Mr. Mason and Mr. Slidell and their secretaries, and send them prisoners on board the United States war vessel near by.

As may readily be understood, when it was known why I had boarded the *Trent*, there was an outburst of rage and indignation from the passengers, who numbered nearly one hundred, many of them Southerners. The captain and the four gentlemen bore themselves with great composure, but the irresponsible lookers-on sang out, "Throw the d—— fellow overboard!" I called on Captain Moir to preserve order, but, for the benefit of the excited passengers, I reminded them that our every move was closely observed from the *San Jacinto* by spy-glasses (she was within hailing distance), that a heavy battery was bearing upon them, and that any indignity to any of her officers or crew then on board might lead to dreadful consequences. This, together with Captain Moir's excellent commanding manner, had a quieting effect.

During this uproar among the passengers, the officer in charge of the *San Jacinto's* boat, not knowing what it meant, and fearing some ill-treatment of me, hurried up with six or eight of the crew. Captain Moir was the first to see this body of armed men, and remonstrated with me at their appearance on the promenade-deck among his passengers, there being many ladies and children among them. I immediately directed the officer to return to his boat and await my orders. I assured him, amidst the noise of his passengers, that the men had come contrary to my instructions. I was really pleased to find the captain so tenacious of his command, for my mind was possessed with the idea that Mr. Mason or Mr. Slidell, or both, would urge Captain Moir to relinquish his command, making it necessary for me to assume it, as in such event my instructions left no opening for me to decline it.

After order had been restored, we discussed the affair more generally, Captain Moir, however, scarcely joining in the conversation—always dignified and punctilious. . . . I carefully avoided giving offense, and confined myself strictly to the duty which had taken me on board. I was anxious that Mr. Slidell and Mr. Mason should not leave any of their luggage behind. Mrs. Slidell having asked me who commanded the *San Jacinto*, I replied, "Your old acquaintance, Captain Wilkes"; whereupon she expressed surprise that he should do the very thing the Confederates were hoping for—something to arouse England; . . . "Really," she added, "Captain Wilkes is playing into our hands!" . . .

After the first uproar had subsided, I sent the boat to Captain Wilkes to say that these gentlemen were all on board, and had objected to being sent to the *San Jacinto*, and that I must use force to accomplish my orders; I asked for a boat to carry them comfortably on board, another for their baggage, and a third to carry stores, which the paymaster's clerk, at Captain Wilkes's order, had already purchased from the steward of the *Trent*, to add to the comfort of the new guests.

When all was ready and the boats were in waiting, I notified both Mr. Mason and Mr. Slidell that the time had come to send them to the *San Jacinto*. They came quietly down to the main-deck, and there repeated that they would not go unless force was used—whereupon two officers, previously instructed, escorted each commissioner to the side, and assisted them into the comfortable cutter sent especially for them. . . .

When all was finished I went on board the *San Jacinto* and reported to Captain Wilkes that I had not taken the *Trent* as a prize, as he had instructed me to do, giving certain reasons, which satisfied him; for he replied, "inasmuch as you have not taken her, you will let her go" or "proceed on her voyage." . . . The reasons I assigned to Captain Wilkes for my action were: First, that the capture of the *Trent* would make it necessary to put a large prize crew (officers and men) on board, and thus materially weaken our battery for use at Port Royal; secondly, that as there were a large number of women and children and mails and specie bound to various ports, the capture would seriously inconvenience innocent persons and merchants; so that I had determined, before taking her, to lay these matters before him for more serious consideration.

I gave my real reasons some weeks afterward to Secretary Chase, whom I met by chance at the Treasury Department, he having asked me to explain why I had not literally obeyed Captain Wilkes's instructions. I told him that it was because I was impressed with England's sympathy for the South, and felt that she would be glad to have so good a ground to declare war against the United States. Mr. Chase seemed surprised, and exclaimed, "You have certainly relieved the Government from great embarrassment, to say the least."

I returned immediately to the *Trent* and informed Captain Moir that Captain Wilkes would not longer detain him, and he might proceed on his voyage. The steamers soon separated, and thus ended one of the most critical events of our civil war.

—FAIRFAX, "Captain Wilkes's Seizure of Mason and Slidell"

6. "SHALL IT BE LOVE, OR HATE, JOHN?"

Few American poets were better known in England, or more respected, than James Russell Lowell. "Jonathan to John"—one of the famous Biglow

Papers—*was Lowell's criticism of the British reaction to the* Trent *affair, but it covered broad ground. Widely read in America, it long retained its popularity, but needless to say it never achieved a comparable popularity with that people to whom it was directed.*

Jonathan to John

It don't seem hardly right, John,
  When both my hands was full,
To stump me to a fight, John,—
  Your cousin, tu, John Bull!
    Ole Uncle S. sez he, "I guess
    We know it now," sez he,
"The Lion's paw is all the law,
    Accordin' to J. B.,
    That's fit for you an' me!"

You wonder why we're hot, John?
  Your mark wuz on the guns,
The neutral guns, thet shot, John,
  Our brothers an' our sons:
    Ole Uncle S. sez he, "I guess
    There's human blood," sez he,
"By fits an' starts, in Yankee hearts,
    Though 't may surprise J. B.
    More 'n it would you an' me." . . .

When your rights was our wrongs, John,
  You didn't stop for fuss,—
Britanny's trident prongs, John,
  Was good 'nough law for us.
    Ole Uncle S. sez he, "I guess,
    Though physic 's good," sez he,
"It does n't foller thet he can swaller
    Prescriptions signed 'J. B.,'
    Put up by you an' me."

We own the ocean, tu, John:
  You mus'n' take it hard,
Ef we can't think with you, John,
  It's jest your own back yard.
    Ole Uncle S. sez he, "I guess
    Ef *thet's* his claim," sez he,
"The fencin'-stuff 'll cost enough
    To bust up friend J. B.,
    Ez wal ez you an' me!" . . .

We give the critters back, John,
    Cos Abram thought 't was right;
It warn't your bullyin' clack, John,
    Provokin' us to fight.
        Ole Uncle S. sez he, "I guess
        We've a hard row," sez he,
"To hoe jest now; but thet, somehow,
      May happen to J. B.,
      Ez wal ez you an' me!"

We ain't so weak an' poor, John,
    With twenty million people,
An' close to every door, John,
    A school-house an' a steeple.
        Ole Uncle S. sez he, "I guess
        It is a fact," sez he,
"The surest plan to make a Man
      Is, think him so, J. B.,
      Ez much ez you or me!" . . .

We know we've got a cause, John,
    Thet's honest, just, an' true;
We thought 't would win applause, John,
    If nowheres else, from you.
        Ole Uncle S. sez he, "I guess
        His love of right," sez he,
"Hangs by a rotton fibre o' cotton:
      ·There's natur' in J. B.,
      Ez wal ez in you an' me!"

The South says, "*Poor folks down!*" John,
    An' "*All men up!*" say we,—
White, yaller, black, an' brown, John:
    Now which is your idee?
        Ole Uncle S. sez he, "I guess
        John preaches wal," sez he;
"But, sermon thru, an' come to *du*,
      Why, there's the old J. B.
      A-crowdin' you an' me!"

Shall it be love, or hate, John?
    It's you thet's to decide;
Ain't *your* bonds held by Fate, John,
    Like all the world's beside?
        Ole Uncle S. sez he, "I guess
        Wise men forgive," sez he,
"But not forgit; an' some time yit
      Thet truth may strike J. B.,
      Ez wal ez you an' me!"

God means to make this land, John,
   Clear thru, from sea to sea,
Believe an' understand, John,
   The *wuth* o' bein' free.
    Ole Uncle S. sez he, "I guess
    God's price is high," sez he;
"But nothin' else than wut he sells
    Wears long, an' thet J. B.
    May larn, like you an' me!"
      —LOWELL, *Poems*

7. COMMONS DEBATES THE RECOGNITION OF THE CONFEDERACY

By two proclamations of April 19 and April 27, 1861, Lincoln had established a blockade of the Confederacy. Was this blockade legally binding? In international law a blockade must be real and effective; a mere "paper" blockade need not be observed. Yet in fact the little United States Navy of 1861 was wholly unable to impose an effective blockade on a dozen or more major ports and several thousand miles of coast line. Britain might, therefore, have taken the position that there was no legal blockade. But to have done so would almost certainly have precipitated war, and Britain neither wanted nor was ready for war. Furthermore Britain was herself a maritime power, dependent on the blockade as an instrument of war; a strict interpretation of blockading might very well redound to her serious disadvantage later on. Lord John Russell, therefore, promptly accepted the blockade.

Southern sympathizers were unwilling to let the matter rest at that. They agitated for a review of the whole blockade question, and for recognition of the Confederacy as a sovereign state. The most prominent of them were Sir John Gregory and William Lindsay. In March 1862 Gregory touched off a debate on the blockade which ended in his total discomfiture. Nothing daunted, Lindsay raised the whole question once again in June 1862. The greatest shipowner in England, Lindsay exercised considerable influence in business circles and, as he was from the Midlands, seemed to speak with peculiar propriety for the starving workingmen of Lancashire. After a trip to Paris and talks with Emperor Napoleon Lindsay returned to London and in June gave notice of a motion to recognize the Confederacy. Then early in July came the news of Lee's victories on the Peninsula and the moment seemed right for pushing the motion to conclusion. The debate ranged over the whole field of relations with the American belligerents. In the end Lindsay was forced to withdraw his motion.

Benjamin Moran, from whose invaluable diary this story is taken, was Secretary of the American Legation in London. His diary is chiefly notable for its acidulous comments on Minister Charles Francis Adams and on his son Henry Adams, as well as on all other Americans who failed to appreciate the merits of Benjamin Moran.

Sat. 19 July, '62. Last evening being the time fixed for the discussion of Lindsay's motion for the recognition of the Rebels, I was sent down to the House by Mr. Adams' direction to observe the feeling and report the proceedings. On going there at about 5 o'clk I found the Commons had adjourned to meet at 6. I went at the appointed hour. There was a very large gathering of strangers extending all through St. Stephen's porch, and filling up nearly the whole of the outside lobby of the House. Among those who were lounging in the hall or corridor leading from the grand central vestibule to the Commons, was Geo. McHenry. This recreant northern man displayed much servility towards the door keepers and policemen, and had a good deal of the mean guilty look of a sheep-stealing dog. He observed me, as I did him, but as I always detested the fellow, I treated him as if I was unaware of his presence. Just as the House again met, the crowd of anxious visitors increased and much confusion followed at the doors. The gate-keepers then increased their already very large stock of insolence and ill-manners, until they became unbearable.

At this time the rebel Mason came up attended by Williams, our late Minister at Constantinople, Geo. McHenry and two or three vulgar looking confederates, whose appearance and manners were not favorable to their modest pretensions to be considered as specimens of the only gentlemen in America. Mason and Williams are both coarse, gross, ponderous, vulgar looking men, and on this occasion they did not show to the best advantage. They were badly dressed. Williams always was a sloven. Last night his shirt front was crumpled and stained with tobacco spit and his trousers were unbuttoned. Mason was impudent—which he mistakes for dignity—and wore a *dress* coat with a black satin vest. Linsey-woolsey don't answer here. The rough boor who keeps the door spoke to them in a loud insolent commanding tone and ordered them back. But while they were parleying Gregory, their champion, came out and in his peculiarly offensive and whining tone said he had orders for the floor for his friend Mr. Mason and suite. The *suite* however being large was not admitted to the privilege he demanded, McHenry and the rest of the mean little rebels being sent into the Speaker's gallery, while Gregory conducted his friends Mason and Williams to seats on the floor under the gallery. I soon followed, and having the privilege of either going into the Diplomatic Gallery or on the floor decided for the floor for the time. Mason sat near the gangway in front and Williams behind.

An ineffectual attempt having been made to induce Lindsay to withdraw his motion, that gentleman rose and began his speech. He opened by striking off every offer of *recognition* and fell back on simple mediation, without referring to hostilities. He is a wretched speaker and soon drove half the members of a very full House away. For years I have entertained great respect for the intelligence and dignity of the English House of Commons, but after hearing the vulgar misrepresentations of Lindsay on the United States last night, welcomed by applause, I can no longer even respect it. His speech, if a blundering utterance of a long tissue of naked falsehoods, can so be called, was simply an insult to intelligence and reason. I thought old Mason was

Illustrated London News

British Reinforcements for Canada

The Cotton Famine, Mottram, near Manchester

ashamed of his advocate. He openly lied about the tariff, and had evidently been crammed by the rebels. After an hour's abuse of us, and his reasons therefore, he wound up by saying that independently of all these, he desired the disruption of the American Union, as every honest Englishman did, because it was too great a Power and England sh'd not let such a power exist on the American continent. Old Mason spat tobacco more furiously at this than ever, and covered the carpet. I thought that if he had a particle of manly feeling left he would blush at the contempt there expressed for him by his champion. For there was in it, a positive declaration that the South was nothing to him, and that he was only trying to array one section against the other for the destruction of both in order to feed the envy of England.

I watched carefully the effect of this speech. At first it was cordially welcomed, but it soon became evident that there was a growing doubt in the House about even *Mediation!* The tories cheered the most. This revealed their policy. I gave Mr. Forster my private telegram giving the denial to the reported capitulation of McClellan & he circulated it. The dates were conclusive, & I began to fear they wouldn't adopt the motion, for after the open abuse of us by Lindsay, and the approval it met by the House, I wanted the resolution passed. It seemed to me that fear of us, and fear alone, was the check to action. There was a lull after Lindsay sat down. Gregory and he, as well as some of the tories went over to Mason. I went up to the Diplomatic Gallery, and Mr. P. Taylor, the new member of Leicester began to speak.

This gentleman was jeered at first, but by perseverance he got a hearing. I observed Palmerston, who seemed to be quietly asleep on the Treasury bench with his hat over his eyes when Lindsay was speaking, but was not, turn and look enquiringly at Taylor. The tories behaved like blackguards. They showed their love of free-speech by trying to put down everybody not of their way of thinking. Mr. Taylor however persevered, and under a great deal of provocation made an eloquent but an indiscreet speech. The popularity, or respect entertained for a speaker, is always evinced in the House by full or empty benches. Mr. Taylor soon brought back the crowd that hobbling Lindsay drove away and he was met both by applause and condemnation. He said the war was between Freedom and Slavery, which was met with loud cries of No, No! and jeers. He also said that mediation was an insult and would lead to war. This was also cried down. And when he mentioned the name of honest Abraham Lincoln, the burst of horse laughter and ridicule that greeted it, was a disgrace to the age. The act itself was bad enough in all conscience, but the manner and tone of the expression were even more offensive. Mr. Taylor was equal to the occasion, and met the guffah of this intelligent assembly of honest and refined English gentlemen with a declaration that shamed them to silence. "Yes," said he "I say honest Abraham Lincoln—a name that will be remembered and honored when all the smooth tongued diplomats and statesmen of the day are forgotten." He also told them that their hostility was hatred of America—that slavery was the cause of the rebellion—and that English advocacy of the rebels was an abandonment of that hostility to slavery that had ever been the characteristic of Englishmen in modern times. The jeers to this were feeble, as the truth it contained was felt. Mr. Taylor quoted most effectually from J. Stuart Mill, and made the most of the point so gained.

Lord A. Vane-Tempest, a dissipated and unprincipled young nobleman spoke next. His manner is that of his class and his speech was like Lindsay's, composed of falsehood and abuse. I thought he was drunk, and so did the House, for he came near falling over the back of the bench in front of him on several occasions. He described the slave-drivers as gentlemen, and the soldiers of the Republic as mercenaries. Went over the old slanders about America insulting England, taking good care to charge to the present Administration all the faults of past cabinets, and wound up with an insult to Mr. Taylor. Vane Tempest is bloated from drink, & would be in the workhouse if he were not a Lord—but being a Lord he is in the English House of Commons. He was a good deal cheered by the tories; and the current of their policy, which until last night they have carefully concealed, was seen to flow with the rebels.

Mr. Forster spoke next. He made a brief but telling speech. Palmerston and Gladstone looked up at him and the tories faintly applauded. I had prepared him with some facts to refute Lindsay, and he used them. He showed that the North had always taxed itself to protect sugar, cotton, tobacco and rice, and that South Carolina never once mentioned tariffs or taxation in her Declaration of Independence. Lindsay had said that odious northern taxation was the cause of the rebellion. But after all, I don't know that it was worth while to notice the fellow. Great respect was paid to Mr. Forster's speech and it did good. By this time the rebel story of McClellan's capitulation had been exploded and their cause was growing palpably weaker.

The tories had however prepared themselves to expound their policy and Mr. Whitesides [Whiteside], the Attorney General for Ireland under Lord Derby in '58, was selected as their mouth-piece. That the proceeding had been pre-arranged is confirmed by the fact that Lord Derby himself came in to hear Mr. Whiteside's speech. Being in the lobby just before Mr. Whitesides began I met the Earl of Derby going into the Commons. D'Israeli usually represents the tories in all great debates in the Lower House, but on this occasion he had evidently declined the task. This fact, and Whiteside's selection, are further proof of prearrangement. He began very deliberately and delivered what was evidently a prepared speech. He is an able eloquent Irish orator and speaks with great force. The tories cheered his references to the supposed failure of Republican institutions loudly, and he belabored us soundly but politely. At times he was severe, but he was never vulgar. One can hear polite slander with a better grace than he can coarse abuse. He was terribly sarcastic at times, but rarely truthful. In fact both classes of the rebel advocates seemed conscious that they could only carry their point by falsehood, and appeals to prejudice. His phillipics at times were savage and were hailed with laughter. Being a tall fine, venerable and powerful man, with considerable action and oratorical force,—rare qualities in England,—

and yet no ranter, he soon had the House with him. He spoke from the floor and therefore had room for movement. His modified Irish accent sounded well when I forgot in my admiration of the orator the subject of his eloquence; but it sent a chill crawling over me when I recollected myself and recalled the fact that its tones were pleading the cause of slavery against freedom. Mr. Forster came up to me while he was speaking and said "You see now where the tories are." I did and was glad of it. They had thrown off the cloak and fixed their position. It was an able speech but altho' well received, its admirers seemed to be more noisy than determined. They were whistling to keep their courage up.

Gregory followed in his insipid way with a lot of platitudes, and expressions of confidence that "this House" would adopt the resolutions; but was not very happy.

There was a pleasant young gentleman whom I did not know in the gallery at my side with whom I had been in conversation during the evening, and who up to this time had thought the vote would be favorable. He however had, like me, been a close observer of the effects of the speeches and the changes in the feeling of the House, and agreed that there would be either no vote or a defeat. I expressed my regret. He knew my sentiments and said he would feel like me if he were a northerner. While we were talking Palmerston, who had nearly all night preserved his sleepy appearance, rose. He was heartily welcomed, and in three minutes settled the matter adversely to the rebels. It was half-past one in the morning, that old man—now 78 years of age—had been for seven hours and a half a listener to the debate, and had heard every word, as all close observers saw, notwithstanding his attitude of sleep, and altho he tottered when he got up, his brain was clear and he delivered the best speech I ever heard from his lips. Silence was accorded him at first—applause and approval at last. His remarks showed that he had watched every action and heard every sentiment of the speakers, and in quoting them he neither misrepresented them nor attributed to any one sentiments that had been uttered by another. He said mediation meant war, and thought the Gov't could manage the affair without going that far, or wounding the feeling of a sensitive, and struggling people. That speech closed the debate, and altho' Fitzgerald spoke afterwards, his remarks amounted to nothing and Lindsay withdrew his motion.

As I came away I met Mason alone, looking sullen and dejected. He has a bad face. In a minute he was joined by Gregory, both evidently disappointed, and putting his arm lovingly round the Irishman's waist the slaveholder and the Briton stalked off to solace their minds and forget their disappointment in the consolations incident to smoking a cigar.

—WALLACE AND GILLESPIE, eds., *The Journal of Benjamin Moran*

8. PALMERSTON AND RUSSELL DISCUSS INTERVENTION

Although the Government had defeated Lindsay's motion, it continued to consider the propriety of an offer of mediation to the American belliger-

ents. *By the autumn of 1862 the American situation appeared to justify such
a move. McClellan had been defeated on the Peninsula; Lee had whipped
Pope at Second Bull Run, and now Lee's victorious hosts were invading the
North with every prospect of success. Pressure from Napoleon, too, was
mounting. In mid-September 1862 the Prime Minister, the Viscount Palmerston and the Foreign Secretary, Lord John Russell, corresponded about the
next move. Both appeared to favor mediation. Then came the news of
Antietam—a Union victory after all. Palmerston had sober second thoughts,
and the mediation movement died as far as the Government was concerned.*
      Here are the crucial letters that passed between Palmerston and Russell.

94 Piccadilly: September 14, 1862

My dear Russell,—The detailed accounts given in the 'Observer' to-day
of the battles of August 29 and 30 between the Confederates and the Federals show that the latter got a very complete smashing; and it seems not
altogether unlikely that still greater disasters await them, and that even
Washington or Baltimore may fall into the hands of the Confederates.

If this should happen, would it not be time for us to consider whether
in such a state of things England and France might not address the contending parties and recommend an arrangement upon the basis of separation?
      —Yours sincerely,

PALMERSTON.

Gotha: September 17, 1862

My dear Palmerston,—Whether the Federal army is destroyed or not, it
is clear that it is driven back to Washington, and has made no progress in
subduing the insurgent States. Such being the case, I agree with you that the
time is come for offering mediation to the United States Government, with a
view to the recognition of the independence of the Confederates. I agree
further, that, in case of failure, we ought ourselves to recognise the Southern
States as an independent State. For the purpose of taking so important a step,
I think we must have a meeting of the Cabinet. The 23rd or 30th would suit
me for the meeting.

We ought then, if we agree on such a step, to propose it first to France,
and then, on the part of England and France, to Russia and other powers, as
a measure decided upon by us.

We ought to make ourselves safe in Canada, not by sending more troops
there, but by concentrating those we have in a few defensible posts before
the winter sets in.

J. RUSSELL

Broadlands: September 23, 1862

My dear Russell,—Your plan of proceedings about the mediation between
the Federals and Confederates seems to be excellent. Of course, the offer
would be made to both the contending parties at the same time; for, though
the offer would be as sure to be accepted by the Southerns as was the proposal
of the Prince of Wales by the Danish Princess, yet, in the one case as in the

other, there are certain forms which it is decent and proper to go through.

A question would occur whether, if the two parties were to accept the mediation, the fact of our mediating would not of itself be tantamount to an acknowledgment of the Confederates as an independent State.

Might it not be well to ask Russia to join England and France in the offer of mediation? . . .

We should be better without her in the mediation, because she would be too favourable to the North; but on the other hand her participation in the offer might render the North the more willing to accept it.

The after communication to the other European powers would be quite right, although they would be too many for mediation.

As to the time of making the offer, if France and Russia agree,—and France, we know, is quite ready, and only waiting for our concurrence— events may be taking place which might render it desirable that the offer should be made before the middle of October.

It is evident that a great conflict is taking place to the north-west of Washington, and its issue must have a great effect on the state of affairs. If the Federals sustain a great defeat, they may be at once ready for mediation, and the iron should be struck while it is hot. If, on the other hand, they should have the best of it, we may wait awhile and see what may follow.— Yours sincerely,

PALMERSTON.

—WALPOLE, The Life of Lord John Russell

October 2

My dear Russell,

I return you Granville's letter which contains much deserving of serious consideration. There is no doubt that the offer of Mediation upon the basis of Separation would be accepted by the South. Why should it not be accepted? It would give the South in principle the points for which they are fighting. The refusal, if refusal there was, would come from the North, who would be unwilling to give up the principle for which they have been fighting so long as they had a reasonable expectation that by going on fighting they could carry their point. The condition of things therefore which would be favourable to an offer of mediation would be great success of the South against the North. That state of things seemed ten days ago to be approaching. Its advance has been lately checked, but we do not yet know the real course of recent events, and still less can we foresee what is about to follow. Ten days or a fortnight more may throw a clearer light upon future prospects.

As regards possible resentment on the part of the Northerns following upon an acknowledgment of the Independence of the South, it is quite true that we should have less to care about that resentment in the spring when communication with Canada was open, and when our naval force could more easily operate upon the American coast, than in winter when we are cut off from Canada and the American coast is not so safe.

But if the acknowledgment were made at one and the same time by England, France and some other Powers, the Yankees would probably not seek a quarrel with us alone, and would not like one against a European Confederation. Such a quarrel would render certain and permanent that Southern Independence the acknowledgment of which would have caused it.

The first communication to be made by England and France to the contending parties might be, not an absolute offer of mediation but a friendly suggestion whether the time was not come when it might be well for the two parties to consider whether the war, however long continued, could lead to any other result than separation; and whether it might not therefore be best to avoid the great evils which must necessarily flow from a prolongation of hostilities by at once coming to an agreement to treat upon that principle of separation which must apparently be the inevitable result of the contest, however long it may last.

The best thing would be that the two parties should settle details by direct negotiation with each other, though perhaps with the rancorous hatred now existing between them this might be difficult. But their quarrels in negotiation would do us no harm if they did not lead to a renewal of war. An armistice, if not accompanied by a cessation of blockades, would be all in favour of the North, especially if New Orleans remained in the hands of the North.

The whole matter is full of difficulty, and can only be cleared up by some more decided events between the contending armies.

PALMERSTON.

—ADAMS, Great Britain and the American Civil War

9. "AN ERROR, THE MOST SINGULAR AND PALPABLE"

The great surprise of the diplomatic battle was Gladstone's Newcastle speech of October 7, 1862. By that time the Cabinet had pretty well decided neither to intervene nor to offer mediation. Gladstone was Chancellor of the Exchequer, and presumably supported the Government policy. Yet at Newcastle he said, "Jefferson Davis and other leaders of the South have made an army; they are making, it appears, a navy; and they have made what is more than either, they have made a nation." By British political standards this was clearly an improper speech to make. A few days later the Home Secretary, Sir George Cornwall Lewis, said at Hereford that the Government did not contemplate any change of policy, thus in effect repudiating Gladstone. Gladstone himself later confessed that this speech was one of the great errors of his career. We give his apology, written in July 1896.*

I HAVE yet to record an undoubted error, the most singular and palpable, I may add the least excusable of them all, especially since it was committed so late as in the year 1862, when I had outlived half a century. In the autumn of that year, and in a speech delivered after a public dinner at Newcastle-

---

* From Morley: *The Life of William Ewart Gladstone*, Vol. II. Copyright 1903 by The Macmillan Company, 1931 by Mary O. Morley, and used with the permission of The Macmillan Company and Mr. Guy E. Morley.

upon-Tyne, I declared in the heat of the American struggle that Jefferson Davis had made a nation, that is to say, that the division of the American Republic by the establishment of a Southern or secession state was an accomplished fact. Strange to say, this declaration, most unwarrantable to be made by a minister of the crown with no authority other than his own, was not due to any feeling of partizanship for the South or hostility to the North. The fortunes of the South were at their zenith. Many who wished well to the Northern cause despaired of its success. The friends of the North in England were beginning to advise that it should give way, for the avoidance of further bloodshed and greater calamity. I weakly supposed that the time had come when respectful suggestions of this kind, founded on the necessity of the case, were required by a spirit of that friendship which, in so many contingencies of life, has to offer sound recommendations with a knowledge that they will not be popular. Not only was this a misjudgment of the case, but even if it had been otherwise, I was not the person to make the declaration. I really, though most strangely, believed that it was an act of friendliness to all America to recognise that the struggle was virtually at an end. I was not one of those who on the ground of British interests desired a division of the American Union. My view was distinctly opposite. I thought that while the Union continued it never could exercise any dangerous pressure upon Canada to estrange it from the empire—our honour, as I thought, rather than our interest forbidding its surrender. But were the Union split, the North, no longer checked by the jealousies of slave-power, would seek a partial compensation for its loss in annexing, or trying to annex, British North America. Lord Palmerston desired the severance as a diminution of a dangerous power, but prudently held his tongue.

That my opinion was founded upon a false estimate of the facts was the very least part of my fault. I did not perceive the gross impropriety of such an utterance from a cabinet minister, of a power allied in blood and language, and bound to loyal neutrality; the case being further exaggerated by the fact that we were already, so to speak, under indictment before the world for not (as was alleged) having strictly enforced the laws of neutrality in the matter of the cruisers. My offence was indeed only a mistake, but one of incredible grossness, and with such consequences of offence and alarm attached to it, that my failing to perceive them justly exposed me to very severe blame. It illustrates vividly that incapacity which my mind so long retained, and perhaps still exhibits, an incapacity of viewing subjects all round, in their extraneous as well as in their internal properties, and thereby of knowing when to be silent and when to speak.

I am the more pained and grieved, because I have for the last five-and-twenty years received from the government and people of America tokens of goodwill which could not fail to arouse my undying gratitude. When we came to the arbitration at Geneva, my words were cited as part of the proof of hostile *animus*. Meantime I had prepared a lengthened statement to show from my abundant declarations on other occasions that there was and could be on my part no such *animus*. I was desirous to present this statement to the arbitrators. My colleagues objected so largely to the proceeding that I desisted. In this I think they probably were wrong. I addressed my paper to the American minister for the information of his government, and Mr. Secretary Fish gave me, so far as intention was concerned, a very handsome acquittal.

And strange to say, *post hoc* though perhaps not *propter hoc*, the United States have been that country of the world in which the most signal marks of public honour have been paid me, and in which my name has been the most popular, the only parallels being Italy, Greece, and the Balkan Peninsula.

—MORLEY, *The Life of William Ewart Gladstone*

10. JOHN BRIGHT DEPLORES THE POLICY OF HIS GOVERNMENT

Cobden, Forster, and Bright were the triumvirate who fought most effectively for the cause of the North, and of the three it was the Quaker Bright whose influence went farthest. Perhaps the greatest figure in the nineteenth-century reform movement in Britain, Bright had fought and triumphed against the Corn Laws, espoused religious, humanitarian, and electoral reform, opposed the Crimean War, and now championed the Union, in and out of Parliament. Henry Adams thought that in the House itself Forster was a more effective advocate of the Union cause, but with the country at large it was Bright's eloquent voice that had greatest influence.

Here is a letter from Bright to his friend Charles Sumner written just three days after Gladstone's "vile" speech.

Llandudno, North Wales, October 10, 1862

DEAR MR. SUMNER,—I was very glad to receive your last letter containing much interesting information on the cotton question. I sent it and the letters, or copies of letters it contained to Mr. Cobden. It is quite clear that your Government was right in not sending an expedition to Texas, when it was a question whether it could keep a footing in Virginia.

I write to you from a feeling of anxiety. You will see what is being said here by public men who speak on your question, and most of all, and worst of all, by your old acquaintance and friend, Mr. Gladstone. He has made a vile speech at Newcastle, full of insulting pity for the North, and of praise and support for the South. He is unstable as water in some things. He is for union and freedom in Italy, and for disunion and bondage in America. A handful of Italians in prison in Naples, without formal trial, shocked his soul so much that he wrote a pamphlet, and has made many speeches upon it; but he has no word of sympathy or of hope for the four millions of the bondsmen of the South! I have known for months past that he talked of an European remonstrance, or mediation, or recognition, or some mischief of that kind, but I did not expect that he would step out openly as the defender and eulogist of Jeff. Davis and his fellow conspirators against God and man. He has spoken, as you will see by the time you receive this, and what he has said will encourage the friends of the South here to encreased exertions to promote something hostile to your Government and people. Palmerston and Russell, I fear, will not need much pressure to induce them to do anything they dare do on behalf of the permanent disruption of your Union.

Now, if I may trouble you again, I want you to write fully and frankly to me, that I may know what is possible and what is likely. If the "proclamation" means anything it means that you will preserve the Union, even tho' it involve a social revolution in the South and the transformation of four millions of slaves into as many laborers and peasants. If you destroy the armed force of the South still you will have a population deeply exasperated and disloyal, and government in their States must be difficult if not impossible. If the black nation can be made a population for the Union, then to hold the South may not be impossible; but without them, I see immeasurable difficulties in your path. Is the North prepared for all the hazards and for all the confusion which for a time such a course may render inevitable; and will the Government be thoroughly supported by all the free States in such a policy? I conclude from the fact that the New York Herald has not dared to condemn the proclamation, that it meets with the support of your people. If the border States should not take fright at it, it seems to me calculated to be a powerful lever in future operations against the revolt. On these points we have, as yet, scarcely received any information, and I look for further tidings with great anxiety.

. . . I talk with men daily, and try to influence opinion in favor of the right; and before long I may have to speak in public on its behalf. I want you to tell me, if you can what I may hope for, and what I may believe, that I may have my faith corrected or strengthened. Will the North persist? Will it grapple with the slavery devil and strangle it? May I believe that your country will be held together?

I begin to believe that another crop of cotton from slave labor will never again be grown on your Northern continent. Terribly as this would make me and mine and multitudes here to suffer, I cannot wish it otherwise. . . .

John Bright

Surely that childish project of removing the black people from America will cease to be talked about. It damages the character of your President and Government.

—Letter from John Bright to Charles Sumner

11. THE ENGLISH PRESS CONDEMNS THE EMANCIPATION PROCLAMATION

It is commonly believed that it was the Emancipation Proclamation that turned the tide of opinion in Britain. There is some truth in this, for that proclamation gave the war a new character. It was no longer a war for Union alone or—as the opposition called it—for Empire. Now it was also a war for Freedom. It is of some interest, however, to note that the immediate reaction of a substantial part of the English press was decidedly hostile to the Proclamation and to the policy which it announced.

We have been able to include here merely two of the many critical editorials on the Proclamation. The first is from the Times, *the most powerful paper in Britain and perhaps in the world; the second from* Blackwood's Edinburgh Magazine.

A. "This Is a Very Sad Document"

IT is rarely that a man can be found to balance accurately mischief to another against advantage to himself. President Lincoln is, as the world says, a good-tempered man, neither better nor worse than the mass of his kind— neither a fool nor a sage, neither a villain nor a saint, but a piece of that common useful clay out of which it delights the American democracy to make great Republican personages. Yet President Lincoln has declared that from the 1st of January next to come every State that is in rebellion shall be, in the eye of Mr. Lincoln, a Free State. After that date Mr. Lincoln proposes to enact that every slave in a rebel State shall be for ever after free, and he promises that neither he, nor his army, nor his navy will do anything to repress *any* efforts which the Negroes in such rebel States may make for the recovery of their freedom.

This means, of course, that Mr. Lincoln will, on the 1st of next January, do his best to excite a servile war in the States which he cannot occupy with his arms. He will run up the rivers in his gunboats; he will seek out the places which are left but slightly guarded, and where the women and children have been trusted to the fidelity of coloured domestics. He will appeal to the black blood of the African; he will whisper of the pleasures of spoil and of the gratification of yet fiercer instincts; and when blood begins to flow and shrieks come piercing through the darkness, Mr. Lincoln will wait till the rising flames tell that all is consummated, and then he will rub his hands and think that revenge is sweet. This is what Mr. Lincoln avows before the world that he is about to do.

Now, we are in Europe thoroughly convinced that the death of slavery must follow as necessarily upon the success of the Confederates in this war as the dispersion of darkness occurs upon the rising of the sun; but sudden and forcible emancipation resulting from "the efforts the Negroes may make for their actual freedom" can only be effected by massacre and utter destruction. Mr. Lincoln avows, therefore, that he proposes to excite the Negroes of the Southern plantations to murder the families of their masters while these are engaged in the war. The conception of such a crime is horrible. The employment of Indians sinks to a level with civilized warfare in comparison with it; the most detestable doctrines of Mazzini are almost less atrocious; even Mr. Lincoln's own recent achievements of burning by gunboats the defenceless villages on the Mississippi are dwarfed by this gigantic wickedness. The single thing to be said for it is that it is a wickedness that holds its head high and scorns hypocrisy. It does not pretend to attack slavery as slavery. It launches this threat of a servile rebellion as a means of war against certain

States, and accompanies it with a declaration of general protection to all other slavery.

Where he has no power Mr. Lincoln will set the Negroes free; where he retains power he will consider them as slaves. "Come to me," he cries to the insurgent planters, "and I will preserve your rights as slaveholders; but set me still at defiance, and I will wrap myself in virtue, and take the sword of freedom in my hand, and, instead of aiding you to oppress, I will champion the rights of humanity. Here are whips for you who are loyal; go forth and flog or sell your black chattels as you please. Here are torches and knives for employment against you who are disloyal; I will press them into every black hand, and teach their use." Little Delaware, with her 2000 slaves, shall still be protected in her loyal tyranny. Maryland, with her 90,000 slaves, shall "freely accept or freely reject" any project for either gradual or immediate abolition; but if Mississippi and South Carolina, where the slaves rather outnumber the masters, do not repent, and receive from Mr. Lincoln a licence to trade in human flesh, that human flesh shall be adopted by Mr. Lincoln as the agent of his vengeance. The position is peculiar for a mere layman. Mr. Lincoln, by this proclamation, constitutes himself a sort of moral American Pope. He claims to sell indulgences to own votaries, and he offers them with full hands to all who will fall down and worship him. It is his to bind, and it is his to loose. His decree of emancipation is to go into remote States, where his temporal power cannot be made manifest, and where no stars and stripes are to be seen; and in those distant swamps he is, by a sort of Yankee excommunication, to lay the land under a slavery interdict. . . .

As a proof of what the leaders of the North, in their passion and their despair, would do if they could, this is a very sad document. As a proof of the hopelessness and recklessness which prompt their actions, it is a very instructive document. We gather from it that Mr. Lincoln has lost all hope of preserving the Union, and is now willing to let any quack try his nostrum. As an act of policy it is, if possible, more contemptible than it is wicked. It may possibly produce some partial risings, for let any armed power publish an exhortation to the labouring class of any community to plunder and murder, and there will be some response. It might happen in London, or Paris, or New York. That Mr. Lincoln's emancipation decrees will have any general effect bearing upon the issue of the war, we do not, however, believe. The Negroes have already abundantly discovered that the tender mercies of the Northerners are cruelties. The freedom which is associated with labour in the trenches, military discipline, and frank avowals of personal abhorrence momentarily repeated does not commend itself to the Negro nature. General Butler could, if he pleased, tell strange stories of the ill success of his tamperings with the Negroes about New Orleans.

We do not think that even now, when Mr. Lincoln plays his last card, it will prove to be a trump. Powerful malignity is a dreadful reality, but impotent malignity is apt to be a very contemptible spectacle. Here is a would-be conqueror and a would-be extirpator who is not quite safe in his seat of government, who is reduced to such straits that he accepts a defeat as a glorious escape, a capitulation of 8000 men as an unimportant event, a drawn battle as a glorious victory, and the retreat of an invading army which retires laden with plunder and rich in stores as a deliverance. Here is a President who has just, against his will, supplied his antagonists with a hundred and twenty guns and millions of stores, and who is trembling for the very ground on which he stands. Yet, if we judged only by his pompous proclamations, we should believe that he had a garrison in every city of the South. This is more like a Chinaman beating his two swords together to frighten his enemy than like an earnest man pressing on his cause in steadfastness and truth.

—*The Times*, October 7, 1862

B. "Monstrous, Reckless, Devilish"

The past month has brought us to the veritable crisis of the great civil war in America. Brought to bay upon their own soil, the Federals in desperation have invoked to their aid the unutterable horrors of a servile war. With their armies baffled and beaten, and with the standards of the rebel army again within sight of Washington, the President has at length owned the impossibility of success in fair warfare, and seeks to paralyse the victorious armies of the South by letting loose upon their hearths and homes the lust and savagery of four million Negroes. The die is cast. Henceforth it is a war of extermination. The North seeks to make of the South a desert—a wilderness of bloodshed and misery; for thus only, now, does it or can it hope to overcome the seceding Confederacy.

Monstrous, reckless, devilish as the project is, we believe it will not succeed. But it at least marks the crisis and turning-point of the war. It shows that the North has shot its last bolt,—the effects of which we do not yet see, but beyond which there is no other. It proves what every one in this country was loth to believe, that rather than let the Southern States be independent, rather than lose their trade and custom, the North would league itself with Beelzebub, and seek to make a hell of half a continent. In return, this atrocious act justifies the South in hoisting the black flag, and in proclaiming a war without quarter against the Yankee hosts. And thus, within the bosom of civilisation, we are called upon to contemplate a war more full of horrors and wickedness than any which stands recorded in the world's history.

When a crisis so manifest and so terrible has been reached in this most melancholy of all civil wars, it is natural that at least something like a crisis should arise amongst the slow-moving minds of her Majesty's Ministers. If they cannot yet agree to act upon their opinions, each member of the Cabinet, we should think, must at least have arrived at some definite opinion of his own. Three weeks ago it was rumoured that before the end of the month Lord Lyons would return to his post at Washington, bearing with him the definite decision of her Majesty's Government. Simultaneously, or immediately in the wake of this rumour, there came Mr Gladstone's speech at Newcastle, where, amid the applause of his audience, he declared that the people of the Southern States were now to be regarded as a NATION. . . .

When Mr Gladstone spoke thus, so plainly and so strongly, it seemed as if the previous rumours were correct, and that before the month was ended the Southern Confederacy would be officially recognised by the British Government as an independent State. But in a few days more, another member of the Cabinet—as is not unusual with that eminently harmonious body—declared himself of an entirely different opinion. . . .

In a moral point of view, there cannot be two opinions in this country as to the President's proclamation. To employ such a means of hostility as a Negro insurrection is simply infamous. In a political point of view we regard it as the greatest mistake which the North has committed. True, the policy of the North has been slowly approximating to this result: it is a natural climax to the mad policy which has animated the North from the beginning. It is the consummation of the mistakes of the North. Union in any shape is now doubly impossible. It remains to be seen, also, whether the temporary accord which the proclamation has established in the North is not on the surface only, and whether the present lull of dissension will not give way ere long to dissensions still more formidable. In the border States of Kentucky, Tennessee, and Missouri, the proclamation cannot fail to excite new and formidable opposition to the Federal Government; while the Confederate States, now menaced with untold horrors, will put forth their whole strength to keep the danger at a distance, and to roll back the war from their frontiers with the fury of desperation.

—*Blackwood's Edinburgh Magazine*, November 1862

12. MANCHESTER WORKINGMEN STAND BY THE UNION

One of the moving and—as it has turned out—one of the historic interchanges of Anglo-American history came when the workingmen of Manchester, most of them thrown out of work by the cotton shortage, addressed a letter to President Lincoln assuring him of their support now that the war was clearly directed to the abolition of slavery. Lincoln's reply was one of his most felicitous efforts.

A. "WE ARE TRULY ONE PEOPLE"

December 31, 1862

To Abraham Lincoln, President of the United States:

As citizens of Manchester, assembled at the Free-Trade Hall, we beg to express our fraternal sentiments toward you and your country. We rejoice in your greatness as an outgrowth of England, whose blood and language you share, whose orderly and legal freedom you have applied to new circumstances, over a region immeasurably greater than our own. We honor your Free States, as a singularly happy abode for the working millions where industry is honored. One thing alone has, in the past, lessened our sympathy with your country and our confidence in it—we mean the ascendency of politicians who not merely maintained Negro slavery, but desired to extend and root it more firmly.

Since we have discerned, however, that the victory of the free North, in the war which has so sorely distressed us as well as afflicted you, will strike off the fetters of the slave, you have attracted our warm and earnest sympathy. We joyfully honor you, as the President, and the Congress with you, for many decisive steps toward practically exemplifying your belief in the words of your great founders: "All men are created free and equal." You have procured the liberation of the slaves in the district around Washington, and thereby made the centre of your Federation visibly free. You have enforced the laws against the slave-trade, and kept up your fleet against it, even while every ship was wanted for service in your terrible war. You have nobly decided to receive ambassadors from the Negro republics of Hayti and Liberia, thus forever renouncing that unworthy prejudice which refuses the rights of humanity to men and women on account of their color. In order more effectually to stop the slave-trade, you have made with our Queen a treaty, which your Senate has ratified, for the right of mutual search. Your Congress has decreed freedom as the law forever in the vast unoccupied or half unsettled Territories which are directly subject to its legislative power. It has offered pecuniary aid to all States which will enact emancipation locally, and has forbidden your Generals to restore fugitive slaves who seek their protection. You have entreated the slave-masters to accept these moderate offers; and after long and patient waiting, you, as Commander-in-Chief of the Army, have appointed to-morrow, the first of January, 1863, as the day of unconditional freedom for the slaves of the rebel States.

Heartily do we congratulate you and your country on this humane and righteous course. We assume that you cannot now stop short of a complete uprooting of slavery. It would not become us to dictate any details, but there are broad principles of humanity which must guide you. If complete emancipation in some States be deferred, though only to a predetermined day, still in the interval, human beings should not be counted chattels. Women must have the rights of chastity and maternity, men the rights of husbands, masters the liberty of manumission. Justice demands for the black, no less than for the white, the protection of law—that his voice be heard in your courts. Nor must any such abomination be tolerated as slave-breeding States, and a slave market—if you are to earn the high reward of all your sacrifices, in the approval of the universal brotherhood and of the Divine Father. It is for your free country to decide whether any thing but immediate and total emancipation can secure the most indispensable rights of humanity against the inveterate wickedness of local laws and local executives.

We implore you, for your own honor and welfare, not to faint in your providential mission. While your enthusiasm is aflame, and the tide of events runs high, let the work be finished effectually. Leave no root of bitterness to spring up and work fresh misery to your children. It is a mighty task, indeed, to reörganize the industry not only of four millions of the colored race, but of five millions of whites. Nevertheless, the vast progress you have made in the short space of twenty months fills us with hope that every stain on your freedom will shortly be removed, and that the erasure of that foul blot upon civilization and Christianity—chattel slavery—during your Presidency will cause the name of Abraham Lincoln to be honored and revered by posterity. We are certain that such a glorious consummation will cement Great Britain to the United States in close and enduring regards. Our interests, moreover, are identified with yours. We are truly one people, though locally separate. And if you have any ill-wishers here, be assured they are chiefly those who oppose liberty at home, and that they will be powerless to stir up quarrels between us, from the very day in which your country becomes, undeniably and without exception, the home of the free.

Accept our high admiration of your firmness in upholding the proclamation of freedom.

—MOORE, ed., *The Rebellion Record*

B. "AN INSTANCE OF SUBLIME CHRISTIAN HEROISM"

January 19, 1863

To the Working-Men of Manchester:

I have the honor to acknowledge the receipt of the address and resolutions which you sent me on the eve of the new year. When I came, on the 4th of March, 1861, through a free and constitutional election to preside in the Government of the United States, the country was found at the verge of civil war. Whatever might have been the cause, or whosoever the fault, one duty, paramount to all others, was before me, namely, to maintain and preserve at once the Constitution and the integrity of the Federal Republic. A conscientious purpose to perform this duty is the key to all the measures of administration which have been and to all which will hereafter be pursued. Under our frame of government and my official oath, I could not depart from this purpose if I would. It is not always in the power of governments to enlarge or restrict the scope of moral results which follow the policies that they may deem it necessary for the public safety from time to time to adopt.

I have understood well that the duty of self-preservation rests solely with the American people; but I have at the same time been aware that favor or disfavor of foreign nations might have a material influence in enlarging or prolonging the struggle with disloyal men in which the country is engaged. A fair examination of history has served to authorize a belief that the past actions and influences of the United States were generally regarded as having been beneficial toward mankind. I have, therefore, reckoned upon the forbearance of nations. Circumstances—to some of which you kindly allude—induce me especially to expect that if justice and good faith should be practised by the United States, they would encounter no hostile influence on the part of Great Britain. It is now a pleasant duty to acknowledge the demonstration you have given of your desire that a spirit of amity and peace toward this country may prevail in the councils of your Queen, who is respected and esteemed in your own country only more than she is by the kindred nation which has its home on this side of the Atlantic.

I know and deeply deplore the sufferings which the working-men at Manchester, and in all Europe, are called to endure in this crisis. It has been often and studiously represented that the attempt to overthrow this government, which was built upon the foundation of human rights, and to substitute for it one which should rest exclusively on the basis of human slavery, was likely to obtain the favor of Europe. Through the action of our disloyal citizens, the working-men of Europe have been subjected to severe trials, for the purpose of forcing their sanction to that attempt. Under the circumstances, I cannot but regard your decisive utterances upon the question as an instance of sublime Christian heroism which has not been surpassed in any age or in any country. It is indeed an energetic and reinspiring assurance of the inherent power of truth and of the ultimate and universal triumph of justice, humanity, and freedom. I do not doubt that the sentiments you have expressed will be sustained by your great nation; and on the other hand, I have no hesitation in assuring you that they will excite admiration, esteem, and the most reciprocal feelings of friendship among the American people. I hail this interchange of sentiment, therefore, as an augury that whatever else may happen, whatever misfortune may befall your country or my own, the peace and friendship which now exist between the two nations will be, as it shall be my desire to make them, perpetual.

Abraham Lincoln.
—*Complete Works of Abraham Lincoln*

13. "COUNT" GUROWSKI RAGES AGAINST THE ENGLISH

Every student of the Civil War knows the venomous Gurowski Diary, but few use it, for it is highly unreliable. It is, however, reliable enough as a reflection of personal opinion, and it is as such that excerpts from it are included here.

Count Adam Gurowski—the propriety of his title was always a little dubious—was born in the Palatinate of Kaliz in Poland, and by his twentieth year had been expelled for revolutionary activities. He returned to Poland to help organize a revolution against Russia and on the failure of that uprising fled to Paris where he was condemned to death in absentia. He wrote on Polish history, studied at Berlin and Heidelberg, lectured at the University of Berne, and in 1849 came to the United States. During the Civil War he served as a translator in the State Department, and from this unsatisfactory vantage point watched what he considered the mismanagement of the war. He was particularly bitter about British official policy, and in this he reflected faithfully enough a considerable segment of American opinion. The Decembrist to whom Gurowski refers is, of course, Louis Napoleon, who came to power through the coup of December 1851. Gurowski is at his worst in this Diary; he is at his uncertain best in his perceptive America and Europe.

Dec. 7 [1862].—The European wiseacres, the would-be statesmen, whether in or out of power, especially in England, and that opprobrium of our century, the English and the Franco-Bonapartist press, have decided to do all that their clever brains can scheme towards preventing this noble American people from working out its mighty and beneficent destinies, and from elaborating and making more glorious than ever its own already very glorious history. As well might the brainless and heartless conspirators against human progress and human liberty endeavor to arrest the rotation of a planet by the stroke of a pickaxe.

Dec. 30.—Those foreign caterwaulings against Butler. England, in 1848-9, whipped women in Ireland, and how many thousands have been murdered by the *Decembriseur?* And the Russian minister joining in this music. A shame for him and for his government!

Dec. 30.—Poor Greeley looks for intervention, mediation, arbitration; and selects Switzerland for the fitting arbitrator! How little—nay—nothing at all, he knows about Switzerland and the Swiss! Stop! stop! respectable old man!

Jan. 5 [1863].—European rulers, wiseacres, meddlers, humbugs, traitors, demons, diplomats, assert that they must interfere here because European interests suffer by the war. Indeed! You have the whole old continent and Australia to boot, and about nine hundreds millions of population; can you not organise yourself so as not to depend from us? And if by your misrules, etc., our interests were to suffer, you would find very strange any complaint made on our part. Keep aloof with your good wishes, and with your advices, and with your interference. You may burn your noses, and even lose your little scalps. You robbers, murderers, hypocrites, surrounded by your liveried lackeys, you presumptuous, arrogant curses of the human race, stand off, and let these people whose worst criminal is a saint compared to a *Decembriseur*—let this people work out its destinies, be it for good or evil.

January 15.—The noble and lofty voice of the genuine English people, the voice of the working classes, begins to be heard. The people re-echo the key-note struck by a J. S. Mills, by a Bright, a Cobden, and others of like pure mind and noble heart. The voice of the genuine English people resounds altogether differently from the shrill *falsetto* with which turf hunters, rent-roll devourers, lords, lordlings, and all the like shams and whelps try to intimidate the patriotic North, and comfort the traitors, the rebels.

January 16.— . . . Sumner will believe that his letters to English old women will change the minds of the English semi-pirates. Sumner is a little afraid of losing ground with the English guardians of civilization. Sumner is full of good wishes, of generous conceptions, and is the man for the millennium. Sumner lacks the keen, sharp, piercing appreciation of common events. And thus Sumner cannot detect that England makes war on our commerce, under the piratic flag of the rebels.

April 2.—Official, lordish, Toryish England, plays treason and infamy right and left. The English money lenders to rebels, the genuine owners of rebel piratical ships, are anxious to destroy the American commerce and to establish over the South an English monopoly. All this because *odiunt dum metuant* the Yankee. You tories, you enemies of freedom, your time of reckoning will come, and it will come at the hands of your own people. You fear the example of America for your oppressions, for your rent-rolls.

April 6.—The people feel how the treason of the English evil wishers slowly extends through its organs. By Butler, Wade, Grimes and others, the people ask for non-intercourse with the English assassin, who surreptitiously, stealthily under cover of darkness, of legal formality, deals, or attempts to deal, a deadly blow. The American sentimentalists strain to the utmost their soft brains, to find excuses for English treason.

English lordlings, scholars, moralists of the Carlyleian mental perversion comment Homer, instead of being clear sighted commentators of what passes under their noses. The English phrase-mongering philanthropists all with joy smacked their bloody lips at the, by them ardently wished and expected downfall of a noble, free and self-governing people. Tigers, hyenas and jackals! clatter your teeth, smack your lips! but you shall not get at the prey.

—Gurowski, *Diary*

14. RICHARD COBDEN REJOICES IN THE EMANCIPATION PROCLAMATION

Cobden, with Bright, was the leader of the English liberals in the mid-nineteenth century. A wealthy manufacturer, he abandoned business to agitate against the Corn Laws and was chiefly instrumental in obtaining their repeal. In Parliament he proved an eloquent spokesman for liberal and humanitarian causes, strongly opposing the Crimean War, intervention in China, and espousing, like Bright, free trade and electoral reform. Twice offered posts in the Cabinet, he twice refused. Worn out with his public labors Cobden died in 1865, but not before he had rendered signal service to the cause of Anglo-American unity; it is not an accident that the Carnegie Endowment has made Cobden's birthplace, Dunford House, an international shrine.

This letter, like Bright's, is addressed to Charles Sumner.

Athenaeum Club, London, 13 Feby., 1863

Private

My dear Sumner.

If I have not written to you before it is not because I have been indifferent to what is passing in your midst. I may say sincerely that my thoughts have run almost as much on American as English politics. But I could do you no service, and shrunk from occupying your overtaxed attention even for a moment. My object in now writing is to speak of a matter which has a practical bearing on your affairs.

You know how much alarmed I was from the first lest our government should interpose in your affairs. The disposition of our ruling class, and the necessities of our cotton trade, pointed to some act of intervention and the indifference of the great mass of our population to your struggle, the object of which they did not foresee and understand, would have made intervention easy indeed popular if you had been a weaker naval power. This state of feeling existed up to the announcement of the President's emancipation Policy. From that moment our old anti-slavery feeling began to arouse itself, and it has been gathering strength ever since. The great rush of the public to all the public meetings called on the subject shows how wide and deep the sympathy for personal freedom still is in the hearts of our people. I know nothing in my political experience so striking as a display of spontaneous public action as that of the vast gathering at Exeter Hall when without one attraction in the form of a popular orator the vast building, its minor rooms and passages and the streets adjoining were crowded with an enthusiastic audience. That meeting has had a powerful effect on our newspapers and politicians. It has closed the mouths of those who have been advocating the side of the South.

And I now write to assure you that any unfriendly act on the part of our government, no matter which of our aristocratic parties is in power, towards your cause is not to be apprehended. If an attempt were made by the government in any way to commit us to the South, a spirit would be instantly aroused which would drive our government from power. This I suppose will be known and felt by the Southern agents in Europe and if communicated to their government must I should think operate as a great discouragement to them. For I *know* that those agents have been incessantly urging in every quarter where they could hope to influence the French and English governments the absolute necessity of *recognition* as a means of putting an end to the war. Recognition of the South, by England, whilst it bases itself on Negro slavery, is an impossibility, unless indeed after the Federal government have recognized the Confederates as a nation.

So much for the influence which your emancipation policy has had on the public opinion of England. But judging from the tone of your press in America it does not seem to have gained the support of your masses. About this however I do not feel competent to offer an opinion. Nor, to confess the truth, do I feel much satisfaction in treating of your politics at all. There appears to me great mismanagement I had almost said incapacity in the management of your affairs, and you seem to be hastening towards financial and economical evils in a manner which fills me with apprehension for the future.

When I met Fremont in Paris two years ago just as you commenced this terrible war I remarked to him that the total abolition of slavery in your northern Continent was the only issue which could justify the war to the civilized world. Every symptom seems to point to this result. But at what a price is the Negro to be emancipated! I confess that if then I had been the arbiter of his fate I should have refused him freedom at the cost of so much white men's blood and women's tears. I do not however blame the North. The South fired the first shot, and on them righteously falls the malediction that "they who take the sword shall perish by the sword." Believe me,

Yours very truly

R. COBDEN

—E. L. PIERCE, contrib., "Letters of Richard Cobden to Charles Sumner"

15. ENGLISH ARISTOCRATS ORGANIZE FOR SOUTHERN INDEPENDENCE

The mediation crisis of 1862 had been successfully surmounted by An-tietam, and by the Emancipation Proclamation. Yet the Confederate cause appeared by no means hopeless, and agitation for some form of intervention persisted. More and more, however, that agitation took on a class character; it was supported by the aristocracy and the great shipbuilders and textile manufacturers. A London Confederate States Aid Association had been or-ganized in 1862, but had died a lingering death. Early in 1863 it was sup-planted by a Southern Independence Association, whose Constitution we reproduce here. The most interesting thing about this otherwise curious organization is its list of sponsors. It appealed, as the Index *pointed out, to "persons of rank and gentlemen of standing." It was this association that called forth Goldwin Smith's devastating "Letter to a Whig Member," one of the most powerful of all defenses of the Union cause.*

SOUTHERN INDEPENDENCE ASSOCIATION OF LONDON

Public opinion is becoming enlightened upon the disruption of the late United States, and upon the character of the war which has been raging on the American continent for nearly three years. British subjects were at first hardly able to realize a federation of States each in itself possessed of sover-eign attributes; while deriving their views of American history from New York and New England, they ascribed the secession of the Southern States to pique at a lost election, and to fear for the continuance of an institution peculiarly distasteful to Englishmen. Assurances were rife from those quar-ters that the movement was the conspiracy of a few daring men, and that a strong Union sentiment existed in the seceding States, which would soon assert its existence under stress of the war.

Gradually the true causes of the disruption have made themselves more and more manifest. The long-widening and now insuperable divergence of character and interests between the two sections of the former Union has been made palpable by the facts of the gigantic struggle. Their wisdom in council, their endurance in the field, and the universal self-sacrifice which has characterized their public and their private life, have won general sym-pathy for the Confederates as a people worthy of, and who have earned, their independence.

On the other hand, the favorable judgment which Englishmen had long cherished as a duty towards that portion of the United States which they imagined most to resemble the Mother Country has met with many rude shocks from the spectacles which have been revealed in that land of governmental tyranny, corruption in high places, ruthlessness in war, untruthfulness of speech, and causeless animosity towards Great Britain. At the same time the Southerners, who had been very harshly judged in this country, have manifested the highest national characteristics, to the surprise and admiration of all.

Public men are awakening to the truth that it is both useless and mischievous to ignore the gradual settlement of Central North America into groups of States, or consolidated nationalities, each an independent Power. They feel that the present attempt of the North is in manifest opposition to this law of natural progress, and they see that the South can never be reunited with the North except as a conquered and garrisoned dependency; whilst the Northern States, if content to leave their former partners alone, are still in possession of all the elements of great and growing national power and wealth.

Our commercial classes are also beginning to perceive that our best interests will be promoted by creating a direct trade with a people so enterprising as the Confederates, inhabiting a land so wide and so abundant in the richest gifts of Providence, and anxious to place themselves in immediate connection with the manufacturers and consumers of Europe.

In short, the struggle is now felt to be, according to Earl Russell's pregnant expression, one for independence on the part of the South, and for empire on the part of the North; for an independence, on the one hand, which it is equitable for themselves and desirable for the world they should achieve; for an empire, on the other hand, which is only possible at the price of the first principles of Federal Republicanism, and whose establishment by fire and sword, and at a countless cost of human life on both sides, would be the ruin of the Southern States. These, surely, are reasons which invoke the intervention of other Powers, if intervention be possible, in the cause of common humanity.

Therefore, not in enmity to the North, but sympathizing with the Confederates, the Southern Independence Association of London has been formed, to act in concert with that which is so actively and usefully at work in Manchester. . . .

The Association will also devote itself to the cultivation of friendly feelings between the people of Great Britain and of the Confederate States; and it will, in particular, steadily but kindly represent to the Southern States that recognition by Europe must necessarily lead to a revision of the system of servile labor unhappily bequeathed to them by England, in accordance with the spirit of the age, so as to combine the gradual extinction of slavery with the preservation of property, the maintenance of the civil polity, and the true civilization of the Negro race.

> The Most Noble the Marquis of Lothian
> The Most Noble the Marquis of Bath
> The Lord Robert Cecil, M.P.

The Lord Eustace Cecil
The Right Honourable Lord Wharncliffe
The Right Honourable Lord Campbell
The Hon. C. Fitzwilliam, M.P.
The Honourable Robt. Bourke
Edward Akroyd, Esq., Halifax
Colonel Greville, M.P.
W. H. Gregory, Esq. M.P.
T. C. Haliburton, Esq. M.P.
A. J. B. Beresford Hope, Esq.
W. S. Lindsay, Esq. M.P.
Wm. Scholefield, Esq. M.P.
James Spence, Esq., Liverpool
William Vansittart, Esq. M.P.
—Goldwin Smith, *Letter to a Whig Member*

16. MINISTER ADAMS POINTS OUT THAT THIS IS WAR

The last diplomatic crisis between Britain and the United States threatened to be the most serious. As early as 1861 the Confederate government had dispatched Captain Bulloch to England to contract for the construction of commerce-destroyers in British shipyards. English law, and the Proclamation of Neutrality, forbade this, but it was relatively easy to evade the prohibition by juggling the ownership papers.

Thus the Confederates were able to build the Florida *and the* Alabama *in England; the subsequent depredations of these ships laid the basis for the* Alabama *claims. That the* Alabama *was being built for the Confederacy was common knowledge, but when Adams protested it, he was met with the assertion that there was no legal proof of Confederate ownership!*

Even more serious was the Confederate plan to build ironclad rams in British yards. Contracts for these were placed with the Laird brothers, for delivery in the summer of 1863, and construction was soon under way at Birkenhead. If these should get away the prospects for American commerce were black; there were no United States ships that could stand up to them and, as Captain Gustavus Fox, Assistant Secretary of the Navy, wrote, "it is a question of life and death." Adams took energetic action, laying before Russell evidence of Confederate ownership. Russell was not satisfied, and Adams supplied him with additional evidence, which he found only partly persuasive.

Meantime other influences were more persuasive. One was the Congressional Act of March 1863 authorizing Lincoln to issue letters of marque to merchantmen: the victims would obviously be English vessels. Another was the combination of Gettysburg and Vicksburg.

On September 3 Russell ordered the ironclads to be detained. Adams did not know this, and two days later he sent this famous letter with its somewhat ambiguous threat of war. The letter was not essential, but it helped. In

October the ironclads were seized by the British government, and subsequently purchased and commissioned in the British Navy.

*This was the last episode that seriously troubled Anglo-American relations
during the war. The combination of Union success on the battlefields and in
the coastal waters and of the Emancipation policy persuaded the British
government to a far more friendly attitude toward the North. The one
thing that continued to exacerbate the relations of the two countries was the
ravages of the cruisers* Alabama, Shenandoah *and* Florida. *After the war
(1872) the* Alabama *Claims Commission found the British government remiss
in allowing these ships to escape and required Britain to pay the United States
damages of fifteen and one-half million dollars.*

Legation of the United States, London, September 5, 1863

My Lord,

At this moment, when one of the iron-clad war-vessels is on the point
of departure from this kingdom on its hostile errand against the United
States, I am honoured with the reply of your Lordship to my notes of the
11th, 16th, and 25th of July and of the 14th of August. I trust I need not
express how profound is my regret at the conclusion to which Her Majesty's
Government have arrived. I can regard it no otherwise than as practically
opening to the insurgents free liberty in this kingdom to execute a policy
described in one of their late publications in the following language:—

"In the present state of the harbour-defences of New York, Boston,
Portland, and smaller Northern cities, such a vessel as the 'Warrior' would
have little difficulty in entering any of those ports, and inflicting a vital
blow upon the enemy, The destruction of Boston alone would be worth a
hundred victories in the field. It would bring such a terror to the 'blue-noses'
as to cause them to wish eagerly for peace, despite their overweening love of
gain which has been so freely administered to since the opening of this war.
Vessels of the 'Warrior' class would promptly raise the blockade of our ports,
and would, even in this respect, confer advantages which would soon repay
the cost of their construction."

It would be superfluous in me to point out to your Lordship that this is
war. No matter what may be the theory adopted of neutrality in a struggle,
when this process is carried on in the manner indicated from a territory and
with the aid of the subjects of a third party, that third party, to all intents
and purposes, ceases to be neutral. Neither is it necessary to show that any
Government which suffers it to be done fails in enforcing the essential conditions of international amity towards the country against whom the hostility
is directed. In my belief it is impossible that any nation retaining a proper
degree of self-respect could tamely submit to a continuance of relations so
utterly deficient in reciprocity. I have no idea that Great Britain would do
so for a moment.

After a careful examination of the full instructions with which I have
been furnished in preparation for such an emergency, I deem it inexpedient
for me to attempt any recurrence to arguments for effective interposition in

the present case. The fatal objection of impotency which paralyzes Her Majesty's Government seems to present an insuperable barrier against all further reasoning. Under these circumstances I prefer to desist from communicating to your Lordship even such further portions of my existing instructions as are suited to the case, lest I should contribute to aggravate difficulties already far too serious. I therefore content myself with informing your Lordship that I transmit by the present steamer a copy of your note for the consideration of my Government, and shall await the more specific directions that will be contained in the reply.

CHARLES FRANCIS ADAMS
—State Papers, North America

XVI

Songs the Soldiers Sang

It is *no accident that the motorized armies of the First and Second World Wars inspired so few songs, and sang so few. The Civil War armies were not mechanized; soldiers marched afoot, and as they marched they sang. No other war has provided us with so many songs, or so many that have retained their popularity for so long—marching songs like "Tramp, Tramp, Tramp," inspirational songs like "The Battle Hymn of the Republic," patriotic songs like "Bonnie Blue Flag," humorous songs like "Goober Peas," sentimental songs like "Lorena."*

There was little organized entertainment in the Civil War—the Sanitary Commission had other things to do than entertain soldiers—so the soldiers amused themselves, often by communal singing, and we know that many of these songs were sung around the campfires of Union and Confederate armies. The folks back home sang, too, gathering around the pianos now appearing in increasing numbers in American parlors.

Only a few of these songs—a selection from hundreds—need any explanation. Most of them can be assigned, with some assurance, to particular authors, and sometimes to composers; others are of disputed origin; others still seem to have come spontaneously from the soldiers themselves. Many of them are preserved for us in variant forms.

This selection is designed to suggest what the soldiers, and their families, actually sang. Patriotic poems—the "Barbara Frietchie" and "Little Giffen of Tennessee" type—are omitted. Some songs were popular in particular regions, or with particular armies, or enjoyed only fleeting popularity; others, like "Lorena," seem to have been equally popular North and South, East and West, with soldiers and with civilians.

1. DIXIE

The most famous and most widely sung of all Civil War songs, "Dixie" actually antedated the war by two years. Nor was it, originally, a Southern song. It was composed by an Ohioan, Dan Emmett, and first sung in Mechanics' Hall on Broadway in April 1859. The origin of the name "Dixie" is obscure, but it was used by Emmett himself in another song composed shortly before "Dixie Land." The song caught on at once and, with the coming of secession, swept the South, where numerous other—and supposedly more appropriate—words were attached to it. It was played at Davis' inauguration as

561

provisional President in Montgomery, Alabama, in February 1861. Yet it was never wholly a Southern song; it is worth remembering that when Lincoln was serenaded after the surrender of Lee he came out on a White House balcony and asked the band to play "Dixie"—now once again a national tune.

Daniel Decatur Emmett is remembered as "the father of the Negro Minstrelsy." He had composed "Old Dan Tucker" in 1830, at the age of fifteen, and thereafter poured out a succession of popular songs for his troupe: "Root, Hog, or Die," "Jordan is a Hard Road to Travel," "High Daddy," and many others well known in their day. He wrote both the words and the music for "Dixie."

I wish I was in de land ob cotton,
Old times dar am not forgotten,
   Look away, look away, look away, Dixie Land!
In Dixie Land whar I was born in,
Early on one frosty mornin',
Look away, look away, look away, Dixie Land!

    CHORUS—Den I wish I was in Dixie—
           Hooray, hooray!
           In Dixie land I'll take my stan'!
           To lib an' die in Dixie
             Away, away,
          Away down south in Dixie
             Away, away,
          Away down south in Dixie.

Ole Missus marry "Will-de-Weaber,"
William was a gay deceber
   Look away, look away, look away, Dixie Land!
But when he put his arm around 'er
He smiled as fierce as a forty-pounder
   Look away, look away, look away, Dixie Land!—CHORUS

His face was sharp as a butcher's cleaber,
But dat did not seem to grieb 'er,
   Look away, look away, look away, Dixie Land!
Ole Missus acted de foolish part,
An' died for a man dat broke her heart,
   Look away, look away, look away, Dixie Land!—CHORUS

Now, here's a health to de next ole Missus,
An' all de gals dat want to kiss us,
   Look away, look away, look away, Dixie Land!
But if you want to drive 'way sorrow,
Come an' hear dis song to-morrow,
   Look away, look away, look away, Dixie Land!—CHORUS

Dar's buckwheat cakes an' Injun batter,
Makes you fat, or a little fatter,
 Look away, look away, look away, Dixie Land!
Den hoe it down and scratch your grabble,
To Dixie's Land I'm bound to trabble,
 Look away, look away, look away, Dixie Land!—CHORUS
         —DANIEL D. EMMETT

2. THE BONNIE BLUE FLAG

"The Bonnie Blue Flag" came out of New Orleans. It was written and first sung by Harry McCarthy, who needed a new song to fill out an act at the Varieties Theatre, in September 1861; the tune was that of an old Irish song, "The Jaunting Car." From New Orleans it spread quickly throughout the South, becoming, in the end, the most popular of Southern marching songs next to "Dixie." When Butler was in command in New Orleans he arrested and fined Blackmar, its publisher, and threatened to fine any one who sang this song 25 dollars. As with so many Civil War songs there are many versions, and many variations in the text.

We are a band of brothers, and native to the soil,
Fighting for the property we gained by honest toil;
And when our rights were threatened, the cry rose near and far:
Hurrah for the bonnie Blue Flag that bears a single star!
 Hurrah! hurrah! for the bonnie Blue Flag
 That bears a single star.

As long as the Union was faithful to her trust,
Like friends and like brothers, kind were we and just;
But now when Northern treachery attempts our rights to mar,
We hoist on high the bonnie Blue Flag that bears a single star.

First, gallant South Carolina nobly made the stand;
Then came Alabama, who took her by the hand;
Next, quickly Mississippi, Georgia, and Florida—
All raised the flag, the bonnie Blue Flag that bears a single star.

Ye men of valor, gather round the banner of the right;
Texas and fair Louisiana join us in the fight.
Davis, our loved President, and Stephens, statesmen are;
Now rally round the bonnie Blue Flag that bears a single star.

And here's to brave Virginia! the Old Dominion State
With the young Confederacy at length has linked her fate.
Impelled by her example, now other States prepare
To hoist on high the bonnie Blue Flag that bears a single star.

Then here's to our Confederacy; strong we are and brave,
Like patriots of old we'll fight, our heritage to save;
And rather than submit to shame, to die we would prefer;
So cheer for the bonnie Blue Flag that bears a single star.

Then cheer, boys, cheer, raise the joyous shout,
For Arkansas and North Carolina now have both gone out;
And let another rousing cheer for Tennessee be given,
The single star of the bonnie Blue Flag has grown to be eleven!
    Hurrah! hurrah! for the bonnie Blue Flag
    That bears a single star.

                   —HARRY MCCARTHY

3. JOHN BROWN'S BODY

This, the most widely sung of Federal songs, is apparently a genuine folk song. No one knows its precise origin, or its author. The tune was taken from a Negro melody popular in the Carolina low country, where it was sung to the refrain

        Say, brothers, will you meet us?
        On Canaan's happy shore?

The words have been assigned to Thomas B. Bishop; the adaptation of the words to the familiar tune to James E. Greenleaf of the Boston Light Artillery, and to a Mr. Gilmore who played it before the 12th Massachusetts Volunteers. Perhaps the most popular variation was "We'll Hang Jeff Davis on a Sour Apple Tree."

John Brown's body lies a-mould'ring in the grave,
John Brown's body lies a-mould'ring in the grave,
John Brown's body lies a-mould'ring in the grave,
    His soul is marching on.

    CHORUS: Glory! Glory Hallelujah!
              Glory! Glory Hallelujah!
              Glory! Glory Hallelujah!
              His soul is marching on.

He's gone to be a soldier in the army of the Lord!
    His soul is marching on.—CHORUS

John Brown's knapsack is strapped upon his back.
    His soul is marching on.—CHORUS

His pet lambs will meet him on the way,
    And they'll go marching on.—CHORUS

They'll hang Jeff Davis on a sour apple tree,
    As they go marching on.—CHORUS

Now for the Union let's give three rousing cheers,
    As we go marching on.
      Hip, Hip, hip, hip, Hurrah!—CHORUS
            —THOMAS B. BISHOP (?)

4. ALL QUIET ALONG THE POTOMAC

Both the author and the composer of this song, so popular with both armies and both peoples, were New Yorkers. Inspired by the oft-repeated headline in the newspapers in 1861, "All Quiet Along the Potomac," with a little notice underneath—"A Picket Shot"—Ethel Lynn Beers composed this poem and published it in Harper's Magazine *in November 1861 under the title "The Picket Guard." Later it was claimed by the fabulous Major Lamar Fontaine of the Confederate Army. The music has been credited to both Henry Coyle and to J. Dayton, both of the 1st Connecticut Artillery, but it seems clearly to have been composed by the famous poet, journalist, and musician, James Hewitt—who at the time was drilling recruits in Richmond, Virginia.*

"All quiet along the Potomac," they say,
    "Except now and then a stray picket
Is shot, as he walks on his beat to and fro,
    By a rifleman hid in the thicket.
'Tis nothing—a private or two now and then
    Will not count in the news of the battle;
Not an officer lost—only one of the men,
    Moaning out, all alone, the death-rattle."

All quiet along the Potomac to-night,
    Where the soldiers lie peacefully dreaming;
Their tents in the rays of the clear autumn moon,
    Or the light of the watch-fire, are gleaming.
A tremulous sigh of the gentle night-wind
    Through the forest leaves softly is creeping;
While stars up above, with their glittering eyes,
    Keep guard, for the army is sleeping.

There's only the sound of the lone sentry's tread,
    As he tramps from the rock to the fountain,
And thinks of the two in the low trundle-bed
    Far away in the cot on the mountain.
His musket falls slack; his face, dark and grim,
    Grows gentle with memories tender,
As he mutters a prayer for the children asleep,
    For their mother; may Heaven defend her!

The moon seems to shine just as brightly as then,
    That night, when the love yet unspoken
Leaped up to his lips—when low-murmured vows
    Were pledged to be ever unbroken.
Then drawing his sleeve roughly over his eyes,
    He dashes off tears that are welling,
And gathers his gun closer up to its place,
    As if to keep down the heart-swelling.

He passes the fountain, the blasted pine-tree,
    The footstep is lagging and weary;
Yet onward he goes, through the broad belt of light,
    Toward the shade of the forest so dreary.
Hark! was it the night-wind that rustled the leaves?
    Was it moonlight so wondrously flashing?
It looked like a rifle . . . "Ha! Mary, good-bye!"
    The red life-blood is ebbing and plashing.

All quiet along the Potomac to-night;
    No sound save the rush of the river;
While soft falls the dew on the face of the dead—
    The picket's off duty forever!
                                    —ETHEL LYNN BEERS

5. MARCHING ALONG

This was a favorite with the soldiers of the Army of the Potomac: the name of the "leader" was changed—pretty frequently as it turned out—to fit the facts. William Bradbury was, in his day, one of the most distinguished of American composers. A student of the great Lowell Mason, he was instrumental in introducing music into the schools, put out a number of singing books, and contributed richly to American psalmody. Among his better known songs are "Just as I Am" and "He Leadeth Me."

The army is gathering from near and from far;
The trumpet is sounding the call for the war;
McClellan's our leader, he's gallant and strong;
We'll gird on our armor and be marching along.

CHORUS: Marching along, we are marching along,
            Gird on the armor and be marching along;
            McClellan's our leader, he's gallant and strong;
            For God and our country we are marching along.

The foe is before us in battle array,
But let us not waver, or turn from the way;
The Lord is our strength, and the Union's our song;
With courage and faith we are marching along.—CHORUS

Our wives and our children we leave in your care;
We feel you will help them with sorrow to bear:
'Tis hard thus to part, but we hope 't won't be long:
We'll keep up our heart as we're marching along.—Chorus

We sigh for our country, we mourn for our dead;
For them now our last drop of blood we will shed;
Our cause is the right one—our foe's in the wrong;
Then gladly we'll sing as we're marching along.—Chorus

The flag of our country is floating on high;
We'll stand by that flag till we conquer or die;
McClellan's our leader, he's gallant and strong;
We'll gird on our armor and be marching along.—Chorus
—William Batchelder Bradbury

6. MARYLAND! MY MARYLAND!

This best known of all state songs was written, appropriately enough, by a native of Baltimore. James Ryder Randall had gone to New Orleans in 1859 to clerk in a ship broker's office. The following year he took a position as tutor in English at Poydras College, a Creole school in Pointe Coupee Parish, and he was there when he read the story of the attack on the 6th Massachusetts as it forced its way through Baltimore. That night he wrote "Maryland! My Maryland!" and sent it to the New Orleans Delta, where it was printed in the issue of April 26. The Misses Cary of Baltimore adapted the words to the familiar music of "O Tannenbaum," and it became one of the favorite marching songs of the Confederacy.

The despot's heel is on thy shore,
   Maryland!
His torch is at thy temple door,
   Maryland!
Avenge the patriotic gore
That flecked the streets of Baltimore,
And be the battle queen of yore,
   Maryland! My Maryland!

Hark to an exiled son's appeal,
   Maryland!
My mother State! to thee I kneel,
   Maryland!
For life and death, for woe and weal,
Thy peerless chivalry reveal,
And gird thy beauteous limbs with steel,
   Maryland! My Maryland!

Thou wilt not cower in the dust,
 Maryland!
Thy beaming sword shall never rust,
 Maryland!
Remember Carroll's sacred trust,
Remember Howard's warlike thrust,—
And all thy slumberers with the just,
 Maryland! My Maryland!

Come! for thy shield is bright and strong,
 Maryland!
Come! for thy dalliance does thee wrong,
 Maryland! .
Come to thine own heroic throng,
Stalking with Liberty along,
And chaunt thy dauntless slogan song,
 Maryland! My Maryland!

Dear Mother! burst the tyrant's chain,
 Maryland!
Virginia should not call in vain,
 Maryland!
She meets her sisters on the plain—
"*Sic semper!*" 'tis the proud refrain
That baffles minions back again,
 Maryland! My Maryland!

I hear the distant thunder-hum,
 Maryland!
The Old Line's bugle, fife, and drum,
 Maryland!
She is not dead, nor deaf, nor dumb—
Huzza! she spurns the Northern scum!
She breathes! she burns! she'll come! she'll come!
 Maryland! My Maryland!
       —JAMES R. RANDALL

7. YE CAVALIERS OF DIXIE

This song was sung to the tune of "Ye Mariners of England"—a difficult tune which relegated the song largely to the stage.

Ye Cavaliers of Dixie!
Who guard the Southern shores,
Whose standards brave the battle storm
Which o'er our border roars
Your glorious sabers draw once more,

And charge the Northern foe;
And reap their columns deep,
And reap their columns deep,
And reap their columns deep.

CHORUS: Where the raging tempests blow,
               Where the raging tempests blow,
               And the iron hail in floods descends,
               And the bloody torrents flow.

Ye Cavaliers of Dixie!
Though dark the tempest lower,
What arms will wear the tyrant's chains
What dastard heart will cower?
Bright o'er the night a sign shall rise
To lead to victory!
And your swords reap their hordes,
Where the battle tempests blow;
Where the iron hail in floods descends,
And the bloody torrents flow.—CHORUS

The South! she needs no ramparts,
No lofty towers to shield;
Your bosoms are her bulwarks strong,
Breastworks that never yield!
The thunder of your battle blades
Shall sweep the servile foe;
While their gore stains the shore,
Where the battle tempests blow;
Where the iron hail in floods descends,
And the bloody torrents flow.—CHORUS

The battle-flag of Dixie
With crimson field shall flame;
Her azure cross and silver stars
Shall light her sons to fame!
When peace with olive branch returns,
That flag's white folds shall glow
Still bright on every height,
When storm has ceased to blow,
And the battle tempests roar no more;
Nor the bloody torrents flow.—CHORUS
                              —BENJAMIN F. PORTER

8. STONEWALL JACKSON'S WAY

A whole volume could be compiled of poetic tributes to the great Stone-
wall; if not the best this is certainly the liveliest, and its tune one of the most

melodious. The author, John W. Palmer, was a Baltimore-born physician who had been in the Gold Rush, sailed to Hawaii, taken part in the Second Burmese War, and settled in New York as journalist, poet and playwright. When the war came Palmer went to Richmond, where, for a time, he was correspondent for the New York Tribune. *Later he served on the staff of General Breckinridge. "Stonewall Jackson's Way" was written at the Battle of Antietam.*

Come, stack arms, men! Pile on the rails,
   Stir up the camp-fire bright;
No matter if the canteen fails,
   We'll make a roaring night.
Here Shenandoah brawls along,
There burly Blue Ridge echoes strong,
To swell the brigade's rousing song
   Of "Stonewall Jackson's Way."

We see him now—the old slouched hat
   Cocked o'er his eye askew,
The shrewd, dry smile, the speech so pat,
   So calm, so blunt, so true.
The "Blue-Light Elder" knows 'em well;
Says he, "That's Banks—he's fond of shell;
Lord save his soul! we'll give him"—well,
   That's "Stonewall Jackson's way."

Silence! ground arms! kneel all! caps off!
   Old Blue-Light's going to pray.
Strangle the fool that dares to scoff!
   Attention! it's his way.
Appealing from his native sod,
In *forma pauperis* to God—
"Lay bare thine arm, stretch forth thy rod!
   Amen!" That's "Stonewall's way."

He's in the saddle now. Fall in!
   Steady! the whole brigade!
Hill's at the ford, cut off—we'll win
   His way out, ball and blade!
What matter if our shoes are worn?
What matter if our feet are torn?
"Quick-step! we're with him before dawn!"
   That's "Stonewall Jackson's way."

The sun's bright lances rout the mists
   Of morning and by George!
Here's Longstreet struggling in the lists,
   Hemmed in an ugly gorge.

Pope and his Yankees, whipped before,
"Bay'nets and grape!" near Stonewall roar;
"Charge, Stuart! Pay off Ashby's score!"
Is "Stonewall Jackson's way."

Ah! maiden, wait and watch and yearn
For news of Stonewall's band!
Ah! widow, read with eyes that burn
That ring upon thy hand.
Ah! wife, sew on, pray on, hope on!
Thy life shall not be all forlorn.
The foe had better ne'er been born
That gets in "Stonewall's way."
—John Williamson Palmer

9. THE BATTLE HYMN OF THE REPUBLIC

It can hardly be doubted that this is the one great song to come out of the Civil War—the one that transcends that particular conflict and embraces every great moral crusade.

Julia Ward Howe was the daughter of a New York banker and wife of the famous Massachusetts reformer, Samuel Gridley Howe. She early made a name for herself in Boston circles by her essays and poems and by her zealous advocacy of abolition and woman's rights. The following excerpts tell how she came to write the "Battle Hymn," and give a glimpse of the meaning of the song to Union prisoners.

A. Writing "The Battle Hymn of the Republic"

I DISTINCTLY remember that a feeling of discouragement came over me as I drew near the city of Washington. I thought of the women of my acquaintance whose sons or husbands were fighting our great battle, the women themselves serving in the hospitals, or busying themselves with the work of the Sanitary Commission. My husband was beyond the age of military service, my eldest son but a stripling; my youngest was a child of not more than two years. I could not leave my nursery to follow the march of our armies; neither had I the practical deftness which the preparing and packing of sanitary stores demanded. Something seemed to say to me, "You would be glad to serve, but you cannot help any one; you have nothing to give, and there is nothing for you to do." Yet, because of my sincere desire, a word was given me to say, which did strengthen the hearts of those who fought in the field and of those who languished in the prison.

We were invited one day to attend a review of troops at some distance from the town. While we were engaged in watching the maneuvers, a sudden movement of the enemy necessitated immediate action. The review was discontinued, and we saw a detachment of soldiers gallop to the assistance of a small body of our men who were in imminent danger of being surrounded and cut off from retreat. The regiments remaining on the field were ordered to march to their cantonments. We returned to the city very slowly, of necessity, for the troops nearly filled the road. My dear minister was in the carriage with me, as were several other friends. To beguile the rather tedious drive, we sang from time to time snatches of the army songs so popular at that time, concluding, I think, with:

> John Brown's body lies a-moldering in the ground;
> His soul is marching on.

The soldiers seemed to like this and answered back, "Good for you!" Mr. Clark said, "Mrs. Howe, why do you not write some good words for that stirring tune?" I replied that I had often wished to do this but had not as yet found in my mind any leading toward it.

I went to bed that night as usual and slept, according to my wont, quite soundly. I awoke in the gray of the morning twilight, and as I lay waiting for the dawn, the long lines of the desired poem began to twine themselves in my mind. Having thought out all the stanzas, I said to myself, "I must get up and write these verses down, lest I fall asleep again and forget them." So with a sudden effort I sprang out of bed and found in the dimness an old stump of a pen which I remembered to have used the day before. I scrawled the verses almost without looking at the paper. I had learned to do this when, on previous occasions, attacks of versification had visited me in the night and I feared to have recourse to a light lest I should wake the baby, who slept near me. I was always obliged to decipher my scrawl before another night should intervene, as it was only legible while the matter was fresh in my mind. At this time, having completed my writing, I returned to bed and fell asleep, saying to myself, "I like this better than most things that I have written."

The poem, which was soon after published in the *Atlantic Monthly* [February 1862], was somewhat praised on its appearance, but the vicissitudes of the war so engrossed public attention that small heed was taken of literary matters. I knew and was content to know that the poem soon found its way to the camps, as I heard from time to time of its being sung in chorus by the soldiers.

—Howe, *Reminiscences*

B. The Battle Hymn of the Republic

Mine eyes have seen the glory of the coming of the Lord:
He is trampling out the vintage where the grapes of wrath are stored;
He hath loosed the fateful lightning of his terrible swift sword:
    His truth is marching on.

I have seen Him in the watch fires of a hundred circling camps;
They have builded Him an altar in the evening dews and damps;
I can read His righteous sentence by the dim and flaring lamps.
    His day is marching on.

I have read a fiery gospel writ in burnished rows of steel:
"As ye deal with my contemners, so with you my grace shall deal;
Let the Hero, born of woman, crush the serpent with his heel,
    Since God is marching on."

He has sounded forth the trumpet that shall never call retreat;
He is sifting out the hearts of men before his judgment seat:
Oh! be swift, my soul, to answer Him! be jubilant, my feet!
    Our God is marching on.

In the beauty of the lilies Christ was born across the sea,
With a glory in His bosom that transfigures you and me:
As He died to make men holy, let us die to make men free,
    While God is marching on.   —JULIA WARD HOWE

C. "THE BATTLE HYMN OF THE REPUBLIC" IN LIBBY PRISON

Among the singers of the "Battle Hymn" was Chaplain McCabe, the fighting chaplain of the 122d Ohio Volunteer Infantry. He read the poem in the "Atlantic," and was so struck with it that he committed it to memory before rising from his chair. He took it with him to the front, and in due time to Libby Prison, whither he was sent after being captured at Winchester. Here, in the great bare room where hundreds of Northern soldiers were herded together, came one night a rumor of disaster to the Union arms. A great battle, their jailers told them; a great Confederate victory. Sadly the Northern men gathered together in groups, sitting or lying on the floor, talking in low tones, wondering how, where, why. Suddenly, one of the Negroes who brought food for the prisoners stooped in passing and whispered to one of the sorrowful groups. The news was false: there had, indeed, been a great battle, but the Union army had won, the Confederates were defeated and scattered.

Like a flame the word flashed through the prison. Men leaped to their feet, shouted, embraced one another in a frenzy of joy and triumph; and Chaplain McCabe, standing in the middle of the room, lifted up his great voice and sang aloud,—

"Mine eyes have seen the glory of the coming of the Lord!"

Every voice took up the chorus, and Libby Prison rang with the shout of "Glory, glory, hallelujah!"

The victory was that of Gettysburg. When, some time after, McCabe was released from prison, he told in Washington, before a great audience of loyal people, the story of his war-time experiences; and when he came to that night in Libby Prison, he sang the "Battle Hymn" once more. The effect was magical; people shouted, wept, and sang, all together; and when the song was ended, above the tumult of applause was heard the voice of Abraham Lincoln, exclaiming, while the tears rolled down his cheeks,—

"Sing it again!"   —RICHARDS AND ELLIOTT, *Julia Ward Howe*

10. WE ARE COMING, FATHER ABRAHAM

The losses in the Peninsular campaign were so heavy that Lincoln on July 2, 1862, appealed to the states to raise "three hundred thousand more" soldiers. It was in response to this appeal that James Sloan Gibbons, the New York abolitionist, wrote "We Are Coming, Father Abraham"—an assertion which, as it turned out, was overconfident.

Gibbons was a Philadelphia Quaker who in the thirties moved to New York and simultaneously entered banking and reform, becoming one of the staunchest supporters of the American Anti-Slavery Society. During the draft riots of 1863 his house was sacked. The music for this song was composed by Stephen Foster, then living in poverty and obscurity in New York City.

> We are coming, Father Abraham, three hundred thousand more,
> From Mississippi's winding stream and from New England's shore;
> We leave our ploughs and workshops, our wives and children dear,
> With hearts too full for utterance, with but a silent tear;
> We dare not look behind us, but steadfastly before:
> We are coming, Father Abraham, three hundred thousand more!
>
> If you look across the hill-tops that meet the northern sky,
> Long moving lines of rising dust your vision may descry;
> And now the wind, an instant, tears the cloudy veil aside,
> And floats aloft our spangled flag in glory and in pride,
> And bayonets in the sunlight gleam, and bands brave music pour,
> We are coming, Father Abraham, three hundred thousand more!
>
> If you look all up our valleys where the growing harvests shine,
> You may see our sturdy farmer boys fast forming into line;
> And children from their mother's knees are pulling at the weeds,
> And learning how to reap and sow against their country's needs;
> And a farewell group stands weeping at every cottage door:
> We are coming, Father Abraham, three hundred thousand more!
>
> You have called us, and we're coming, by Richmond's bloody tide
> To lay us down, for Freedom's sake, our brothers' bones beside,
> Or from foul treason's savage grasp to wrench the murderous blade,
> And in the face of foreign foes its fragments to parade.
> Six hundred thousand loyal men and true have gone before:
> We are coming, Father Abraham, three hundred thousand more!
>
> —JAMES SLOAN GIBBONS

11. THE BATTLE-CRY OF FREEDOM

This song, like "We Are Coming, Father Abraham," was written in response to Lincoln's appeal for troops. George F. Root, who wrote both the words and the music, was, with his friend and colleague Henry Clay Work, the most prolific and successful of Northern Civil War song writers, author of the ever popular "Tramp, Tramp, Tramp," "The Vacant Chair," "Just Before the Battle, Mother," and others. He had taught at the Boston Academy of Music and the New York Normal Institute before going to Chicago, in 1859, to open a music store. "The Battle-Cry of Freedom" was written for a rally at Court House Square in Chicago; the famous Hutchinson family of singers carried it throughout the North.

There were two versions of this song—the so-called "rallying" version and the "battle-song" version. The better-known "rallying" song is given here; the first verse of the "battle-song" is as follows:

> *We are marching to the field, boys, we're going to the fight,*
> *Shouting the battle-cry of freedom;*
> *And we bear the glorious stars for the Union and the right,*
> *Shouting the battle-cry of freedom.*

If we are to believe Mrs. Pickett one version of the song was equally popular in the Confederacy.

> Yes, We'll rally round the flag,
> Boys, we'll rally once again,
> Shouting the battle-cry of Freedom,
> We will rally from the hillside, we'll gather from the plain,
> Shouting the battle-cry of Freedom.
>
> CHORUS: The Union forever,
>   Hurray! boys, Hurrah!
>   Down with the traitor, up with the star;
>   While we rally round the flag boys, rally once again,
>   Shouting the battle-cry of Freedom.
>
> We are springing to the call of our Brothers gone before,
> Shouting the battle-cry of Freedom;
> And we'll fill the vacant ranks with a million freemen more,
> Shouting the battle-cry of Freedom.—CHORUS
>
> We will welcome to our numbers the loyal, true and brave,
> Shouting the battle-cry of Freedom;
> And altho' they may be poor, not a man shall be a slave,
> Shouting the battle-cry of Freedom.—CHORUS
>
> So we're springing to the call from the East and from the West,
> Shouting the battle-cry of Freedom;
> And we'll hurl the rebel crew from the land we love the best,
> Shouting the battle-cry of Freedom.—CHORUS
>
>   —GEORGE F. ROOT

12. TRAMP, TRAMP, TRAMP

This song, also by George Root, was even more popular with the soldiers than "The Battle-Cry of Freedom." It is a shining example of the sentimentalism of the Civil War generation, but it is worth noting that it has retained its popularity to this day, largely because of its lively tune.

In the prison cell I sit,
    Thinking, mother dear, of you,
And our bright and happy home so far away,
    And the tears they fill my eyes,
Spite of all that I can do,
    Tho' I try to cheer my comrades and be gay.

CHORUS: Tramp, tramp, tramp, the boys are marching,
        Oh, cheer up, comrades, they will come,
      And beneath the starry flag we shall breath the air again,
        Of freedom in our own beloved home.

In the battle front we stood
    When the fiercest charge they made,
And they swept us off a hundred men or more,
    But before we reached their lines
They were beaten back dismayed,
    And we heard the cry of vict'ry o'er and o'er.—CHORUS

So within the prison cell
    We are waiting for the day
That shall come to open wide the iron door,
    And the hollow eye grows bright,
And the poor heart almost gay,
    As we think of seeing friends and home once more.—CHORUS
                           —GEORGE F. ROOT

13. JUST BEFORE THE BATTLE, MOTHER

Here is another song from the adept pen of George Root. Better than most songs it lent itself to parody, one of the most widely sung of which ran:

Just before the battle, mother,
I was drinking mountain dew.
When I saw the Rebels marching,
To the rear I quickly flew.

It was widely sung in both armies, but appeared to be more popular in the South than in the North.

Just before the battle, mother,
I am thinking most of you;
While upon the field we are watching,
With the enemy in view.
Comrades brave are 'round me lying,
Filled with thoughts of home and God;
For well they know upon the morrow
Some will sleep beneath the sod.

CHORUS: Farewell, mother, you may never
Press me to your heart again;
But, oh, you'll not forget me, mother,
If I'm numbered with the slain.

Oh! I long to see you, mother,
And the loving ones at home;
But I'll never leave our banner
'Till in honor I can come.
Tell the enemy around you
That their cruel words, we know,
In every battle kill our soldiers
By the help they give the foe.—CHORUS
—GEORGE F. ROOT

14. TENTING TONIGHT

Like so many Civil War songs this one was almost equally popular on both sides. It was written by a New Hampshire singer, Walter Kittredge, who in 1861 had published a compilation of Union songs. Unable to find a publisher for "Tenting Tonight," he sang it himself in the army, and soon, despite its palpable defeatism, it had immense vogue.

We're tenting tonight on the old camp ground,
Give us a song to cheer our weary hearts,
A song of home, and the friends we love so dear.

CHORUS: Many are the hearts that are weary tonight,
Wishing for the war to cease;
Many are the hearts looking for the right
To see the dawn of peace.
Tenting tonight, tenting tonight,
Tenting on the old camp ground.

We've been tenting tonight on the old camp ground,
Thinking of days gone by, of the loved ones at home
That gave us the hand, and the tear that said "good-bye!"—CHORUS

We are tired of war on the old camp ground,
Many are dead and gone, of the brave and true
Who've left their homes, others been wounded long.—CHORUS

We've been fighting today on the old camp ground,
Many are lying near; some are dead
And some are dying, many are in tears.

LAST CHORUS: Many are the hearts that are weary tonight,
              Wishing for the war to cease;
              Many are the hearts looking for the right,
              To see the dawn of peace.
              Dying tonight, dying tonight,
              Dying on the old camp ground.
                              —WALTER KITTREDGE

15. WEEPING, SAD AND LONELY

The author of this lachrymose song, Charles Sawyer, wrote a number of sentimental pieces including one tear-jerker, "Who Will Care for Mother Now?" which inspired an equally doleful reply, "Do Not Grieve for Thy Dear Mother." So depressing was "Weeping, Sad and Lonely" that some officers forbade its singing. Yet it was immensely popular on both sides. "There is nothing in this sentimental song," says Charles C. Eggleston, "that enables one to read the riddle of its remarkable popularity. It has no poetic merit; its rhythm is commonplace, and the tune to which it was sung was of the flimsiest musical structure, without even a trick of melody to commend it. Yet the song was more frequently sung, on both sides, than any other, the Southern soldiers inserting 'gray' for 'blue.' . . . Men chanted it on the march, and women sang it to piano accompaniment in all houses."

No introduction is necessary for the three songs that follow this one. They express perfectly the cloying sentimentalism of the Civil War years; they remind us, too, how young were most of the soldiers who fought in the war, and how heavy were the casualties—heavier proportionately than in any other war which the United States has fought.

A. WEEPING, SAD AND LONELY

Dearest love, do you remember
    When we last did meet,
How you told me that you loved me,
    Kneeling at my feet?
Oh! how proud you stood before me
    In your suit of blue,
When you vow'd to me and country
    Ever to be true.

CHORUS: Weeping, sad and lonely,
            Hopes and fears how vain!
            Yet praying,
            When this cruel war is over,
            Praying that we meet again.

When the summer breeze is sighing
   Mournfully along;
Or when autumn leaves are falling,
   Sadly breathes the song.
Oft in dreams I see thee lying
   On the battle plain,
Lonely, wounded, even dying,
   Calling, but in vain.—CHORUS

If amid the din of battle,
   Nobly you should fall,
Far away from those who love you,
   None to hear your call—
Who would whisper words of comfort?
   Who would soothe your pain?
Ah! the many cruel fancies
   Ever in my brain.—CHORUS

But our country called you, darling,
   Angels cheer your way:
While our nation's sons are fighting,
   We can only pray.
Nobly strike for God and liberty,
   Let all nations see
How we love the starry banner
   Emblem of the free.—CHORUS
                —CHARLES C. SAWYER

B. THE FADED COAT OF BLUE

My brave lad he sleeps in his faded coat of blue;
In a lonely grave unknown lies the heart that beat so true;
He sank faint and hungry among the famished brave,
And they laid him sad and lonely within his nameless grave.

CHORUS: No more the bugle calls the weary one,
            Rest noble spirit, in thy grave unknown!
            I'll find you and know you, among the good and true,
            When a robe of white is giv'n for the faded coat of blue.

He cried, "Give me water and just a little crumb,
And my mother she will bless you through all the years to come;
Oh! tell my sweet sister, so gentle, good and true,
That I'll meet her up in heaven, in my faded coat of blue."—Chorus
—J. H. McNaughton

C. The Vacant Chair

We shall meet but we shall miss him,
　There will be one vacant chair;
We shall linger to caress him
　While we breathe our evening prayer.
When a year ago we gathered,
　Joy was in his mild blue eye;
But a golden cord is severed,
　And our hopes in ruins lie.

Chorus: We shall meet but we shall miss him,
　　　　There will be one vacant chair;
　　　　We shall linger to caress him,
　　　　When we breathe our evening prayer.

At our fireside sad and lonely,
　Often will the bosom swell
At remembrance of the story
　How our noble soldier fell;
How he strove to bear our banner
　Through the thickest of the fight
And uphold our country's honor
　In the strength of manhood's might.—Chorus
—George F. Root

D. Sleeping for the Flag

When the boys come home in triumph, brother,
With the laurels they shall gain;
When we go to give them welcome, brother,
We shall look for you in vain.
We shall wait for your returning, brother,
You were set forever free;
For your comrades left you sleeping, brother,
Underneath a Southern tree.

Chorus: Sleeping to waken in this weary world no more;
　　　　Sleeping for your true lov'd country, brother,
　　　　Sleeping for the flag you bore.

You who were the first on duty, brother,
When "to arms" your leader cried,—
You have left the ranks forever,
You have laid your arms aside,
From the awful scenes of battle, brother,
You were set forever free;
When your comrades left you sleeping, brother,
Underneath the Southern tree.—CHORUS

—HENRY CLAY WORK

16. MARCHING THROUGH GEORGIA

Few other Civil War songs have had the enduring popularity of this, and probably no other has spread so widely over the globe. The Japanese played it when they entered Port Arthur, the British sang it in India, it was included in a British Soldiers' Songbook in the First World War, and was played and sung by British and Americans alike in the Second World War.

Henry Clay Work was the son of an abolitionist who had suffered imprisonment for his work on the underground railway in Illinois; he himself was active not only in antislavery but in temperance work as well, and among his better-known songs is the memorable "Father, Dear Father, Come Home with Me Now."

Bring the good old bugle, boys, we'll sing another song—
Sing it with a spirit that will start the world along—
Sing it as we used to sing it, fifty thousand strong,
While we were marching through Georgia.

CHORUS: "Hurrah! Hurrah! we bring the jubilee!
Hurrah! Hurrah! the flag that makes you free!"
So we sang the chorus from Atlanta to the sea,
While we were marching through Georgia.

How the darkeys shouted when they heard the joyful sound!
How the turkeys gobbled which our commissary found!
How the sweet potatoes even started from the ground,
While we were marching through Georgia.—CHORUS

Yes, and there were Union men who wept with joyful tears,
When they saw the honored flag they had not seen for years;
Hardly could they be restrained from breaking forth in cheers,
While we were marching through Georgia.—CHORUS

"Sherman's dashing Yankee boys will never reach the coast!"
So the saucy rebels said, and 'twas a handsome boast.
Had they not forgot, alas! to reckon with the host,
While we were marching through Georgia?—CHORUS

So we made a thoroughfare for Freedom and her train,
Sixty miles in latitude—three hundred to the main;
Treason fled before us, for resistance was in vain,
While we were marching through Georgia.—CHORUS
                              —HENRY CLAY WORK

17. MISTER, HERE'S YOUR MULE

No introduction is needed for this and the following four items. They remind us that Americans of the Civil War generation, for all their sentimentalism, were able to laugh at themselves—and at others. "Mister, Here's Your Mule" was particularly popular in the Western armies. "Do They Miss Me in the Trenches," written by J. W. Naff of the 3rd Louisiana Infantry, is a parody on "Do They Miss Me at Home." The vicissitudes of fighting in the Army of the Potomac inspired the wry "We Are the Boys of Potomac's Ranks," rehearsing the defeat of one Union general after another in the mud and forests of northern Virginia. It was sung to the tune of "When Johnny Comes Marching Home." The "goober peas" of Pender's song are, of course, peanuts. "Grafted into the Army" is something of a take-off both on the draft and on the boys who tried, in vain, to avoid it.

A. MISTER, HERE'S YOUR MULE

A farmer came to camp, one day, with milk and eggs to sell,
Upon a mule who oft would stray to where no one could tell,
The farmer, tired of his tramp, for hours was made a fool
By ev'ryone he met in camp, with "Mister, here's your mule."

CHORUS: Come on, come on, come on, old man, and don't be made a fool,
              I'll tell the truth as best I can,
              John Morgan's got your mule.

His eggs and chickens all were gone before the break of day,
The mule was heard of all along—that's what the soldiers say;
And still he hunted all day long—alas! the witless fool—
While ev'ry man would sing the song, "Mister, here's your mule."—CHORUS

The soldiers now, in laughing mood, on mischief were intent,
They toted muly on their backs, around from tent to tent;
Through this hole and that they pushed his head, and made a rule
To shout with humorous voices all, "Mister, here's your mule."—CHORUS

Alas! one day the mule was missed, ah! who could tell his fate?
The farmer, like a man bereft, searched early and searched late;
And as he passed from camp to camp, with stricken face, the fool
Cried out to ev'ryone he met, "Oh, Mister, where's my mule?"—CHORUS
                              —AUTHOR UNKNOWN

B. Do They Miss Me in the Trenches?

Do they miss me in the trench, do they miss me
When the shells fly so thickly around?
Do they know that I've run down the hill-side
To look for my hole in the ground?
But the shells exploded so near me,
It seemed best for me to run;
And though some laughed as I crawfished,
I could not discover the fun.

I often get up in the trenches,
When some Yankee is near out of sight,
And fire a round or two at him,
To make the boys think that I'll fight.
But when the Yanks commence shelling,
I run to my home down the hill;
I swear my legs never will stay there,
Though all may stay there who will.

I'll save myself through the dread struggle,
And when the great battle is o'er,
I'll claim my full rations of laurels,
As always I've done heretofore.
I'll say that I've fought them as bravely
As the best of my comrades who fell,
And swear most roundly to all others
That I never had fears of a shell.
—J. W. Naff

C. We Are the Boys of Potomac's Ranks

We are the boys of Potomac's ranks,
  Hurrah! Hurrah!
We are the boys of Potomac's ranks,
We ran with McDowell, retreated with Banks,
And we'll all drink stone blind—
Johnny, fill up the bowl.

We fought with McClellan, the Rebs, shakes, and fever,
  Hurrah! Hurrah!
We fought with McClellan, the Rebs, shakes, and fever,
But Mac joined the navy on reaching James River,
And we'll all drink stone blind—
Johnny, fill up the bowl.

They gave us John Pope, our patience to tax,
  Hurrah! Hurrah!
They gave us John Pope, our patience to tax,
Who said that out West he'd seen naught but *gray backs,*
And we'll all drink stone blind—
Johnny, fill up the bowl.

He said his headquarters were in the saddle,
  Hurrah! Hurrah!
He said his headquarters were in the saddle,
But Stonewall Jackson made him skedaddle—
And we'll all drink stone blind—
Johnny, fill up the bowl.

Then Mac was recalled, but after Antietam,
  Hurrah! Hurrah!
Then Mac was recalled, but after Antietam
Abe gave him a rest, he was too slow to beat 'em,
And we'll all drink stone blind—
Johnny, fill up the bowl.

Oh, Burnside, then he tried his luck,
  Hurrah! Hurrah!
Oh, Burnside, then he tried his luck,
But in the mud so fast got stuck,
And we'll all drink stone blind—
Johnny, fill up the bowl.

Then Hooker was taken to fill the bill,
  Hurrah! Hurrah!
Then Hooker was taken to fill the bill,
But he got a black eye at Chancellorsville,
And we'll all drink stone blind—
Johnny, fill up the bowl.

Next came General Meade, a slow old plug,
  Hurrah! Hurrah!
Next came General Meade, a slow old plug,
For he let them get away at Gettysburg,
And we'll all drink stone blind—
Johnny, fill up the bowl.

                        —Author Unknown

D. Goober Peas

Sitting by the roadside on a summer day,
Chatting with my messmates, passing time away,
Lying in the shadow underneath the trees,
Goodness, how delicious, eating goober peas!

CHORUS: Peas! Peas! Peas! Peas! eating goober peas!
    Goodness, how delicious, eating goober peas!

When a horseman passes, the soldiers have a rule,
To cry out at their loudest, "Mister, here's your mule,"
But another pleasure enchantinger than these,
Is wearing out your grinders, eating goober peas!—CHORUS

Just before the battle the General hears a row,
He says, "The Yanks are coming, I hear their rifles now,"
He turns around in wonder, and what do you think he sees?
The Georgia militia eating goober peas!—CHORUS

I think my song has lasted almost long enough.
The subject's interesting, but the rhymes are mighty rough,
I wish this war was over, when free from rags and fleas,
We'd kiss our wives and sweethearts and gobble goober peas!—CHORUS

           —A. PENDER

E. GRAFTED INTO THE ARMY

Our Jimmy has gone for to live in a tent,
They have grafted him into the army;
He finally pucker'd up courage and went,
When they grafted him into the army.
I told them the child was too young, alas!
At the captain's fore-quarters, they said he would pass—
They'd train him up well in the infantry class—
So they grafted him into the army.

CHORUS: Oh, Jimmy farewell!
    Your brothers fell
    Way down in Alabarmy;
    I tho't they would spare a lone widder's heir,
    But they grafted him into the army.

Drest up in his unicorn—dear little chap;
They have grafted him into the army;
It seems but a day since he sot in my lap,
But they grafted him into the army.
And these are the trousies he used to wear—
Them very same buttons—the patch and the tear—
But Uncle Sam gave him a bran new pair
When they grafted him into the army.—CHORUS

Now in my provisions I see him revealed—
They have grafted him into the army;
A picket beside the contented field,
They have grafted him into the army.
He looks kinder sickish—begins to cry—
A big volunteer standing right in his eye!
Oh what if the ducky should up and die,
Now they've grafted him into the army?—Chorus

—Henry Clay Work

18. LORENA

Almost forgotten now, "Lorena" was the most widely sung and the most popular of Civil War songs, and justly so, for, except for some of Stephen Foster's, no song of this decade had a lovelier melody. As with so many Civil War songs, the origin of "Lorena" is obscure. It has been assigned to one H. D. L. Webster, as early as 1850, but John Wyeth, historian of Forrest and author of With Sabre and Scalpel, *gives it a different history:*

"As we passed a home of the Trappist Brotherhood, Lieutenant Frank Brady entertained us by singing Lorena, a war-time poem which had been set to music and was then very popular. He told us that the author of the poem was an inmate of this Trappist home. If this were so, and the self-imprisoned brother heard the sweet voice of the cavalier as he sang 'The Years creep slowly by, Lorena' what sad and tender memories it must have awakened."

The years creep slowly by, Lorena,
The snow is on the grass again;
The sun's low down the sky, Lorena,
The frost gleams where the flowers have been,
But the heart throbs on as warmly now,
As when the summer days were nigh;
Oh, the sun can never dip so low,
Adown affection's cloudless sky.
The sun can never dip so low,
Adown affection's cloudless sky.

A hundred months have passed, Lorena,
Since last I held that hand in mine;
And felt the pulse beat fast, Lorena,
Tho' mine beat faster far than thine.
A hundred months, 'twas flow'ry May,
When up the hilly slope we climbed,
To watch the dying of the day
And hear the distant church bells chime.
To watch the dying of the day
And hear the distant churchbells chime.

We loved each other then, Lorena,
More than we ever dared to tell;
And what we might have been, Lorena,
Had but our lovings prospered well—
But then, 'tis past, the years are gone,
I'll not call up their shadowy forms;
I'll say to them, "lost years, sleep on!
Sleep on! nor heed life's pelting storms."
I'll say to them, "lost years, sleep on!
Sleep on! nor heed life's pelting storms."

The story of that past, Lorena,
Alas! I care not to repeat
The hopes that could not last, Lorena,
They lived, but only lived to cheat.
I would not cause e'en one regret
To rankle in your bosom now;
For "if we *try*, we may forget,"
Were words of thine long years ago.
For "if we *try*, we may forget,"
Were words of thine long years ago.

Yes, these were words of thine, Lorena,
They burn within my memory yet;
They touched some tender chords, Lorena,
Which thrill and tremble with regret.
'Twas not thy woman's heart that spoke;
Thy heart was always true to me;
A duty, stern and pressing, broke
The tie which linked my soul with thee.
A duty, stern and pressing, broke
The tie which linked my soul with thee.

It matters little now, Lorena,
The past is in the eternal Past,
Our heads will soon lie low, Lorena,
Life's tide is ebbing out so fast.
There is a Future! O thank God!
Of life, this is so small a part!
'Tis dust to dust beneath the sod;
But there, *up there*, 'tis heart to heart.
'Tis dust to dust beneath the sod;
But there, *up there*, 'tis heart to heart.
                              —H. D. L. WEBSTER (?)

19. WHEN JOHNNY COMES MARCHING HOME

*This song, more commonly associated with the Spanish-American War,
originated in the Civil War, but just when we do not know. It has been*

assigned to Father Louis Lambert, "the American Newman," who served as chaplain of the 18th Illinois Infantry, but the better claim seems to be that of the extraordinary Patrick Sarsfield Gilmore, Butler's bandmaster in New Orleans and organizer of the gigantic Peace Jubilee of 1869 which employed a chorus of ten thousand and an orchestra of one thousand pieces. The melody itself has entered deeply into American music: Burnet Tuthill wrote a series of variations on it for piano and wind instruments, and Roy Harris composed his American Overture *on its theme.*

When Johnny comes marching home again, hurrah, hurrah!
We'll give him a hearty welcome then, hurrah, hurrah!
The men will cheer, the boys will shout,
The ladies they will all turn out,

CHORUS: And we'll all feel gay when Johnny comes marching home.
   And we'll all feel gay when Johnny comes marching home.

The old church bell will peal with joy, hurrah, hurrah!
To welcome home our darling boy, hurrah, hurrah!
The village lads and lassies say,
With roses they will strew the way,

CHORUS: And we'll all feel gay when Johnny comes marching home.

Get ready for the Jubilee, hurrah, hurrah!
We'll give the hero three times three, hurrah, hurrah!
The laurel wreath is ready now
To place upon his loyal brow,

CHORUS: And we'll all feel gay when Johnny comes marching home.

Let love and friendship on that day, hurrah, hurrah!
Their choicest treasures then display, hurrah, hurrah!
And let each one perform some part,
To fill with joy the warrior's heart,

CHORUS: And we'll all feel gay when Johnny comes marching home.
   And we'll all feel gay when Johnny comes marching home.
        —PATRICK S. GILMORE (?)